T0190181

Lecture Notes in Computer Science 13477

More information about this series at https://link.springer.com/bookseries/558

Barbara Göbl · Erik van der Spek ·
Jannicke Baalsrud Hauge · Rod McCall (Eds.)

Entertainment Computing – ICEC 2022

21st IFIP TC 14 International Conference, ICEC 2022
Bremen, Germany, November 1–3, 2022
Proceedings

 Springer

Editors
Barbara Göbl ⓘ
University of Vienna
Vienna, Austria

Erik van der Spek ⓘ
Eindhoven University of Technology
Eindhoven, The Netherlands

Jannicke Baalsrud Hauge ⓘ
Royal Institute of Technology
Södertälje, Sweden

BIBA – Bremer Institut für Produktion und
Logistik GmbH
Bremen, Germany

Rod McCall ⓘ
Luxembourg Institute of Science
and Technology
Esch-Sur-Alzette, Luxembourg

ISSN 0302-9743   ISSN 1611-3349 (electronic)
Lecture Notes in Computer Science
ISBN 978-3-031-20211-7   ISBN 978-3-031-20212-4 (eBook)
https://doi.org/10.1007/978-3-031-20212-4

This Springer imprint is published by the registered company Springer Nature Switzerland AG
The registered company address is: Gewerbestrasse 11, 6330 Cham, Switzerland

Preface

We are proud to present the conference proceedings of the 21st edition of the IFIP International Conference on Entertainment Computing (ICEC 2022) in this edited LNCS volume. The conference was hosted by "BIBA - Bremer Institut für Produktion und Logistik an der Universität Bremen" in Bremen, Germany, during November 1–3, 2022. As the longest lasting and prime scientific conference in the area of Entertainment Computing, ICEC brings together researchers and practitioners with diverse backgrounds in order to connect, share, and discuss both recent and potential future developments in this field. Considering the broad range of topics represented in our three keynotes, 35 papers, four workshops, and one tutorial, ICEC 2022 served as a lively forum for multidisciplinary exchange to advance our understanding of Entertainment Computing and all related areas.

Overall, we received a total of 72 submissions from authors in Europe, Asia, North and South America, and Oceania. The works collected in this volume discuss latest findings in the fields of Entertainment Tools and Methods, Serious Gameplay, Game Communities, Player Behaviour and Analysis, Game Experience, and Art and Entertainment. All papers underwent double blind peer review with an average of 3.2 reviews per paper. This resulted in 13 accepted full papers, 13 work-in-progress papers, two student competition papers, and three workshop papers. Additionally, a special track presented seven peer-reviewed papers in the fields of Digital Arts and Health, discussed in a workshop hosted by IFIP Working Group (WG) 14.7. Three further workshops were organized on the topics of Social and Ethical Issues in Entertainment Computing (WG 14.5), Interactive Immersive Entertainment (WG 14.6), and Current Opportunities and Challenges of Digital Game-based Learning (WG 14.8).

We would like to express our gratitude to everyone who supported us in hosting this year's conference and ensuring the high quality of the presented proceedings. We thank all members of the Program Committee, composed of 91 experts from 29 different countries, for their hard work. We would also like to thank all the Organizing Committee members who contributed their valuable time and insights. Many thanks also go to the International Federation for Information Processing (IFIP), the ICEC Steering Committee, and our local organizers. Without all this support, this conference would not have been possible.

September 2022

Barbara Göbl
Erik van der Spek
Jannicke Baalsrud Hauge
Rod McCall

Organization

General Chairs

Jannicke Baalsrud Hauge   KTH Royal Institute of Technology, Sweden, and
BIBA Bremen, Germany

Rod McCall   Luxembourg Institute of Science and Technology,
Luxembourg

Program Committee Chairs

Barbara Göbl   University of Vienna, Austria

Erik van der Spek   Eindhoven University of Technology,
The Netherlands

Work in Progress Chairs

Jorge C. S. Cardoso   University of Coimbra, Portugal

Dimitry Alexandrovsky   University of Bremen, Germany

Tutorials Chair

Esteban Clua   Federal Fluminense University, Brazil

Workshop Chairs

Heinrich Söbke   Bauhaus-Universität Weimar, Germany

Paula Alexandra Silva   University of Coimbra, Portugal

Interactive Entertainment/Experiential Works Chair

Moritz Quant   BIBA Bremen, Germany

Student Competition Chairs

Thiago Porcino   Dalhousie University, Canada

Jaime Garcia   University of Technology Sydney, Australia

Doctoral Consortium Chairs

Helmut Hlavacs	University of Vienna, Austria
Simone Kriglstein	Masaryk University, Czech Republic, and AIT Austrian Institute of Technology GmbH, Austria

Publicity Chair

Aleksandra Himstedt	BIBA Bremen, Germany

Local Organization

Sundus Fatima	BIBA Bremen, Germany
Moritz Quandt	BIBA Bremen, Germany
Heiko Duin	BIBA Bremen, Germany
Jakob Baalsrud Hauge	Hochschule Bremen, Germany

Steering Committee

Licinio Roque	University of Coimbra, Portugal
Jannicke Baalsrud Hauge	KTH Royal Institute of Technology, Sweden, and BIBA Bremen, Germany
Esteban Clua	Federal Fluminense University, Brazil
Jorge C. S. Cardoso	University of Coimbra, Portugal
Rainer Malaka	University of Bremen, Germany
Erik van der Spek	Eindhoven University of Technology, Netherlands

Program Committee

Matthew Barr	University of Glasgow, UK
Nicole Basaraba	Maastricht University, The Netherlands
Regina Bernhaupt	Eindhoven University of Technology, The Netherlands
Ioannis Bikas	University of Bremen, Germany
Fernando Birra	Universidade NOVA de Lisboa, Portugal
Nicholas Bowman	Texas Tech University, USA
Joseph Alexander Brown	Brock University, Canada
Carlos Caires	University of Saint Joseph, Macao
Elin Carstensdottir	University of California, Santa Cruz, USA
Joao Cordeiro	Portuguese Catholic University, Portugal
Nuno Correia	Universidade NOVA de Lisboa, Portugal
Drew Davidson	Carnegie Mellon University, USA

Mara Dionisio	Madeira Interactive Technologies Institute, Portugal
Ralf Doerner	RheinMain University of Applied Sciences, Germany
Heiko Duin	BIBA Bremen, Germany
Kai Erenli	UAS BFI Vienna, Austria
Gerald Estadieu	University of Saint Joseph, Macao
Bruno Feijo	Pontifical Catholic University of Rio de Janeiro, Brazil
Pablo Figueroa	Universidad de los Andes, Colombia
Mateus Finco	Universidade Federal do Rio Grande do Sul, Brazil
Mikael Fridenfalk	Uppsala University, Sweden
Florian Gnadlinger	University of Applied Sciences HTW Berlin, Germany, and Masaryk University, Czech Republic
Stefan Goebel	TU Darmstadt, Germany
Pedro Gonzalez Calero	Universidad Politécnica de Madrid, Spain
Noriko Hanakawa	Hannan University, Japan
Robin Horst	RheinMain University of Applied Sciences, Germany
Jun Hu	Eindhoven University of Technology, The Netherlands
Yuqi Hu	University of Nottingham Ningbo China, China
Hiroyuki Iida	JAIST, Japan
Naoya Isoyama	Nara Institute of Science and Technology, Japan
Jinyuan Jia	Tongji University, China
Hao Jiang	Zhejiang University, Ningbo, China
Philipp Jordan	University of Hawaii at Manoa, USA
Fares Kayali	University of Vienna, Austria
Mohd Nor Akmal Khalid	Japan Advanced Institute of Science and Technology, Japan
Chris Kiefer	University of Sussex, UK
Christoph Klimmt	Hanover University of Music, Drama, and Media, Germany
Kei Kobayashi	Nagoya City University, Japan
Troy Kohwalter	Universidade Federal Fluminense, Brazil
Sara Kunz	Portuguese Catholic University, Portugal
Mei-Kei Lai	Macao Polytechnic University, Macao
Danielle Langlois	Masaryk University, Czech Republic
Michael Lankes	University of Applied Sciences Upper Austria, Hagenberg, Austria
Jingya Li	Beijing Jiaotong University, China

Qingde Li	University of Hull, UK
Sheng Li	Peking University, China
Bingjian Liu	University of Nottingham Ningbo China, China
Penousal Machado	University of Coimbra, Portugal
Hung Mai Cong	Kyoto University, Japan
Panos Markopoulos	Eindhoven University of Technology, The Netherlands
Filipa Martins de Abreu	CITAR, Portugal
Andre Miede	Hochschule für Technik und Wirtschaft des Saarlandes, Germany
Michela Mortara	CNR-IMATI, Italy
Wolfgang Mueller	University of Education Weingarten, Germany
Satoshi Nakamura	Meiji University, Japan
Ryohei Nakatsu	Kyoto University, Japan
Andrés Adolfo Navarro Newball	Pontificia Universidad Javeriana, Cali, Colombia
Carla Patrão	Instituto Politécnico de Coimbra, Portugal
Andre Perrotta	CITAR, Portugal
Johannes Pfau	Universität Bremen, Germany
Maria Popescu	Carol I National Defence University, Romania
Kjetil Raaen	Høyskolen Kristiania, Norway
Theresa-Marie Rhyne	Independent Consultant, USA
Teresa Romeo	Universidade NOVA de Lisboa, Portugal
Licinio Roque	University of Coimbra, Portugal
Che Mat Ruzinoor	Universiti Putra Malaysia, Malaysia
Anthony Savidis	University of Crete and ICS-FORTH, Greece
Andreas Scalas	CNR-IMATI, Italy
Mariana Seiça	University of Coimbra, Portugal
Nikitas Sgouros	University of Piraeus, Greece
Yang Shen	Beijing Normal University, China
Dirk Snyman	North-West University, South Africa
Edirlei Soares de Lima	Universidade Europeia, Portugal
Ioana Andreea Stefan	Advanced Technology Systems, Romania
Matthias Steinböck	University of Vienna, Austria
Elif Surer	Middle East Technical University, Turkey
Cristina Sylla	University of Minho, Portugal
Laszlo Szecsi	Budapest University of Technology and Economics, Hungary
Daniel Thalmann	Ecole Polytechnique Fédérale de Lausanne, Switzerland
Joseph Timoney	Maynooth University, Ireland
Mai Xuan Trang	Phenikaa University, Vietnam
Kai Tuuri	University of Jyväskylä, Finland

Contents

Art and Entertainment

Game Communities

Workshops and Tutorials

Game Experience

AstraVerse: Establishing a Culturally Sensitive Framework for Integrating Elements from Mythological Backgrounds

Sai Siddartha Maram[(✉)] [iD], Johannes Pfau[iD], Reza Habibi[iD],
and Magy Seif El-Nasr[iD]

University of California, Santa Cruz, CA, USA
{samaram,jopfau,rehabibi,mseifeln}@uscc.edu

Abstract. Game designers often refer to sources of inspiration for creating new characters and narratives, with cultural and mythological references being a prominent choice for orientation. This however implicitly entails the importance of preventing the misuse of mythological or religious references to respect affiliated groups and believers. In this paper, we present a three-step framework to augment the ability of designers to create innovative characters using mythology as an inspiration while addressing and avoiding cultural backlash. The efficacy of the framework is verified by implementing the framework on Hindu Mythology. We present qualitative and quantitative findings which indicate that characters designed using the framework report significantly higher appraisal from a Hindu population than controversial portrayals of Hindu deities from actually shipped games.

Keywords: Game design · Character design · Co-design · Culture

1 Introduction

With trends of game design and development moving towards more agile approaches, it becomes challenging for game designers to constantly produce unique characters, narratives and mechanics. Olesen reports how it is common to hear from video game designers in agile environments that they find it difficult to generate ideas for narratives and inspiration for character design [31]. Considering established literature in the field of design, inspiration is one of the main factors for generating new ideas within game development [9,25,36,46]. According to Hagen [19], one of the most popular sources of inspiration is mythology as to help in designing new characters.

Drawing from mythology makes for a frequent occurrence within the gaming industry, but has not had much discussion in academia [12,48]; especially Roman and Greek mythology have commonly been utilized to create characters [16]. Successful known titles include gods and characters transplanted from various mythologies [4,30,41,42,45]. Not only does the mere transplantation of gods

© IFIP International Federation for Information Processing 2022
Published by Springer Nature Switzerland AG 2022
B. Göbl et al. (Eds.): ICEC 2022, LNCS 13477, pp. 3–17, 2022.
https://doi.org/10.1007/978-3-031-20212-4_1

(in this context: the usage of literal characters from established belief or mythology) create a pragmatical upper cap on the number of characters a designer can draw from, but the adulteration of actual religious figures can arguably bear potential for controversy and cultural offense.

There have been numerous controversies over transplanting gods into video games, such as *Hanuman: The Boy Warrior* [4], where the literal depiction of an important Hindu figure was perceived as nothing but denigration; or *Faith Fighter* [26], where multiple gods from world religions compete in brawl combat and especially Muhammad had to be censored, as Islamic belief prohibits the depiction of gods. These controversies revolve around how certain religious groups find the concept of "controlling gods through a joy-stick" or them "being inflicted damage" as offensive [1,2,43]. It becomes essential to realize that creating immersive experiences can not come at the cost of cultural sensitivity. This urges the need for a set of regulations or a framework for designers that allows drawing inspiration for characters from mythology without transplanting the worshipped iconography and twisted narrative. The contributions of this paper include:

- A three-step framework that allows game designers to prevent transplanting gods from mythology and support the creation of new yet culturally sensitive characters.
- An implementation of the proposed framework on Hindu mythology that proves the framework's efficacy as well as the publication of a taxonomy of game mechanics inspired from Hindu mythology.

2   Related Work

2.1   Cultural Affordances in Games

Social scientists view games as a new form of cultural expression, and collective behavior [10,18]. Seif El-Nasr *et al.* specifically expound how even video games are subjected to cultural and religious perception [15]. Convincing narratives and the diminishing line between graphics and reality have made games successful in influencing people [21]. This diminishing line makes it important to study cultural affordances in games. We pay attention to religion since it has been established how video games can create reflection on understanding religion [10]. Twisting actual narratives for game mechanics might influence perceptions and alter religious facts for players [10]. Consider the game *Hanuman the Boy Warrior* [4]. The game requires Hanuman (protagonist) to explore a forest and fight demons. The character re-spawns with the message "You have failed" every time the character falls into water. This is a twist to religious beliefs where Hanuman is considered immortal and has extraordinary aquatic abilities. Vasalou *et al.* reinforce how cultural sensitivity is essential in Serious games and mentions the importance of culturally authentic narratives [44]. The impetus of this work is to help designers design novel and culturally sensitive characters using elements from mythology as inspiration.

2.2   Theology and Gaming

Ferdig mentions how religion can either be found explicitly or implicitly in games [17]. Above that, interactions between religion, new media and games have been discussed frequently [6,13,20,33,34,38]. Radde-Antweiler *et al.* and Detweiler provide a detailed account of how historically, various theologists have studied the influence of new media and games on how religion is being shaped in the modern world [13,33]. Vsisler's work studies the perception of the Arab region, and how Islamic communities are perceived by players due to their representation in video games [38]. Their findings show how representation in games, unfortunately, has stereotyped communities to players and emphasizes how cultural and theological representation is an important point of discussion. Most work in religion and games has revolved around studying the effects of video games on religious perception. To our knowledge, there is no discussion on how religion can inspire designers develop new mechanics and characters, which is a gap this paper addresses.

2.3   Game Design Frameworks and Taxonomies

Taxonomies provide a way to organize and classify themes and concepts [3]. Researchers have established taxonomies on various concepts such as game mechanics [29], death and rebirth [11], bugs [22], player modelling [39], games for health [14,24], platformer games [40]. Frameworks for Serious Game design [8], Motion-Based Games [27], Collaborative Games [23] discuss design guidelines for different classifications of games. Previous work constituted discussions on formal design procedures and rules but does not discuss religion and cultural affordances. This work offers a case study on how the proposed taxonomy helps identify game mechanics from a specific culture and uses these mechanics to help designers build interesting yet appropriate characters and narratives.

3   AstraVerse Framework

This framework can be broken down into three steps as follows:

- Mythological Derivation: Establishing the taxonomy of mythological references.
- Generative Step: Facilitating the creation of new characters using the taxonomy.
- Evaluative Step: Evaluating generated characters on (a) creative and (b) cultural scales.

3.1   Mythological Derivation

The goal of the first step is to compile a taxonomy based on the particular mythological background. In order to develop this taxonomy, we first identify various game elements that might benefit from this mythological influence [37].

These primarily boil down – but are not limited – to character visualization, narrative, character abilities, in-game items or collectables, exploration, and combat mechanics. From the chosen mythology, we refer to cultural literature, internet threads and individual experts in mythology to identify popular mythological elements of interest. Finally, we construct nomenclature and visual iconography that can inspire game mechanics as well as characters and other elements.

3.2   Generative and Evaluative Steps

The generative step aim at verifying if the developed taxonomy allows the creation of characters. Designers – independent from the constructors of the taxonomy – are presented with the taxonomy and are requested to create new characters (participatory design). The evaluative step then verifies if the newly developed characters are deemed as creative and culturally valid. A feasible audience to review these with regards to creativity and novelty might arguably be senior game designers. The cultural validity however should be verified by performing qualitative and quantitative studies using participants that identify with or are familiar with the cultural backdrop associated with the particular mythology.

4   Applying the Framework on Hindu Mythology

The backlash certain games received from Hindu religious groups [1,2,43] renders Hindu mythology an appropriate benchmark to verify if characters inspired from Hindu mythology can create engaging characters while still being culturally valid.

In order to showcase and evaluate a use case taxonomy (c.f. Sect. 4.1) and investigate the general capabilities of the proposed framework (c.f. Section 3), we organized a participatory design workshop. The participants of this workshop were introduced to the taxonomical elements outlined in Tables 1, 2, 3 and 4 with visual guiding of characters from Figs. 1 and 2. After that, they were requested to design a narrative and describe as well as sketch the visualized game character(s). The following section tackles taxonomical elements constructed from the framework (step 1 of the framework), whereas the subsequent section presents designers creating new characters using the taxonomy (step 2 of the framework) and finally qualitative remarks and interpretations from senior game designers (step 3(a) of the framework) about these creations, as well as assessments of cultural and religious appropriateness from a population with Hindu background (step 3 (b) of the framework).

4.1   Mythological Derivation [Step 1]: Establishing a Taxonomy on Mythological Hindu Characters and Mythical Objects

Hindu mythology discusses and presents a wide range of gods. We refer to works from Bansal [5] and Hindu epics such as the Mahabharata and Ramayana to identify characters and artifacts. Apart from these, we utilized popular illustrated mythological comics such as *Amar Chitra Katha*, internet forums as *TvTropes* [28], and popular Hindu Mythology YouTube channels such as *KidsOne* to aid building the taxonomy. The attributes, narrative and game mechanics these avatars inspire have been separated from their nomenclature and visual iconography, presented in Tables 1, 2, 3 and split into groups according to the classification by Parrinder [32].

We also identify elements which help the narrative flow and complete the core game loops. These may entail ways to heal characters, collectables or ways to transport around locations/maps involved in the narrative. Eventually, we derive a collection of mythological objects from Hindu mythology and how they could be used in game loops (c.f. Table 4).

4.2 Generative Step [Step 2]: Facilitating the Creation of Characters from the Established Hindu Taxonomy

For the participatory design workshop, we recruited three amateur game designers from a game design program (Masters degree) at <University of California, Santa Cruz>. None of the participants identified as Hindus, and only one of them claimed to be partially aware of Hindu mythology. The following procedure was used in the workshop:

- Take informed consent and introduce them to the context of the workshop i.e. to generate game narratives, design, sketch, or narrate visualized game characters using a taxonomy.
- The researcher educates the participant on the developed taxonomy in Sect. 4.1.
- With the introduced knowledge and ideas, the participant is requested to design and visualize game characters.

4.3 Constructed Outcomes from Generative Step

This section comprises the outcomes (transcribed from narration) of the Participatory Design from participants P1, P2 and P3 in terms of narrative creations and possible visual representations of these, derived as concept art during the workshop.

P1: "A Cosmic Time Portal".

- **Narrative:** *"A hiker slips down the mountain and falls into a celestial portal connecting the ancient times. He falls down to the armoury of celestial weapons. He is thrown back to the current day with the weapons stuck to him forever. The portal also throws ancient Asuars and powerful demons back into the modern day setting"*
- **Visualization :** *"In my game I would like to build a massive female villain. I might have a three headed villain like Ravan (Row 17 Table 2) and have a extreme size like Kumbakaran (Row 18 Table 2). I will also arm her with Nature Powers like Krishna (Row 8 Table 1). Each head controlling different aspects of nature"*. A visual representation is presented Fig. 3.

Table 1. Understating attributes and characteristics of dashavatara

Sr no.	Avatar name	Avatar description	Genre of narrative	Usable game mechanics
The Serial Number in the table indicates the Visual representation in Fig. 1				
1	Matsya	In the zoomorphic version the avatar is a fish with the horn. In the anthropomorphic version the upper half is human and the lower half resembles a fish	Saves creation from a great flood. (Similar to flood myths across cultures), Recovers ancient scriptures by defeating a horse headed demon	Underwater speed due to fish fins, Underwater strength, Mythical horn
2	Kurma	In the zoomorphic version the avatar is a turtle. In the anthropomorphic version the upper half is human and the lower half resembles the shell of a turtle	Carries the weight of the world on the shell, Acts as a axis in mythology to churn a mythical cosmic ocean	Underwater agility due to turtle fins, Extreme focus and stability, Extreme strength, Hard protective shell
3	Varaha	The Varaha avatar has a boar head and a human torso as lower half	Goes to the depth of a cosmic ocean to lift Goddess Earth with tusks. Defeats fierce demons who imprison Goddess Earth	Agility in both water and land, Extreme speed, Mythical and sharp tusks, Boar face, Four hands
4	Narasimha	The avatar is visualized with a Lion head and human lower half	The avatar defeats a smart demon with mythical abilities	Extreme strength, Lion face, Lion like sharp claws and sharp teeth., Four hands, Carries a mace, Cosmic conch and Rotating sharp disk
5	Vamana	This avatar is visualized as a dwarf carrying an umbrella and jug of water	The avatar stops a demon king from performing supreme sacrifices and restore the heavens to the Hindu King of Gods	Mutable in size(Dwarf to Giant), Mythical powers (Chants, Spells), Carries a protective umbrella, Magic water
6	Parushurama	This avatar is visualized as a powerful Saint	The avatar is credited to bring order and peace by defeating unjust kings who were ruling land with tyranny and greed	Fierce warrior, Yields the axe, Skilled in arms, Knowledge on how wield to celestial weapons, Extreme aggression, Skilled in rituals and academic knowledge
7	Rama	This Avatar is visualized as a Prince	The avatar is credited of defeating a powerful 10 headed demon Ravana. This avatar is the central protagonist of the Hindu Epic "Ramayana"	Skilled archer, Discipline, Kind, Academically strong, Celestial bow, Celestial and divine arrows
8	Krishna	This avatar is visualized as a Prince	The avatar defeats his Uncle, The avatar is a pivotal character of the Hindu Epic "Mahabharata"	Skilled warrior, Yields the rotating cosmic flame disc, Yields celestial weapons and shields, Academically strong, Mutable in size, Mythical powers, Great rapport with animals and nature, Multiple arms, Master flute player
9	Buddha	This avatar is visualized a monk	The primary purpose of this avatar was to teach morals and principles	Academically strong, Great orator, Peace loving, Calm
10	Kalki	A person riding a mythical white horse and carrying a long sword	The avatar is supposed to eliminate human human race and restart cycle of life	Swift, Skilled swordsmen, Mythical horse, Flaming sword

Table 2. Understanding Attributes and Characteristics of Characters from the Mahabharata and Ramayana

Sr no.	Avatar name	Avatar description	Genre of narrative	Usable game mechanics
The Serial Number in the table indicates the Visual representation in Fig. 1				
11	Arjuna	This avatar is visualized as a prince	The son of the King of gods. He is the best archer in Hindu Mythology. He yields all celestial weapons. There are instances where Arjuna is also portrayed as a eunuch	Plethora of celestial weapons, Infinite arrow quiver, Cosmic bow, Indestructible chariot
12	Karna	This avatar is visualized as a prince	The son of the Sun god. Karna is a great archer second to Arjuna. Karna is considered to be radiant and bright as the sun	Indestructible golden armor, Radiant earrings reflecting Solar radiation, Cosmic bow, Loyalty, Recipient of many curses
13	Bheema	This avatar is visualized as a prince	The son of Wind God. Has the strength of 1000 elephants. Feared among Giants and Asuras	Extreme strength, Yields of the cosmic mace, Pride in strength, Affection towards loved ones
14	Duryodhana	This avatar is visualized as a prince	Prime antagonist in the Mahabharata. Is know for his extreme greed. Is a mighty warrior and ranks among the greatest wrestlers	Extreme pride and cunning, Iron body in the upper half, Fragile Lower half the body, Extremely experienced wrestler, Death grip
15	Gatotkach	This avatar is visualized as a friendly demon	The son of Bheema (Row 13). Is a mighty warrior with magical powers	Magical illusions, Mutable size, Multiplied powers at nightfall
16	Hanuman	Has anthropomorphic iconography. Avatar is visualized with a Monkey head, human lower half and has a Monkey Tail	The avatar is the son of the wind god. Student of the Sun god and the principle associate of Rama (Row 7 Table 1). Blessed as one of the immortals in Hindu mythology	Fierce warrior, Yields the mace, Extreme strength, Extreme loyalty, Capable of flight, Skilled in academic knowledge
17	Ravana	This Avatar is visualized as the king of Sri Lanka with ten heads	He is the central antagonist of the Hindu Epic "Ramayana". Has his soul in his navel, making him invincible at the rest of his body. Mighty with 10 heads and has knowledge to many celestial weapons	Skilled warrior and fierce commander, Extreme pride and lust, Great devotee of certain Gods, Access to celestial and cosmic weapons, Academically strong, Posses aerial flight machines
18	Kumbakaran	This avatar is visualized as an extremely large giant	He is a massive asura who is known to squash enemies to pulp. He is slow and has ferocious appetite. Sleeps for 6 months of the year and awake the other 6 months	Extreme strength, Slow maneuver, Can be only hit by celestial weapons, High Energy drain
19	Shiva	Is one of the supreme Gods in Hindu Mythology. Has a serpent around the neck and the moon in the form of a crescent locked in the hair	Is labelled as the god of destruction. His dark blue color is attributed to carrying a dangerous poison in his throat to save humanity	Third eye whose opening leads to annihilation, Trident, Hour glass shaped drum which causes cosmic vibration, Serpent neck, Commander of God Soldiers, Lunar Control

Table 3. Understanding attributes and characteristics of gods of various qualities and elements

Sr no.	Avatar name	Avatar description	Genre of narrative	Usable game mechanics
		The Serial Number in the table indicates the Visual representation in Fig. 2		
20	Saraswati	This avatar is visualized as a goddess	The goddess is treated as the goddess of education	Music powers (Carries the instrument Veena), Purifying powers, Highest educational knowledge, Resides in a white lotus, Travels in a white swan
21	Lakshmi	This avatar is visualized as a goddess	The goddess is the spouse of Lord Vishnu (source of Table 1) and is has incarnations along with the Dashavatara (Table 1)	Giver of wealth, fortune, Power of maya ("illusion"), Giver of agriculture, fertility, health, courage
22	Bhoodevi	This avatar is visualized as a woman	This goddess is treated as Mother Earth	Strength (carries the weight of living beings), Earth control powers (rotation, tunnels), Landmass control (earthquakes, avalanches)
23	Durga	There have been many popular representation of this goddess These range from two arms, to 10 arms carrying various weapons	This goddess is considered one of the most powerful deity in Hindu mythology	Has a lion as a vehicle, Carries discs, mace, bows, swords, conch in certain representations, Creates powerful Illusions
24	Surya	This avatar is a radiant human	This god is treated as the Sun God	Solar flames, Extreme gravity, Controls day and night, Extreme speed (Rides a chariot with 7 horses)
25	Vayu	This avatar is visualized the as a human with Wind capabilities	This god is the controller of Air, Wind and gases	Flying abilities and Extreme speed, Can control winds (Storms, Tornado's)
26	Agni	This avatar is visualized as a human engulfed in flames	The God Agni is the representation of Fire	Symbolically represents Fire, Receives damage from rain and aqua avatars, Huge appetite (burns down forests), Guardians of Divine weapons
27	Varuna	This avatar is visualized the as a human with Aqua capabilities	This god is the king of the oceans and aquatic life	Extreme underwater abilities Commander of the Sea animals Ocean Control (Tsunamis, Cyclones, Gateways)
28	Ganesha	God with a human torso and Elephant head	This is the god on removing all obstacles and education	Strength, Devotion and high patience, Magical elephant tusks and elephant trunk, Slow Movement, A jewellery adorned Rat as a transport vehicle
29	Garuda	He has a human body and face. The mouth is modified to the shape of an eagle. Garuda has a huge wingspan	Garuda has been discussed in Hindu mythology on multiple occasions. Garuda is the vehicle of Lord Vishnu for most of his Avatars (Table 1)	Aerial ability, Cosmic speeds, Large wingspan, Commands over eagles, Consumes snake as prey, High loyalty

Table 4. Understanding Mythical Objects and their Role in Game Loops

Sr no.	Game loop element	Item name	Abilities
1	Shields	Karan Kavach, Shiv Kavach, Bramha Kavach	The Karan Kavach is the Armour given to Karna (Row 12 Table 2) by the Sun god. The armour is a supreme armour and the one who wears it is invincible at battle. The Shiv Kavach could only be destroyed by the BramhaAstra (Row 6 Table 4). Shields can be introduced in game loops as collectables whose effects span over a time period. Shields can also be introduced as inbuilt character abilities with a cooling period once used
2	Flags	Garuda Flag, Indra Flag, Hanuman Flag, Kaama Flag	Flags act as collectables in a game loop. These collectables can act as short term abilities. The Garuda Flag is a reflection of speed, The Indra flag is a symbol of authority, The Hanuman Flag is powerful flag which resits incoming celestial weapons, Tha Kaama Flag is the flag of love
3	Healing Herbs and Elixirs	Sanjeevani, Amrit	It is common for protagonists and other character during game play to loose health. Healing herbs such as the Sanjeevni and Amrit have narrative references in Hindu mythology to restore life and health
4	Transport	Garuda, Surya Vimana, Hansa Vimana, Pushpaka Vimana, Tripurajit Vimana	The term Vimana is analogus to flight. Hindu mythology had references to Vehicles which broke the time space barrier. The Surya vimana is a golden Chariot with 7 White horses (each corresponding to one day of the week). The Hansa Vimana is a White chariot guided by swans. The Pushpaka Vimana is a chariot of Ravana (Row 17 Table 2). The Tripurajit Vimana is cosmic Chariot used by Shiva (Row 19 Table 2). Garuda is a Eagle with a huge wingspan capable of flying through the cosmos
5	Elemental Weapons	BhumaAstra (Earth), AgniAstra (Fire), VayuAstra (Wind), VarunaAstra (Water)	The BhumaAstra is a weapon capable of shattering the earth and digging tunnels. The AgniAstra is a fire emitting weapon. The VayuAstra is told to travel at great speeds. The VarunaAstra is capable of unleashing large water bodies on avatars, fires
6	Cosmic Weapons 1	Bramhastra, Trishul, Sudarshana Chakra, Vajra	The Bramhastra is an extremely powerful weapon capable of destroying armies and cities. The Trishul is the weapon of Shiva (Row 19 Table 2). Visually similar to the trident. Sudarshana Chakra is a disc which travels at cosmic speeds to behead enemies and return to the owner once done. The Vajra is analogus to the mighty thunderbolt
7	Cosminc Weapons 2	PashpataAstra, NarayanaAstra, BrahmashirshaAstra, RudraAstra	The PashupataAstra is one of the irresistible weapons, which requires high skill to use. The NarayanaAstra is a weapon which showers weapons from the sky upon enemies. The shower can only be stopped once the enemy bows to the power of the weapon and disarms themselves. The BrahmshirshaAstra is an advanced version of the BramhaAstra and is said to cause four times more damage. The RudraAstra translates to the Furious Weapons, it is the only weapon which can counter a BramhaAstra
8	Cosmic Weapons 3	NagaPasha, GarudaAstra, Sammohanastra, Prajnastra	The NagaPasha is a weapon dedicated to the Snake Gods. The weapon releases serpents to attack the enemies. This can be countered by the GarudaAstra, which summons Garuda (Row 4 Table 4) the eagle, which sweeps the serpents. The SammohanaAstra intoxicates enemies, while the PrajnaAstra recovers them from the intoxication
8	Cosmic Bows	Gandeeva, Sharanga, Vijaya, Pinaka	Not all bows can handle Cosmic Weapons. These are a few bows have been used by various characters in Hindu mythology. The typical Characteric of these bows include high string tension, Multiple strings, made from celestial wood from alternate dimensions
9	Cosmic Swords	Nandaka, Chandrahas	The Nandaka is the sword of the Dahsavatars. The Chandrahas translates to "crescent" in Hindu mythology there has been references where the crescent of the Moon acts as a sword for the Gods

Fig. 1. Visual representation of characters discussed in Table 1 and Table 2.

Fig. 2. Visual representation of characters discussed in Table 3

Fig. 3. Character visualization of participant 1

Fig. 4. Character visualization of participant 2.

Fig. 5. Character visualization of participant 3.

P2: "Mystique Musician".

- **Narrative:** *"The narrative is linked to African tribes and their freedom struggle against colonial empires. A young girl has music has her genre of attacks. She is a black musician who evolves as levels in the game progress. She yields all mythical instruments mentioned in the taxonomy (Row 20 Table 4, Row 8 Table 1 and Row 19 Table 2)."*
- **Visualization:** *"I am thinking of giving the protagonist multiple arms like Narasimha (Row 4 Table 1) and Varaha (Row 3 Table 1). The character will unlock more arms and more weapons as the levels progress"*. A visualization of this character is shown in Fig. 4

P3: "War of the Elements".

- **Narrative.** *"It is important that people are bought aware of climate changes. In my game I want to make use of Natural elements in Hindu Mythology such a Lunar control, Sun energy and Wind energy to show players how the lack of either of them leads to trouble. I want characters in my game to control nature"*

– **Visualization.** *Like Shiva (Row 19 Table 2) has a moon in his forehead. The crescent of the moon can act as a sword facing terrestrial enemies. While fighting aqua characters the moon would glow to be a dull disc to cause low tide. A negotiating character would be a character with earth capabilities (Row 22 Table 3) or solar capabilities since they would have a greater gravitational pull."* A Visual Representation is presented in Fig. 5.

4.4   Creative Evaluation [Step 3(a)]: Evaluating the Creative Dimension of Workshop Outcomes

Procedure. First, the produced narratives and characters (c.f. Section 4.3, Sects. 4.3 and 4.3) were presented to two senior game designers to evaluate the creative and novelty element of the creations. We recorded these interviews and asked them to quantify their estimation as well.

Measures. For measuring creativity and novelty, we asked the senior game developers to judge items (on a scale of 5) based on Brookhart's rubric [7]. On top of this, the interviewees were asked to comment on the particular narratives qualitatively.

Participants. In total, $(n_a = 2)$ senior game developers (those with 3+ years of Game Production experience) assessed the creative quality of the creations.

Results of Creative Evaluation. Table 5 contains the quantitative assessment of senior game designers towards the produced characters. Furthermore, we asked them to elaborate on their scores. Judge 1, who scored Participant 2 the highest (in terms of cumulative points compared to other participants), shared - *"The combination of mythical influence on historical freedom wars is fascinating, ranging from colonial invasions, musical warfare and finally introducing mythical physical characteristics. The other idea (Participant 1) had mythical power from both ends, while here it is more the mythical powers of the hero taking on huge armies in different conditions."*

Judge 2 had appreciative feedback on Participant 3's work - *"I really like the idea of a mutable moon sword causing tides and that being the primary way it fights. That feels really cool. The character also being made of bushes and trunk as hair is also an interesting combination."*

4.5   Cultural Evaluation [Step 3(b)]: Evaluating the Cultural Validity of Workshop Outcomes

Procedure. Students with a Hindu background were presented Fig. 3, 4, 5 as well as depictions[1] of a Hindu goddess that raised controversial discussions in

---

[1] A reference to the image depicting the representation of Kali from the game SMITE can be found at https://images.news18.com/ibnlive/uploads/2012/07/kalismite.jpg.

the multiplayer online battle arena game *SMITE* [42]. Participants were asked to comment on the representation in SMITE as well as on the images produced by our taxonomy qualitatively, which was later classified by structuring content analysis.

Measures. Regarding the cultural assessment, participants were surveyed using semi-structured interviews on their appraisal and statements towards both visualizations.

Participants. In total, ($n_b = 39$) students were recruited through a call for participation from online Indian Communities at <University Name> for the cultural appropriateness evaluation. From the recruited student participants, 92.9% identified as Hindus (3.6% Atheists and 3.6% Jains). All of the participants claimed to be aware of Hindu mythology and the most of them also knew other mythologies, most popularly Greek (69%).

Table 5. Quantitative Evaluation [7] of Designed Characters and Narratives in Sect. 4.3 by Experienced Game Designers

	Judge 1			Judge 2		
	P1	P2	P3	P1	P2	P3
Variety of ideas and contexts	3	5	3	3	3	4
Variety of sources	4	4	3	4	3	3
Combining ideas	4	5	4	4	3	4
Communicating something new	3	5	4	3	3	3

Results of Cultural Evaluation. Participants were shown a representation of Goddess Kali from the game *SMITE*. The Hindu-affiliated participants had mixed opinions on the representation with 10% of them being *"offended"* by the portrayal. Another 10% of the participants claimed the representation is *"Perfectly normal"*. Around 20% of them were not offended but claimed *"they were not comfortable"* with such a visualization. The majority of 53% claimed *"they might be okay with such a representation, but know people who would be offended"*. Also, participants qualitatively reinforced that (P9): *"Kali presented like this, people here in <USA> might find it amusing. If you are planning to launch in India, be ready for controversies and only criticism. "*

After presenting *SMITE's* representation of Goodess Kali, we asked participants to comment on characters from Fig. 3, 4, 5. For Fig. 3, 76% of the students felt the characters were *"Perfectly Normal"* and 10% of the students shared *"they might be okay with such a representation, but people who would be offended"*. A 5% reported *"they are not comfortable"* and 3% of the participants felt the representation was *offensive*. With reference to this, (P19) interpreted the result that

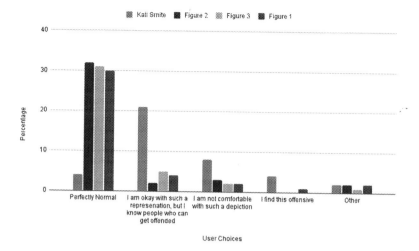

Fig. 6. Quantitative results reflecting cultural acceptance of characters from SMITE and generated characters as part of the study shown in Fig. 3, 4, 5

"Three heads makes me think of Ravana but he had ten [heads]. Also Reminds me of Lord Brahma with his multiple heads but it doesn't strike as an instant connection."

For Fig. 4, 82% of the participants felt the characters were *"Perfectly Normal"* and only 5% shared *"they might be okay with such a representation, but know people who would be offended"*. No participant responded to be *"offended"* and only 7% of the participants shared *"they were not comfortable"*. In reference to Fig. 4, (P2) declared: *"I find this art more artistic rather than something offensive. Even if it's explicitly implying that the art has taken some elements from Hindu mythology, I still find it creative and something joyful, a person who is enjoying music. I can't see how this art is gonna be offensive to people."*

For Fig. 5, 79% of the participants felt the characters were *"Perfectly Normal"* and 12% of them shared *"they might be okay with such a representation, but people who would be offended"*. 5% reported *"they were not comfortable"*. No participant responded to be *offended*. (P6) added that *"healing herbs reminds me of Sanjeevani from Ramayana. There are many mythological aspects here, like the hair represents vegetation and the solar shield representing the Surya Vamsha."*

5   Results and Discussion

Fig. 6 reveals an arguably positive trend in cultural acceptance of characters when built using the provided framework. To investigate this effect, we calculated statistical significance utilizing Wilcoxon rank sum tests on the ordinally ranked response categories between the *SMITE* example and each of the characters produced within our workshop [47]. For measuring the impact of these comparisons, we additionally computed effect sizes r after Rosenthal [35]. As hypothesized, the *SMITE* portrayal of Kali produced significantly higher indications of offensiveness than the characters of Fig. 4 ($p < 0.05, r = 0.79$), Fig. 5 ($p < 0.05, r = 0.83$) and Fig. 3 ($p < 0.05, r = 0.74$); all showing large effect sizes.

Even if the perceived creativity and novelty of characters are always subjective and dependent on the target population that would play such a game, senior game designers approved the potential of the taxonomy to construct innovative characters by means of inspiration and combination. *SMITE's* version of Kali raised considerably more rejections than endorsement. This highly contrasts the feedback that characters produced by our taxonomy received, with most of the responses judging all three of them as perfectly normal, none or only single mentions of offense and only minor doubts of the appropriateness for peers within the Hindu community. Statistical significances with large effect sizes throughout all comparisons further strengthen the potential of our approach.

6   Future Work and Conclusion

In the next iteration of the work, we plan to use standard UX research methods such as Grounded Theory and Card sorting to create the taxonomy. We plan to have a larger participatory design workshop for creating characters (to eliminate any creative bias). In the future, we seek to come up with metrics to determine upper limits on how much a designer can borrow from a taxonomy and prevent misuse by accidentally creating characters which might be perceived as culturally insensitive characters.

In this paper, we presented a framework which allows designers to draw inspiration from mythological references while maintaining cultural validity. As a case study, we build a taxonomy using the proposed framework over Hindu mythology to help designers create culturally sensitive characters. To showcase that the framework supports the creation of creative and novel characters, we discussed outcomes from a study where game designers used a taxonomy constructed from the framework to build novel characters. These created characters were evaluated on the lines of creativity and cultural sensitivity. The outcomes of these evaluations supported our hypothesis of allowing designers to create creative, culturally inclusive and immersive characters using the proposed taxonomy. We believe, the scope of the is paper is not limited to Hindu mythology and is equally valid for other mythologies.

Acknowledgments. The research team would like acknowledge and thank all the participants and senior designers for taking part in our study. We would also like to acknowledge and thank the University of California, Santa Cruz for their support.

References

1. Religious groups protest game for its depiction of kali- technology news, firstpost (2012). https://www.firstpost.com/tech/news-analysis/religious-groups-protest-game-for-its-depiction-of-kali-3603945.html

2. Alexander, L.: Hindu statesman criticizes sony's hanuman: Boy warrior (2009). https://www.gamasutra.com/php-bin/news_index.php?story=23280

3. Antle, A.N., Wise, A.: Getting down to details: using learning theory to inform tangibles research and design for children. Interact. Comput. **25**(1), 1–20 (2013)

4. Aurona Technologies: Hanuman the Boy Warrior (2009)

5. Bansal, S.P.: Hindu gods and goddesses. Smriti Books (2005)

6. Bornet, P., Burger, M.: Religions in play: games, rituals, and virtual worlds, vol. 2. Theologischer Verlag Zürich (2012)

7. Brookhart, S.M.: How to create and use rubrics for formative assessment and grading. Ascd (2013)

8. Buchanan, L., Wolanczyk, F., Zinghini, F.: Blending bloom's taxonomy and serious game design. In: Proceedings of the International Conference on Security and Management (SAM), p. 1. The Steering Committee of The World Congress in Computer Science, Computer (2011)

9. Bunian, S., Li, K., Jemmali, C., Harteveld, C., Fu, Y., Seif El-Nasr, M.S.: Vins: Visual search for mobile user interface design. In: Proceedings of the 2021 CHI Conference on Human Factors in Computing Systems, pp. 1–14 (2021)

10. Campbell, H.A., Wagner, R., Luft, S., Gregory, R., Grieve, G.P., Zeiler, X.: Gaming religionworlds: why religious studies should pay attention to religion in gaming. J. Am. Acad. Relig. **84**(3), 641–664 (2016)

11. Cuerdo, M.A.M., Melcer, E.F.: " i'll be back": A taxonomy of death and rebirth in platformer video games. In: Extended Abstracts of the 2020 CHI Conference on Human Factors in Computing Systems, pp. 1–13 (2020)

12. De Wildt, L., Aupers, S.: Playing the other: role-playing religion in videogames. Europ. J. Cult. Studies **22**(5–6), 867–884 (2019)

13. Detweiler, C.: Halos and avatars: Playing video games with god. Westminster John Knox Press (2010)

14. Dormann, C.: Toward ludic gerontechnology: a review of games for dementia care. DiGRA/FDG (2016)

15. El Nasr, M.S., Al-Saati, M., Niedenthal, S., Milam, D.: Assassin's creed: A multicultural read. Loading... **2**(3) (2008)

16. Evangelopoulou, O., Xinogalos, S.: Myth troubles: an open-source educational game in scratch for Greek mythology. Simul. Gaming **49**(1), 71–91 (2018)

17. Ferdig, R.E.: Developing a framework for understanding the relationship between religion and videogames. Online-Heidelberg J. Relig. Internet **5** (2014)

18. Grieve, G.P., Campbell, H.A.: Studying religion in digital gaming. a critical review of an emerging field. Online-Heidelberg J. Relig. Internet **5** (2014)

19. Hagen, U.: Where do game design ideas come from? invention and recycling in games developed in sweden. In: DiGRA Conference (2009)

20. Heidbrink, S., Knoll, T.: Online-Heidelberg journal of religions on the internet/5 religion in digital games: multiperspective and interdisciplinary approaches. Online-Heidelberg J. Relig. Internet (2014)

21. Von der Heiden, J.M., Braun, B., Müller, K.W., Egloff, B.: The association between video gaming and psychological functioning. Front. Psychol. **10** 1731 (2019)

22. Lewis, C., Whitehead, J., Wardrip-Fruin, N.: What went wrong: a taxonomy of video game bugs. In: Proceedings of the fifth international conference on the foundations of digital games, pp. 108–115 (2010)

23. Loparev, A., Egert, C.A.: Toward an effective approach to collaboration education: A taxonomy for game design. In: 2015 IEEE Games Entertainment Media Conference (GEM), pp. 1–4. IEEE (2015)

24. McCallum, S., Boletsis, C.: Dementia games: a literature review of dementia-related serious games. In: Ma, M., Oliveira, M.F., Petersen, S., Hauge, J.B. (eds.) SGDA 2013. LNCS, vol. 8101, pp. 15–27. Springer, Heidelberg (2013). https://doi.org/10.1007/978-3-642-40790-1_2

25. Mete, F.: The creative role of sources of inspiration in clothing design. Int. J. Cloth. Sci. Technol. **18**(4) 278–293 (2006)

26. Molleindustria: Faith Fighter (2009)

27. Mueller, F., Isbister, K.: Movement-based game guidelines. In: Proceedings of the Sigchi Conference on Human Factors in Computing Systems, pp. 2191–2200 (2014)

28. Multiple: Hindu mythology / myth, https://tvtropes.org/pmwiki/pmwiki.php/Myth/HinduMythology

29. Nacke, L.E., Grimshaw, M.: Player-game interaction through affective sound. In: Game sound technology and player interaction: Concepts and developments, pp. 264–285. IGI global (2011)

30. Ninja Theory: Hellblade: Senua's Sacrifice (2017)

31. Olesen, J.F.: Design processes in game jams: Studies of rapid design processes. In: Extended Abstracts Publication of the Annual Symposium on Computer-Human Interaction in Play, pp. 723–726. CHI PLAY '17 Extended Abstracts, Association for Computing Machinery, New York, NY, USA (2017). https://doi.org/10.1145/3130859.3133226

32. Parrinder, E.G.: Avatar and incarnation (1982)

33. Radde-Antweiler, K.: Religion is becoming virtualised. introduction the the special issue on religion in virtual worlds. Online-Heidelberg Journal of Religions on the Internet: Vol. 03.1 Being Virtually Real? Virtual Worlds from a Cultural Studies' Perspective (2008)

34. Radde-Antweiler, K., Waltmathe, M., Zeiler, X.: Video gaming, let's plays, and religion: The relevance of researching gamevironments. Gamevironments (1) (2014)

35. Rosenthal, R., Cooper, H., Hedges, L., et al.: Parametric measures of effect size. Handbook Res. Synth. **621**(2), 231–244 (1994)

36. Sbai, O., Elhoseiny, M., Bordes, A., LeCun, Y., Couprie, C.: DesIGN: design inspiration from generative networks. In: Leal-Taixé, L., Roth, S. (eds.) ECCV 2018. LNCS, vol. 11131, pp. 37–44. Springer, Cham (2019). https://doi.org/10.1007/978-3-030-11015-4_5

37. Sicart, M.: Defining game mechanics. Game Studies **8**(2), 1–14 (2008)

38. Šisler, V.: Digital arabs: representation in video games. Europ. J. Cult. Studies **11**(2), 203–220 (2008)

39. Smith, A.M., Lewis, C., Hullett, K., Smith, G., Sullivan, A.: An inclusive taxonomy of player modeling. University of California, Santa Cruz, Tech. Rep. UCSC-SOE-11-13 (2011)

40. Smith, G., Cha, M., Whitehead, J.: A framework for analysis of 2d platformer levels. In: Proceedings of the 2008 ACM SIGGRAPH Symposium on Video Games, pp. 75–80 (2008)

41. Supermassive Games: Until Dawn (2015)

42. Titan Forge Games: Super Metroid (2019)

43. Usher, W.: Smite offends hindus, catholics, jews, with porno-style depiction of kali (Jul 2012), https://www.cinemablend.com/games/SMITE-Offends-Hindus-Catholics-Jews-With-Porno-Style-Depiction-Kali-44645.html

44. Vasalou, A., Khaled, R., Gooch, D., Benton, L.: Problematizing cultural appropriation. In: Proceedings of the first ACM SIGCHI Annual Symposium on Computer-Human Interaction in Play, pp. 267–276 (2014)

45. Vigil Games: Darksiders (2010)
46. Wallace, S., et al.: Sketchy: drawing inspiration from the crowd. Proc. ACM Human-Comput. Interact. **4**(CSCW2), 1–27 (2020)
47. Wilcoxon, F.: Individual comparisons by ranking methods. In: Kotz, S., Johnson, N.L. (eds) Breakthroughs in Statistics Breakthroughs in statistics, pp. 196–202. Springer (1992). https://doi.org/10.1007/978-1-4612-4380-9_16
48. de Wildt, L., Apperley, T.H., Clemens, J., Fordyce, R., Mukherjee, S.: (re-) orienting the video game avatar. Games Cult. **15**(8), 962–981 (2020)

Comfortably Numb? Violent Video Games and Their Effects on Aggression, Mood, and Pain-Related Responses

Gary L. Wagener(✉) [ID] and André Melzer [ID]

University of Luxembourg, 11 Prte des Sciences, 4366 Esch-sur-Alzette, Luxembourg
gary.wagener@uni.lu

Abstract. In contrast to findings that violent video game (VVG) exposure has a desensitizing effect on empathy and physiological reactivity to scenes of violence [1], no desensitization was found for player responses to pain stimuli in three lab experiments. Compared to a non-violent game, VVG exposure neither affected physiological responses, nor participants' self-reports of perceived pain caused by thermal stress. In addition, the level of game immersion did not affect pain perception, pain tolerance, or aggressive behavior (study 3). In contrast, violent game preference was associated with lower reports of perceived proximal pain, distal pain, and greater antisocial behavior. However, all studies confirmed the detrimental effect of VVG on emotion: participants reported lower positive and greater negative affect after playing the violent compared to the nonviolent game. In sum, the present findings speak against a generalized desensitization effect of VVG on the player. Rather, our findings further support the notion of pain and pain-related responses as complex and multidimensional, modulated by individual, physiological, and contextual factors [2].

Keywords: Violent video games · Desensitization · Pain · Pain perception · Mood

1 Introduction

The impressive economic and social success of video games as well as their potential effects has put the medium under extensive scientific scrutiny. In fact, whether violent video games (VVG) cause negative effects on player emotion, cognition and behavior has led to fierce debates among scholars [3–8]. In the light of the popularity and availability of video games (VG), the great interest of parents, stakeholders, and the general public about their potential effects, but also regarding current discussions about stable and consistent findings in psychology, replications, and meaningful advancements of existing approaches are inevitable to overcome simplifications and over-generalization of results on the effects of VVG.

© IFIP International Federation for Information Processing 2022
Published by Springer Nature Switzerland AG 2022
B. Göbl et al. (Eds.): ICEC 2022, LNCS 13477, pp. 18–38, 2022.
https://doi.org/10.1007/978-3-031-20212-4_2

1.1 Violent Video Games and Aggression Desensitization

According to the General Aggression Model (GAM; [9]), VVG exposure can have short-term and long-term effects on aggression. Short-term exposure to VVG can influence a person's affect, arousal, or cognition, increasing the likelihood that the person will behave aggressively [9, 10]. In contrast, long-term exposure to VVG may in turn influence individual factors, leading to a desensitization effect, increased trait aggression or the reinforcement of attitudes and beliefs towards aggression [10].

The present study addresses findings of a desensitizing effect of VVG exposure. Desensitization is characterized as a decrease in the psychological and physiological response to a stimulus after continuous exposure [11]. Compared to non-violent games, playing VVG has been reported to reduce physiological and/or neurological arousal as well as emotional responding [11–13]. However, desensitization caused by VVG is believed to affect internal processes as well as social interactions. Violence in video games has been reported to increase aggressive behavior, reduce feelings of empathy in the players, and increase aggressive affect [1, 10]. Regarding the latter, feelings like hostility, anger, and a sense for vengeance are increased after VVG exposure [10] which also negatively impacts mood, increasing negative affect and decreasing positive affect [14–16]. Regarding feelings of empathy, participants that were exposed to VG violence showed reduced automatic emotional reactions to harm befalling someone else [17, 18]. For children and adolescents, VVG exposure is assumed to increase the risk of desensitization, possibly affecting aggression levels and decreasing prosocial behavior [19].

1.2 Violent Video Games and Pain Desensitization

Another likely candidate for the desensitizing effects of violence in VG is pain. Pain denotes a complex concept that is modulated by individual, physiological, and contextual factors [2]. Moreover, pain has individual as well as social aspects. Based on the assumptions in the GAM, the potentially numbing and the emotion desensitizing effect of playing VVG should result in stimuli perceived as less painful, both for pain directed to the self (i.e., proximal pain) and above all pain observed in others (i.e., distal pain). The latter is also affected by reduced empathic responses after VVG exposure [1]. For example, studies have shown that exposure to VVG leads to increased desensitization, reducing physiological and emotional reactions to stimuli [10, 11]. The present study therefore tested whether playing VVG has a desensitizing effect on participants' pain responses.

Regarding the role of VG in improving health-related outcomes, a meta-analysis confirmed the pain distracting effect of playing VG [20]. To date, however, only few studies have tested the effects of playing VG on pain perceptions directly. In one study, the so-called cold-pressor test was conducted, in which participants hold their hand in ice-cold water for as long as possible while taking out paper clips [21]. The experience of immersion during gameplay was crucial for pain sensitivity (Study 2): Compared to solving a non-immersive puzzle game, having played a first-person 3-D game led to greater pain tolerance (as indicated by the greater number of paperclips retrieved from ice-cold water), as well as greater indifference towards people depicted as experiencing displeasure. The authors attributed their findings to the desensitizing effect to pain in oneself and in others [21]. Stephens and Allsop [22] found that playing a VVG not only increased aggressive feelings and arousal (as indicated by heart rate), but also pain tolerance. Compared to a golf video game (i.e., the non-violent game), participants that had played a first-person shooter game found ice-cold water less painful (i.e., increased pain tolerance), as indicated by the longer time they held their hand in ice-cold water. The authors attribute this finding to the hypoalgesic effect of the emotional response that accompanies raised state aggression [22].

VVG exposure is thought to have a desensitizing effect not only on proximal pain but also on distal pain perception. In an event-related potential study [23], participants with no habitual experience in violent gaming showed reduced empathic responses to painful images after playing a VVG for 40 min. Participants with habitual violent gaming experience showed a desensitization effect to painful images already before gameplay. They also showed no additional decrease in empathic response to painful images after gameplay. The authors suggested that habitual violent gamers down-regulate their negative-emotional arousal to better perform in-game [23].

1.3 Hypotheses

Theoretically, then, players should become desensitized to aggression in their cognitive, physiological, and emotional responses after continuous exposure to VVG. For example, regarding desensitization in physiological response, Bartholow et al. reported that VVG exposure reduced event-related brain potentials which in turn predicted aggressive behavior in male adults, even when controlling for trait-aggression [11].

Therefore, three experimental studies tested the hypotheses that VVG exposure leads to reduced proximal (H1) and distal (H2) pain perception. In addition, VVG exposure is expected to increase pain tolerance (H3), increase aggressive behavior (H4), decrease physiological reactions to pain stimuli (H5), and decrease mood (H6).

Study 1 tested these hypotheses in a between-subjects lab experiment. Study 2 used the same basic design, trying to replicate findings with different methods to increase validity. Study 3 introduced the additional factor of immersion into the study design.

2 Study 1

Study 1[1] tested the relationship between VVG exposure and proximal pain perception, aggressive behavior, and mood. It was hypothesized that in contrast to playing a non-violent VG, playing a VVG decreases proximal pain perception, increases aggressive behavior, and decreases mood.

2.1 Methods

Participants. Participants ($N = 66$; 50% females; $M_{age} = 22.92$; $SD = 2.88$) were recruited at the University of Luxembourg. They indicated how much they played VG

---

[1] All three studies presented were accepted for ethics approval at the University of Luxembourg.

during typical weekdays, weekends, and holidays (1 = never; 2 = less than 1 h; 3 = 1–2 h; 4 = 2–3 h; 5 = more than 3 h). On average, participants played VG on a low to medium level ($M = 1.83$; $SD = .99$).

Pain Perception, Pain Tolerance, and Aggressive Behavior. Pain was induced using the cold pressor test (CPT). A container (size in cm: 60 x 40 x 18) was filled with cold water (4 °C) controlled by the immersion cooler Julabo FT200. To measure pain tolerance, participants held their hand up to the forearm in the cold water for as long as possible. Time was kept using a stopwatch. To measure pain perception, participants verbally rated their pain level every 15 s using a numerical rating scale (0 = no pain to 10 = worst possible pain, [24]). To measure aggressive behavior, they assigned a minimum time requirement in the CPT for the next participant. For ethical reasons, the maximum duration for the CPT was set to three minutes.

Target Games. Participants played both games on the Wii game console on a 46″ flatscreen. For the violent condition, *Manhunt 2* was chosen due to its high violence ratings. Participants controlled the game character, a patient who tries to escape from a closed psychiatric ward by killing people who get in his way. Participants in the non-violent condition played *Wii Sports Resort*, which includes a variety of sports games. Both games were chosen as they were easy to play but challenging.

Mood. Mood was assessed at two points in time with the positive and negative affect subscales of the PANAS [25] Each subscale comprises ten adjectives (e.g., active, guilty) that were rated on a 5-point scale (1 = not at all to 5 = extremely) on how strongly the person feels about each adjective. Internal consistency before gameplay was good for positive affect (Cronbach's $\alpha = .82$) and negative affect ($\alpha = .88$). The second measurement was done immediately after gameplay. The items were given in a different, randomized order. Again, the internal consistency was good for positive affect ($\alpha = .83$) and for negative affect ($\alpha = .89$).

Trait Aggression. To assess trait aggression, the Aggression Questionnaire [26] that includes the subscales for physical aggression (8 items), anger (6 items), and hostility (6 items) was used in its German version [27]. The items were rated on a 4-point scale (1 = I strongly disagree to 4 = I strongly agree). The combined scale for trait aggression showed good internal consistency ($\alpha = .80$).

Violent Video Games Preference. A novel five-item scale was designed for violent video game preference. Participants indicated how much they prefer and appreciate violent content in video games. Each item started with "I prefer games..." and were related to, among other factors, the motivation to intentionally behave antisocially in games (i.e., "...where I can hurt or kill others"), and to dominate others (i.e., "...that contain scenes of power and domination"). The scale had very good internal consistency ($\alpha = .85$).

Pain Sensitivity. To measure trait pain sensitivity, five items of the Pain Sensitivity Questionnaire (PSQ; [28]) were used. Participants were presented with five imaginary situations (e.g., "imagine that you burn your tongue on a hot drink") and rated the pain they would experience during these situations on a scale from $0 =$ no pain to $10 =$ worst possible pain. The PSQ had good internal consistency ($\alpha = .76$).

Empathy. To measure the relationship between empathy and pain perception, three of the four subscales of the German version of the Interpersonal Reactivity Index (IRI; [29, 30], namely empathic concern (e.g., "I often have tender, concerned feelings for people less fortunate than me"), perspective taking (e.g., "I sometimes try to understand my friends better by imagining how things look from their perspective"), and fantasy (e.g., "when I am reading an interesting story or novel, I imagine how I would feel if the events in the story were happening to me"). Each subscale was measured with four items on a 4-point-scale ($1 =$ strongly disagree to $4 =$ strongly agree). The combined scale for trait-empathy had acceptable internal consistency ($\alpha = .67$).

Manipulation Check. To check if conditions were in fact perceived differently, participants rated two items on game content (e.g., "How brutal would you rate the game you just played"). Furthermore, they were asked about any difficulties with the game controls. Participants rated the items on a 5-point scale ($1 =$ not at all to $5 =$ very much).

Procedure. After participants gave their informed consent, they were alternately assigned by gender to one of two conditions (violent condition vs. non-violent condition). Afterwards, participants provided demographic data, rated the PANAS items, indicated their gaming habits, and rated the IRI items, followed by the Trait Aggression Questionnaire and the PSQ. Next, participants played one of two video games according to their experimental condition for 15 min. After gameplay, participants first rated the PANAS items again and answered the control items for their game perception. Finally, the CPT was performed. Participants were told that they had to hold their hand in the cold water as long as possible. Next, as a measure of aggressive behavior, participants had to indicate a time requirement in the CPT for the next participant as a measure of aggressive behavior. Finally, participants were remunerated, thanked for their participation, and debriefed. The entire experiment lasted for about 30 min.

2.2 Results

All analyses were performed with IBM SPSS versions 25 and 27. The significance level was set at $p < .05$. Bonferroni correction for multiple comparisons was consistently applied in all three studies.

Control Variables. In the CPT, there was no gender difference for pain perception, $F(1, 60) = 1.49, p = .227, \eta^2p = .02$. There were also no differences between conditions with regard to trait empathy, trait pain sensitivity, trait aggression, or gaming experience, $ps \geq .136$. Personality traits did not correlate with pain perception, or pain tolerance, $ps \geq .118$. Only VVG preference significantly correlated with trait empathy ($r = .25, p = .041$), trait aggression ($r = .40, p = .001$), and aggressive behavior ($r = .32, p < .001$).

The manipulation check confirmed that the game conditions were perceived differently. Participants rated the violent game as more brutal ($M = 4.27; SD = 1.01$) than the non-violent game ($M = 1.00; SD = 0.00$), $F(1, 64) = 347.53, p < .001, \eta^2 = .84$.

Furthermore, VVG preference was correlated with change in positive affect (T2-T1) ($r = .27, p = .031$), pain tolerance ($r = .28, p = .026$), and proximal pain perception ($r = -.28, p = .025$).

Hypotheses. A one-way ANOVA with condition as between-subjects variable (violent vs. non-violent condition) and proximal pain perception (pain ratings during CPT) as dependent variable tested H1. However, there was no significant effect, $F(1, 62) < 0.01$, $p = .974, d < .01$. Next, a one-way ANOVA with time in the CPT as dependent variable tested H3. Again, there was no significant effect, $F(1, 64) = 1.97, p = .166, d = .35$. Means and standard deviations are displayed in Table 1.

To test H4, a one-way ANOVA was calculated with condition as between-subjects factor and time in the CPT allotted to the next participant as dependent variable, but did not reveal a significant effect, $F(1, 64) = 0.04, p = .835, d = .05$.

Finally, two mixed-measures ANOVA tested H6. Again, condition served as between-subjects factor, and positive affect (PA score at T1 vs. PA score at T2) and negative affect (NA score at T1 vs. NA score at T2) served as within-subjects factors, respectively. Regarding positive affect, there was no significant within-subjects effect or between-subjects effect, $p \geq .10$. However, the interaction between condition and PA score was significant, $F(1, 60) = 23.11, p < .001, \eta^2 p = .28$. Contrasts revealed that for participants who played the violent game there was a significant decrease in positive affect from T1 to T2, $F(1, 28) = 14.94, p = .001, \eta^2 p = .35$, see Fig. 1. In contrast, participants who played the non-violent game had a significant increase in positive affect, $F(1, 32) = 7.31, p = .011, \eta^2 p = .19$. For the negative affect, there was a significant within-subjects effect, $F(1, 62) = 13.80, p < .001, \eta^2 p = .18$, and a significant between-subjects effect, $F(1, 62) = 13.07, p = .001, \eta^2 p = .17$. However, the interaction between condition and the within-subjects factor of NA score was also significant, $F(1, 62) = 24.45, p < .001, \eta^2 p = .28$. Separate analysis showed that the negative affect increased for participants who played the violent game, $F(1, 30) = 22.62, p < .001, \eta^2 p = .43$. This was not the case for participants who played the non-violent game, $F(1, 32) = 1.81$, $p = .188, \eta^2 p = .05$.

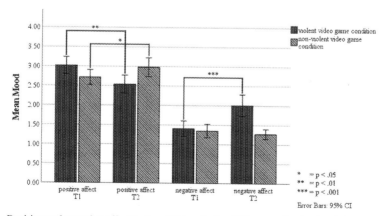

Fig. 1. Positive and negative affect before (T1) and after (T2) gameplay in the violent video game condition and the non-violent video game condition in study 1.

Table 1. Means and standard deviations for positive and negative affect at T1 and T2 as well as proximal pain perception and pain tolerance in the two game conditions in study 1.

Measure	Violent condition		Non-violent condition	
	M	SD	M	SD
Positive affect T1	3.06	0.60	2.72	0.55
Positive affect T2	2.52	0.55	2.98	0.69
Negative affect T1	1.44	0.50	1.35	0.49
Negative affect T2	1.99	0.68	1.27	0.35
Proximal pain perception	6.91	1.65	6.92	1.61
Pain tolerance (with exclusions)	88.65	65.48	96.41	71.49
Pain tolerance (without exclusions)	101.45	81.50	133.42	102.52
Aggressive Behavior (time allotted to next participant in CPT)	48.94	55.41	46.55	35.55

To test if gender influenced the effect of VVG exposure on pain tolerance, a two-way ANOVA was calculated with gender and condition (violent vs. non-violent) as between-subjects factors and time in the CPT as dependent variable. Results did not show any significant main or interaction effects, $Fs \leq .82$, $ps \geq .370$, $\eta^2 p \leq .02$.

Furthermore, an additional ANCOVA was run to test for the effect of condition (violent vs. non-violent condition) on pain tolerance (time in the CPT), including pain sensitivity (PSQ score) as covariate. The main effect of condition on pain tolerance did not reach the level of significance, $F(1,54) = .02$, $p = .884$, $\eta^2 p < .001$. Pain sensitivity was also not a significant predictor of pain tolerance, $F(1, 54) = 1.79$, $p = .187$, $\eta^2 p = .03$. Means and standard deviations are displayed in Table 2.

Table 2. Means and standard deviations for pain tolerance, PSQ score, as well as Pain tolerance at the covariate mean level of PSQ

Measure	Violent condition		Non-violent condition	
	M	SD	M	SD
Pain tolerance	90.40	65.85	96.41	71.49
Pain tolerance at PSQ = 3.88	91.98	12.49	94.65	13.17
PSQ score	3.94	1.65	3.59	1.40

2.3 Discussion

As expected, there was a significant effect of VVG play on mood, decreasing positive affect and increasing negative affect. However, VVG play did not significantly affect pain tolerance in the CPT, proximal pain perception, or aggressive behavior. Can the absence of a desensitization effect be replicated, or was it just due to the use of inappropriate methods?

3 Study 2

Study 2 included different measures for pain and aggressive behavior. Pain tolerance and perception were assessed with the Medoc Pathway Pain and Sensory Evaluation System (see below). Heart rate variability (HRV) indicated the activity of the autonomic nervous system, with higher HRV relating to greater pain inhibition capacity [31]. The Competitive Reaction Time Task (CRTT) measured aggressive behavior.

3.1 Methods

Participants. A total of 64 participants ($M_{age} = 27.57$; $SD = 11.57$) took part in study 2 (50% females) at the University of Luxembourg. As in study 1, participants indicated how much they played video games ($M = 2.22$; $SD = 1.23$). They also rated their gaming experience (1 = not experienced, 2 = somewhat inexperienced, 3 = somewhat experienced, 4 = experienced). On average, participants were experienced on a medium level ($M = 2.38$; $SD = 1.11$). Again, participants rated the five items for violent video game preference ($\alpha = .91$).

Pain Tolerance and Proximal Pain Perception. To assess pain tolerance, pain stimuli were applied via a heat thermode. There were 9 trials, each lasting five seconds with an increase of 1 °C per trial. The first heat stimulus was set at 42 °C and the maximum heat stimulus was set at 50 °C. Between trials, the thermode immediately cooled to 32 °C. For each trial, participants rated their perceived pain on a 10-point numerical rating scale (0 = no pain and 10 = worst possible pain) [24]. If a participant rated a pain stimulus as 10, the task was immediately discontinued. Individual pain tolerance was the sum of the trials the participants had completed until they gave a maximum pain rating (10) or until all 9 trials were completed.

Competitive Reaction Time Task. The CRTT is a flexible and powerful tool to assess the effect of aggression-eliciting stimuli [32]. For the task, participants were told that they would play a game against a pretend opponent who, unbeknownst to the participants, did not actually exist. In each of the nine rounds of the task, participants were told to press a key as quickly as possible when the green box on the monitor turned red. If the opponent was faster, the participants were exposed to a noise blast between 50 and 105 decibels through headphones. Prior to each round, participants indicated the amplitude and duration of the noise blast for their opponent if the opponent lost the round (aggressive behavior). The number of wins and defeats was determined in advance without the participants knowing. In the first round, the participants always lost.

Heart Rate Variability. HRV was measured with two electrocardiography electrodes using a heart rate belt connected via Bluetooth to an iPad. One electrode was placed under the upper right clavicle and the other electrode was placed above the hip on the left side of the body. Data was collected with the app HRV Logger and transferred to Artiifact [33] for further analyses. Here, the root mean square of successive differences (RMSSD) for the time domain and the absolute power of the high frequency-band (HF; 0.15–0.40 Hz) for the frequency domain were used [34]. RMSSD reflects beat-to-beat HRV and is robust against influential factors like respiration and is correlated to HF. RMSSD and HF are reliable measures for parasympathetic activity [34], which typically indicates the bodily functions when a person is at rest. Baseline HRV was assessed during the five minutes it took participants to answer questionnaire items, during gameplay, and during the pain perception task.

Target Games. Participants played the same games as in study 1 for 15 min.

Mood, Trait Aggression, Empathy, Pain Sensitivity. Violent Video Game Preference. Study 2 used the same measures as in study 1. Mood was again assessed at two time points with the PANAS scales [25]. The internal consistency before gameplay was good for positive affect ($\alpha = .85$) and acceptable for negative affect ($\alpha = .67$). For the post-measurement, the internal consistency was excellent both for positive affect ($\alpha = .91$) and negative affect ($\alpha = .91$). The German version of the Aggression Questionnaire [27] measured trait-aggression which showed very good internal consistency ($\alpha = .85$). The combined scale for trait empathy that included the three subscales for emotional concern, fantasy, and perspective taking from the German version of the IRI [30] had good internal consistency ($\alpha = .82$). With regard to participants' inherent pain sensitivity, the PSQ-scale [28] showed an acceptable internal consistency ($\alpha = .67$). Finally, the violent video game preference scale had excellent internal consistency ($\alpha = .91$).

Manipulation Check. Game perception was measured with four novel items (e.g., "How brutal would you rate the game you just played?"; $\alpha = .87$). Another item tested if game mechanics or the effects of the controls of the game influenced participants (i.e., "How difficult was it for you to control the game?"). Items were rated on a 4-point scale (1 = not at all to 4 = very much).

Procedure. After participants gave informed consent, they provided demographic information and rated the items of the questionnaire. In the meantime, baseline HRV was assessed. Then, participants were randomly assigned to one of the two conditions (violent condition vs. non-violent condition) and played for 15 min. During gameplay, the second HRV measurement was recorded. After gameplay, participants first rated the PANAS items again and filled in the control items for game perception. Then, the task for pain perception and tolerance was applied together with the third HRV measurement. Next, participants completed the CRTT task. Finally, they were remunerated, thanked for their participation, and debriefed. The entire study took about 45 min.

3.2 Results

Control Variables. There were no significant group differences for trait aggression, empathy, pain sensitivity, or for the effect of game controls $ps \geq .102$. In contrast, there was a significant difference between the two conditions on game perception, Welch's $F(1, 32.36) = 240.64$, $p < .001$, $\eta^2 = .80$. As expected, participants rated the VVG as significantly more brutal, more morally questionable, felt more guilt, and felt that they dealt out more pain in the game ($M = 2.85$; $SD = 0.66$) than the non-violent game ($M = 1.02$; $SD = 0.10$).

In the CRTT, males ($M = 5.75$, $SD = 1.92$) behaved significantly more aggressively than females ($M = 3.71$, $SD = 2.45$), $F(1, 62) = 13.71$, $p < .001$, $\eta^2 = .18$. There was also a gender effect for duration in the CRTT, with males ($M = 5.05$; $SD = 2.19$) choosing longer durations of noise blasts than females ($M = 3.36$, $SD = 2.18$), $F(1, 62) = 9.59$, $p = .003$, $\eta^2 = .13$. However, no other gender effect was significant, $ps \geq .115$.

Aggressive behavior (CRTT intensity) was correlated with gaming experience, $r = .35$, $p = .005$, trait aggression, $r = .29$, $p = .021$, and pain perception, $r = -.25$, $p = .043$. Interestingly, trait empathy was positively related to gaming experience, $r = .35$, $p = .005$.

Violent video game preference was positively correlated with intensity ($r = .43$, $p < .001$) and duration ($r = .49$, $p < .001$) in the CRTT only, but not to proximal pain perception, mood, HRV, or pain tolerance ($ps \geq .124$).

Hypotheses. To test H3, two one-way ANOVAs were calculated with game condition as independent variable, and pain perception (i.e., mean of pain ratings) and pain tolerance (i.e., sum of pain induction trials) as dependent variables, respectively. Game conditions did not differ for pain perception or pain tolerance, $ps \geq .520$. Means and standard deviations are shown in Table 2.

To test H4, a one-way ANOVA was calculated with condition as independent variable, intensity in the CRTT, and duration in the CRTT as dependent variables. There was no significant difference between conditions for CRTT intensity or CRTT duration, $ps \geq .620$ (Table 3).[2]

Table 3. Means and standard deviations in the two game conditions for CRTT intensity, CRTT duration, pain perception, and pain tolerance in study 2.

Measure	Violent condition		Non-violent condition		Group Differences		
	M	SD	M	SD	Test	p	η^2
CRTT Intensity	4.88	2.72	4.58	2.10	$F = 0.25$	.621	< .01
CRTT Duration	4.34	2.57	4.07	2.09	$F = 0.22$	.641	< .01
Pain Perception	5.28	1.82	5.00	1.58	$F = 0.42$	.518	.01
Pain Tolerance	8.22	1.69	8.44	0.91	$F = 0.42$	.520	.01

---

[2] As noted by a reviewer, as there were significant gender differences in the CRTT gender should be included as a covariate. Therefore, additional ANCOVAs were computed with gender as a covariate. Again, there were no significant effects of VVG exposure on aggressive behavior in the CRTT ($p \geq .771$).

To test H5, a mixed ANOVA was calculated with condition as between-subjects variable, and RMSSD and HF as within-subjects variables. There was no significant between-subjects effect, $F(1, 39) = 2.89$, $p = .097$, $\eta^2 p = .07$, but a significant within-subjects effect for RMSSD, $F(1.72, 66.99) = 8.92$, $p = .001$, $\eta^2 p = .19$. Mauchly's test of sphericity was significant (Mauchly's $W = .84$, $p = .033$) and therefore the Greenhouse-Geisser correction ($\varepsilon = .86$) was applied. Within-subjects contrasts confirmed a significant decrease in RMSSD from baseline ($M = 44.18$; $SD = 26.41$) to RMSSD during gameplay ($M = 34.31$; $SD = 19.94$), $F(1, 39) = 7.82$, $p = .008$, $\eta^2 p = .17$, and from gameplay to pain perception ($M = 45.57$; $SD = 21.81$), $F(1, 39) = 20.31$, $p < .001$, $\eta^2 p = .34$. More importantly, there was a significant interaction effect between condition and RMSSD change from gameplay to pain perception task. Only participants who played the VVG had a significant increase in RMSSD from gameplay to pain perception task, $F(1, 39) = 5.24$, $p = .028$, $\eta^2 p = .12$ (see Fig. 2). For HF, there was also a significant within-subjects effect for HF, $F(2, 78) = 7.15$, $p = .001$, $\eta^2 p = .16$. During gameplay ($M = 0.04$, $SD = 0.02$), there was a significant decrease in HF compared to baseline ($M = 0.04$, $SD = 0.03$), $F(1, 39) = 4.45$, $p = .041$, $\eta^2 p = .10$, whereas HF significantly increased from gameplay to the pain perception task ($M = 0.05$; $SD = 0.03$), $F(1, 39) = 15.62$, $p < .001$, $\eta^2 p = .29$ (see Fig. 3). There was no significant interaction effect, $F(2, 78) = 1.36$, $p = .262$, $\eta^2 p = .03$ or between-subjects effect, $F(1, 39) = 2.25$, $p = .142$, $\eta^2 p = .06$.

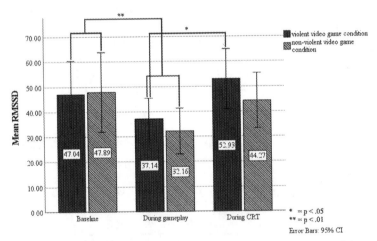

Fig. 2. Mean RMSSD in the VVG condition and the non-violent video game condition at baseline (T1), during gameplay (T2) and during CRTT (T3) in study 2.

Finally, two mixed-measures ANOVA tested H6. Condition served as between-subjects factor, and positive affect (PA score at T1 vs. PA score at T2) and negative affect (NA score at T1 vs. NA score at T2) were the within-subject factors, respectively. For positive affect, only the interaction between condition and PA score was significant, $F(1, 62) = 4.17$, $p = .045$, $\eta^2 p = .06$, but separate analyses did not reveal any significant effects, $ps \geq .130$. For negative affect, there was a significant within-subjects effect, $F(1, 62) = 5.50$, $p = .022$, $\eta^2 p = .08$, indicating a significant increase in negative affect from

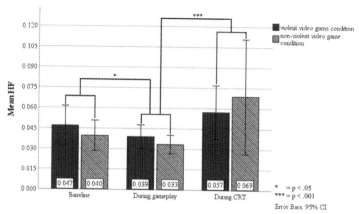

Fig. 3. Mean HF in the VVG condition and the non-violent video game condition at baseline (T1), during gameplay (T2) and during CRTT (T3) in study 2.

T1 ($M = 1.32$; $SD = 0.33$) to T2 ($M = 1.48$; $SD = .63$), and a significant between-subjects effect, $F(1, 62) = 14.33$, $p < .001$, $\eta^2p = .19$. More importantly, the interaction effect between condition and the within-subjects factor of NA score was significant, $F(1, 62) = 10.58$, $p = .002$, $\eta^2p = .15$. Separate analysis showed that participants who played the violent game showed a significant increase in negative affect from T1 ($M = 1.32$; $SD = 0.33$) to T2 ($M = 1.76$; $SD = 0.78.$), $F(1, 31) = 8.65$, $p = .006$, $\eta^2p = .22$, see Fig. 4. In the non-violent game condition, there was no significant within-subjects effect for NA score from T1 ($M = 1.27$; $SD = .27$) to T2 ($M = 1.20$; $SD = 0.20$), $F(1, 31) = 2.19$, $p = .149$, $\eta^2p = .07$.

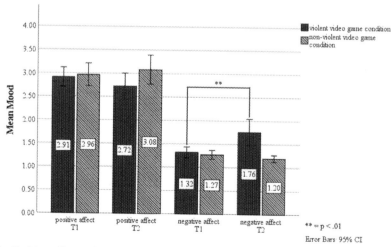

Fig. 4. Positive affect and negative affect in the VVG condition and the non-violent video game condition at the beginning of the experiment (T1) and after gameplay (T2) in study 2.

3.3 Discussion

Study 2 confirmed the results of study 1, using different outcome measures. There were no significant effects of VVG play on aggressive behavior, pain perception, or on pain tolerance. Again, VVP play lead to increased negative effect. In study 2, however, VVG play had no influence on positive affect. Since the level of immersion in the game mediates the effects of VVG [35], study 3 was conducted to replicate the results of the first two studies and test the level of immersion as an additional factor.

4 Study 3

The level of immersion in the game mediates the effects of VVG [35] and influences pain sensitivity [21]. Therefore, participants played either a violent-immersive, a non-violent-immersive or a non-violent-non-immersive video game in study 3.

4.1 Methods

Participants. Study 3 involved 75 participants ($M_{age} = 27$; $SD = 10.06$; 42% females). Participants indicated to play VG on a medium level ($M = 2.22$; $SD = 1.23$).

Pain Perception. To measure distal pain perception, participants rated the level of pain they perceived in pictures. The pictures were pilot tested with $N = 50$ student participants. Each of the 15 neutral pictures and 17 pain-related pictures of the IAPS (International Affective Picture System; [36]) were rated on a numerical pain rating scale from 0 (=no pain) to 10 (=worst possible pain) [24]. From these pictures, 10 neutral ($\alpha = .76$) and 10 pain-related pictures ($\alpha = .92$) with the highest reliabilities were chosen. A dependent sample t-test showed that the pain-related pictures were rated as significantly more painful ($M = 7.11$, $SD = 1.89$) than the neutral pictures ($M = 0.30$, $SD = 0.52$), $t(49) = 26.01, p < .001, d = 4.91$. In study 3, participants rated these 20 items in randomized order on the same numerical pain rating scale used in the pilot study. Proximal pain perception was again measured with the CPT (see study 1).

Heart Rate Variability. Again, there were three heart rate measurement times during the study. Data from T1 served as a baseline, data from T2 were collected during game-play, and data from T3 were recorded during the CPT. Due to technical difficulties, T1 data for four participants could not be used.

Mood, Trait Aggression, Pain Sensitivity. Study 3 used the same measures as studies 1 and 2. Mood was again assessed at two timepoints with the PANAS [25]. In study 3, the internal consistency at t1 was very good for positive affect ($\alpha = .86$) and acceptable for negative affect ($\alpha = .63$). For t2, the internal consistency ranged from very good to excellent for the positive ($\alpha = .92$) and negative affect ($\alpha = .87$). The two subscales for anger and hostility from the German version of the Aggression Questionnaire [34] were combined to general trait aggression, which showed very good internal consistency ($\alpha = .85$). The PSQ was again used to measure participants' inherent pain sensi-tivity [35] and had acceptable internal consistency ($\alpha = .69$).

Target Games. In the violent condition, *Sniper Elite III* for the PlayStation4 was used due to its high violence ratings (age rating label "PEGI 18") and high level of immersion. In *Sniper Elite III*, the player shoots down enemy WW2 soldiers as a sniper. The game contains explicit graphical representations of extreme violence and blood. In the non-violent immersive condition, the racing game *Mario Kart 8* was played on the Wii U console. In the non-violent non-immersive condition, *Yoshi's Fruit Cart* for the Wii U was chosen as it is neither violent nor immersive. The game required participants to draw line paths with the Stylus so that the game character Yoshi can collect points (i.e., fruits). All the three games had simple controls that were easy to explain to participants.

Empathy. Trait empathy was measured using the two subscales for emotional concern and perspective taking from the German version of the IRI [30]. The combined scale had good internal consistency ($\alpha = .73$). In addition to the IRI, media-based empathy (MBE; [37]) was used to measure the ability of participants to feel empathy for fictitious characters (4 items; e.g., "Media reports about what is happening in the world are very close to me."), as well as their ability to immerse themselves in VG (5 items; e.g., "I experience very strong feelings when I play good video games."). The items were rated on a five-point Likert scale ($1 = I$ strongly disagree to $5 = I$ strongly agree; $\alpha = .83$).

Manipulation Check. Game perception was measured with five items on competition, frustration, time pressure, brutality, and immersion. The items (e.g., "how brutal would you rate the game you just played?") were rated on a 5-point scale ($1 = $ not at all to $5 = $ very much). The scale showed good internal consistency ($\alpha = .74$).

Procedure. After participants gave informed consent, the electrodes for HRV assessment were applied. Then, questions on demographics, trait empathy, trait pain sensitivity were answered, and the PANAS items rated. Next, participants were randomly assigned to one of the three game conditions. After familiarizing themselves with the game controls, they played for 15 min. Then, participants rated the PANAS items again and the items for trait aggression. Next, the CPT was administered. Then, the pictorial stimuli were shown to assess distal pain perception. Finally, participants were remunerated, thanked and debriefed. The experiment took about 45 min.

4.2 Results

Control Variables. There were no significant differences between conditions for trait empathy, trait aggression, media-based empathy, or pain sensitivity, $ps \geq .37$. Also, there were no differences between the genders, $ps \geq .40$.

Hypotheses. The between-subjects ANOVA that tested the differences between the three game conditions for proximal pain perception (H1) showed no significant effect, $F(2, 72) = 0.25, p = .783, \eta^2 p = .01$. Neither the ANOVA on distal pain perception (H2) nor the comparison of conditions in terms of pain tolerance (H3) revealed significant effects, $p \geq .433$. Means and standard deviations are displayed in Table 4.

Table 4. Means and standard deviations in the different game conditions for proximal pain perception, distal pain perception, and pain tolerance in study 3.

Measure	Violent condition		Non-violent-immersive condition		Non-violent-non-immersive condition	
	M	*SD*	*M*	*SD*	*M*	*SD*
Proximal Pain Perception	6.48	1.12	6.30	2.21	6.63	1.42
Distal Pain Perception	7.87	1.74	8.10	0.99	7.81	1.24
Pain Tolerance	91.80	58.22	100.60	62.62	78.20	63.13

Next, two repeated-measures ANOVAs tested if VVG exposure influenced mood (H6). Condition served as between-subjects factor, whereas positive affect (PA score at T1 vs. PA score at T2) and negative affect (NA score at T1 vs. NA score at T2) were the within-subject factors, respectively. No significant effects were found, $p \geq .085$. However, separate analyses showed that there was a significant decrease in positive mood for participants who played the violent game, $F(1, 23) = 8.87$, $p = .007$, $\eta^2 p = .28$, see Fig. 5. There was no significant difference in mood after playing the non-violent-immersive or the non-violent-non-immersive video game, $Fs \leq .33$, $ps \geq .592$, $\eta^2 p \leq .01$. For negative affect, there was only a significant interaction effect, $F(2, 71) = 6.79$, $p = .002$, $\eta^2 p = .16$. Separate analysis showed a significant increase in negative affect for participants who had played the violent game, $F(1, 23) = 12.51$, $p = .002$, $\eta^2 p = .35$, which was not the case in the other conditions, $Fs \leq 1.39$, $p \geq .249$, $\eta^2 p \leq .06$. Means and standard deviations are displayed in Table 5.

Two additional ANCOVAs with pain sensitivity (PSQ score) as covariate were calculated. There were no significant effects on pain tolerance (time in the CPT) or proximal pain perception, $p \geq .15$. Pain sensitivity did not predict pain tolerance, $F(26, 26.70)$, $p = .970$, $\eta^2 p = .49$, but proximal pain perception, $F(26, 29.97) = 2.58$, $p = .007$, $\eta^2 p = .691$.

To test H5, a mixed ANOVA was calculated with RMSSD and with HF as within-subjects factors and condition as between-subjects factor. For RMSSD, Mauchly's test of sphericity was significant ($p < .001$) and so the Greenhouse-Geisser correction was applied ($\varepsilon = .83$). The analysis revealed a significant within-subjects effect for RMSSD, $F(1.66, 119.49) = 5.19$, $p = .011$, $\eta^2 p = .07$, with a significant increase in RMSSD from gameplay ($M = 39.17$; $SD = 20.78$) to when participants did the CPT ($M = 43.70$; $SD = 22.83$), $F(1, 72) = 5.66$, $p = .020$, $\eta^2 p = .07$. However, there was no significant between-subjects effect or interaction effect, $p \geq .430$ (see Fig. 6). For HF, Mauchly's test of sphericity was significant ($p < .001$) and so the Greenhouse-Geisser correction was applied ($\varepsilon = .77$). The analysis revealed no significant effects $p \geq .083$.

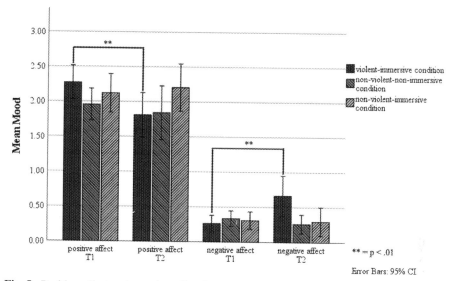

Fig. 5. Positive affect and negative affect in the three game conditions at the beginning of the experiment (T1) and after gameplay (T2) in study 3.

Table 5. Means and standard deviations for positive and negative affect at T1 and T2 across the three conditions in study 3.

Measure	Violent condition		Non-violent-immersive condition		Non-violent-non-immersive condition	
	M	*SD*	*M*	*SD*	*M*	*SD*
Positive affect T1	2.27	0.58	2.12	0.67	1.96	0.55
Positive affect T2	1.81	0.75	2.20	0.82	1.84	0.93
Negative affect T1	0.26	0.28	0.31	0.28	0.34	0.27
Negative affect T2	0.66	0.68	0.30	0.50	0.26	0.33

4.3   Discussion

Again, VVG play significantly affected mood, leading to decreased positive affect and increased negative affect. However, like study 1 and 2, there were no significant effects of VVG play on pain-related indicators. In addition, level of immersion had no effect on the results for the outcome variables.

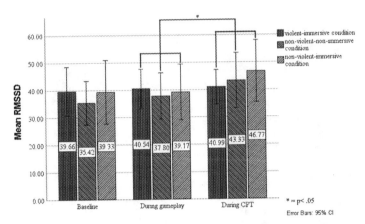

Fig. 6. Mean RMSSD at baseline, during gameplay, and during the CPT across the three conditions in study 3.

5   General Discussion

Does playing VVG increase aggression while numbing and desensitizing pain? Three lab experiments tested the effects of VVG on pain-related indicators and aggressive behavior. The empirical results of the present studies are clear: there were no significant effects of direct VVG exposure on behavioral data of aggressive behavior, pain tolerance, or pain perception. In contrast, the VVG preference of participants was associated with higher pain tolerance and lower proximal pain perception in study 1, and VVG preference was associated with higher trait aggression and higher aggressive behavior in study 2. We may speculate that people with higher trait aggression and those who behave more aggressively are drawn more toward VVG and in-game depictions of violence. Notwithstanding this, at least the present findings suggest that VVG exposure itself does not lead to an increase in aggressive behavior or to desensitization.

All three studies confirmed the negative effect that VVG play has on mood. Compared to a nonviolent VG participants in the VVG condition felt significantly worse after playing—their positive affect decreased, while negative affect increased. This finding is in line with prior research that showed VVG effects on mood [15, 38].

Pain is a complex and multidimensional construct, modulated by individual, physiological, and contextual factors [2]. Based on the findings from the present studies, it appears that physiological factors as well as personality traits dominate pain responses. Perhaps the gaming episode in the present studies was too weak as contextual factor to show any effect on pain perception or pain tolerance. In contrast, individual factors affected pain tolerance, pain perception, and aggressive behavior. Significant gender differences were found on aggressive behavior in study 1, with males being more aggressive than females. Personality traits (i.e., trait aggression, trait pain sensitivity, and violent video game preference) were related to pain tolerance, pain perception, and positive affect (study 1), and to aggressive behavior (study 2). Although some authors assume that situational factors influence aggression more than personality factors [39], this was not the case in the present studies. Similar to the presented results, other studies also show that personality factors rather than game violence are associated with aggression [40]. Markey and Markey concluded that personality factors and personal predispositions moderate negative VVG effects, thus making some individuals more vulnerable to VVG effects than others [41]. In addition, personality factors are related to both VVG preferences and VVG exposure [42, 43] and can moderate physiological reactions to VVG exposure [44]. Thus, when confronted with VG violence, individuals without these predispositions should not show an increase in aggression or desensitization.

In study 2, HRV (RMSSD and HF) significantly decreased from baseline to gameplay and increased again to during the CRTT across both conditions. In study 3, HRV (RMSSD) significantly increased from gameplay to the CPT for participants across all gaming conditions. This shows that participants experienced decreased parasympathetic activity during gameplay, but higher parasympathetic activity after gameplay, possibly representing greater tension during and a reduction in tension after gameplay. This is in line with previous research showing an increase in parasympathetic activity after VVG play [45]. However, there were no significant differences between participants playing a violent or a non-violent game. Furthermore, research has shown that parasympathetic activity is decreased during the experience of pain [31]. This was also not the case in the present study as RMSSD increased during the CPT for participants in study 3. It is unclear why playing a VG decreased parasympathetic activity in study 2, and if HRV increased during the CRTT due to the prior gaming effects or due to the nature of the CRTT or other variables. Future studies should incorporate explicit measures that in addition to objective physiological measures to disentangle these findings, assess the perceived physiological states of participants.

Playing a VG can indeed lead to a decrease in pain perception [21, 22, 46, 47]. It is possible that the assumed distractive, hypoalgesic effects of playing VG is independent of violent content. In the presented studies, however, there was no control condition in which participants did not play a VG. Therefore, it cannot be ruled out that playing VG generally leads to desensitization to pain. Based on the present findings, we can only conclude that the content of the game, violent or not, has no pain-related effects.

Regarding limitations, the large variability in the present student-dominated samples with only a few VG enthusiasts may have contributed to the lack of pain-related effects detected. Sample sizes with few "hardcore gamers" might not be sufficient to detect small effects that would be expected for the desensitization effects of VVG [10].

Another limitation of the present studies lies in their design. The games used in the present studies varied greatly regarding content, game design, graphical appearance, and game controls. Future studies should limit these potentially influential factors by using more comparable target games, or ideally, by using passages (nonviolent vs. violent) from the same game. Moreover, although some authors have argued that even short-term exposure to VVG can lead to desensitization [17], playing a violent game for only 15 min might be too short to influence later aggression, pain perception, or pain tolerance measures. Future studies should therefore increase playing time to increase the generalizability and reliability of findings.

In summary, the present results are consistent with findings that exposure to VG violence does not have a desensitization effect on aggression [48, 49], pain perception

[50, 51], or empathic response [52]. However, the effects of violent games may be moderated by specific personality factors not tested here that make people more susceptible to the effects, increasing the likelihood of desensitization, aggression and pain tolerance, while at the same time decreasing pain perception and empathic concern. Future studies should therefore take a closer look into the moderating role of personality factors on the effects of (violent) video games on the players.

References

1. Calvert, S.L., et al.: The American psychological association task force assessment of violent video games: science in the service of public interest. Am. Psychol. **72**, 126–143 (2017). https://doi.org/10.1037/a0040413
2. Melzack, R.: Evolution of the neuromatrix theory of pain. In: The Prithvi Raj Lecture: Presented at the Third World Congress of World Institute of Pain, Barcelona 2004. Pain Practice. 5, pp. 85–94 (2005). https://doi.org/10.1111/j.1533-2500.2005.05203.x
3. Bushman, B.J., Huesmann, L.R.: Twenty-five years of research on violence in digital games and aggression revisited: a reply to. Eur. Psychol. **19**, 47–55 (2014). https://doi.org/10.1027/1016-9040/a000164
4. Bushman, B.J., Gollwitzer, M., Cruz, C.: There is broad consensus: media researchers agree that violent media increase aggression in children, and pediatricians and parents concur. Psychol. Pop. Media Cult. **4**, 200–214 (2015). https://doi.org/10.1037/ppm0000046
5. Ferguson, C.J.: Pay no attention to that data behind the curtain: on angry birds, happy children, scholarly squabbles, publication bias, and why betas rule metas. Perspect Psychol Sci. **10**, 683–691 (2015). https://doi.org/10.1177/1745691615593353
6. Ferguson, C.J.: Aggressive video games research emerges from its replication crisis (Sort of). Current Opinion in Psychology **36**, 16 (2020)
7. Ferguson, C.J., Colwell, J.: Understanding why scholars hold different views on the influences of video games on public health: opinions on video game influences on public health. J Commun. **67**, 305–327 (2017). https://doi.org/10.1111/jcom.12293
8. Scharrer, E., Kamau, G., Warren, S., Zhang, C.: Violent video games DO promote aggression. 28
9. Allen, J.J., Anderson, C.A., Bushman, B.J.: The general aggression model. Curr. Opin. Psychol. **19**, 75–80 (2018). https://doi.org/10.1016/j.copsyc.2017.03.034
10. Anderson, C.A., et al.: Violent video game effects on aggression, empathy, and prosocial behavior in Eastern and Western countries: a meta-analytic review. Psychol. Bull. **136**, 151–173 (2010). https://doi.org/10.1037/a0018251
11. Bartholow, B.D., Bushman, B.J., Sestir, M.A.: Chronic violent video game exposure and desensitization to violence: behavioral and event-related brain potential data. J. Exp. Soc. Psychol. **42**, 532–539 (2006). https://doi.org/10.1016/j.jesp.2005.08.006
12. Engelhardt, C.R., Bartholow, B.D., Kerr, G.T., Bushman, B.J.: This is your brain on violent video games: neural desensitization to violence predicts increased aggression following violent video game exposure. J. Exp. Soc. Psychol. **47**, 1033–1036 (2011). https://doi.org/10.1016/j.jesp.2011.03.027
13. Gentile, D.A., Swing, E.L., Anderson, C.A., Rinker, D., Thomas, K.M.: Differential neural recruitment during violent video game play in violent- and nonviolent-game players. Psychol. Pop. Media Cult. **5**, 39–51 (2016). https://doi.org/10.1037/ppm0000009
14. Hartmann, T., Vorderer, P.: It's okay to shoot a character: moral disengagement in violent video games. J. Commun. **60**, 94–119 (2010). https://doi.org/10.1111/j.1460-2466.2009.01459.x

15. Lee, E.-H., et al.: The effects of video games on aggression, sociality, and affect: a meta-analytic study. KOSES. **23**(4), 41–60 (2020). https://doi.org/10.14695/KJSOS.2020.23.4.41

16. Mathiak, K.A., Klasen, M., Weber, R., Ackermann, H., Shergill, S.S., Mathiak, K.: Reward system and temporal pole contributions to affective evaluation during a first person shooter video game. BMC Neurosci. **12**, 66 (2011). https://doi.org/10.1186/1471-2202-12-66

17. Bushman, B.J., Anderson, C.A.: Comfortably numb: desensitizing effects of violent media on helping others. Psychol Sci. **20**, 273–277 (2009). https://doi.org/10.1111/j.1467-9280.2009.02287.x

18. Funk, J.B., Baldacci, H.B., Pasold, T., Baumgardner, J.: Violence exposure in real-life, video games, television, movies, and the internet: is there desensitization? J. Adolesc. **27**, 23–39 (2004). https://doi.org/10.1016/j.adolescence.2003.10.005

19. Brockmyer, J.F.: Desensitization and violent video games. Child Adolesc. Psychiatr. Clin. N. Am. **31**, 121–132 (2022). https://doi.org/10.1016/j.chc.2021.06.005

20. Primack, B.A., et al.: Role of video games in improving health-related outcomes. Am. J. Prev. Med. **42**, 630–638 (2012). https://doi.org/10.1016/j.amepre.2012.02.023

21. Weger, U.W., Loughnan, S.: Virtually numbed: Immersive video gaming alters real-life experience. Psychon. Bull. Rev. **21**(2), 562–565 (2013). https://doi.org/10.3758/s13423-013-0512-2

22. Stephens, R., Allsop, C.: Effect of manipulated state aggression on pain tolerance. Psychol Rep. **111**, 311–321 (2012). https://doi.org/10.2466/16.02.20.PR0.111.4.311-321

23. Miedzobrodzka, E., van Hooff, J.C., Konijn, E.A., Krabbendam, L.: Is it painful? playing violent video games affects brain responses to painful pictures: an event-related potential study. Psychology of Popular Media. **11**, 13–23 (2022). https://doi.org/10.1037/ppm0000290

24. Karcioglu, O., Topacoglu, H., Dikme, O., Dikme, O.: A systematic review of the pain scales in adults: which to use? Am. J. Emerg. Med. **36**, 707–714 (2018). https://doi.org/10.1016/j.ajem.2018.01.008

25. Watson, D., Anna, L., Tellegen, A.: Development and Validation of Brief Measures of Positive and Negative Affect: The PANAS Scales. 8

26. Buss, A.H., Perry, M.: The Aggression Questionnaire. 8

27. Herzberg, P.Y.: Faktorstruktur, Gütekriterien und Konstruktvalidität der deutschen Übersetzung des Aggressionsfragebogens von Buss und Perry. Zeitschrift für Differentielle und Diagnostische Psychologie. **24**, 311–323 (2003). https://doi.org/10.1024/0170-1789.24.4.311

28. Ruscheweyh, R., Marziniak, M., Stumpenhorst, F., Reinholz, J., Knecht, S.: Pain sensitivity can be assessed by self-rating: Development and validation of the Pain Sensitivity Questionnaire. Pain **146**(1-2), 6574 (2009)

29. Davis, M.H.: Measuring individual differences in empathy: evidence for a multidimensional approach. J. Pers. Soc. Psychol. **44**, 113–126 (1983). https://doi.org/10.1037/0022-3514.44.1.113

30. Paulus: (2009)

31. Forte, G., Troisi, G., Pazzaglia, M., Pascalis, V.D., Casagrande, M.: Heart rate variability and pain: a systematic review. Brain Sci. **12**, 153 (2022). https://doi.org/10.3390/brainsci12020153

32. Warburton, W.A., Bushman, B.J.: The competitive reaction time task: the development and scientific utility of a flexible laboratory aggression paradigm. Aggr Behav. **45**, 389–396 (2019). https://doi.org/10.1002/ab.21829

33. Kaufmann, T., Sütterlin, S., Schulz, S.M., Vögele, C.: ARTiiFACT: a tool for heart rate artifact processing and heart rate variability analysis. Behav Res. **43**, 1161–1170 (2011). https://doi.org/10.3758/s13428-011-0107-7

34. Shaffer, F., Ginsberg, J.P.: An overview of heart rate variability metrics and norms. Front. Public Health. **5**, 258 (2017). https://doi.org/10.3389/fpubh.2017.00258

35. Lull, R.B., Bushman, B.J.: Immersed in violence: presence mediates the effect of 3D violent video gameplay on angry feelings. Psychol. Pop. Media Cult. **5**, 133–144 (2016). https://doi.org/10.1037/ppm0000062
36. Lang, P.J., Bradley, M.M., Cuthbert, B.N.: International affective picture system (IAPS): affective ratings of pictures and instruction manual. Technical report A-8. University of Florida, Gainesville, FL (2008)
37. Happ, C., Pfetsch, J.: Medienbasierte Empathie (MBE): Entwicklung eines Instruments zur Erfassung empathischer Reaktionen bei Mediennutzung. Diagnostica **62**, 110–125 (2016). https://doi.org/10.1026/0012-1924/a000152
38. Saleem, M., Anderson, C.A., Gentile, D.A.: Effects of prosocial, neutral, and violent video games on college students' affect: violent video games and students' affect. Aggr Behav. **38**, 263–271 (2012). https://doi.org/10.1002/ab.21427
39. Hasan, Y., Eldous, H.: The role of personality traits and situational factors as determinants of aggression. TOPSYJ. **13**, 282–288 (2020). https://doi.org/10.2174/1874350102013010282
40. Winkel, M., Novak, D.M., Hopson, H.: Personality factors, subject gender, and the effects of aggressive video games on aggression in adolescents. J. Res. Pers. **21**, 211–223 (1987). https://doi.org/10.1016/0092-6566(87)90008-0
41. Markey, P.M., Markey, C.N.: Vulnerability to violent video games: a review and integration of personality research. Rev. Gen. Psychol. **14**, 82–91 (2010). https://doi.org/10.1037/a0019000
42. Greitemeyer, T.: Everyday sadism predicts violent video game preferences. Personality Individ. Differ. **75**, 19–23 (2015). https://doi.org/10.1016/j.paid.2014.10.049
43. Greitemeyer, T., Sagioglou, C.: The longitudinal relationship between everyday sadism and the amount of violent video game play. Personality Individ. Differ. **104**, 238–242 (2017). https://doi.org/10.1016/j.paid.2016.08.021
44. Wagener, G.L.: Presented at the (2020)
45. Ivarsson, M., Anderson, M., Åkerstedt, T., Lindblad, F.: Playing a violent television game affects heart rate variability. Acta Paediatr. **98**, 166–172 (2009). https://doi.org/10.1111/j.1651-2227.2008.01096.x
46. Barcatta, K., Holl, E., Battistutta, L., van der Meulen, M., Rischer, K.M.: When less is more: investigating factors influencing the distraction effect of virtual reality from pain. Front. Pain Res. **2**, 800258 (2022). https://doi.org/10.3389/fpain.2021.800258
47. Gupta, A., Scott, K., Dukewich, M.: Innovative technology using virtual reality in the treatment of pain: does it reduce pain via distraction, or is there more to it? Pain Med. **19**, 151–159 (2018). https://doi.org/10.1093/pm/pnx109
48. Goodson, S., Turner, K.J., Pearson, S.L., Carter, P.: Violent video games and the P300: no evidence to support the neural desensitization hypothesis. Cyberpsychol. Behav. Soc. Netw. **24**, 48–55 (2021). https://doi.org/10.1089/cyber.2020.0029
49. Read, G.L., Ballard, M., Emery, L.J., Bazzini, D.G.: Examining desensitization using facial electromyography: violent videogames, gender, and affective responding. Comput. Hum. Behav. **62**, 201–211 (2016). https://doi.org/10.1016/j.chb.2016.03.074
50. Gao, X., Pan, W., Li, C., Weng, L., Yao, M., Chen, A.: Long-time exposure to violent video games does not show desensitization on empathy for pain: an fmri study. Front. Psychol. **8**, 650 (2017). https://doi.org/10.3389/fpsyg.2017.00650
51. Kühn, S., Kugler, D., Schmalen, K., Weichenberger, M., Witt, C., Gallinat, J.: The myth of blunted gamers: no evidence for desensitization in empathy for pain after a violent video game intervention in a longitudinal fMRI study on non-gamers. Neurosignals **26**, 22–30 (2018). https://doi.org/10.1159/000487217
52. Szycik, G.R., Mohammadi, B., Münte, T.F., te Wildt, B.T.: Lack of Evidence That neural empathic responses are blunted in excessive users of violent video games: an fMRI study. Front. Psychol. **8**, 174 (2017). https://doi.org/10.3389/fpsyg.2017.00174

Discovering the Motivational Constitution of 'Playing Games for Fun'

Kai Tuuri[1]([✉])([ID]) and Jukka Vahlo[1,2]([ID])

[1] Department of Music, Art and Culture Studies, University of Jyväskylä,
P.O. Box 35, 40014 Jyväskylä, Finland
krtuuri@jyu.fi
[2] School of Economics, Centre for Collaborative Research, University of Turku,
20014 Turku, Finland
julavi@utu.fi

Abstract. Regardless of its all-encompassing and ubiquitous nature, game and play researchers have often steered away from applying fun as a research concept. If a concept seems to be associated with everything, it logically follows that the concept lacks explanatory power. In this paper, we do not merely settle for the blunt conclusion that fun is not an interesting research concept. Rather we start to explore the phenomenon of fun by approaching it through three lenses: motivation to play, gameplay experience, and psychological need satisfaction. By analyzing two large survey samples collected in Finland (N = 879) and South-Korea (N = 1519), we cluster survey participants into player types according to their gameplay motivations. It is revealed that all players are more motivated by fun than by other need-based gaming motives, but also that a significant minority of players are only motivated by fun. By studying player preferences of the player types, it is furthermore highlighted that these *Fun-Seekers* generally dislike most gameplay activities and differ from other player types also regarding their genre play habits. Practical and theoretical implications of these findings are discussed.

Keywords: Fun · Gameplay · Motivation · Self-determination

1 Introduction

Video games are fun. However oversimplified this argument may be, it gets continuously repeated both in the ongoing cultural discourse on video games as well as in industrial and academic accounts of them. It is very commonplace to just state that "I play games just for fun" or that "games are nothing but good fun". Just to give an example of the importance of fun in the academic discussion, in

This work has been funded by Business Finland (projects 9214/31/2019 and 864/31/2016), Academy of Finland (Centre of Excellence in Game Culture Studies, project n:o 312397), and supported by Kinrate Analytics Ltd, a private company specialized in player market analytics.

© IFIP International Federation for Information Processing 2022
Published by Springer Nature Switzerland AG 2022
B. Göbl et al. (Eds.): ICEC 2022, LNCS 13477, pp. 39–46, 2022.
https://doi.org/10.1007/978-3-031-20212-4_3

his book about game-based learning, Marc Prensky [6] has listed twelve characteristics of video games that contribute to their ability to be engaging. The very first of them states that games are essentially a form of fun. However, as an academic concept, "fun" is highly ambiguous in its meaning, and the understanding of the concept rarely gets elaborated in papers discussing or utilizing this concept in research [14]. Our focus in this work-in-progress paper is on shedding more light on *fun as a reason to play games*. While also acknowledging how the concept might refer to certain types of games and features of gameplay, we are here primarily interested in describing fun in motivational terms. Instead of settling for a singular concept of fun, our intention is to discover the motivational constitution of this concept. That is, what kind of motives to play games and motivational factors of gameplay are associated with fun.

Already at the dawn of video game research, Chris Crawford [2] has discussed the potential differences between asking "why do people play games in general?" and "what makes a game more fun than another?" According to Crawford, the key difference lies between the motivating and enjoyment factors of games. Admitting an inevitable dependence between the two, motivating factors refer to the reasons for approaching games (even the ones without much enjoyment but, e.g., a good exercise) while enjoyment factors help people to choose between games on the basis of fun, that is, the gameplay and sensory based gratification it offers. However, in order to be fun, a game must sufficiently satisfy the approach motivations of the player [2]. On the basis of such a formulation, fun clearly is a criterion for game choice and for continued play, but it is not necessarily to be seen as a genuine approach motivation to play games. This formulation, however, leaves much room for clarifying the relationship between motivation and fun, especially in regards to studying what kind of things in gameplay constitute fun in terms of motivational approach towards games.

The terms "fun" and "enjoyment" are frequently considered synonyms in the literature [14]. In particular, enjoyment and pleasure emphasize positive connotations of fun. But such a meaning should not be restricted to superficial aspects of the concept, as even the most serious things in life (especially the ones we are passionate about) give us enjoyment and make us return to the corresponding activities [6]. On the other hand, "fun" can also promote negative connotations, for example, when understood in more frivolous terms of amusement or ridicule [6]. However, one should note that in regard to play, pleasures are merely not submissive to (superficial) fun and happiness, since engagement with play opens up a whole spectrum of variations of pleasure in the world [10]. How should we then conceptualize these engaging things in life that promote substantial pleasure and enjoyment for people? We may look for answers to this question in Ryan and Deci's [7] influential *Self-Determination Theory* (SDT). It is a macro-theory of human motivation and organismic growth, with a focus on curiosity and explorative behavior as a manifestation of intrinsic motivation.

According to the SDT [7], three basic psychological needs (autonomy, competence and relatedness) energize motivational processes and promote harmonious development of the human organism within the world. Satisfaction of the basic need for actualizing one's autonomic self is considered to be the primary element of this theory, essentially referring to activities that embrace one's spontaneous curiosity, interest and free will. This seems to align well with notions that the disposition of having "fun" is essentially a voluntary (intrinsically motivated) attitude of perceiving situations as enjoyable (e.g., [1]), as well as with game research literature emphasizing players' participation in game experiences as being characteristically voluntary and autonomous (e.g., [4,5,12]). The models of game motivation research are also typically built upon the premise of an autonomous player (e.g., [9,15]). In addition to autonomy, the basic needs of competence and relatedness also provide potential approaches. For example, as the flow-theory [3] proposes, the balance between a player's skills and a game's challenges should arguably result in pleasurable experiences relating to one's competence. Tamborini et al. [13] have established that enjoyment indeed derives from the satisfaction of SDT needs, which however, do not necessarily include a purely pleasure-driven search for enjoyment.

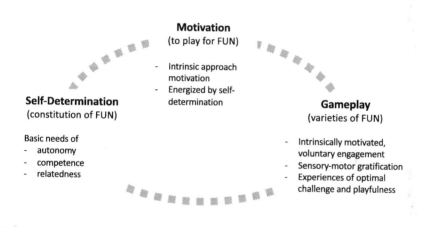

Fig. 1. The circle of fun, incorporating the perspectives of Motivation, Gameplay experience and Self-Determination.

In this study we conceptualize the SDT basic needs satisfaction as the self-reflective ways how fun is in general constituted in personal life. Self-determination thus provides an approach for scrutinizing both the varieties of pleasure afforded by gameplay and fun as a motivational disposition (see Fig. 1). Furthermore, this approach opens up a possibility to utilize three "lenses" in conceptualizing fun in terms of (1) motivation, (2) situated gameplay experience, and (3) reflective constitution of the self. On the basis of two survey datasets, we will next report a brief empirical investigation of how "fun" appears as a factor of gameplay motives and preferences through these three lenses.

2   Methods

Two large survey samples were collected within the ongoing project from Finland (N = 879) and from South-Korea (N = 1519) in cooperation with two market research companies. Both of the data collection processes were designed to produce samples that would represent the age (ages from 18 to 65) and gender distribution of the said countries. Prior to making any analyses, a total of 52 survey responses were removed from the Finnish sample and 131 from the Korean sample as these respondents were identified as outliers. After the data cleaning process, the Finnish sample consisted of 827 respondents (49.0% male, 51.0% female, mean age 41.4) and the Korean sample of 1,388 respondents (50.4% male, 49.6% female, mean age 39.1).

Both of the surveys included the Intrinsic Motivations to Gameplay (IMG) inventory, the Gameplay Activity inventory (GAIN), a 17-item inventory on video game genre play, a five-item inventory on preferred game modes (e.g., single-player computer games, multiplayer mobile games), and demographic questions. The 15-IMG is a SDT compatible five-factor inventory on motives to play digital games [15]. It assesses general gaming motives of *Autonomy* ($\alpha = 0.92$), *Competence* ($\alpha = 0.89$), *Relatedness* ($\alpha = 0.89$), *Immersion* ($\alpha = 0.91$), and *Fun* ($\alpha = 0.90$). The 15-GAIN is a five-factor construct that measures players' preferences in gameplay activity types of *Aggression* ($\alpha = 0.88$), *Caretaking* ($\alpha = 0.83$), *Coordinate* ($\alpha = 0.83$), *Exploration* ($\alpha = 0.85$), and *Management* ($\alpha = 0.88$). The GAIN was applied in the study as it informs us about game choice and game enjoyment [16], whereas the IMG instrument has been developed and validated precisely for investigating approach motivations to play video games at large.

We made an exploratory cluster analysis with Stata 16.2 software in order to explore how the motivational factor of Fun was related to other play motives (i.e., approach factors) and furthermore to gameplay preferences (i.e., enjoyment factors), genre play habits, and player demographics. For this purpose, we generated factor sum variables for each of the five IMG dimensions and proceeded to do a cluster analysis based on these motive factors. The number (k) of clusters was identified by investigating scree plots generated from the within sum of squared (WSS) and its logarithm [log(WSS)] for cluster solutions between 2 and 20 clusters. A solution of eight clusters was found to be the most prominent, and therefore we conducted a nonhierarchical k-means cluster analysis with Euclidean distance for $k = 8$.

3   Results

As a result of the cluster analysis, it was first found that Fun had the highest mean sum of the five IMG-based motive factors across all clusters. We then standardized the values for all of the five factor sums by each cluster and found that the effect size between the Fun factor and the second most highest ranged from small ($d = 0.23$) to huge ($d = 1.94$) and that this approach generated, in principle, player clusters that were very motivated, reasonably motivated, slightly motivated, and amotivated to play videogames. Differently put, by initially generating clusters based on sum variables, the results did not inform us much about the motivational profiles as the k-means procedure identified the clusters based

Table 1. The six-cluster solution. Reporting standardized factor sums and direct factors sum.

	Immersive	Autonomous	Challenger	Fun-Seeker	Social	Competitive
N	199	623	392	566	229	201
Standardized						
Relatedness	0.03	−0.84	0.27	0.14	1.43	1.07
Competence	−0.61	0.34	0.75	−0.73	−0.57	0.29
Immersion	1.10	−0.15	0.10	−0.10	0.07	−0.28
Fun	−0.88	−0.12	−0.22	0.85	−0.49	−1.24
Autonomy	0.37	0.76	−0.89	−0.17	−0.43	0.16
Factor sums						
Relatedness	2.47	1.82	2.14	1.72	3.39	3.29
Competence	2.74	3.39	3.29	1.95	2.49	3.43
Immersion	3.50	2.38	2.16	1.68	2.39	2.43
Fun	3.24	3.66	3.26	3.53	3.29	3.02
Autonomy	3.39	3.53	1.99	2.16	2.50	3.24
Motive average	3.07	2.95	2.57	2.21	2.81	3.08

on *how motivated players were* instead of being able to generate insight into *what motivates them* to play games.

To overcome this issue, another approach to k-means clustering was taken. Prior to making the analysis, the five factor sum variables were now standardized for each survey participant. By doing so, we excluded from the cluster analysis information about to what degree a participant was motivated to play games in general and based the analysis only on what factors motivated them the most and the least in comparison to their own motivation mean value. The scree plots suggested a solution of six clusters, and a k-means clustering was made accordingly. The six clusters are reported in Table 1.

Of the six clusters, only Cluster 4 was identified as based on its players desire to play video games because of *Fun*. Participants of Cluster 1 were grouped together, because of the *Immersion* and *Autonomy* motive whereas *Autonomy* and *Competence* were both relatively high motives for the second player cluster. The *Competence* motive was the most important motivational factor for Cluster 3. And finally both Cluster 5 and Cluster 6 were motivated by *Relatedness*. Cluster 6 had the lowest value for *Fun* of the six clusters.

However, when we observed the non-standardized factor sums it was revealed that *Fun* had the highest mean value not only for Cluster 4 but also for Cluster 2. The significance of the *Fun* motive was evident also when taking into account that Cluster 2 and Cluster 4 were clearly the two largest clusters with 623 and 566 participants. Next we calculated GAIN factor sums, genre playing habit means, game mode preferences, and descriptive statistics for demographics for the six clusters (Table 2).

Participants of the *Immersive* cluster had the highest mean preference for *Exploration, Aggression, Caretaking*, and *Management* of the six player clusters.

Table 2. Descriptive GAIN, genre play, game mode, and playtime statistics for the six clusters.

	Immersive	Autonomous	Challenger	Fun-Seeker	Social	Competitive
N	199	623	392	566	229	201
Aggression	2.71	2.26	2.10	1.81	2.47	2.5
Caretaking	2.69	2.36	2.40	2.11	2.42	2.44
Coordinate	2.49	2.31	2.24	1.87	2.39	2.53
Exploration	3.28	3.02	2.69	2.38	2.87	2.86
Management	2.93	2.64	2.30	2.02	2.56	2.70
GAIN average	2.82	2.52	2.34	2.04	2.54	2.62
Action	2.22	1.70	1.70	1.49	2.02	2.19
Action-adventure	2.44	1.77	1.76	1.50	1.81	2.06
Racing	2.36	1.94	1.98	1.89	2.51	2.46
Puzzle	2.72	3.04	3.08	3.04	2.81	2.78
RPG	2.62	1.88	1.92	1.60	2.28	2.31
Simulation	2.38	1.83	1.77	1.68	1.97	2.11
Sports	2.18	1.65	1.79	1.59	2.02	2.31
Strategy	2.45	1.87	1.91	1.69	2.38	2.50
Platformer	2.33	1.78	1.89	1.71	1.95	2.09
Genre average	2.21	1.72	1.77	1.58	1.94	2.09
Single-player PC/console games	2.98	3.15	2.68	2.70	2.66	2.78
Single-player mobile games	3.05	3.32	3.04	3.24	2.97	2.94
Co-op PC/console games	2.76	2.26	2.24	2.13	2.67	2.77
Multiplayer PC/console games	2.54	2.15	2.03	1.88	2.64	2.71
Multiplayer mobile games	2.40	2.09	2.08	1.88	2.52	2.53
PC play hours/week	2.91	2.62	2.17	2.11	3.69	3.18
Console play hours/week	1.79	1.36	0.82	0.90	0.72	1.19
Mobile play hours/week	3.53	3.79	4.36	4.23	4.26	3.55

They also had the highest mean value for genre play, meaning that they played more genres than players of the other clusters. They played action games, action-adventure games, role-playing games, simulations, and platform games more than other players. The *Immersive* players had the highest weekly mean play hours on console play (1.8 h), and lowest mean age (35.9 years, 57% male). The cluster was under-represented in the Finnish sample.

The *Autonomous* players had the second highest preference average for *Exploration*, and they reported the highest preference for single-player computer and console play, and single-player mobile play. The puzzle genre was their favorite. They were the oldest player cluster (42.6 years, 50% male), and they were over-represented in Finland. The *Challenger* player type (40.1 years, 54% female) had the highest preference for the puzzle genre and they played mobile games each week for 4.4 h, which was the highest value of the player clusters. They were equally represented in both countries.

The *Fun-Seeker* was only motivated to play because of *Fun*. They also did not prefer any of the gameplay activity types but instead had the lowest preferences for all of the five factors of the six player clusters. Furthermore, they had the lowest game genre average, but they played puzzle games almost as much as the *Challenger* type. They also had the second highest weekly play hours for mobile gaming, and the second highest preference average for single-player mobile games after the *Autonomous* type. A total of 57% of this player type were female players. It was equally represented in both countries, and the mean age of the cluster was 40.5 years.

Finally, the *Social* and the *Competitive* player clusters were both motivated by *Relatedness*. They both enjoyed *Exploration* to a similar extent, and they both reported high scores for the racing game genre. The *Competitive* also had a relatively high score for sports games, and the highest score for strategy games of the six clusters. They both enjoyed multiplayer computer and console games more than the other clusters. The *Social* player type had the highest weekly computer play hours of the clusters, followed by the second highest hours of the *Competitive* type. Both of these clusters were over-represented in South-Korea. A total of 56% of the *Social* cluster were male players, but this was overshadowed by the *Competitive* player type which consisted of 60% of males.

If we consider together the two clusters (*Autonomous* and *Fun-Seeker*) that had the highest mean sums for the *Fun* motive, we can note that these two clusters covered 53.8% of all players included in the study. These two clusters shared similar game preferences and interests as both of them preferred the puzzle genre and single-player experiences. On the same note, the clusters that had the highest *Relatedness* motive for game play had notably lower *Fun* motive scores. This raises a question about a possible tension between the social motive to play when compared to playing just for *Fun*.

4   Concluding Statements

To a large part, the results of the present investigation seem to agree with the general expectations that playing games is fun, people play games because of the fun, and that such fun associates with the voluntariness of gameplay. In the results of the first cluster analysis, fun in particular appeared as an all-encompassing and ubiquitous motivational orientation, which would arguably incorporate expectations of gameplay gratifications and motivational factors in a diffuse manner. Due to this ubiquitous nature, following Crawford's [2] line of thought, it seems difficult to treat fun as the same level of motive as the more discrete need-based IMG motives overtaken by it. Rather, fun could be considered as more like a general game gratification orientation.

The second cluster analysis, however, offered much more defined results revealing a six cluster solution, in which only one of the clusters (25.6% of the players) was solely based on a general fun-seeking game gratification orientation. Thus, the players represented by this Fun-seeker cluster appear purely as gratification seekers, while with the other clusters, fun appears to be more defined and needs-based. The results support Tamborini et al.'s [13] model that makes a distinction between the deeper, SDT needs-based and the more superficial and hedonistic-driven orientations towards enjoyment. Furthermore, the results are in line with Ryan et al.'s [8] conceptual distinction between hedonistic and eudai-monic approaches to human well-being, which in particular proposes that the latter approach indeed can be characterized in SDT-based motivational terms.

The question remains: what are the qualities of game gratification that are preferred by the Fun-Seekers? Our results indicate that they prefer logical prob-lem solving and other game mechanics and interaction types typical of mobile puzzle games. In future studies this issue could be further investigated by includ-ing scrutiny of gameplay challenge dimensions, as well as focusing more on the performative ways of pleasure constitution. The latter approach could, for exam-ple, include a particular focus on the vitality forms [11] of the actions of gameplay as an immediate arousal of pleasure within sensory-motor interaction experience.

References

1. Bisson, C., Luckner, J.: Fun in learning: The pedagogical role of fun in adventure education. J. Exp. Educ. **19**(2), 108–112 (1996)
2. Crawford, C.: The art of computer game design. Osborne/McGraw-Hill, Berkeley, California (1984)
3. Csikszentmihalyi, M.: Flow: the psychology of optimal experience. Harper & Row, New York (1990)
4. Goffman, E.: Encounters. Two Studies in the Sociology of Interaction. Mansfield Centre, CT: Martino Publishing (1961)
5. Huizinga, J.: Homo Ludens: A Study of the Play-Element in Culture. Routledge, United Kingdom (1949)
6. Prensky, M.: Digital Game Based Learning. McGraw-Hill, New York (2001)
7. Ryan, R., Deci, L.: Intrinsic and extrinsic motivations: classic definitions and new directions. Contemp. Educ. Psychol. **25**, 54–67 (2000)
8. Ryan, R., Huta, V., Deci, L.: Living well: A self-determination theory perspective on eudaimonia. J. Happiness Stud. **9**(1), 139–170 (2008)
9. Sherry, J.L., Lucas, K., Greenberg, B.S., Lachlan, K.: Video game uses and gratifi-cations as predictors of use and game preference. In: Vorderer, P., Bryant, J. (eds.) Playing Video Games. Motives, Responses, and Consequences, pp. 213–224. New York: Routledge, Taylor & Francis Group (2006)
10. Sicart, M.: Play Matters. MIT Press, Cambridge, MA, London (2014)
11. Stern, D.N.: Forms of vitality: Exploring dynamic experience in psychology, the arts, psychotherapy, and development. Oxford University Press (2010)
12. Suits, B.: The Grasshopper. Games, Life and Utopia. Peterborough: Broadview Press (1978)
13. Tamborini, R., Bowman, N.D., Eden, A., Grizzard, M., Organ, A.: Defining media enjoyment as the satisfaction of intrinsic needs. J. Commun. **60**(4), 758–777 (2010)
14. Tisza, G., Markopoulos, P.: FunQ: measuring the fun experience of a learning activity with adolescents. Curr. Psychol. 1–21 (2021). https://doi.org/10.1007/s12144-021-01484-2
15. Vahlo, J., Hamari, J.: Five-Factor Inventory of Intrinsic Motivations to Gameplay (IMG). In Proceedings of the 52nd Hawaii International Conference on System Sciences, pp. 2476–2485 (2019)
16. Vahlo, J., Smed, J., Koponen, A.: Validating gameplay activity inventory (GAIN) for modeling player profiles. User Model. User Adap. Inter. **28**, 425–453 (2018)

Towards an Understanding of How Players Make Meaning from Post-Play Process Visualizations

Erica Kleinman[1(✉)], Jennifer Villareale[2], Murtuza Shergadwala[1],
Zhaoqing Teng[1], Andy Bryant[1], Jichen Zhu[3], and Magy Seif El-Nasr[1]

[1] University of California Santa Cruz, Santa Cruz, CA, USA
{emkleinm,mshergad,zhteng,mseifeln}@ucsc.edu, a@andybryant.com
[2] Drexel University, Philadelphia, PA, USA
jmv85@drexel.edu
[3] IT University of Copenhagen, Copenhagen, Denmark
jicz@itu.dk

Abstract. Player-facing, retrospective gameplay visualizations help players track progress and learn from others. Visualizations of a user's step by step process, may be able to advance retrospective visualization. However, we currently do not know how players make meaning from process visualizations of game data. In this work, we take a first step towards addressing this gap by examining how players make meaning from process visualizations of other players' gameplay. We identify two interpretation methods comprised of six techniques and discuss what these results mean for future use of player-facing process visualizations.

Keywords: Post-game visualization · Process visualization · Visualization interpretation · Interpretation techniques · User studies

1 Introduction

The last decade has seen an increased interest in player-facing post-game visualizations [5,5,15,21,29,43,44,50]. Recent work has, however, revealed that existing visualizations do not often provide enough causal information for players to make connections between their actions and the outcomes they experienced [23]. Process visualizations, which present human process as a sequence of actions taken [3,30,37,41,42,45,46], appear well suited to preserving causal information. Player-facing, post-play process visualizations are, however, rare and typically included as a secondary feature to a visualization of another type [1,24,32]. As such, they are rarely the focus of research, and we know little about how players extract meaning from them, which is necessary to ensure that we design and implement them in appropriate and effective ways.

B. Göbl et al. (Eds.): ICEC 2022, LNCS 13477, pp. 47–58, 2022.
https://doi.org/10.1007/978-3-031-20212-4_4

In this paper, we take the first steps to address this gap by examining how players make sense of post-play process visualizations of others' gameplay in the context of an educational game. In particular, our research question is: "What interpretation techniques do players use to make sense of process visualizations of others' gameplay?" We chose to focus on having participants interpret other players' data due to the significant role that reviewing the gameplay of others' plays in learning how to play games [36]. To answer this question, we conducted a qualitative study with 13 players of the game *Parallel* [49], prompting them to make sense of other players' gameplay through a process visualization. Results revealed six interpretation techniques that players leverage to extract meaning from game data. We also identified two general sense-making methods for post-play process visualizations: *the induction method* and *the framing method*. Based on these results, we present and discuss four general design implications that should be considered in future design and development.

2   Related Work

To date, most player-facing gameplay visualizations feature either aggregate [5,15] or spatio-temporal data [1,24,44]. Aggregate visualization techniques use visual elements such as percentages, graphs, and charts [5,15,29]. However, such visualizations do not preserve granular strategic information [20], making it difficult for players to determine where they may have made a mistake. Spatio-temporal visualizations, in contrast, present granular, action by action, data, superimposed atop a game map [1,22,24,44]. However, when scaled, spatio-temporal visualizations often remove granular data, and instead focus on movement over time [44]. While informative, these visualizations loses much of the causal information.

These drawbacks created a space that process visualizations began to fill. In other domains, review of process has been valuable for optimizing human workflows [40,41] and learning [27,28]. In games, graph-based process visualizations are used for game analytics and user experience research [2,3,9,16–18,20,30,45]. Player-facing process visualizations, in contrast, are typically designed as timelines depicting the ordering of actions taken over the course of a game [1,22,24,32]. However, these timelines are often secondary features attached to another visualization system [1,24]. As such they are often not the focus of research. This results in a lack of knowledge about how players extract insights from process visualizations, which is necessary for informed design.

Understanding how users make sense of data is pivotal for the design of player-facing visualizations. While there is a lot of work in InfoVis [10,34,35,47], in the context of games such work is sparse. Previous work investigated this question in spatio-temporal visualization [22] and demonstrated that making meaning from visualized game data requires unique investigation. However, to the best of our knowledge, no one has specifically investigated this question in the context of process visualizations.

3 Methodology

Parallel is a puzzle game designed to teach parallel programming concepts [19, 39, 49]. We chose to conduct our research with an educational game, because retrospective visualizations are already common in digital learning contexts [4, 43, 50]. We chose *Parallel* for this study as it is complex enough for players to demonstrate various approaches to solving problems, yet simple enough for players to become comfortable with gameplay quickly.

Using the visualization tool Glyph [30], we generated a process visualization (see Fig. 1) based on 15 key strategic *Parallel* gameplay actions. Each node in Glyph's network graph represented a different in-game action and a link between two nodes indicated that at least one player in the community transitioned between those two actions. Individual player trajectories within this visualization can be highlighted as seen in Fig. 1.

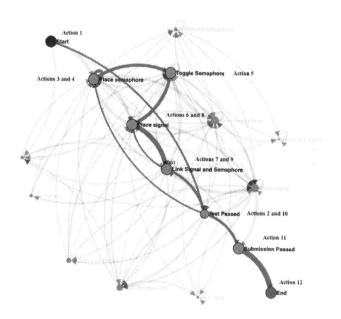

Fig. 1. An screen shot of the process visualization, with player 8's sequence highlighted.

13 undergraduate computer science students were recruited from universities in the United States, as they represent the target population for *Parallel* [49]. Gameplay took from 30 to 60 min. Players then signed up for data-driven retrospective interviews [8] conducted over Zoom.

3.1 Interview Protocol

Prompt Design. Based on previous work [22, 34, 38] we recognized two types of interpretation techniques: interaction techniques used to extract information from the visualization and cognitive techniques used to make sense out of that information. To ensure that we elicited techniques in both categories, we developed two prompts:

1. Could you describe this player's actions using the visualization? ("interaction prompt")
2. Can you say why you think the player played the way they did? ("cognitive prompt")

Procedure. A slide deck was prepared and presented to each participant during the interview. One researcher led the interview, screen-sharing the slide deck, while two others remained silent and recorded, in text, what the participant said.

The first slide contained a visualization of the participant's own data. On this slide, the lead researcher gave the participant basic instructions on how to read the visualization. The next slide contained a visualization of another participant, who played similarly to the interviewee. The last slide contained a visualization of another participant, who played differently than the interviewee. While displaying the second and third slides, the lead researcher asked the prompts described above. Interviews lasted about 30 min and participants received a 50$ gift card.

3.2 Data Analysis

Interview data was analyzed using a two-step, iterative thematic analysis protocol [13,33]. The first step of the analysis identified the specific interpretation techniques that players used. Two researchers, separately, performed open coding on the interview responses. The unit of analysis was a player's response to a prompt. They then met and discussed their initial codes to generate a code book of six interpretation techniques. The researchers then performed an inter-rater reliability check using Cohen's Kappa [7] on 30% [6] of the data. The codes achieved an IRR score of .87, indicating very strong agreement [25].

The second step identified the overall process of making sense of the data. The two researchers separately analyzed each prompt response and marked which of the six interpretation strategies were used and in what order. The researchers then reconvened and discussed their findings. They identified two methods for engaging the interpretation techniques and performed a second inter-rater reliability check, again on 30% of the data set [6]. The method codes achieved an IRR score of .74, indicated strong agreement [25]. One researcher then labeled the remainder of the data set with the method codes.

4 Results

The six interpretation techniques are shown in Table 1.

Table 1. The six interpretation techniques identified based on analysis of players' interaction with the community visualizations and brief definitions.

Interpretation Technique	Definition
Reading the Visualization to Collect Information	The participant read the data that appeared in the visualization but did not extrapolate on it
Identifying Patterns to Inform Inferences: Sequential Pattern	The participant identified a pattern related to the ordering of data-points
Identifying Patterns to Inform Inferences: Frequency Pattern	The participant identified a pattern related to the amount of data-points
Making a Comparison to Guide Pattern Identification	The participant compares the data of the other player to their own experience to better make sense and extract patterns
Making an Inference to Understand the Other Player: Approach or Strategy	The participant makes an inference regarding the subject's intentions behind the actions they took
Making an Inference to Understand the Other Player: Understanding or Expertise	The participant makes an inference regarding the subject's knowledge or comprehension of the gameplay

Reading the Visualization to Collect Information. Participants would try to collect information from the visualized data as a precursor to making connections between data points. For example, P9 reads the trajectory of another player, stating "They do start, test passed, sub failed, they place the semaphore, then maybe they toggle it, they place the signal, they link, maybe they move it around." Notably, reading the visualization would often encompass a read-through of the entire sequence, suggesting that participants were engaging this method to gain a holistic overview of the data. This is illustrated by P0 who said "it looks like they placed and moved semaphores and placed signals, linked some together, ran a submission, stopped the submission, placed another semaphore, maybe moved it again, toggled it, and then maybe toggled a different one, ran it, a test passed, and then the submission passed." Notably, participants did not always read the visualization, many jumped to identifying patterns.

Identifying Patterns to Inform Inferences. Participants would make general statements about the characteristics of the data. We saw two types of patterns that participants would identify:

- **Sequential Pattern**: Refers to the participant identifying patterns in the ordering of actions. For example, P3 noticed that "[the other player] repeats that process of toggling then placing then linking". Recognition of these patterns is facilitated by the sequential nature of the visualization and it would likely be harder to recognize such patterns otherwise.
- **Frequency Pattern**: Refers to the participant identifying a pattern regarding the number of actions taken. For example, P0 said: "They move a limited

number of times, but they ran the submission a lot because it looks like they stopped it a lot."

We observed that pattern recognition would lead to inferences regarding the players who generated the data. For example, P8 described "They seem to jump back and forth a lot. They were probably thinking through a lot of their placement and movement."

Making a Comparison to Guide Pattern Identification. Comparison did not always occur, but when it did, players would typically compare patterns in peers' gameplay to patterns in their own. For example, P0 said "They use the stop submission button, that's interesting, I don't think I used it at all." Often, participants would use comparison as a way to guide the identification of additional patterns. This is well illustrated by P1 "Once they laid down a solution they would test it and see if it failed or not. Whereas I don't remember doing as much testing." Here, the participant has identified a pattern in which the subject would lay down a solution then test it. They compare this to their own gameplay, in which they did not test as much. Such comparison can help them identify more patterns (what else did the other player do differently?) and begin to generate a more formal inference.

Making an Inference to Understand the Other Player. As discussed above, inferences were informed by identified patterns within the data, which were sometimes guided by comparison. We observed inferences to be focused primarily on the player, which differs from previous work [22]. We observed two types of inferences:

- **Approach or Strategy:** Refers to the participant making an inference about subject's plan execution. For example P10 said "They saw that the test passed so their aim was to try and generalize the solution." Here, P10 infers a strategic decision that the player made (trying to generalize their solution) as a way of explaining an observed pattern in the data (that the player did not immediately submit after their test passed and instead took other actions).
- **Understanding or Expertise:** Refers to the participant making an inference about what the subject knows about the task or subject. For example P11 said "I would say they probably came in with a good idea about how they were going to do the level before they started playing [since] they're very calculated, they rarely jump back and forth between states." Here, the participant has developed an image in their mind regarding the expertise of the other player (that they had a good idea of what they were going to do) that can be used to explain an observed pattern in their data (that they rarely go back to previously visited states).

4.1 Sense-Making Methods

The interpretation techniques connect to one another to form a process for making sense of the data. We refer to this process as a *sense-making method*. We identify two general methods for sense-making for post-play process visualizations for games, seen in Fig. 2 and described in detail below:

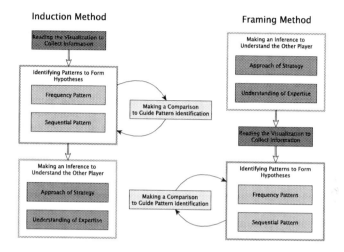

Fig. 2. The sense-making methods we observed in terms of the ordering of interpretation techniques.

Induction Method: This method represents an approach in which players began their sense-making process by *reading the visualization*. They would then *identify patterns* in the data, and use *comparison*, if necessary, to generate an understanding of gameplay events. This would culminate in an *inference* about the other player. An example of this method is demonstrated by P7: first, they read the visualization, stating "Ran a test and it passed then worked to place the items in one sequence, and then the test failed, and then in another they stopped it again." They follow this with recognition of a frequency pattern, stating "It looks like they placed a lot". Finally, they offer an explanation, stating "they probably deleted [the signals and semaphores] instead of moving them."

Framing Method: When participants used this method, they first made *inferences* about the other player, often based on visually apparent details, e.g., length of the trajectory. They would then switch to collecting information, first *reading the visualization*, then using one or both *pattern identification* techniques and *comparison*, to generate hypotheses that justified and supported their initial inference. An example of this method is demonstrated by P12: they begin with an inference of the other player's strategy (or lack thereof), stating "I would think that this player kind of did stuff at random, I'm not sure if there was a process that they used." They follow this by reading the visualization to collect information, stating "It seems like [they're] going from start and then placing a semaphore [then] going from test passed to stopping submission and moving a signal". They follow this with identification of a sequential pattern (or lack thereof), stating "It doesn't look like this graph had a lot of iterative processes. It's a little jumbled up."

5 Discussion and Implications

It becomes apparent that inferences facilitate players' ability to extract actionable insights from data. This finding is similar to what has been discussed in InfoViz work regarding mental models of data [26,47,48]. Unlike InfoViz work, the inferences here inform a mental model of the individual who produced the data rather than the data itself, similar to what was seen by Kleinman et al. in their study of spatio-temporal post-play visualization [22]. Further, in this work we see the presence of a sense-making method that begins with the inference and then collects data to enforce it. This may have been encouraged by the nature of the visualization, from which surface level information, such as length of trajectory, could be quickly extracted and used to reach a preemptive conclusion.

This suggests that process visualizations, which present data in a holistic manner, may encourage players to make assumptions about the data up front. However, there is the very real possibility that these up-front assumptions can lead to inaccurate inferences. **Thus, process visualizations for post-play analysis should consider incorporating design elements that can inform players' up-front assumptions and guide them towards correct initial inferences.** One way to accomplish this could be the grouping or labeling actions inside a visualization to indicate what they mean.

Further, while previous work discusses users adjusting frames and hypotheses [22,26], participants in our study who used the framing method did not make adjustments. In fact, it seemed that they rarely uncovered information that they recognized as contradictory to their inference. Based on our results, we hypothesize two reasons for this. The first reason is related to the participants' familiarity with the game. In our study, participants had no prior experience with *Parallel*. As a result, they likely lack the domain knowledge necessary to recognize gameplay strategies in the data. **Thus, process visualizations may aid players best if they are not displayed until the player has become more familiar with the game.**

The second reason is related to the abstraction of the data. The presentation of the gameplay data as a trajectory of actions may have been too abstract. Including game state, recognized as important to understanding context [22], information in the process visualization could have helped players better understand what they were observing. **Thus, retrospective process visualizations should consider incorporating game state information, to ensure that players are able to correctly interpret the context behind each action.** This implication, along with the previous one, can help ensure that the player is equipped to correct misunderstandings about the data.

Additionally, the inclusion of comparison, as shown in the results, is not discussed in the previous work by Kleinman et al. [22], where players were not shown their own data. This suggests that the inclusion of a player's own data is likely to spark comparison between themselves and others. Using comparison between self and others has been explored in the domain of personal informatics, though usually within the context of a user understanding their own data through the comparison [11,31]. Here the comparison was used to understand the other player, as finding the differences in how the other player behaved compared to oneself gave participants an anchor point to begin understanding the rest of their experience.

This suggests that process visualizations can leverage comparison to help players more quickly identify connected patterns and reach inferences. **Thus, process visualizations in post-play contexts should consider highlighting how the player's own data compares to and differs from the data of the subject of analysis.** This does, however, raise questions about the potential risks of prompting comparison among players, as previous work has demonstrated that players who under-perform can become discouraged when prompted to compare themselves to high-performing players [12]. Thus, process visualizations may wish to only permit comparison against other players with similar skill levels or quality of performance.

6   Limitations

We acknowledge that this study was performed on a small sample size (n = 13). However, we did see saturation in the data at 7 participants and argue that this sample size aligns with those seen in similar work [14,22]. We additionally recognize that we only looked at a single game, only at the analysis of others' data, and that the nature of the visualization itself likely influenced our results. As such, more work is needed to ensure the generalizability of the findings. With this in mind we present this work as a first step towards understanding how players make sense of process visualizations of others' data during post-play analysis.

7   Conclusion

In this work, we take a first step towards understanding how players make sense of process visualizations during post-play analysis. Through a 13-participant qualitative user study, we identified six interpretation techniques that players used to make sense of process visualizations and two methods for sense-making. We discuss the implications of these findings on the use of player-facing process visualizations in post-play analysis.

Acknowledgements. This work is supported by the national Science Foundation (NSF) under Grant #1917855. The authors would like to thank all past and current members of the project.

References

1. Afonso, A.P., Carmo, M.B., Gonçalves, T., Vieira, P.: Visualeague: player performance analysis using spatial-temporal data. Multimedia Tools Appl. **78**(23), 33069–33090 (2019)
2. Ahmad, S., et al.: Modeling individual and team behavior through spatio-temporal analysis. In: Proceedings of the Annual Symposium on Computer-Human Interaction in Play, pp. 601–612 (2019)
3. Andersen, E., Liu, Y.E., Apter, E., Boucher-Genesse, F., Popović, Z.: Gameplay analysis through state projection. In: Proceedings of the Fifth International Conference on the Foundations of Digital Games, pp. 1–8 (2010)
4. Bodily, R., et al.: Open learner models and learning analytics dashboards: a systematic review. In: Proceedings of the 8th International Conference on Learning Analytics and Knowledge, pp. 41–50 (2018)
5. Bowman, B., Elmqvist, N., Jankun-Kelly, T.: Toward visualization for games: theory, design space, and patterns. IEEE Trans. Visual Comput. Graphics **18**(11), 1956–1968 (2012)
6. Campbell, J.L., Quincy, C., Osserman, J., Pedersen, O.K.: Coding in-depth semistructured interviews: problems of unitization and intercoder reliability and agreement. Sociol. Methods Res. **42**(3), 294–320 (2013)
7. Cohen, J.: A coefficient of agreement for nominal scales. Educ. Psychol. Measur. **20**(1), 37–46 (1960)
8. El-Nasr, M.S., Durga, S., Shiyko, M., Sceppa, C.: Data-driven retrospective interviewing (ddri): a proposed methodology for formative evaluation of pervasive games. Entertainment Comput. **11**, 1–19 (2015)
9. El-Nasr, M.S., Nguyen, T.H.D., Canossa, A., Drachen, A.: Game Data Science. Oxford University Press (2021)
10. Endert, A., Hossain, M.S., Ramakrishnan, N., North, C., Fiaux, P., Andrews, C.: The human is the loop: new directions for visual analytics. Journal of intelligent information systems **43**(3), 411–435 (2014)
11. Epstein, D., Cordeiro, F., Bales, E., Fogarty, J., Munson, S.: Taming data complexity in lifelogs: exploring visual cuts of personal informatics data. In: Proceedings of the 2014 Conference on Designing Interactive Systems, pp. 667–676 (2014)
12. Esteves, J., Valogianni, K., Greenhill, A.: Online social games: the effect of social comparison elements on continuance behaviour. Inform. Manage. **58**(4), 103452 (2021)
13. Gavin, H.: Thematic analysis. Understanding research methods and statistics in psychology, pp. 273–282 (2008)
14. Halabi, N., Wallner, G., Mirza-Babaei, P.: Assessing the impact of visual design on the interpretation of aggregated playtesting data visualization. In: Proceedings of the Annual Symposium on Computer-Human Interaction in Play, pp. 639–650 (2019)
15. Hazzard, E.: Data visualization in games (2014). https://erikhazzard.com/blog/game-development/data-visualization-in-games
16. Horn, B., Hoover, A.K., Barnes, J., Folajimi, Y., Smith, G., Harteveld, C.: Opening the black box of play: Strategy analysis of an educational game. In: Proceedings of the 2016 Annual Symposium on Computer-Human Interaction in Play, pp. 142–153. ACM (2016)

17. Javvaji, N., Harteveld, C., Seif El-Nasr, M.: Understanding player patterns by combining knowledge-based data abstraction with interactive visualization. In: Proceedings of the Annual Symposium on Computer-Human Interaction in Play (2020)
18. Jemmali, C., Kleinman, E., Bunian, S., Almeda, M.V., Rowe, E., Seif El-Nasr, M.: Maads: Mixed-methods approach for the analysis of debugging sequences of beginner programmers. In: Proceedings of the 51st ACM Technical Symposium on Computer Science Education, pp. 86–92 (2020)
19. Kantharaju, P., Alderfer, K., Zhu, J., Char, B., Smith, B., Ontanón, S.: Tracing player knowledge in a parallel programming educational game. arXiv preprint arXiv:1908.05632 (2019)
20. Kleinman, E., et al.: "and then they died": Using action sequences for data driven, context aware gameplay analysis. In: International Conference on the Foundations of Digital Games. FDG '20, Association for Computing Machinery, New York, NY, USA (2020)
21. Kleinman, E., El-Nasr, M.S.: Using data to "git gud": A push for a player-centric approach to the use of data in esports (2021)
22. Kleinman, E., Preetham, N., Teng, Z., Bryant, A., Seif El-Nasr, M.: "what happened here!?" a taxonomy for user interaction with spatio-temporal game data visualization. Proceedings of the ACM on Human-Computer Interaction 5(CHI PLAY), 1–27 (2021)
23. Kleinman, E., Shergadwala, M.N., Seif El-Nasr, M.: Kills, deaths, and (computational) assists: Identifying opportunities for computational support in esport learning. In: CHI Conference on Human Factors in Computing Systems. CHI '22, Association for Computing Machinery, New York, NY, USA (2022). https://doi.org/10.1145/3491102.3517654
24. Kuan, Y.T., Wang, Y.S., Chuang, J.H.: Visualizing real-time strategy games: The example of starcraft ii. In: 2017 IEEE Conference on Visual Analytics Science and Technology (VAST), pp. 71–80. IEEE (2017)
25. Landis, J.R., Koch, G.G.: The measurement of observer agreement for categorical data. biometrics, pp. 159–174 (1977)
26. Lee, S., Kim, S.H., Hung, Y.H., Lam, H., Kang, Y.a., Yi, J.S.: How do people make sense of unfamiliar visualizations?: A grounded model of novice's information visualization sensemaking. IEEE Trans. Visualization Computer Graphics 22(1), 499–508 (2015)
27. Lin, X., Hmelo, C., Kinzer, C.K., Secules, T.J.: Designing technology to support reflection. Educa. Tech. Research Dev. 47(3), 43–62 (1999)
28. Loh, B., Radinsky, J., Russell, E., Gomez, L.M., Reiser, B.J., Edelson, D.C.: The progress portfolio: Designing reflective tools for a classroom context. In: Proceedings of the SIGCHI Conference on Human Factors in Computing Systems, pp. 627–634 (1998)
29. Medler, B.: Player dossiers: Analyzing gameplay data as a reward. Game Studies 11(1) (2011)
30. Nguyen, T.H.D., El-Nasr, M.S., Canossa, A.: Glyph: Visualization tool for understanding problem solving strategies in puzzle games. In: FDG (2015)
31. Puussaar, A., Clear, A.K., Wright, P.: Enhancing personal informatics through social sensemaking. In: Proceedings of the 2017 CHI Conference on Human Factors in Computing Systems, pp. 6936–6942 (2017)
32. RPGLogs, L.: Warcraft logs (2013–2021). https://www.warcraftlogs.com/
33. Saldaña, J.: The coding manual for qualitative researchers. Sage (2015)

34. Sandouka, K.: Interactive visualizations: A literature review. MWAIS 2019 Proceedings. p. 8 (2019)
35. Shneiderman, B.: The eyes have it: A task by data type taxonomy for information visualizations. In: Proceedings 1996 IEEE Symposium on Visual Languages, pp. 336–343. IEEE (1996)
36. Sjöblom, M., Hamari, J.: Why do people watch others play video games? an empirical study on the motivations of twitch users. Comput. Hum. Behav. **75**, 985–996 (2017)
37. Temkin, B.D.: Mapping the customer journey. Forrester Res. **3**, 20 (2010)
38. Valiati, E.R., Pimenta, M.S., Freitas, C.M.: A taxonomy of tasks for guiding the evaluation of multidimensional visualizations. In: Proceedings of the 2006 AVI Workshop on Beyond time and Errors: Novel Evaluation Methods for Information Visualization, pp. 1–6 (2006)
39. Valls-Vargas, J., Zhu, J., Ontañón, S.: Graph grammar-based controllable generation of puzzles for a learning game about parallel programming. In: Proceedings of the 12th International Conference on the Foundations of Digital Games, pp. 1–10 (2017)
40. Van Der Aalst, W.: Process mining: overview and opportunities. ACM Trans. Manage. Inform. Syst. (TMIS) **3**(2), 1–17 (2012)
41. Van Der Aalst, W., et al.: Process Mining Manifesto. In: Daniel, F., Barkaoui, K., Dustdar, S. (eds.) BPM 2011. LNBIP, vol. 99, pp. 169–194. Springer, Heidelberg (2012). https://doi.org/10.1007/978-3-642-28108-2_19
42. van der Aalst, W., Adriansyah, A., van Dongen, B.: Causal nets: a modeling language tailored towards process discovery. In: Katoen, J.-P., König, B. (eds.) CONCUR 2011. LNCS, vol. 6901, pp. 28–42. Springer, Heidelberg (2011). https://doi.org/10.1007/978-3-642-23217-6_3
43. Villareale, J., F. Biemer, C., Seif El-Nasr, M., Zhu, J.: Reflection in game-based learning: A survey of programming games. In: International Conference on the Foundations of Digital Games, pp. 1–9 (2020)
44. Wallner, G., Kriglstein, S.: Visualizations for retrospective analysis of battles in team-based combat games: A user study. In: Proceedings of the 2016 Annual Symposium on Computer-Human Interaction in Play, pp. 22–32 (2016)
45. Wallner, G.: Play-graph: A methodology and visualization approach for the analysis of gameplay data. In: FDG, pp. 253–260 (2013)
46. White, S.A.: Introduction to bpmn. Ibm Cooperation **2**(0), 0 (2004)
47. Yi, J.S., ah Kang, Y., Stasko, J., Jacko, J.A.: Toward a deeper understanding of the role of interaction in information visualization. IEEE transactions on visualization and computer graphics **13**(6), 1224–1231 (2007)
48. Yi, J.S., Kang, Y.a., Stasko, J.T., Jacko, J.A.: Understanding and characterizing insights: how do people gain insights using information visualization? In: Proceedings of the 2008 Workshop on BEyond time and errors: novel evaLuation methods for Information Visualization, pp. 1–6 (2008)
49. Zhu, J., et al.: Programming in game space: how to represent parallel programming concepts in an educational game. In: Proceedings of the 14th International Conference on the Foundations of Digital Games, pp. 1–10 (2019)
50. Zhu, J., El-Nasr, M.S.: Open player modeling: Empowering players through data transparency. arXiv preprint arXiv:2110.05810 (2021)

Entertainment Tools and Methods

Plot Composition by Mapping Situation Calculus Schemas into Petri Net Representation

Edirlei Soares de Lima[1,2]([✉]) [iD], Antonio L. Furtado[3] [iD], Bruno Feijó[3] [iD], and Marco A. Casanova[3] [iD]

[1] IADE, Universidade Europeia, Av. D. Carlos I 4, 1200-649 Lisbon, Portugal
edirlei.lima@universidadeeuropeia.pt
[2] UNIDCOM/IADE, Av. D. Carlos I 4, 1200-649 Lisbon, Portugal
[3] Department of Informatics, PUC-Rio, R. Marquês de São Vicente 225, Rio de Janeiro, Brazil
{furtado,casanova}@inf.puc-rio.br

Abstract. In this paper we propose a new plot composition method based on situation calculus and Petri net models, which are applied, in a complementary fashion, to a narrative open to user co-authorship. The method starts with the specification of situation calculus schemas, which allow a planning algorithm to check if the specification covers the desired cases. A Petri net is then automatically derived from the schemas in a second phase, guiding interactive plot generation and dramatization. The applicability of the proposed method is validated through the implementation of an interactive storytelling system capable of representing the generated Petri net models using 2D graphics and animations.

Keywords: Petri net · Situation calculus · Interactive storytelling · Plot generation · Dramatization

1 Introduction

Readers enjoy a far more pleasant experience with narratives in which they are invited to participate as co-authors. This claim is convincingly expressed by Umberto Eco [8], when talking of "open works" and "works in movement," i.e., works that deliberately leave decisions on the meaning of specific passages to the care of the reader. However, this ideal, which is hard to satisfy in book format, only now is truly reachable through interactive narratives developed for digital environments.

The most popular approach to interactive narrative, especially in narrative-driven games (e.g., Heavy Rain (2010) and Detroit Become Human (2018) by Quantic Dream), is the branching technique (also known as branching path stories [16]). In this technique, the player makes a choice at each branching point. The writer usually builds a rigid structure of branching points through a manually authored process without any consistency check. User decisions involve choosing which way to proceed at branching points, thus leading, knowingly or not, to a subsequent outcome. To identify such branching points, designers usually use Petri nets [3, 23], a graphically structured modeling technique for dynamic systems [22].

© IFIP International Federation for Information Processing 2022
Published by Springer Nature Switzerland AG 2022
B. Göbl et al. (Eds.): ICEC 2022, LNCS 13477, pp. 61–75, 2022.
https://doi.org/10.1007/978-3-031-20212-4_5

A more suitable and robust approach is to treat a narrative as an application process where, instead of a single linear plot, the designers (authors) define a fixed repertoire of predefined event-producing operations containing preconditions and post-conditions. These conditions enforce the intended conventions and preserve consistency when the users (readers performing as co-authors) are allowed to decide. Postconditions consist of facts asserted or retracted as the consequence of executing the operator. And as we argue in this paper, situation calculus [15] is a suitable modeling strategy that can exploit backward-chaining plan generation based on the operators above mentioned (e.g., using STRIPS [11]) to show what specific plots can emerge.

This paper presents a new plot composition method that combines both modeling techniques in a *complementary* fashion. We consider Petri nets from the perspective of event logs, as proposed by Wil van der Aalst [1]. Our method starts with specifying situation calculus schemas for a chosen process application. It then automatically derives a Petri net representation from these schemas, which is informative enough to be employed for interactive plot generation and dramatization. The method is analogously applicable to information system domains, where business transactions can be treated in the same way as narrative plots.

The contribution of our work is twofold. First, we shed light on the complementarity between situational calculus and Petri nets. Second, we have taken the process of composing interactive plots to a more robust and semantically consistent level. In our approach, situation calculus is used at specification time, enforcing integrity constraints, and checking if the specification allows all desirable use cases while disallowing undesirable cases. In the final step, the automatically generated Petri net allows visualizing the processes and effectively executing them.

The paper is organized as follows. Section 2 discusses related work. Section 3 presents our approach to deriving a Petri net model from a situation calculus model in a narrative domain. Section 4 explores the application of the proposed method in a fully implemented interactive storytelling system. Finally, concluding remarks are the object of Sect. 5.

2 Related Work

Situation calculus [15] provides a second-order logic method to formalize state transitions caused by event-producing operations. Petri nets, in turn, are commonly utilized in Process Mining work [1] for obtaining an implicit model of an application, by discovering the partial order requirements prevailing on a significant number of traces extracted from an execution log. For example, in [14], Petri net synthesis is preceded by a preliminary activity mining algorithm.

From [1] we borrowed and used in our first experiments [19] the simple introductory case of a request processing application, represented by a Petri net. When specifying the trial by combat application that serves as a running example in the present paper, we were able to end up with a structurally analogous Petri net representation, thus favoring the claim [6] that serious and entertainment applications can be treated by the same modelling formalisms.

Research involving situation calculus and Petri net formalisms includes in special [24], which proposes a formal ontology that highlights the correspondence between a sequence of actions starting from an initial state in situation calculus, and a sequence of transition firings starting from an initial node in a Petri net. However, the aforementioned work focuses only on the analysis of structural properties of Petri nets and situation calculus models.

The relations between Petri nets and automated planning were also explored in previous research, such as [13], where a method to transform planning graphs into Petri nets is presented and used to demonstrate that Petri net unfolding, a form of partial order reduction, can be used to recognize independent planning subproblems. The transformation of Petri net models into planning problems was also explored in [2], which is the inverse of the process discussed in this paper. Plans are modelled as Petri nets in [25] and plans are used to produce workflows in [10] (re-calling that Petri nets can be viewed as a particular form of workflow).

Petri nets were also applied in interactive storytelling contexts. Riedl et al. [23] uses a specialized type of Petri net, called colored Petri net, to allow authors to manually model interactive narratives as a process in which multiple players can navigate through different narrative scenes. During dramatization, their system uses an execution algorithm that monitors for situations in which the Petri net fails to account for player actions. When a failure situation is identified, a planning algorithm is used to generate new narrative events to restore the integrity of the Petri net. In this paper, instead of relying on manually authored Petri nets, we focus on the automatic process of mapping situation calculus schemas into Petri net models.

Petri nets are also commonly used as modelling tools to design narratives and character behaviors in games. An example of work that employs manually authored Petri nets to represent narrative plots is presented by Balas et al. [3], which uses hierarchical Petri nets to define branching narratives for games. Lee and Cho [17] also proposed a quest generation method for games where quests are modeled as Petri nets, which are activated during a game session according to characters' goals and the current world state. A similar approach is explored by El-Sattar [9], who uses Petri nets as a state-based model to design narrative plots. The use of Petri nets to model and control individual characters in an interactive storytelling context is also explored by Brom and Abonyi [4], who utilize manually designed Petri nets to represent the narrative of the game.

Although Petri nets have been previously explored as a structure to represent narrative plots, most of the previous research focus on the use Petri nets as a modelling tool to allow authors to design interactive narratives. In this paper, we follow a different approach and focus on plot composition by automatically mapping situation calculus schemas into Petri net representations that are suitable for interactive dramatization.

3 From Situation Calculus to Petri Net Models

3.1 The Basic Situation Calculus Model

Situation calculus is a logical language used to represent and reason about dynamic worlds, which has been successfully applied to a variety of domains and problems, including narrative generation [6]. According to Kowalski [15], situation calculus, as a logic program, can be compactly expressed by the following two clauses, which define what sentences P hold in the situation $result(A, S)$ that is the result of the transition from state S by an action of type A:

$$holds(P, result(A, S)) \leftarrow happens(A, S) \wedge initiates(A, S, P)$$
$$holds(P, result(A, S)) \leftarrow happens(A, S) \wedge holds(P, S) \wedge \neg terminates(A, S, P)$$

noting that the second clause of this second-order logic formulation avoids the exponential proliferation of first-order logic clauses, which constitutes the so-called frame problem by eliminating the need to specify every class of facts (P) that are *not* affected by the execution of an operation (A).

In turn, these situation calculus clauses suggest an elementary plan-generator, which can be thus expressed in natural language:

- A fact F holds if it is true in the initial state;
- F holds if it is added as one of the effects of an operation Op, and the preconditions of Op hold at the current state;
- F holds after the execution of an operation Op if it did already hold at the current state and if it is not deleted as one of the effects of Op.

and then translated into a Prolog program:

```
holds(Fact, [start]) :- initial_state(Fact), !.
holds(Fact, [Operation | Current_state]) :- added(Fact, Operation),
                                    precond(Operation, Current_state).
holds(Fact, [Operation | Current_state]) :- not deleted(Fact, Operation),
                                    holds(Fact, Current_state).
```

Although this elementary program is able to handle overly simple cases, such as the well-known monkey-and-bananas problem, it must be considerably expanded for practical usage, such as proposed in [5, 7].

As a general starting point to apply situation calculus in storytelling domains, one must specify static and dynamic schemas, which include the classes of facts that will eventually populate states, a set of facts describing the initial state, and a fixed repertoire of event-producing operations for performing state changes in conformance with the applicable integrity constraints. Each operation is defined in terms of pre-conditions, which consist of conjunctions of positive and/or negative terms expressing facts, and any number of post-conditions, consisting of facts to be asserted or retracted as the effect of executing the operation (cf. The STRIPS model [11]).

As an illustration, we shall concentrate on a simple narrative incident taken and adapted from the film *Excalibur*, directed, produced, and co-written by John Boorman in 1981. The incident can be thus summarized:

Sir Gawain accuses Queen Guinevere of adultery. A trial by combat is announced, there being two candidate knights to claim the Queen's innocence: Lancelot, a worthy knight, famous for his many victories, and Perceval, who would be no less reputed in the future, but at that time still had little combat experience. The Queen would be vindicated if her defender could defeat the accuser, otherwise she would be condemned. The trial could be reinitiated if a last-minute replacement of defender chanced to occur.

The entities involved in the incident and their properties are specified through a static schema:[1]

```
entity(person, pn).
entity(knight, kn).
attribute(knight, strength).
attribute(knight, loyal).
entity(accuser, an).
entity(defendant, dn).
attribute(defendant, has_defender).
entity(defender, dn).
entity(challenger, cn).
entity(offense, on).
relationship(accusation, [defendant, offense]).
attribute(accusation, vindicated).
attribute(accusation, condemned).
relationship(encounter, [challenger, defender]).
attribute(encounter, winner).
```

The event-producing operations are defined in a dynamic schema. For example, the operator for the *combat* event is defined below, noting that the V parameter identifies the winner, who can be either the accuser or the defending knight, depending on their strength:

```
operation(combat(A, K, D, O, V)).
precond(combat(A, K, D, O, V), (accusation(D, O), challenger(A),
        defender(K), strength(K, Sk), strength(A, Sa),
        if(Sk > Sa, V = K, V = A))).
added(encounter(A, K), combat(A, K, D, O, V)).
added(winner([A, K], V), combat(A, K, D, O, V)).
added(defendant(D), accuse(A, D, O)).
```

In order to conduct experiments, an initial state must be introduced, indicating the instances of the entity classes and the specific initial values of their properties:

```
person('Guinevere').
knight('Lancelot').
loyal('Lancelot', true).
strength('Lancelot', 200).
knight('Perceval').
loyal('Perceval', true).
strength('Perceval', 100).
knight('Gawain').
loyal('Gawain', false).
strength('Gawain', 150).
offense(murder).
offense(adultery).
```

Described in this fashion, the well-intentioned but still immature Perceval would stand no chance to defeat Gawain when playing the role of defender. This default result is evidenced in the plan-generated plot below, in which the last parameter of the combat operation (in boldface) indicates the winner:

---

[1] A complete description of the static and dynamic schemas used in this example is available at: http://www.icad.puc-rio.br/~logtell/petri-net/schemas-trial-by-combat.pdf.

```
accuse(Gawain, Guinevere, adultery), enter_challenger(Gawain, Guinevere,
adultery), enter_beginner_defender(Perceval, Guinevere, adultery), com-
bat(Gawain, Perceval, Guinevere, adultery, Gawain), condemn(Guinevere,
adultery).
```

On the contrary, Lancelot had what was required to triumph, thereby establishing the Queen's innocence:

```
accuse(Gawain, Guinevere, adultery), enter_challenger(Gawain, Guinevere,
adultery), enter_worthy_defender(Lancelot, Guinevere, adultery), com-
bat(Gawain, Lancelot, Guinevere, adultery, Lancelot), vindi-
cate(Guinevere, adultery).
```

Both for serious and for entertainment applications, the situation calculus model leads to the verification, by applying plan-generation, whether the proposed specification allows all desirable use cases and effectively disallows those which transgress the intended conventions [6]. On the other hand, the Petri net model, like other workflow engines, can be designed to run in a tightly restrictive mode, with the additional asset of the explicit determination of the workable sequences and of the branching points open to the user's choice – which strongly suggests that it is particularly qualified for the dramatization of interactive narratives.

In this paper, we argue that the two models are complementary to each other, to the point that the Petri net representation can be generated from the situation calculus model, over which an execution method, analogous to the standard token-based Petri net method, can be operated.

3.2   Deriving a Petri Net from a Situation Calculus Model

In the semi-formal terminology employed in this paper, a Petri net is a graph with two kinds of nodes: *places* (round nodes, either empty or containing exactly one token) and *transitions* (square nodes representing operations).[2]

We define a Petri net *edge* as triple (Op_1, Pn, Op_2), with two (operational) transition nodes (Op_1 and Op_2) and an intervening place node (Pn). Petri net edges are positioned so as to express a partial ordering in the execution of events, which may follow each other in linear sequences, possibly branching to form and-forks, or-forks, and-joins, and or-joins. We shall also consider a simple case of backward loop, allowing to return to a previous position and try different branching options.

Our approach to generate a Petri net model is based on the observation that the ordering requirements of a Petri net can be derived from the situation calculus model. The first basic consideration is that there exists an edge connecting (through a Pn node) Op_1 and Op_2 if the post-conditions of Op_1 have a non-empty intersection with the pre-conditions of Op_2. There is also an edge from Op_1 to Op_2 if some post-condition of Op_1 cancels some post-condition of Op_2 (thus causing a backward loop, whereby Op_2 can be retried).

Forks occur when there are edges leading from an Op node into two or more nodes $Op_1, Op_2, ..., Op_n$. A fork is an or-fork if $Op_1, Op_2, ..., Op_n$ contain either incompatible pre-conditions or redundant post-conditions. Incompatibility typically results from

---

[2] A comprehensive and still useful classic survey of the Petri net formalism is provided in [21].

conflicting value comparisons as well as from logic opposition (*P* vs. not *P*). In addition, we consider any pair Op_i and Op_j incompatible if the execution of one of them would be rendered impossible by the execution of the other, which might happen if the pre-conditions of one of these operations require *P* (or not *P*), whereas the post-conditions of the other produce the deletion of *P* (or, respectively, the addition of *P*). A fork is an and-fork if none of these situations holds.

Joins occur when there are edges from two or more nodes Op_1, Op_2, ..., Op_n into a single node *Op*. A join is an or-join if Op_1, Op_2, ..., Op_n contain redundant post-conditions, or post-conditions that cancel the post-conditions of *Op* (which induces a backward loop enabling *Op* to be retried). A join is an and-join if none of these situations holds.

By thus considering the presence of edges, as well forks and joins, we have a method to automatically generate a clausal representation of the Petri net corresponding to a given situation calculus specification.

In order to illustrate the results of our method, we shall return to the trial by combat example described in the previous section. By applying our method, we obtain the clausal representation below describing the edges of the Petri net. The one-letter operation labels provide a useful abbreviation, commonly employed in process mining [1] to represent transactions as parameter-less *traces*.

```
(∅, start, a:accuse(a, d, o))
(a:accuse(a, d, o), s(1), b:enter_worthy_defender(k, d, o))
(a:accuse(a, d, o), s(1), c:enter_beginner_defender(k, d, o))
(a:accuse(a, d, o), s(2), d:enter_challenger(a, d, o))
(b:enter_worthy_defender(k, d, o), s(3), e:combat(a, k, d, o, v))
(c:enter_beginner_defender(k, d, o), s(3), e:combat(a, k, d, o, v))
(d:enter_challenger(a, d, o), s(4), e:combat(a, k, d, o, v))
(e:combat(a, k, d, o, v), s(5), f:reinitiate_trial(a, k, d, o, v))
(e:combat(a, k, d, o, v), s(5), g:vindicate(d, o))
(e:combat(a, k, d, o, v), s(5), h:condemn(d, o))
(f:reinitiate_trial(a, k, d, o, v), s(1), b:enter_worthy_defender(k, d, o))
(f:reinitiate_trial(a, k, d, o, v), s(1), c:enter_beginner_defender(k,d,o))
(f:reinitiate_trial(a, k, d, o, v), s(2), d:enter_challenger(a, d, o))
(g:vindicate(d, o), end, ∅)
(h:condemn(d, o), end, ∅)
```

The detected cases of or-forks and or-joins are listed below:

```
Or-forks:
accuse(a, d, o) → enter_worthy_defender(k, d, o),
                 enter_beginner_defender(k, d, o)
combat(a, k, d, o, v) → condemn(d, o),
                        vindicate(d, o),
                        reinitiate_trial(a, k, d, o, v)
reinitiate_trial(a, k, d, o, v) → enter_worthy_defender(k, d, o),
                                  enter_beginner_defender(k, d, o)
Or-joins:
combat(a, k, d, o, v) ← enter_worthy_defender(k, d, o),
                        enter_beginner_defender(k, d, o)
enter_beginner_defender(k, d, o) ← accuse(a, d, o),
                                   reinitiate_trial(a, k, d, o, v)
enter_worthy_defender(k, d, o) ← accuse(a, d, o),
                                 reinitiate_trial(a, k, d, o, v)
enter_challenger(a, d, o) ← accuse(a, d, o)
                            reinitiate_trial(a, k, d, o, v)
```

Once the clausal representation is generated, a visual representation of the Petri net can be created, as shown in Fig. 1.

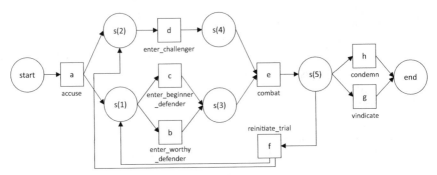

Fig. 1. Petri net drawn from the clausal representation derived from the situation calculus model.

Operations coming from and-forks can be executed in any order. In addition, they might be executed in parallel to simulate narrative events taking place at the same time. As a preliminary consideration, note that, by construction, or-forks stem from place nodes, and or-joins always converge to a single place node. Since place nodes can contain at most one token, or-type branching is restricted – as should be expected – to the selection of a single option. In contrast, and-forks stem from operation nodes, and and-joins converge to an operation node. Differently from place nodes, operation nodes are able to emit tokens to all outgoing place nodes (one token for each).

The generated Petri net is ready to be executed in order to establish the plot for an interactive narrative. According to the standard token-based Petri net process, executing a Petri net begins by placing a token in the start place node. The place node is then <u>activated</u> which signifies that the token is consumed, and the single operation node attached to the start node is <u>enabled</u>. In the next steps, successive place nodes are activated after receiving tokens from enabled nodes, and some operation node to which all incoming place nodes are active (i.e., contain a token) is chosen to be enabled. The process ends when some operation node connected to the end place node is reached.

An interactive trace-generation program that allows users to traverse through the Petri net generated for the trial by combat is available online at:

http://www.icad.puc-rio.br/~logtell/petri-net/trial-by-combat/.

4 Interactive Storytelling Application

In order to validate the applicability of our method, we implemented a full interactive storytelling system capable of representing the generated Petri net models using 2D graphics and animations.

4.1 System Architecture

The architecture of our interactive storytelling system is based on a client-server model (Fig. 2), where the server is responsible for the generation of the plot (Petri net model) and the client handles the dramatization of the story. On the server-side, the Network Manager receives plot requests from clients and uses the Prolog implementation described in the previous sections to generate a Petri net, which is then sent to clients for dramatization. On the client-side, the Drama Manager interprets and controls the execution of the Petri net by sending action requests to virtual Actors. The process of composing scenes for dramatization (i.e., selecting the Actors and Locations to show) is performed by the Scene Composer, which is constantly being informed by the Drama Manager about the type of scene being dramatized.

User interaction is handled by the Interaction App module, which is implemented as a mobile app that uses a Convolutional Neural Network classifier to identify hand-draw sketches (see [20] for more details about the sketch recognition process). Once a sketch is recognized, its identification class is sent to the Interaction Server through a TCP/IP network message. The Interaction Server module is responsible for receiving and interpreting the sketch classes sent by clients. Two interaction modes are supported: (1) single user mode, in which the first valid user sketch received by the system is immediately used as the interference choice to be incorporated into the story; and (2) voting mode, in which the Interaction Server collects all users' sketches during a certain time and then selects one through a voting process.

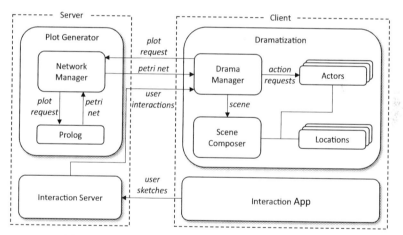

Fig. 2. Architecture of our interactive storytelling system.

Multiple programming languages were used in the implementation of our interactive storytelling system. As described in the previous sections, the process of generating plots in the Petri net model is implemented in Prolog. However, the Plot Generator also includes an additional module called Network Manager, which is implemented in C# and provides network communication capabilities to the system, allowing us to implement the plot generation process as a service provided by a network server. On the client-side, the dramatization system is implemented in Lua[3] using the Löve 2D framework,[4] which provides the graphical functionalities needed to create visual representations for the story. The interaction process is implemented in Java as an Android app, which communicates with a Web service implemented in PHP. See [12] for more details about the design of the sketch-based interaction system.

The Petri net representation of the plot created by the Plot Generator consists of a directed graph $G = (V, E)$, where V is a set of nodes $\{v_1, v_2, ..., v_n\}$ and E is a set of edges $\{e_i = (v_i, v_j), ..., e_m = (v_k, v_w)\}$. Each node v_i is a pair (id_i, ev_i), where id_i is a unique name that identifies the node v_i and ev_i is an event description in a predicate format for *transition* nodes (e.g., accuse(a,d,o)), or the constant nil for *place* nodes (as described in Sect. 3.2, places are nodes that can contain tokens and transitions are nodes that represent operations).

When encoding the Petri net to be sent to the dramatization system, the graph is simplified as a set of edges, where each edge is represented in the format $[id_i: ev_i, id_j: ev_j]$. For example, the initial edges of the Petri net generated for the trial by combat (connecting nodes *start*, *a*, *s(1)*, and *s(2)*, as illustrated in Fig. 1), can be described as:

```
[start:nil, a:accuse(a, d, o)]
[a:accuse(a, d, o), s(1):nil]
[a:accuse(a, d, o), s(2):nil]
```

4.2 Interactive Dramatization

The process of dramatizing the Petri net representation of the plot involves a simple step-wise algorithm that controls the execution of the story by updating a list of active events according to a standard token-based execution approach. As described in Algorithm 1, function Execute-PetriNet-Step receives by parameter a Petri net PN and a list C with the nodes that were executed in the previous step of the algorithm (for the first step: C={start}). The algorithm performs all the operations to activate place nodes and transition nodes for a single iteration of the execution process. The narrative events associated with activated transition nodes are added to set A, which is returned when the execution of the iteration ends. The set of narrative events returned by a single call of function Execute-PetriNet-Step represents the parallel events that take place during a certain point of the narrative. When the dramatization of these events ends, function Execute-PetriNet-Step can be called again to obtain the next narrative events for dramatization. If an empty set is returned, the narrative ends.

---

[3] Lua is a well-known programming language developed at the Pontifical Catholic University of Rio de Janeiro, Brazil (http://www.lua.org/).

[4] https://love2d.org/.

Algorithm 1. Petri net execution algorithm.

```
1.    function Execute-PetriNet-Step(PN, C)
2.       A = Ø;
3.       for each node V in C do
4.          if PN[V] is a PLACE then
5.             N = number of edges in PN[V];
6.             if N is greater than 0 then
7.                if N is 1 then
8.                   S = first edge in PN[V];
9.                else
10.                  S = get selected edge from PN[V] based on user interaction;
11.               end
12.               TA = get number of tokens available in parent nodes of PN[S];
13.               TN = get indegree of PN[S];
14.               if TA is greater or equal than TN then
15.                  Consume TN tokens from the parent nodes of PN[S];
16.                  Add S to A;
17.               end
18.            end
19.         else if PN[V] is a TRANSITION then
20.            for each edge E in PN[V] do
21.               if PN[E] is a PLACE then
22.                  Add a token to place PN[E];
23.                  L = Execute-PetriNet-Step(PN, {E});
24.                  for each node W in L do
25.                     Add W to A;
26.                  end
27.               end
28.            end
29.         end
30.      end
31.      return A;
32.   end
```

All the assets used for dramatization (e.g., character animations, background images, and audio files) are defined in a library manually constructed for the domain of a specific story. The context library is a 5-tuple $L = (\gamma, \alpha, \beta, \delta, \pi)$, where:

- γ is a set that defines the actors of the story. Each actor has a name and a set of actions, which are represented by animations in a sprite sheet format;
- α defines the locations of the story. Besides associating each location with a background image and a soundtrack, it also defines a set of waypoints where actors can be placed during the scene composition process;
- β defines the characters' dialogs (text and audio);
- δ is a set that defines the interaction points of the story. Each interaction point is associated with a set of interactive objects, which are represented by the classes of sketches that can be used by users to interact at each interaction point. The interaction points also include a set of instructions to guide the user during the interaction;
- π establishes values for the variables present in the events of the Petri net.

In our implementation, the context library is defined in an XML file. The library used for the trial by combat example is available at: http://www.icad.puc-rio.br/~logtell/petri-net/context-trial-by-combat.xml.

During the dramatization of the story, our system generates 2D animations in real time according to the actions performed by the virtual actors. An automatic virtual camera maintains the active actors always centered in the image frame while they move around the virtual world. When more than one actor is involved in the action, the camera will target the center of the scene, which is calculated based on the positions of all characters that are participating in the event.

User interaction occurs at or-fork nodes of the Petri net. When a node of this type is activated, users are instructed by the virtual characters to interact by drawing specific objects in the interaction app. The instructions are defined in the context library and comprise a set of phases (text and audio), which are repeated until the user draws a valid object (single user interaction mode) or during a certain time frame (voting interaction mode). When the user's choice is identified, the corresponding transition node is selected to be activated (as indicated in line 10 of Algorithm 1). An example of a user interaction moment for the trial by combat is illustrated in Fig. 3, showing the user's decision whether to help Gawain or Perceval, in the combat by drawing a spear or a sword (i.e., the weapons used by each character). A complete video demonstration of the trial by combat example is available at:

https://www.youtube.com/watch?v=qI2TeBrhycc.

(a)   (b)

Fig. 3. User interaction moment in the trial by combat: (a) shows the dramatization system instructing the user to draw a spear to assist Gawain or a sword to help Perceval; and (b) shows that the user chose to draw a sword in the interaction app.

5   Concluding Remarks

We claim that our research thus far has already revealed the advantages of the complementary use of situation calculus and Petri nets. The situation calculus model is most convenient to start with, allowing to investigate through a planning algorithm the appropriateness of the initial specification.

On the other hand, mapping the situation calculus schemas into the graphic structure of a Petri net permits the identification of the points where the narrative process proceeds along branching sequences, so as to recognize and explicitly annotate the occurrence of forks, joins and loops. This kind of information is most helpful to guide interactive plot generation/dramatization and is indispensable if dramatization is done by putting together video-recorded sequences [18], given that scene transition often poses nontrivial adjustment problems that cannot be left to be solved at runtime.

In addition, one must recall the relevance of this method to game design [16], where multiple-ending and branching path storytelling mark increasingly advanced stages in the interactivity spectrum, with remarkable examples, such as the Mass Effect trilogy (BioWare, 2007–2012) and The Witcher trilogy (CD Projekt RED, 2007–2015). Due to their predictability, handcrafted branching narrative structures are still dominant in the game industry. However, we believe that more open approaches to interactive story-telling, such as our method, can expand the boundaries of game narratives towards new forms of interactive experiences. The situation calculus used at the specification stage of our approach gracefully deals with unpredictability because the complete sequence of outcomes is not explicit in the set of operators but can be easily verified.

Much work, however, remains to be done. As a proof of concept, we initiated this project working upon an oversimplified example. Accordingly, we do not claim that the current prototype can handle all problems associated with more complex applications and intricate Petri net schemes. For instance, Petri net loops caused by iterative actions have not been considered. Also, we could enrich the information kept at each Petri net node by collecting user behavior data during a run and analyzing them to regulate the branching options. Another essential future investigation is to address non-deterministic events, i.e., events that can have more than one outcome. Finally, we also plan to explore authoring systems to support story writers, and to conduct comprehensive user satisfaction tests involving writers (i.e., authors) and players (i.e., co-authors) in future works.

Acknowledgements. We want to thank CNPq (National Council for Scientific and Technological Development) and FINEP (Funding Agency for Studies and Projects), which belong to the Ministry of Science, Technology, and Innovation of Brazil, for the financial support.

References

1. Aalst, W.V.D.: Process mining. Commun. ACM **55**(8), 76–83 (2012). https://doi.org/10.1145/2240236.2240257
2. Agostinelli, S., Maggi, F.M., Marrella, A., Mecella, M.: Verifying petri net-based process models using automated planning. In: Proceedings of the 2019 IEEE 23rd International Enterprise Distributed Object Computing Workshop (EDOCW), pp. 44–53. IEEE Press, New York (2019). https://doi.org/10.1109/EDOCW.2019.00021
3. Balas, D., Brom, C., Abonyi, A., Gemrot, J.: Hierarchical petri nets for story plots featuring virtual humans. In: Proceedings of the Fourth AAAI Conference on Artificial Intelligence and Interactive Digital Entertainment (AIIDE'08), pp. 2–9. AAAI Press, Menlo Park (2008)
4. Brom, C., Abonyi, A.: Petri-nets for game plot. In: Proceedings of AISB Artificial Intelligence and Simulation Behaviour Convention **3**, pp. 6–13 (2006)
5. Ciarlini, A.E.M., Barbosa, S.D.J., Casanova, M.A., Furtado, A.L.: Event relations in plan-based plot composition. Computers in Entertainment **7**(4), 55 (2009). https://doi.org/10.1145/1658866.1658874

6. Ciarlini, A.E.M., Casanova, M.A., Furtado, A.L., Veloso, P.A.S.: Modeling interactive storytelling genres as application domains. J. Intelligent Inf. Systems **35**(3), 347–381 (2010). https://doi.org/10.1007/s10844-009-0108-5

7. Ciarlini, A.E.M., Pozzer, C.T., Furtado, A.L., Feijó, B.: A logic-based tool for interactive generation and dramatization of stories. In: Proceedings of the International Conference on Advances in Computer Entertainment Technology (ACE 2005), pp. 133–140. ACM Press, New York (2005). https://doi.org/10.1145/1178477.1178495

8. Eco, U.: The Open Work. Harvard University Press, Cambridge (1989)

9. El-Sattar, H.K.H.A.: A new framework for plot-based interactive storytelling generation. In: Proceedings of the 2008 Fifth International Conference on Computer Graphics, Imaging and Visualisation, pp. 317–322. IEEE Press, New York (2008). https://doi.org/10.1109/CGIV.2008.50

10. Fernandes, A., Ciarlini, A.E.M., Furtado, A.L., Hinchey, M.G., Casanova, M.A., Breitman, K.K.: Adding flexibility to workflows through incremental planning. Innovations Syst. Softw. Eng. **3**(4), 291–302 (2007). https://doi.org/10.1007/s11334-007-0035-y

11. Fikes, R.E., Nilsson, N.J.: A new approach to the application of theorem proving to problem solving. Artif. Intell. **2**(3–4), 189–208 (1971). https://doi.org/10.1016/0004-3702(71)90010-5

12. Gheno, F., Lima, E.S.: História viva: a sketch-based interactive storytelling system. In: Proceedings of the XX Brazilian Symposium on Computer Games and Digital Entertainment (SBGames 2021), pp. 116–125. SBC, Porto Alegre (2021)

13. Hickmott, S., Rintanen, J., Thiebaux, S., White, L.: Planning via petri net unfolding. In: Proceedings of the 20th International Joint Conference on Artificial intelligence, pp. 1904–1911. AAAI Press, Menlo Park (2007)

14. Kindler, E., Rubin, V., Schäfer, W.: Process mining and petri net synthesis. In: Eder, J., Dustdar, S. (eds.) BPM 2006. LNCS, vol. 4103, pp. 105–116. Springer, Heidelberg (2006). https://doi.org/10.1007/11837862_12

15. Kowalski, R., Sadri, F.: Reconciling the event calculus with the situation calculus. J. Logic Programming **31**(1–3), 39–58 (1997)

16. Lebowitz, J., Klug, C.: Interactive Storytelling for Video Games: A Player-Centered Approach to Creating Memorable Characters and Stories. Focal Press, Waltham (2011)

17. Lee, Y.-S., Cho, S.-B.: Dynamic quest plot generation using Petri net planning. In: Proceedings of the Workshop at SIGGRAPH Asia (WASA '12), pp. 47–52. ACM Press, New York (2012). https://doi.org/10.1145/2425296.2425304

18. de Lima, E.S., Feijó, B., Furtado, A.L.: Video-based interactive storytelling using real-time video compositing techniques. Multimedia Tools Appl. **77**(2), 2333–2357 (2017). https://doi.org/10.1007/s11042-017-4423-5

19. Lima, E.S., Furtado, A.L., Feijó, B., Casanova, M.A.: A note on process modelling: combining situation calculus with petri nets. Technical Report 01/2022, Department of Informatics, PUC-RIO, Rio de Janeiro (2022). https://doi.org/10.17771/PUCRio.DImcc.59758

20. Lima, E.S., Gheno, F., Viseu, A.: Sketch-based interaction for planning-based interactive storytelling. In: Proceedings of the XIX Brazilian Symposium on Computer Games and Digital Entertainment (SBGames 2020), pp. 348–356. IEEE Press, New York (2020). https://doi.org/10.1109/SBGames51465.2020.00029

21. Peterson, J.L.: Petri nets. ACM Comput. Surv. **9**(3), 223–252 (1977). https://doi.org/10.1145/356698.356702

22. Peterson, J.L.: Petri Net Theory and the Modeling of Systems. Prentice Hall, Upper Saddle River (1981)

23. Riedl, M., Li, B., Ai, H., Ram, A.: Robust and authorable multiplayer storytelling experiences. In: Proceedings of the Seventh AAAI Conference on Artificial Intelligence and Interactive Digital Entertainment (AIIDE'11), pp. 189–194. AAAI Press, Menlo Park (2011)

24. Tan, X.: SCOPE: A situation calculus ontology of Petri Nets. In: Proceedings of 6th International Conference of Formal Ontology in Information Systems, Toronto, Canada, pp. 227–240 (2010)
25. Ziparo, V.A., Iocchi, L., Nardi, D., Palamara, P.F., Costelha, H.: Petri net plans - a formal model for representation and execution of multi-robot plans. In: Proceedings of the 7th International Conference on Autonomous Agents and Multiagent Systems (AAMAS 2008), pp. 79–86 (2008)

Upward Influence Tactics: Playful Virtual Reality Approach for Analysing Human Multi-robot Interaction

Cornelia Gerdenitsch[1(✉)], Matthias Weinhofer[2], Jaison Puthenkalam[1], and Simone Kriglstein[1,2,3]

[1] AIT Austrian Institute of Technology GmbH, Vienna, Austria
{cornelia.gerdenitsch,jaison.puthenkalam}@ait.ac.at
[2] Faculty of Computer Science, University of Vienna, Vienna, Austria
matthias.weinhofer@univie.ac.at
[3] Masaryk University, Brno, Czech Republic
kriglstein@mail.muni.cz

Abstract. The interest, the potential, and also the technical development in artificial intelligence assistants shows us that these will play an essential role in the future of work. Exploring the interaction and communication between human and artificial intelligence (AI) assistants forms the basis for the development of trustworthy and meaningful AI-based systems. In this paper we focused on the question how humans react to AI - more precisely, AI gents as robots - that act to influence human behavior and emotions by using two upward influencing tactics: Ingratiating and Blocking. For this purpose, we developed a playful virtual reality approach that creates a leader-subordinate relationship between humans and the AI agents in a factory environment. We explore how humans react to those agents. Among other things, we found that behaviors that are seen as likable in humans are perceived as distracting in robots (e.g., compliments used by the ingratiating tactic). Further, robots were perceived as a group and not as individuals. Our findings showed us directions and open questions which need to be investigated in future work investigating human-multi-robot interaction at the workplace.

Keywords: Virtual reality · Robot · Leadership · Influence tactics · Human robot interaction

1 Introduction

Let's imagine a fully automated production line in which a large number of industrial robots handle all manual tasks. The role of the human is to control and monitor the machines. In our specific scenario, a single human works with multiple robots and has authority/power. If we now compare this human multi-robot

B. Göbl et al. (Eds.): ICEC 2022, LNCS 13477, pp. 76–88, 2022.
https://doi.org/10.1007/978-3-031-20212-4_6

system with the relationships between humans in organizations, this corresponds to a leadership situation; the human is the leader and the robots are the subordinates. We now ask how the use of influence tactics, such as those used by employees towards managers, affects humans when used by robots. To address this question, we simulated this scenario in a virtual reality (VR) environment.

In this paper, we present our findings from this VR-based factory environment that creates a leader-subordinate relationship consisting of a human as the leader and multiple robots as the subordinates. Using artificial intelligence, we equipped the robots with upward influence tactics - tactics used by employees to steer the leader in a particular direction [5]. These involve the *ingratiation* tactic - showing approval or praise - and the *blocking* tactic - threatening to work more slowly or become uncooperative. We chose a playful approach with challenges and earnable 'credits' to support the user's interaction with the robots over time. The use of a virtual environment also allows us to safely simulate the factory floor and be free in the design of the robots. An evaluation was conducted to obtain feedback on the designed VR environment and to gain initial insight into how users respond to the robots.

2   Related Work

The way interactions between humans and robots take place in industrial workplaces is described as coexistence (working side by side), cooperation (working on the same product on different tasks) or collaboration (working together on one task) [1]. In this context, robots and humans are work colleagues operating on a similar hierarchical level. However, when authority and power is given to the human who is tasked with instructing and supervising the robots, this is similar to a leader-subordinate relationship; the leader is a human and the subordinates are robots.

Although most research on leadership focuses on the behavior of leaders (i.e., leadership styles; [25]) and how they influence their subordinates, leadership is not an exclusively one-way process. Rather, leadership can be from both sides [28]. Subordinates can influence leaders in the form of upward influence tactics [12,20,24,32]. By bringing the interpersonal influence theory [16] to the organizational setting, Kipnis and colleagues [23] identified a categorization of eight influence tactics including assertiveness, ingratiation, rationality, sanctions, exchange, upward appeals, blocking and coalitions. Since than these tactics have been extended by several authors including [15,32]. The use of a specific tactic depends on a number of contextual and individual factors. Individuals differ for instance in the influence tactic they apply. For instance, one may use self-promotion to obtain a job promotion another one ingratiation [20].

Tactics can be separated into soft - such as ingratiation - and hard - such as assertiveness - ones [14]. For this research we selected one soft and one hard tactic. The tactic *Ingratiation* is shown when employees use compliments to flatter their leaders in order to be treated better or to gain a more positive reputation [19,20,32]. Using ingratiation as influence tactic has a positive effect on performance assessment and extrinsic success [20]. *Blocking*, on the other hand, is formulating a threat of becoming uncooperative if demands are not met, such as working more slowly or ignoring the instructor [5]. Upward influence tactics have been shown not only to affect performance on the job [20] but also to affect the quality of the relationship between leaders and subordinates. In particular, it has been shown that upward influence tactics affect the extent to which leaders favor some subordinates over others in their decisions, as the tactics affect mutual respect [9]. Also, Falbe and Yukl [13], demonstrated that a single soft tactic is more effective than a singly hard tactic.

The interaction between humans and robots have been researched for instance in terms of the appearance of robots [18] and their nonverbal [30] or verbal communication [29]. Further it has been highlighted that the perceived formal authority of a robot influences human behavior. Particularly, it has been shown that robots that are perceived as peers are more persuasive than those with formal authority [31]. Recent research investigates the interaction between humans and multiple robots that are either represented by teams [6,27] or swarms [22]. In this context, the design of the motions of the robot swarm [22] and the interface design of the remote control through which the robot swarm can be instructed [7,26] has been explored so far.

Within this work, we contribute to existing research by exploring how humans experience the interaction with multi-robots when these show behavior that is intended to influence them. In this context, we use artificial intelligence to model autonomous behavior in a way that robots can act independently to some extend.

3 Approach

A VR factory environment was developed using Unreal Engine 4 [11]. In this virtual environment the user acts as a leader of factory workers, that are represented by virtual robot-like characters. In the following sections we describe the robot avatar, the virtual environment and interaction modes, the task of the game, and the robot behavior.

3.1 Robot Avatar

We used Blender 2.8 [4] to create and animate the robot avatar. Based on previous evidence and animation guidelines [33] initial designs were created. A pretest was conducted with 22 participants to gain first feedback from users (Fig. 1 A to E). Within an online survey we asked those users to assess all designs regarding likability, reliability, trustworthiness, competence, intelligence, perceived threat and innocence on a Likert scale from 1 (lowest) to 5 (highest). Participants were then asked to select their most preferred design and rate which variant of the head, body, and eyes design they liked best. The feedback from the participants indicated a preference to designs A and C. We decided to implement design A, since the participants perceived this design as more likeable, trustworthy and

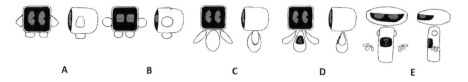

Fig. 1. Initial robot designs (A-E) from two perspectives (front and side), that have been subject to pre-testing.

innocent compared to design C. We argue that these properties may help the bonding between the user and robots.

The final robot design comprised humanoid characteristics including a face, legs and arms (see Fig. 2). In particular, the robot avatar is a white cube with a display which shows two eyes. The arms and legs are white cones. Humanoid robots are preferred in interactions as they garner more trust [8]. Further, it was shown that personality traits were more likely to be attributed to them compared to non-humanoid designs [8]. To represent emotions through facial expressions, the robot was designed with a large head and eyes (see Fig. 3). Previous research highlight facial expressions as a essential feature of a communicative robot [2,21]. To make robots distinguishable in the virtual environment, colored armlets (blue, red, pink, yellow, green) and numbers (1 to 5) on the backside of the robot are used.

Fig. 2. Final design of the robot from three perspectives (front, side, back).

3.2   Virtual Environment and Interaction Modes

The factory environment is designed to be open and on a single level. Two rooms were designed: a leader's office and a factory floor (see Fig. 4). A glass wall is located between the two spaces, through which the robots movements can be observed. The leader's office serves to represent the player's status and authority as a manager. Artifacts such as a large desk and office decorations

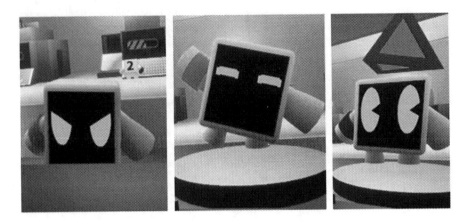

Fig. 3. Three emotional expressions: angry, happy, neutral. Right image: A robot transporting an item on its head, which was picked up from the material supply machine.

(a plant, an abstract painting, and a cup) are used to support this. By moving the head, the player could overlook the entire factory floor.

Goods were produced on the factory floor. Five robots operated three machines that produced one of three different goods: tetrahedrons, cubes and dodecahedrons. Each good was assigned to a machine, graphically represented at the top of the machines. A good can only be produced if the corresponding machine has at least one source material stored. Thus, in a first step, materials must be picked up from the material supply by a robot and brought to the machine. The status of production is displayed on the machine by a progress bar. When a product is finished, it appears at the left side of the machine. A robot then needs to pick the good up and bring it to a fume hood. An image above their heads indicate which good a robot is carrying at the moment.

Interaction in the virtual environment is realized through point and click operations via the VR-controllers. The interaction with the robots is realized through a terminal placed on the leaders desk (see Fig. 5). Four pages are implemented. On the first one the user finds a summary about the actual progress; how many goods have been produced so far. The second one lists all robots. After selecting one robot a third page automatically appears. Tasks can then be assigned to the selected robot. Tasks are i) operating on one of the machines, ii) supplying the machine with materials, iii) collecting all produced goods (robots autonomously seek out finished goods and carry them to the flume hub), and iv) calling robot to the office. Finally, the fourth page summarises the robots' communication. When a robot is attending the office, it formulates requests and thoughts which are depicted at this terminal page.

Fig. 4. Examples from the environment. Left: The place from the player (desk, a display, coffee cup and a plant) and the view to the factory room with the five robots. Robot 2 is operating the machine producing cubes, and robot 5 is operating the machine producing dodecahedrons. Right: A conversation between the player and a robot.

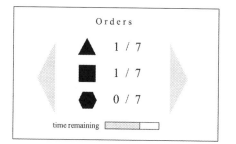

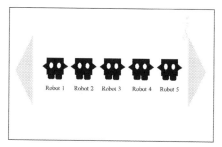

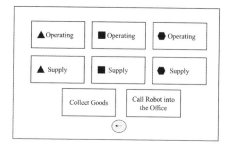

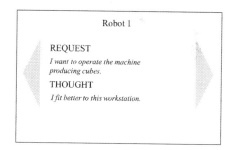

Fig. 5. Terminal.

3.3 Task of the Game

The task of the game is the production of a certain amount of goods within a given time limit. Both aspects can be configured at the beginning of the game, with a default setting of seven tetrahedrons, seven cubes, and seven dodecahedrons to be produced within ten minutes. In order to manage this challenge, the player has to assign robots to specific operations. Credits are awarded to the player whenever a produced good was 'delivered' (sucked into the fume hood). The current status of produced goods and the time remaining is shown at the terminal.

The game session was split in two phases, each of which accounted for half of the defined time. In phase one, the robots follow orders from the players without interacting. In phase two, robots start interacting with the player. They walk in front of the glass wall and wave to the player as a request to come into the office. The player can then decide to let the robot in or not. When the robot is let in, it moves in front of the desk and stands on a marked spot, which then moves up and brings the robot up to desk height. Now the robot can express a request (e.g., 'I want another task') which is shown at the terminal. The player can then comply with the request (e.g. assigning a different task to the robot) or not. Then the robot leaves the office and continues work, with it's behavior adapted based on the player's reaction.

3.4   Robot Behavior

Robots are equipped with one of two types of behavior - *Ingratiating* or *Blocking* - which can be selected at the beginning of the game. We used a behaviour tree system provided by Unreal Engine 4 [10] to model this behavior. This tree was supplemented by additional sub-behaviour trees that would account for autonomous behaviour. Further the behaviour trees were supplemented with the ability to cycle through a variety of facial expressions for the robot, both randomly and context sensitive.

Robots are able to formulate 'requests' and 'thoughts'. Requests concern the task they have been assigned to, and want to have changed (e.g. 'I would like to produce X instead of Y'). Thoughts are represented by compliments in the ingratiating group and threats (of deliberately worse performance if requests are not met) in the blocking group. The sequence and combination of requests and thoughts followed a predefined repeating storyboard. Robots showing the ingratiating behavior follow a repeating four-step pattern of *thought* → *thought* → *request* → *both* (thought and request). Thus, in 75% of the contacts, ingratiating robots formulate thoughts, while in 50% an actual request is formulated. This specific pattern was used in order to establish these robots as being more interested in positive rapport (communicated via thoughts) rather than making demands (communicated via requests). Inversely, robots that are equipped with the blocking behavior follow a cycle with a strong focus on demands: *both* (thought and request) → *request* → *both* → *request*. Thus, in 50% of the contacts robots formulate thoughts, while in 100% requests are formulated. When these requests were not met, they had a random chance of displaying uncooperative behaviours, in particular laying down their work or slowing down work speed.

Every 30–40 seconds one of the robots attempt to make contact with the player in a predefined order (robot 1, robot 3, robot 5, robot 2, and finally robot 4). Thus, players would thus receive about six autonomous contact attempts within five minutes (default setting of phase 2). Further, the interaction cycle would be completed at least once.

4   Evaluation

4.1   Method

We conducted a study with ten participants aged between 25 and 60. Participants were randomly assigned to one of the two influence tactics. In the *Ingratiating* condition there were three female and two male participants, while in the *Blocking* condition there were three male and two female participants. All participants were able to familiarize themselves with the environment and managed the game and inputs without any major problems.

The study lasted about 30 min and was organized in four steps: First, participants were provided with a written instruction with a possibility to discuss technical questions afterwards. After that, the VR glasses were put on and the participants could explore the environment (without robots) and get used to the controllers. Then the gameplay started, with a time limit was set to ten minutes. During gameplay, participants were observed and their comments were noted. Since the game action was simultaneously displayed on a screen connected to the computer running the virtual environment, observation was possible. At the end, we conducted an interview and asked the following questions: *Please describe the assignment/job you were given, How did you perceive your role as leaders?, How did you perceive the robots?, What influenced your decisions to grant or dismiss a robot's request?, How do you describe working with the robots?, What strategy did you use to complete the task?, Can you describe what factors led to your success or failure?,* and *What did playing the game feel like from a technical/haptic standpoint?*

4.2   Findings

At the beginning participants started to establish a game strategy to meet the challenge. Three strategies were observed: In the "one type of goods at a time" strategy, two robots are assigned to a machine for production and supply and another one to goods collection. No adaptations are made, with the purpose of finishing the production of the first good first before continuing with the other ones. Four users followed this strategy, two of which expressed boredom towards the end of the first phase. Another four users employed a "parallel processing" strategy. Here, one robot is assigned to each of the three machines. Another robot has to collect the produced goods and bring them to the fume hood, and the last one supplies all machines with needed material. Finally, in the chaotic approach, the assignments of robots are changed constantly with no discernible reasoning. Two participants used this chaotic approach.

One observation across all participants was that users are activated and excited during the gameplay. This activation further increases in the second phase once the robots start interacting. In this phase, some participants also expressed irritation with these interactions interfering with their strategy.

None of the participants achieved the goal of 7×3 collected goods within ten minutes. Participants felt that the failure was their own fault, as they failed to properly manage the robots which resulted in a lack of organisation. At the same time, some participants saw the robots as capable of the necessary agency. In particular in the blocking condition, two users mentioned to have completely relinquished control to the robots at some point, granting every request thereafter. The reason given was that they thought that the robots would know best what steps had to be taken to manage the factory successfully.

Regarding the robots' appearance, all participants reacted positively to the robots' design and their animations, with nine stating that they perceived their cuteness as appealing and four commenting that the animations made the robots likeable. The greeting/waving animation displayed by the robots when entering the office was perceived as a polite.

In terms of the robots' behavior, nine participants expressed a preference for the robots to be more autonomous and require less direct instruction. Also the randomly displayed emotional expressions have been mentioned several times. Participants mentioned feeling insecure about their own behavior and performance which they perceived to possibly have caused these emotions. For instance, participants formulated worry about having done something incorrectly or performing poorly as a supervisor when a robot displayed an angry or unsatisfied face.

One observation during the game was that participants did not differentiate between the individual robots - instead robots were perceived as a unit. Numbers on the back and colored armlets were used to differentiate between the robots. However, these markers were only used for giving commands and seems to have not lead to participants differentiating between the robots in other aspects - for instance by having a favor for one or another. This also led to the consequence that actions of a single robot 'affected' all the other ones.

Ingratiating Influence Tactic. Participants from the *Ingratiating* group accepted on average 87.5% of the robot requests. The most often given reasons for this were that the requests fit the game strategy anyway, as well as that there was no obvious reason to refuse the request. Once the robots started acting autonomously and interacting with the player, participants showed stress and hectic behavior. This disrupted the game strategies that had been built up in the first phase, and participants then tended to focus on interacting with the robots and to process them as quickly as possible. When asked, *How did you perceive your role as a leader?* participants indicated that their role was relatively low-stress and only became slightly more stressful when the robots began to act autonomously. Two participants in the group were amused or felt complimented by the positive messages from the robots. However, four out of five expressed dissatisfaction that the robots left their work to give encouragement. Participants mentioned that the robots should only interrupt their work when they were not assigned a task or after all tasks were completed. The expressed dissatisfaction with the robots increased with each message that did not contain a specific request.

Blocking Influence Tactic. Participants from the *Blocking* group accepted on average 81% of robot's requests. Two players who approved all of the requests indicated that they assumed that the robots would likely know which actions were best to achieve the stated goals. Therefore, they left the decision-making power to the robots and approved each request from the robots. In response to the question *How did you perceive your role as a supervisor?* all five participants indicated that they found their role stressful. It is worth noting that users did not describe any particular phase as stressful, which distinguishes their descriptions from those of the *Ingratiating* group, where only the second phase was described as stressful. A further observation was that the participants did not seem to notice the robots acting on their threats if their demands were not met (e.g. by becoming slower over time). Instead participants perceived the robots to be acting in a positive and friendly way. Three participants further mentioned not wanting to disappoint the robots and wanting to be a good and friendly boss for them.

5 Discussion

In the present study we used VR to simulate a human multi-robot interaction at an industrial workplace analogous to a leader-subordinate relationship. A evaluation of the virtual simulation yielded insights that should guide further developments and research.

Power and Ability: The user as a leader had the power and authority to give instructions to the robots, but preferred to have the robots do the tasks autonomously with less direct instruction. It was generally assumed that the robot has the necessary ability and can best decide for itself how the challenge can be met. This was expressed through a desire to hand over tasks to the technology. We recommend for future studies to investigate what is associated with this desire. Themes can be for instance, the perception of one's own skills and that of the robots, issues of responsibilities or previous experiences in human-robot interactions.

Individual Robot within a Swarm: We found indications that robots are seen as a group rather than as individual entities. Robots were not afforded individuality, and actions of a single robot affect the robots as a whole. One explanation could be the design of the robots, which was not distinctive enough. Also, forming relationships with individual robots would require more time than we used in the present study. Likewise leader-subordinate relationship form over time by recurrent interactions. Future work could explore if relationships with single robots emerge when interacting with them on a daily basis. It would also be interesting to investigate design principles that support this evolving process. For instance, previous research highlight that body movement and gestures [17], and dimensions of anthropomorphism [3] convey affect. In addition, individual facial expressions (instead of random ones for all) can support individual robot bonding and discrimination.

Influence Tactics: It appeared that users were irritated when the robots started to interact. The reaction to the robot behaviors showed peculiarities. We found, for example, that behaviors that are considered likeable in humans are considered annoying in robots. Participants were irritated and, over time, annoyed when robots approached them to make friendly statements. Behaviours like compliments were perceived as distracting rather than likable. Also blocking behavior was attributed to own mistakes rather than to inappropriate behavior by the robot. Despite initial findings on how robots can exert influence, this was limited to the formulation of very simple requests and thoughts. Future research should focus more on communication and investigate different forms of it.

6   Conclusion

In this paper, we explored the interaction between humans and multiple AI-driven robots in an industrial setting. We placed participants in a VR environment in the role of a manager (in a leader role) managing a group of robots (in a subordinate role) that were equipped with upward influencing tactics. We discovered that behaviours like compliments were perceived as distracting rather than likable. Furthermore, despite differences in appearance, the robots were perceived as a group rather than individuals, and actions of one robot could influence the perception of others. These and other initial findings described in this paper showcase promising areas for future research to explore the relationship between humans and multi AI-driven robots in the context of work.

Acknowledgements. This work is supported by the Austrian Research Promotion Agency (FFG) within the project "Virtual Skills Lab" (FFG No. 872573) and the project "MED1stMR" (Medical First Responder Training using a Mixed Reality Approach featuring haptic feedback for enhanced realism) funded by the H2020 program (Grant Agreement No. 101021775).

References

1. Aaltonen, I., Salmi, T., Marstio, I.: Refining levels of collaboration to support the design and evaluation of human-robot interaction in the manufacturing industry. Procedia CIRP **72**, 93–98 (2018). https://doi.org/10.1016/j.procir.2018.03.214
2. Bartneck, C., Kanda, T., Mubin, O., Al Mahmud, A.: Does the design of a robot influence its animacy and perceived intelligence? Int. J. Soc. Robot. **1**(2), 195–204 (2009)
3. Bartneck, C., Kulić, D., Croft, E., Zoghbi, S.: Measurement instruments for the anthropomorphism, animacy, likeability, perceived intelligence, and perceived safety of robots. Int. J. Social Robot. **1**, 71–81 (2009). https://doi.org/10.1007/s12369-008-0001-3
4. Blender Foundation: Blender 2.8 (2022). www.blender.org/download/releases/2-80 Accessed Jan 12 2022
5. Blickle, G.: Einflusstaktiken von mitarbeitern und vorgesetztenbeurteilung: Eine prädiktive feldstudie. [employee influence tactics and supervisor evaluation: a predictive field study.]. Zeitschrift für Personalpsychologie 1 (2003). https://doi.org/10.1026//1617-6391.2.1.4

6. Chan, W.P., et al.: Design and evaluation of an augmented reality head-mounted display interface for human robot teams collaborating in physically shared manufacturing tasks. J. Hum.-Robot Interact. (2022). https://doi.org/10.1145/3524082
7. Chen, J.Y.C., Haas, E.C., Barnes, M.J.: Human performance issues and user interface design for teleoperated robots. IEEE Transactions on Systems, Man, and Cybernetics, Part C Appl. Rev. **37**(6), 1231–1245 (2007). https://doi.org/10.1109/TSMCC.2007.905819
8. Choudhury, A., Li, H., Greene, C., Perumalla, S.: Humanoid robot-application and influence. Archives Clin. Biomed. Res. **2**, 198–227 (2018). https://doi.org/10.26502/acbr.50170059
9. Clarke, N., Alshenalfi, N., Garavan, T.: Upward influence tactics and their effects on job performance ratings and flexible working arrangements: the mediating roles of mutual recognition respect and mutual appraisal respect. Hum. Resour. Manage. **58**(4), 397–416 (2019). https://doi.org/10.1002/hrm.21967
10. Epic Games Inc.: Behavior trees (2004-2022), docs.unrealengine.com/4.27/en-US/InteractiveExperiences/ArtificialIntelligence/BehaviorTrees. Accessed Jan 12 2022
11. Epic Games Inc.: Unreal engine (2004-2022). https://www.unrealengine.com/en-US Accessed Jan 12 2022
12. Epitropaki, O., Martin, R.: Transformational-transactional leadership and upward influence: the role of relative leader-member exchanges (rlmx) and perceived organizational support (pos). Leadersh. Q. **24**(2), 299–315 (2013). https://doi.org/10.1016/j.leaqua.2012.11.007
13. Falbe, C.M., Yukl, G.: Consequences for managers of using single influence tactics and combinations of tactics. Acad. Manage. J. **35**(63) (1992). https://doi.org/10.5465/256490
14. Farmer, S., Maslyn, J., Fedor, D., Goodman, J.: Putting upward influence strategies in context. J. Organ. Behav. **18**, 17–42 (1997). https://doi.org/10.1002/(SICI)1099-1379(199701)18:1⟨17::AID-JOB785⟩3.0.CO;2-9
15. Ferris, G., Judge, T., Rowland, K., Fitzgibbons, D.: Subordinate influence and the performance rating process; test and a model. Organ. Behav. Hum. Decis. Process. **58**, 101–135 (1994). https://doi.org/10.1006/obhd.1994.1030
16. Gardner, W.L., Martinko, M.J.: Impression management in organizations. J. Manag. **14**(2), 321–338 (1988). https://doi.org/10.1177/014920638801400210
17. Ginevra, C., Villalba, S.D., Camurri, A.: Recognising human emotions from body movement and gesture dynamics. Affective Computing and Intelligent Interaction, pp. 71–82 (2007). https://doi.org/10.1007/978-3-540-74889-2_7arXiv:9780.20139
18. Goetz J, Kiesler S, P.A.: Matching robot appearance and behavior to tasks to improve human-robot cooperation. In: IEEE International Work Robot Human Interact Communication, vol. 11, 575–608 (2003). https://doi.org/10.1109/ROMAN.2003.12517960
19. Gordon, R.A.: Impact of ingratiation on judgments and evaluations: a meta-analytic investigation. J. Personality Social Psychol. **71**(54) (1996). https://doi.org/10.1037/0022-3514.71.1.54
20. Higgins, C.A., Judge, T.A., Ferris, G.R.: Influence tactics and work outcomes: A meta-analysis. J. Organ. Behav. **24**(1), 89–106 (2003). http://www.jstor.org/stable/4093798
21. Kao, Y.H., Wang, W.J.: Design and implementation of a family robot. In: 2015 12th International Joint Conference on Computer Science and Software Engineering (JCSSE), pp. 251–256. IEEE (2015)

22. Kim, L.H., Follmer, S.: Ubiswarm: Ubiquitous robotic interfaces and investigation of abstract motion as a display. Proc. ACM Interact. Mob. Wearable Ubiquitous Technol. **1**(3) (2017). https://doi.org/10.1145/3130931, https://doi.org/10.1145/3130931

23. Kipnis, D., Schmidt, S.M., Wilkinson, I.: Intra-organizational influence tactics: explorations in getting one's way. J. Appl. Psychol. **65**(4), 440–452 1980. https://doi.org/10.1037/0021-9010.65.4.440

24. Lee, S., Han, S., Cheong, M., Kim, S.L., Yun, S.: How do i get my way? a meta-analytic review of research on influence tactics. Leadersh. Q. **28**(1), 210–228 (2017). https://doi.org/10.1016/j.leaqua.2016.11.001

25. Lowe, K.B., Kroeck, K.G., Sivasubramaniam, N.: Effectiveness correlates of transformation and transactional leadership: a meta-analytic review of the mlq literature. Leadersh. Q. **7**, 385–425 (1996). https://doi.org/10.1016/S1048-9843(96)90027-2

26. Lunghi, G., Marin, R., Di Castro, M., Masi, A., Sanz, P.J.: Multimodal human-robot interface for accessible remote robotic interventions in hazardous environments. IEEE Access **7**, 127290–127319 (2019). https://doi.org/10.1109/ACCESS.2019.2939493

27. Ma, L.M., IJtsma, M., Feigh, K.M., Pritchett, A.R.: Metrics for human-robot team design: A teamwork perspective on evaluation of human-robot teams. J. Hum.-Robot Interact. (2022). https://doi.org/10.1145/3522581

28. Madigan, C., Johnstone, K., Way, K.A., Capra, M.: How do safety professionals' influence managers within organizations? a critical incident approach. Saf. Sci. **144**, 105478 (2021)

29. Marin Vargas, A., Cominelli, L., Dell'Orletta, F., Scilingo, E.P.: Verbal communication in robotics: A study on salient terms, research fields and trends in the last decades based on a computational linguistic analysis. Front. Comput. Sci. **2** 591164 (2021). https://doi.org/10.3389/fcomp.2020.591164

30. Saunderson, S., Nejat, G.: How Robots Influence Humans: a survey of nonverbal communication in social human–robot interaction. Int. J. Soc. Robot. **11**(4), 575–608 (2019). https://doi.org/10.1007/s12369-019-00523-0

31. Saunderson, S.P., Nejat, G.: Persuasive robots should avoid authority: The effects of formal and real authority on persuasion in human-robot interaction. Science robotics 6, eabd5186 (2021). https://doi.org/10.1126/scirobotics.abd5186

32. Schriesheim, C.A., Hinkin, T.R.: Influence tactics used by subordinates: a theoretical and empirical analysis and refinement of the kipnis, schmidt, and wilkinson subscales. J. Appl. Psychol. **75**, 246–257 (1990)

33. Thomas, F., Johnston, O.: The illusion of life: Disney animation. Hyperion New York (1995)

OptimizingMARL: Developing Cooperative Game Environments Based on Multi-agent Reinforcement Learning

Thaís Ferreira[1(✉)], Esteban Clua[1], Troy Costa Kohwalter[1], and Rodrigo Santos[2]

[1] Universidade Federal Fluminense, Niteroi, Brazil
thais_ferreira@id.uff.br, {esteban,troy}@ic.uff.br
[2] Universidade Federal do Estado do Rio de Janeiro, Rio de Janeiro, Brazil
rps@uniriotec.br

Abstract. Intelligent agents are critical components of the current game development state of the art. With advances in hardware, many games can simulate cities and ecosystems full of agents. These environments are known as multi-agent environments. In this domain, reinforcement learning has been explored to develop artificial agents in games. In reinforcement learning, the agent must discover which actions lead to greater rewards by experimenting with these actions and defining a search by trial and error. Specifying when to reward agents is not a simple task and requires knowledge about the environment and the problem to be solved. Furthermore, defining the elements of multi-agent reinforcement learning required for the learning environment can be challenging for developers who are not domain experts. This paper proposes a framework for developing multi-agent cooperative game environments to facilitate the process and improve agent performance during reinforcement learning. The framework consists of steps for modeling the learning environment and designing rewards and knowledge distribution, trying to achieve the best environment configuration for training. The framework was applied to the development of three multi-agent environments, and tests were conducted to analyze the techniques used in reward design. The results show that the use of frequent rewards favors the emergence of essential behaviors (necessary for the resolution of tasks), improving the learning of agents. Although the knowledge distribution can reduce task complexity, dependency between groups is a decisive factor in its implementation.

Keywords: Multi-agent reinforcement learning · Cooperative environments · Games

This work is supported by CAPES and FAPERJ.

B. Göbl et al. (Eds.): ICEC 2022, LNCS 13477, pp. 89–102, 2022.
https://doi.org/10.1007/978-3-031-20212-4_7

1 Introduction

The use of Artificial Intelligence (AI) techniques in electronic games has been notably explored in recent years [15,19]. This trend can be explained by the constant advances in research, the evolution in hardware and processing, and the consumer market demands. Reinforcement Learning (RL) [10] is an AI technique that has been largely applied and tested in games [20]. In RL, agents learn through rewards. If the agent receives a positive reward, it begins to understand that this behavior is beneficial. Similarly, if it receives a negative reward, it understands that something is wrong and looks to avoid this behavior. Through these rewards, the agent can learn, so the reward design must be carried out effectively, especially in multi-agent environments, where the distribution of rewards should favor collaboration among agents.

Understanding the whole process of multi-agent reinforcement learning is not a simple task. Although many works explore the Multi-Agent Reinforcement Learning (MARL) domain [2,4,5,9,16,18,19,21], the focus is not on game development but rather on creating new environments or algorithms. These environments are scaled for testing in specific domains with a focus on the performance of the algorithms used [1,8,11,12]. Exploring the MARL domain in game development is extremely important and can bring new perspectives and approaches. Moreover, designing rewards for the best agent learning is not an easy task, and it is necessary to explore and present methods around this challenge.

In this context, we propose the *OptimizingMARL*, a framework for cooperative game environments development based on MARL. The framework brings practices that guide the development and configuration of cooperative multi-agent environments looking for the best performance in agent training. This performance is related to the use of dense rewards (frequent rewards) to encourage the emergence of essential behaviors - those necessary to solve the tasks and the problem. It is possible to identify how the reward design influences the agents' training performance and which strategies are best for each environment developed through the experiments performed. Furthermore, the framework consists of steps for modeling the learning environment, enabling macro understanding of RL and game elements.

This paper is organized as follows: Sect. 2 outlines related work. Section 3 presents the *OptimizingMARL*. Section 4 describes the conducted experiments, presenting the development of the environments applying the framework and the analysis of the results. Finally, Sect. 5 concludes this work, listing contributions, limitations, and future work.

2 Related Work

In the context of MARL, many works explore the use of new algorithms to improve agent learning performance [1,8,11,12]. Foerster et al. [5] present the COMA algorithm that uses the same centralized network for all agents, with the agents' shared observations and actions as input. COMA uses the centralized network to estimate how much each agent influenced the expected value. Each agent learns via a modeled reward that compares the overall reward to the received when that agent's action is replaced by a default action [5].

Cohen et al. [3] introduce MA-POCA (*Multi-Agent Posthumous Credit Assignment*), a new algorithm that is very similar to COMA, but is capable of training groups of agents to solve tasks in which individual agents can be removed or introduced during the episode. Iqbal and Sha [7] present the MAAC algorithm that trains decentralized policies in multi-agent settings using a centralized network capable of sharing and selecting relevant information for each agent at every instant. While these works test the algorithms in environments that simulate games, the focus is not on game development. This works does not specify how the reward design was performed, as the focus is on the results and performance of each algorithm.

Through the literature review, we found only one study by Zhao et al. [22] that most closely resembles our proposal. Zhao et al. [22] present a hierarchical approach for training agents by breaking complex problems into a hierarchy of easy learning tasks to achieve near-human behavior and a high level of skill in team sports games. The authors first train the agents against other easy-level agents and then make the level more difficult once the agent has learned the basics. For the training, they use a proprietary tool they call *Simple Team Sports Simulator (STS2)*. It simulates a 2D soccer environment, in which the state space consists of the coordinates of the players, their speeds, and an indicator of who has the ball.

The authors run tests with agents in 1 vs 1 and 2 vs 2 matches using the PPO [14], DQN [13], and Rainbow [6] algorithms. Through the analysis of the results, the authors concluded that sparse score-based rewards are not sufficient to train the agents even at a high level, which requires the application of a more refined reward design.

Following the proposal of Zhao et al. [22], we seek to improve agent performance in MARL. However, our focus is on modeling the elements of MARL and on reward design. We propose an easy and more practical way to create multi-agent environments that enables a macro understanding of RL elements in the context of a cooperative multi-agent game environment.

3   The Framework OptimizingMARL

Training intelligent agents in cooperative game environments may not be a simple task. The process requires a series of steps and procedures such as specifying the agents, designing rewards, and developing the environment. Moreover, designing rewards that enable faster learning is not trivial, making the process of creating a multi-agent environment optimized for training difficult. To simplify and optimize the process of building and training intelligent agents in cooperative game environments, we propose the *OptimizingMARL*, which comprises three macro-steps: (1) conceptual modeling of the learning environment;

(2) reward design and knowledge distribution; and (3) the creation of the environment. Figure 1 illustrates the macro-steps of *OptimizingMARL* and the next subsections explain them in detail.

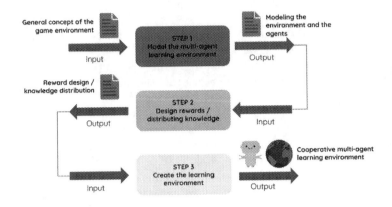

Fig. 1. Overview of the macro steps of the *OptimizingMARL*.

3.1   Model the Multi-agent Learning Environment

In this step, we conceptually specify game and RL elements (e.g., agents, environment). The **concept of the game/environment** provides critical information about the goals and tasks that the agents must accomplish and about the objects that will be present in the environment (e.g., objects that the agents can interact with, obstacles, enemies). The **environment** consists of the place where agents will interact and make decisions. The environment must have the necessary characteristics and objects for the agents to interact and solve their tasks. We can create a document specifying all the objects (and their properties) that must be present in the environment. We define the **scenario objects** - those that are part of the game, such as items, enemies, and obstacles, that the agents will interact with - and the **objects' characteristics** - each object of the scenario has its properties such as colliders, texture, physics, among others.

The **agent** is the actor that observes and performs actions in the environment. An agent must have a **observation space** - the agent collects its observations about the state of the world before making decisions - and **actions**. Finally, there is the reward signal. The reward signal should not be given all the time, but only when the agent performs an action that is good or bad for solving the problem. The reward signal is how the goals are communicated to the agent, so it needs to be configured so that maximizing the reward generates the desired optimal behavior. The next subsection presents the *OptimizingMARL* step related to reward design and the possibility of knowledge distribution based on this design.

3.2   Design Rewards and Distributing Knowledge

The reward is primal in RL and it works as an incentive mechanism, telling the agent what is correct or not. The RL agent's goal is to maximize the total reward received during an execution episode. The reward is immediate and defines the characteristics of the problem to be faced by the agent [17]. To know at what times to reward agents, it is essential that developers have mastery of the problem to be solved in the environment. It is common to have the necessary knowledge about the environment in games. However, depending on the complexity of the environment and the tasks, the projection of rewards may not be trivial or easy to visualize. Therefore, the *OptimizingMARL* comprises a set of activities for understanding the problem to be solved in the environment and for designing rewards. The steps consist of understanding the agents' goals as well as the tasks required to solve the problem. Figure 2 presents the flow of activities.

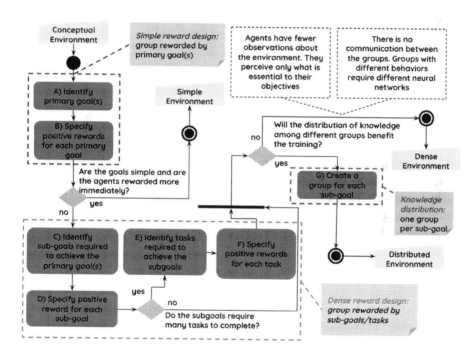

Fig. 2. Activity flow of the reward project/knowledge distribution of the *Optimizing-MARL*.

Simple Reward Design. It starts by identifying the primary goals (activity A) through the conceptual modeling of the environment. The primary goals are directly related to the main problem that the group of agents needs to solve. After their identification it specifies a reward for each of these primary goals (activity B). The reward design is complete, and the environment can begin to be modeled if the group gains rewards so that they can learn the behaviors essential to solving the problem. However, if the goals are still complex and the rewards are still sparse, this can hinder the agents' learning, causing training to take longer. Therefore, it is necessary to design dense rewards so that the group gains rewards more frequently to encourage the emergence of essential behaviors. We define these behaviors as those indispensable to solving the task.

Dense Reward Design. To define dense rewards, it is first necessary to identify the sub-goals derived from the primary goals (activity C). A reward is specified for each of these sub-goals (activity D). Therefore, the group gains rewards more frequently, learning essential behaviors more immediately. If the agents still need to do many tasks to achieve these sub-goals, it is interesting to identify these tasks (activity E) and reward the group for each task performed (activity F). Rewards for primary goals, sub-goals, and tasks should follow a value hierarchy. The group should be rewarded discretely for completing tasks while completing sub-goals will be rewarded more heavily until they complete the primary goal (higher reward value). Therefore, it prevents agents from getting "stuck" just completing tasks instead of progressing and solving the main problem of the environment. After step D (or F), if the knowledge distribution is not suitable for the situation, we end the process and generate a conceptual environment with dense rewards. Otherwise, we proceed to activity (G) and specify a group for each sub-goal following the dense reward design.

Knowledge Distribution. It is necessary to analyze whether the distribution of knowledge will favor training in the environment after specifying the rewards for sub-goals (and optionally the tasks). This step consists in creating a group for each sub-goal. Since each group has a specific goal, the agents may have fewer insights into the environment. After creating a group for each sub-goal, we generate the distributed conceptual environment.

3.3   Create the Learning Environment

The environment development step is the last step of the process. The development consists of creating the necessary elements in the scenario, the agents, programming their behaviors, indicating what to do when an agent is restarted, specifying its sensors, configuring the algorithms and the neural network parameters, and providing the rewards when necessary, among other activities. Unlike the previous two stages, the environment creation step is more specific, as it depends on the platform being used for agent development and training.

4   Experiments

The experiments were developed using the Unity ML-Agents Toolkit [20]. The flexibility of Unity enables the creation of tasks to complex 3D strategy games, physics-based puzzles, or multi-agent competitive games. Unlike other research platforms, Unity is not restricted to any specific gameplay genre or simulation, making it a general platform. We use the MA-POCA [3], a new algorithm designed to train groups of agents to solve tasks.

We performed tests for three configurations of the same environment: simple environment, based on a simple reward design (1), dense environment, which has a dense reward design (2), and a distributed environment, which has a knowledge division among different groups (3). In all experiments the agents perceive the environment through ray cast sensors. These sensors can perceive an element through a tag every time a ray intersects an object. If the tag of that object is specified in the sensor, the agent can perceive this object. ML-Agents Toolkit provides a fully connected neural network model to learn from those observations.

Figure 3 shows the three environments developed and used in the tests. The first environment (left) was not created entirely by us. This environment comes with Unity-ML agents, but we made changes to the environment and followed the steps in the framework to get the three possible configurations. The following subsections describes each environment in more details and our respective findings.

Fig. 3. Dungeon Escape environment (left); Color Balls (center); Wild World (right).

4.1 Dungeon Escape Environment

In the Dungeon Escape environment, the agents cooperate to escape from a dungeon before the dragon escapes through the portal. The agents need to defeat the dragon, get a key that was dropped, and open the door. The agents must collect the sword and hit the dragon to defeat the dragon. From this concept of the Dungeon Escape environment, we use the framework to model the learning environment (step 1). It defines the scenario objects (e.g., the agents, the dragon, the door, the key, the sword) and their properties (e.g., colliders, texture). After that, we applied step 2 of the *OptimizingMARL* following the activities to obtain the three configurations for the environment (simple, dense, and distributed). Figure 4 shows the designed reward and distributed knowledge activities. Finally, we create the learning environment (step 3).

In step 2, we first identify the primary goal, which is to escape from the dungeon. Then we reward the group when they achieve this goal. Since we applied

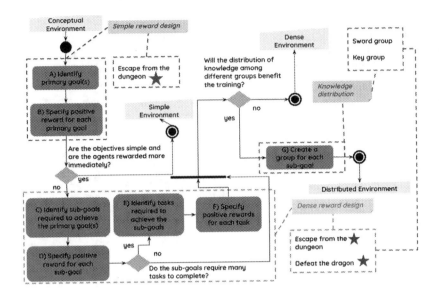

Fig. 4. Dungeon Escape environment rewards and knowledge distribution project.

only the steps related to the simple reward design, this environment is the simple reward environment (1). We continue following the activities to develop the dense reward environment (2). We identify the sub-goal needed to achieve the primary goal: defeat the dragon. Now the group gets rewarded when they defeat the dragon and when they escape from the dungeon. Since the environment is relatively simple, we decided not to divide the sub-goal into tasks and reward the group for them. But this is at the discretion of the development team.

We continue following the activities to develop the environment (3). Once we have identified the sub-goals, we can create an agent type responsible for each of these sub-goals. So we specify an agent type responsible for picking up the sword and defeating the enemy, and another agent type responsible for collecting the key and opening the door. So we will have two groups in this environment.

In both simple (1) and dense (2) environments, there is one group composed of six agents. All agents have the same behavior. The group gains a reward only when an agent escapes from the dungeon. In the distributed environment (3), the agents are divided into two groups, each composed of three agents. The *sword_group* is responsible for collecting the sword and defeating the dragon. This group gain a positively reward only when it defeats the dragon. The *key_group* is responsible for collecting the key that the dragon drops and for opening the door. This group gain a positively rewarded only when it effectively opens the door. The *sword_group* does not perceive the key, the door, or who has the key. The *key_group* does not perceive the sword, nor who has the sword.

Figure 5 presents the results for all environments: (1) simple reward design, (2) dense reward design, and (3) knowledge distribution. The maximum average reward that can be obtained by a group in all environments is 1.0. For analysis purposes, we perform knowledge distribution even though it is not suitable for this environment due to one group's dependence on the other.

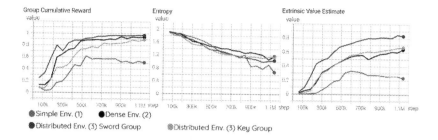

Fig. 5. Results for the three environments in Dungeon Escape experiment.

The cumulative reward group is the mean cumulative episode reward overall agents and should increase during a successful training session. Observing the cumulative reward graph, it is evident that the use of dense rewards (2, green line) improves learning performance if compared to the simple environment (1, red line). In the distributed environment (3), the *sword_group* (light blue line) obtained high rewards. From the graph, the dependency between the groups is clear. The *sword_group* was able to get more rewards because it depends only on itself. The *key_group* (pink line) got smaller rewards because to complete their goal they need the *sword_group* to complete theirs first. The key group gets more rewards as the *sword_group* learns.

Entropy is related to how random the decisions of the model are. It should slowly decrease in a successful training session. It occurred for all environments, meaning that the models make less random decisions during the sessions training. The extrinsic value estimate is the mean value approximation for all states visited by the agent. Once these values have converged to the optimal state values, then the optimal policy can be achieved, which should increase during a successful training session. The *sword_group* in environment 3 presented higher values when compared to the others environments. In this way, this group can obtain the optimal policy in fewer steps.

Through the analysis, we can conclude that dense sub-goal reward design is the best option for the Dungeon Escape environment. Although the *sword_group* in environment 3 shows better learning, the *key_group* was disadvantaged by the dependency between the groups. In addition, specifying the dense rewards for this environment takes less time than specifying two different agent types for each group.

4.2   Color Balls Environment

In the Color Balls environment, the agents need to get all fifteen balls to the goal (green area). To catch a ball of a specific color, the agent must wear the same color uniform. To put on the uniform, the agent needs to get on one of the colored squares. To change the color of the uniform, only climb the square of the desired color. When the agent owns a ball, it cannot change its uniform. We applied the framework to develop the three configurations of the same environment.

In the simple (1) and dense (2) environments, there is one group with ten agents. In environment 1, the group is positively rewarded when it completes the primary goal, which is when all fifteen balls are placed into the green area. In environments 2 and 3, the group is positively rewarded for each ball placed in the green area. In environment 3, the agents do not need to correlate the ball color with the uniform color they are wearing because each group has a specific color. The agents only need to understand that they need to be wearing their uniforms to collect the ball.

Figure 6 shows the results for the three environments. For better visualization, the graph shows the results of red group in environment 3. All groups in this environment have the same behavior, where the only difference is that each one perceives the ball and the square in the color of its group. For comparison, the maximum average reward that can be obtained by the groups is 5.0 in all environments. As expected, the simple environment (orange line) showed low group reward value because agents are failing to complete the tasks before time runs out. The entropy showed a slight decay but less when it is compared to the other environments. Since agents fail to accumulate rewards, the model continues to work on bad policies, and the estimated value for all states does not increase.

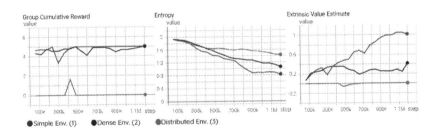

Fig. 6. Results for the three environments in color balls experiment.

This environment is challenging because agents need to understand that they can only pick up a ball if they are wearing the same color uniform. In this case, the vector of observations has an integer variable that corresponds to the color of the ball ($1 =$ yellow, $2 =$ red, $3 =$ white, $4 =$ purple, and $5 =$ blue). Thus, it is necessary to associate the variable value with the tag in the raycast sensor, making learning more difficult. The group's performance improved greatly with the design of the dense rewards (blue line). In environment 2, the group is rewarded for each ball placed in the green area. More immediate reward facilitates the association between the uniform color (integer variable) and the ball tag (string in the raycast sensor).

In environment 3, we changed the integer variable to boolean, indicating whether the agent wore the uniform or not. In addition, the agents have decreased their perceptions and no longer need to associate the colors with the balls. Each group has a specific color and the agents need to put on their uniform, pick up the balls, and place them in the goal. This environment showed the best results, reaching the maximum reward starting at 480k steps. For the value estimate, the groups in environment 3 presented higher values when compared to environments 1 and 2. As such, the groups can obtain the optimal policy in fewer steps.

The analysis allowed us to conclude that distributing knowledge is the best option for the Color Balls environment. The groups in this environment have the same perceptions and behavior, making the knowledge distribution a simple task. The main change is in the vector of observations that starts working with a boolean variable instead of an integer.

4.3   Wild World Environment

In this environment, the agents of a village must survive for an "indeterminate" amount of time in a hostile environment. It means that while the agents keep reaching the goals, they can accumulate rewards until the maximum number of steps in the episode is reached. These goals consist of: making food to feed all the villagers, keeping the fireplaces lit to fight the cold and prevent the villagers from getting hypothermia, and fighting the ferocious wolves that reside in the forest near the village and can attack the villagers. We applied the *Optimizing-MARL* to develop the three configurations of the environment (simple, dense, and distributed).

In the simple (1) and dense (2) environments, there is one group consisting of fifteen agents. In environment 1, the group is positively rewarded when it completes the primary goals: prepare food, light fire, and defeat a wolf. In environment 2, the group is positively rewarded when it reaches the primary goals (higher reward) and sub-goals (small reward): plant vegetables, take wood, and equip the sword.

In environment 3, the agents are distributed into three groups. The *food_group* is responsible for collecting seed, planting the vegetables, harvesting the vegetables, and preparing the food (higher reward). This group is positively rewarded when it plants vegetables (small reward) and prepares the food. The *fire_group* is responsible for equipping ax, taking wood, and lighting the fire (higher reward). This group is positively rewarded when it takes the wood (small reward) and light the fire. The *wolf_group* is responsible for equipping the sword and defeating a wolf. This group is positively rewarded when it equips the sword (small reward) and defeats a wolf (higher reward).

Figure 7 shows the results for the three environments. The *wolf_group* in environment 3 is the only one that has a reward limit. This group gains rewards when an agent equips a sword and when an agent defeats a wolf. However, the number of swords and wolves is finite, making the maximum reward 36 per episode. Regarding the group cumulative reward, the simple environment (dark blue line) presents the lowest values. This can be easily explained because the group is rewarded only when it achieves its primary goals. The problem is that for an agent to achieve one of these goals, it needs to perform a series of tasks beforehand.

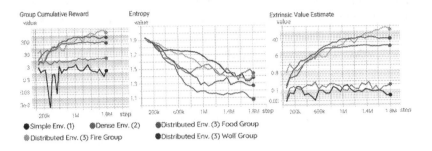

Fig. 7. Results for the three environments in wild world experiment.

The group in environment 2 shows a huge improvement over the previous group. The sub-goal reward encourages agents to complete the primary goals in stages. The *food_group* and *fire_group* groups in environment 3 were also able to achieve high rewards. However, even with fewer perceptions about the environment, the cumulative reward did not show much improvement compared to the group in environment 2. The *wolf_group* kept the accumulated reward around 15 (36 is the maximum value), showing no great improvement or worsening.

The entropy fell for all groups, although it fell more sharply in the *food_group* in environment 3, indicating less random decisions. For the value estimate, the group in environment 2 and the *food_group* and *fire_group* in environment 3 presented higher values when compared to the others. In this way, the groups can obtain the optimal policy in fewer steps.

From the analysis, we can conclude that dense sub-goal reward design is the best option for the Wild World environment. The *wolf_group* in environment 3 cannot perform well. Also, specifying the dense rewards for this environment takes less time than specifying three different agent types for each group.

5   Conclusion

In this paper, we introduced a framework to develop multi-agent environments for cooperative games. The proposed framework addresses the design of dense rewards for emergence of essential behaviors and the knowledge distribution. Through the framework it is possible to design environments aiming to improve the agents' training performance.

Based on the analysis of the results, we can conclude that: (i) dense rewards favor the emergence of essential behaviors, improving agent learning; (ii) knowledge distribution can decrease task complexity. The Color Balls environment showed better results with knowledge distribution. It happened because the task became less complex. Instead of associating the value of the integer variable with the ball tag, the agents now have to understand that if they are in uniform (boolean variable is true), they can pick up the ball; (iii) the dependency of the groups is an important factor in the knowledge distribution. In the Dungeon Escape environment, the key group showed lower results compared to the sword group due to their dependency. In the Survival, Color Balls and Wild World environments (*food_group* and *fire_group*), the groups showed very similar results, evidencing the importance of independence; and (iv) the framework allows the development of an environment in order to improve the learning performance of agents in multi-agent environments.

The main limitation of this work is the number of environments built and used for testing. At the time this paper was written, we had not yet developed environments that brought more elaborate challenges and incorporated different game mechanics. As future work, we intend to: (i) carry out new tests to analyze the impact of individual rewards (the agent is rewarded and not the group) on the performance of the group as a whole; (ii) build more complex environments; and (iii) seek a way to add communication between groups for environments with distributed knowledge.

Acknowledgments. The authors would like to thank NVIDIA, CAPES and FAPERJ for the financial support.

References

1. Bellemare, M.G., Naddaf, Y., Veness, J., Bowling, M.: The arcade learning environment: an evaluation platform for general agents. J. Artif. Intell. Res. **47**(1), 253–279 (2013)
2. Berner, C., et al.: Dota 2 with large scale deep reinforcement learning (2019)
3. Cohen, A., et al.: On the use and misuse of absorbing states in multi-agent reinforcement learning (2021)
4. Foerster, J., Assael, Y., Freitas, N., Whiteson, S.: Learning to communicate with deep multi-agent reinforcement learning. In: Proceedings of the 30th International Conference on Neural Information Processing Systems, pp. 2145–2153. NIPS'16, Curran Associates Inc. (2016)
5. Foerster, J., Farquhar, G., Afouras, T., Nardelli, N., Whiteson, S.: Counterfactual multi-agent policy gradients. In: Proceedings of the AAAI Conference on Artificial Intelligence, vol. 32, pp. 2974–2982. AAAI (2018)
6. Hessel, M., et al.: Rainbow: Combining improvements in deep reinforcement learning. In: Proceedings of the 32nd AAAI Conference on Artificial Intelligence, vol. 32, pp. 3215–3222. PKP Publishing Services Network (2018)
7. Iqbal, S., Sha, F.: Actor-attention-critic for multi-agent reinforcement learning. In: Proceedings of the 36th International Conference on Machine Learning, pp. 2961–2970. PMLR 97, Long Beach, California (2019)
8. Johnson, M., Hofmann, K., Hutton, T., Bignell, D.: The malmo platform for artificial intelligence experimentation. In: Proceedings of the 25th International Joint Conference on Artificial Intelligence, pp. 4246–4247. IJCAI'16, AAAI Press (2016)
9. Jorge, E., Kågebäck, M., Johansson, F., Gustavsson, E.: Learning to play guess who? and inventing a grounded language as a consequence (2016)

10. Kaelbling, L., Littman, M., Moore, A.: Reinforcement learning: a survey. J. Artif. Intell. Res. **4**, 237–285 (1996)
11. Kempka, M., Wydmuch, M., Runc, G., Toczek, J., Jaśkowski, W.: Vizdoom: A doom-based ai research platform for visual reinforcement learning. In: IEEE Conference on Computational Intelligence and Games (CIG), pp. 1–8 (2016)
12. Mnih, V., et al.: Playing atari with deep reinforcement learning (2013)
13. Mnih, V., et al.: Human-level control through deep reinforcement learning. Nature **518**, 529–533 (2015)
14. Schulman, J., Wolski, F., Dhariwal, P., Radford, A., Klimov, O.: Proximal policy optimization algorithms (2017)
15. Summerville, A., et al.: Procedural content generation via machine learning (pcgml). IEEE Trans. Games **10**(3), 257–270 (2018)
16. Sunehag, P., et al.: Value-decomposition networks for cooperative multi-agent learning based on team reward. In: Proceedings of the 17th International Conference on Autonomous Agents and MultiAgent Systems. pp. 2085–2087. AAMAS '18, International Foundation for Autonomous Agents and Multiagent Systems, Richland, SC (2016)
17. Sutton, R., Barto, A.: Reinf. Learn.: Introduction. MIT Press, London, England (2018)
18. Vidhate, D., Kulkarni, P.: Enhanced cooperative multi-agent learning algorithms (ecmla) using reinforcement learning. In: 2016 International Conference on Computing, Analytics and Security Trends (CAST), pp. 556–561. IEEE (2016)
19. Vinyals, O., et al.: Grandmaster level in Starcraft II using multi-agent reinforcement learning. Nature **575**, 350–354 (2019)
20. Yannakakis, G., Togelius, J.: Artificial Intelligence and Games. Springer (2018). https://doi.org/10.1007/978-3-319-63519-4
21. Zhang, Q., Zhao, D., Lewis, F.: Model-free reinforcement learning for fully cooperative multi-agent graphical games. In: 2018 International Joint Conference on Neural Networks (IJCNN), pp. 1–6. IEEE (2018)
22. Zhao, Y., Borovikov, I., Rupert, J., Somers, C., Bierami, A.: On multi-agent learning in team sports games. In: Proceedings of the 36th International Conference on Machine Learning (ICML) (2019)

Game Engine Comparative Anatomy

Gabriel C. Ullmann[1]([✉]), Cristiano Politowski[1], Yann-Gaël Guéhéneuc[1], and Fabio Petrillo[2]

[1] Concordia University, Montreal, QC, Canada
g_cavalh@live.concordia.ca, c_polito@encs.concordia.ca,
yann-gael.gueheneuc@concordia.ca
[2] École de Technologie Supérieure, Montreal, QC, Canada
fabio.petrillo@etsmtl.ca

Abstract. Video game developers use game engines as a tool to manage complex aspects of game development. While engines play a big role in the success of games, to the best of our knowledge, they are often developed in isolation, in a closed-source manner, without architectural discussions, comparison, and collaboration among projects. In this work in progress, we compare the call graphs of two open-source engines: Godot 3.4.4 and Urho3D 1.8. While static analysis tools could provide us with a general picture without precise call graph paths, the use of a profiler such as Callgrind allows us to also view the call order and frequency. These graphs give us insight into the engines' designs. We showed that, by using Callgrind, we can obtain a high-level view of an engine's architecture, which can be used to understand it. In future work, we intend to apply both dynamic and static analysis to other open-source engines to understand architectural patterns and their impact on aspects such as performance and maintenance.

Keywords: Game engines · Game engine architecture · Game development

1 Introduction

Game engines allow developers to create games in an agile and standardized way. While there is a wide array of free, open-source engines, many large studios choose to develop proprietary solutions to be used internally. Famous examples of this approach are Frostbite[1], id Tech[2], and RAGE[3]. There are also popular closed-source engines available publicly, such as Unity and Source [11].

When writing a proprietary engine, developers are able to customize it to fulfill performance or feature requirements of a certain game or game genre,

---

[1] https://www.ea.com/frostbite.
[2] https://arstechnica.com/gaming/2018/08/doom-eternal-reveals-new-powers-puts-hell-back-on-earth/.
[3] https://www.inverse.com/gaming/gta-6-leaks-new-rage-engine.

© IFIP International Federation for Information Processing 2022
Published by Springer Nature Switzerland AG 2022
B. Göbl et al. (Eds.): ICEC 2022, LNCS 13477, pp. 103–111, 2022.
https://doi.org/10.1007/978-3-031-20212-4_8

which may give them an edge on competitors. As a downside, however, this development process hinders exchange of information that could be beneficial to the entire game development community. According to [12], "almost all relevant game engines are closed source which means that particularities on implementation of certain functionalities are not available to developers. The only way for a developer to understand the way certain components work and communicate is to create his/her own computer game engine".

Developers may also find obstacles when creating a game engine from scratch, especially due to a lack of standards on how high-level architecture components should be created and related for this kind of system. Even though books have been published on the topic of game engine architecture [4–6], according to [1], often these publications "tend to only briefly describe the high-level architecture before plunging straight down to the lowest level and describing how the individual components of the engine are implemented". Furthermore, they mention that "such literature offers an excellent source of information for writing an engine, but provides little assistance for designing one when the requirements are different from the solution described".

We believe game engines would benefit from experience exchanges with other projects of the same kind. A comparative analysis would allow us to identify commonalities and propose points of improvement to existing engines. In this work in progress, we compare the call graphs of two open-source engines, Godot and Urho3D, considering these aspects.

The Callgrind profiling tool is used to generate these call graphs, which reflect the execution of a base game project produced with each engine. By comparing the call graphs, we aim to observe the main components of each engine and how responsibilities are divided among them.

While static analysis tools could provide us with a general picture without precise call graph paths, we chose to use a profiler because it allows us to view the call order, frequency, and the number of CPU cycles taken by each method. As a result of this analysis, we will answer the following questions: Are game engine designs similar? If so, how similar are they? Our hypothesis is that game engines follow a similar design and architectural structure.

We show that producing a high-level architecture view of the engine is possible using a profiling tool and that it is a way to get insights into an engine's design. In future work, we will compare these architectures with those proposed by researchers, both through static and dynamic analysis. We will study how design choices made in each case may influence performance, maintenance, and the range of games that can be produced with a given engine.

2   Related Work

Several works compare game engines concerning ease of use [3], available tools and target platforms, and also to determine which are more suitable for a given platform [9] or game genre [10]. However, these comparisons are made from a game developer point of view and do not encompass details related to engine design or implementation. Other works focus on proposing architecture to fulfill a specific requirement, such as low-energy consumption for mobile devices [2]. Novel distributed architectures have also been proposed [7,8].

In our work, we compare Godot and Urho3D, not simply in terms of what features are available and in what situations they fit best, but also looking at how engine subsystems (e.g., graphics, audio, physics, etc.) are organized, initialized and in which ways they interact and relate.

3 Approach

3.1 Overview

Our approach consists of five steps. First, we selected C++ engines available on Github (more details on Sect. 3.2) and cloned their repositories. Following the documentation or running scripts provided by the developer, we compiled them. Using the engine's editor, we created a new project, setting up the minimum necessary to make it run. We will hereby call this our "base game"[4]. A Godot project demands at least one scene object to run, which can be created via the engine's editor. Urho3D, on the other hand, has no editor: one must create a .cpp file and include Urho3D's library to create a new project. We can run the game loop by calling the *Start* method, no scene creation needed.

We then ran the base game's packaging process, which allows us to obtain an executable that can be analyzed by the profiler. In the case of Urho3D, there is no packaging, only .cpp file compilation. Normally the code would be compiled in release mode, with all optimizations in place, but in our case, we changed the packaging settings to obtain an executable with debug symbols.

We ran Callgrind on the base game executable to obtain the list of all calls made by the program, which it saves into a log file. Using KCachegrind, we converted this Callgrind log into a visual representation of the program's execution, a call graph. Class and method names in the graph guided our analysis since they helped us understand the responsibilities of each component.

3.2 Engine Selection

We searched for all repositories on GitHub filtering by topic (*game-engine*) and language (C++). We chose to consider only C++ since this is one of the most popular languages for game engine development [11]. After that, we selected 15 projects and ordered them by number of stars and forks. We then proceeded to clone and build each one of them, starting by those with the highest sum of stars and forks. At the time of writing of this paper, we managed to compile and produce a running executable for two of these engines: Godot and Urho3D.

---

[4] https://github.com/gamedev-studies/engine-profiling-projects/tree/master/BaseGame.

3.3   Engine Compilation and Analysis

We cloned the GitHub repositories for Godot and Urho3D, working with the latest version at the time for each: commit *feb0d* at the *master* branch for Urho3D and commit *242c05* at the *3.4.3-stable* branch for Godot.

Following the instructions in the documentation, we compiled Godot export templates for Linux (we used Ubuntu 20.04.4 LTS), both in release and debug modes. These are binary files containing engine code compiled for a specific target platform. Before generating an executable for any Godot project, we must link these templates to the project via the editor's GUI. We created a Godot base game, generated the executable, and then ran it with Callgrind for 30 s.

4   Godot's Call Graph

We verified that the first tasks Godot executes upon running a game are registering classes and initializing a window (Fig. 1). Since our base game is running on Ubuntu, Godot calls the X11 windowing system. After getting a window instance, the engine then proceeds to call methods to create a scene. Once ready, a notification is sent into the engine's message queue. According to the engine documentation, the *MessageQueue* class is "a thread-safe buffer to queue set and call methods for other threads"[5].

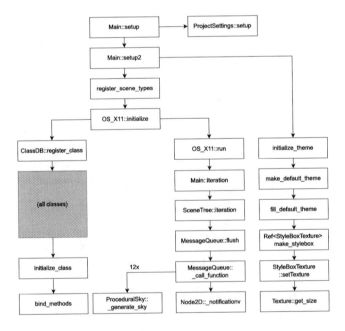

Fig. 1. Godot's base game call graph, showing which methods are called.

---

[5] https://docs.godotengine.org/en/stable/development/cpp/custom_godot_servers.html.

Also during startup, Godot's calls methods to set up its GUI theme system[6], such as *initialize_theme*, even though in our base game it is not being used. Similarly, a *ProceduralSky::_generate_sky* method is called repeatedly even though no sky is drawn. According to Godot's documentation[7], this class procedurally generates a sky object, which is "stored in a texture and then displayed as a background in the scene". Since no textures are loaded into the base game, nothing is drawn, but the sky generation method is called and updated anyway.

To validate our approach, we compared Godot's call graph with a "layers of abstraction" diagram posted on Twitter by Godot's creator Juan Linietsky[8]. This comparison can be seen in Fig. 2. Searching by class names, we found matches for all classes, even though the names were not the same (e.g. *PhysicsServer* and *Physics2DServer*).

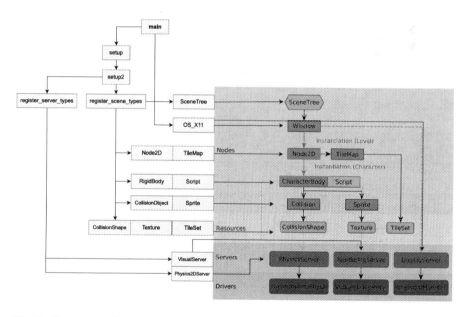

Fig. 2. Comparison between the call graph for Godot base game and diagram of "layers of abstraction" by Juan Linietsky

The most notorious difference is the class described by Linietsky as *Window*. There is no class with this name on Godot's code base. We believe, however, that he referred to windowing systems in general and therefore decided to simply use the term *Window* since his diagram was platform-agnostic.

Also regarding the windowing system, we found no class named *DisplayServer* on the call graph. To understand what part of our call graph corresponds to this

---

[6] https://docs.godotengine.org/en/stable/classes/class_theme.html.

[7] https://docs.godotengine.org/en/stable/classes/class_proceduralsky.html.

[8] https://twitter.com/reduzio/status/1506266084420337666.

class, we used method names as a reference. Inspecting the source code, we determined that methods *get_singleton* and *has_feature* from the *DisplayServer* class were called by the *ProjectSettings* class, which is instantiated by the first *setup* method. In the base game's graph, we found this same method name being called by a class named *OS*.

5   Urho3D's Call Graph

Differently from Godot, Urho3D initializes its graphics object first and only then calls DSL (Simple DirectMedia Layer) and X11 to open a window, as shown in Fig. 3. However, they both initialize UI-related code even though there is no UI to draw, and register all game object classes even though they are not instantiated.

Furthermore, our attention was drawn to the fact that, while Urho3D calls one initialization method per class, Godot calls *Main::setup* and *Main::setup2*. These apparently redundant calls are justified by the developer as a way to separate low and high level "singletons and core types"[9]

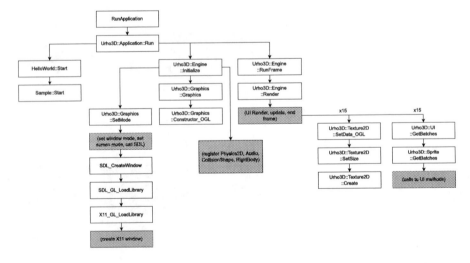

Fig. 3. Urho3D's base game call graph, showing which methods are called.

6   Comparing Godot and Urho3D

In terms of similarities, both Godot and Urho3D have the same features present in the most widely used game engines, such as graphics, audio, and physics. Both engines register all game object classes upon startup and initialize graphics systems, even though there is nothing more than an empty window to draw.

---

[9] Line 342 at https://github.com/godotengine/godot/blob/3.4/main/main.cpp.

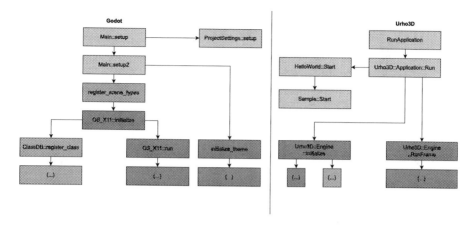

Fig. 4. Division of responsibility on Godot and Urho3D: initialization methods (orange), class registration (red) and graphics (blue). Call tree ramifications omitted for brevity. (Color figure online)

On the other hand, the engines run graphics and window initialization in different orders. Godot creates the window first, Urho3D does the opposite and uses the DSL library to manage the interaction with X11. Godot has a scene manager and internal messaging system which are initialized even in a simple project such as the base game. Urho3D initializes only graphics and UI in this case.

7   Discussion

We can use call graphs to visualize the division of responsibilities inside the engines during initialization. They also provide an overview of the most important subsystems and at which moment they are registered and called.

However, these observations do not give us deep insights into architectural patterns and design choices for specific subsystems that could be useful for game engine developers. To obtain this knowledge, we will generate dynamic and static call graphs, as well as C++ #include graphs for each subsystem in the future.

While comparing the engines, we also identified project and runtime environment conditions that could make the profiler generate the call graph differently. These are important to note since they may change our overall view of the architecture.

Operating System: There is a possibility that if we ran the profiler on a Windows or Android version of the same base games, we would obtain a different call graph. Each platform has its own system calls, GUI and data types, so the engines account for this by adding platform-specific code. If the call graph would be largely different, this difference could indicate that code evolution and maintainability are compromised.

Active Features: Important class or method names may not be present in the graphs because they have not been called during the analyzed run. The base game only calls methods from the engine "core" and not others referring to more specific features (e.g., networking methods, which would be needed in a multiplayer game).

Other Means of Analysis: Results could vary when running our base game with other profilers such as `gprof` or `gperftools`. Furthermore, while dynamic analysis can provide us with a precise call graph, it only represents a given run of the program and is therefore only a partial view.

8   Conclusion

In this work in progress, we showed that producing a high-level architecture view of an engine is possible with the use of a profiler, such as Callgrind, which generates engine call graphs. We compared Godot 3.4.4 and Urho3D 1.8 not only by looking at the engine's subsystems but also in which order and frequency they are called, which would not be possible by applying static analysis alone.

As for the research question "are game engine designs similar?", we concluded that Godot and Urho3D have a similar feature set and therefore could be used to create the same types of games. Their features are the same present in most widely used game engines, but they divide responsibilities and call them in the code in different ways. Also, we identified that both engines initialize subsystems even though they are not used (e.g. UI). While this may consume resources, it seems to be the right choice since these systems are often used.

In future work, we intend to compare different open-source engine call graphs, starting with Unreal Engine 5, to understand what architectural design patterns are most frequently applied to them and how similar they are among engines. Also, we will compare these architectures with those proposed by researchers, using static and dynamic analysis, to understand the impact of design on engine performance, maintenance, and feature richness.

Acknowledgements. The authors were partially supported by the NSERC Discovery Grant and Canada Research Chairs programs.

References

1. Anderson, E.F., Engel, S., Comninos, P., McLoughlin, L.: The case for research in game engine architecture. In: Proceedings of the 2008 Conference on Future Play: Research, Play, Share, Future Play 2008, New York, USA, pp. 228–231. Association for Computing Machinery. event-place: Toronto, Ontario, Canada (2008)
2. Christopoulou, E., Xinogalos, S.: Overview and comparative analysis of game engines for desktop and mobile devices. Int. J. Serious Games 4(4), 21–36 (2017)
3. Dickson, P.E., Block, J.E., Echevarria, G.N., Keenan, K.C.: An experience-based comparison of unity and unreal for a stand-alone 3D game development course. In: Proceedings of the 2017 ACM Conference on Innovation and Technology in Computer Science Education, Bologna Italy, pp. 70–75. ACM, June 2017

4. Eberly, D.H.: 3D game engine design: a practical approach to real-time computer graphics, 2nd edn. Elsevier/Morgan Kaufmann, Amsterdam, Boston (2007)
5. Gregory, J.: Game engine architecture, third edn . Taylor & Francis, CRC Press, Boca Raton (2018)
6. Lengyel, E.: Foundations of game engine development. Terathon Software LLC, Lincoln, California (2016)
7. Maggiorini, D., Ripamonti, L.A., Zanon, E., Bujari, A., Palazzi, C.E.: SMASH: A distributed game engine architecture. In: 2016 IEEE Symposium on Computers and Communication (ISCC), Messina, Italy, pp. 196–201. IEEE, June 2016
8. Marin, C., Chover, M., Sotoca, J.M.: Prototyping a game engine architecture as a multi-agent system. Západočeská univerzita. In: Computer Science Research Notes (2019)
9. Pattrasitidecha, A.: Comparison and evaluation of 3D mobile game engines. Master's thesis, Chalmers University of Technology (2014)
10. Pavkov, S., Frankovic, I., Hoic-Bozic, N.: Comparison of game engines for serious games. In: 2017 40th International Convention on Information and Communication Technology, Electronics and Microelectronics (MIPRO), Opatija, Croatia, pp. 728–733. IEEE, May 2017
11. Politowski, C., Petrillo, F., Montandon, J.E., Valente, M.T., Guéhéneuc, Y.-G.: Are game engines software frameworks? a three-perspective study. J. Syst. Softw. **171**, 110846 (2021)
12. Sršen, M., Orehovački, T.: Developing a game engine in c# programming language. In: 2021 44th International Convention on Information, Communication and Electronic Technology (MIPRO), pp. 1717–1722 (2021)

Design of an Extended Reality Collaboration Architecture for Mixed Immersive and Multi-surface Interaction

Thiago Porcino$^{(\boxtimes)}$ ⓘ, Seyed Adel Ghaeinianⓘ, Juliano Franzⓘ,
Joseph Mallochⓘ, and Derek Reillyⓘ

Graphics and Experiential Media Lab, Dalhousie University, Halifax, NS, Canada
{thiago,adelghaeinian}@dal.ca
https://gem.cs.dal.ca/

Abstract. EXtended Reality (XR) is a rapidly developing paradigm for computer entertainment, and is also increasingly used for simulation, training, data analysis, and other non-entertainment purposes, often employing head-worn XR devices like the Microsoft HoloLens. In XR, integration with the physical world should also include integration with commonly used digital devices. This paper proposes an architecture to integrate head-worn displays with touchscreen devices, such as phones, tablets, or large tabletop or wall displays. The architecture emerged through the iterative development of a prototype for collaborative analysis and decision-making for the maritime domain. However, our architecture can flexibly support a range of domains and purposes. XR designers, XR entertainment researchers, and game developers can benefit from our architecture to propose new ways of gaming, considering multiple devices as user interfaces in an immersive collaborative environment.

Keywords: Extended reality · Immersive visualization · XR Architecture · Augmented reality · Mixed reality

1 Introduction

We have seen rapid development and increased public interest in mixed reality technologies in recent years [3] in areas such as training, analytics, and entertainment. In 2021, the augmented reality (AR), virtual reality (VR), and mixed reality (MR) market was valued at 30.7 billion U.S. dollars and it is expected to reach close to 300 billion by 2024 [23].

Head-worn displays (HWDs) are one way to achieve immersive mixed reality or virtual reality. These devices usually consist of electronic displays and lenses that are fixed over the head toward the eyes of the user. HWDs are used in various domains including games and entertainment [24], military [19], education [1], therapy [4], and medicine [12].

While some HWDs are themselves mobile devices (in that they are not tethered to a desktop PC), there is a lack of tools that assist in integrating augmented reality HWDs (such as HoloLens) and other single-user mobile devices

© IFIP International Federation for Information Processing 2022
Published by Springer Nature Switzerland AG 2022
B. Göbl et al. (Eds.): ICEC 2022, LNCS 13477, pp. 112–122, 2022.
https://doi.org/10.1007/978-3-031-20212-4_9

(like phones or tablets) with shared devices such as large wall or tabletop displays. In this paper, we present a novel architecture that integrates multiple AR HWDs with a shared large display (a tabletop display in our prototype) and with handheld touchscreen devices such as phones or tablets. AR HWDs are a natural component of multi-system collaborative environments, as they can provide personalized and/or *ad hoc* extensions to interaction and visualization: for example, a visual representation can be extended beyond or above a tabletop display, gestures and head orientation can become part of a shared interface, and 3D representations of inter-device communication become possible.

While the focus of the developed prototype in this work is geospatial data analysis and visualization within a collaborative decision making context, the proposed architecture readily extends to other areas, and in particular entertainment-focused XR applications such as games that integrate with shared displays, such as an interactive mixed reality board game or puzzle.

Furthermore, our architecture allows researchers to prototype and study visualizations and interaction techniques that integrate modern HWDs and interactive touchscreens in the general case or in applied contexts such as entertainment, games, training and simulation, immersive analytics, and more.

This paper is organized as follows: Sect. 2 describes the related work; Sect. 3 details the iterative design and development of our prototype, leading to the proposed architecture. We then outline future work and current limitations in Sect. 4, and conclude in Sect. 5.

2 Related Work

Multi-system collaborative environments require flexibility of computation, data, interaction, and visualization [9, 16]. The general idea is that devices should be dynamically reconfigurable according to a desired or emergent objective. Any multi-system collaborative environment that incorporates AR HWDs should allow for these devices to be flexibly added to, removed from, and configured for the system.

Salimian et al. [21] proposed IMRCE, a Unity toolkit for immersive mixed reality collaboration. In this work, users interact with shared 3D virtual objects using touchscreens, in VR, or in mixed reality configurations. IMRCE connects mixed groups of collocated and remote collaborators, and was designed to support rapid prototyping of mixed reality collaborative environments that use hand and position tracking as data. IMRCE was evaluated with groups of developers who developed simple prototypes using the toolkit, and with end users who performed collaborative tasks using it[20]. While IMRCE was compared against a base Unity development environment, other competitive toolkits such as TwinSpace [18], SoD-Toolkit [22], KinectArms [8], or Proximity [14], were not considered, in part due to IMRCE's embedding within Unity3D.

Huh et al. [10] introduce an architecture in which multiple AR/VR clients can collaborate in a shared workspace in a decentralized manner. Their architecture has two data categories: the data stored in the database (based data) and shared among users, and the user's data (extension data), which are a modified version of the standard data common to all users. Their architecture facilitates immersive XR collaboration between clients while the network connection is not stable enough using distributed databases and decentralized web technologies.

Ran et al. [17] focus on rendering virtual objects around a common virtual point (in the virtual world). They developed a system called SPAR (Spatially Consistent AR). According to the authors, AR apps have issues of high latency, spatial drift, and spatial inconsistency of the virtual assets distributed over time and users. In other words, the virtual objects aren't rendered simultaneously and with the exact position for all involved users. For this reason, SPAR attends as a new method for communication and computation of AR devices. They worked with an open-source AR platform (Android) instead of closed popular ones such as Apple and Microsoft because their code cannot be changed for tests. Authors mentioned they decreased the total latency by 55% and spatial inconsistency by up to 60% compared to the communication of off-the-shelf AR systems.

In summary, the related works take different approaches to integrate systems for collaboration. IMRCE [21], SPAR [17], and Huh's architecture [10] are the three works closest to our own. However, in IMRCE [21] content is limited to presentation in virtual reality, while in SPAR [17] immersive augmented reality content was not integrated with other devices, such as a tabletop display. Our platform supports both diverse hardware platforms and diverse forms of content and channels of content presentation. Furthermore, Huh et al. [10] designed a decentralized XR architecture quite similar to our architecture concerning AR processing and visualization. However, they do not include shared screens in their architecture. Unlike other works, in our system, collaborators can work around a shared display (SD) or use tablets, HWDs, or screen touchable devices.

3   Materials and Methods

The software framework presented in this paper was originally developed to support collaborative monitoring, analysis, and decision-making involving maritime data. The resulting system combines a shared tabletop display with tablet displays and AR HWDs used by multiple users. A cloud-based repository provides data from multiple sources to our interfaces. These data are used to generate 2D geospatial visualizations presented on the tabletop display, which are augmented by 3D visualizations in augmented reality. Tablet displays permit individual collaborators to query and constrain the data visualization on both their personal HWD and the shared tabletop display. The tablet interface lets individuals query structured data visually, either through touch-based interaction with query primitives on the tablet, interactive selection and filtering of the geospatial visualization on the tabletop, or direct manipulation of 3D objects via the AR HWD. The querying system is built on top of SPARQL [15], a query language for structured databases commonly used by data-driven AI systems.

We used the Unity 3D game engine as the primary development framework to produce the XR content. The first reason was that Unity 3D is a powerful game engine that allows the creation of rich interactive AR/MR/VR/XR experiences (such as games or simulations) for mobile devices. Second, we adopt the idea of exploring the multi-player gaming concept for asset communication between the server and clients in our AR solution. We used a library for multi-player network communication (Photon Engine) and developed the server-side (Shared Server or SS) and a client-side (AR Room). The AR Room can be described as a set of clients that can connect to the server or Shared Server (SS).

Moreover, we propose the following architecture (illustrated in Fig. 1) to integrate the SD with multiple HoloLens' and tablets. The developed applications were constructed using Unity 3D as game engine for 3D models, interaction, and AR communication, which includes Photon Engine for AR multi-player behaviors between SS and clients inside the AR Room. Moreover, we used React [7] and Leaflet [5] for the web-based SD application and SPARQL for database access. We divided our architecture in 5 entities.

- **Shared Display (SD)** - The SD entity represents a shared physical display with the visualization application embedded. The SD has a web-based application developed in React using the Mapbox API [2] to show the Map and AR 3D objects. The SD sends the Map's latitude/longitude boundaries, zoom, orientation, and rotation information to the SS in real-time (each interaction in the SD is shared among other connected devices). The SD can also display a unique QR code for calibrating the coordinate systems used by the augmented reality layer (Illustrated in the "AR Room" box in Fig. 1). The SD application can customize the visualization by selecting specific data using a visual query builder to consult the data source through SS.
- **Shared Server (SS)** - the SS is responsible for converting lat/long data received from the database to the relative position in AR context, processing these data, transforming the selection into a structured data file (JSON), and sharing this data with other devices connected to the SS' network (i.e., Table, Database, and Augmented Reality Content). The SS also receives input queries from the SD (Fig. 1) and any other connected devices and if necessary converts them to SQL. The SS instantiates the corresponding AR 3D object to show in augmented reality on the HoloLens. In each HoloLens we have an Client App that is connected to the SS by a AR Room layer. All AR 3D objects are available to visualized by clients inside the AR Room layer.
- **AR Room** - In this layer, each AR client is synchronized with the SS. Every AR 3D object spawned by SS can be visualized by one or more clients. Client interactions with AR objects can be visualized privately or shared with the entire network. For example, invoking an AR menu is visualized privately on the local client only, whereas spawned AR Objects resulting from the first interaction might be visualized by other connected clients.

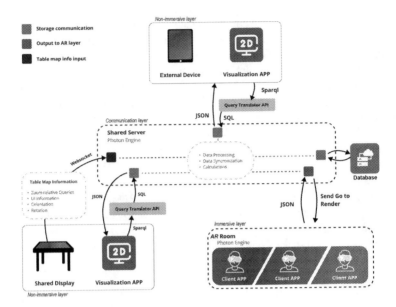

Fig. 1. The overall architecture. Data arrives from the right (Database), and is processed by Shared Server (SS). The user can interact with the system via a physical Shared Display (SD) (by physical touching gestures, such as clicking, pinching, pan, zooming) or augmented reality (making gestures on air in a AR context and wearing a HoloLens). AR devices (HoloLens) and new non-immersive devices (such as tablets or smartphones) can connect to the SS and see data in XR or non-immersive visualizations.

- **External Device** - In this entity, external devices can connect to SS using the same or similar built applications as the SD. While SD is responsible for communicating with SS and sending SD information (such as zoom, orientation, and screen size), the new device can send queries to request data and the results in real time. This allows to users to avoid using the shared table to consult data if they wish, and the 2D application does not need to follow the same structure as the shared visualization on the SD.
- **Query Translator API** - The query API supports and translates between different query representations (currently SQL, SPARQL, and a custom structured visual query language). This intermediate API ensures that our architecture retains the flexibility to work with different software and their particular query languages.

3.1 2D Visualization

The 2D visualization application consists of three parts, the map visualization, the visual query builder, and the text query editor where users can write their valid SPARQL queries on the query editor (see on top-right on Fig. 2) and see respective query visuals on the visual query builder. Moreover, the result from both queries (visual or text) allows users to visualize selection areas on the map and their respective assets (2D objects linked to the specific latitude and longitude coordinates). The 2D visualization app supports real-time updates, which means the visual query builder, text query editor, and the map have event listeners and triggers to update the visualization during users interactions (e.g., when a user is selecting a region by visual query builder, they see the results on the visualization area instantly). Additionally, to enable AR devices to see holographic visualization aligned with the SS, we put a QR Code in the application to support the alignment by AR Devices. AR Devices can use this QR Code as a world reference to calculate the relative size and position to align their AR content.

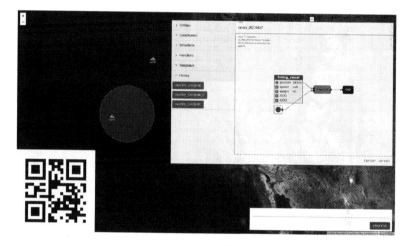

Fig. 2. Shared Display (SD) application developed in React. At the bottom left, a QR code is used to align the AR visualization with the SD. At the top right is the visual query builder, where the user can make data selection in real-time and see the results on the SD.

On top of the map layer (illustrated in Fig. 2), we implemented an Interaction Layer (IL). On the IL, the user can interact with the map using touches, drag and drops, zoom, pans, tangible object placements, or AR interactions using AR tools (e.g., HoloLens).

We pass direct interaction data between the SD and the 2D Application using TUIO [11] over a socket connection. This protocol is commonly used for multi-touch surfaces and supports both touch and interaction using tangible objects. The IL can process information received from AR clients through their specific web-socket connection, and the updates are reflected in the visual query and the map in real-time.

More detailed, to synchronize the SD application and AR clients, the 2D Application sends the visual query data, the map boundaries of the visible region in SS (north-west and south-east coordinates in latitude and longitude), and the map current zoom level to the AR clients through SS. We adopted web sockets with JSON-formatted messages to perform this communication between SD and SS.

3.2   AR Visualization

As outlined above, the AR application consists of two layers: a shared server (SS) and the AR Room. The SS is responsible for communicating with the database and making conversions, for example:

– Converting latitude and longitude to the Unity coordinate system. We used Mapbox SDK [13] for converting the geographic coordinate system (GCS) from our data source to Unity' coordinate system in meters.
– Computing coordinate system transformations between tabletop display and the AR visualization.
– Sending the information to Client-render layer (AR Room), which means the application responsible for generating the augmented reality in each connected AR client.

Second, the AR Room, which is responsible for rendering in each connected AR client (Client App) the real-time data processed to the virtual environment (including all game objects). This strategy was adopted to avoid high latency in the Client App (See on bottom-right on Fig. 1). The main duties of each client App are:

– Allows user to interact with objects, all interactions are computed in each client, individually.
– Render the content in AR.

In that sense, different AR clients can connect to the SS and they do not need to recalculate conversions that were already made by the SS. This enables the AR clients see the same virtual environment in collaborative way.

To make this network communication between SS and AR Room, we adopt the Photon Engine SDK [6]. Photon is a base layer for multiplayer games and higher-level network solutions. This plugin for Unity solves issues such as matchmaking and fast network communication using a scalable approach. Basically, Photon enable to create a shared-room where each client APP can connect and get the same information from server. Additionally, both (SS and Client APP) are Unity applications but with distinct duties.

In summary, each element in AR visualization are created and processed by SS, and multiple instances of Client-render connected to the SS' shared AR room can see and interact with the same AR content (Fig. 3).

Furthermore, we implemented some interactions in an augmented reality app (Client APP) for the able user in the decision-making process during our solution. The first one is the query selection (at left in Fig. 4), where the user can see an augmented reality arch connector between the world map selection on SD

Fig. 3. Users are interacting with the SD wearing HoloLens. The HoloLens first-person vision of augmented reality interaction over the SD at the left. A third person of the user interacting with both systems is on the right.

visualization in 2D (built in the query builder) and the 2D object that represent this selection on query builder. In the other interaction (Fig. 4, at the right), the user is grabbing an instance of an augmented reality object to show to others or get more information about the specific vessel.

Fig. 4. The user selects a piece of vessel information (the user can grab and drag a the AR object to use this element to get more details about the selected vessel).

4   Future Work and Limitations

While the presented architecture is finished and can fit in distinct contexts, the developed prototype is under development, and there are still many challenges to overcome. Although this prototype is not a final solution, we believe this work can contribute to other researchers giving insights and directing them to develop multiple-system XR experiences for different purposes (analysis, entertainment, simulations) and fields (health, military, educational, games).

While our study case is related to a non-entertainment context, we designed our architecture to support numerous application contexts for analysis, simulation, or entertainment applications (such as XR gaming experiences). In other words, our proposed architecture is flexible in terms of application context and field.

Besides, we are still limited in terms of developed interactions. Currently, we are working to produce more interactions among systems. While the already developed interactions can be a good study case, we realized we need to design more AR interactions before starting the usability tests phase with users.

For this reason, the next step of this project is to conduct a user-experimental set of tests and a profound study about user behaviors in our XR interaction interfaces. We also intend to include design thinking techniques to help us construct a memorable experience for the final user of this project. Moreover, it is necessary to conduct an in-depth evaluation of users' behaviors using our solution and evaluate how this solution contributes to the decision-making process in naval organizations.

5   Conclusion

We presented an architecture to integrate augmented reality with physical SD in this work. We implemented this solution to facilitate the decision-making processes in naval organizations under monitoring vessels' role. Moreover, we develop SD and AR device systems that allow multiple users to collaborate using immersive devices (e.g., HoloLens) or non-immersive such as tablets or smartphones.

Besides, we designed and implemented different ways to visualize data (e.g., visual query builder, touchable gestures, AR gestures). In other words, our novel architecture enables multiple users to see the request and see data in an immersive or non-immersive way using particular devices (AR devices, tablets, and shared displays, which include tabletop and other touchable screens). In terms of flexibility, our architecture allows users to add or remove the immersive layer without affecting the visualization for other users. While the SD is the main non-immersive layer and is dependent on visualization, external non-immersive devices are not dependent and can be connected or disconnected at any time without affecting the visualization.

Furthermore, our proposed architecture works with a layer (Shared Server or SS) that helps to avoid unnecessary computational processing in HoloLens (concerning the limited hardware' memory and graphical processing). Moreover, the interaction of multiple users using immersive and non-immersive devices can produce rich discussion among users.

We believe our architecture and prototype can help XR designers and researchers to propose new visualizations in immersive environments that combine multiple devices to facilitate decision-making processes for different purposes (simulation, education, gaming, or analysis).

References

1. Ahir, K., Govani, K., Gajera, R., Shah, M.: Application on virtual reality for enhanced education learning, military training and sports. Augmented Hum. Res. **5**(1), 7 (2020)
2. Cadenas, C.: Geovisualization: integration and visualization of multiple datasets using mapbox. California Polytechnic State University (2014)
3. Calvelo, M., Piñeiro, Á., Garcia-Fandino, R.: An immersive journey to the molecular structure of sars-cov-2: Virtual reality in covid-19. Comput. Struct. Biotech. J. **18**, 2621–2628 (2020)
4. Carrión, M., Santorum, M., Benavides, J., Aguilar, J., Ortiz, Y.: Developing a virtual reality serious game to recreational therapy using iplus methodology. In: 2019 International Conference on Virtual Reality and Visualization (ICVRV), pp. 133–137. IEEE (2019)
5. Crickard III, P.: Leaflet. js essentials. Packt Publishing Ltd. (2014)
6. Exit Games Inc: Realtime intro | photon engine. https://doc.photonengine.com/en-us/realtime/current/getting-started/realtime-intro. (Accessed 22 Apr 2022)
7. Gackenheimer, C., Paul, A.: Introduction to React. Apress, Berkeley, CA (2015). https://doi.org/10.1007/978-1-4842-1245-5
8. Genest, A.M., Gutwin, C., Tang, A., Kalyn, M., Ivkovic, Z.: Kinectarms: a toolkit for capturing and displaying arm embodiments in distributed tabletop groupware. In: Proceedings of the 2013 Conference on Computer Supported Cooperative Work, pp. 157–166 (2013)
9. Herz, D., Lee, P., Lutz, L., Stewart, M., Tuell, J., Wiig, J., et al.: Addressing the needs of multi-system youth: Strengthening the connection between child welfare and juvenile justice. In: Center for Juvenile Justice Reform, pp. 1–69 (2012)
10. Huh, S., Muralidharan, S., Ko, H., Yoo, B.: Xr collaboration architecture based on decentralized web. In: The 24th International Conference on 3D Web Technology, Web3D 2019, p. 1–9. , Association for Computing Machinery, New York, NY, USA (2019). https://doi.org/10.1145/3329714.3338137,https://doi.org/10.1145/3329714.3338137
11. Kaltenbrunner, M., Bovermann, T., Bencina, R., Costanza, E., et al.: Tuio: A protocol for table-top tangible user interfaces. In: Proceedings of the The 6th Int'l Workshop on Gesture in Human-Computer Interaction and Simulation, pp. 1–5. Citeseer (2005)
12. Kühnapfel, U., Cakmak, H.K., Maaß, H.: Endoscopic surgery training using virtual reality and deformable tissue simulation. Comput. Graph. **24**(5), 671–682 (2000)
13. Linwood, J.: Getting started with the Mapbox SDK. In: Build Location Apps on iOS with Swift, pp. 165–178. Apress, Berkeley, CA (2020). https://doi.org/10.1007/978-1-4842-6083-8_11
14. Marquardt, N., Diaz-Marino, R., Boring, S., Greenberg, S.: The proximity toolkit: prototyping proxemic interactions in ubiquitous computing ecologies. In: Proceedings of the 24th Annual ACM Symposium on User Interface Software and Technology, pp. 315–326 (2011)
15. Pérez, J., Arenas, M., Gutierrez, C.: Semantics and complexity of sparql. ACM Trans. Database Syst. (TODS) **34**(3), 1–45 (2009)
16. Powers, J.D., Edwards, J.D., Blackman, K.F., Wegmann, K.M.: Key elements of a successful multi-system collaboration for school-based mental health: In-depth interviews with district and agency administrators. Urban Rev. **45**(5), 651–670 (2013)

17. Ran, X., Slocum, C., Tsai, Y.Z., Apicharttrisorn, K., Gorlatova, M., Chen, J.: Multi-user augmented reality with communication efficient and spatially consistent virtual objects. In: Proceedings of the 16th International Conference on emerging Networking EXperiments and Technologies, pp. 386–398 (2020)
18. Reilly, D.F., Rouzati, H., Wu, A., Hwang, J.Y., Brudvik, J., Edwards, W.K.: Twinspace: an infrastructure for cross-reality team spaces. In: Proceedings of the 23nd Annual ACM Symposium on User Interface Software and Technology, pp. 119–128 (2010)
19. Rizzo, A., et al.: Virtual reality goes to war: A brief review of the future of military behavioral healthcare. J. Clin. Psychol. Med. Settings **18**(2), 176–187 (2011)
20. Salimian, H., Brooks, S., Reilly, D.: Mp remix: Relaxed wysiwis immersive interfaces for mixed presence collaboration with 3d content. In: Proceedings of the ACM Human-Computer Interaction 3(CSCW), Nov 2019. https://doi.org/10.1145/3359207
21. Salimian, M., Brooks, S., Reilly, D.: Imrce: A unity toolkit for virtual co-presence. In: Proceedings of the Symposium on Spatial User Interaction, pp. 48–59 (2018)
22. Seyed, T., Azazi, A., Chan, E., Wang, Y., Maurer, F.: Sod-toolkit: A toolkit for interactively prototyping and developing multi-sensor, multi-device environments. In: Proceedings of the 2015 International Conference on Interactive Tabletops & Surfaces, pp. 171–180 (2015)
23. Statista, A.: The statistics portal. Web site (2021). https://www.statista.com/statistics/591181/global-augmented-virtual-reality-market-size/
24. Studios, B.G.: The elder scrolls v: Skyrim. Bethesda Game Studios (2015)

Player Behavior and Analysis

Mental Wear and Tear: An Exploratory Study on Mental Fatigue in Video Games Using the Example of League of Legends

Ioannis Bikas[1], Johannes Pfau[2]([✉]) [iD], Bastian Dänekas[1], and Rainer Malaka[1] [iD]

[1] University of Bremen, Bibliothekstraße 1, 28359 Bremen, Germany
{bikasio,daenekba,malaka}@uni-bremen.de
[2] University of California, 1156 High Street, Santa Cruz, USA
jopfau@ucsc.edu

Abstract. Playing video games has become a major factor of spending leisure time. As competitive and e-sports games grow in popularity and size, demands of complexity, time investment and cognitive strain to acquire proficiency and keep up with competitors grow with them. Fundamental psychological work stresses the detrimental impact of sinking extensive amounts of time into tasks onto mental health and capabilities to perform in those tasks. However, the effects of prolonged task execution without adequate rest in self-imposed leisure environments (e.g. video games) are largely under-investigated. We therefore seek to investigate these effects as well as their related consequences in the highly competitive scene of e-sports games. Prolonged task execution in tasks that are primarily of a cognitive nature is usually not associated with physical strain or physical fatigue. We therefore primarily investigate effects on cognitive capabilities, like the onset of mental fatigue, as well as mental well-being. Over the course of seven weeks, we monitored the playing routines of League of Legends players and tracked measures of mental fatigue before and after sessions. Together with qualitative remarks, explanations and attitudes towards playing, time investment and skill acquisition, we gathered player reports showing significantly deteriorated moods and dispositions to playing as well as high indications of mental fatigue based on significant occurrences of related symptoms. Additionally, we analyzed the matches played by the participants during the study period and found a gaussian-like distribution of performance relative to the number of successively played matches. We discuss associated problems and propose ideas for methods facilitating more time-efficient alternatives of video game skill acquisition.

Keywords: Mental fatigue · Video games · E-sports · Game survey

This research is funded by the Klaus Tschira Stiftung.

© IFIP International Federation for Information Processing 2022
Published by Springer Nature Switzerland AG 2022
B. Göbl et al. (Eds.): ICEC 2022, LNCS 13477, pp. 125–139, 2022.
https://doi.org/10.1007/978-3-031-20212-4_10

1   Introduction

The video games industry has grown to unprecedented success with competitive games and e-sports covering a considerable share of the revenue[1]. Competitive online multiplayer games like League of Legends (3.5 million daily players)[2] DotA 2 [34] (640,000 daily players)[3] and Counter Strike: Global Offensive [33] (890,000 daily players)[4] display unrivaled daily player numbers in particular. These games prominently feature competitive matchmaking modes where players can compete for rank. Reaching a high rank is a desirable goal for many players and often requires a lot of time and dedication to achieve. An intuitive strategy to pursue this is to increase playtime in order to facilitate improvement (in skill as well as rank). It is known in psychology and sports that executing tasks for prolonged periods of time without adequate rest leads to exhaustion and a decrease in performance. In contrast to traditional sports, it seems unlikely that playing video games causes any considerable physical exhaustion. Therefore, interest shifts to effects on cognitive abilities and mental well-being. One particular effect that is mainly related to prolonged task execution is that of mental fatigue [4]. Mental fatigue describes a change in the mental state of a person caused by sustained task performance in cognitive tasks. This change is typically marked by subjective feelings of tiredness, a decline in task performance and a loss of motivation to continue work on the task [19,20,26]. However, whether video games induce mental fatigue is currently under-investigated. As relevant factors concerning performance in video games, mental fatigue has been found to affect attention [3], executive control [20], manual dexterity and anticipation timing [9], decision making and accuracy [32], as well as reaction time [15] (more detailed explanations in Sect. 2). Attention also plays an integral role in skill acquisition as does the ability to distinguish relevant from irrelevant information [17]. Since mental fatigue has been shown to negatively impact both abilities [3,21], it is feasible to assume that it could impair skill acquisition as well. With the above in mind, mental fatigue impairs functions related to performance as well as learning and could thus mean that the intuitive approach of embracing the "grind" (i.e. playing as much as possible) to facilitate skill gain or improve rank is a suboptimal strategy. Moreover, sitting for prolonged periods of time is known to pose health risks [10] and prolonged computer use may contribute to musculoskeletal injury of the neck and upper extremities [7]. Thus, increasing playtime to gain proficiency may not only be ineffective but may also increase risk for the above mentioned health issues. If more effective approaches could be established, this increase in risk may be entirely unnecessary. This paper seeks to investigate whether there is evidence that players of video games experience any of the above mentioned effects. This could establish a basis for further

---

[1] https://newzoo.com/insights/articles/the-games-market-in-2021-the-year-in-numbers-e-sports-cloud-gaming/.

[2] https://webtribunal.net/blog/league-of-legends-player-count/#gref.

[3] https://steamcharts.com/app/570.

[4] https://steamcharts.com/app/730.

exploration of possible effects on player performance and learning (as opposed to perceived effects) and the development of more effective training techniques as well as guidelines for better performance in video games. These developments could likely be extended to comparable digital domains (e.g. surgery using digital interfaces and minimally invasive techniques). Thus, the following research questions are formulated:

- Do indications exist that playing demanding video games for prolonged periods of time may induce mental fatigue (or general fatigue)?
- Are players aware of possible health risks related to computer use over prolonged periods of time?
- Do players attempt to save time by using techniques that make learning more effecient and are they interested in using such techniques?

To approach answering these research questions, we tracked twelve League of Legends [29] players over seven weeks using a two-part questionnaire assessing symptoms of mental fatigue and general fatigue. Additionally, a follow-up survey collected 20 responses to achieve a better understanding of the players' general perception regarding the topic. This exploratory pre-study found significant indications for the onset of both fatigue and mental fatigue after play sessions of League of Legends as perceived by the participants. Participants confirmed increases in playtime to be their main method to gain rank and proficiency and showed an awareness for the existence of specialised training techniques. Physical and mental strain were reported to be common experiences when playing (with some even experiencing gaming-related injuries). Additionally, participants stated a willingness to use efficient training or learning techniques as an alternative to just playing. This work contributes to games user research by recording and observing game-related effects, such as mental fatigue, that may suppress training and skill acquisition, as well as to the areas of (psychological) health and video games, as mentioned effects can arguably impact a player's well-being and condition

2   Related Work

Mental fatigue describes a change in the mental state of a person caused by sustained task performance in cognitive tasks over prolonged periods of time. This change is typically marked by subjective feelings of tiredness, a decline in task performance and a loss of motivation to continue work on the task [19, 20, 26]. Mental fatigue is commonly encountered in everyday life when work on cognitively demanding tasks is required. This is usually resolved by taking a break from the task - an intuitive step since tiredness and loss of motivation occur. Still, mental fatigue has been found to be one of the most frequent causes for accidents in the workplace [2, 25]. The detrimental effects on performance associated with mental fatigue are multifaceted in nature.

Boksem et al. showed changes in the efficiency of attentional mechanisms that lead to a decrease in the ability to ignore irrelevant information while identifying relevant information due to mental fatigue [3]. Faber et al. where an evaluation of ERP (event-related potentials) data collected during their experiment confirmed this [21]. It should be noted that stimulus-driven attention was largely unaffected while goal-driven attention decreased significantly. This means that highly automated behavior can be sustained over long periods of time even in spite of the onset of mental fatigue while unexpected situations that require flexible goal-driven responses become less feasible. Linden et al. investigated the effects of mental fatigue on executive control [20]. Executive control can be defined as a basic cognitive process responsible for goal-directed behavior including attention, task switching and functions used to keep goals and goal-related information in mind [1,8,18]. Their studies showed a decrease in the ability to generate and test goal-oriented hypotheses in subjects affected by mental fatigue. Planning ability in general was also found to decrease which was shown by a significant increase in the time needed to execute the first move in the Tower of London tests. The effects of mental fatigue on performance have been observed in multiple different domains. Duncan et al. found that mental fatigue negatively impacts manual dexterity and anticipation timing in trained adults [9]. Negative impacts on decision making and accuracy have been observed in soccer, basketball and table tennis [32]. Basketball players in particular have been shown to suffer from a decline in technical performance when under the effects of mental fatigue [27]. Reaction time has also been found to be affected [15]. Even highly physical endeavours such as endurance sports and swimming showed a decline in performance due to mental fatigue [22,23,28,35]. Lastly, Fortes et al. found that as little as 30 min of playing video games causes mental fatigue and impairs decision-making in amateur boxers [13].

3   Study

7-Week Study: To investigate whether players experience symptoms of mental fatigue (or general fatigue) when playing strenuous games for prolonged periods of time, we asked twelve participants to fill out a two-part questionnaire before and after their play sessions once a week over a period of seven weeks. We chose League of Legends as the target game because it is known to be difficult and popular. The period of seven weeks was chosen to make the results more resistant to both outside influences like general fatigue at a specific day and game-related factors like losing streaks or particularly close games. The study was advertised via email among the students of the affiliated University (redacted for submission) and additionally distributed in gaming-focused Discord communities in order to better reach the target group of regular League of Legends players. Recipients were encouraged to further distribute the information to reach as many players as possible. As a reward for finishing the study, Riot Points vouchers valued at 20 Euro each were advertised in an attempt to decrease the possible number of participants who may drop out because of the length of the study.

Follow-Up Survey: To gain additional insights into the general perception players have on performance and skill acquisition in video games, a follow-up survey was conducted using ten questions (see Sect. 3.1). This survey was distributed in online gaming communities via Discord and also used for semi-structured interviews with four of the participants of the 7-week study. Recipients were encouraged to further distribute the survey.

3.1 Measures

Two-part Questionnaire used in the 7-Week Study: Due to the lack of an established and evaluated questionnaire that assesses non-pathological mental fatigue for tasks comparable to competitive gaming, the first part of the questionnaire aims to address the most common symptoms of mental fatigue through five questions rated on 5-point Likert scales:

1. How much aversion do you feel towards continuing playing right now?
2. How would you rate your ability to further concentrate on playing right now?
3. How tired do you feel right now?
4. How would you rate the effort of playing the game right now?
5. How would you rate your motivation to do your best in another match right now?

These questions are directly drawn from the most pronounced symptoms of mental fatigue as described by the related work [4,19,20,26]. The second part features 40 items taken from the shortened Profile of Mood States (POMS) [14] which were also rated on 5-point Likert scales. These items are used to scan for signs of general fatigue and changes in mood.

Follow-up Survey: To gain more insight into the players' general conception regarding skill acquisition in games, performance in games, fatigue in games, common session lengths and willingness to use techniques to gain proficiency more efficiently, semi-structured interviews using ten guiding questions have been conducted. The guiding questions are the following:

Q1: What do you think is the most important factor when it comes to getting good at a game?
Q2: Did you ever use any kind of technique to get better at a game more quickly/efficiently? (If so, what did you do and did it work?)
Q3: If you had the goal to get a high rank in League of Legends as quickly as possible, what would be your approach?
Q4: What do you think professional players do differently from regular players in order to become significantly better at the game?
Q5: What do you consider a gaming session of average length?
Q6: What do you consider a long gaming session?
Q7: Given unlimited time to play League of Legends, can you think of any consequences that would have?
Q8: How do you think your performance changes during a gaming session?

Q9: Do you sometimes feel fatigued or tired after playing? (Does that happen every time or only under certain circumstances?)

Q10: Did you ever experience any gaming-related physical pains or aches?

3.2   Participants

In total, twelve participants took part in the seven-week study. Of these twelve, seven had to be sorted out because they did not produce usable data sets (did not fill out the questionnaires before and after a session but randomly on different days) or because they quit the study preemptively (without submitting any data at all). Of the remaining five participants, four agreed to voluntarily supply demographic data. Information on gender was optional and collected according to best practices with the following options: woman, man, non-binary, prefer not to disclose, prefer to self-describe (open text box). They were split evenly between male and female with an average age of 25. Two of them stated to play every day while the other two stated to play almost every day. Additionally, 20 participants took part in the follow-up survey that was conducted after the seven-week study period had ended.

4   Results

7-Week Study: Results of part one of the questionnaire (five questions aimed at mental fatigue symptoms) are significant for four out of five questions. Using a signed-rank Wilcoxon test for paired values [38], answers given before and after a play session were compared for each question respectively. Participants felt significantly more aversion to continue playing after their session ($p < 0.01$, $W = 39$, Cohen's $d = 1.15$ [6]), rated their ability to further concentrate on playing significantly lower ($p < 0.01$, $W = 36.5$, $d = 1.22$), felt significantly more tired ($p < 0.01$, $W = 26$, $d = 0.96$) and rated their motivation to do their best in the game significantly lower ($p < 0.01$, $W = 4$, $d = 1.68$) as compared to before they started playing. Participants did not rate the effort of playing the game to be significantly higher. Using a signed-rank Wilcoxon test for paired values, results of part two of the questionnaire (shortened 40 item POMS) were compared using the same methodology. Results were significantly higher for the items in Table 1 after a play session while Table 2 outlines the POMS items that were found to be significantly lower than before.

For the remaining POMS items, no significant changes could be found (Tense, Angry, Proud, On Edge, Grouchy, Ashamed, Hopeless, Uneasy, Restless, Annoyed, Discouraged, Resentful, Nervous, Miserable, Bitter, Anxious, Helpless, Satisfied, Bewildered, Furious, Worthless, Forgetful, Vigorous, Uncertain about Things, Bushed and Embarrassed). It should be noted that the participants had a 45% average win rate over the duration of the study. To investigate whether the players' perception corresponds to an actual decline in performance, the matches played by the participants during the study period were grouped into streaks. Note that we were able to use the data of all 12 participants for this step. We

Table 1. Shortened POMS items significantly higher after playing.

Item	p-Value	W	Cohen's d
Worn out	$p < 0.01$	16	$d = 1.24$
Unhappy	$p < 0.01$	7	$d = 0.9$
Confused	$p < 0.01$	8	$d = 0.65$
Sad	$p < 0.01$	6	$d = 0.7$
Unable to Concentrate	$p < 0.01$	19	$d = 0.93$
Fatigued	$p < 0.01$	21.5	$d = 0.87$
Exhausted	$p < 0.01$	34.5	$d = 1.07$
Weary	$p < 0.01$	9	$d = 0.64$

Table 2. Shortened POMS items that were found to be significantly lower after playing.

Item	p-Value	W	Cohen's d
Lively	$p < 0.01$	35	$d = 1$
Active	$p < 0.01$	13	$d = 1.24$
Competent	$p < 0.01$	20.5	$d = 1.19$
Confident	$p < 0.01$	12	$d = 1.2$
Full of Pep	$p < 0.01$	5	$d = 0.77$
Energetic	$p < 0.01$	21	$d = 1.15$

define a match streak as any number of matches that have been played with no more than 20 min break in-between them. 20 min were chosen as a threshold for several reasons: The Riot data base offers game start times (the moment the players enter the match and can move their character) instead of the time a player entered the queue to find another match or the time a player found a new match. Champions (playable Characters) need to be picked and banned before each match which takes up to 10 min[5]. Moreover, receiving match rewards and commending teammates for good conduct as well as chatting with the players of both teams and possibly reporting players for bad conduct is another source of delay between matches. In the given data set, streaks of the following length were present: two, three, four, five. With regards to the win rate within those streaks the following has been found: Streaks of length one (241 wins, 294 losses) showed a 45% win rate, streaks of length two (48 wins, 60 losses) showed a 44.4% win rate and streaks of length three (28 wins, 29 losses) showed a 49% win rate. Moreover, streaks of length four (31 wins, 25 losses) showed a 55.4% win rate and streaks of length five (8 wins, 17 losses) showed a decline to 32% win rate.

---

[5] https://leagueoflegends.fandom.com/wiki/Draft_Pick#Champion_Selection.

Follow-up Survey: In total, 20 people completed the follow-up survey. Outcomes for each particular question were classified and analyzed after structured content analysis [24]. This means similar answers to the ten questions (Q1–10) presented in Sect. 3.1 were counted and combined into categories. When asked about the most important factor to become good at a game, 52% of the answers dealt with time investment (practice, time, patience) while 32% of the answers dealt with analysis of gameplay (one's own gameplay or professional gameplay) in order to learn from mistakes or gain new knowledge. 76% of the participants stated that they do use techniques to get better at games more effectively with 52% of the answers including watching professional gameplay or guides. Three of the participants used mechanical training (last-hitting in League of Legends and an aim trainer for shooters), reporting it to be successful, while two emphasized the importance of analysing replays to identify bad habits. When asked about their approach to gain a high rank in a game as quickly as possible, the most common answers revolved around time investment (playing as much as possible with a 30% share) and efficiency (focusing on a small amount of champions with a 15% share). This is consistent with their thoughts on how professional players become significantly better at games with the most common answers being vast amounts of playtime (41%) and regular analysis of gameplay (22%). Ambition and so called fundamentals (some kind of implicit knowledge or understanding about the workings of a game that can't be gained easily) were also expressed twice. When asked about the length of their average gaming sessions, answers showed considerable differences spanning from 40 min to six hours (M = 2.34, SD = 1.41). Similarly, perceptions of what a long gaming sessions is ranged from as low as 50 min to up to twelve hours (M = 4.625, SD = 3.361). To our surprise, 40% of the participants only considered sessions of five or more hours as long. Given unlimited time to play a game, the most common consequences named were decline in physical health (30%), boredom (23%) and decline in mental health (20%) while 13% of the answers related to conflicts with other aspects of life (social life, work, university etc.). When asked about changes in their performance during a gaming session, 48% of the answers reported a decline of performance over time. Moreover, 20% of the participants stated to require a warm-up phase to reach peak performance and 16% said their performance is dependent on their mood. Fatigue after playing was experienced by 85% of the participants with 50% of the answers stating long play sessions as the primary reason and 25% referring to losing streaks. When asked about gaming-related pains or aches, 55% of participants stated to not have experienced anything. Among the other participants, hand and wrist pain was the most common problem (55% of the answers) with the rest of the answers being evenly spread between headaches, back pain, eye strain, thumb arthritis and carpal tunnel syndrome. One participant reported to require medical care to get rid of their problem. Lastly, when asked if they would be willing to use exercises or techniques *instead* of playing if it reduced the time needed to become proficient at a game, 70% of the participants answered affirmatively.

5   Discussion

The results of the initial questionnaire show significant changes in four of the five most reported symptoms of mental fatigue: significantly increased aversion to continue the task, significantly lower perceived ability to concentrate on the task, significantly increased perceived tiredness and significantly lower willingness to do one's best. This could indicate the onset of mental fatigue during play sessions of League of Legends and is likely extendable to other demanding and/or competitive video games. The results of the shortened POMS support this by showing significant changes in categories relevant to fatigue and the ability to perform since participants reported to be worn out, fatigued, unable to concentrate, exhausted and weary. Additionally, participants reported to be less lively, less active, less full of pep and less energetic. This could have implications for general player behavior in competitive settings since "grinding" out matches to gain rank could be a lot less effective than it might intuitively appear to be. It could also be relevant for competitive e-sports events and their organisation. The common practice of having the grand finals of a tournament (reaching already multi-million dollar prize pools such as in the case of DotA 2's International) at the same day as the losers bracket leading up to it might put the team that has to go through multiple matches on the same day before reaching the finals at a significant disadvantage due to fatigue-related decline of performance. Interestingly, participants did not rate the effort of playing the game to be significantly higher after playing which couldn't support our initial hypothesis. However, a bias for people to perceive actions that align with their self-concordant goals to be easier (even if more effort is invested) could explain this result [37]. There could also be a self-serving bias [12] against stating that playing a game takes effort since this could negatively reflect on how the player's competence is perceived. Still, even if these observations are not related to mental fatigue as defined by the related work, they still indicate that playing a competitive game like League of Legends for prolonged periods of time may cause fatigue in general. This could be an important insight, not only in the context of games, but other strenuous digital domains that require high performance over long periods of time like surgeries using digitally controlled equipment or security-related activities like flight monitoring. Note that a positive correlation between video game skill and surgical skill has already been observed [31], suggesting that other transfers between these domains may be possible. Lastly, players reported to be significantly more sad and unhappy while feeling less competent and confident. This could be explained well by the participant's average win rate of 45% during the study period. While it seems intuitive to assume that a representative sample should show a 50% win rate on average, it should be stressed that this is just a snapshot of the players' performance during the study period. Interestingly, average win rates seem to be below 50% in general for the lower half of the ranks[6]. Since these ranks are populated by around 80% of the player base[7], win rates below 50% appear to be the norm rather than an exception. The results of the follow-up survey provide insight into the participant's general perception about performance and skill acquisition in League of Legends. According to the participants, the most important factor related to improvement is time investment as it was the most common answer when asked directly, when asked about their approach to gain rank quickly and when asked about the reason why professional players become significantly better. They were nevertheless aware that techniques could be used to make improvement more effective as analysis of gameplay was the second most common answer to Q1 and Q3 while focusing their efforts on a small number of champions to be more time-efficient was the second most common answer to Q2. Interestingly, diminishing returns in terms of skill acquisition when simply adding more playtime or quality of practice were no concerns, since only one person planned to avoid playing too much due to performance decline even though almost half of the participants reported a decline of performance over time (48%) as an answer to Q8. The only answer related to quality was the emphasis of playing in a high-level environment as the third most common answer to explain how professional players become significantly better. This indicates that the participants judge the main difference between a good and an average player to be a quantitative discrepancy in playtime. Yet, 76% of them used techniques to improve in a more specific way instead of using the same time to simply play more. Usage of mechanical training techniques (which were perceived to be successful), map awareness reminders and guides to gain knowledge further indicate that participants think improvements can be made by subdividing general gameplay into a set of specific skills that can in turn be addressed in a specific manner and shows a willingness to use such tools. With average gaming sessions between 1.5 and 3 h, participants showed a willingness to invest a considerable amount of time into the game. The majority of participants reported to experience fatigue after playing, with 50% of them pointing to session length and 25% to losing streaks as the main cause. Additionally, 45% of participants reported experiences with physical pain caused by gaming including hand and wrist pain, injuries, headaches and back pain. It seems that some kind of (perceived) mental and physical strain in certain areas is relatively common among the participants when playing. This is supported by the answers to Q7 (unlimited time to play the game and its supposed consequences) with decline in physical and mental health making up 50% of the answers. This is an interesting result since the participants main approach to gain proficiency is to increase their playtime even though they simultaneously associate increases in playtime with mental and physical strain. More effective and efficient methods of skill acquisition that save time but still produce tangible results could be a solution to this problem. A demand among the participants for such a solution

---

[6] https://www.somebits.com//~nelson/lol-stats-notebooks-2016/
    League+of+Legends+win+rates+by+tier.html.

[7] https://www.esportstales.com/league-of-legends/rank-distribution-percentage-of-players-by-tier.

also exists since 70% answered affirmatively when asked if they would make use of techniques to improve more efficiently instead of just playing. The players' perception regarding a decline in performance relative to the length of their gaming session was supported by their win rates. While streaks of one, two and three successive matches showed win rates below 50% (45%, 44.4% and 49% respectively), streaks of length four suddenly increased to 55.4%. Interestingly, the increase in win rate between streaks of one, two, three and four matches corresponds to the participants mention of a perceived warm-up phase. Streaks of five successive matches showed a considerable drop in win rate to 32%. This could imply that a point of optimal performance is reached during a play-session after which performance declines. Still, more data needs to be analyzed to gain insight into this aspect. With regards to our research questions the following can be inferred: Playing demanding video games for prolonged periods of time leads to perceived fatigue with significant indications for the onset of mental fatigue. In our sample, win rates decline considerably for sessions of more than three successive matches. Players use techniques like revision, mechanical practice tools, analysis of professional gameplay and guides to make skill acquisition more efficient while being aware of possible health risks associated with increased playtime. Finally, players are willing to use efficient methods *instead* of playing to gain proficiency.

6 Limitations and Future Work

The results of this work are mainly restricted due to the low number of participants. Even though the results are significant for almost all categories related to mental fatigue (with the exception of no increase in perceived effort) and fatigue in general, it is difficult to see them as anything other than indicative. Furthermore, the data collected describes the players' perceptions. This does not provide any information on whether these perceptions are rooted in an actual decline of performance. Even though the participants match data showed a clear decline in win rate relative to the number of successively played matches, it is unclear which aspects of performance were compromised and how strongly each individual participant's performance declined during these matches. A follow-up study with more participants and analysis of match performances on a larger scale is planned to confirm and extend these findings. If individual match performances can be found to decline relative to time played without adequate rest, this could have implications for fairness in e-sports tournaments (as discussed in Sect. 5). Such a detrimental effect on performance would also make the exploration of structured training methods as well as guidelines for optimal performance in this domain particularly important. If effective, these methods could support players in their e-sports endeavours and additionally decrease the risk of gaming-related injuries as well as health and mental health issues by lowering requirements of play time to achieve the same (or possibly better) results. Limitations also apply to the recruitment process. Gaming focused community discord servers were used as the primary venue to advertise the study in an attempt to preserve ecological validity by reaching actual players from the chosen target group. Albeit difficult to achieve, recruiting players from all the different regions and from all the different ranks (representing skill levels) in equal amounts would facilitate more representative results. Another limitation for this study is the game of choice. Even though the results are likely extendable to other competitive or strenuous games, more genres need to be investigated to really confirm this assumption. Additionally, the multiplayer as well as the team aspect could influence how strongly players fatigue. Studies with single-player games are needed to make the results more relevant for digital domains that require one person to work on a non-competitive task (e.g. flight monitoring or surgery). With regards to future work, it is also unclear whether the same training methods and performance guidelines will necessarily apply to games in other genres. Further improvements are possible regarding the measures used in this study. A fully validated questionnaire for detecting mental fatigue in players of video games specifically would have produced much stronger evidence. To our knowledge, such a questionnaire unfortunately does not exist. Even though this paper argues that mental fatigue might have a negative effect on performance in video games due to its effects on cognitive functions (described in Sect. 2), more empirical evidence is needed to confirm this conjecture. A follow-up study investigating the behavior of performance metrics relative to uninterrupted playtime as mentioned before is thus essential. Since participants stated a demand for techniques and structured methods to improve more efficiently at video games, identification and evaluation of such techniques will be explored in future work. Mental practice and deliberate practice (as defined by Ericsson et al. [11]) are both interesting areas that have been found to be beneficial in other areas like traditional sports or music [5, 16, 30, 36]. Lastly, the digital nature of video games allows the development and use of integrated practice tools for skill acquisition that could make effective practice more seamless and enjoyable. Digital tools could be used to improve feedback, visualize player performance, indicate optimal play patterns, supply gameplay related information on demand or even analyze player performance automatically to detect weaknesses and suggest areas of improvement. Development and evaluation of such tools could not only make skill acquisition in video games more effective but also more accessible, sustainable and fun.

7   Conclusion

Video games are one of the most popular leisure activities in the world. People are willing to spend large amounts of time playing these games, especially in the case of competitive games like League of Legends. Playing long sessions without rest seems to be a popular method to gain rank and proficiency in such games. Since this requires considerable amounts of time, concerns related to the effectiveness of this method are valid. It is known in other fields that executing tasks for prolonged periods of time leads to fatigue and mental fatigue in particular, which can in turn negatively impact performance as well as learning.

This exploratory study found significant indications for the onset of both fatigue and mental fatigue after play sessions of League of Legends as perceived by the participants together with a considerable decline in win rate when playing five matches in succession. Additionally, participants not only confirmed increases in playtime to be their main method to gain rank and proficiency but also showed an awareness for the existence of specialised training techniques and reported physical and mental strain to be a common experience when playing (with some even experiencing gaming-related injuries). Lastly, participants stated a willingness to use efficient training or learning techniques instead of playing if they enabled them to save time.

Acknowledgements. We would like all participants. This research is funded by the Klaus Tschira Stiftung. One author is funded by the James S. McDonnell Foundation (Grant Title: A Methodology for Studying the Dynamics of Resilience of College Students).

References

1. Anderson, J.R., Bellezza, F.S.: Rules of the Mind. Psychology Press, London (2009)
2. Baker, K., Olson, J., Morisseau, D.: Work practices, fatigue, and nuclear power plant safety performance. Hum. Factors **36**(2), 244–257 (1994). https://doi.org/10.1177/001872089403600206. pMID: 8070790
3. Boksem, M.A., Meijman, T.F., Lorist, M.M.: Effects of mental fatigue on attention: an ERP study. Cogn. Brain Res. **25**(1), 107–116 (2005). https://doi.org/10.1016/j.cogbrainres.2005.04.011, https://www.sciencedirect.com/science/article/pii/S0926641005001187
4. Boksem, M.A., Tops, M.: Mental fatigue: costs and benefits. Brain Res. Rev. **59**(1), 125–139 (2008)
5. Charness, N., Tuffiash, M., Krampe, R., Reingold, E., Vasyukova, E.: The role of deliberate practice in chess expertise. Appl. Cogn. Psychol. **19**(2), 151–165 (2005)
6. Cohen, J.: Statistical Power Analysis for the Behavioral Sciences. Routledge, Milton Park (2013)
7. Cook, C., Burgess-Limerick, R., Chang, S.: The prevalence of neck and upper extremity musculoskeletal symptoms in computer mouse users. Int. J. Ind. Ergonomics **26**(3), 347–356 (2000). https://doi.org/10.1016/S0169-8141(00)00010-X, https://www.sciencedirect.com/science/article/pii/S016981410000010X
8. Duncan, J., Emslie, H., Williams, P., Johnson, R., Freer, C.: Intelligence and the frontal lobe: the organization of goal-directed behavior. Cogn. Psychol. **30**(3), 257–303 (1996). https://doi.org/10.1006/cogp.1996.0008
9. Duncan, M.J., Fowler, N., George, O., Joyce, S., Hankey, J.: Mental fatigue negatively influences manual dexterity and anticipation timing but not repeated high-intensity exercise performance in trained adults. Res. Sports Med. **23**(1), 1–13 (2015)
10. Dunstan, D.W., Howard, B., Healy, G.N., Owen, N.: Too much sitting-a health hazard. Diabetes Res. Clin. Pract. **97**(3), 368–376 (2012)
11. Ericsson, K.A., Krampe, R.T., Tesch-Römer, C.: The role of deliberate practice in the acquisition of expert performance. Psychol. Rev. **100**(3), 363 (1993)
12. Forsyth, D.R.: Self-serving bias (2008)

13. Fortes, L.S., et al.: Playing videogames or using social media applications on smartphones causes mental fatigue and impairs decision-making performance in amateur boxers. Appl. Neuropsychol. Adult, 1–12 (2021)

14. Grove, R., Prapavessis, H.: Abbreviated poms questionnaire (40 items), November 2013

15. Habay, J., et al.: Mental fatigue and sport-specific psychomotor performance: a systematic review. Sports Med. 1–22 (2021). https://doi.org/10.1007/s40279-021-01429-6

16. Isaac, A.R.: Mental practice: does it work in the field? Sport Psychol. **6**(2), 192–198 (1992)

17. Johnson, A., Proctor, R.W.: Skill Acquisition and Training: Achieving Expertise in Simple and Complex Tasks. Routledge, Taylor & Francis Group (2017)

18. Jong, R.: An intention-activation account of residual switch costs. Control Cogn. Process. **18**, 356–376 (2000)

19. Linden, D.: The urge to stop: the cognitive and biological nature of acute mental fatigue (2011)

20. Linden, D., Frese, M., Meijman, T.: Mental fatigue and the control of cognitive processes: effects on perseveration and planning. Acta Psychol. **113**, 45–65 (2003). https://doi.org/10.1016/S0001-6918(02)00150-6

21. Lorist, M.: How mental fatigue affects visual selective attention. Front. Hum. Neurosci. **5** (2011). https://doi.org/10.3389/conf.fnhum.2011.207.00261

22. Marcora, S.M., Staiano, W., Manning, V.: Mental fatigue impairs physical performance in humans. J. Appl. Physiol. **106**(3), 857–864 (2009)

23. Martin, K., Meeusen, R., Thompson, K.G., Keegan, R., Rattray, B.: Mental fatigue impairs endurance performance: a physiological explanation. Sports Med. **48**(9), 2041–2051 (2018)

24. Mayring, P., Fenzl, T.: Qualitative Inhaltsanalyse. In: Handbuch Methoden der empirischen Sozialforschung, pp. 633–648. Springer, Wiesbaden (2019). https://doi.org/10.1007/978-3-658-21308-4_42

25. McCormick, F., Kadzielski, J., Landrigan, C.P., Evans, B., Herndon, J.H., Rubash, H.E.: Surgeon fatigue: a prospective analysis of the incidence, risk, and intervals of predicted fatigue-related impairment in residents. Arch. Surg. **147**(5), 430–435 (2012). https://doi.org/10.1001/archsurg.2012.84

26. Meijman, T.F.: Mental fatigue and the efficiency of information processing in relation to work times. Int. J. Ind. Ergon. **20**(1), 31–38 (1997). https://doi.org/10.1016/S0169-8141(96)00029-7, https://www.sciencedirect.com/science/article/pii/S0169814196000297

27. Moreira, A., Aoki, M.S., Franchini, E., da Silva Machado, D.G., Paludo, A.C., Okano, A.H.: Mental fatigue impairs technical performance and alters neuroendocrine and autonomic responses in elite young basketball players. Physiol. Behav. **196**, 112–118 (2018)

28. Penna, E.M., et al.: Mental fatigue impairs physical performance in young swimmers. Pediatric Exerc. Sci. **30**(2), 208–215 (2018)

29. Riot Games: League of Legends. Game [PC], riot Games, Los Angeles, California, USA, October 2009

30. Ross, S.L.: The effectiveness of mental practice in improving the performance of college trombonists. J. Res. Music Educ. **33**(4), 221–230 (1985)

31. Rosser, J.C., et al.: The impact of video games on training surgeons in the 21st century. Arch. Surg. **142**(2), 181–186 (2007)

32. Sun, H., Soh, K.G., Roslan, S., Wazir, M.R.W.N., Soh, K.L.: Does mental fatigue affect skilled performance in athletes? a systematic review. PLoS ONE **16**(10), e0258307 (2021)

33. Valve: Counter-Strike: Global Offensive. Game [PC,PS3,XBox360], valve, Bellevue, Washington State, USA, August 2012

34. Valve: Dota2. Game [PC], valve, Bellevue, Washington State, USA, July 2013

35. Van Cutsem, J., Marcora, S.: The effects of mental fatigue on sport performance: an update. In: Motivation and Self-regulation in Sport and Exercise, pp. 134–148. Routledge (2021)

36. Ward, P., Hodges, N.J., Starkes, J.L., Williams, M.A.: The road to excellence: deliberate practice and the development of expertise. High Ability Stud. **18**(2), 119–153 (2007)

37. Werner, K.M., Milyavskaya, M., Foxen-Craft, E., Koestner, R.: Some goals just feel easier: self-concordance leads to goal progress through subjective ease, not effort. Pers. Individ. Differ. **96**, 237–242 (2016). https://doi.org/10.1016/j.paid.2016.03.002, https://www.sciencedirect.com/science/article/pii/S0191886916301477

38. Wilcoxon, F.: Individual comparisons by ranking methods. In: Kotz, S., Johnson, N.L. (eds.) Breakthroughs in statistics, pp. 196–202. Springer, New York (1992). https://doi.org/10.1007/978-1-4612-4380-9_16

Difficulty Pacing Impact on Player Motivation

William Rao Fernandes[✉][iD] and Guillaume Levieux[iD]

Conservatoire National des Arts et Metiers, CEDRIC, Paris, France
{william.fernandes,guillaume.levieux}@cnam.fr

Abstract. Challenge, and thus difficulty, is one of the main factors of enjoyment and motivation in video games. To enhance the players' motivation, many studies rely on Dynamic Difficulty Adjustment model in order to follow a difficulty curve. However, few authors worked on the shape of the difficulty curve itself. Our goal in this paper is to evaluate how players react to different difficulty curves. We use four different difficulty curves, including two flat curves and two curves with different baseline and peak levels. We test those curves on 67 students of a video games school while playing a First-Person Shooter game. Our study shows that curves with peaks have the strongest impact on players' motivation.

1 Introduction

Whether when studying video games or psychology, motivation is an important part of the literature. In fact, many studies on video games are using psychology theories in order to enhance the players' motivation [8,19,20,29]. Many of these studies try to design a difficulty curve that matches the Flow Theory, as the flow state is known as a mental state where players are strongly focused [27]. This is considered as an engaging moment, providing a positive feeling between arousal and control. The flow theory states that difficulty should be neither too hard nor too easy, matching the player skills, and that other interesting states can be obtained by slightly unbalancing difficulty. However, there are no scientific studies on what kind of difficulty curve might enhance the players' motivation even more. The only articles we found are from game designers who share their point of view about their industrial experiences [11,31,34].

The goal of this paper is to design different difficulty curves in order to enhance the players' motivation. Then, by using these curves in a video game, compare the players' actual motivation for each curve. To do so, we will use a Dynamic Difficulty Adjustment (DDA) model which can follow any difficulty curve [28].

The paper starts with a literature review of difficulty and motivation, which help us shape our DDA model. However, few authors have experimentally studied difficulty curves shapes, but there exists theoretical models and design good

© IFIP International Federation for Information Processing 2022
Published by Springer Nature Switzerland AG 2022
B. Göbl et al. (Eds.): ICEC 2022, LNCS 13477, pp. 140–153, 2022.
https://doi.org/10.1007/978-3-031-20212-4_11

practices that can help us to design our difficulty curves and to form our hypotheses. Then we detail our experiment, present our results and finally discuss them.

2   Difficulty and Motivation

Many authors consider challenge as one of the core features of video games' enjoyment. Ryan et al. study intrinsic motivation and apply Self-Determination Theory to video games. They show how enjoyment is related to the feeling of competence, which relies on an optimal level of challenge, and thus, on the game's difficulty [29]. Jesper Juul's definition of video games states that a video game has quantifiable outcomes, influenced by the players' effort. This definition puts challenge as part of the very nature of a game, as the level of challenge mainly drives the effort the players have to put in the game. Juul also provided insight on how failure, and thus difficulty, is one of the core aspects of video game enjoyment and learning progression [17,18]. Malone considers that video games are captivating because they provide challenge, foster the player's curiosity and propose a rich fantasy [25]. Malone explains that challenge is directly related to the game's difficulty and corresponds to the uncertainty for the players to reach the game's goals. Lazzaro proposes a four factor model, where *Hard Fun* is related to the feeling of overcoming difficult tasks [20]. Sweetser et al. see also challenge as one of the most fundamental part of their Game Flow framework [32].

The work of Sweetser et al. stems from Mihaly Csikszentmihalyi's Theory of Flow [27], who has been trying to figure out the properties of activities showing a strong, intrinsic ability to motivate. Csikszentmihalyi research states that these activities provide *perceived challenges, or opportunities for action, that stretch (neither over matching nor underutilizing) existing skills* [27]. Such a flow state has been shown to be globally amplified by the use of a basic difficulty adjustment system [3]. A study of large population of players in two commercial games confirm that players prefer specific levels of difficulty [1].

In order to enhance the motivation of the player, many studies focused on Dynamic Difficulty Adjustment (DDA) models. DDA models are used to automatically change the difficulty parameters of a game, based on the players' skills, in order to keep the players entertained. Many DDA models are using data representing the player's performance. The $+/-\ \delta$ algorithm, for instance, can start with no data and only use the player's last success or failure to converge to what we may call a *balanced* difficulty state, where the player has a 0.5 probability to fail [28]. Constant used this algorithm to adapt the difficulty of three games based on logical, motor and sensory difficulties [8]. This algorithm is also used in the famous game Crash Bandicoot [12]. DDA algorithms can be specific to a game genre, like the Rubber Band artificial intelligence (AI), used for sport or racing games, that will adjust the difficulty by comparing the position of the enemies and the player [37]. We also have more advanced models, using learning algorithms to adapt the difficulty like Andrade with Q-learning [2], dynamic scripting [30], or Monte Carlo Tree Search [9,14,16]. In a previous research, we developed a simple DDA algorithm that needs few data points [28]. The model is using both $+/-$ δ algorithm and logistic regression. The $+/-$ δ algorithm is used to gather enough data until the logistic regression is accurate enough, which let the model estimate the parameters needed to provide the targeted failure probability.

Difficulty is thus a fundamental aspect of video games, and the progression of difficulty seems to be one of the many ways that video games can keep us motivated and concentrated for long period of times. One way to enhance motivation using difficulty is by designing difficulty curves that represent how difficulty will change over time. By shaping the difficulty curve, designers can decide when to challenge the players, when to give them rest, gradually increasing or decreasing difficulty or creating difficulty peaks. The difficulty curves can also be used by a DDA model, as presented previously. However, there is little to none literature about how to design a good difficulty curve. We thus focus on the difficulty curve's shape, in order to provide experimental evidence of their impact on player's motivation.

3   Difficulty Curves

As we said, difficulty is thought over time. Games rarely have the same difficulty level from the beginning to the end [1]. One way to plan the pace of difficulty is to design a difficulty curve that will drive the game's difficulty during the game session [6]. According to some game designer and also proposed by [21], a good difficulty curve will start low in difficulty, gradually raising the difficulty until a specific event occurs. Then, difficulty can be lowered to let the players enjoy their success, and then gradually increase again to repeat the pattern [11, 31,34]. Often, the difficulty curve will match the introduction of new gameplay mechanics that the player will have to master in order to move forward. That is the case for The Legend of Zelda, an iconic game from Nintendo [26]. The players will get a new item at the beginning of a dungeon, meaning that they will need to learn new skills. This leads to a difficulty peak. Then, as the players explore the dungeon, they will improve their skills, which translate to the difficulty going down. Finally, the players will face the dungeon master, a new peak of difficulty. Getting out of the dungeon, the new item will allow players to reach new parts of the game map, that were not accessible, or unlock shortcuts, and difficulty is thus going down. But these new parts of the game maps may lead to stronger enemies, new dungeons, and thus the difficulty goes up again.

Allart et al. worked on the impact of two games difficulty curves on player retention. The data comes from two industrial games, Rayman Legends and Tom Clancy's: The Division [1]. They showed that difficulty is by itself an explanatory variable of player retention, and that players tend to prefer higher levels of difficulty. It is to note that both games have almost always a probability of failure under the balanced difficulty of 50%. They have also shown that people prefer lower difficulty at the beginning, which confirm the self-efficacy theory [5]. This paper also shows that difficulty peaks are present in Ubisoft games [1]. It is shown that players enjoy difficulty peaks when the game is not punitive like Rayman Legends, which comforted us for our experimentation, as difficulty curves and difficulty peaks seemed at least as important as overall difficulty.

Loftus studied why gamers are attracted to video games [23]. At this time, players mainly played paying arcade games. Players were rewarded by a high score when playing well, and had to pay when losing in order to keep their progression. The main goal of game designers was to have a difficulty hard enough, so the players lose a lot, but they feel like they can beat the game, so they keep playing. The path to success is reachable but close to failure, and the players might regret their decisions afterward [13]. Regret is a way to make the players try again where they failed, because they were close to the success they wanted. To apply that idea of regret, we can use difficulty curves with some peaks of difficulty. By doing so, we challenge the players to higher difficulty than they are used to, which lead to a greater reward when they clear the level.

Weiner described that people react with positive emotions if they feel like their actions are the cause of success [35]. However, Weiner showed that people will feel less positive emotions if the task is too easy, which confirms that the task difficulty is a variable we need to take into account. We can apply that to video games, as the players will feel less satisfied winning a game if they know that the game difficulty was set to easy [24]. Klimmt decided to let the players know in which difficulty they were during his experimentation. However, Klimmt found out that players enjoyed the game more with a lower difficulty, when they had very few failures [19]. It is to note that players had 10 min of gameplay, which leads us to suggest that the first contact with the game should be with a low difficulty. The idea of positive emotion linked to success is also found in a more advance form of the Flow theory, where the authors seek to propose tasks with a difficulty lower than the people skills in order to put people in different positive emotional states [27].

Linehan et al. focused on four mainstream puzzle games, Portal, Portal 2, Braid and Lemmings. They analyzed the data from these games in order to understand why people were attracted to them. For all the games, the same pattern is used. The beginning of the game is really simple, as players need to learn the basic mechanics. Then each time the game includes a new mechanics, they have some time to familiarize with it with a low difficulty puzzle before getting to a more challenging level of difficulty [22].

Following our literature review, we have three major point to design a difficulty curve. The first one is the starting difficulty. Following Linehan et al., as well as Bandura's self-efficacy theory, each of our curves will start low [5, 22].

The second point is the difficulty level. We can follow the flow and suggest a curve that goes up to 50% chance of winning because, as we saw it in the literature review of difficulty and motivation, it is widespread. This will be our balanced curve that we will name *Flow* Curve as it simply follows the goal of matching the player skills. To test the difference with difficulty level, we designed an 80% chance of winning curve, as players might prefer a lower difficulty [19]. This will be our*Low* Curve.

The third point is the presence or absence of difficulty peaks. We found in the literature review of the difficulty curves that making difficulty peaks is pleasing for the players [11,31,34]. We designed two more difficulty curves, with the same baseline as the first two, but adding high difficulty peaks that reach 80% chances of failure. We thus add the *Low Peaks* and the *Flow Peaks* curves.

Figure 1 shows the shape of each of the curves we designed for the experiment.

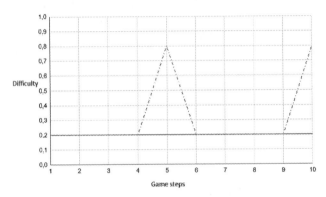

(a) *Low* difficulty curves.

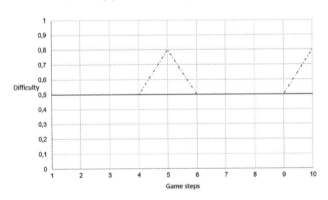

(b) *High* difficulty curves.

Fig. 1. Designed difficulty curves

The continuous orange curves are flat curves, while the dotted violet ones are curves with difficulty peaks. Difficulty peaks appear at every five rounds of the game, with a failure probability of 0.8.

4 Experimentation

4.1 Hypotheses

Lomas et al. study leads us to suppose that the game difficulty can lead players to a lack of motivation if they know they are playing on low difficulty [24]. We thus chose not to explicitly show the current game's difficulty. Then we start following the root of the flow theory, with a difficulty that matches the player's skills. This is however contradictory with Klimmt et al. study, that shows that player might prefer lower difficulty as they provide more positive feedbacks, [19]. The first hypothesis that we will put to test will thus be that the Flow curve, which offers a difficulty corresponding to the player's skill, might be more appreciated than the Low curve.

We are using a game that is not punitive. We will present the game in the Methodology section. In this game, losing leads the players to another try at a similar task, the only difference between the failed task and the new one will be the task difficulty. The players will face the same enemy, in the same arena, with the same items. In this context, following [1] discussion, we believe that the difficulty curves with peaks will be more appreciated, because they will bring more satisfaction if the player succeeds when the difficulty is high, but they will feel very little frustration if they fail, because they can directly start playing again without loss of progress.

Finally, our last hypothesis is the grouping of the first two other hypotheses, which is that the Flow Peaks curve will be the most appreciated of the four curves.

1. The Flow curve is more appreciated than the Low curve;
2. The curves with peaks are more appreciated;
3. The Flow Peaks curve is more appreciated than the others.

4.2 Methodology

In this paper and following Levieux and Aponte et al., we consider that an estimation of the game's difficulty is very close to the estimation of players' performance, that we define as their failure probability [4,21]. As shown in Fig. 1, the curves represent the failure probability at each try.

We modified a Unity First-Person Shooter (FPS) mini-game to make it a one versus one arena game [33]. The Fig. 2 is a screenshot during a play session. In this game, the player can move forward, backward, left and right, and can move the camera using the mouse. We only used one type of weapon, in order to reduce the variability for this experiment. We modified the level design and enemy AI so that the player will fight in an arena versus an AI-controlled enemy. The AI will patrol the map and, when it sees the player, will start to follow them and shoot them. Each time the player beats the enemy, a new enemy respawns, and we refill the player's health. If the player dies, we destroy the enemy, then respawn the player and a new enemy. The AI has different parameters that change according to the difficulty. We can change its movement speed, shooting speed, shooting range, and player detection range.

We use a DDA model developed in a previous research to follow our difficulty curve [28]. This DDA model allows us to follow any difficulty curve using as few data points as possible. It can be used on many game types, allows a developer to set the game's difficulty to any level within approximately two minutes of playtime. In order to roughly estimate the difficulty as quickly as possible, the model drives a single metavariable to adjust the game's difficulty. As described, the game difficulty depend on the game's variables which are the enemy moving speed, shooting speed, shooting range and detection range. It starts with a simple $+/-\delta$ algorithm to gather a few data points, and then uses logistic regression to estimate the players' failure probability when the smallest required amount of data has been collected.

Fig. 2. Game screenshot. The player is aiming at the enemy

The experience has three phases. The first one is a questionnaire about the player's gaming habits and self-efficacy profile. This questionnaire has been used in an experimentation on Players' confidence [7], but we removed the last part on risk aversion. It is to note that this questionnaire is in French, as our participants are all French-speaking people.

The second part is the game session. Participants will have to play for at least 10 min and up to 20 min. At the start of the session, we pick a random difficulty curve between our four curves. During the game session, the player will face an AI-controlled enemy in an arena fight. When 5 min pass, a button appears on the top right of the screen, asking if the player is bored. If the player clicks on it, the game will select another difficulty curve. After 5 more minutes from the click, the button will reappear. Clicking again on the button will end the game session. We brief the players before the game session about the button, so they cannot miss it while playing. By doing this, we want to register a playtime, and consider that the playtime is a way to indirectly evaluate the players' motivation.

No matter how the game session ended, by clicking the buttons or by playing 20 min, the player will enter the third phase of the test, and fill is the Game Experience Questionnaire or GEQ [15] that has been translated into French. The experimentation sessions took place at LeCNAM ENJMIN, a video game school [10]. Most students there play video games and use 3D software, so our participants already know how to navigate a 3D world and play a FPS with a PC setup. Indeed, learning these skills on a 20 min game session would not be representative of a real play session.

5   Results

Sixty-seven participants played our shooter game (55 male and 12 female) with a mean age of 23 ($\sigma = 3.24$). Participants played for at least 10 min, and up to 20 min, with a mean playtime of 17 min and 40 s.

We estimate the DDA model's quality for each participant. To do so, we calculate the ratio of the number of prediction errors to the total number of predictions for each play session. We decided to remove extreme values, using the interquartile range (IQR) of the statistical dispersion of the model's quality[1]. We removed 8 participants with a too high prediction error ratio. We checked the players' performance by calculating the mean difficulty of their tries, in order to detect if some players did not understand the rules of the game, or on the contrary, if they found an exploit that would lead them to victory at each try. But we did not find any abnormal data.

We have three hypotheses to test, using the data we collected. Our first hypothesis concerns the baseline difficulty of the curves. We are thinking that participants will enjoy the game more with a higher difficulty level, that will put them in the flow state or arousal state. Those two states should motivate the players or at least make them play longer, which means that we expect participants to play longer on the Flow curve and Flow Peaks curve.

Our second hypothesis, following the literature, is that participants played longer on curves with difficulty peaks. We also expect participants to play longer on high difficulty curves, and on difficulty curves with peaks. Combining these two statements, we expect the Flow Peaks curve to be the more appealing curve of all four.

In order to check our hypotheses, we checked for each participant how long they played on the first curve, before clicking on the button for the first time. Because the player could click on a button to tell us when they are getting bored, we use the playtime as an estimation of the player enjoyment of the game for this curve. As shown by Fig. 3, most of the participants who had the Flow curve played less, meaning they pressed the button earlier, while participants with Low, Low Peaks and Flow Peaks curves played longer before pressing the button.

---

[1] To find the extreme value, we get the upper extremity of the dispersion: Quartile 3 + 1,5*IQR.

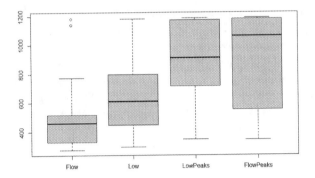

Fig. 3. Playtime of the participants on the first curve chosen

Table 1. P-value of the Wilcoxon Rank Sum tests comparing the playtime for each couples of curves. The Flow Curve is significantly lower than the two curves with peaks, no matter the overall difficulty. * for p <0.05, ** for p <0.01

	Low	Low peaks	Flow
Low peaks	0.07	X	X
Flow	0.1	0.03*	X
Flow peaks	0.06	0.8	0.008**

To validate that visual data, we did several Wilcoxon Rank Sum tests, each time testing a specific curve's playtime versus the three others [36]. As we can see on Fig. 2, we got significant results while testing the Flow versus the Flow Peaks curve, which partially validate our hypothesis that players prefer difficulty curves with peaks. However, we don't have the same results with the Low curve versus the Low Peaks curve. To further test our hypothesis regarding curves with peaks versus flat curves, and high difficulty curves versus low difficulty curves, we compared the participants' playtime on the different curves, grouping the data two by two. The first one are Low difficulty curves and High difficulty curves, but as we can see on Fig. 3, the graphical result is not as we expected.

We did a Wilcoxon Rank Sum test to check if the high difficulty versus low difficulty had some significant results, but they were not with a p-value of 0.16, which means our hypothesis on the game being more appealing when the difficulty is higher is wrong. We will discuss this result in the next section.

The second comparison was between curves with peaks and flat curves, which is our second hypothesis. Players seem to play longer on the curves with peaks, as seen in Fig. 4, supporting our hypothesis.

To fully validate this hypothesis, we made another Wilcoxon Rank Sum test using for each curve the playtime data and grouping the flat curves together and the curves with peaks together, with p-value ≈ 0.003, rejecting the null hypothesis and thus supports us with our hypothesis.

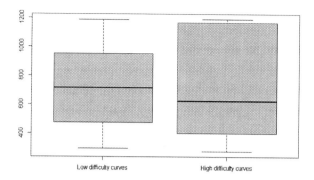

Fig. 4. Playtime of the participants, High difficulty vs Low difficulty Results are not significant with a p-value of the Wilcoxon test ≈ 0.16. This means that overall difficulty did not contribute to the players' motivation in our experiment.

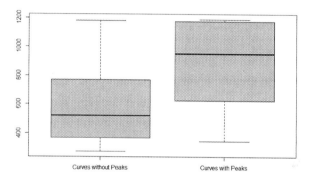

Fig. 5. Playtime of the participants, Peaks vs no Peaks. Wilcoxon Rank Sum test p $\approx$ 0.003 : difficulty peaks did contribute to the players' motivation in our experiment.

To sum up, our results do not validate our hypothesis for the high difficulty. However, Flow Peaks and Low Peaks are the two curves with the longest playtime, and the data validate our hypothesis that people will prefer curves with peaks. In addition, Flow Peaks curve is the one with the longest playtime. However, we cannot affirm that the Flow Peaks curve is the most appealing of the four curves. It is to note that we were wrong saying that the Flow Curve would be more appealing than both the Low and Low Peaks curve.

We decided to check the data from the GEQ in order to see if the player's experiences matches our results. The GEQ is composed of 7 components that we can class in two categories:

1. Positive components: Competence, Sensory and Imaginative Immersion, Flow, Challenge, Positive affect
2. Negative components: Tension/Annoyance, Negative Affect

Table 2. Significant location shift of the Wilcoxon Rank Sum test comparing the results from the GEQ for each couples of curves. The flow curve is significantly lower than the two curves with peaks for the Competence and the positive components.

Competence	Flow	Positive	Flow
Low Peaks	−5*	Low Peaks	−5**
Flow Peaks	−3*	Flow Peaks	−3*

Regarding our hypotheses, we are expecting that players who had a curve with peaks have higher positive score than the players who had flat curve, as well as lower negative score.

Using the data from the GEQ, we check the score of each component for each participant. We compare each curve with the three others for each component. We have significant results on the Competence and the Positive components for the Flow versus the Flow Peaks. The participants playing on the flow curve felt less positive emotion with a p-value ≈ 0.03 at the Wilcoxon Rank Sum test and less competence with a p-value ≈ 0.05 than the participants playing on the flow peaks curve. The other significant results are on the Positive and Competence components for the Flow versus Low Peaks. Again the participants felt less competence on the flow curve, with a p-value ≈ 0.03 and less positive emotion with a p-value ≈ 0.007. The Table 2 regroup the Location Shift for each significant results. It supports the results on the playtime and the hypothesis that people prefer difficulty curves with peaks.

6   Discussion

Our results confirmed that our participants preferred difficulty curves with peaks of difficulty. However, our participants are mainly gamers and they are all students. We decided to pass the experiment in a game development school to get rid of some bias like the learning of using a keyboard and mouse to play a game and the learning of basic FPS mechanics. This population is also close to the target population of FPS games. But our results are only valid for this game and this population, and we would like to replicate this experiment on a different public. The target public could be casual gamers for instance, maybe with different results.

As we said, we used a FPS game, mainly because it is a type of game based on motor skills, with a short period of learning, as the participants could learn the few mechanics of the game, the player's mobility, the gravity, the shooting rate, the reloading time, and the game's map in a couple of minutes, which let them play at their best potential afterward. FPS game are very often competitive. Our result might come from the fact that some of our participants are regular FPS players, and they may have taken the experiment as a competition. We cannot affirm that the same population of players will react the same on an adventure game like Zelda, and testing the same population on this type of game, would be very interesting. There exist different form of difficulty, and it would be very interesting to test the impact of difficulty curves on logical difficulty, for instance [4,8,21].

The FPS game we used is a one versus one battle arena game, which is a subcategory for FPS games. The players spawn in a small arena with a unique enemy. When the player fails, they simply respawn, and the game continues, thus failure is not punitive, but merely a quick negative feedback of the players failure to overcome the challenge. As Allart discussed, the punitive aspect of failure might influence the impact of difficulty on motivation. When a game proposes a difficult challenge that takes a long time to beat and must be restarted on failure, it creates tension, but failure can be much more frustrating, changing the impact of difficulty on motivation.

7   Conclusion

In this paper, we propose an experiment on difficulty curves. Many authors use difficulty curves in order to enhance the players' motivation, but few studies the impact of difficulty curves on the players.

For our experiment, we test a population of students as they played a simple battle arena FPS. This game is using a DDA model in order to adapt the difficulty to the players abilities, following a specific difficulty curve. Each participant played with one of four difficulty curves that we designed, to test the impact of base level and presence of difficulty peaks.

Results show the that players might prefer difficulty curves with peaks over flat ones. It is to note that we thought that the Flow curve would be the most enjoyed, but it seems to be the least preferred curve of all four. Thus, using a DDA model that is able to perfectly balance difficulty with player level, and thus simply aim for, a flat 50% chances of losing might not be the best idea for a FPS game.

Acknowledgement. This research is part of the *Programme d'investissement d'avenir E-FRAN* project *DysApp*, conducted with *Caisse des Dépôts* and supported by the French Government.

References

1. Allart, T., Levieux, G., Pierfitte, M., Guilloux, A., Natkin, S.: Difficulty influence on motivation over time in video games using survival analysis. In: Proceedings of the 12th International Conference on the Foundations of Digital Games, p. 2. ACM (2017)
2. Andrade, G., Ramalho, G., Santana, H., Corruble, V.: Extending reinforcement learning to provide dynamic game balancing. In: Proceedings of the Workshop on Reasoning, Representation, and Learning in Computer Games, 19th International Joint Conference on Artificial Intelligence (IJCAI), pp. 7–12 (2005)

3. Ang, D., Mitchell, A.: Comparing effects of dynamic difficulty adjustment systems on video game experience. In: Proceedings of the Annual Symposium on Computer-Human Interaction in Play, pp. 317–327. ACM (2017)
4. Aponte, M.V., Levieux, G., Natkin, S.: Measuring the level of difficulty in single player video games. Entertainment Comput. **2**(4), 205–213 (2011)
5. Bandura, A.: Self-efficacy: toward a unifying theory of behavioral change. Psychol. Rev. **84**(2), 191 (1977)
6. Byrne, E.: Game level design, vol. 6. Charles River Media Boston (2005)
7. Constant, T., Levieux, G.: Dynamic difficulty adjustment impact on players' confidence. In: Proceedings of the 2019 CHI Conference on Human Factors in Computing Systems, CHI 2019, pp. 463:1–463:12 (2019)
8. Constant, T., Levieux, G., Buendia, A., Natkin, S.: From objective to subjective difficulty evaluation in video Games. In: Bernhaupt, R., Dalvi, G., Joshi, A., Balkrishan, D.K., O'Neill, J., Winckler, M. (eds.) INTERACT 2017. LNCS, vol. 10514, pp. 107–127. Springer, Cham (2017). https://doi.org/10.1007/978-3-319-67684-5_8
9. Demediuk, S., Tamassia, M., Raffe, W.L., Zambetta, F., Li, X., Mueller, F.: Monte carlo tree search based algorithms for dynamic difficulty adjustment. In: 2017 IEEE Conference on Computational Intelligence and Games (CIG), pp. 53–59, August 2017. https://doi.org/10.1109/CIG.2017.8080415
10. ENJMIN: École nationale du jeu et des médias interactifs numériques, https://enjmin-en.cnam.fr/. Accessed 11 July 2022
11. Frazer: level design and difficulty curves (2017). http://www.teaboygames.com/2017/06/14/level-design-and-difficulty-curves/. Accessed 16 Sep 2020
12. Gavin, A.: Making crash bandicoot part 6 (2011). https://all-things-andy-gavin.com/2011/02/07/making-crash-bandicoot-part-6. Accessed 06 Sep 2018
13. Gilovich, T., Medvec, V.H.: The experience of regret: what, when, and why. Psychol. Rev. **102**(2), 379 (1995)
14. Hao, Y., He, S., Wang, J., Liu, X., Huang, W., et al.: Dynamic difficulty adjustment of game AI by MCTS for the game Pac-Man. In: Natural Computation (ICNC), 2010 Sixth International Conference on, vol. 8, pp. 3918–3922. IEEE (2010)
15. IJsselsteijn, W., De Kort, Y., Poels, K.: The game experience questionnaire. Eindhoven: Technische Universiteit Eindhoven, pp. 3–9 (2013)
16. Ishihara, M., Ito, S., Ishii, R., Harada, T., Thawonmas, R.: Monte-carlo tree search for implementation of dynamic difficulty adjustment fighting game AIs having believable behaviors. In: 2018 IEEE Conference on Computational Intelligence and Games (CIG), pp. 1–8. IEEE (2018)
17. Juul, J.: Fear of failing? the many meanings of difficulty in video games. Video Game Theor. reader **2**, 237–252 (2009)
18. Juul, J.: The Art of Failure: an Essay on the Pain of Playing Video Games. MIT Press, Cambridge (2013)
19. Klimmt, C., Blake, C., Hefner, D., Vorderer, P., Roth, C.: Player performance, satisfaction, and video game enjoyment. In: ICEC, pp. 1–12 (2009)
20. Lazzaro, N.: Why we play games: four keys to more emotion without story (2004)
21. Levieux, G.: Mesure de la difficulte des jeux video. Ph.D. thesis, Paris, CNAM (2011)
22. Linehan, C., Bellord, G., Kirman, B., Morford, Z.H., Roche, B.: Learning curves: analysing pace and challenge in four successful puzzle games. In: Proceedings of the first ACM SIGCHI annual symposium on Computer-human interaction in play, pp. 181–190 (2014)
23. Loftus, G.R., Loftus, E.F.: Mind at play. Basic Books, Inc, The psychology of video games (1983)

24. Lomas, J.D., Koedinger, K., Patel, N., Shodhan, S., Poonwala, N., Forlizzi, J.L.: Is difficulty overrated? the effects of choice, novelty and suspense on intrinsic motivation in educational games. In: Proceedings of the 2017 CHI Conference on Human Factors in Computing Systems, pp. 1028–1039 (2017)
25. Malone, T.W.: Heuristics for designing enjoyable user interfaces: lessons from computer games. In: Proceedings of the 1982 Conference on Human Factors in Computing Systems, pp. 63–68. ACM (1982)
26. Miyamoto, S., Nakago, T., Tezuka, T.: The legend of Zelda. Kyoto, Japan, Nintendo (1986)
27. Nakamura, J., Csikszentmihalyi, M.: The Concept of Flow. In: Flow and the Foundations of Positive Psychology, pp. 239–263. Springer, Dordrecht (2014). https://doi.org/10.1007/978-94-017-9088-8_16
28. Rao Fernandes, W., Levieux, G.: δ-logit?: dynamic difficulty adjustment using few data points. In: van der Spek, E., Göbel, S., Do, E.Y.-L., Clua, E., Baalsrud Hauge, J. (eds.) ICEC-JCSG 2019. LNCS, vol. 11863, pp. 158–171. Springer, Cham (2019). https://doi.org/10.1007/978-3-030-34644-7_13
29. Ryan, R.M., Rigby, C.S., Przybylski, A.: The motivational pull of video games: a self-determination theory approach. Motiv. Emot. 30(4), 344–360 (2006)
30. Spronck, P., Sprinkhuizen-Kuyper, I., Postma, E.: Difficulty scaling of game AI. In: Proceedings of the 5th International Conference on Intelligent Games and Simulation (GAME-ON 2004), pp. 33–37 (2004)
31. Strachan, D.: Making difficulty curves in games (2018). http://www.davetech.co.uk/difficultycurves. Accessed 16 Sep 2020
32. Sweetser, P., Wyeth, P.: GameFlow: a model for evaluating player enjoyment in games. Comput. Entertainment (CIE) 3(3), 3–3 (2005)
33. Unity: Fps microgame. https://learn.unity.com/project/fps-template. Accessed 15 Sep 2020
34. Vazquez, R.: How tough is your game? creating difficulty graphs (2011). https://www.gamasutra.com/view/feature/134917/how_tough_is_your_game_creating_.php. Accessed 05 May 2020
35. Weiner, B., Heckhausen, H., Meyer, W.U.: Causal ascriptions and achievement behavior: a conceptual analysis of effort and reanalysis of locus of control. J. Pers. Soc. Psychol. 21(2), 239 (1972)
36. Wilcoxon, F.: Individual comparisons by ranking methods. In: Kotz, S., Johnson, N.L. (eds.) Breakthroughs in Statistics, pp. 196–202. Springer, New York (1992). https://doi.org/10.1007/978-1-4612-4380-9_16
37. Yasuyuki, O., Katsuhisa, S.: Racing game program and video game device (2003). https://patents.google.com/patent/US7278913. Accessed 18 Sep 2018

Toward Dynamic Difficulty Adjustment with Audio Cues by Gaussian Process Regression in a First-Person Shooter

Xiaoxu Li[1], Marcel Wira[1], and Ruck Thawonmas[2]([✉]) [ID]

[1] Graduate School of Information Science and Engineering, Ritsumeikan University,
1-1-1 Nojihigashi, Kusatsu, Shiga 525-8577, Japan
{gr0557hs,gr0556sp}@ed.ritsumei.ac.jp
[2] College of Information Science and Engineering, Ritsumeikan University,
1-1-1 Nojihigashi, Kusatsu, Shiga 525-8577, Japan
ruck@is.ritsumei.ac.jp

Abstract. This study presents an in-game audio-cue setting approach using Gaussian Process Regression (GPR) to provide dynamic difficulty adjustment (DDA) in a first-person shooter game. A novel difficulty-recommendation method is proposed to set our GPR goal for a better personalized audio cue setting. Recent studies showed that audio cues could give the player significant affective changes and influence the player's performance. In addition, other studies showed that it is effective to train the player's in-game ability by adjusting audio cues. However, no research has used audio cues as the primary factor in determining game difficulty. Experimental results show that our game can reach a recommended difficulty within a few plays.

Keywords: Game · First-person shooter · Audio cues · Dynamic difficulty adjustment · Gaussian process regression

1 Introduction

Audio/audio cues are effective in influencing players' affective states [1–4]. In addition, there exist several previous studies reporting that changes in a player's affective state would influence their gaming experience [5], game ability [3,6], and mental health [7]. However, no studies directly used audio cues as the main element to implement the dynamic difficulty adjustment (DDA). DDA is a method to adjust game difficulty based on a player's performance. In this paper, we propose a difficulty-recommendation method and an efficient approach that uses

Supplementary Information The online version contains supplementary material available at https://doi.org/10.1007/978-3-031-20212-4_12.

Gaussian Process Regression (GPR) to automatically adjust the game difficulty with audio cues toward the recommended goal. This should ensure the resulting GPR goal to provide a more tailored and appropriate recommendation on audio cue settings to the player and our DDA approach to adapt quickly to each player.

There are two contributions from this work. First, the recommended GPR goal will suggest a better difficulty setting for the targeted player compared with our Baselines introduced in Sect. 4. Second, audio cues are being deployed as a significant parameter of DDA to adjust the game difficulty for the first time, which may show an alternative sound design for the audio cues.

2   Related Work

2.1   Audio Cues

Game audio includes background music, ambiance and audio cues. We expect that DDA with audio cues can help the player improve their game ability, self-efficacy, and confidence. Previous studies showed that audio affects the player's affective state and further influences their in-game choices [1], tension-anxiety level, and experiences [4]. Ribeiro et al. reported that a high audiovisual thematic cohesion would give the player a better game experience and positive affect [2]. Hence, it is worth making better use of audio cues to help our players during gaming time in many aspects. For example, audio cues could train players' gaming abilities on a first-person shooter (FPS) game [8] and were designed for the visually impaired [9]. Despite all the advantages of audio cues, there is no existing study on audio cues as a central element for DDA. In this paper, we choose enemy-audio-cue volume as our main element for DDA since the previous study showed that players need to pay attention to the increase and decrease of the audio cue volume of, for example, footsteps and gunfire for precisely locating the enemy [8].

2.2   GPR

In recent years, Bayesian Optimization (BO) has been used as a promising method for DDA. It can be used to quickly model and optimally predict to adjust the game's difficulty for a specific player. With BO, the standard and powerful way to derive a probabilistic model is GPR, a non-parameteric model for regression analysis of data. An existing study by Khajah et al. [10] used BO methods to design games like Flappy Bird and Spring Ninja that maximize user engagement. More recently, in González-Duque et al. [11], a method for fast game content adaptation was proposed that uses GPR for level generation in Sudoku and a Roguelike game.

3   Methodology

3.1   Difficulty Recommendation

In the literature, a recommended difficulty was usually set at a 50:50 win-loss ratio [12]. However, it is not a good choice in our case, where we do not want the player to repeat the same game level in an FPS game. The following shows why we do not use a 50:50 win-loss ratio as our GPR goal. We would need to ask players to play the same game level multiple times for us to be able to find the 50:50 win-lose ratio. And if so, audio cues would be less relevant to the game's difficulty because the player might remember the map associated with such a level.

Regarding the DDA goal, no previous study pointed out the relationship between player performance and audio cues. In addition, the best audio cue settings should be different for different games and players. Therefore, using a predetermined DDA goal set for all the players would be of less practicality in our work.

Hence, in this sub-section, we propose a method for recommending a difficulty goal to set in-game audio cues as our difficulty element in an FPS game with different game levels. Here, a difficulty goal is defined as "the performance we expect the player to have when the player plays the game." A promising difficulty goal should have the following characteristics.

- The player will not feel too easy or too difficult when playing a level that meets a given difficulty goal, which is in analogy to the aforementioned goal with a 50:50 win-loss ratio.
- It is a personalized goal.

Assume that we know the performance of a player of interest for every difficulty setting available in the game. A candidate difficulty goal would be an average between the best performance and the worst performance, and a difficulty setting where the player's performance is nearest to this difficulty goal should be exposed to the player. However, focusing solely on the player's performance may lead to a problem. For example, Fig. 1: Case 1 shows a scenario in which the player's performance has only two values, 1 at difficulty setting #1 and 0 at the rest. In this case, the average between the best and worst performances is 0.5, so any difficulty setting from #1 to #19 can be selected.

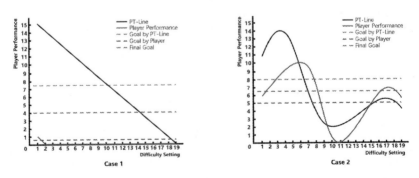

Fig. 1. Case 1: Goal by PT-Line: 7.5/Goal by Player: 0.5/Final Goal: 4 and Case 2: Goal by PT-Line: 8/Goal by Player: 5/Final Goal: 6.5

Algorithm 1 GPR Goal Recommendation

Input: $C_{Best}, C_{Worst}, T_{Best}, T_{Worst}$
Output: G_{Final}
$\quad G_{Player} = w_1 C_{Best} + (1 - w_1)C_{Worst}$
$\quad G_{PT-Line} = w_2 T_{Best} + (1 - w_2)T_{Worst}$
$\quad G_{Final} = w_3 G_{Player} + (1 - w_3)G_{PT-Line}$

However, when the knowledge of the average performance of test players at such difficulty settings is given, shown as the PT-Line in the figure, one would argue to deploy a specific difficulty setting, such as #19, since the player's performance equals the average performance of the test players.

At the same time, this figure also demonstrates that the PT-Line may differ much from the player performance line. Therefore, depending entirely on the PT-Line for goal setting is also unfriendly to the player.

To derive a more player-friendly difficulty goal, Final Goal in the figure, we balance the player performance line and the PT-Line. Case 2 in Fig. 1 depicts a more general scenario. The algorithm to derive the difficulty goal is given in Algorithm 1.

In this algorithm, C_{Best} and C_{Worst} denote the best and worst performances of the current player; T_{Best} and T_{Worst} denote the best and worst performances of the PT-Line created by the all test players' data with 2nd-degree polynomial regression; and w_1, w_2, and w_3 are adjusting coefficients whose values range from 0 to 1, which give room to game designers/developers to emphasize the more important terms according to their thoughts.

Since PT-Line is a pre-designed performance line, we can derive it in many different ways. In this paper, as shown above, we use our test player data to fit a line as our PT-line with 2nd-degree polynomial regression. We think it is more robust and reasonable for our data set because we infer that the relationship between our difficulty element and performance is a quadratic function, which is discussed in Sect. 4.

In this work, GPR allows us to obtain C_{Best} and C_{Worst} when the player's actual performance is at least obtained at one of the difficulty settings. In addition, all the adjusting coefficients are empirically set to 0.5.

3.2 Difficulty Setting with GPR

Given G_{Final}, we then use GPR to determine a difficulty setting or, more specifically, the audio setting of enemy-audio-cue volume in this work that would make the current player's performance close to G_{Final}. This is summarized in Algorithm 2.

In this algorithm, PT is PT-Line. PC represents the current player's data set, in the form of a set of tuples (i, p_i) consisting of audio setting i and the player's performance at this audio setting, and f_{cur} is a GPR model that returns the current player's predicted performance P for a given audio setting AS.

Algorithm 2 DDA with Audio cues by GPR

Input: PT
Output: AS

$T_{Best}, T_{Worst} = max(PT), min(PT)$
$PC = \{\}$
$G_{Final} = 1/2(T_{Best} + T_{Worst})$
$AS = PT^{-1}(G_{Final})$
$P = Game(AS)$
$MP = |P - G_{Final}|$
$i = 1$
Initialize f_{cur}
while $i \leq MaxIterations$ **and** $MP \geq Threshold$ **do**
    Append (AS, P) to PC
    Fit f_{cur} with PC
    $C_{Best}, C_{Worst} = max(f_{cur}), min(f_{cur})$
    $G_{Final} = GPR\ Goal\ Recommendation(C_{Best}, C_{Worst}, T_{Best}, T_{Worst})$
    $AS = f_{cur}^{-1}(G_{Final})$
    $P = Game(AS)$
    $MP = |P - G_{Final}|$
end while

The model is initialized with non-zero mean kernel functions having the mean individually set to the values on PT-Line at respective audio settings. If there are multiple returning AS candidates from f_{cur}^{-1}, one will be randomly selected.

However, if our player has already played the level with the recommended AS, a random level ranging from the index of $AS \pm j$ will be chosen, where j empirically set to 5. If such levels have also been already played, a random level that the player has never played will be chosen.

To validate our model performance MP at iteration (or each game play) i, we use the following equation where $Game(AS_i)$ is the performance of the player playing the game while being exposed to the audio setting at iteration i.

$$MP_i = |Game(AS_i) - G_{Final}| \qquad (1)$$

Note that the closer MP is to zero, the better the prediction.

4   Experiment and Result

We collected performance data from 40 players who played an originally developed FPS game, modified from an FPS template provided by Unreal Engine 4, for five levels. In this game, as audio cues, each level is assigned a different and fixed audio volume setting of either 0%, 25%, 50%, 75%, or 100% for its AI enemies[1] The clear time of a level by a player was used as the player's performance metric.

---

[1] Demo videos: https://tinyurl.com/FPSaudioCues.

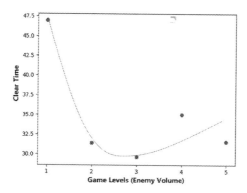

Fig. 2. Relationship between clear time and enemy volume

Figure 2 shows the average performance at each level, superimposed with a regression line obtained with 2nd-degree polynomial regression. It can be seen that the relationship between enemy-audio-cue volume and player completion time is a quadratic function. To examine the effectiveness of our DDA approach, we used the aforementioned regression line to synthesize the average performances of those players at 101 levels from 0% to 100% volume settings with a step size of 1. For performance comparison, we used three baseline algorithms as follows:

Baseline 1: Have the player play all the levels whose indices are divisible by 10 (in total, 11 levels)

Baseline 2: Have the player play all the levels whose indices are divisible by 5 (in total, 21 levels)

Baseline 3: Have the player play all the levels whose indices are divisible by 2 (in total, 51 levels)

In each of the above baseline algorithms, among the played levels, the level that has the player's performance nearest to G_{Final} will be selected. In addition, we used a mechanism similar to four-fold cross-validation to divide the 40 players into 30 test players whose data form PT and 10 current players whose individual data are used for assessing each DDA algorithm per fold. In our approach, the RBF kernel with a length scale of 7 and an output variance of 1 was empirically used in GPR, and *Threshold* was empirically set to 1. For each current player, Algorithm 2 was run for 10 trials.

Table 1 shows the results of each approach in terms of the average (AVG) and the standard deviation (STD) of MP for all the players and 10 trials. This table shows that, given the same number of plays (iterations), our DDA approach outperforms respective baseline algorithms. Figure 3 shows AVG and STD of MP from our DDA at each iteration. From this figure, one can find that the average MP decreases quickly in the first 20 iterations and then gradually moves toward 1, the threshold deployed in Algorithm 2.

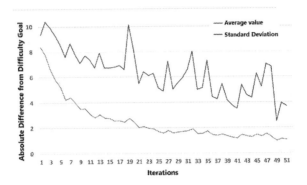

Fig. 3. AVG and STD of MP at each iteration

Table 1. Comparsion between ours and baselines

	Ours	Ours	Ours	Baseline 1	Baseline 2	Baseline 3
	11	21	51	11	21	51
	Iterations	Iterations	Iterations	Plays	Plays	Plays
AVG	3.085	2.032	1.037	7.762	6.112	3.573
STD	7.367	5.486	3.681	10.944	7.586	6.359

5 Conclusions and Future Work

We proposed a novel difficulty-recommendation method for DDA implemented by GPR. At the same time, this method was used in an FPS game with audio cues as the primary factor. With our difficulty-recommendation method, players are not required to play a single level numerous times until the right difficulty setting is personally found. Therefore, it could be expected that their enjoyment would be retained during such a period. In addition, we infer that the relationship between enemy-audio-cue volume and player performance is a quadratic function for our game, which may provide new insight into audio cue design. Our experiment showed that GPR's performance in reaching our difficulty goal for audio cue setting is better than the three baselines in our FPS game.

In the future, we will find whether our difficulty-recommendation method and the inferred relationship between audio cues and player performance are universal and applicable to other FPS games. Secondly, we will investigate how our difficulty recommendation method will function as player abilities change. Thirdly, we will conduct user studies to better understand our players' feelings about recommended difficulty goals. Next, we will look at more game performance metrics like life points, resource use, and other audio cue aspects such as attenuation. Finally, we will look into using audio cues as a parameter for DDA in other types of games like Roguelikes, fighting, or car racing games.

Acknowledgment. JingYi Gao from Tokyo Polytechnic University contributed to this work by providing game modifications. Ratchanon Nobnop from our laboratory contributed to this work with technical support.

References

1. Felix, A., King, C.L., Gunawan, A.A.S.: Audio Influence on Game atmosphere during various Game Events. Proc. Comput. Sci. **179**, 222–231 (2021)
2. Ribeiro, G., Rogers, K., Altmeyer, M., Terkildsen, T., Nacke, L.E.: Game atmosphere: effects of audiovisual thematic cohesion on player experience and psychophysiology. In: Proceedings of the Annual Symposium on Computer-Human Interaction in Play on Proceedings, pp. 107–119 (2020)
3. Tuuri, K., Koskela, O., Vahlo, J., Tissari, H.: Identifying the impact of game music both within and beyond gameplay. In: Baalsrud Hauge, J., C. S. Cardoso, J., Roque, L., Gonzalez-Calero, P.A. (eds.) ICEC 2021. LNCS, vol. 13056, pp. 411–418. Springer, Cham (2021). https://doi.org/10.1007/978-3-030-89394-1_33
4. Cassidy, G., MacDonald, R.: The effects of music choice on task performance: a study of the impact of self-selected and experimenter-selected music on driving game performance and experience. Music. Sci. **13**, 357–386 (2009)
5. Liu, C., Agrawal, P., Sarkar, N., Chen, S.: Dynamic difficulty adjustment in computer games through real-time anxiety-based affective feedback. Int. J. Hum. Comput. Interact. **25**, 506–529 (2009)
6. Cowan, B., Kapralos, B., Collins, K.: Does improved sound rendering increase player performance? a graph-based spatial audio framework. IEEE Trans. Games **13**, 263–274 (2020)
7. Dechant, M., Poeller, S., Johanson, C., Wiley, K., Mandryk, R.L.: In-game and out-of-game social anxiety influences player motivations, activities, and experiences in MMORPGs. In: Proceedings of the 2020 CHI Conference on Human Factors in Computing Systems on Proceedings, pp. 1–14 (2020)
8. Johanson, C., Mandryk, R.L.: Scaffolding player location awareness through audio cues in first-person shooters. In: Proceedings of the 2016 CHI Conference on Human Factors in Computing Systems, pp. 3450–3461 (2016)
9. Oren, M.A.: Speed sonic across the span: building a platform audio game. In: CHI 2007 Extended Abstracts on Human Factors in Computing Systems on Proceedings, pp. 2231–2236 (2007)
10. Khajah, M.M., Roads, B.D., Lindsey, R.V., Liu, Y.-E Mozer, M.C.: Designing engaging games using Bayesian optimization. In: Proceedings of the 2016 CHI Conference on Human Factors in Computing Systems, pp. 5571–5582 (2016)
11. González-Duque, M., Palm, R.B., Risi, S.: Fast game content adaptation through bayesian-based player modelling. In: 2021 IEEE Conference on Games (CoG), pp. 01–08 (2021)
12. Constant, T., Levieux, G.: Dynamic difficulty adjustment impact on players' confidence. In: Proceedings of the 2019 CHI Conference on Human Factors in Computing Systems, pp. 1–12 (2019)

Playstyles in Tetris: Beyond Player Skill, Score, and Competition

Stéphanie Mader[✉] and Eloïse Tassin

Conservatoire National des Arts et Métiers, CNAM-CEDRIC, ILJ, 292, Rue Saint Martin, Paris, France
stephanie.mader@cnam.fr
https://cedric.cnam.fr

Abstract. In this study, we looked at playstyles in Tetris in order to explore how players construct meaning in abstract video games. To do this, we looked at playstyles that go beyond metrics related to player skill, score and competition. Indeed, non-expert playstyle are often neglected in playstyle studies, but construction of meaning can also occur in non-competitive playstyles. We logged the play of 31 Tetris players and used Principal Component Analysis to model their playstyles. In doing so, we discovered 4 distinct playstyles that we present in this paper.

Keywords: Playstyles · Player models · Game logs · Telemetry · Tetris

1 Introduction

In this paper, we present preliminary results from our work modelling the playstyles of Tetris players. Playstyle can be defined as the way someone plays a specific video game. Most video games provide degrees of freedom in their interactions, giving options to players to tailor their experience in this possibility space through their playstyle [1,12]. Beyond this, players can also define their own goals while playing, sometimes subverting the game. Tekofsky et al. define playstyle as "any (set of) patterns in game actions performed by a player." [11].

This study is part of a research project exploring how players construct meaning while playing abstract video games. For this, we created 3 variations of the game Tetris, a widely popular arcade action-puzzle video game. We changed a

This study is part of a project supported by Région Ile-de-France (Appel DIM-RFSI 2020). The authors thank everyone whose work on the transdisciplinary Tetris-20 project indirectly contributed to this publication: Vinciane Zabban, Fanny Georges, Leticia Andlauer, Sophie Bemelmans, Elisa Massip. The authors would also like to thank Nicolas Piñeros for kindly helping us to conduct part of our study at the Ludomaker gamelab.

Published by Springer Nature Switzerland AG 2022
B. Göbl et al. (Eds.): ICEC 2022, LNCS 13477, pp. 162–170, 2022.
https://doi.org/10.1007/978-3-031-20212-4_13

few game rules to provide a different game experience and meaning. Even though the gameplay of Tetris seems constricted, through 6 preliminary interviews and observations of players, we found out they played more diversely than expected. Only one of them was playing as intended by the designer and interpreted the meanings. This prompted us to model playstyles as an important criteria to analyse how playstyle and meaning creation interacted in such video games.

Many studies have been done on Tetris; the studies about playstyle focus on player skill and score [5,10]. These studies distinguish between expert and novice players but do not analyse novice players in details. We observed that playstyle studies on other games also neglected non-competitive players [2,9,11].

As construction of meaning can also occur in non-competitive and novice playstyles, we looked at playstyles metrics beyond those related to player skill, score and competition. In this paper, we present the results of this first exploration. We extracted the game logs of 31 players of Tetris totalling 110 games played among three different Tetris variations and then used Principal Component Analysis on 23 quantitative variables and 4 qualitative variables.

2   Background

Since Bartle's typology of MUD players in 1996 [1], many approaches have been used to model players such as typology of play preferences from surveys [12], profiles based on psychological models [8], or player skill model [7]. Here, we focus on approaches using primarily game logs to study playstyles. Apart from the practicality of having access to game logs, one challenge lies in the large amount of data generated by game logs. Players data need to be aggregated into variables calculated from the addition of small game events or accumulated through time. Moreover, Karpinskyj et al., in their survey of video game personalisation techniques, noted that game logs alone only produced objective facts about events in the game and were difficult to use for more interpretative analysis [4]. This challenge of interpreting data has also been noted by Drachen et al. in their comparative studies of clustering methods for game logs. The authors even used the method capability at providing interpretable behavioral profiles as their main comparison criteria between clustering techniques [3]. Indeed, Principal Component Analysis (PCA) with clustering techniques such as k-means can be used to define groups of players, but the resulting groups can be more or less easy to interpret, and in our case, to translate into playstyle.

Some studies about playstyles use game logs and clustering techniques but the authors either defined the main playstyles beforehand, or did not provide interpretation of the profiles. Bialas et al. linked playstyles of Battlefield 3 to cultural differences [2], Tekofsky et al. tried to correlate playstyle with the player age [11], and Norouzzadeh Ravari et al. used PCA to study playstyles of expert players of Starcraft [9]. Those studies provide important results about what influences or not playstyles, but they feature a top-down approach to playstyles and their objects of study are competitive multiplayer video games. Resulting in analysis and playstyles weighted towards player skill, score and winning strategy.

If Tetris can be played as a competitive multiplayer video game, our study concentrates on its use as a solo video game. Tetris has been used in numerous studies from different disciplines. A few of them use in-game data logging to profile players generally to feed a dynamic difficulty adjustment algorithm with the objective of helping the player reach an optimal experience or flow (see [6] or [10] for examples). We found one Tetris study using a method similar to ours; Lindstedt and Grey studied how to distinguish between expert and novice players using PCA on game logs [5]. They identified three main components connected to scoring: disarray, 4-line planning, decide-move-placed.

Regarding the current literature on the topic, the main originality of our work is that we aim at discovering non-competitive Tetris playstyles. Indeed, if most game definitions include some notions of challenges and conflicts, players do not always abide by those rules. As a result, their playstyle can be more diverse than expected even in a seemingly simple arcade action-puzzle game such as Tetris. Current studies analysing playstyles appear to overlook player agency to determine their own play objective and success independently of the score and game rules. Playstyle being the manner players play a game, we argue the importance of not equating playstyle to skill. Skill is about player ability to do something well, and is, along challenge, difficulty, and their connections to learning and flow, an important and vastly studied topic. Competitive playstyles allow to categorise and describe the manners players play to win or score, but those are not the only kind of playstyles. In this study, our objective is to explore the existence of playstyles in Tetris beyond player skill and competition.

3   Tetris and Our Variations

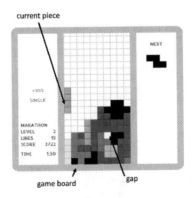

Fig. 1. Screenshot of the Tetris game used in this study.

In Tetris (Fig. 1), the player stacks pieces (also called tetrominos or zoids) until they loose because a piece can not be placed entirely in the game board, or win because they reach a specific objective of time, score, or number of lines depending on the game mode. A piece is always composed of 4 blocks (or squares) and there are 7 different pieces. If the player can stack the pieces to have one or more complete lines, they disappear, give points that accumulate in a score (depending on the number of lines done among other parameters), and the blocks above come down the same number of lines. Players can leave gaps in the game board that they will need to clean to make lines. The piece they control comes down automatically at a linear speed that augments each time they pass a level by making 10 lines. Players can only rotate the piece (right or left), translate/shift it (right or left), or make it descend more quickly (soft drop) or instantly (hard drop). An episode starts at the appearance of a piece and ends when the piece is placed on the game board. A game or a run encompasses everything from the appearance of the first piece to the win or loss of the player, forcing them to restart a run if they want to continue playing. Clearing 4 lines at the same time is called a 4-line or a Tetris, it requires the use of the bar-shaped piece.

Technically, the Tetris game is in html5/javascript based on an open-source Tetris by Choogmin Lee[1] and can be played within a web browser. It already featured a standard Tetris mode using a **7-bag** randomizer, a way to distribute pieces that mimics a bag in which one of each piece has been put and then distributed one after the other. This system is used to provide randomization while maintaining a balanced distribution between the 7 different type of pieces. We developed **notNice**, a variation in which the game stops providing the player with bar-shaped pieces when the player is ready to complete a 4-line, then provides two bars consecutively once a 4-line is no longer possible. All other aspects are identical to the 7-bag variation. Then, we developed **covExplore**, inspired by the Covid-19 crisis and the complexity of dealing with propagation while maintaining an activity (here stacking pieces). Some blocks of the pieces are colored in green and can infect neighboring blocks. Most of them will heal, become immune and take a blue color. Some others will become very sick (colored in red), a few of them will die and disappear from the game board, leaving a gap.

We implemented a logging system. When a piece appears, an AJAX query is sent to a PHP page to save all the logs of the previous episode; player's actions and game state variables such as the game board data. This information is serialised for the AJAX query and saved in a MySQL database.

4   Method

Our sample was of 31 persons, 22 who identified as women, 9 as men. They were between 20 and 57 years old (avg: 30, std deviation of approx. 10.5). The observations took place over 4 days at two different French universities. Participants were voluntary students, teachers, researchers and administrative staff. The entire protocol consisted of a questionnaire comprising steps in which the participants had to play the different variations of Tetris and answer questions

---

[1] https://github.com/clee704/tetris-html5.

after each run about the changes they perceived. Direct observations of their playstyle were made and most of the participants were interviewed after. For this study, we used primarily data from the game logs and some observations to facilitate the cluster interpretation. For each variation, the player is allowed to play as many times as they wish. In total, 110 runs were analysed (standard 7-bag: 35, notNice: 38, covExplore: 37). Three runs have been excluded because the game logging did not work properly on them.

In order to identify different playstyles, we decided to use Principal Component Analysis or PCA, a method for data analysis which transforms a set of linked variables into a smaller set. We first cleaned and treated the game logs using the R language. We aggregated the data per runs and computed variables usually used in Tetris game stats such as keys per pieces.

As we are interested in playstyles and not winning strategies, the indicators regarding inputs and strategy were divided by the number of episodes, lines or inputs (depending on the variable) giving us a frequency. This made sure the duration or number of pieces played in each run would not impact the results. The quantitative variables selected can be classified in different categories:

- **Game board**: minimum and maximum height, total number of gaps, height mean absolute deviation
- **Inputs**: left and right shifts, left and right rotations, soft and hard drops, keys pressed per pieces (KPP), keys pressed per second (KPS), missed inputs (when a key is pressed that is not part of the controls)
- **Strategy**: number of combos (combos: succession of episodes with lines completed), number of 4-line, number of 4-line per pieces, number of B2B (back-to-back: two 4-line in a row)
- **Scoring**: pieces dropped per second (PPS), gravity (piece descend speed), maximum level, final score and number of lines
- Time delay between a piece apparition and the first input

The qualitative variables used to explain the clusters are the player's id, the run number, which variation is played and how the run ended (player quit the run, timer ended or game over).

We visualised the results using the R-package Factoshiny[2]. It reduces the variables by itself and allowed us to manipulate the data in order to understand it better. This package also automatically edits a report with the different clusters highlighted with the PCA.

5   Results

Using the PCA method is useful to reduce the dimensionality of several quantitative data while capturing the greatest amount of variance in the data. We can then discover and define clusters in the dimensions PCA highlighted. Clusters

---

[2] http://factominer.free.fr/graphs/factoshiny.html.

can be characterised because they differ from the average. We will thus first present an average run of our sample and then describe the different playstyles.

In an average run of our sample, the board has a mean minimum height of 4.04 blocks and a mean maximum height of 8.80 blocks with a height mean absolute deviation of 1.80 block. Knowing that the game board has a height of 20 blocks, it implies that the game board stays mainly below the middle. This run would also have an average of 9.91 gaps left in the game board (means of gaps present per episode). The mean time delay between the apparition of the piece and the first input would be of approximately 1.03 second. The mean inputs frequency is an average of 1.41 key per second and approximately 5.66 inputs for landing a piece. 0.26 piece are placed per second (around a piece every 3.85 seconds). The average run has a score of 5395 points. With median analysis, an average run would total no 4-line but a combo every 10 lines in average. With input frequency analysis, we know that a little more than half of the inputs are left and right shifts.

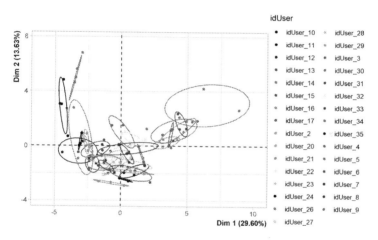

Fig. 2. Individuals factor map created using Factoshiny. One color per individual. (Color figure online)

The first two dimensions of the analysis express 43.23% of the total dataset variance. This value is strongly greater than the reference value of 16.23%[3] and the variability explained by this plane is thus highly significant. We studied the first 6 dimensions of the PCA with a cumulative percentage of variance of 76.26%. Each dimension defines two or three clusters that we will present. Since the data is related to runs, the clusters qualify runs and not players directly. However, the Wilks test p-value reveals that for each dimension, the variable factors are best separated on the plane by player's id (see Fig. 2 for a graphic visualisation). It is therefore acceptable to infer that each Tetris player has their

---

[3] Reference value: the 0.95-quantile of the variance percentages distribution obtained by simulating 9000 data tables of equivalent size on the basis of a normal distribution.

	Characteristics	High values	Low values
1	Gaps left, high KPP, few lines	Soft drops, KPP, gaps, left rotation, missed inputs, KPS, max. height, height mean absolute deviation	Right rotation, lines, left shift, right shift, level, score, combos
2	Slow play, very few gaps, low game	Soft drops, time delays, KPP, lines	Max. height, min. height, gaps, PPS, KPS, hard drops
3	Fast, meaningful inputs, clean, low game, use of 4-line	PPS, score, max. level, KPS, hard drops, 4-line per pieces, 4-line, gravity, lines	Time delay, soft drops, min. height, gaps, max. height, KPP
4	Fast, lots of gaps left, high game	Min. height, max. height, gaps, hard drop, KPS, PPS, left shift	Soft drop, time delay
5	Voluntary defeats	Height mean absolute deviation, PPS	Left shift, right shift, lines, KPP, KPS, hard drops
6	Voluntary defeats after some time	Hard drops, height mean absolute deviation, PPS, KPS	Lines, 4-line, 4-line per piece
7	4-lines strategy	B2B, 4-line per piece, 4-line, gravity, score, level	Time delay
8	Left rotation	Left rotation, gravity, score, level	Time delay
9	Shifts and low game	Right shift, KPP, left shift, missed inputs	Max. height, combos, min. height, level

Fig. 3. 9 clusters highlighted through PCA, variables sorted from strongest to weakest.

own playstyle. This same Wilks test shows that the different variations and the run number do not seem to have a significant impact on the clusters. We decided that a cluster can be qualified as a playstyle if the data is collected from someone who plays already knowing the mechanics. Therefore if one discovers the game, it cannot be qualified as a playstyle. Similarly, if one loses on purpose, it is not a playstyle because the person did not "play".

The observations we made during the experiment allowed us to know that the first cluster (8 runs, 2 players) contains two participants who never played Tetris before and had no idea what the aim of the game was. The second (7 runs, 4 players), third (6 runs, 4 players) and fourth (4 runs, 2 players) clusters have the potential to be qualified as playstyles because they indicate ways of using the inputs and managing the board. The fifth cluster (2 runs, 1 player) consists only of two runs from a person who did not play at all for their second and third runs. They made the pieces go straight down until they lost. We find these runs again in the sixth cluster (5 runs, 4 players), along with other runs ended prematurely by the player after some time. The seventh cluster (4 runs, 3 players) is 4-line oriented and could also qualify as a playstyle. The two last clusters show the limits of our method. The eighth cluster (2 runs, 1 player) was created for one person who used exclusively the left rotation. The last cluster (3 runs, 3 players) is representative of several runs but the variables do not seem explicit enough to sketch a playstyle. The Fig. 3 sums up the different clusters found with the PCA.

6   Discussion and Limitations

In this study, four of the clusters can be qualified as playstyles: cluster 2, 3, 4, 7. Cluster 2 describes a slow and precise way of playing with a tendency to clean the game field. Cluster 3 encompasses people who played fast with a few inputs for each pieces, left little to no gaps and made 4-line. Cluster 4 includes runs where people played fast but with a high board containing gaps. Finally, cluster 7 encompasses runs where 4-lines were picked in priority.

Even if the majority of clusters makes sense with our direct observation, they do not all translate into a playstyle. If it is interesting that the clustering did capture new players (cluster 1) and players voluntarily loosing their run (clusters 5 and 6), we need more data to deepen the analysis. For instance, a few players used both hands on the keyboard making them use the inputs differently, but they do not appear as their own category. Most of them would also have preferred to play with a game controller as it was their usual way of playing. Forcing them to use a keyboard may have had an effect on how they approached the game.

Aggregating the data into runs mean that we miss precise moments during the game. Players may change strategy depending on the height of the game or react to certain pieces for example. Defining those moments and analysing how players change their behavior or not would be of interest to better understand different playstyles. Another area of improvement is the board analysis as seen in the work of Lindstedt and Grey. We have the data for the board and intend to add those data to later works. Our sample size is too small to generalise the playstyles we found and we only got 3 players scoring 4-lines. Finally, if we found different non-competitive playstyles, the PCA was not able to capture very unusual playstyles such as the participant trying to draw a dog on the board. We may need to use a top-down approach for such case.

Even if we found that few players showed different playstyles for different runs, those were not linked to the variations played. This may be explained by the limited amount of runs played for each variations. In a later study, we need to make them play more runs to see if players identify the changes and adapt their playstyle after a few runs are played.

7   Conclusion

If challenge and strategies to win are very important topics of video game design and development, they cannot encompass the diversity of playstyles found in video games as they tend to exclude from their analysis playstyles not oriented toward winning. Indeed, those profiles tend to be grouped into a broad category of novice players. However, players often give themselves different goals than the one given by the game and those are not well reflected in current studies.

In this paper, we showed that Principal Component Analysis on variables extracted from game logs could return relevant clusters of playstyles. This is still a work-in-progress research: the 4 playstyles we found will need more work to be demonstrated and we should find new ones in the future. However, the general approach and those first results are encouraging. In order to explore to what extent the way players make sense of their experience is dependant on their playstyle, we now need to compare data from the questionnaires and interviews with the playstyles. But before that, we will recruit more participants to deepen and validate the modelling of Tetris playstyles beyond skill, score and competition.

References

1. Bartle, R.: Hearts, clubs, diamonds, spades: Players who suit muds. J. MUDs Res. **1**(1), 19 (1996)
2. Bialas, M., Tekofsky, S., Spronck, P.: Cultural influences on play style. In: 2014 IEEE Conference on Computational Intelligence and Games, Dortmund, Germany, pp. 1–7. IEEE, Aug 2014. https://doi.org/10.1109/CIG.2014.6932894, http://ieeexplore.ieee.org/document/6932894/
3. Drachen, A., Thurau, C., Sifa, R., Bauckhage, C.: A comparison of methods for player clustering via behavioral telemetry. arXiv preprint arXiv:1407.3950 (2014)
4. Karpinskyj, S., Zambetta, F., Cavedon, L.: Video game personalisation techniques: A comprehensive survey. Entertainment Comput. **5**(4), 211–218 (2014). https://doi.org/10.1016/j.entcom.2014.09.002, https://www.sciencedirect.com/science/article/pii/S1875952114000342
5. Lindstedt, J.K., Gray, W.D.: Distinguishing experts from novices by the Mind's Hand and Mind's Eye. Cognitive Psychol. **109**, 1–25 (2019). https://doi.org/10.1016/j.cogpsych.2018.11.003, https://linkinghub.elsevier.com/retrieve/pii/S0010028518300756
6. Lora, D., Sánchez-Ruiz, A.A., González-Calero, P.A., Gómez-Martín, M.A.: Dynamic Difficulty Adjustment in Tetris. In: Proceedings of the Twenty-Ninth International Florida Artificial Intelligence Research Society Conference (2015)
7. Mader, S., Natkin, S., Levieux, G.: How to analyse therapeutic games: the player/game/therapy model. In: Herrlich, M., Malaka, R., Masuch, M. (eds.) ICEC 2012. LNCS, vol. 7522, pp. 193–206. Springer, Heidelberg (2012). https://doi.org/10.1007/978-3-642-33542-6_17
8. Nacke, L.E., Bateman, C., Mandryk, R.L.: BrainHex: A neurobiological gamer typology survey. Entertainment Comput. **5**(1), 55–62 (2014)
9. Norouzzadeh Ravari, Y., Bakkes, S., Spronck, P.: Playing styles in StarCraft. In: European GAME-ON Conference on Simulation and AI in Computer Games (2018)
10. Spiel, K., Bertel, S., Kayali, F.: Not another Z piece!: Adaptive Difficulty in TETRIS. In: Proceedings of the 2017 CHI Conference on Human Factors in Computing Systems, Denver Colorado USA, pp. 5126–5131. ACM (May 2017). https://doi.org/10.1145/3025453.3025721, https://dl.acm.org/doi/10.1145/3025453.3025721, zSCC: 0000013
11. Tekofsky, S., Spronck, P., Goudbeek, M., Plaat, A., van den Herik, J.: Past our prime: a study of age and play style development in Battlefield 3. IEEE Trans. Comput. Intell. AI in Games **7**(3), 292–303 (2015). https://doi.org/10.1109/TCIAIG.2015.2393433, http://ieeexplore.ieee.org/document/7012062/
12. Yee, N.: Motivations for play in online games. CyberPsychol. Behav. **9**(6), 772–775 (2006)

A Matter of Closeness: Player-Avatar Relationships as Degree of Including Avatars in the Self

Daniel Possler[1]($\boxtimes$) (iD), Natascha N. Carnol[1], Christoph Klimmt[1] (iD), Ina Weber-Hoffmann[1], and Arthur A. Raney[2] (iD)

[1] Department of Journalism and Communication Research, Hanover University of Music, Drama and Media, Expo Plaza 12, 30539 Hannover, Germany
Daniel.Possler@ijk.hmtm-hannover.de

[2] School of Communication, Florida State University, Tallahassee, FL 32306-2664, USA

Abstract. The relationship between players and their avatars was found to be critical to game use and effects. Past scholarship has, thus, explored the various player-avatar relationships (PARs) that can emerge during gaming. We argue that the Inclusion-of-Other-in-the-Self principle from the social-psychological Self-Expansion Model provides a fruitful theoretical perspective to systematize and explain the structure of the diverse PAR types. Based on the model, we define a PAR as inclusion of the avatar into the player's self. The more characteristics of the avatar are included, the more a player adopts the perspective of and feels close to the avatar. We draw on in-depth interviews with 32 players from Germany and the U.S. to explore how PARs can be systematized based on the Self-Expansion Model. Consistent with the model, we found that the heterogeneity of PARs can be organized by a distance/closeness continuum. Five types of PARs were extracted from the data, ranging from functional relationships to weak or strong (para)social relationships to selective or complete identification. We discuss how this typology and the Self-Expansion Model can advance game research.

Keywords: Video games · Avatars · Identification · Parasocial relationships

1 Introduction

Avatars are essential elements of most modern video games [1]. As representations of players in the game [2], they constitute a central means by which users influence the state of a game [1]. Moreover, avatars allow players to represent and experiment with their identity [3, 4] and can serve as rich narrative devices [5]. Consequently, players' relationships with their avatars were found to be critical to video game use and effects, affecting inter alia players' motivations [4, 6], their style of playing (e.g., pro- vs. antisocial gaming [7]), entertainment experiences [8] and outcomes such as aggression [9].

Supplementary Information The online version contains supplementary material available at https://doi.org/10.1007/978-3-031-20212-4_14.

Given the centrality of player-avatar relationships (PARs), game scholars extensively studied what types of PARs emerge during gaming; inter alia to guide future game development [e.g., 10]. As video game players usually control their avatars, the relationship between them has often been described as identification [11]—a psychological 'merger' between player and avatar [12, 13]. However, research has also shown that players sometimes perceive avatars as separate social beings [6, 14]. Consequently, PARs can emerge that mirror parasocial relationships between users and characters in linear media [15, 16] or even social relationships between 'real' people [1, 6].

Considerable progress has been made in organizing this variety of possible PARs [e.g., 1, 6, 17, 18]. However, it remains a challenge to systematize and explain the structure of the diverse PAR types from a cohesive theoretical standpoint. We argue that the Inclusion-of-Other-in-the-Self idea from the Self-Expansion Model [19–21] provides such a unified theoretical perspective that can explain a rich variation of PARs. Results of in-depth interviews with 32 players demonstrate the utility of this theoretical account to systematize PARs.

2   Theoretical Approaches to Player-Avatar Relationships

2.1   Status Quo

Based on prior conceptualizations, PARs can broadly be defined as involvement with the media character [22] and be described as players' cognitive, affective, behavioral and motivational engagement with their avatars [23]. This involvement can take a wide variety of different forms [1]. One attempt to organize this variation is the differentiation between dyadic and monadic understandings [12].

Dyadic approaches such as parasocial relationships [24] or character liking [25] describe media users as observers of media characters. Relationships to characters occur when users develop interest or emotions towards a character [25, 26], but the character is perceived as a (seemingly) autonomous entity different from the user. *Monadic concepts*, in contrast, assume that "through interactivity [...] video games (partly) override the distance between media user and media character" [12]: As players control their avatar, they temporarily feel *to be* the avatar [11, 13, 27]. For example, the monadic notion of identification proposed by Klimmt and colleagues [12] suggests that players temporarily integrate parts of the avatar's identity in their own self-concept, which may be metaphorized as a melting of player and avatar during play [4, 28].

Valuable progress beyond this juxtaposition was achieved by Banks [6, 17] and Banks and Bowman [1, 14, 18, 29]. They identified four archetypes of PARs: Accordingly, avatars can be perceived (1) as mere objects, (2) as virtual extensions of the players ("avatar-as-me" [6]), (3) as symbiotes, used to create new personas, or (4) as distinct entities that allow 'real' social interactions [6, 17]. An important insight from this research is that players sometimes perceive their avatars as authentic social others, resulting in PARs that represent 'real' social relationships. Moreover, this research showed that the possible range of PARs also includes modes that do not match a conventional understanding of 'relationship' at all, as players may view their avatars as non-social, functional game elements (i.e., objects that help them to win the game) [30].

Banks and Bowman also showed that the PAR archetypes can be organized as a continuum of sociality, ranging from non-social (i.e., avatar as object) to fully social relationships (i.e., avatar as distinct social agent) [1, 6, 14]. A number of ludic and social qualities were identified that vary across the four archetypes [6, 14, 18, 29]. These qualities include anthropomorphic autonomy (i.e., perceiving the avatars as authentic social entities), emotional closeness, critical concern regarding the game's authenticity (i.e., evaluating the internal consistency and coherence of the game world), and sense of control over the avatar [1, 18, 29].

In sum, game researchers have identified a variety of different PAR types. However, explaining and systematizing the various PAR forms from a cohesive theoretical standpoint remains challenging. For example, both monadic and dyadic relationship concepts assume that players adopt the avatars' perspective, but attribute this experience to different mechanisms (i.e., psychological melting in monadic [12] and empathy in dyadic relationships [26]). Moreover, the present state of research hardly explains how the relationship between a player and an avatar transitions over time from one PAR type to another. How, for instance, can empathy in dyadic PARs turn into full perspective taking (i.e., identification)? We argue that viewing PARs from the perspective of the Inclusion-of-Other-in-the-Self principle [19–21] can resolve these open questions.

2.2 The Inclusion-of-Other-In-The-Self Principle

The Inclusion-of-Other-in-the-Self principle has been suggested in the Self-Expansion Model [19–21]. This model aims to explain experiences and behaviors in close social relationships [19]. Put simply, the model proposes that human beings have a fundamental self-expansion motivation—a drive to increase their resources, perspectives, and identities [19, 20]. One way to satisfy this motivation is to form close relationships because in such relationships people include the resources, perspectives, and identities of others in their selves (Inclusion-of-Other-in-the-Self principle) [19–21]. Hence, in a close relationship, the cognitive construction of the self and the other overlaps [19]. For example, various studies showed that people treat the other's resources and outcomes (i.e., failures and successes) like their own, have problems cognitively differentiating between themselves and the other, and extend self-related biases to the other [19, 20]. Against this background, Aron and colleagues [31] argue that the *'closeness'* of a relationship represents the degree to which the other is included in the self. The stronger one's self overlaps with the self of the other, the closer the relationship is perceived.

2.3 PAR as Inclusion of the Avatar in the Self

We suggest that understanding players' involvement with their avatars from the perspective of the Inclusion-of-Other-in-the-Self principle can bridge the different PAR concepts and contributes to answer the questions raised above. A PAR can be understood as inclusion of the avatar in the player's self. The stronger this inclusion, the closer the relationship should be experienced [31]. This notion corresponds well with *monadic* PAR concepts [11]. Most notably, Klimmt and colleagues [12] suggested that during identification players' self-concept is temporarily altered as users *include* characteristics of their avatars' identity in their self-concept. Further consistent with the principle [31], identification was often theorized to be selective: The amount of avatar characteristics that are included in the self can vary substantially [12].

The principle also seems well suited to explain *dyadic PARs* such as parasocial or fully social relationships [6, 15], as the Self-Expansion Model was originally developed to describe social relationships in which people remain separate entities [19]. But even in dyadic relationships people seem to include the resources and perspective of the other in the self and share the other's emotions [19, 20]. The principle can thus explain how empathy for game avatars emerges in dyadic PARs. Finally, it can also explain how PARs evolve and shift over time: The more avatar characteristics are integrated in the player's self, the more a PAR should evolve from a dyadic to a monadic form.

In line with these assumptions, Shedlosky-Shoemaker et al. [32] found that people indeed include fictional characters in their selves while using linear media. Other research has suggested that players also include avatars in their selves while gaming, and this process is stronger the more players are emotionally attached, feel similar to and embodied in avatars [33]. While these results are promising, the systematization of PARs along the degree of perceived closeness—the experiential quality of including other in the self [31]—requires further investigation. Specifically, we argue that closeness increases from dyadic to monadic relationships as people include avatars to a stronger degree in their selves. However, others argued that closeness should be the highest in dyadic, fully social relationships [1, 18]. Moreover, it is unknown how perceiving an avatar as a mere object fits into the closeness continuum. Hence, in the present contribution, we aim to explore how PARs can be systemized along the quality of closeness. We ask:

- RQ: How can players' relationships with their game avatars be systematized along the characteristic of 'closeness', defined as the inclusion of the avatar in the self?

3   Method

Qualitative in-depth interviews with 32 players (see table A in the electronic supplementary material) from Germany (n = 19) and the United States (n = 13) were conducted. Interviewers were trained communication students, and the respondents were recruited in their peer group (German participants) as well as in a university class and a recreational center (U.S. participants). To maximize diversity, we recruited participants of different age (17–34 years), gender (5 female participants) and self-ascribed gamer identity (casual gamer: n = 11; regular gamer: n = 4; heavy gamer: n = 7; hardcore gamer: n = 7; n/s: n = 3).

The semi-structured interviews were based on a flexible guideline that allowed maintaining an open and dialogue-like situation. Players were asked inter alia about the process of selection and customization of a video game avatar. Moreover, the interview guideline addressed experiential traces of PARs. The questions dealt with how participants interact with avatars and experience relationships with them in general but also focused on monadic and dyadic relationships in particular. The interviews were conducted face-to-face or, as an exception, via videoconference and lasted between 14 and 51 min. All interviews were audio-recorded and fully transcribed.

A qualitative content analysis [34] was conducted involving three steps. (1) At first, all passages portraying experiences of PARs were identified. Coding was guided by a rather broad definition of PARs ("involvement with an avatar"; see Sect. 2.1). (2) In the next step, we followed a semi-deductive approach to classify the types of PARs portrayed in these passages. Initial codes were based on the theoretically derived distinction between functional ("absence of involvement with an avatar" [6]), dyadic ("involvement with an avatar separated from the player") or monadic relations ("involvement with an avatar including a (partly) merge of identities"). This rather broad categorization of PAR types was inductively refined during multiple codings of the full material. (3) Finally, the characteristics of the identified PAR types were analyzed to explore their differences. Codes were generated inductively. A particular focus was on the perceived closeness of the relationships and on experiential traces of including the avatar in the self. All steps were conducted separately by two researchers, and differences were discussed to improve intersubjectivity of interpretations.

4 Results

4.1 A Distance-Closeness Continuum

Respondents described several characteristics of the relationship with their avatars. Among them, the closeness to the avatar was mentioned most often. Closeness was usually described as feeling related to (e.g., R 04, 22, 31), connected with (e.g., R 06, 21, 23, 24, 25, 29, 30, 31), being attached to or emotionally involved with the avatar (e.g., R 25, 27, 32). Even respondents who denied having a relationship with their avatar referred to (a lack of) closeness to describe their experience (e.g., R 01, 14). For example, respondent 14 answered the question if he had experienced a relationship with an avatar: *"Not at all, actually I would say I'm quite distanced from the avatar that I play"*. Thus, in line with the Inclusion-of-Other-in-the-Self principle [31], specific degrees of player-avatar closeness emerged as central quality of PARs.

Many PARs that we categorized as dyadic relationships were experienced as rather close (e.g., R 36: *"[The avatars] are really quite close. Yeah, you can empathize with them"*). However, in descriptions that were categorized as monadic relationships, the bond between player and avatar seemed to be even closer (e.g., R 06, 25, 27), as the avatar was not experienced as a separate individual (e.g., R 25: *"I don't view them as another person, I view them as an extension of myself"*). In contrast to this closeness, some participants underlined their distance to their avatars by talking about the relationship in a functional way (e.g., R 01, 04, 22, 23). A statement by respondent no. 29 on the interchangeability of avatars illustrates this: *"I didn't feel very attached to my own character especially since I was in the mind-set of 'Okay, I'm going to make a different profile after I am done with this'"*. Several participants reported changes in the quality of their PAR in the course of play. For example, respondent no. 28 explained that the formation of a PAR involves multiple steps in which the relation is becoming closer, including getting to know the avatar and developing an affection for her/him/it.

The results are consistent with previous research that found substantial differences between PAR experiences [1, 6, 18]. Moreover, the findings correspond to the Inclusion-of-Other-in-the-Self principle [31] by highlighting that gamers may go through relationship experiences from very high interpersonal distance to very high closeness to their avatar, and degrees of distance/closeness may evolve over time. Finally, monadic PARs were characterized as being closer than dyadic PARs. Thus, it seems reasonable to systematize the diversity of PARs on a continuum among their inherent level of player-avatar closeness.

4.2   In-Depth Findings: Five Types of PARs and Related Experiences

In-depth coding served to expand the continuum of closeness into a model of five types of PARs.

Functional PAR: Some players reported to have no emotional link to the controlled avatars, but rather perceived them as a "*playing piece*" (R 01). For example, one participant stated that he sometimes lets his avatar die just for fun (R 01). Other gamers compared their treatment of their avatars to playing cards (R 18) or chess (R 03), thus emphasizing the "tool" aspect over a (para)social experience. Moreover, this form of PAR is governed by an achievement orientation. Players' stance towards their avatars is "*just to control them*" (R 24), to use them effectively for achieving in-game goals. Thus, the functional PAR corresponds to past findings revealing players' instrumental, non-social perspective on avatars [6, 30]. No evidence was found that players integrate avatars' resources, perspectives, or identities in their self in a functional PAR.

Empathy-based Dyadic PAR: The second type of PAR that emerged from the analysis is based on empathy. Several respondents said they perceive their avatars as independent entities but become emotionally involved by witnessing what happens to them in the game (R 04: "*You most often have knowledge of the emotional life of the protagonist, and hence they are very close*"). Based on the Self-Expansion Model [19], this process implies including the avatar's perspective in the player's self. In line with the model [19, 20], participants reported to experience the avatar's outcomes as their own to some degree and mirror his/her/its emotions. Specifically, compassion (e.g., R 08, 09) or empathy (e.g., R 01, 04, 05, 06, 07) were frequently mentioned. Moreover, due to the emotional bond, players' treatment of their avatars is determined by positive actions like "*cheering*" (R 05) or caring for them (R 20: "*It's like I kind of want to be protective of him*"). Besides, during instances of failure, players hold the avatar (but not necessarily themselves) responsible (e.g., R 27). In sum, it seems that players indeed include their avatars' perspectives in their selves in this type of PAR, but avatars and players remain sufficiently separate entities so that players still remain observers.

Intensive Dyadic PAR: In some interviews, a pattern of dyadic PARs emerged that could be described as a strong emotional bond or even intimacy (e.g., being "*on fire*" for the avatar, R 30). In this type, the avatar is experienced as a close other—like a good friend (e.g., R 04, 32), which resembles parasocial or fully social relationships [6, 26]. This close interpersonal connection can last beyond the gaming episode. For example, respondent no. 10 declared: "*And at the end, when it's all over, you think,* *now I want to know what he [the avatar] does after the game"*, a description suggesting similarity to parasocial break-ups [35]. The emotional bond seems to originate from avatars' strong appeal to the players. Respondents reported to appreciate the avatars for certain characteristics such as being a *"hero saving the world"* (R 21) or for being a *"nice guy"* (R 01). This attraction seems to motivate players to maintain a coherent positive image of the avatar. Participants mentioned that they try to behave like the avatars would do, although it would not correspond to their normal gaming behavior (e.g., R 01, 31). Just like in theatrical role-play, they try not to damage the authenticity and appeal of the avatars by acting in an inappropriate way (e.g., R 6, 16, 26). Thus, it seems, that in this type of PAR, players include the avatar's perspective and identity to an even closer degree in their self than in the empathy-based PAR.

Selective Identification: In statements related to the fourth type of PAR found in the analysis, participants reported that the boundaries between their selves and the avatars begin to blur as they identify with characteristics of the avatars that are similar to their own (R 6, 17, 30, 31). Moreover, they mentioned idealized character traits or abilities (e.g., the *"ability to do martial arts"* R 24) as dimensions on which they preferred to identify (e.g. R 2, 3, 5, 19, 24). This also includes evil character traits, as long as they are perceived attractive (R 13). Such reports resonate well with concepts of identification [11, 12] and are empirical manifestations of including an avatar's characteristics in the self. For example, respondent no. 26, thinking of avatars he feels related to, mentioned that *"having humor, having like adventure, having charm (…) is the kind of person you would want to hang out with in real life. And (…) you are controlling them and actually being them"*. To facilitate this experience, players have reported that they sometimes design the avatar to reflect their own selves. Compared to the intensive dyad PAR, participants who identify on a selective level reported less frequently to orientate their in-game behavior on the appreciated characteristics of the avatar in a sense of acting (*"what he would do"*; R 31). They rather stated to follow their own intentions (R 30: *"what-I-feel-is-the-right decision"*; also: R 06, 10, 21, 31). Thus, players absorb attributes of the avatars and/or adjust their controlling of the avatar so that the avatar mirrors attributes of the player (*"avatar-as-me"* [6]). Hence, the selective identification type represents the transition from dyadic to monadic PARs [12]. Moreover and extending the Inclusion-of-Other-in-the-Self principle [19–21], it seems that during video game identification players sometimes include (or project) their own self 'in the avatar'.

Shift of Identity: Reports related to the closest PAR type that emerged from the analysis describe a (temporary) shift of identity. The feeling of 'being' the avatar (e.g., R 02, 06, 13. 19, 28, 31) with all her/his/its goals and perspectives (e.g., R 21, 23, 26) was described for example by respondent no. 28: *"his daughter is on a ship […] you are supposed to save her. And I got really heated like: '[…] Get the hell away from my daughter!'"*. In this extreme type of PAR, participants reported to feel even closer than in selective identification, most likely because their temporary self-concept rests on avatar attributes rather than on their own selves (R 26: *"I really was becoming the character"*). Hence, this PAR can be described as total inclusion of the avatar in the player's self. As a result, the gamers reported a strong responsibility for in-game actions and related consequences (e.g., R 06, 10, 12, 21). In a combat game context, this means that *"blood [is] on the player's hands"* (R 10). This also implies that through identity shifts, game avatars allow players experiencing entirely new situations firsthand (e.g., R 31: moral dilemmas) or explore possible selves (e.g., R 31: 'being' a sports star; also: R 21, 25). Such experiences can even impact players' life outside virtual worlds (e.g., R 21: "'*Link*' *kind of made me more courageous*"). Hence, this closest form of PARs seems to allow players the most to enlarge their identities—to expand their selves [19, 20].

5   Discussion

The present study reapproaches the diversity and complexity of video game player-avatar relationships (PARs). Our respondents described their PARs in ways that mirror different accounts of monadic, dyadic and functional PARs that have been proposed in the literature [1, 6, 11–13, 15, 17, 18, 29, 30].

As a key contribution, the study demonstrates that the diversity of PAR types can be explained based on the Inclusion-of-Other-in-the-Self principle [19–21]. In line with this idea [31], varying degrees of perceived 'closeness' to the avatar emerged as central quality of PARs in the interviews. Moreover, it was found that functional, dyadic and monadic PARs could be organized on a continuum from high player-avatar distance to high player-avatar closeness (see Sect. 4.1). In-depth coding revealed further experiential and behavioral traces of players' inclusion of the avatar in their selves. In the *functional* PAR players separate themselves completely from the avatars. In contrast, in dyadic relationships (*empathic* or *intense dyadic PAR*) they incorporate the avatars' perspectives and identities into their selves and, thus, treat the avatars' outcomes as their own, leading to intense empathic responses. These are precisely the experiences that have frequently been described in research on the Self-Expansion Model [19, 20].

In video games, however, the adoption of an avatar's characteristics, perspectives, and identities can go even further to the point of partial (*selective identification*) or complete identification of the player with the avatar (*shift of identities*). This temporal alteration of players' self-concept [12], thus, extends the intensity of including others in the self, usually found in social relationships in the material world [19, 20]. Metaphorically speaking, player's self and the avatar totally overlap in an intense monadic PAR (*shift of identities*). Interestingly, participants' statements illustrated that these merger experiences with the avatar can begin either on the end of the player or on the end of the avatar. In some cases, players seem to be impressed by the idealized attributes of an avatar and import such desirable attributes into their temporary self-perception—this marks the mode of identification explicated by Klimmt et al. [12] and others [4, 13, 28] and mirrors the Inclusion-of-Other-in-the-Self idea [19–21]. In other cases, however, the merger of identities process starts with the players, particularly their intention to design avatars in a way that mirrors their own salient characteristics such as appearance or morality. In contrast to identification via change of the player's self-concept, this could be described as identification via avatar creation, as digital 'cloning' of the player. The latter would converge with notions of similarity identification or homophily, whereas the former corresponds to notions of wishful identification [11]. Both subtypes of monadic PARs should hence be investigated further and may lead to new insights into playing motivations, avatar customization [3, 30] and gaming effects.

To answer our RQ, Fig. 1 illustrates how the identified PAR types can be systematized along the characteristic of 'closeness', defined as the inclusion of the avatar in the player's self. Based on the Inclusion-of-Other-in-the-Self (IOS) Scale [36], the degree of overlap between players and avatars is symbolized by more or less overlapping pairs of circles. This distance/closeness continuum could at first sight be understood as the degree of involvement [23] with avatars. However, very high involvement in the sense of avatars being highly relevant to players was found for both dyadic and monadic PARs, so distance versus closeness is not necessarily the same as involvement. Rather the PAR experiences found in the in-depth analysis (see Sect. 4.2) suggest that the continuum indeed represents how strongly the avatars' perspectives and identities are included in players' self. Moderate inclusion will result in dyadic PARs, but these may still come with great emotional involvement just as monadic PARs. Hence, it is reasonable to differentiate the closeness from the involvement dimension.

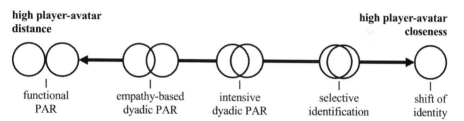

high player-avatar distance

high player-avatar closeness

| functional PAR | empathy-based dyadic PAR | intensive dyadic PAR | selective identification | shift of identity |

Fig. 1. Systematization of PAR types based on the metaphor of the IOS scale [36]

Future research is needed to further investigate the findings reported here. At first, our study should be replicated with an even more diverse sample (e.g., more female players). In addition, it should be examined whether the identified continuum of PAR types is genre independent. As an initial exploration, we categorized which games participants in this study referred to when talking about the five PARs (see Table B in the electronic supplementary material). We found that participants experienced the five PARs in almost every genre. Thus, the continuum seems rather genre independent, but more research on this subject is needed.

Moreover, the applicability of the Self-Expansion model [19–21] to PARs should be further investigated. First, a quantitative survey in which players are asked to recall a recently controlled avatar seems useful. Based on the IOS Scale [36] and other established measures of player-avatar interactions [4, 18], the relationship between closeness and PAR types could be further investigated. Second, longitudinal studies, such as those already conducted in the context of the Self-Expansion Model [19], seem valuable to investigate the development of PARs over time. Third, experimental studies in which the relationship between avatars and players is manipulated seem promising as well.

In addition, future research could examine the transferability of findings on the Self-Expansion Model to PARs. Specifically, various predictors of including others in the self have been identified [19]. Studying those in the context of games might help scholars explain the formation of PARs and guide game development [10]. Another promising approach for future research is to study how close PARs help to satisfy players' self-expansion motivation. According to the Self-Expansion Model, human beings want to grow as a person, and including others in the self is one way to accomplish this [19–21]. Our results suggest that intensely close PARs (i.e., *shift of identities*) are well suited for self-expansion. Thus, investigating the self-expansion effects of PARs may provide insights into how video games can facilitate growth and self-realization—effects that increasingly attract the attention of games researchers [37]. In sum, we believe that incorporating the perspective of the Self-Expansion Model to avatars contributes to explaining the centrality of player-avatar relationships for game use and effects.

References

1. Bowman, N.D., Banks, J.: Player-avatar identification, relationships, and interaction: Entertainment through asocial, parasocial, and fully social processes. In: Vorderer, P., Klimmt, C. (eds.): The Oxford Handbook of Entertainment Theory. pp. 689–716. Oxford University Press, New York (2021). https://doi.org/10.1093/oxfordhb/9780190072216.013.36
2. Nowak, K.L., Fox, J.: Avatars and computer-mediated communication: a review of the definitions, uses, and effects of digital representations on communication. RCR. 6, 30–53 (2018). https://doi.org/10.12840/issn.2255-4165.2018.06.01.015
3. Bessière, K., Seay, A.F., Kiesler, S.: The ideal elf: identity exploration in world of warcraft. Cyberpsychol. Behav. Soc. Netw. 10, 530–535 (2007). https://doi.org/10.1089/cpb.2007.9994
4. van Looy, J., Courtois, C., de Vocht, M., de Marez, L.: Player identification in online games: validation of a scale for measuring identification in MMOGs. Media Psychol. 15, 197–221 (2012). https://doi.org/10.1080/15213269.2012.674917
5. Jørgensen, K.: Game characters as narrative devices. a comparative analysis of dragon age: origins and mass effect 2. EJCGC 4(2), 315–331 (2010). https://doi.org/10.7557/23.6051
6. Banks, J.: Object, me, symbiote, other: a social typology of player-avatar relationships. First Monday 20 (2015). https://doi.org/10.5210/fm.v20i2.5433
7. Bowman, N.D., Schultheiss, D., Schumann, C.: "I'm attached, and I'm a good guy/gal!": how character attachment influences pro- and anti-social motivations to play massively multiplayer online role-playing games. Cyberpsychol. Behav. Soc. Netw. 15, 169–174 (2012). https://doi.org/10.1089/cyber.2011.0311
8. Hefner, D., Klimmt, C., Vorderer, P.: Identification with the player character as determinant of video game enjoyment. In: Ma, L., Rauterberg, M., Nakatsu, R. (eds.) ICEC 2007. LNCS, vol. 4740, pp. 39–48. Springer, Heidelberg (2007). https://doi.org/10.1007/978-3-540-74873-1_6
9. Lin, J.-H.: Identification matters: a moderated mediation model of media interactivity, character identification, and video game violence on aggression. J. Commun. 63, 682–702 (2013). https://doi.org/10.1111/jcom.12044
10. Wang, H., Ruan, Y.-C., Hsu, S.-Y., Sun, C.-T.: Effects of game design features on player-avatar relationships and motivation for buying decorative virtual items. In: DiGRA'19 - Proceedings of the 2019 DiGRA International Conference: Game, Play and the Emerging Ludo-Mix. http://www.digra.org/wp-content/uploads/digital-library/DiGRA_2019_paper_161.pdf
11. Downs, E., Bowman, N.D., Banks, J.: A polythetic model of player-avatar identification: synthesizing multiple mechanisms. Psychol. Pop. Media Cult. 8, 269–279 (2019). https://doi.org/10.1037/ppm0000170
12. Klimmt, C., Hefner, D., Vorderer, P.: The video game experience as "true" identification: a theory of enjoyable alterations of players' self-perception. Commun. Theory 19, 351–373 (2009). https://doi.org/10.1111/j.1468-2885.2009.01347.x
13. Ratan, R.A.: Self-Presence, explicated: body, emotion, and identity extension into the virtual self. In: Luppicini, R. (ed.): Handbook of Research on Technoself. pp. 322–336. Information Science Reference, Hershey (2013)

14. Banks, J., Bowman, N.D.: Avatars are (sometimes) people too: linguistic indicators of parasocial and social ties in player-avatar relationships. New Media Soc. **18**, 1257–1276 (2014). https://doi.org/10.1177/1461444814554898

15. Kavli, K.: The player's parasocial interaction with digital entities. In: Lugmayr, A. (ed.): Proceeding of the 16th International Academic MindTrek Conference. pp. 83–89 (2012). https://doi.org/10.1145/2393132.2393150

16. Schmierbach, M., Limperos, A.M.: Virtual justice: testing disposition theory in the context of a story-driven video game. J. Broadcast. Electron. Media **57**, 526–542 (2013). https://doi.org/10.1080/08838151.2013.845828

17. Banks, J.: Human-technology relationality and self-network organization: players and avatars in World· of Warcraft, Colorado State University, Fort Collins (2013). http://hdl.handle.net/10217/80931

18. Banks, J., Bowman, N.D., Lin, J.-H.T., Pietschmann, D., Wasserman, J.A.: The common player-avatar interaction scale (cPAX): expansion and cross-language validation. Int. J. Hum Comput Stud. **129**, 64–73 (2019). https://doi.org/10.1016/j.ijhcs.2019.03.003

19. Aron, A., Lewandowski, G.W., Mashek, D., Aron, E.N.: The self-expansion model of motivation and cognition in close relationships. In: Simpson, J., Campbell, L. (eds.): The Oxford Handbook of Close Relationships. pp. 90–115. Oxford University Press, New York (2013). https://doi.org/10.1093/oxfordhb/9780195398694.013.0005

20. Aron, A., McLaughlin-Volpe, T., Mashek, D., Lewandowski, G., Wright, S.C., Aron, E.N.: Including others in the self. Eur. Rev. Soc. Psychol. **15**, 101–132 (2004). https://doi.org/10.1080/10463280440000008

21. Aron, A., Aron, E.N., Tudor, M., Nelson, G.: Close relationships as including other in the self. J. Pers. Soc. Psychol. **60**, 241–253 (1991). https://doi.org/10.1037/0022-3514.60.2.241

22. Brown, W.J.: Examining four processes of audience involvement with media personae: transportation, parasocial interaction, identification, and worship. Commun. Theory **25**, 259–283 (2015). https://doi.org/10.1111/comt.12053

23. Wirth, W.: Involvement. In: Bryant, J., Vorderer, P. (eds.) Psychology of Entertainment, pp. 199–213. Lawrence Erlbaum Associates, Mahwah (2006)

24. Horton, D., Wohl, R.: Mass communication and para-social interaction. Psychiatry **19**, 215–229 (1956). https://doi.org/10.1080/00332747.1956.11023049

25. Raney, A.A.: Expanding disposition theory: reconsidering character liking, moral evaluations, and enjoyment. Commun. Theory **14**, 348–369 (2004). https://doi.org/10.1111/j.1468-2885.2004.tb00319.x

26. Klimmt, C., Hartmann, T., Schramm, H.: Parasocial interactions and relationships. In: Bryant, J., Vorderer, P. (eds.) Psychology of entertainment, pp. 291–313. Lawrence Erlbaum Associates, Mahwah (2006)

27. Lewis, M.L., Weber, R., Bowman, N.D.: "They may be pixels, but they're my pixels": developing a metric of character attachment in role-playing video games. Cyberpsychol. Behav. **11**, 515–518 (2008). https://doi.org/10.1089/cpb.2007.0137

28. Li, D.D., Liau, A.K., Khoo, A.: Player-Avatar Identification in video gaming: concept and measurement. Comput. Hum. Behav. **29**, 257–263 (2013). https://doi.org/10.1016/j.chb.2012.09.002

29. Banks, J., Bowman, N.D.: Emotion, anthropomorphism, realism, control: validation of a merged metric for player–avatar interaction (PAX). Comput. Hum. Behav. **54**, 215–223 (2016). https://doi.org/10.1016/j.chb.2015.07.030

30. Trepte, S., Reinecke, L.: Avatar creation and video game enjoyment: effects of life-satisfaction, game competitiveness and identification with the avatar. J. Media Psychol. **22**, 171–184 (2010). https://doi.org/10.1027/1864-1105/a000022

31. Aron, A.P., Mashek, D.J., Aron, E.N.: Closeness as including other in the self. In: Mashek, D.J., Aron, A.P. (eds.) Handbook of closeness and intimacy, pp. 27–41. Lawrence Erlbaum Associates Publishers, Mahwah (2004)
32. Shedlosky-Shoemaker, R., Costabile, K.A., Arkin, R.M.: Self-Expansion through fictional characters. Self and Identity 13(5), 556–578 (2014). https://doi.org/10.1080/15298868.2014.882269
33. Mancini, T., Sibilla, F.: Can the avatar become part of the player's identity? Presented at the 26th Annual Conference of the International Society for Research on Identity (Poster) (2019)
34. Mayring, P.: Qualitative content analysis. Forum Qualitative Sozialforschung / Forum: Qualitative Social Research. 1, (2000). https://doi.org/10.17169/FQS-1.2.1089
35. Cohen, J.: Parasocial break-up from favorite television characters: the role of attachment styles and relationship intensity. J. Soc. Pers. Relat. 21, 187–202 (2004). https://doi.org/10.1177/0265407504041374
36. Aron, A., Aron, E.N., Smollan, D.: Inclusion of other in the self scale and the structure of interpersonal closeness. J. Pers. Soc. Psychol. 63, 596–612 (1992). https://doi.org/10.1037/0022-3514.63.4.596
37. Daneels, R., Bowman, N.D., Possler, D., Mekler, E.D.: The 'eudaimonic experience': a scoping review of the concept in digital games research. MaC. 9(2), 178–190 (2021). https://doi.org/10.17645/mac.v9i2.3824

Serious Gameplay

Through Troubled Waters: A Narrative Game for Anger Regulation

Jiaqi Li, Sotirios Piliouras[✉], Semma Raadschelders,
Vivian Imani Dap, Claudia Alessandra Libbi,
and Marcello A. Gómez-Maureira

Leiden University, Rapenburg 70, 2311 EZ Leiden, The Netherlands
{j.li.21,s.piliouras,s.l.raadschelders,v.i.dap}@umail.leidenuniv.nl

Abstract. Emotion regulation, such as one's ability to attenuate the negative impacts of anger, is an important skill that requires recognizing related emotions and knowing appropriate responses. This work presents *Through Troubled Waters* (TTW), a narrative-based video game that allows people to explore and experiment with different anger coping mechanisms in a playful environment. We describe how the design of the game aims to support players in recognizing, labeling, and responding to emotions related to anger. A pilot study with 18 participants was conducted to assess important game mechanics such as dialogue choices and the collection of 'strategy cards'. Our findings show that participants were able to effectively communicate about the anger coping strategies that were presented in the game and potentially reflect on their own strategies. Additionally, more than half of the participants reported the desire to adjust their current anger coping styles. This suggests the potential use of TTW and this type of serious gaming as a supporting tool for emotional intelligence education and mental health interventions.

Keywords: Anger coping strategies · Video games · Emotion regulation · Anger regulation · Storytelling · Serious games

1 Introduction

Emotional intelligence plays a crucial role in many aspects of a person's life, such as at school or work and in their personal relationships [13,16] - thus, it is a necessary aspect of functioning in society [15]. Emotional intelligence includes a range of knowledge and skills, such as the ability to understand, express and regulate emotion [42]. These skills are connected to each other. When expressing emotion, we are sending signals to others to communicate our emotional states, which can benefit us by receiving assistance [42]. The knowledge about how to

---

J. Li, S. Piliouras, S. Raadschelders and V.I. Dap—Contributed equally to this study.

© IFIP International Federation for Information Processing 2022
Published by Springer Nature Switzerland AG 2022
B. Göbl et al. (Eds.): ICEC 2022, LNCS 13477, pp. 185–199, 2022.
https://doi.org/10.1007/978-3-031-20212-4_15

cope with emotion is highly related to emotion regulation, which has been an important topic in the field of psychology for years [10,42]. Emotion regulation refers to the ability to monitor, evaluate and modify emotional reactions [43], and can help us maintain a more stable emotional state and achieve our goals in everyday life [6].

There is evidence that serious games are an effective tool in improving mental health [14,26] either as stand-alone interventions or as part of psychotherapy [12]. Previous research has used serious games and gamification in the field of emotion regulation (e.g., Pacella and López-Pérez's study on children's regulation strategy tendencies [32]). Storytelling in games has been used to enhance empathy and emotion understanding and showed promising results [40,41]. Similarly, card games have been used as a tool to understand emotional expression, recognize facial expressions, and learn to cope with emotions [20,27,49]. Additionally, games can be used for experience-based learning, which has several advantages. For example, games are frequently designed to be highly interactive and require players to apply what they have learned as part of their game experience. Experience-based learning using games is also often perceived as more fun and therefore motivates learners to be active participants [19]. Studies such as these reveal the potential of games to support the development of emotional intelligence.

The present study focuses on supporting players in better regulating their emotions - specifically *anger*. Anger is considered to be a commonly suppressed and sometimes unrecognized emotion despite being easily triggered [8,31,34]. The suppression of anger can amplify the emotional pain as well as the sensitivity to its experience [29,34]. A model of six anger coping strategies has been proposed [28], which includes *anger-out*: direct expression of anger in an aggressive manner; *diffusion*: deflection of anger to another stimulus or activity; *avoidance*: leaving a situation and suppressing the feeling of anger; *support seeking*: seeking support in others; *assertion*: expressing constructively the anger or solving the angering event and *rumination*: coping with anger by repeatedly deliberating over its cause.

For anger regulation, previous research explored and confirmed the efficacy of games in eliciting anger in research settings [46,47]. For example, when being unfairly treated in the *Ultimatum Game*, players were found to experience feelings of anger and to use different coping strategies to regulate their emotions during gameplay [46]. However, their study only focused on two broad categories of anger regulation instead of six specific anger regulation strategies [28]. Furthermore, by only asking players to retrospectively describe their coping strategies and subjectively applying a category label, inaccuracies and biases may have affected the results [5,21,48].

This study aims to address these limitations by **examining all six anger coping strategies (four of which are implemented in a pilot study) and asking players to consciously think about different ways of coping with anger as part of a game.** For this purpose we created *Through Troubled Waters* (TTW), a narrative-based video game that allows players to explore and experiment with different anger coping mechanisms. It is an adaptation of the prototype of *When Life Gives You Lemons* (WLGYL), a video game designed in a separate study to support autistic girls in their socio-emotional development [27]. WLGYL addressed a broader range of target learning goals that were specific to its target audience, which was also involved in co-designing the game. Although emotional learning was already part of the game conceptually, the implementation was still incomplete with room for expansion and improvement. The present study kept a number of key features from WLGYL, but changed the content to only focus on emotional learning and coping strategies, as well as broadening the target audience.

Taking into account the effects of video games on learning [19,36], we anticipate that players will gain a better understanding of anger coping strategies after having played TTW. Furthermore, previous studies have suggested that games could trigger self-reflection in players [11,22,23] and potential behavior changes [4,17,22]. We therefore explore whether a game in which players choose to act according to anger coping strategies will cause reflection or even changes of their own anger regulation strategies in their own life. The central objectives of this study are to examine whether an anger coping game can get players to:

1. better understand different ways of anger regulation (direct goal of the game);
2. self-reflect and change their anger coping habits (indirect goal of the game).

2   Game Design

Providing the plethora of existing research tools in the intersection of serious gaming and mental health, we opted to use an already existing game as a starting point. This was done with the purpose of utilizing some earlier researched game features for emotional skills as a base to build on the more specific goals of anger regulation. We chose to adapt WLGYL as it addressed these relevant matters to our research (i.e., emotion) and the code was available to us for modification. Furthermore, it was expected that a narrative-based game would be a good choice to achieve positive effects in changing behaviors [50]. The game was developed in Unity [2] as game engine, using Yarn Spinner [3] to create dialogue and branching narratives. It was built for WebGL targets and deployed to Github Pages so it could be played in the supported internet browsers. In the game development, we adopted the applied games engagement model [25] which supported more intentional design decisions to ensure integration of the serious purpose (anger management) to the game systems. The decisions we made during the design process will be described below.

2.1   Original Game: *When Life Gives You Lemons* (WLGYL)

A number of features from WLGYL were kept, as they were conductive to the aims of our present study. For example, we used most of WLGYL's assets, such as the world map and characters, as well as the pixel art and friendly ('cute') design, because of its aesthetic appeal to players and reminiscent of games that players have enjoyed in the past [30,39]. TTW also retained WLGYL's island setting and story theme, since going to a summer camp and being introduced to new people is a commonly familiar concept that offers opportunities for new experiences and incidents triggering anger [38].

Furthermore, we decided to maintain that players make choices during gameplay. In WLGYL it was a key feature to give players a sense of autonomy [27], which was also important for TTW as it can increase players' immersion and enjoyment [37]. The original card collection feature, whereby players are rewarded with informative cards related to target skills during in-game scenarios, was modified to include (newly designed) cards specific to anger regulation. The aim was to reinforce learning about new anger coping strategies, directly mapping it to our research objective - under the assumption that cards would be an engaging way to introduce emotion regulation concepts. Players can learn more about their own anger coping habits by noticing which cards they have collected and used (see Fig. 1) with the goal of inducing self-reflection and behavior change upon potential new realizations.

Fig. 1. Unlocking a new card (left) and the card as shown in inventory (right).

2.2   Modified Game: *Through Troubled Waters* (TTW)

In the modified game[1], players decide on the ways that they want to cope with anger through making choices in anger-triggering events. We removed elements of the game that were not related to our research objectives, such as the player's stats and energy bar, phone interactions and the tasks list.

Regarding the game scenarios, we wrote a new story that focuses on several anger-triggering events that happen to the player character (PC). Players can engage in dialogue with non-player characters (NPCs) as in the original game, but their in-dialogue choices are specifically related to the PC's anger coping

---

[1] The Unity source code for the game can be found here https://osf.io/etxu7/?view_only=f8e01202eabf4fb4b22a9394603170a2.

Fig. 2. Dialogue during the second scenario of the game and choosing how to react to an anger triggering event.

Fig. 3. Player exploring the island.

behavior. See Fig. 2 for an example of the dialogues. Considering the limited scope of this game as an experimental exploration, four anger coping strategies were selected out of the total six strategies and are provided throughout the game for players to choose from. *Avoidance* and *anger-out* were chosen as the two extremes in the anger -in/-out spectrum. We further included *support seeking* as a frequently used strategy with high stability and *diffusion* as a novel factor in the anger responding model that is not close to either end of the spectrum [28].

When choosing, the players earn a card that corresponds to the selected anger coping strategy. This aims to fulfill the direct objective of this research: **players learn the name and description of an anger coping strategy and see an example of how the strategy may be used in a social setting.** Previously collected strategy cards can be used in subsequent dialogues to apply the strategies through the given choices. When not engaged in dialogue, the player can walk around the island to explore it, adding to the feeling of autonomy [37] (see Fig. 3). Once the player is ready to continue the story, they can enter a new scenario by talking to one of the NPCs.

3   Method

We conducted a pilot study to examine if we could find supporting evidence that our design choices in TTW would succeed in achieving the research objectives. The experiment process, the involved research instruments and the data analysis are described in the following sections.

3.1   Measurements

To measure participants' preference for anger coping strategies, we use the behavioral Anger Response Questionnaire (BARQ), a validated measure of the six anger coping strategies (see introduction). All six of the factors are covered by 6–7 items, which contribute to a total number of 37 items. The items describe how people could react when they feel angry and the choice is made on a 5-point frequency scale, from 1 (rarely) to 5 (very frequently).

In addition to the questionnaire, we also conducted interviews to investigate the participants' understanding and self-awareness of anger coping strategies. Interviews were semi-structured, allowing for open answers while keeping a consistent structure. The interview consisted of 8 questions covering three topics that are directly related to the research goals. The first section focused on the participant's emotion activation and relatability to the main character. Finding out about the experienced emotions and identification with the character was considered necessary in estimating the validity of the following questions. The second section was aimed to check the participant's recall and understanding of anger coping strategies within the game. Finally, the third section examined the participant's level of self-reflection on anger coping strategies as a result of their game experience and their will to make changes related to the strategies in the future.

3.2   Sampling and Experiment Procedure

Participants were chosen using convenience sampling, only including young adults and teenagers. No other inclusion criteria (e.g., presence of anger issues) were applied. The experiment procedure consisted of three stages. Before starting, participants were asked to provide their consent to the collection of data from the questionnaire and the audio recording of their interview. Participants were informed that all data would be stored anonymously in a safe location and used only for this research. In the first stage of the experiment, participants would fill in the BARQ questionnaire, which is referred to as the pre-game questionnaire in this paper. All questionnaires in this study were sent and filled out online through Qualtrics [1]. In the second stage, the participants would play the game, which was available online. There was no pre-defined duration of the game. The participants were asked to play until reaching the end of the game, which was clearly stated in the game through an 'ending' message. The third stage consisted of retaking the same BARQ questionnaire (i.e., the post-game questionnaire) and performing the interview. The whole experiment process was designed to last between 30–60 min.

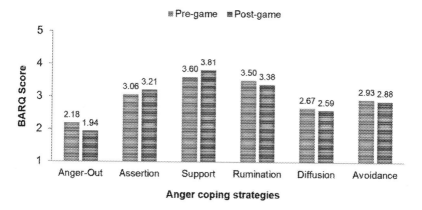

Fig. 4. The average BARQ score for each strategy (N = 18). Support = Support-Seeking.

3.3 Data Analysis

Concerning the BARQ results, items that belonged to the same coping strategy category were grouped and averaged. This was done for both the pre- and post-game questionnaire. A paired Samples T-Test was performed in order to examine the possible differences in the average scores for each strategy between the two questionnaires. For the interview analysis, brief notes were made during the interview procedure to highlight the key answers by the participants. These notes were revised and adjusted afterwards, with the help of interview recordings. Finally, the answers were categorized and quantified. For example, for the question "What anger coping strategies did you experience in the gameplay? Could you describe them?", the answers were processed by counting the number of times that an anger coping strategy was recalled and described correctly. A correct answer did not have to match the wording exactly, but needed to express a similar meaning as the sample description provided in the game. Since this process can be subject to the evaluators' judgment, two researchers processed each answer independently and when there was a difference in their judgment, the specific interview answer would be marked and discussed within the whole research team to reach an agreement. The insight that was obtained from the quantification process was then further studied in a qualitative way by looking back to the participants' more detailed answers and the results obtained from the questionnaires.

4   Results

Eighteen people participated in this study, most of which were bachelor or master students. Eight of them were surveyed and interviewed face-to-face while ten of them were surveyed and interviewed via a videoconferencing tool. The actual play time of the participants until reaching the end of the game was 8–15 min.

Table 1. Descriptive statistics and t-test results for pre- and post-game BARQ scores (N=18).

Strategy	Time	Mean	SD	t	df	p	Cohen's d
Anger-out	Pre-game	2.18	0.73	3.16	17	**0.01***	0.75
	Post-game	1.94	0.77				
Assertion	Pre-game	3.06	0.97	−1.47	17	0.16	−0.35
	Post-game	3.21	0.89				
Support seeking	Pre-game	3.60	0.43	−1.70	17	0.11	−0.40
	Post-game	3.81	0.50				
Rumination	Pre-game	3.50	0.82	1.12	17	0.28	0.27
	post-game	3.38	0.90				
Diffusion	Pre-game	2.67	1.00	0.77	17	0.45	0.18
	Post-game	2.59	1.04				
Avoidance	Pre-game	2.93	0.85	0.49	17	0.63	0.12
	Post-game	2.88	0.81				

* Significant at alpha of 0.05

4.1   Quantitative Results

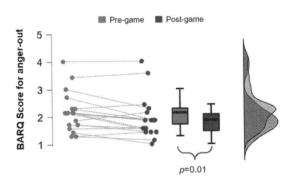

Fig. 5. A rain cloud plot of the anger-out scores before and after the game in 18 participants. The plot combines a cloud of points, box plot and a violin plot.

Figure 4 shows the average BARQ scores of each strategy in both the pre- and post-game questionnaires. When the participants completed this survey for the first time, support-seeking and rumination received the highest score (3.60 and 3.50, respectively), while auger-out was reported as the least frequently used strategy by participants (2.18).

After playing the game, the most and least frequently used strategies were still the same, although there were minor changes in their average scores, such as the support-seeking score (from 3.60 to 3.81) and the anger-out score (from 2.18 to 1.94). See Table 1 for each strategy's mean and standard deviation results[2].

A paired sample t-test showed that there was a significant difference in participants' reported frequency of using anger-out strategy between the pre-game questionnaire (M = 2.18, SD = 0.73) and post-game questionnaire (M = 1.94, SD = 0.77); t(17) = 3.16, p = 0.01. Figure 5 shows a rain cloud plot of the changes in scores after playing the game.

4.2   Qualitative Results

Emotion Activation and Relatability to the Character: When being asked if they could describe what emotions the main character felt during the whole game, 88.9% of participants mentioned anger. They also reported emotions besides anger, such as happiness and excitement.

Answers about emotions that the participants themselves felt during gameplay varied. 27.8% reported that they felt anger to some extent, such as (quoted verbatim): "Most of time I felt anger", "I thought the player is supposed to feel angry. I felt a bit angry but not so much because it felt not so real. I tried to feel like the character, especially in the last fight. I had a similar experience." Some of them reported neutral emotions or even relaxation or amusement: "I was pretty calm and relaxed cause I know it's a game."

44.4% of participants confirmed that they could relate to the main character (Q:"How does the character relate to you?"), answering e.g.: "Yes, even though the choices were quite limited compared to the questionnaire. I felt that I could easily get in the shoes of the character.", "We related a lot because they did everything I told them to.", "Yeah, I have been on summer camps. Shared experiences." However, there were 27.8% of participants having experienced no or low level of relatedness. One participant commented: "I wouldn't say we are the same at all. In those situations I would simply not care." "I don't feel identified with the character because it's a boy and not much background. I was from more of an observer perspective." 27.8% of participants had answers somewhere in the middle between "yes" and "no". Their replies showed that while they felt in control of the character, the choices provided by the game did not allow them to accurately represent their actual choice, reducing the amount they could relate. An example for such a reply is: "Not entirely. Some choices did reflect what I would do but it wasn't the exact reaction I would go for."

Understanding of the Strategies (Direct Goal): Participants generally indicated that emotion regulation was not a new topic to them. 88.9% of participants reported that they had heard theories about how to deal with emotions like anger before playing this game. When asked about which anger coping strategies they had experienced in the game play, all of them mentioned the avoidance strategy, and 94.4% of participants experienced support-seeking in their game

---

[2] More detailed results can be found here https://osf.io/etxu7/?view_only=f8e0120 2eabf4fb4b22a9394603170a2.

journey. Anger-out and Diffusion were also mentioned by some participants (50% and 38.9%, respectively). When mentioning the strategies, the participants could describe the strategies in their own words and understand how a strategy works. As an example, one answer was: "First, seeking help: finding someone that I am comfortable to talk with and open up. Second, focus on working: playing dodge ball-ignoring the situation and trying to forget it..." Some participants also mentioned that they would like to choose some other strategies, rather than the ones provided as options in the game. For example: "For the last one I think there should have been more options, (such as) approaching people in a normal manner." "I would have probably found the middle ground between the answers."

Self-reflection and Change (Indirect Goal): When asked which anger coping strategies the participants used in real life, 72.2% mentioned avoidance and 66.7% mentioned support seeking. While participants were not new to the presented coping strategies, some were not aware that reactions were actually a recognized strategy. One participant said: "I haven't framed them so much as strategies. For myself I haven't seen seek for help as a technical strategy for my anger. It's more unconscious."

27.8% of participants indicated that they would likely not apply any of the game's coping strategies to their real life, e.g. because "the system I have in place is working just fine and is serving me well." 55.6% of participants suggested they might try some strategy that they did not use often in the past or make some changes to the way they reacted to the angering event. For example: "Maybe I would try to be more active when coping with anger... maybe talking about it more, or confront the person... something I would like to try in my life." 27.8% of participants stated that this game gave them a chance to reflect on their own anger-coping strategies: "I think most of them are something that I usually do in my life. I didn't feel anything new. But the game helped me to organize my strategies. In the first survey I didn't know that clear, but in the second survey I was more clear to think about my own strategies." "I use a lot avoidance, so during the game I was questioning myself how good or bad it is." "In the game I realized that avoidance can also be a behavior of oppression to yourself, and so that it can also have negative results."

5   Discussion

To examine the effectiveness of this game in achieving the two research objectives (whether an anger coping game can get players to 1. better understand different ways of anger regulation; 2. self-reflect and change their anger coping habits), we first verified its efficacy in creating anger-triggering contexts in which anger regulation could be elicited. According to the interview results, when playing the game, most of the participants indeed recognized that the player character felt anger, the target emotion, in the game scenarios. This result confirmed the previous research findings [46, 47] of the effectiveness of games in providing such a context where emotions could be triggered and perceived by players. It is worth mentioning that participants further identified other emotions besides anger, such as happiness or excitement, since the PC was starting a new journey and making new friends. This suggests that the perception of in-game emotions is similar to the emotion perception in real life contexts, where individuals often feel more than a single emotion at the same time [9] and different individuals might have different reactions to the same event [45]. These findings indicate that there might potentially exist a good ecological validity in this study, especially if compared to strict experimental isolation, like removing all elements that are not directly related to anger provocation [33]. Higher ecological validity implies a better generalization of our experimental findings to the real world [24].

For the first research objective (direct game goal), from the interview results we can see that this anger-coping game, which successfully placed players in anger-triggering events, could help players to better understand different ways of responding to anger in related game scenarios. During the interview, participants were able to describe the strategies they used in the game and how those strategies worked, even for strategies that they hadn't recognized as an anger coping response before. In general, participants showed an understanding of different forms of anger responding and connected the styles that appeared in the game to their real life experience. While this, overall, indicates a positive result regarding our goal, it is worth exploring whether the interview itself also contributed to the process of learning in future research.

For the second research objective (indirect game goal), the majority of participants reported that the game helped them either reflect on their anger-coping behavior or develop a motivation to make changes to it. This result was expected based on related studies where a positive influence of games were found in promoting awareness and behavior change [4,11,17,22,23]. Based on pre- and post tests using the BARQ, we found evidence that the game affected the frequency with which participants would use different anger coping styles. One significant change was the reduction in using the anger-out strategy. This is possibly explained by results from the interview, which indicate that angering in-game situations made participants more aware that they disliked confronting people in such cases. Instead, they often preferred seeking support for their character and indicated that the game helped them feel more certain about this choice, possibly leading to the increased perceived usage of support-seeking in participants' real life (though this change was not statistically significant). Interestingly, a difference was observed in the BARQ scores of assertion and rumination, which were not provided as option strategies in the game. It is possible that the absence of the participants' preferred strategy in the provided options of a scenario triggered them to think about these two missing strategies. This finding further supports the effects of this game in triggering self-reflection and connecting in-game scenarios to real life experiences.

One additional insight is the players' relatedness to their game character. According to previous research, when players feel closely related to their character in the game, they could enjoy the game more, be more immersed [18,44] and be more motivated to play serious games [7,35]. From the interview results, we noticed different levels of relatedness to the character among our participants, which depended on the degree of similarity participants felt to their character and the degree of choice control (also mentioned in previous research [7]). Some participants found similarities in what the character was experiencing compared to their own past experiences. On the other hand, for participants who considered themselves as calmer or more mature, the game character's age was an issue - not allowing them to fully relate to a teenager character in a summer camp. This is consistent with previous findings on player identification (i.e., character appearance or personality traits could affect players' identification) [18,44]. Regarding choice control, one complaint was that the personally preferred coping strategy, or the ability to combine strategies, was not offered as an option in the game. This contributed to lowering the participant's sense of relatedness to the character's experience [7]. To improve relatedness, future development efforts could consider involving multiple character profiles for players to choose from, or provide more customization to better align the context of the PC with that of the player [44]. A bigger game experience consisting of more scenarios and all anger regulation strategies would allow the use of the cards multiple times, further improving the players' feeling of control [7,44]. To reinforce the reflection aspect, additional insight into their anger coping habits could be provided by showing which cards are used most frequently. Additionally, we only collected data from participants right after playing the game. In order to study long-term affects, multiple questionnaires and interviews should be taken over a longer period of time.

6   Conclusion

In this study, a video game has been adapted to focus on anger regulation and make players think about and choose their preferred anger response styles in specific anger-triggering scenarios. For the research objectives, (1) the interview results showed that this game can support players to better understand different anger coping styles, especially for the styles that were not recognized by the participants as strategies before (direct goal of the game); (2) both the questionnaire and interview results revealed some changes of participants' perception as well as preference of the usage of different anger coping strategies. After playing the game and experiencing anger responding scenarios, participants knew better about how they usually cope with angering events and what they want to change for better anger responses in their future life (indirect game goal). The finding that participants were able to recall and sufficiently explain a considerable amount of anger coping strategies featured in the game highlights the potential use of TTW as an educational tool for emotional intelligence. The triggered self-reflection and desire for behavior change that was observed on some participants further suggests the potential of this game as a powerful tool for mental health interventions such as therapy. Finally, provided that anger is just one of the various emotions, TTW and the insights from this study can be useful for research on other types of emotion regulation in the future.

References

1. Qualtrics survey software. https://www.qualtrics.com/. (Accessed 7 May 2022)
2. Unity. https://unity.com/. (Accessed 7 May 2022)
3. Yarn spinner. https://yarnspinner.dev/. (Accessed 7 May 2022)
4. Baranowski, T., Buday, R., Thompson, D.I., Baranowski, J.: Playing for real: video games and stories for health-related behavior change. Am. J. Prev. Med. **34**(1), 74–82 (2008)
5. Barrett, L.F.: The relationships among momentary emotion experiences, personality descriptions, and retrospective ratings of emotion. Pers. Soc. Psychol. Bull. **23**(10), 1100–1110 (1997)
6. Bernardini, S., Porayska-Pomsta, K., Smith, T.J.: Echoes: An intelligent serious game for fostering social communication in children with autism. Inf. Sci. **264**, 41–60 (2014)
7. Blumberg, F.C., Almonte, D.E., Anthony, J.S., Hashimoto, N.: Serious games: What are they? what do they do? why should we play them. In: The Oxford Handbook of Media Psychology, pp. 334–351 (2013)
8. Cassiello-Robbins, C., Barlow, D.H.: Anger: The unrecognized emotion in emotional disorders. Clin. Psychol. Sci. Pract. **23**(1), 66 (2016)
9. Charles, S.T., Piazza, J.R., Urban, E.J.: Mixed emotions across adulthood: When, where, and why? Curr. Opin. Behav. Sci. **15**, 58–61 (2017)
10. Cheong, Y.-G., Khaled, R., Holmgård, C., Yannakakis, G.N.: Serious games for teaching conflict resolution: modeling conflict dynamicsSerious games for teaching conflict resolution: modeling conflict dynamics. In: D'Errico, F., Poggi, I., Vinciarelli, A., Vincze, L. (eds.) Conflict and Multimodal Communication. CSS, pp. 449–475. Springer, Cham (2015). https://doi.org/10.1007/978-3-319-14081-0_21
11. Dormann, C., Whitson, J.R., Neuvians, M.: Once more with feeling: Game design patterns for learning in the affective domain. Games Culture **8**(4), 215–237 (2013)
12. Eichenberg, C., Schott, M.: Serious games for psychotherapy: A systematic review. Games Health J. **6**(3), 127–135 (2017)
13. Eisenberg, N., et al.: The relations of regulation and emotionality to problem behavior in elementary school children. Dev. Psychopathol. **8**(1), 141–162 (1996)
14. Fleming, T.M.: Serious games and gamification for mental health: current status and promising directions. Front. Psych. **7**, 215 (2017)
15. Gardner, H.E.: Intelligence reframed: Multiple intelligences for the 21st century, Hachette UK (2000)
16. Goleman, D.: Emotional intelligence: Why it can matter more than IQ. Bloomsbury Publishing (1996)
17. Granic, I., Lobel, A., Engels, R.C.: The benefits of playing video games. Am. Psychol. **69**(1), 66 (2014)
18. Hefner, D., Klimmt, C., Vorderer, P.: Identification with the player character as determinant of video game enjoyment. In: Ma, L., Rauterberg, M., Nakatsu, R. (eds.) ICEC 2007. LNCS, vol. 4740, pp. 39–48. Springer, Heidelberg (2007). https://doi.org/10.1007/978-3-540-74873-1_6
19. Hromek, R., Roffey, S.: Promoting social and emotional learning with games: "it's fun and we learn things". Simulation Gaming **40**(5), 626–644 (2009)
20. Jayman, M., Ventouris, A.: Dealing children a helping hand with book of beasties: the mental wellness card game. Educ. Child Psychol. **37**(4), 69–80 (2020)

21. John Bernardin, H., Thomason, S., Ronald Buckley, M., Kane, J.S.: Rater rating-level bias and accuracy in performance appraisals: The impact of rater personality, performance management competence, and rater accountability. Hum. Resour. Manage. **55**(2), 321–340 (2016)
22. Kaufman, G., Flanagan, M., Seidman, M.: Creating stealth game interventions for attitude and behavior change: An "embedded design" model. In: Persuasive Gaming in Context, p. 73 (2015)
23. Khaled, R.: Questions over answers: Reflective game design. In: Cermak-Sassenrath, D. (ed.) Playful Disruption of Digital Media. GMSE, pp. 3–27. Springer, Singapore (2018). https://doi.org/10.1007/978-981-10-1891-6_1
24. Kihlstrom, J.F.: Ecological validity and "ecological validity". Perspectives on Psychol. Sci. **16**(2), 466–471 (2021)
25. Kniestedt, I., Lefter, I., Lukosch, S., Brazier, F.M.: Re-framing engagement for applied games: A conceptual framework. Entertainment Comput. **41**, 100475 (2022). https://doi.org/10.1016/j.entcom.2021.100475, www.sciencedirect.com/science/article/pii/S1875952121000720
26. Lau, H.M., Smit, J.H., Fleming, T.M., Riper, H.: Serious games for mental health: are they accessible, feasible, and effective? a systematic review and meta-analysis. Front. Psych. **7**, 209 (2017)
27. Libbi, C.A.: When Life Gives You Lemons: Designing a Game With and For Autistic Girls. Master's thesis, MSc Thesis University of Twente (2021)
28. Linden, W., Hogan, B.E., Rutledge, T., Chawla, A., Lenz, J.W., Leung, D.: There is more to anger coping than "in" or "out". Emotion **3**(1), 12 (2003)
29. Memedovic, S., Grisham, J.R., Denson, T.F., Moulds, M.L.: The effects of trait reappraisal and suppression on anger and blood pressure in response to provocation. J. Res. Pers. **44**(4), 540–543 (2010)
30. Ohkura, M. (ed.): Kawaii Engineering. SSCC, Springer, Singapore (2019). https://doi.org/10.1007/978-981-13-7964-2
31. Osgood, J.M., Quartana, P.J.: An overview of anger: A common emotion with a complicated backstory (2021)
32. Pacella, D., López-Pérez, B.: Assessing children's interpersonal emotion regulation with virtual agents: The serious game emodiscovery. Comput. Educ. **123**, 1–12 (2018)
33. Parsons, S.: Authenticity in virtual reality for assessment and intervention in autism: A conceptual review. Educ. Res. Rev. **19**, 138–157 (2016)
34. Quartana, P.J., Burns, J.W.: Painful consequences of anger suppression. Emotion **7**(2), 400 (2007)
35. Rahimabad, R.M., Rezvani, M.H.: Identifying factors affecting the immersion and concentration of players in serious games. In: 2020 International Serious Games Symposium (ISGS), pp. 61–67. IEEE (2020)
36. Rodríguez, A., et al.: Gameteen: new tools for evaluating and training emotional regulation strategies. Annu. Rev. Cybertherapy Telemed. **2012**, 334 (2012)
37. Ryan, R.M., Rigby, C.S., Przybylski, A.: The motivational pull of video games: A self-determination theory approach. Motiv. Emot. **30**(4), 344–360 (2006)
38. Schafer, E.D.: Using psychological science to improve summer camp staff training. Child Adolesc. Psychiatr. Clin. N. Am. **16**(4), 817–828 (2007)
39. Silber, D.: Pixel art for game developers. CRC Press (2015)
40. Skaraas, S.B., Gomez, J., Jaccheri, L.: Playing with empathy through a collaborative storytelling game. In: Clua, E., Roque, L., Lugmayr, A., Tuomi, P. (eds.) ICEC 2018. LNCS, vol. 11112, pp. 254–259. Springer, Cham (2018). https://doi.org/10.1007/978-3-319-99426-0_26

41. Skaraas, S.B., Gomez, J., Jaccheri, L.: Tappetina's empathy game: a playground of storytelling and emotional understanding. In: Proceedings of the 17th ACM Conference on Interaction Design and Children, pp. 509–512 (2018)
42. Southam-Gerow, M.A., Kendall, P.C.: Emotion regulation and understanding: Implications for child psychopathology and therapy. Clin. Psychol. Rev. **22**(2), 189–222 (2002)
43. Thompson, R.A.: Emotion regulation: A theme in search of definition. Monogr. Soc. Res. Child Devel. **59**, 25–52 (1994)
44. Turkay, S., Kinzer, C.K.: The effects of avatar-based customization on player identification. In: Gamification: Concepts, Methodologies, Tools, and Applications, pp. 247–272. IGI Global (2015)
45. Vansteelandt, K., Van Mechelen, I., Nezlek, J.B.: The co-occurrence of emotions in daily life: A multilevel approach. J. Res. Pers. **39**(3), 325–335 (2005)
46. Vögele, C., Sorg, S., Studtmann, M., Weber, H.: Cardiac autonomic regulation and anger coping in adolescents. Biol. Psychol. **85**(3), 465–471 (2010)
47. Wang, N., Marsella, S.: Introducing EVG: An emotion evoking game. In: Gratch, J., Young, M., Aylett, R., Ballin, D., Olivier, P. (eds.) IVA 2006. LNCS (LNAI), vol. 4133, pp. 282–291. Springer, Heidelberg (2006). https://doi.org/10.1007/11821830_23
48. Wherry, R.J., Sr., Bartlett, C.: The control of bias in ratings: A theory of rating. Pers. Psychol. **35**(3), 521–551 (1982)
49. Yamamoto, M.: Development of regulation of emotional expression in young children: The relationship between understanding of real emotions and facial expressions in a card game. Annu. Bull. Grad. Sch. Educ. Tohoku Univ. **5**, 43–54 (2019)
50. Zhou, C., Occa, A., Kim, S., Morgan, S.: A meta-analysis of narrative game-based interventions for promoting healthy behaviors. J. Health Commun. **25**(1), 54–65 (2020)

Incorporating the Theory of Attention in Applied Game Design

Isabelle Kniestedt[1]([✉]), Stephan Lukosch[2], Milan van der Kuil[3], Iulia Lefter[1], and Frances Brazier[1]

[1] TPM, Delft University of Technology, Delft, The Netherlands
ikniestedt@gmail.com
[2] HIT Lab NZ, University of Canterbury, Christchurch, New Zealand
[3] Trimbos-instituut, Utrecht, The Netherlands

Abstract. Whereas entertainment games are capable of creating deeply rewarding and emotional experiences, applied game projects often result in products that, while potentially effective, are lacking in many other aspects of the user experience. This may be due to the fact that the focus of most design approaches for applied games lies primarily on the use of game mechanics, neglecting other aspects of design that aim to shape and influence the player's emotional journey. This article provides an exploratory effort in a different approach to creating applied games, namely through the design of user attention and by integrating the theory of attention into applied game design practice. This approach is tested in two ongoing applied game projects, from which preliminary guidelines for applied game researchers and practitioners are proposed.

Keywords: Applied games · Serious games · Game design · Attention

1 Introduction

The design of games for non-entertainment purposes (referred to as 'applied' games in this article) is a continued topic of discussion within academic discourse. Frameworks for applied game design, intended to support the development of such games, tend to focus on defining conceptual factors that play a role in the design process [44]. Some factors are well understood, such as the importance of defining the learning content (i.e., the intended skills or knowledge to be gained) [3,10,23] or defining the intended user's existing needs, interests, experience and skills [9]. Connections have also been made between these aspects and the intended design of the applied game. It has, for example, been suggested that a game genre (e.g., 'strategy' or 'action adventure') should be chosen following previously established needs [3,29,46]. This, in turn, should then lead to the inclusion of genre-appropriate rules and game mechanics [44].

© IFIP International Federation for Information Processing 2022
Published by Springer Nature Switzerland AG 2022
B. Göbl et al. (Eds.): ICEC 2022, LNCS 13477, pp. 200–213, 2022.
https://doi.org/10.1007/978-3-031-20212-4_16

Games offer players agency through actions – it is one of the primary factors that sets them apart from other forms of media [21]. As such, it is not surprising that applied game design efforts tend to focus on mechanics (i.e., actions that can be taken to interact with the game world) and their corresponding systems (e.g., feedback mechanisms) [38]. This type of approach has resulted in work focused on establishing the value of specific mechanics and their effect within an applied game or for a specific audience (e.g., [16,18,35,36], with the goal of creating an easy to use 'catalogue' of mechanics that can be applied to any purpose. This is not unlike gamification efforts, however, where the same game elements are applied to any context [17]. Similar to how gamification has been criticised for oversimplifying how games function [20] by mistaking incidental properties of games (e.g., leaderboards, points) for primary features (i.e., complex, meaningful interaction) [4], this article argues that applied game design approaches singularly focused on mechanics risk falling into the same trap. The result of such approaches are games that similarly ignore important aspects of the player's emotional experience.

With the entertainment game industry producing vast amounts of easily accessible games, resulting in a growing game literacy among audiences, overly simplistic game designs may not remain engaging (and, thus, effective in achieving their purpose) in the future [7]. For this reason, applied game practitioners should continue to adopt knowledge and techniques from entertainment game design. Naturally, there are many approaches to game design. This article provides an exploratory attempt to incorporate one such an approach, and does so by **mapping and adopting the theory of attention** from entertainment game design to that of applied games.

One popular design approach within entertainment games has been that of design 'lenses' [37], which can be used to evaluate design decisions from different perspectives at various stages of development. **This article proposes a new lens for applied games: the lens of attention.** Within games, attention can be directed through design decisions [5]. These range from granular decisions, such as the presentation of feedback or design of user interfaces, to more comprehensive choices that determine the structure of the game.

The following section provides an **overview of the underlying theory of attention**, and how it factors into game design. This theory is then used to **extend existing models of applied game design and engagement**, and used to **guide design discussions in two applied game projects**. From these discussions, the article outlines **preliminary guidelines to designing applied games with attention**.

2   Related Work

'Attention' refers to a sustained focus of cognitive resources on information while filtering extraneous information [40]. It is considered a basic function that is a precursor to all other cognitive functions. Particularly important to the subject of this article are *reflexive attention* and *selective attention*, as well as the related term of *vigilance*.

Reflexive attention, also known as stimulus-driven attention, describes a person's ability to respond to specific sensory stimuli [33]. It is driven by the properties of objects (e.g., movement or sound) and is a largely autonomous process—attention is drawn to such stimuli whether a person wants to or not. Selective attention refers to the aspect of attentional processing that is under a person's control [13]. Attention is a limited resource - a person cannot pay attention to everything at once or for an unlimited time. Vigilance refers to the ability to respond to events in the environment, which decreases over time as a result of fatigue due to cognitive load [33]. Techniques such as switching attention to another stimulus can mitigate these negative effects.

Attention plays a role in game design in many ways. The most established is in that of user interface (UI) design, and how information is presented to the player [2,37]. Important information is shown in the player's direct view, accompanied by sound and visual indicators to draw (reflexive) attention. Less critical elements are distributed at the edges of the screen to let a player focus on them if required (selective attention). Designers may also shape the environment, use lighting, or place objects to alert players to specific areas of the game, elicit curiosity, or guide them towards goals [15]. While important, this use of attention is not the primary focus of this article. Instead, this section will introduce two other aspects in which attention plays an important role, which have not yet been incorporated into applied game design: **areas of involvement** and **balance and rhythm**.

2.1   Areas of Involvement

Calleja [5] proposes **six general areas of involvement within a video game**; ludic (gameplay), spatial, kinaesthetic (movement), narrative, shared (social), and affective (emotional). Games provide a combination of these areas, and attention shifts between them from moment to moment. Kinaesthetic involvement (i.e., involvement from the act of controlling an avatar) may be dominant during a challenging platforming section, but shifting to affective involvement when appreciating the view. Deciding when to heal during a combat encounter or reading enemy attack patterns are examples of ludic involvement, while the player is also still concerned with dodging incoming attacks (kinaesthetic). In such moments, the player's attention is more likely to be 'saturated', and they are unlikely to admire the scenery. **When and how to shift the player's attention is essential in structuring the game experience.** For example, developers at CDProjekt Red devised a '40-second rule' when developing *The Witcher 3* [6], determining through play tests that players should see something of interest (e.g., a pack of deer, opponents, an NPC) every 40 s of exploring the world in order to stay engaged [39]. A more simplified version of the areas [26] is that of **gameplay** (ludic, spatial, and kinaesthetic), **social** (narrative and shared), and **affective** (emotional experience) (Fig. 1).

Different areas of attention are considered more or less effective than others in *capturing* **and** *maintaining* **attention** [26] Mechanics, controls, and spatial design pose an entry barrier that players need to invest time and

Fig. 1. In *Zelda: BotW* [32] the player's attention frequently shifts between, e.g., affective (a beautiful vista), gameplay (learning controls), and social (meeting an NPC).

energy in. Mechanics that are deep enough, however, can maintain attention for a long time. Narratives and characters neither capture nor hold attention very well; while people are drawn to them, it is challenging to write them in a way that are both quickly understood and remain interesting [1]. Finally, elements aiming at affective involvement capture attention well (e.g., through art style, music, and sound design), but are less likely to hold attention unless the game offers other elements of substance.

Depending on the game, the balance between the areas of involvement varies. A platforming game may not involve many narrative or social aspects, while a game focused on creating an affective experience through sound and visuals may have simple mechanics. However, it is reasonable to say that a balance is usually required in creating a unified experience [37].

2.2 Balance and Rhythm

Attention factors into game design in two major ways; in repeatedly capturing a player's attention from moment to moment (reflexive) and in maintaining that attention by offering depth within and variety between game areas (selective). It is furthermore necessary to be aware of overloading the player cognitively through too much information (vigilance), or under-stimulating them by staying within one area for too long. Designing with this knowledge in mind leads to the creation of rhythm or the 'emotional beat' in a game [27,37].

Flow theory states that a pleasant state of enjoyment is reached when a person's skill and the challenges provided by a task are in balance. This theory is often used in relation to games, as games are considered suitable vehicles for inducing a flow state [41]. It would be incorrect to assume, however, that games simply provide a stream of challenges that continuously matches the player's skill level. Modern games provide a wide variety of experiences, including moments of (extreme) challenge. This can be highly entertaining, memorable, and engaging. The popularity [34] of the recent release *Elden Ring* [14] - a game developed by FromSoftware, a studio notorious for creating difficult games - provides a good example of this. In games like this, moments of high intensity (e.g., an encounter with a seemingly insurmountable enemy) are balanced with moments of respite (e.g., exploring, crafting, interacting with characters). This is the case within the overarching game structure (in which major enemy encounters are balanced with longer sections of exploration, affective experiences, and other or lower-intensity gameplay) and on a more granular level, such as in the design of specific areas. **Together, these moments form the 'rhythm' of the game, offering memorable highs and lows in the player's experience.**

There is no universal standard for what this rhythm should be and it will vary depending on the game. Missions in *Uncharted 3* [30], for example, follow a three-act structure similar to movies [26,27]. Naturally, there are also games that aim for a pleasant 'middle' experience, in which a player never has the feeling that they can't overcome the obstacles presented to them. Examples of these are zen-like games (e.g., *Flow* [42] or *Flower* [43]), puzzle games (e.g., *Monument Valley* [45]), or simulation games (e.g., *Animal Crossing* [31] or *Stardew Valley* [8]). However, it is important to note is that, even in these experiences, there are still variations in attention demand and a switching of attention between different areas (e.g., talking to characters, admiring visuals or music, movement, or (light) combat mechanics).

These are only some examples in which attention is manipulated through design in order to shape a player's experience. Game designers use everything at their disposal, including mechanics, environments, motion, stories, characters, lighting, visuals, and sound to grab and hold a player's attention, to offer depth and variation, and to structure and balance the player experience. This happens on different levels, both in the overall game structure and from moment to moment. In doing so, **designers take care not to saturate players with different types of information, but rather use the various aspects of design to enforce a defined and coherent player experience.**

2.3   Attention in Applied Games

Attention is not a novel concept in the applied game literature. As mentioned previously, it has been used in relation to UI design and the presentation of information [44]. Outside of this, however, it has primarily been used to explain other concepts, such as immersion [19]. Attention is considered a first level of, or stepping stone towards higher levels of immersion, but not core to game design.

One exception is the Applied Games Engagement Model (AGEM) [25]. AGEM differentiates between **game systems**, and **everything that is meant to fulfil an intentional, non-entertainment (applied) purpose.** This may include **elements external to the game**, such as the physical environment and facilitators. **Together, they form the entire game experience.** Attention is directed through design decision and shifts between the game systems and the applied purpose. In general, there should be a sense of **overlap** between the two, although the overlap may vary throughout the game. At times, attention may be directed away from the game systems altogether to facilitate moments of reflection.

The theory proposed by AGEM is similar to the theory of attention for applied games, in which a player's attention is guided between areas of attention. It is, however, a theoretical model that has not yet been tested in practice. This article addresses this gap and assesses the extent to which the model is fruitful in practice.

3   Implementation

To design the game systems of an applied game, this article presumes that the theory of attention outlined in Sect. 2 can be of use, as long as the applied purpose is taken into account. This section describes how this was done in practice. Stakeholders from two applied game projects (Fig. 2) participated in guided design discussions. Both projects were ongoing at different institutions; they were not 'created' for this article. Each of the projects had gone through a design and development cycle, resulting in a prototype. The projects were then continued by different people than the original developers. The new developers identified issues with the existing design. During the discussions, they used the theory of attention to address these perceived issues. In the interest of scope, this article does not go into detail on the design of the games, but only uses examples to illustrate how the theory was applied. The two cases provided here were selected based on convenience and availability. However, the projects presented can be considered representative of a larger selection of applied gaming projects.

3.1   Case 1: Virtual Reality (VR) Person-Centred Care (PCC)

The first case study has been developed by the Trimbos-institute, with the aid of an external applied game development studio. It is VR training software for health workers caring for people with dementia. It aims to train players in person-centred care [11] by placing them in the role of a carer working in a nursing home. During the game, the player is presented with narrative scenarios that are to be resolved by choosing one of several options. One the options is considered to be the only correct answer based on the principles of person-centred care. Players are informed of how successful they are at the end of the scenario through a score, and given further relevant information on the topic of person-centred care. Throughout the game, players complete several, primarily text-based, scenarios. The game utilises a realistic 3D art style, using sound and simple animations to emphasise the actions of the characters.

The project was inactive for some time until it was picked up by a new stakeholder. Issues with the original design were primarily related to the game being "not very much like a game". Especially the allocation of points and restrictive nature of the scenarios were considered inadequate for the subject matter. The new stakeholder was intent on developing the game further, but had few specific ideas on how to approach it.

3.2   Case 2: When Life Gives You Lemons (WLGYL)

The second case study was developed as part of a MSc graduation project [28]. WLGYL is a 2D role-playing game (RPG) aimed at teaching girls with autism

Fig. 2. Screenshots from the case study prototypes of PCC (left) and WLGYL (right).

about emotions and social skills. The game was designed with input from psychologists and the target audience in multiple co-design sessions. In the game, the player takes the role of a young girl going on a summer camp, where her task is to make new friends. She does so by exploring the camp and talking to other characters. Talking to characters presents the player with narrative scenarios, in which a player needs to make choices. The scenarios encourage the player to explore the effects of choices to learn about different types of social interaction. Each interaction is rewarded with an 'emotion card' (e.g., 'anger') that provides information on that emotion.

The project was picked up by another group of MSc students to continue development and test it. The existing prototype was not completely functional and had limited content. The new group (advised by the previous developer, their supervisors, and a research group of psychologists) also determined that the initial game's design was too complex: trying to teach or improve emotion regulation and social skills. They limited the scope of the game to anger coping mechanisms. However, at this point they were facing difficulties managing the input from several sources, and assessing the impact of their design decisions.

3.3   The Lens of Attention

The Lens of Attention was applied to both of these cases according to a fixed procedure. First, **the existing design was mapped** in line with a given set of conceptual factors from applied game models (e.g., the learning content [3,22,46], the physical space [25], the role of facilitators [3,25], additional media [12] and infrastructure [23]). The existing game mechanics and systems were similarly identified. The **intended overlap between purpose and game systems was then determined** [25]. The third step was to **evaluate the game systems for how they mediated interaction with the purpose.** This was done by **relating them to the areas of involvement**, to see how they aimed to *capture and hold attention*, offered *variety and balance*, and *directed attention towards the purpose.*

In WLGYL, multiple stakeholders were involved and discussed these aspects with each other. In PCC, with a single stakeholder, the investigator had a more prominent role. All discussions were collaborative, however – the investigator prompted the stakeholders to consider certain topics and trigger reflection. Visual aids were used in the form of a (physical or digital) whiteboard to which both investigator and stakeholder(s) could add information (Fig. 3). Discussion was kept open for stakeholders to ask questions, amend prompts to suit their needs, or add thoughts and ideas that had not been asked about specifically. Similarly, the investigator could add or adjust questions and topics of discussion when the situation called for it.

3.4 Design Discussions

Discussions were held both online and in person, and lasted a total of several hours for each project. The primary investigator of this article held discussions with one or several stakeholders of the applied game project. The stakeholders were first introduced to the lens of attention. Then, this theory was applied to the existing design.

Discussions began with discussing and defining the existing game concepts. The stakeholders determined the games' goals and target audience. This, in turn, lead to discussion on metrics of success that could be used to determine whether the game is successful in achieving those goals. Despite both projects having gone through a significant design and development phase, discussion of these topics unearthed several points of confusion or disagreement. In particular, the question of **context** (i.e., play conditions, physical environment, and facilitators) had not been considered before. In both cases, the games were assumed to be standalone products, used by their target audience seemingly 'just because'. In PCC, this raised the question of whether healthcare workers would autonomously decide to put on a VR headset (either at home or in the workplace) to learn about person-centred care, or what would keep them from doing so. A similar discussion took place in WLGYL on the question of whether the game should be used together with a therapist. In these discussions, the point of **time and frequency** came up, that is, how often and how long the game was envisioned to be played. This had not been a point of consideration in either project, yet led to extensive discussion on the design implications of various decisions and how the context could be more meaningfully integrated into the game's design. For example, in PCC the option of integrating the game in existing (non-game) training programs teaching person-centred care was discussed. This type of group setting would make VR a less valid option, unless the functionality to project the player's view unto a screen for a group to follow along was added. In both case studies, the importance of **reflection** was an important element of these discussions as well, and whether the games would benefit from being played over multiple sessions, allowing players to put what they had learned into action and reflect on it. In WLGYL, mechanics such as a character being used to help the player reflect on their past week (in the case of weekly play sessions) were discussed, as well as other mechanics to further trigger moments of introspection by the player.

Part of mapping the original design was to establish where there was overlap between applied purpose and game systems. Both games had a clear

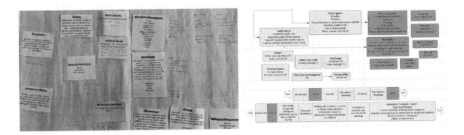

Fig. 3. Work-in-progress of the visual aids used during discussions.

overlap between the purpose and systems within the narrative scenarios - players were exposed to the educational content through the story and characters, and made choices within these sections. The areas of involvement were those of social involvement and, to an extent, gameplay. In the remainder of the design, however, the overlap was very limited.

WLGYL had included moments of exploration to the narrative sections. Although this did not have much overlap with the purpose, it did introduce rhythm into the game structure by switching attention to a different type of gameplay and allowing for moments of 'down time'. Additions similar to this were discussed in the context of PCC, to bring variety to the experience, as well as to provide players agency to learn about the characters and to make informed choices.

While both games used gameplay and social involvement to some extent, **affective involvement had either been neglected or completely undefined**. Art styles were chosen either for realism (PCC) or to be appealing to the target demographic (WLGYL). WLGYL had some thoughts on the emotions they wanted players to feel (e.g., anger and relief), but had not yet given thought to how to elicit such emotions through their visual design. PCC had not much considered the emotions of the player prior to the discussion, even though the target audience experiences deep and varied emotions when dealing with their clients. In both cases, discussions on affective involvement led to amendments to the original design. For example, WLGYL considered **how the use of the game's aesthetics could enforce the emotional experience**, by emphasising what characters (including the player) were meant to emote. For example, in addition to informing the player through text, they also considered shrinking the character portrait when they felt uncertain or insecure, or enlarging them using animations and changes in colour to convey anger.

Both games used some form of points as feedback method for the player. PCC provided the player with stars based on how well they performed in a scenario. In WLGYL, in addition to points, the player could collect emotion cards. Although these provide some information, they had no other function in the game. In many applied games, points also serve as a motivator for improvement. In both of the games studied in the context of this article, however, the stakeholders were not happy with the utilitarian approach in the original design. Through discussion, it became clear that this was, at least in part, due to the sensitive or emotional topics the games address. In this context, it felt too simple and not nuanced enough to judge a player's performance through points. The stakeholders also questioned whether players would experience the intended reflection on their own behaviour on the basis of points as a primary mechanism of feedback. In PCC, it was considered likely that, rather than reflecting on the scenarios and their content, players would simply be motivated to find the 'correct' answer to gain a good score [20].

Discussions around this topic focused on **contextualising the feedback given to the player**. In WLGYL, stakeholders decided to use the emotion cards as a gameplay mechanism, by allowing the player to use previously collected cards and 'put them into practice' in subsequent conversations. This elevated the cards from a form of feedback to an active component in the game's mechanics, allowing for further integration of the purpose. They also considered changes to the game's progress screen, visualising the extended effects of the player's decisions on how skilled they became in different coping strategies and the overall camp atmosphere.

A similar discussion took place for PCC. The consequences of person-centred care go well beyond the 'performance' of the practitioner. Rather than a simple score, decisions by the player in PCC could show the impact on the happiness of people with dementia, as well as the impact on the player character's well-being. On the other hand, spending more time with a client could negatively impact other factors, such as being able to finish other tasks, increasing pressure on colleagues. Incorporating such elements in the feedback would not only make the benefits of practising person-centred care more tangible to the player, they also could inspire reflection beyond the educational information offered by the game, and spark discussion outside the game environment (e.g., about aspects of a department preventing practitioners from working more person-centred, like time and budget). Such ideas were not completely fleshed out within the design discussions, as both the investigator and stakeholder lacked the necessary knowledge on the topic. However, such topics were considered **particularly suitable to discuss in a co-design session with the target audience and other stakeholders**.

4 Discussion

Both the case studies described in Sect. 3 started out from a consideration of mechanics, as is in line with many applied game design frameworks. This approach did not result in perfect designs. While this is expected (the first iteration of an idea is rarely the last), it also left the stakeholders unsure how to diagnose the issues and how to continue development. While different issues were diagnosed in both cases, **the lens of attention helped to identify that there was a lack of connection between the different aspects that, together, form a player's experience: gameplay, social and, particularly, affective involvement.**

The lens of attention provided a tool for reflection, that opened the door to new discussion and design ideas. Any decisions resulting from the discussions would need to be tested upon implementation. Doing so was outside the scope of this article. Games are generally developed through an iterative process. The lens of attention could be a recurring tool within applied game development, used to assess the design after each moment of testing to identify new issues and evaluate whether the previous decisions ended up working as intended.

The games discussed in this article are similar in design to other applied games developed for comparable purposes. Based on the experience gained in discussion these projects, the following preliminary guidelines can thus be proposed:

Consider Context, Including Play Time and Frequency: Even with care and consideration, it is possible that aspects of a design are not clearly defined or properly considered, or that they are simply overlooked. Of particular importance in the case studies was to consider the games in their larger context, and the potential necessity of designing moments of built-in reflection. Increased understanding of the game's context also served as inspiration for design, and a basis for structuring co-design efforts.

Map the Overlap: Mapping the game's intended elements or sections of gameplay helped to visualise where there was a lack of meaningful integration between content and game systems. This exercise in particular helped to identify where perceived issues with the existing design originated from. In the case studies, the lack of overlap was particularly noticeable in the feedback systems. It also made it clear whether and when a game could potentially benefit from (out-of-game) reflection moments, or whether the experience was potentially more monotonous than intended.

Create Balance Using Affective Involvement: The consideration of balancing the different areas of involvement flowed naturally from a mapping of the overlap. A varied experience is required to keep players engaged, able and willing to focus on the learning content. This can be done, not only through the areas of gameplay and social involvement, but that of affective involvement as well. It is recommended to search for aspects of a project's design in which that third area of attention in particular can be better utilised.

Contextualize Feedback and Integrate Context: One way of increasing the affective experience of a game is to integrate the extended effects of the game's learning content. Feedback mechanisms in particular proved to be underutilised in the case studies, despite their potential in increasing reflection and affective involvement.

Finally, it should be noted that not every applied game *needs* to provide a deeper, emotional experience. Many entertainment games are very successful aiming for simple, singular mechanics (e.g., many mobile games, such as *Candy Crush* [24]). As an extension, many applied games can benefit from similar designs, using simple mechanics, bright colours, and feedback points to motivate further play. However, applied games often tackle subjects that would benefit from approaching their design from another perspective. It is for those projects, that this article aims to be of use. The theory presented here does not point to one particular solution or is meant as a 'cook-book'-style approach to game design. Rather, it is **a perspective to be used in conjunction with other methods that should help practitioners and researchers understand the design they are working on**, and give ideas of furthering their design beyond the use of specific mechanics and points to motivate play.

5   Conclusion

This article presented the theory of attention, adapting it from how it has been used in commercial game design, and implementing it in existing theory on applied games. The result is the 'lens of attention' for applied games, based on the AGEM and other models of applied game design. The article explored practical use of the lens through two case studies, helping stakeholders apply the theory to their applied games and reporting the resulting discussions.

The stakeholders expressed positive views towards the use of the theory, stating that it **provided them with new insights and clarified previously undefined concerns about the existing design, made them consider questions and topics that had not previously occurred to them, and opened up the path to new design decisions**.

Naturally, the narrative presented in this article provides limited validation of the theory. Future efforts in this research direction will focus on formulating a practical 'how-to' on the lens of attention, so that it may be applied by more practitioners, developed further, and assessed in different types of situations and in combination with existing design methods.

Applied games find themselves 'competing' with a massive variety of entertainment titles that offer unique and engaging player experiences. Some applied goals can be achieved with fairly simple designs, using tried and established base mechanics. In order for applied games to tackle more complex problems, however, it is essential that their design methods evolve with those of their entertainment counterparts. This article provides some insight into how to achieve this, with the hope that practitioners may continue to develop it and continue to advance the practice of applied game design.

References

1. Bateman, C.: Game writing: Narrative skills for videogames. Bloomsbury Publishing, USA (2021)
2. Bateman, C., Boon, R.: 21st Century Game Design (game development series). Charles River Media, Inc. (2005)
3. Bellotti, F., et al.: Designing serious games for education: from pedagogical principles to game mechanisms. In: Proceedings of the 5th European Conference on Games Based Learning, pp. 26–34. University of Athens Greece (2011)
4. Bogost, I.: Why gamification is bullshit. Gameful wWrld: Approach. Issues Appli. **65**, 65–79 (2015)

5. Calleja, G.: In-game: From immersion to incorporation. MIT Press (2011)
6. CDProjekt Red: The Witcher 3: Wild Hunt. [Nintendo Switch, PlayStation 4, PlayStation 5, Xbox One, Xbox Series X/S, Microsoft Windows] (2015)
7. Chee, C.M., Wong, D.H.T.: Affluent gaming experience could fail gamification in education: a review. IETE Tech. Rev. **34**(6), 593–597 (2017)
8. ConcernedApe: Stardew Valley. [Microsoft Windows, macOS, Linux, PlayStation 4, Xbox One, Nintendo Switch, PlayStation Vita, iOS, Android] (2016)
9. De Freitas, S., Jarvis, S.: A framework for developing serious games to meet learner needs. In: Interservice/Industry Training, Simulation, and Education Conference (I/ITSEC) (2006)
10. De Freitas, S., Neumann, T.: The use of 'exploratory learning'for supporting immersive learning in virtual environments. Comput. Educ. **52**(2), 343–352 (2009)
11. Fazio, S., Pace, D., Flinner, J., Kallmyer, B.: The fundamentals of person-centered care for individuals with dementia. Gerontologist **58**(suppl_1), S10–S19 (2018)
12. Fisch, S.M.: Making educational computer games "educational". In: Proceedings of the 2005 Conference on Interaction Design and Children, pp. 56–61 (2005)
13. Fisher, A., Kloos, H.: Development of selective sustained attention: The role of executive functions. In: Executive Function in Preschool-age Children: Integrating Measurement, Neurodevelopment, and Translational Research, pp. 215–237 (2016)
14. FromSoftware: Elden Ring. [Playstation 4, Playstation 5, Microsoft Windows, Xbox One, Xbox Series X/S] (2022)
15. Gómez-Maureira, M.A., Kniestedt, I., Van Duijn, M., Rieffe, C., Plaat, A.: Level design patterns that invoke curiosity-driven exploration: An empirical study across multiple conditions. In: Proceedings of the ACM on Human-Computer Interaction 5(CHIPLAY), pp. 1–32 (2021)
16. Grund, C.K.: How games and game elements facilitate learning and motivation: A literature review. In: INFORMATIK 2015 (2015)
17. Hamari, J., Koivisto, J., Sarsa, H.: Does gamification work?-a literature review of empirical studies on gamification. In: 2014 47th Hawaii International Conference on System Sciences, pp. 3025–3034. IEEE (2014)
18. Hew, K.F., Huang, B., Chu, K.W.S., Chiu, D.K.: Engaging asian students through game mechanics: Findings from two experiment studies. Comput. Educ. **92**, 221–236 (2016)
19. Hookham, G., Nesbitt, K.: A systematic review of the definition and measurement of engagement in serious games. In: Proceedings of the Australasian Computer Science Week Multiconference, pp. 1–10 (2019)
20. Hung, A.C.Y.: A critique and defense of gamification. J. Interact. Online Learn. 15, 57–72 (2017)
21. Karth, I.: Ergodic agency: how play manifests understanding. In: Engaging with Videogames: Play, Theory and Practice, pp. 205–216. Brill (2014)
22. Kiili, K.: Content creation challenges and flow experience in educational games: The it-emperor case. Internet High. Educ. **8**(3), 183–198 (2005)
23. Kiili, K., De Freitas, S., Arnab, S., Lainema, T.: The design principles for flow experience in educational games. Proc. Comput. Sci. **15**, 78–91 (2012)
24. King: Candy Crush Saga. [iOS, Android, Microsoft Windows Phone, Microsoft Windows, macOS, Linux] (2011)
25. Kniestedt, I., Lefter, I., Lukosch, S., Brazier, F.M.: Re-framing engagement for applied games: A conceptual framework. Entertain. Comput. **41**, 100475 (2022). https://doi.org/10.1016/j.entcom.2021.100475, https://www.sciencedirect.com/science/article/pii/S1875952121000720

26. Lemarchand, R.: Attention, not immersion: Making your games better with psychology and playtesting, the uncharted way (2012). https://www.gdcvault.com/play/1015464/Attention-Not-Immersion-Making-Your
27. Lemarchand, R.: A Playful Production Process: For Game Designers (and Everyone). MIT Press (2021)
28. Libbi, C.: When life gives you lemons: designing a game with and for autistic girls, Aug 2021. http://essay.utwente.nl/88356/
29. Malliarakis, C., Satratzemi, M., Xinogalos, S.: Designing educational games for computer programming: A holistic framework. Electr. J. of e-Learn. **12**(3), 281–298 (2014)
30. Naughty Dog: Uncharted 3: Drake's Deception. [Playstation 3] (2011)
31. Nintendo EAD: Animal Crossing. [Nintendo 64, Nintendo Gamecube] (2001)
32. Nintendo EAD: The Legend of Zelda: Breath of the Wild. [Nintendo Switch, Nintendo Wii U] (2017)
33. O'Donnell, B.F.: Forms of attention and attentional disorders. In: Seminars in Speech and Language, vol. 23, pp. 099–106 (2002)
34. Orland, K.: Putting elden ring's 12 million sales in context (2012). https://arstechnica.com/gaming/2022/03/putting-elden-rings-12-million-sales-in-context/
35. Parnandi, A., Gutierrez-Osuna, R.: A comparative study of game mechanics and control laws for an adaptive physiological game. J. Multimodal User Interfaces **9**(1), 31–42 (2015)
36. Camps-Ortueta, I., González-Calero, P.A., Quiroga, M.A., Gómez-Martín, P.P.: Measuring preferences in game mechanics: Towards personalized chocolate-covered broccoli. In: van der Spek, E., Göbel, S., Do, E.Y.-L., Clua, E., Baalsrud Hauge, J. (eds.) ICEC-JCSG 2019. LNCS, vol. 11863, pp. 15–27. Springer, Cham (2019). https://doi.org/10.1007/978-3-030-34644-7_2
37. Schell, J.: The Art of Game Design: A book of lenses. CRC Press (2008)
38. Sicart, M.: Defining game mechanics. Game Stud. 8(2) (2008)
39. Strickland, D.: Witcher 3's '40 second rule' kept players engaged (2017). https://www.tweaktown.com/news/59420/witcher-3s-40-second-rule-kept-players-engaged/
40. Styles, E.: The psychology of attention. Psychology Press (2006)
41. Sweetser, P., Wyeth, P.: Gameflow: a model for evaluating player enjoyment in games. Comput. Entertain. (CIE) **3**(3), 3–3 (2005)
42. Thatgamecompany: Flow. [Playstation 3, Playstation 4] (2006)
43. Thatgamecompany: Flower. [Playstation 3, Playstation 4, iOS, Microsoft Windows] (2009)
44. Tsita, C., Satratzemi, M.: Conceptual factors for the design of serious games. In: Gentile, M., Allegra, M., Söbke, H. (eds.) GALA 2018. LNCS, vol. 11385, pp. 232–241. Springer, Cham (2019). https://doi.org/10.1007/978-3-030-11548-7_22
45. Ustwo: Monument Valley. [Android, iOS, Microsoft Windows, Microsoft Windows Phone] (2014)
46. Yusoff, A., Crowder, R., Gilbert, L., Wills, G.: A conceptual framework for serious games. In: 2009 Ninth IEEE International Conference on Advanced Learning Technologies, pp. 21–23. IEEE (2009)

Exergames in the GAME2AWE Platform with Dynamic Difficulty Adjustment

Michail Danousis, Christos Goumopoulos$^{(\boxtimes)}$ [ID], and Alexandros Fakis

Department of Information and Communication Systems Engineering, University of the Aegean, 83200 Karlovassi, Samos, Greece
{mdanousis,goumop,alfa}@aegean.gr

Abstract. Exergames can motivate the elderly to exercise as long as they derive pleasure from them. Therefore, the different needs and expectations of older people must be first understood while taking into account their different characteristics both in exergame design phase and actual playing time. In this paper, the GAME2AWE platform is introduced that combines hardware and intelligent software to create personalized gaming experiences aimed at improving the motor and cognitive functionality of the elderly. This work focuses, in particular, on dynamic adaptation mechanisms specified to adjust the difficulty or challenge of a game, according to the players' performance. Dynamic difficulty adjustment provides a solution to configuring the variables that define the difficulty of a game in order to compensate for the abilities of a particular player during a game session. Capturing game and player related information during the gameplay creates datasets which are then used to develop models for estimating the satisfaction of the player while playing. These models are then used to adjust the difficulty variables in order to achieve optimal user satisfaction. The main proposition regarding the model construction is that the prediction of fun can be defined as a function of different attributes which a machine learning method can learn.

Keywords: Exergames · Dynamic difficulty adjustment · Fall risk · Elderly

1 Introduction

Physical activity plays a key role in preventing falls as it reduces the loss of muscle mass and strength and stimulates the body's control. In cases of injury, it is the most effective means of recovery in combination with clinical treatment. In addition, cognitive improvements and mental benefits for the elderly can be achieved through physical activities. Studies show that weekly physical activity can help prevent mild cognitive impairment or prevent its progression to dementia [1].

The technological advancements integrated in devices supporting exercising though games, i.e., exergaming, offer quite promising possibilities for the enhancement of the motor function as well as the cognitive functions, elements very important for the support of the elderly in their daily activities. Exergames using motion detection sensors can provide balance exercises for seniors by implementing games that require appropriate

© IFIP International Federation for Information Processing 2022
Published by Springer Nature Switzerland AG 2022
B. Göbl et al. (Eds.): ICEC 2022, LNCS 13477, pp. 214–223, 2022.
https://doi.org/10.1007/978-3-031-20212-4_17

postures and movement by the player. Similarly, balance platforms equipped with sensors can detect physical strength and visualize balance performance by providing real-time feedback on controlling posture and weight shifting of the elderly [2].

A related study concluded that a six-week training plan on a dynamic balance control platform helped to improve functional balance due to the intervention program by using visual feedback to posture control [3]. Posture control determines a person's ability to maintain an upright posture during a movement. A similar study found that seniors who participated in a six-week exercise program with exergames specifically designed to prevent falls and using motion monitoring systems using Kinect technology could reduce the risk of falls by enhancing overall balance, physical strength and improvement in motor functions [4]. Another study reported a virtual reality treadmill program in which patients who had a stroke completed three 30-min sessions per week for a period of four weeks [5]. Participants showed improvement in balance, gait speed and maximum walking duration.

Although there are plenty of studies that report various positive effects of playing exergames by the elderly, the involved applications typically demonstrate a static approach regarding their content which often leads to foreseeable and neutral gameplay. Pre-gameplay configuration is used which refers to adjusting or modifying the game parameters before the start of each session to adapt the game to the patient's capabilities. In many games, this configuration implies the ability to select a level of difficulty. On the other hand, adaptivity during the gameplay is less explored in practice although it can make games more interesting and personalized.

In this paper we introduce the GAME2AWE platform [6] that combines hardware and intelligent software to create personalized gaming experiences aimed at improving the motor and cognitive functionality of the elderly. The GAME2AWE approach embraces the viewpoint that exercises through games provide significant health benefits for the elderly. Essentially, reinforcing strength and balance through exergames is an effective action to prevent falls. This work focuses, in particular, on dynamic adaptation mechanisms specified to adjust the difficulty or challenge of a game, according to the users' performance in the game. Game performance can be measured, for example, based on in-game scores, completion time and failures.

2 GAME2AWE Platform

2.1 Scope

The GAME2AWE platform is developed in the context of the homonymous research project with the aim to support physical activities through games (exergames) that are suitable for seniors by integrating multiple enabling technologies and intelligent software to create adaptable gaming experiences. The platform combines multiple enabling technologies in terms of Kinect Motion Sensor, Virtual/Augmented Reality and Smart Floor technology, thus providing the user with a greater variety of interactions and exercises. A research study will investigate and validate the effectiveness of the GAME2AWE platform in terms of enhancing physical endurance and reducing the risk of falling among older people. The study will compare exercising with the GAME2AWE platform versus standard care.

Figure 1 illustrates the GAME2AWE system architecture. The Device Layer is responsible for the communication of the external devices with the system. Data collected by the devices are dispatched to the Data Layer for preprocessing and structuring in order to be used by machine learning algorithms. The datasets assembled are then used by the Analysis Layer for the purpose of accepting or rejecting an activity. In the case of the Kinect technology, this layer evaluates the data based on the recorded activities stored in training files using pattern matching algorithms to assess if the user is performing a known activity. It evaluates also a detection confidence and if this is above a defined threshold, it allows the activity to be performed inside the game. In the event of acceptance, activity evidence is perceived by the player via Game Mechanics. The game mechanisms inform the system about the progress of the player in the gameplay in order to make the corresponding adaptation of the game parameters. The Adaptation Layer provides the system intelligence to create adaptable gaming experiences by adjusting the parameters and elements of each game. The Interaction Layer updates graphical elements at the user interface that provide useful/helpful information to the player.

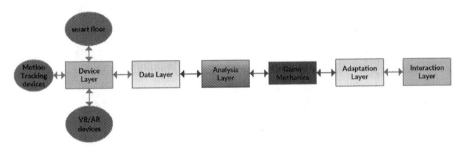

Fig. 1. System architecture.

The Adaptation Layer (AL) is the focus in this work. AL is responsible for tailoring the parameters and elements of each game. A key concern in AL design is to be able to modify the elements that have to do with the difficulty of the game. In addition to the difficulty, AL will determine various elements that play a subordinate role in the game having to do with the emotions they evoke in the player and consequently with the overall experience. Since physical and motor skills as well as cognitive abilities vary among older users, exergames should be able to adjust the difficulty of the game according to their individual skill level. As a result, in the long term the motivation of the players will be enhanced because the game will have the element of challenge. However, this challenge should not leave the players disappointed, or in other words, the goal of the game should be achievable and fun to be fulfilled. An example of how to change the difficulty of a game is to display random components to force players to act differently each time they are playing it.

2.2 Methodology

The design and development of the GAME2AWE platform is based on the principles of human-centered and participatory design, as this approach is particularly suitable for the development of exergames targeting the elderly [7]. The essence of participatory design is the involvement of the end user from the beginning of the development process, organizing a continuous and active user involvement that guides the entire design and development cycle. Based on this approach, the user participates not only as an evaluator when needed, but also as an active member of the development team. This approach is repetitive, where design is subject to evaluation and review at every stage of the development process.

For the development of exergames, an initial list of potential games was assembled in the form of themes, basic features, integration of appropriate exercises and operating rules after analyzing the relevant literature and leveraging on our own relevant experiences [8]. Subsequently, representative scenarios from two game themes ("Life on a Farm" and "Fun Park Tour") were selected to meet the project objectives and presented for feedback to end users and healthcare experts within a focus group. The data collected from the workings of the focus group were analyzed to derive the basic guidelines and to record issues that need attention in the design and implementation of the games [9].

2.3 Example Games

Two example exergames from the "Life on a Farm" theme are presented and will be used also for the discussion on dynamic difficulty adjustment. Both games have been implemented using the Microsoft Kinect motion sensor which allows the user to interact with the computer through the use of gestures, movements and voice commands [10].

Fruit Harvest

The purpose of this game is to harvest as many ripe fruits as possible (e.g., apples, peaches, pomegranates) in a given period of time and place them in baskets on the ground. The game mechanics incorporate a composite movement that serves the purpose of fruit harvesting. The player raises the right hand high to reach the fruit and lowers it to leave the fruit in the basket found on the left side (Fig. 2). Alternatively, the player can raise the left hand to reach the fruit and leave it in the basket on the right side. The avatar displayed on the screen is controlled by the players' motions.

When the fruit appears on the tree it will be green which means it is not ready for harvest. Ripe fruits for harvest will be red. On the other hand, if the ripe fruit stays on the tree for a long time it will rot (turn black) and fall to the ground. Points will be awarded depending on how many fruits the player has collected and placed in the basket. Points will be wasted if green fruits are collected or if the fruits are left to rot.

The level of difficulty will determine the rate at which the fruits will appear and ripen on the tree. A higher level of difficulty will result in more fruits appearing on the tree at the same time and at a faster rate of ripening. An additional challenge at a higher level of difficulty is to have two baskets (in the right and left of the player) and to determine where the picked fruit should be placed. This approach provides on the one hand the potential for cognitive training and on the other hand the possibility for a greater variety of movements and exercises.

This game allows multiple players to participate where players can either work together to collect fruits or compete over who can pick the most fruits. Assistance is provided to the players whenever it is necessary. For example, if the player is idle for a long time, helpful animations are displayed to demonstrate the movements that are awaited to be performed.

The user interface of the game is kept simple and only the essential information and elements are displayed. Consistency is also important and thus the points earned are always displayed on the top right of the screen, whereas the vitality bar is shown on the left side. The latter is a visual element that reflects the physical activity progress based on the movements performed in the gameplay. While harvesting a green fruit negatively affects the cognitive assessment and the earned points at the same time this movement is a physical activity and is reflected positively on the vitality bar.

Fig. 2. "Fruit Harvest" and "Healthy Garden" game screenshots from the "Life on a Farm" theme based on the Kinect motion sensor.

Healthy Garden

In this scenario the player is asked to handle various insects which can either benefit or harm the plants in a garden (Fig. 2). The player is asked to neutralize the harmful insects with stepping movements (i.e., left/right sideway steps and forward/backward steps). Stepping exercises are appropriate for GAME2AWE since it is known that the performance in such exercises can be a good predictor of falls. Furthermore, a repeated training program with stepping exercises for the elderly can improve their balance.

During the game several insects appear on the screen starting with one at a time. Insects can be either useful (e.g., Virgin's pony, bees, wasps, ladybugs, earthworms) or harmful (e.g. fly, dacus, locusts, cockroaches, beetles, mites). Thus, the player depending on the mode of the gameplay is asked to recognize them. The avatar displayed on the screen is a pair of shoes that are moving according to the player's stepping movements. The user interface displays the points and the vitality bar in the same way explained for the "Fruit Harvest" game. Moreover, this game may provide a view of the next insect to appear depending on the difficulty level.

Insects move in different directions and at different positions each time, either to the right or left of the player, or behind or in front of her. The player must perform appropriate stepping movements, either to avoid or to neutralize the insects. The game difficulty depends on factors such as the insect appearance frequency, the insect appearance position and insect category.

3 Dynamic Difficulty Adjustment

3.1 Background

Dynamic difficulty adjustment (DDA) entails the integration of in-game mechanisms that respond to a particular player's abilities over the course of a game session [11]. To maintain balance in the game, DDA approaches should align with a game's fundamental design goals with respect to the experience of a player. To adjust the difficulty of a game in this way, an input is required, which is usually some information linked directly or indirectly with the player. Based on the nature of the input two main categories of DDA techniques are examined in this work:

- **Performance based DDA**: This technique employs game performance metrics as an input for the dynamic adjustment strategies. Performance metrics of a game can be elements like the score, the levels played, the items that have been unlocked, or any other element that the game designer has added into the game that can track the user's performance in some way.
- **Emotional based DDA**: This technique employs the emotional state of the user as input. Extracting the emotional state of a player is a challenging topic. Methods for extracting the emotional state include facial expression recognition [12] and physiological signals (e.g., heart rate, skin conductance level, skin conductance response frequency, and electroencephalogram) [13].

As an example of the first technique, an adaptive mechanism was developed to tune predetermined game parameters in real time in order to improve the "entertainment value" for the player when playing the game [14]. The entertainment value has been extracted from a sample of players that participated in an experimental study via a questionnaire. Each of the participants played 2 games that varied in terms of speed and curiosity. The final dataset consisted of 9 performance-based attributes (score, reaction times, etc.) derived from 137 games and one target class specifying the "entertainment value". After creating the dataset, a machine learning model was trained with the purpose of classifying a player's preference with respect to speed and curiosity. The results showed a model that can predict the preferences of a player during play with an accuracy close to 74%. This model's predictions were used to adjust the speed and curiosity variables during gameplay. The participants on average stated that the adaptive version of the game was more preferable.

As an example of the second technique, a study was performed using the player's reported emotions during the play [13]. The emotions were associated with electroencephalogram and peripheral signals that were extracted during the same playing period. After forming the dataset, a machine learning classifier was trained to be able to detect emotions using the physiological signals with satisfactory accuracy.

3.2 GAME2AWE Approach

Our approach on DDA is applied to the exergames in the "Life on a Farm" theme using the Kinect motion sensor of the GAME2AWE platform. Our DDA method is organized into two parts. The first part focuses on performance based DDA strategies, using as input game data such as scores, frequency of actions, success rate of actions, and others. The second part focuses on emotion based DDA strategies using facial emotion recognition as input. In both parts a prediction model of "Fun" in the gameplay is built, using datasets that are composed of input variables as attributes and the results of two-alternative forced choice (2-AFC) questions regarding "fun" in the gameplay [15], as the label. In both cases an algorithm is built which is tuning the game difficulty (challenge) and predictability variables to maximize players' "Fun", as inspired by a related research [14].

Taking the "Fruit Harvest" game, as an example, the notions of challenge and predictability are defined based on two parameters that are associated with the game mechanics. Challenge is defined by the speed with which the fruits in the tree are changing their state. This is actually controlled by a parameter named "speed", which determines the time in seconds between state changes. Predictability, on the other hand, is defined in terms of the side (or sides) of the tree, that the fruits appear, before changing their state. The parameter controlling this behavior is named "mode". In this game, mode has 3 possible states that represent right, left, and both sides respectively.

Other games, such as the "Healthy Garden" game, use the same notions of challenge and predictability with a different interpretation. Challenge is defined by the speed that an insect appears and disappears in the garden. The speed parameter determines the time from the entrance of an insect to its exit. Predictability (i.e., the mode parameter) is defined, in this case, by the side of the garden that the insect appears (left, right, top and bottom).

As mentioned previously, our first goal is to find a way to predict the "Fun" in the game, as the players are playing. The approach is to initially create a dataset, suitable for training a machine learning model that predicts "Fun" during gameplay, based on in-game performance metrics. This means that the dataset should contain correlations between the performance attributes and the label so that the model can discover them. The performance metrics defined for the example games are: i) *Points (Pts)*; ii) *Vitality Bar percentage (VB%)*; iii) *Correct Actions (CA)*; iv) *Incorrect Actions (IA)*; v) *No Actions when needed (NA)*; vi) *Average Reaction Time ($\mu(Rt)$)*; vii) *Standard Deviation Reaction Time ($\sigma(Rt)$)*; viii)*Successful movements per second (SM)*; ix) *Unsuccessful movements per second (UM)*; x) *IDLE time percentage (IDL%)*.

In the "Fruit Harvest" game, the speed that the fruits change states was defined as the challenge variable, because the sooner the state changes the harder it is for the player to perform the correct actions required timely. Furthermore, the mode of the game was defined as the predictability variable, since this game parameter defines the variety of states and actions the gameplay involves, and thus is associated with increasing or decreasing the predictability factor of the game. A similar approach is also followed for the "Healthy Garden" game with respect to the challenge and predictability variables specification in the corresponding dataset.

During a focus group workshop that was conducted to validate the exergame prototypes [9], the DDA approach was also studied. Each participant was asked to play a pair of games that varied both in challenge and predictability variables for both "Fruit Harvest" and "Healthy Garden" scenarios. After both games were played for both its variations, participants were asked to answer a simple question regarding which of the games was more fun, following the two-alternative forced choice method (2-AFC). Once these responses were paired with the game performance data that were gathered during each game, the final dataset was created. The dataset consisted of the defined game performance metrics, the variables of *Challenge (Chl)* and *Predictability (Prd)*, and the response of the user regarding "*FUN*", as the label (1 = Fun / 0 = Not Fun). An example sample of this dataset is shown in Table 1.

Table 1. Example sample of the dataset for the performance based DDA.

Pts	VB%	CA	IA	NA	M (Rt)	Σ (Rt)	SM	UM	IDL%	Chl	Prd	FUN
25	56	15	7	3	0.97	1.2	26	4	47	8	1	1
20	40	12	8	5	0.95	1.3	23	9	40	9	2	0

A second dataset was assembled to experimentally practice the DDA method that is based on the emotional state of the user. For this purpose, the new "Azure Kinect" sensor is exploited which besides offering body tracking services for capturing gestures and motions it also provides advanced functionality through the "Azure Cognitive Services" platform. Adding cognitive services allows detection and identification of emotions. In particular, leveraging on the "Face API", 8 different emotions (i.e., "*anger*", "*contempt*", "*disgust*", "*fear*", "*happiness*", "*neutral*", "*sadness*" and "*surprise*") can be extracted from the player during the play time. Each one of these emotions can be extracted, along with an accuracy value that ranges from 0 to 1 and represents the confidence with which the face API produced the prediction for a particular recognized emotion. In this context, an example sample of the dataset is shown in Table 2. The dataset, as in the case of performance based DDA, contains also the variables of *Challenge (Chl)* and *Predictability (Prd)*, and the label parameter "*FUN*".

Table 2. Example sample of the dataset for the emotional based DDA.

Anger	Contempt	Disgust	Fear	Happiness	Neutral	Sadness	Surprise	Chl	Prd	FUN
0	0	0	0	1	0	0	0.3	8	1	1
1	0	0	0	0	0.6	0	0	9	2	0

3.3 Building the Fun Prediction Model

The Fun prediction model provides the basis for the DDA approach discussed. An Artificial Neural Network (ANN) model, following the Sequential Feature Selection technique, will be defined. In particular, a learning approach will be used that exploits a Genetic Algorithm to evolve the ANN topology, where vectors of ANN connection weights represent the chromosomes. In this process, a fitting function will be used by the learning mechanism to evaluate the difference between the subjective value of fun as reported by the players and the output value of the model. The main proposition regarding the model construction is that the prediction of fun can be defined as a function of different attributes which a machine learning method can learn.

The dataset for the performance based DDA (Table 1) contains attributes that are linked to the performance of the player, as well as the variables *Challenge* (*Chl*) and *Predictability* (*Prd*), which represent the parameters of speed and mode of the games. These parameters are the only ones that are directly controllable by the game mechanics. This observation, along with the fact that the ANN model that predicts the value of fun based on the dataset attributes, is a differentiable function, leads to the conclusion that using partial derivatives, i.e., the direction to which the *Chl* (i.e., speed parameter) and *Prd* (i.e., mode parameter) should be adjusted, in order to increase the overall fun prediction, can be calculated. Thus, using the gradient ascent algorithm and some predefined values concerning the magnitude of the change in the controllable parameters and the frequency of the change, a DDA algorithm can be deployed. Such an algorithm will be deployed and tested on a sufficient scale during the final evaluation of the GAME2AWE platform in the near future. A similar technique can be also applied with respect to the dataset built for emotional based DDA (Table 2).

4   Conclusions

The GAME2AWE platform aims to deliver exergames that are entertaining and health beneficial to the elderly so that improvements on motor and cognitive functions can be achieved in the most efficient way. The end users point of view is very important regarding the design and implementation of the exergames and this has been resolved following a participatory design approach by involving all relevant stakeholders. Another crucial factor for the successful adoption of the exergames by the targeted users is to match game challenges to the player's skill level during playing time. The adaptation layer of the GAME2AWE platform architecture provides the system intelligence to create adaptable gaming experiences by adjusting the parameters and elements of each game. In this paper, suitable dynamic difficulty adjustment techniques have been specified and a roadmap for implementing an algorithm that can adjust the value of key parameters controlling the game difficulty based on a fun prediction model has been outlined.

Acknowledgements. This research has been co-financed by the European Regional Development Fund of the European Union and Greek national funds through the Operational Program Competitiveness, Entrepreneurship and Innovation, under the call RESEARCH – CREATE – INNOVATE (project code:T2EDK-04785).

References

1. Lautenschlager, N.T., Cox, K., Kurz, A.F.: Physical activity and mild cognitive impairment and Alzheimer's disease. Curr. Neurol. Neurosci. Rep. **10**(5), 352–358 (2010)
2. Martinho, D., Carneiro, J., Corchado, J.M., Marreiros, G.: A systematic review of gamification techniques applied to elderly care. Artif. Intell. Rev. **53**(7), 4863–4901 (2020)

3. Nicholson, V.P., McKean, M., Lowe, J., Fawcett, C., Burkett, B.: Six weeks of unsupervised Nintendo Wii Fit gaming is effective at improving balance in independent older adults. J. Aging Phys. Act. **23**(1), 153–158 (2015)
4. Van Diest, M., Stegenga, J., Wörtche, H.J., Verkerke, G.J., Postema, K., Lamoth, C.J.: Exergames for unsupervised balance training at home: a pilot study in healthy older adults. Gait Posture **44**, 161–167 (2016)
5. Kim, N., Lee, B., Kim, Y., Min, W.: Effects of virtual reality treadmill training on community balance confidence and gait in people post-stroke: a randomized controlled trial. J. Experimental Stroke Translational Medicine **9**(1), 1–7 (2016)
6. GAME2AWE Homepage, https://game2awe.aegean.gr/, last accessed 2022/7/12
7. Brox, E., Konstantinidis, S.T., Evertsen, G.: User-centered design of serious games for older adults following 3 years of experience with exergames for seniors: a study design. JMIR serious games **5**(1), e6254 (2017)
8. Chartomatsidis, M., Goumopoulos, C.: A balance training game tool for seniors using Microsoft Kinect and 3D worlds. In: Proceedings of the 5th International Conference on Information and Communication Technologies for Ageing Well and e-Health, pp. 135–145 (2019)
9. Goumopoulos, C., Chartomatsidis, M., Koumanakos, G.: Participatory design of fall prevention exergames using multiple enabling technologies. In: Proceedings of the 8th International Conference on Information and Communication Technologies for Ageing Well and e-Health, pp. 70–80 (2022)
10. Tashev, I.: Kinect development kit: a toolkit for gesture-and speech-based human-machine interaction. IEEE Signal Process. Mag. **30**(5), 129–131 (2013)
11. Lopes, R., Bidarra, R.: Adaptivity challenges in games and simulations: a survey. IEEE Trans. Computational Intelligence AI in Games **3**(2), 85–99 (2011)
12. Ninaus, M., et al.: Increased emotional engagement in game-based learning–a machine learning approach on facial emotion detection data. Comput. Educ. **142**, 103641 (2019)
13. Chanel, G., Rebetez, C., Bétrancourt, M., Pun, T.: Emotion assessment from physiological signals for adaptation of game difficulty. IEEE Trans. Systems, Man, Cybernetics-Part A: Syst. Humans **41**(6), 1052–1063 (2011)
14. Yannakakis, G.N., Hallam, J.: Real-time game adaptation for optimizing player satisfaction. IEEE Trans. Computational Intelligence AI Games **1**(2), 121–133 (2009)
15. Malone, T.W.: What makes things fun to learn? Heuristics for designing instructional computer games. In: Proceedings of the 3rd ACM SIGSMALL symposium and the first SIGPC symposium on Small systems, pp. 162–169 (1980)

Art and Entertainment

Improvement of Deep Learning Technology to Create 3D Model of Fluid Art

Mai Cong Hung[1(✉)], Mai Xuan Trang[2(✉)], Akihiro Yamada[3], Naoko Tosa[4], and Ryohei Nakatsu[4]

[1] Osaka University, Osaka, Japan
mai.cong.hung.t3f@osaka-u.ac.jp
[2] Phenikaa University, Hanoi, Vietnam
trang.maixuan@phenikaa-uni.edu.vn
[3] Toppan Inc., Tokyo, Japan
akihiro_1.yamada@toppan.co.jp
[4] Kyoto University, Kyoto, Japan
tosa.naoko.5c@kyoto-u.ac.jp, ryohei.nakatsu@design.kyoto-u.ac.jp

Abstract. Art is an essential part of the entertainment. As 3D entertainment such as 3D games is a trend, it is an exciting topic how to create 3D artworks from 2D artworks. In this work, we investigate the 3D reconstruction problem of the artwork called "Sound of Ikebana," which is created by shooting fluid phenomena using a high-speed camera and can create organic, sophisticated, and complex forms. Firstly, we used the Phase Only Correlation method to capture the artwork's point cloud based on the images captured by multiple high-speed cameras. Then we create a 3D model by a deep learning-based approach from the 2D Sound of Ikebana images. Our result shows that we can apply deep learning techniques to improve the reconstruction of 3D modeling from 2D images with highly complicated forms.

Keywords: Fluid art · Sound of Ikebana · 3D reconstruction · Differentiable rendering network · CycleGAN

1 Introduction

Art has been closely connected to human mentality and has been at the center of entertainment since ancient times. In entertainment such as games, the shift from 2D games to 3D games is a recent trend. Therefore, even in the area of art, how to create 3D artworks from 2D artworks such as paintings is an exciting research theme. We tackle this issue in this paper.

One of the authors, Naoko Tosa, created fluid art based on fluid phenomena. One of her representative fluid artworks, called "Sound of Ikebana [1]," is a collection of video artwork originated by her. The artwork is created by shooting Ikebana-like forms, generated by giving sound vibration to various types of liquid, by a high-speed camera of

---

M. C. Hung, M. X. Trang---Equally contributed as co-first authors

B. Göbl et al. (Eds.): ICEC 2022, LNCS 13477, pp. 227–237, 2022.
https://doi.org/10.1007/978-3-031-20212-4_18

2000 frames/second. She tried to express numerous color variations and cultural stories by utilizing liquid materials.

Although the Sound of Ikebana is a 2D video, obtaining the 3D Sound of Ikebana would give a complete and exciting view of the fluid art. However, the current 3D scanning tools cannot capture the high-speed motion of the fluid flows with high quality.

To reconstruct the 3D model of the Sound of Ikebana, we decided to use the generative models in deep learning. Breakthrough technology in generative models of deep learning has been named Generative Adversarial Networks (GANs) [2]. GANs model includes a generator G that learns to generate new data. At the same time, a discriminator D tries to identify whether the generated data lies in the distribution of the latent space or not. The training process can converge even with a small number of training data by performing learning as a zero-sum game between these two networks. Many GANs variations have been developed by modifying the basic configuration. It is natural to consider applying GANs to 3D generative problems. For instance, one might refer to pioneering works on 3D GANs in constructing 3D models of familiar objects [3].

For artworks like the Sound of Ikebana, the absence of 3D training models requires a different technique. The only training data we have are 2D photos, and we need a 2D-to-3D GAN model instead. For a pioneer work of this approach, we refer to the work of GANverse3D [4]. GANverse3D architecture consists of two neural networks that render images. The first one is StyleGAN [5], which constructs a training dataset based on photos of the main object (vehicles, birds, horses…) taken from different angles to generate multi-view images from an input image. The obtained sets of photos from various angles were fed into an inverse graphics neural network that extracts a 3D model of an object from 2D input images.

In the previous work on the 3D modeling of Sound of Ikebana, Tosa et al. obtained the point cloud data of the front-view surface via the Phase Only Correlation method [6]. In this study, we improve the results via a deep learning approach inspired by the idea of GANverse3D. We perform the deformation from an initial untextured mesh into the targeted 3D Sound of Ikebana using the differentiable rendering network DIB-R [7]. In the process, the 2D Sound of Ikebana stylized images of the back-view and side-view of the mesh generated by CycleGAN [8], a GANs variation with the style transfer capability, is used.

This paper consists of the following sections. In Sect. 2, the concept and creation process of the Sound of Ikebana, a fluid art created by Naoko Tosa, one of the authors. Section 3 details the generation of the 3D Sound of Ikebana, including its process and the obtained result. Moreover, Sect. 4 gives the conclusion.

2   Sound of Ikebana

Sound of Ikebana is a media art creation based on fluid dynamics. Fluid dynamics is a physics discipline that studies the behavior of fluid flows. The fluid flows have some properties that inspire artists to create new art. Firstly, the primary reason for this is that the fluid flows are flexible and natural. Therefore, artists might use them to represent various kinds of shapes. Secondly, fluid dynamics is uncertain even if the initial conditions are fixed. Artists might enjoy the unexpected phenomena or chance phenomena of the fluid flows to incorporate something unexpected into their artworks.

Sound of Ikebana is a typical example of fluid arts created by Naoko Tosa, one of the authors. The artist used sound vibration as the primary method to develop fluid arts. Figure 1 illustrates the Sound of Ikebana generation system. A speaker is set with its corn on top, thin rubber is put on it, and viscous fluid such as color paint is put on the thin rubber. Then, the sound vibrates the corn, and the liquid jumps up, creating various forms. At the same time, the created forms are shot by a high-speed camera with 2000 frames per second.

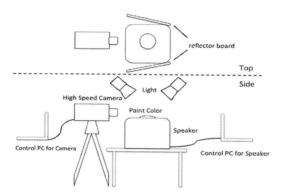

Fig. 1. Sound of Ikebana generation system [1]

While the sound vibration from the speaker controls the initial condition, various color materials make beautiful forms. By carefully choosing the quantity of raw paint and the sound source, the artist successfully created fluid forms that represent the beauty of Japanese Ikebana. The color variations are also considered to express the philosophy of Japanese art, as specific colors are used to represent flowers in each Japanese season and the "Wabi-Sabi" aesthetics in Japanese culture. (Wabi-Sabi is the Japanese sense of beauty, which means "beauty within simplicity.") Figure 2 shows several images from the artwork.

A high-speed camera is an essential tool in this work. As the fluid flows last only for a significantly short time, the artist used a camera of 2000 frames per second to record the fluid flow. After that, the captured video is replayed at a speed of 30 frames per second, or 67 times slower than the actual time. Then people can enjoy beautiful forms that their naked eyes cannot see. In other words, the recorded videos can visualize hidden beauty in physical or natural phenomena, which we cannot enjoy without high technology.

An interesting issue is why Naoko Tosa named the video art "Ikebana," a traditional Japanese flower arrangement. She probably found a similarity between Ikebana and her artwork based on her artistic intuition. Figure 3 shows the similarity between the artwork and the primary form of Ikebana. The primary form of Ikebana is an asymmetric triangle that connects three points of different heights, "core," "sub," and "body" (Fig. 3: left). It is interesting to note that the shapes in the Sound of Ikebana often resemble the form of Ikebana (Fig. 3: right).

Fig. 2. Examples of the Sound of Ikebana by Naoko Tosa

Japanese artists have found beauty in natural phenomena such as rivers and scattered waves and have created artworks. Ikebana artists in the old days probably tried to represent nature minimally and found that an asymmetric triangle is the primary form of nature. While Tosa attempted to find the primary form of nature by using recent high-speed camera technology, she found the same asymmetric triangle in physical or natural phenomena.

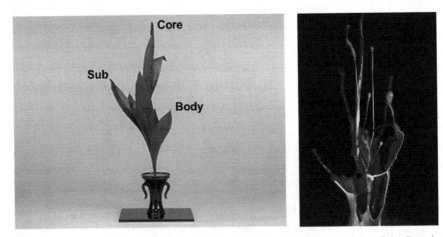

Fig. 3. Left: The basic form of Ikebana (in the public domain). Right: A form of the Sound of Ikebana.

The videos and photos extracted from the Sound of Ikebana are beautiful, but we can only enjoy them from a particular point of view. It is natural to expect to view the complete 3D view of these artworks. If we could do this, we could further investigate the relationship between Ikebana and the Sound of Ikebana. However, the current 3D sensing technologies cannot capture the small-size and fast-moving flows with high quality. Therefore, we need to use some 3D reconstruction techniques from 2D data. In [6], the authors used an image matching technique to extract the point cloud and approximate the 3D mesh from the videos obtained by multiple high-speed cameras. We review this work and improve it. The details are described in the following section.

3 3D Reconstruction of Sound of Ikebana

3.1 Phase only Correlation Method

In the previous work on the 3D modeling of Sound of Ikebana [6], a method using multiple high-speed cameras is introduced. By setting numerous high-speed cameras around the front view of the color materials, one can obtain various photo frames of a fluid flow from multiple viewpoints. Figure 4 illustrates the setting for shooting.

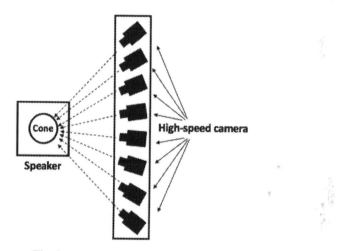

Fig. 4. Multi-camera settings for POC [6]

Then, via the Phase-Only Correlation method [7, 8], these photo frames generate an approximated point cloud of the Sound of Ikebana. Phase-Only Correlation (POC) is an image matching method that uses phase information. The Fourier transform modifies the two images, and a respected POC function is calculated from the transfer spectra. One can obtain an optimal peak model of the POC function when the transformation between two images solely depends on translation. When applying POC to multi-view stereo, k stereo pairs are made from one reference viewpoint and k neighboring viewpoints. POC is utilized to match local windows between each stereo picture. By estimating the coordinates of the 3D points from the peak model of the POC function, the 3D coordinates can be calculated with higher accuracy than conventional methods. This method is effective when the cameras are set in a narrow baseline for complicated shapes like the Sound of Ikebana. Toppan Printing Inc. Has commercialized POC under the name "TORESYS 3DTM". This software performed the 3D modeling of the Sound of Ikebana in [6].

After obtaining the 3D point clouds of the front view of the Sound of Ikebana via POC, the authors in [6] used the Poisson reconstruction method to approximate meshes from these 3D points. Figure 5 shows the 3D reconstruction obtained from the POC and the Poisson reconstruction method. However, these meshes require further manual editing to obtain a clean 3D mesh, so we sought to improve this method.

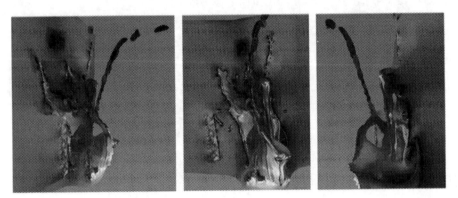

Fig. 5. Examples of 3D Reconstruction by POC and Poisson reconstruction algorithm [6].

When we performed surface reconstruction from the point clouds by the AlphaShape algorithm [9], we obtained surface meshes, as is shown in Fig. 6, which look more similar to the observed Sound of Ikebana. Therefore, we decided to create the 3D Sound of Ikebana models based on the surface meshes obtained by AlphaShape. Since the surface meshes are 2-dimensional manifolds, we consider an approach deforming an initial 3D mesh of a 3-dimensional manifold into an approximated 3D model of the Sound of Ikebana which preserves the fixed surface mesh. We use a deep learning-based method in this task.

Fig. 6. An approximated surface mesh obtained by AlphaShape. Image captured by Meshlab application.

3.2 GANs

GANs (generative adversarial networks) have been an essential topic of deep learning in the last decade. A primary GAN network consists of a generator G and a discriminator D, as shown in Fig. 7. The training process of the network is a minimax game: G tries to generate new data for a training dataset while D tries to evaluate whether a data point is real or fake. The equilibrium state of this game is the point at that G and D could perform their best, and the process does not require extensive training data. Many GANs variations have been developed by modifying the primary mechanism.

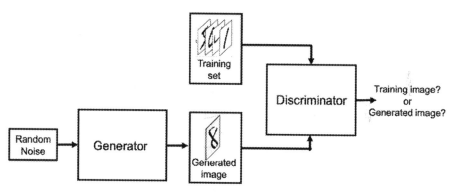

Fig. 7. Basic configuration of GAN ([2])

There are several 3D GANs variations, but we do not have enough 3D data on the Sound of Ikebana at the current level. Therefore, we consider an approach that reconstructs 3D models from 2D images. We refer to the GANverse3D for inspirational work on this task. The authors of GANverse3D use StyleGAN to generate multi-view data from a 2D input image and reconstruct the 3D view by deformation of an initial mesh via the DIB-R network [10], which is included in the Nvidia Kaolin Library [11]. The training process minimizes the loss function consisting of the differences between the multi-view 2D images generated by StyleGAN and the projected 2D images taken around the deforming mesh by the DIB-R network.

Since the Sound of Ikebana is hard to reproduce as fluid flow is uncertain, we could not get enough multi-view data for StyleGAN training. Moreover, we have the approximated 3D surface reconstructed meshes by the POC method and Alpha shape algorithm. So, we could use style transfer to transform the 2D textures of these meshes into the Sound of Ikebana style. Therefore, we use CycleGAN[12] this time. CycleGAN is a set-to-set level transformation network between two data sets as it does not require paired training. The architecture of CycleGAN is illustrated in Fig. 8 [12]. The generator's training process optimizes the minimax game between generators and discriminators. It minimizes the cycle-consistency loss by comparing the difference between an input image and the reconstructed image by combining two generators (from domain A to domain B and domain B).

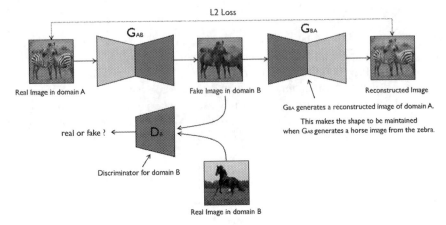

Fig. 8. Basic configuration of CycleGAN ([12])

We use CycleGAN to predict 2D information of the uncaptured flow by transforming 2D projected images taken around the approximated mesh by POC into 2D images of Sound of Ikebana style. The complete process will be discussed in 3.3.

3.3   Improvement of 3D Modeling for Sound of Ikebana

Our experiment includes the following steps, as illustrated in Fig. 9.

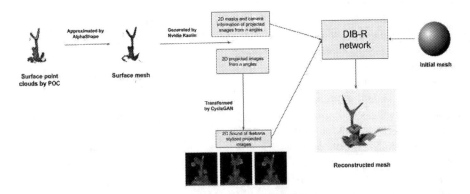

Fig. 9. Our 3D modeling process

Step 1: We use the POC method to obtain the point cloud of the Sound of Ikebana obtained from images with multiple angles.

Step 2: We use the AlphaShape algorithm [9] to reconstruct an approximated surface mesh. We also use Laplacian normalization to smooth out the surface mesh.

Step 3: We use Nvidia Kaolin Application to generate n 2D projected images of the approximated surface mesh from n angles. Here we fix the elevation to be 0 and vary in azimuth. We also obtain n 2D masks and angle information of these images by the Kaolin Application. In our experiment, we set $n = 200$.

Step 4: We perform CycleGAN transformation between the projected images in Step 3 and the captured frame images of the artwork by multiple cameras to obtain Sound of Ikebana stylized projected images. We use these images to predict the texture of the 3-dimensional manifold mesh.

Step 5: We deform an initial mesh (sphere) via the DIB-R network by minimizing the following loss function:

$$L = \lambda_{im}L_{im} + \lambda_{IOU}L_{IOU} + \lambda_{lap}L_{lap} + \lambda_{flat}L_{flat}$$

Here, L_{im} is the standard image reconstruction loss between Ikebana stylized projected images in step 4 and the projected image of the current mesh (the projected angles information obtained in step 2) defined in the RGB color space. L_{IOU} is the intersection-over-union between the ground-truth mask (obtained in step 2) and the rendered mask of the current mesh. L_{lap} and L_{flat} are smooth regularization losses (see [11]). λ_{im}, λ_{IOU}, λ_{lap}, λ_{flat} are hyperparameters. We used these hyperparameters for fine-tuning purposes.

3.4 Results

Following the previous subsection process, we obtain the 3D model of some forms of the Sound of Ikebana, as shown in Fig. 11. The original 2D Sound of Ikebana artworks are shown in Fig. 10.

Fig. 10. Original Sound of Ikebana used in our experiment

The results show that our method has reconstructed well-approximated (in terms of shape and texture) 3D meshes from the point clouds obtained by the POC method. These meshes are 3-dimensional manifolds and are ready to print by 3D printers.

Fig. 11. Examples of 3D Sound of Ikebana obtained by our experiment. Image captured by the NVIDIA Kaolin Application.

This experiment reconstructs the Sound of Ikebana artworks with similar topology to the initial mesh (sphere) as the DIB-R network is topology invariant. We note that the initial mesh should not be too complex as the deformation might be aggressive or collapse. We might use different initial meshes (but not too complex) in the following experiments for the Sound of Ikebana artworks of multiple connected components and multiple holes.

The texture of the meshes is well reconstructed at a certain level but not as smooth as the original Sound of Ikebana artworks. Moreover, if we increase the weight of the smooth normalization losses in Step 5, the meshes would not be well deformed into the expected shapes. We consider using an improvision of CycleGAN to increase the resolution of the style transfer step and improve the smooth normalization losses for a better quality of the textures.

As the cameras need to be set in a narrow baseline so that the POC method could perform better, we only obtain the 2D training data of the front view of the artworks. Our method is limited to predicting the meshes' side view and back view in this experiment. Therefore the inner information of the 3D Sound of Ikebana was not reconstructed in this study and requires advanced technique.

4   Conclusion

We have been creating fluid art that utilizes fluid phenomena, led by Naoko Tosa, one of the authors. A representative fluid art called "Sound of Ikebana" is produced by giving sound vibration to fluid such as color paint and shooting the created forms. We found that Ikebana-like beautiful and organic forms are created through this process. It is an exciting research issue to investigate why there is a similarity between the forms of the

Sound of Ikebana and actual Ikebana. For this purpose, it is desirable to create 3D forms of the Sound of Ikebana to observe the forms of the artwork from various viewpoints.

This paper described our attempt to create "3D Sound of Ikebana" from 2D training images. Our method consists of two phases. In the first phase, we use Phase-Correlation Only method to obtain the point clouds. We use improved deep learning to generate meshes based on the point clouds and the 2D Sound of Ikebana method in the second phase. The results show that this method could generate the 3D Sound of Ikebana of simply-topology.

In the subsequent study, we will study the reconstruction of more complex shapes and the improvement in the smoothness of the textures. We might also consider a new setting of the cameras to obtain more inner structure of the 3D Sound of Ikebana artworks.

Our works are still in the early stage, and in the subsequent research, we will study how to improve the quality of the 3D models of more complex structures. In the future, we will continue exploring the application of 3D materialized fluid art to various areas in our society.

References

1. Tosa, N., Nakatsu, R., Pang, Y.: Creation of media art utilizing fluid dynamics. In: 2017 International Conference on Culture and Computing, pp. 129–135 (2017)
2. Creswell, A., et al.: Generative adversarial networks: an overview. IEEE Signal Process. Mag. **35**(1), 53–65 (2018)
3. Wu, J., et al.: Learning a probabilistic latent space of object shapes via 3d generative-adversarial modeling. Advances in Neural Information Processing Systems, pp. 82–90 (2016)
4. Zhang, Y., et al.: Image GANs meet Differentiable Rendering for Inverse Graphics and Interpretable 3D Neural Rendering. ICLR 2021 (2021)
5. Karras, T., Laine, S., Aila, T.: A style-based generator architecture for generative adversarial networks. CVPR2019 (2019)
6. Tosa, N., et al.: 3D modeling and 3D materialization of fluid art that occurs in very short time. In: 19th IFIP, TC 14 International Conference, pp. 409–421 (2020)
7. Sakai, S. et al.: An efficient image matching method for multi-view stereo. ACCV 2012, LNCS, vol. 7727, pp. 283–296. Springer, Heidelberg (2013). https://doi.org/10.1007/978-3-642-37447-0_22
8. Shuji, S., et al.: Phase-based window matching with geometric correction for multi-view stereo. IEJCE Trans. Inf. Syst. **98**(10), 1818–1828 (2015)
9. Edelsbrunner, H., Kirkpatrick, D.G., Seidel, R.: On the shape of a set of points in the plane. IEEE Trans. Inf. Theory **29**(4), 551–559 (1983)
10. Chen, W. et al.: Learning to predict 3d objects with an interpolation-based differentiable renderer. In: 2017 Neural Information Processing Systems NiPS (2019)
11. Fuji Tsang, C., et al.: Kaolin: A Pytorch Library for Accelerating 3D Deep Learning Research (2022). https://github.com/NVIDIAGameWorks/kaolin
12. Zhu, J., Park, T., Isola, P., Efros, A.A.: Unpaired image-to-image translation using cycle-consistent adversarial networks. In: 2017 IEEE International Conference on Computer Vision (ICCV), pp. 2242–2251 (2017)

Method for Music Game Control Using Myoelectric Sensors

Shuo Zhou(✉) and Norihisa Segawa

Kyoto Sangyo University, Kyoto, Japan
{zhoushuo3,sega}@acm.org

Abstract. In a music game, a player interacts with a piece of music or a type of musical score. The progression of the game is based on the player's actions in time with the music. Many music games have a called timing adjustment function, which optimizes the reaction of the user in advance by adjusting the timing of button presses according to the user's reaction. This study utilizes myoelectric sensors to perform real-time timing adjustments using the degree of fatigue of the user's muscles as an indicator during a music game. By utilizing the changes in myoelectricity when muscles become fatigued, the control of music games can be improved.

Keywords: Game control · EMG · Fatigue · Myoelectric sensor · Music game · Muscles · Timing adjustment · Arduino

1 Introduction

In a music game, a player interacts with a piece of music or a type of musical score. The player performs actions (e.g., pressing buttons, taking steps, operating a controller that resembles a musical instrument) in time with the music. Since the birth of music games, various masterpieces have appeared, and recently, VR-based music games have been developing more and more recently as games that anyone can enjoy playing.

Many music games include a feature called timing adjustment or offset. Timing adjustment is the ability to adjust the timing of button presses earlier or later in the game, depending on the user's reaction, to optimize the response. We know that playing music games for a long time can lead to hand and arm muscle stiffness and fatigue [1]. When we play music games, the discomfort caused by hand fatigue will greatly affect our gaming experience [2]. The negative effects of fatigue can prevent us from achieving a high score in the game. Therefore, when our arms are in a fatigued state, we can also use the timing adjustment feature to reduce the negative impact of muscle fatigue on us as a way to improve our gaming experience. Although the timing adjustment function is very practical

© IFIP International Federation for Information Processing 2022
Published by Springer Nature Switzerland AG 2022
B. Göbl et al. (Eds.): ICEC 2022, LNCS 13477, pp. 238–246, 2022.
https://doi.org/10.1007/978-3-031-20212-4_19

for those music game players. However, the current music games cannot use the timing adjustment function in the middle of the game. Therefore, players will still be affected by the gradual increase of fatigue in the middle of the game.

Electromyogram (EMG) is a bioelectric representation of muscles recorded by electromyography. EMG is essential for evaluating the estimated on-off timing of human skeletal muscles during movement [3] (Fig. 1). A study [4] showed that muscle fiber conduction velocity (CV) is an important physiological parameter for analyzing and evaluating the fatigue of tendons. We can evaluate the CV through EMG [5]. We learned that muscle fatigue can be quantified by assessing the CV in the fatigue state through EMG in the study [6]. As muscle fatigue increases, a decreasing trend in CV can be observed over this period of time.

In this study, we will use a myoelectric sensor to obtain the EMG of the player's hand during the music game [7]. By using the features of muscle fatigue on the EMG, we can calculate and analyze the EMG of the player's hand to know its fatigue state during the game in real-time. Then, we can use the timing adjustment function according to the player's hand fatigue state to offset the impact of fatigue on the game operation to improve the player's experience. This approach allows us to use the timing adjustment function in the middle of the game and adjust it with higher precision.

Currently, the primary research on EMG has been on motion recognition using EMG features for physical recovery training. Our study proposes this approach because we focus on using the relationship between the fatigue level and the EMG signal to control the game. Moreover, because obtaining signals from the EMG to analyze hand movements is accurate, we can improve the use of the timing adjustment function to make players have a better experience in the music game.

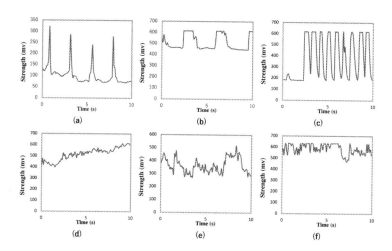

Fig. 1. EMG under different actions. (a) Clap. (b) Hands Up. (c) Press. (d) Handshake. (e) Lifting. (f) Typing.

2   Music Game Control Optimization System

This system measures EMG from the user's hand during a music game and uses the values to control the timing adjustment function, which is an important parameter for controlling a music game.

2.1   System Implementation

Implementation Overview. This system uses a myoelectric sensor to measure muscle potentials from the user in real-time during a game. Next, the measured EMG data is sent to a PC that is programmed to measure the user's fatigue level. The user's fatigue is classified into several levels and paired with the corresponding muscle potentials. The system then adjusts the timing of the music game control decisions based on the user's real fatigue level (Fig. 2).

How to Obtain the EMG of the Hand Muscles. This system continuously acquires myoelectric data as the user plays the game using an Arduino-based program and a myoelectric sensor called MyoWare [8] (Fig. 3). The myoelectric sensor collects electrical signals from the user's hand, and the Arduino program calculates the strength of muscle activity in real-time. The calculated data are then continuously sent to the PC through a USB cable to obtain the user's EMG during the game.

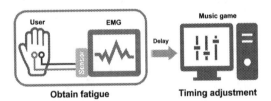

Fig. 2. Music game control optimization system.

Fig. 3. MyoWare

How to Adjust the Timing Judgment Function of the Music Game. Our purpose is to improve the gaming experience by assessing real-time fatigue through the EMG of the user's hands during the game and using the game's timing adjustment function to counteract the effects of fatigue on game control. Because most games in the market cannot utilize the timing adjustment function in the middle of the game, we developed a music game program in Python and associated muscle fatigue with the timing adjustment function. This allows us to implement real-time timing adjustments in the game based on the current muscle fatigue state.

2.2   Sensing Devices for Measuring EMG

We have developed a prototype system of a music game control optimization system. This prototype system is implemented using an Arduino. It can control lamps, switches, and motors connected to boards, thus assisting people with less experience in electronic construction to develop unique creations (Fig. 4(a)). To assess the fatigue level of hand muscles, we need to analyze the EMG during hand movements in real-time. We use the MyoWare muscle electrical signal sensor by applying Mid (red) and End (blue) electrodes to the mid and end of the hand muscle fibers, respectively, and then applying Ref (black) electrodes to skeletal locations unrelated to the muscle under investigation (Fig. 4(b)).

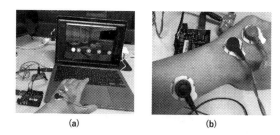

(a)   (b)

Fig. 4. (a) System layout. (b) Configuration of electrodes.

2.3   Evaluation of Muscle Fatigue

In order to evaluate our system, we have to define muscle fatigue. When we measure the electrical signal of the muscle through the MyoWare sensor, we can only obtain the characteristics of the changes in muscle movement on the time axis, where the intensity of the voltage represents the degree of muscle contraction. We know that muscle fiber CV decreases when muscles are fatigued;

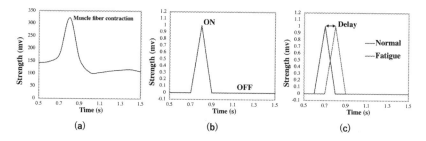

(a)   (b)   (c)

Fig. 5. (a) EMG of muscle fibers during contraction recorded by Arduino. (b) The recorded EMG is processed and set to ON when the muscle is active and OFF when it is inactive. (c) The processed data allowed us to easily observe the delay of muscle fiber contraction in the fatigue state.

therefore, we can assess the degree of muscle fatigue by the delay in the time axis of the electrical signal due to muscle fiber contraction under the same exercise (Fig. 5).

2.4 Music Game

The music game in this study includes some basic functions such as background music, music beat, timing determination, combined statistics, and score statistics (Fig. 6). When the program checks whether the user's hand is in a fatigued state, the system will use the timing adjustment function according to the fatigue level to offset the delay caused by fatigue. For example, if the delay caused by fatigue is 0.1 s, the timing adjustment function will extend the rhythm determination by 0.1 s to offset the delay (Fig. 6(b)(c)).

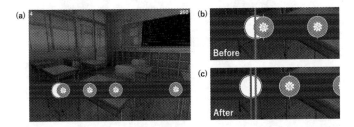

Fig. 6. (a) Custom music game. (b) The judgment line before the timing adjustment function is activated. (c) The judgment line is adjusted to the delay caused by muscle fatigue after activating the timing adjustment function.

3 Evaluation of the Proposed Method

3.1 Experimental Method

We tested the effectiveness of this system using the music games mentioned in the previous sections. In the experimental session, we set up five different musical rhythms. Each rhythm was tested five times with and without the device, respectively. Each rhythm was set to have 80–130 targets. The score and the corresponding completion level were calculated at the end of each test.

This study focused on the effect of hand fatigue on game operation, which we believe was the leading cause of delay in music games. Before wearing the device, we put the hand into a fatigued state by manual procedures. We found that the user's completion rate in the music game decreased substantially after hand fatigue compared to the before (Fig. 7). Thus, we created the delay due to hand fatigue by manual procedures.

In this study, only the authors' data were collected because the study is still a work in progress.

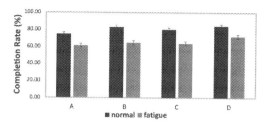

Fig. 7. The average completion rate of each rhythm after manual fatigue. Rhythm A decreased from 74.88% to 61.50%, rhythm B decreased from 83.11% to 64.84%, rhythm C decreased from 80.27% to 63.98%, and rhythm D decreased from 84.38% to 72.19%.

3.2 Experimental Results

The following are the results of our tests of the system using the music game (Fig. 8). We calculated the mean and variance of the completion rates with and without the device at the five rhythms.

A t-test was used to evaluate the system. We observed the following:

– The system improved the average completion rate by 5% compared to the method without the device.

We formulated the following t-test hypotheses.

– Null hypothesis: The method with the device in this system was significantly less effective than the method without the device at the 5% significance level.

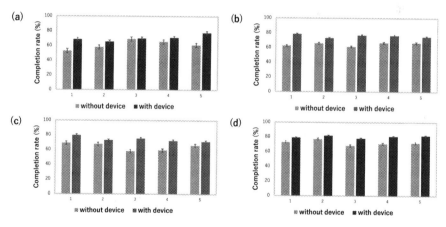

Fig. 8. Average completion rates for each rhythm with and without the device. (a) The average completion rate without equipment was 61.50%, and the average completion rate with equipment was 70.75%. (b) The average completion rate without equipment was 64.84%, and the average completion rate with equipment was 76.15%. (c) The average completion rate without equipment was 63.98%, and the average completion rate with equipment was 74.25%. (d) The average completion rate without equipment was 72.19%, and the average completion rate with equipment was 80.31%.

The mean value of the completion rates of the method with and without the device was equal.

- Counter-hypothesis: The method with the device was significantly more effective than the method without the device at the 5% significance level. The mean of the completion rates of the method with and without the device was different.

The degrees of freedom followed a t-distribution pattern, and the significance level was set at 5% (two-tailed test).

According to the statistical analysis, in test A (Fig. 8(a)), the t-value is -2.637 and the p-value is 0.030; in test B (Fig. 8(b)), the t value is -7.751 and the p-value is 0.005×10^2; in test C (Fig. 8(c)), the t value is -3.794 and the p-value is 0.005; and in test D (Fig. 8(d)), the t value is -5.009 and the p-value is 0.001. When the degree of freedom is 8, the critical t value is 2.306, and the rejection region is $t \leq -2.306$ or $t \geq 2.306$. The test results confirmed that the system with the device was significantly more effective than that without the device at the 5% level of the mean completion rate. In other words, the proposed system improved the mean score by 5% compared to the system without the device.

3.3   Discussion

In this study, we used custom-made music games to simulate a real game environment. The t-test validated the effectiveness of the music game control optimization system using myoelectric sensors. This study was conducted using sensors to obtain the user's EMG and thus counteract the effects of fatigue on physical function by analyzing the user's fatigue level. Therefore, we believe that this system can also be useful in other activities such as sports and musical instrument playing to counteract some of the effects of fatigue on muscle control.

4   Conclusion and Future Work

In this study, we detected players' muscle fatigue in the game in real-time using myoelectric sensors and enabled them to have a better gaming experience through a system designed to counteract the effects of muscle fatigue on game control. This study provides us with an idea: we can improve a player's gaming experience not only through dedicated gaming devices but also by using the player's biological information in the game.

In a future study, we will collect more biological information from the game users for more detailed experiments and analyses to prove the generalizability of the system. Furthermore, considering the individual differences, we will also improve the system by experimenting with more people.

Acknowledgments. This work was supported by JSPS KAKENHI Grant Numbers 20K11780.

References

1. Kanal, V., Brady, J., Nambiappan, H., Kyrarini, M., Wylie, G., Makedon, F.: Towards a serious game based human-robot framework for fatigue assessment. In: Proceedings of the 13th ACM International Conference on Pervasive Technologies Related to Assistive Environments (PETRA '20). Association for Computing Machinery, New York, NY, USA, Article 74, 1–6. https://doi.org/10.1145/3389189. 3398744

2. Asghari Oskoei, M., Hu, H., Gan, J.Q.: Manifestation of fatigue in myoelectric signals of dynamic contractions produced during playing PC games. In: 2008 30th Annual International Conference of the IEEE Engineering in Medicine and Biology Society, pp. 315–318 (2008) https://ieeexplore.ieee.org/document/4649153

3. Merlo, A., Farina, D., Merletti, R.: A fast and reliable technique for muscle activity detection from surface EMG signals. IEEE Trans. Biomed. Eng. 50(3), 316–323 (2003). https://doi.org/10.1109/TBME.2003.808829

4. Schwartz, F.P., Nascimento, F.A.O., Bottaro, M., Celes, R.S.: The behavior of action potential conduction velocity on isokinetic knee extension tests. Annual Int. Conf. IEEE Eng. Med. Biol. 2010, 1348–1351 (2010). https://doi.org/10.1109/ IEMBS.2010.5626751

5. Koutsos, E., Cretu, V., Georgiou, P.: A muscle fibre conduction velocity tracking ASIC for local fatigue monitoring. IEEE Trans. Biomed. Circuits Syst. 10(6), 1119–1128 (2016). https://doi.org/10.1109/TBCAS.2016.2520563

6. Farina, D., Pozzo, M., Merlo, E., Bottin, A., Merletti, R.: Assessment of average muscle fiber conduction velocity from surface EMG signals during fatiguing dynamic contractions. IEEE Trans. Biomed. Eng. 51(8), 1383–1393 (2004). https://doi.org/10.1109/TBME.2004.827556

7. Montoya, M., Henao, O., Muñoz, J.: Muscle fatigue detection through wearable sensors: a comparative study using the myo armband. In: Proceedings of the XVIII International Conference on Human Computer Interaction (Interacción '17). Association for Computing Machinery, New York, NY, USA, Article 30, 1–2 (2004). https://doi.org/10.1145/3123818.3123855

8. MyoWare. www.sparkfun.com/products/18977 Accessed Apr 27 2022

9. Bansal, T., Khan, A.A.: Fatigue Assessment of Bicep Brachii Muscle Using Surface EMG Signals Obtained from Isometric Contraction. In: Proceedings of the 2020 8th International Conference on Communications and Broadband Networking (ICCBN '20). Association for Computing Machinery, New York, NY, USA, 1–8 (2020). doi: 10.1145/3390525.3390533

10. Ebied, A., Awadallah, M., Abbass, M.A., El-Sharkawy, Y.: Upper limb muscle fatigue analysis using multi-channel surface EMG. In: 2020 2nd Novel Intelligent and Leading Emerging Sciences Conference (NILES), pp. 423–427 (2020) https:// doi.org/10.1109/NILES50944.2020.9257909

11. Zhang, G., Morin, E., Zhang, Y., Etemad, S.A.: In:Non-invasive detection of low-level muscle fatigue using surface EMG with wavelet decomposition. In: 2018 40th Annual International Conference of the IEEE Engineering in Medicine and Biology Society (EMBC), pp. 5648–5651 (2018). https://doi.org/10.1109/EMBC.2018. 8513588

12. Zwarts, M.J., Bleijenberg, G., Van Engelen, B.G.M.: Clinical neurophysiology of fatigue. Clin. Neurophysiol. 119(1), 2–10 (2008). https://doi.org/10.1016/j.clinph. 2007.09.126

13. Roberto, M., De Luca, C.J.: New techniques in surface electromyography. Comput. Aided Electromyograph. Expert Syst. **2**, 115–124 (1989)
14. Auccahuasi, W., et al.: Analysis of a mechanism to evaluate upper limb muscle activity based on surface electromyography using the MYO-EMG device. In: Proceedings of the 5th International Conference on Communication and Information Processing (ICCIP '19). Association for Computing Machinery, New York, NY, USA, 144–148 (2019). https://doi.org/10.1145/3369985.3370016
15. Miyata, H., Sadoyama, T., Katsuta, S.: Muscle fiber conduction velocity in human vastus lateralis during isometric contractions–relation to muscle fiber composition–. Jpn. J. Phys. Fitness Sports Med. 34(4), 231–238 (1985). https://doi.org/10.7600/jspfsm1949.34.231

Creation of Fluid Art "Sound of Ikebana" Under Microgravity Using Parabolic Flight

Naoko Tosa[1], Shigetaka Toba[1], Yunian Pang[1], Akihiro Yamada[2], Takashi Suzuki[2], and Ryohei Nakatsu[1(✉)]

[1] Kyoto University, Sakyo, Kyoto 606-8501, Japan
{tosa.naoko.5c,pang.yunian.2c}@kyoto-u.ac.jp,
toba.shigetaka.57z@st.kyoto-u.ac.jp,
ryohei.nakatsu@design.kyoto-u.ac.jp
[2] Toppan Inc., Taito, Tokyo 110-8560, Japan
{akihiro_1.yamada,takashi.suzuki}@toppan.co.jp

Abstract. Art is situated at the center of entertainment; therefore, new art in the future space age is an exciting subject. The authors, led by an artist, have been creating video artwork "Sound of Ikebana," made by giving sound vibration to fluid and shooting it with a high-speed camera. To study its shape under weightlessness, we conducted the generation of the artwork under microgravity realized by parabolic flight. We confirmed that new shapes of the Sound of Ikebana were created. Furthermore, a three-dimensional artwork was created by shooting the phenomenon from multiple viewpoints.

Keywords: Fluid art · Sound of Ikebana · Microgravity · Parabolic flight

1 Introduction

Recently, there have been many topics related to space, such as NASA's landing of an uncrewed spacecraft on Mars in February 2021 [1], Virgin Galactic's Richard Branson and Amazon's Jeff Bezos flying into space of about 100 km in July 2021, a four-day flight to orbit around the earth by four civilians by SpaceX's spacecraft Crew Dragon in September 2021 [2].

Although the day when ordinary people can quickly go out into space is still a long way off, it is necessary to consider our life and society when space travel becomes a reality. How will space travel affect our bodies and spirits in the future when space travel becomes familiar to the general public? It is also necessary to consider how the culture we have built up in our society will change in the space age.

Art has been deeply linked to human spirituality and has been at the center of entertainment since ancient times. Therefore, an essential and exciting theme is what art and entertainment will look like in the space age. What will happen to art and entertainment, how people interact with them in the space age, and whether new art and entertainment that matches the space age will be born are themes that need to be considered now [3].

© IFIP International Federation for Information Processing 2022
Published by Springer Nature Switzerland AG 2022
B. Göbl et al. (Eds.): ICEC 2022, LNCS 13477, pp. 247–255, 2022.
https://doi.org/10.1007/978-3-031-20212-4_20

We are interested in what art will look like in the environment of weightlessness, which is peculiar to space travel. We have been working on producing fluid art [4], which is art using fluid phenomena. Because fluid behavior is different in zero gravity than in normal gravity, we think studying fluid art in zero/microgravity is necessary.

This paper first describes the concept of fluid art that uses the fluid phenomenon, then the details of a representative fluid art called "Sound of Ikebana" will be described. Then the process of the experiment and the produced art will be described, where the artist herself created artworks under the microgravity obtained by the particular flight called "parabolic flight." It also describes an attempt to create a 3D art object from the obtained 2D art video.

2   Related Works

Art generation in the space age is an exciting theme, and multiple projects are being carried out mainly in the United States and Japan. The MIT Media Lab in the United States has launched the "Space Exploration Initiative [5]" to conduct various experiments under zero gravity. Among them is a project to explore the way of art in the space age. For example, in a project conducted by an artist called "Telepresent Drawings in Space," the theme is how to deliver sensations and emotions in outer space to the ground. The trajectory of an object floating under zero gravity is recorded with a sensor. They try to reproduce the trajectory on the ground and make it an artwork.

In Japan, JAXA (Japan Aerospace Exploration Agency) has a Japanese laboratory called "Kibo" on the ISS, which can be used for scientific experiments and experiments of art creation. From 2008 to 2011, the first call for proposals for art creation in space was opened, and nine experiments were conducted in "Kibo" [6]. From 2011 to 2013, eight themes were implemented in the second phase [7].

These studies have great significance as pioneering research on the new art in the space era. However, in these studies, artists did not try to generate art under zero gravity by themselves. On the other hand, in our project led by an artist, the artist herself tried to generate art under microgravity to study the way of art in the space age.

3   Fluid Art "Sound of Ikebana"

3.1   Fluid Art

The behavior of fluid consists of a large part of natural phenomena [8]. Fluids are known to be able to create beautiful shapes under a variety of conditions [9].

As beauty is a fundamental element of art, it is natural to use fluid phenomena as a basic methodology for art creation. One of the authors, Naoko Tosa, has led a project to create "fluid art" by shooting the behavior of fluids with a high-speed camera. High-speed cameras have traditionally been used to capture a variety of phenomena that occur in brief periods, such as the explosion of physical material, etc. On the other hand, we were interested in producing various beautiful organic shapes using fluids. Then, she found it possible to create an Ikebana-like shape (Ikebana is a Japanese flower arrangement) with a fluid such as paint by giving sound vibration. Figure 1 shows the generation system.

When a speaker is placed facing up, a thin rubber film is put on it, a fluid such as paint is placed on the rubber film, and the speaker is vibrated with sound, the paint jumps up and makes various shapes, and the process is shot with a high-speed camera. Here, a high-speed camera of 2000 frames/second is used. A PC connected to the speaker produces various sounds and vibrates the speaker [4].

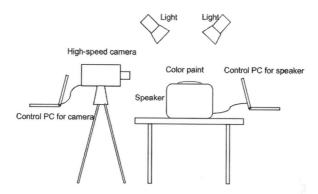

Fig. 1. Fluid art generation system. (©Naoko Tosa)

3.2 "Sound of Ikebana"

Using this environment, we systematically changed sound shape (sine wave, sawtooth wave, etc.), frequency of sound, type of fluid, a viscosity of the fluid, etc., and shot various fluid forms with a high-speed camera. We confirmed that various beautiful Ikebana-like shapes were generated. Tosa created a video art called "Sound of Ikebana [4]" by editing the obtained video image according to the colors of the Japanese seasons. Figure 2 shows several scenes from the artwork. She also used this artwork for projection mapping in Singapore in 2014. Also, in April 2017, as part of Tosa's Japan Cultural Envoy activities, an exhibition was held at Times Square in New York using more than 60 digital billboards [11].

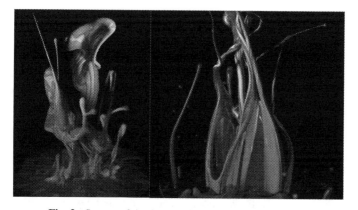

Fig. 2. Scenes of the Sound of Ikebana. (©Naoko Tosa)

4   Microgravity Generation Method

4.1   Parabolic Flight

Parabolic flight means flying on a parabolic flight path [10]. After gaining sufficient speed by a rapid descent, the aircraft is raised, and the thrust is narrowed down to the extent that it compensates for air resistance to perform the parabolic motion. During Parabolic Flight, a microgravity environment of about 10^{-2} to 10^{-3} G can be realized for about 10 to 20 s, so it is used for various microgravity experiments and training of astronauts. One company provides commercial services for parabolic flights [12]. Figure 3 shows the flight curve in parabolic flight and the gravity in each phase.

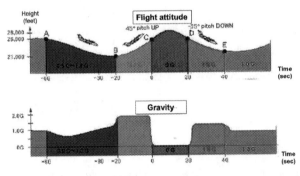

Fig. 3.   Parabolic flight.

4.2   Free-Fall

An alternative method of realizing microgravity is free-fall. When an object falls downward, pulled by gravity, it is in a weightless state. In other words, weightlessness can be achieved by creating a freefall state by dropping things from a high place.

In Japan, the Microgravity Laboratory of Japan (MGLAB) in Toki City, Gifu Prefecture, has a free fall distance of 100 m and a free fall time of 4.5 s. This drop tower was evacuated inside the tower to eliminate air resistance and allow the fall capsule to fall freely [14].

Also, the ZARM microgravity experimental facility, called the Bremen Drop Tower, at the University of Bremen in Bremen, Germany, is well known. Its height is 147 m (actual fall distance is 110 m), and if the falling capsule is dropped in a tower that has been evacuated, the weightlessness for almost 4.7 s is realized [15].

5   Creation of Fluid Art Under Microgravity

5.1   Basic Methodology

To create art under microgravity, we worked on an experiment where the artist took the initiative in creating the Sound of Ikebana under microgravity. Of the parabolic flight and freefall described before, we adopted the parabolic flight, which can generate microgravity for a certain period.

At the same time, in addition to shooting the image of the Sound of Ikebana under microgravity and making it a two-dimensional video art, we challenged an attempt to realize it as a three-dimensional object. The Sound of Ikebana has been evaluated many times as "Japanese" and "Japanese beauty is expressed" [16]. By making the Sound of Ikebana a three-dimensional object, it can be exhibited in various places as three-dimensional art. The shape can be examined from various directions. Then it is possible to receive many people's impressions and comments on why it looks Japanese. Based on this idea, we decided to restore the 3D shape of the Sound of Ikebana and make it into a 3D object using a 3D printer [17].

To realize 3D restoration, researchers have studied a method to create a 3D model based on images taken from multiple directions [18][19]. There are two methods of using multiple still cameras and multiple high-speed video cameras as a shooting method. The method of performing synchronous shooting using multiple still cameras can be developed at a relatively low cost, but the timing of pressing the shutter becomes a problem. We first constructed a system using multiple still cameras and conducted various experiments in this research. However, we found that it is challenging to obtain shooting results that are beautifully shaped depending on the timing of pressing the shutter. Based on the above considerations and preliminary experiments, we decided to conduct an experiment in which shooting is performed using multiple high-speed cameras.

5.2   Sound of Ikebana Creation Using Parabolic Flight

In order to create the Sound of Ikebana during parabolic flight, it is necessary to develop a small-size generation system shown in Fig. 1 to bring on board. Furthermore, to make the Sound of Ikebana into a three-dimensional object, it is necessary to have a system equipped with multiple high-speed cameras. Figure 4 shows the developed generation system. The system uses a high-speed multi-camera system. The camera part has a shooting speed of 2000 frames/second with 2 M pixels. Six units were installed surrounding the speaker. Since a workspace such as setting paint is required, we decided that six high-speed cameras surround the speaker at about 120 to 180°.

a. Front view   b. Side view

Fig. 4. Sound of Ikebana generation system for parabolic flight. (©Naoko Tosa)

In order to create the Sound of Ikebana during the parabolic flight, it is necessary to set paints quickly, drive speakers, and shoot with multiple high-speed cameras. All the participants in the experiment, including the artist Naoko Tosa, are new to parabolic flight. In order to minimize failures in an unfamiliar environment, we installed the generation system in the laboratory and carried out training simulating an actual flight. We practiced setting a new film on the speaker, setting paints on it, driving speakers and starting shooting in synchronization with them, and cleaning after shooting with the same time intervals as the actual flight. By practicing this about 50 times, it was possible to perform each procedure skillfully in a short time. It was possible to create and shoot the Sound of Ikebana almost without failure by following the practiced procedure in the actual parabolic flight.

In an actual parabolic flight, the microgravity of about 20 s was achieved 10 times. Figure 5 shows several scenes of the fluid art creation during the parabolic flight.

a. The airplane used for the parabolic flight   b. The scene when microgravity is realized

c. The scene of the "Sound of Ikebana"
creation under microgravity

Fig. 5. Sound of Ikebana creation scenes during an actual parabolic flight. (©Naoko Tosa)

5.3   Sound of Ikebana Under the Parabolic Flight

As mentioned earlier, one parabolic flight allowed us to experience microgravity ten times. Moreover, the flight was carried out twice over two days. Except for two failures which was caused by the inaccurate timing among the three members, the Sound of

Ikebana was created 18 times. Therefore, obtaining video images of 6 positions x 18 times was possible. Figure 6 shows how the actual Sound of Ikebana images changes as time passes. Also, Fig. 7 shows an example of an image at a specific video moment taken from 6 positions.

Fig. 6. An example of how the Sound of Ikebana changes its shape depending on time. (©Naoko Tosa)

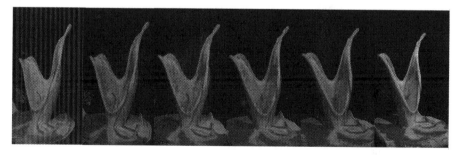

Fig. 7. An example of images shot from multiple positions. (©Naoko Tosa)

We found that the Sound of Ikebana generated under microgravity has the following characteristics compared to the case under normal gravity.

- Under normal gravity, the height at which the paint jumps up is suppressed by gravity. However, under microgravity, as there is no such restriction, the paint jumps higher and creates more extended shapes.
- The paint that jumps up to a certain height under normal gravity starts to fall after that, creating a shape in which the jumping-up paint and the falling paint are mixed and sometimes look messy. However, since the paint does not fall under microgravity, the appearance of jumping and spreading looks more sophisticated.

5.4 Three-Dimensional Materialization of the Sound of Ikebana Under Microgravity

Various studies have been conducted on creating a 3D model from images from multiple viewpoints [18, 19]. Also, there are several commercial software. We used a software called "TORESYS 3D™" commercialized by Toppan Inc. Then, using the obtained 3D model, it is possible to generate a 3D object with a 3D printer. An example of the completed 3D Sound of Ikebana is shown in Fig. 8.

Fig. 8. An example of the 3D Sound of Ikebana created using a 3D printer. (©Naoko Tosa)

6 Conclusion

As the space age arrives, it is essential to consider new art in the new era. One of the authors, artist Naoko Tosa, has created a video artwork called "Sound of Ikebana" based on the fluid phenomenon by giving sound vibration to liquids such as paints and shooting them with a high-speed camera. We are interested in what shape this art would produce under zero/microgravity.

We adopted parabolic flight to create microgravity and conducted an art creation experiment of the Sound of Ikebana, led by Tosa, using parabolic flight. Also, we challenged making the Sound of Ikebana as a 3D object by shooting the phenomenon using multiple high-speed cameras.

Under microgravity, the fluid expands more dynamically and does not fall due to microgravity. Then we obtained more sophisticated, beautiful, and organic shapes of the Sound of Ikebana under microgravity than in ordinary gravity. As a result, we have obtained new 2D and 3D art that expresses the "space-age."

As our future research, we will carry out detailed comparison between two types of the Sound of Ikebana; one created under normal gravity and the other created under microgravity. And we will clarify the difference both from scientific and artistic point of views.

We plan to exhibit this new art as 2D and 3D art so that people can appreciate its original and organic shape. Furthermore, we consider using it for art and the shape of vehicles and architecture in the future society.

Acknowledgment. We thank NAC Inc. For lending us multiple high-speed cameras during the preparation and execution of the parabolic flight, especially to Mr. Yamamoto of NAC for his continuous support.

References

1. Williford, K.H., et al.: The NASA Mars 2020 rover mission and the search for extraterrestrial life. In: Chapter 11, From Habitability to Life on Mars, pp. 275–308. Elsevier (2020)
2. www.spacex.com/human-spaceflight/earth/index.html. Accessed 4 July 2022
3. Murnik, M.: Art in the environment of zero gravity: a sketch. Virtual Creat. **6**(1–2), 67–74 (2016)
4. Pang, Y., Tamai, H., Tosa, N., Nakatsu, R.: Sound of ikebana: creation of media art based on fluid dynamics. Int. J. Human. Social Sci. Educ. **8**(3), 90–102 (2021)
5. https://www.media.mit.edu/groups/space-exploration/overview/. Accessed 4 July 2022
6. https://iss.jaxa.jp/kiboexp/field/epo/pilot/first/. Accessed 4 July 2022. (in Japanese)
7. https://iss.jaxa.jp/kiboexp/field/epo/pilot/second/. Accessed 4 July 2022. (in Japanese)
8. Bernard, P.S.: Fluid Dynamics. Cambridge University Press, Cambridge (2015)
9. Krechetnikov, R., Homsy, G.M.: Crown-forming instability phenomena in the drop splash problem. J. Colloid Interf. Sci. **331**(2), 555–559 (2009)
10. Pang, Y., Zhao, L., Nakatsu, R., Tosa, N.: A study of variable control of sound vibration form (SVF) for media art creation. In: 2017 International Conference on Culture and Computing (2017)
11. http://www.newyorkled.com/___AAABlog/event/times-square-midnight-moment-sound-of-ikebana-spring-naoko-tosa/. Accessed 4 July 2022
12. Shelhamer, M.: Parabolic flight as a spaceflight analog. J. Appl. Physiol. **120**, 1442–1448 (2015)
13. https://www.das.co.jp/en/. Accessed 4 July 2022
14. Tagawa, Y., et al.: Present state of microgravity laboratory of Japan. J. Jpn. Soc. Microgravity Appl **6**(2) (1989)
15. Dreyer, M.: The drop tower bremen. Microgravity Sci. Technol. **22**(4), 461 (2010)
16. Tosa, N., Pang, Y., Yang, Q., Nakatsu, R.: Pursuit and expression of Japanese beauty using technology. Special Issue "The Machine as Artist (for the 21st Century)," Arts J. MDPI **8**(1), 38 (2019)
17. Tosa, N., Yunian, P., Nakatsu, R., Yamada, A., Suzuki, T., Yamamoto, K.: 3D modeling and 3D materialization of fluid art that occurs in very short time. In: Nunes, N.J., Ma, L., Wang, M., Correia, N., Pan, Z. (eds.) ICEC 2020. LNCS, vol. 12523, pp. 409–421. Springer, Cham (2020). https://doi.org/10.1007/978-3-030-65736-9_37
18. Seitz, S.M., Curless, B., Diebel, J., Scharstein, D., Szeliski, R.: A Comparison and evaluation of multi-view stereo reconstruction algorithms. In: Proceedings of International Conference on Computer Vision and Pattern Recognition, pp. 519–528 (2006)
19. Strecha, C., von Hansen, W., Gool, L.V., Fua, P., Thoennessen, U.: On benchmarking camera calibration and multi-view stereo for high-resolution imagery. In: Proceedings of International Conference on Computer Vision and Pattern Recognition, pp. 1–8 (2008)

Design Explorations of Interactive Point Cloud Based Virtual Environments Using Volumetric Capture and Visualisation Techniques

Maximilian Rubin[1]([✉]) [iD], Jorge C. S. Cardoso[2] [iD], and Pedro Martins Carvalho[3] [iD]

[1] University of Coimbra, DEI, Coimbra, Portugal
maximilian@student.dei.uc.pt
[2] University of Coimbra, CISUC, DEI, Coimbra, Portugal
jorgecardoso@dei.uc.pt
[3] University of Coimbra, FCTUC, DArq, Coimbra, Portugal
pmcarvalho@uc.pt

Abstract. This project reports a work-in-progress of the creation of a Virtual Reality experience, based on a memory of the Botanical Garden of the University of Coimbra, using point cloud capture and visualisation techniques. The main goal is the creation of an immersive audio-visual experience that will grasp the *ambiance* of the Botanical Garden along with simulating some of its natural processes. We have developed a high-fidelity prototype for a single location of the Garden and report the results of preliminary usability tests.

Keywords: Virtual Reality · Data capture · Point clouds · Photogrammetry · Audiovisual experience · Immersive media

1 Introduction

Capturing environments and moments in time has always been something humans have been fascinated by – from paintings to analog photography, to digital cameras. We are currently experiencing rapid technological shifts in the ways we can capture and represent reality. The recent hype surrounding the Metaverse [1] is just one of the many examples which will radically change the way we communicate and perceive reality as we know it [2]. Because of this, there has been an influx of new methods and tools to facilitate the emergence of this upcoming digital realm [3–5].

Virtual tours of sites of cultural heritage have generally been achieved either through 360-degree video capture or panoramic imagery due to their accessibility and ease of use [6], however, these methods limit the user's full sense of depth of the image [7]. A solution to overcome this limitation consists of capturing real-world data through

---

Supplementary Information The online version contains supplementary material available at https://doi.org/10.1007/978-3-031-20212-4_21.

B. Göbl et al. (Eds.): ICEC 2022, LNCS 13477, pp. 256–265, 2022.
https://doi.org/10.1007/978-3-031-20212-4_21

3D scanning methods, resulting in a set of data points in space called a point cloud. This point cloud then typically gets passed through a surface reconstruction process, transforming it into a 3D polygon mesh. However, point clouds usually come with a variety of properties and imperfections – turning the surface reconstruction process into a challenging task. This can lead to a "low resolution" appearance that is quite noticeable at close proximity, especially when dealing with large-scale objects or scenes [8]. Nonetheless, by visualising point clouds in their crude and diffuse state, our focus gets taken away from the surface detail of what was captured, allowing our mind to focus more on the atmosphere and tone of the locale. So rather than using computer algorithms to fill in missing surface information with polygons, which are merely an interpolated interpretation of reality, we can take advantage of our brain's innate ability to actively interpret our perceived reality by "filling in the gaps", fabricating the illusion of reality, and thus allowing for a deeper, more authentic connection between the user and the virtual world [9, 10].

This project's main goal is the creation of a visual memory of the Botanical Garden of the University of Coimbra [11], by capturing reality and thus a moment in time that can then be run and visualised in 3D space (through Virtual Reality), in real-time. In addition to serving as a digital backup of the Garden and commemorating its 250th anniversary, this project will also allow anyone to access and experience this location remotely, even in face of restrictions such as ones imposed by pandemics or physical limitations, effectively allowing unlimited visits to this site of cultural heritage [12].

This project will focus on three distinct areas within the Botanical Garden, each of which highlights memorable centenary tree specimens: the *Tilia x europaea,* the *Erythrina Crista-Galli* and the *Ficus Macrophylla* (Fig. 1). These areas will be virtually interconnected, simulating snippets of a memory stroll through the Garden, allowing users to travel from one memory to the next.

As a technology-driven species, we have been slowly losing touch with nature and have become more distant to its life-giving benefits [13]. This project aims to trigger our innate "biophilia" [14] (a term used to describe our affiliation with mother nature, its positive impact on our mental health and our overall well-being), not as a tool to substitute nature itself, but rather as a tool to enhance it. To achieve this, we will simulate some of the area's natural processes usually hidden to the naked eye, with the aim of invoking a sense of inquisitiveness within our users. These natural processes will be simulated over our point clouds and will consist of the tree's vascular systems and underground root networks, following the premise that if we can observe the processes of nature in VR, we'll become more conscious of its inner workings in real life. Here we will study if a point cloud based VR experience of nature can transmit similar positive psychological benefits of actual nature.

Finally, this project aims to provide multiple visualisation mediums (a desktop version, 360-degree videos, and a VR version) to improve audience reach, whilst also granting the ability to free-roam within our virtual environment. Regarding the VR version, a rather optimistic yet feasible goal is to include the Oculus Quest 2, by taking advantage of its experimental Passthrough API [15], thus theoretically allowing for a mixed reality *"in-situ"* variant, where users would be able to interact within the real environment whilst observing its hidden natural processes and/or experience lost heritage features. To our knowledge, this has not yet been achieved in the context of nature.

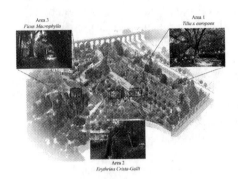

Fig. 1. Illustration of the Botanical Garden depicting the centenary tree specimens. Adapted from: «https://www.facebook.com/media/set/?set=a.424667424214088&type=3»

2 Related Work

From a research of existing relevant works, a set of three cases were selected: *Memories of Tsukiji*, by Ruben Frosali, *Shinjuku*, by Benjamin Bardou and *In the Eyes of the Animal*, by Marshmallow Laser Feast.

   Memories of Tsukiji [16] is an immersive art experience that explores what was formerly the world's largest fish market. Tokyo's Tsukiji inner market shut its doors permanently on October 6th, 2018, and has been completely demolished due to its ageing buildings. Ruben Frosali and his team took the task to recreate the fish market and all of its history, digitally, but instead of following the conventional photo realistic simulation approach to cultural heritage, as in creating the closest 3D mesh replica possible, they decided to explore the fragmented nature of photogrammetry's dense cloud generation process. The photorealism is still there, relatively speaking, however, its semi-abstract spatial data does a compelling job of evoking feelings of a memory lost in time. Memories tend to be quite personal and subjective, but in *Memories of Tsukiji*, the audience all end up falling into the same memory spectrum, the same way when families gather around to view photo albums, they all gain shared memories. While Ruben and his team were performing live, the audience was able to use a controller in the middle of the room to interact with the installation and dynamically change the scene projected on the wall by looking in different directions.

   Shinjuku [17] is another project which explores the depth of our perception and memories. Created by art director and filmmaker Benjamin Bardou, *Shinjuku* embraces a more surreal side to volumetric capture which takes us on a walk through Tokyo's Shinjuku district. Available as both an interactive VR experience (HTC Vive) and a video preview, *Shinjuku's* concept mixes point clouds with force induced particle systems to create a heavily fragmented and dynamic environment. Being part of his Megalopolis project, which aims to explore the theme of memories in modern cities through different visual and immersive variations (short films and VR sets), *Shinjuku's* non-linear narrative was specifically designed to evoke the experience of the city dweller. In this context, the use of photogrammetry, with all its imperfections and shattered aesthetic, is to be seen as a kind of memorial restitution. Benjamin also played with the idea of merging memories into one experience, by creating a dreamscape where users can fall into an ethereal realm of shared memories and access the collective unconscious. Although similar to *Memories of Tsukiji*, *Shinjuku* can perhaps be considered more chaotic in terms of its visual representation due to all the force fields and visual effects used, however it still manages to effortlessly encompass the sense of accessing a memory in time.

Finally, Marshmallow Laser Feast explores the line between the virtual and the real, exploring emerging technologies and embedding them into live interactive and immersive environments. By employing a point cloud based pointillist aesthetic in real-time multisensory VR experiences, they are able to explore visual perspectives beyond the reach of the human senses. *In the Eyes of the Animal* [18] takes you on a journey through nature's food chain by putting you in the eyes of four distinct animals (a mosquito, a dragonfly, a frog and an owl) which inhabit the Grizedale Forest, near the Lake District of Northwest England. Scientific facts were taken from each one of these species which were then applied to construct a completely speculative visual narrative for each animal. A prominent incentive behind the creation of their project was to challenge our overly human-centric vision of the world, by shifting our perspective and showing us that we do, in fact, cohabitate with an extremely complex and advanced natural world. This is something that further inspired the development of our project: to create a tool to enable us to detach ourselves from our somewhat artificial day-to-day lives, by opening new sources of compassion and interest for the natural world.

These three projects consist of pre-rendered videos and real-time immersive VR experiences. However, the latter are quite demanding, hardware-wise, usually take place in short lived localised exhibitions and typically follow a predetermined route within their virtual worlds, thus limiting the users' ability for full control within the virtual setting.

3   Development Pipeline

Our development pipeline followed three high-level phases: Data Acquisition, Data Processing and Project development.

The first phase, Data Acquisition, consists of capturing the required data from the Botanical Garden, this includes photogrammetric data capture together with binaural audio recordings.

During the second phase, Data Processing, captured data will be analysed, cleaned up and refined to ensure that these data get effectively transformed into rich point clouds. To achieve this, Agisoft Metashape [19] is used (a software that performs photogrammetric processing of digital images and generates 3D spatial data), along with CloudCompare [20] (a 3D processing software used for editing point cloud data). The Project Development phase consists of merging all the previously collected and refined data into Unity's game engine [21], with the aim of creating our desired immersive experience. This phase explores user interactivity, sound design and particle systems to further enhance its audio-visual and immersive factors. After having completed these steps, preliminary quality and performance tests are run to make sure the project runs smoothly with minimal framerate drops and visual/auditory anomalies.

Finally, the produced immersive experience is then adjusted to run in compatibility for a VR headset.

These three main phases are not necessarily executed sequentially, but rather iterated as we refine the process.

4 Prototype: *Tilia x europaea*

Our goal is to create an audiovisual interactive and immersive experience of three chosen areas containing centenary trees of the Botanical Garden (the *Tilia x europaea*, the *Erythrina Crista-Galli* and the *Ficus Macrophylla*), where users will be able to traverse these three areas seamlessly. However, our current prototype consists of a single area: the centenary *Tilia x europaea* tree [22]. For this prototype, we explored different visual representations of our point cloud, different approaches to represent some of the natural processes associated with tree's biology, interactions that allow users to directly influence the behaviour of the experience, sound, and locomotion and traversal through the different areas.

4.1 Point-Cloud Representation

We explored three point cloud rendering methods to find a sweet spot between visual fidelity and computational performance. First we tried rendering our point cloud as a static object with a specific point size, however, these points would become large at close proximity thus negatively impacting the visual dream-like aesthetic we were looking for (Fig. 2). To solve this, we rendered each point as "pixel absolute" so that each point would only occupy the size of a screen pixel (Fig. 3). We then experimented using Unity's visual effect graph to render and animate our point cloud, here we explored its continuous point burst feature with the addition of force fields. This method resulted in some interesting visuals dominated by roiling textures (Fig. 4), however, we quickly noticed how computationally heavier this rendering method was compared to the first method, for this reason we chose the pixel absolute, more photo realistic, approach.

Fig. 2. (Left): Points with a set point size.   **Fig. 3.** (Mid): Points rendered as "pixel absolute".   **Fig. 4.** (Right): Visual effect graph render with force fields.

4.2 Representation of Natural Processes

We then took on the challenge of animating the tree's vascular system and underground root network, using botanical visual references [23] as well as its apparent surface roots. Here we initially tried using Unity's visual effect graph with particle emitters to simulate these systems, however, we had a difficult time controlling its form, resulting in a less than desirable result (Fig. 5). To solve this, we created SDFs (Signed Distance Fields) from 3D generated models of the tree's trunk, branches, and root system using Unity's SDF bake tool (Fig. 6). Particle systems were then encapsulated within the volumes of the SDFs, resulting in a more realistic simulation (Fig. 7). After this, we implemented a "conform to body" effect, using the user's position to lightly attract the particles contained within the SDF's in a magnetic fashion – creating a synergistic play between the two.

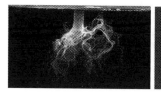  

Fig. 5. (Left): Visual effect graph of a root simulation.

Fig. 6. (Mid): SDF of a root system.

Fig. 7. (Right): Resulting combination of SDF's and particle systems.

4.3 Interactions

To further explore user interactivity, we decided to bring the tree's leaves "to life" (Fig. 8). We achieved this by isolating as many leaves as possible from our point cloud, then proceeded to transform these data into two texture files (containing position and colour data), we then used these as data inputs within a separate visual effect graph particle system. This system works by constantly spawning leaf particles with a small force applied to their positive y-axis. Each point has a random lifetime between two and four seconds and each point's size is determined by a curve of an inverted parabola over its lifetime. Moreover, we also implemented a sphere collider container within the user's view (camera), allowing users to collide and interact with the leaf particles to emulate the traditional experience of touching the tree's leaves.

Fig. 8. Screen-Captures of the interactive leaf particle system.

4.4 Sound

When it comes to sound design, our goal consists of creating an immersive dynamic audio environment with spatial sound for each area, however, for this prototype we merely incorporated a 360-degree speaker placeholder situated in the centre of the scene, which emits a recorded ambient soundtrack of the area.

4.5 Locomotion and Area Traversal

Finally, two modes of locomotion were developed for our area: a keyboard & mouse mode and a gamepad controller mode.

As our main goal consists of capturing three areas of the Garden, we had to think of a way of interconnecting these areas. We initially attempted to merge multiple point clouds into a single scene, but this resulted in performance issues, forcing us to distribute each area into separate scenes. To overcome this, we implemented two exits situated at either extremity of our captured area, coinciding with existing pathways of the captured space. These exits allow users to travel from one area to another and were initially programmed using trigger colliders, however, after a few tests we decided a more gradual and interactive approach was necessary. To achieve this, we developed a script that constantly calculates the user's position from the exits and gradually fades-out the scene depending on how close the user is to the given exits, allowing for a smoother transition to the next area (Fig. 9).

Fig. 9. Visual representation of the fade-out system.

5 Evaluation

Although the Botanical Garden immersive experience is still a work-in-progress, we wanted to perform preliminary tests with participants external to our team to understand how people would react to the immersive environment. During a high-school visit to our University, we ran in-person playtests on sixteen students. Each participant explored two variants of our virtual environment: one variant used a keyboard and mouse (with a fixed altitude) to move and explore the environment; the second variant, used a gamepad controller (with the ability to fly). During these tests we recorded user analytics, including play time and user position and orientation in the virtual environment. We later asked our participants to answer a short feedback questionnaire where they were asked to describe their experience in five words, what variant they preferred (keyboard or gamepad controller), and lastly, a line for comments and/or suggestions.

The average play time for the keyboard and mouse was 53 seconds whilst the gamepad controller was 62 seconds. The most popular words were *"Realistic"* (11.8%), *"Fun"* (11.8%), *"Interesting"* (9.4%) and *"Incredible"* (7.1%). Two thirds of the participants preferred the gamepad controller over the keyboard and mouse, however, this factor could be linked to the young demographic and further tests ought to be performed on a wider audience.

In terms of user position tracking and despite the area having a central focal point (being the tree), we noticed that most users ended up exploring the entire space, as can be seen in the user position trackers (Fig. 10). Furthermore, we noticed that most of our participants had the urge to travel to the next area, wanting to see more.

Finally, some users managed to bypass the set boundaries of our area, which is something which will have to be examined and corrected.

In general, these preliminary results show a positive evaluation and have provided enough feedback for us to continue to expand and improve our virtual world.

Fig. 10. User position trackers of all users: the trails representing the user's travelled course, whilst the arrows represent the user's viewing direction.

6 Conclusion and Future Work

The objective of this project is to develop an audio-visual experience based on three distinct locations of the Botanical Garden of the University of Coimbra, whose goal is to be made compatible with three visualisation mediums (a desktop version, 360-degree videos, and a VR version). We have currently developed a high-fidelity desktop prototype of one of the three areas which has recently passed through usability tests with positive results. Our next goal is to capture and add the other two areas to our project, that will then be made compatible with the remaining visualisation mediums mentioned above. Once we complete our virtual environment, additional usability and user experience iterations will be performed to help identify areas for improvement and optimisation.

Link to Shared Google Drive folder containing supplementary material (2.28 GB): https://drive.google.com/file/d/1Eh_Nsl_rqxkziyYhjF3QsKchYK0gN_27/view? usp=sharing.

References

1. Lee, L.H., et al.: All one needs to know about metaverse: a complete survey on technological singularity, virtual ecosystem, and research agenda (2021). https://www.researchgate.net/pub lication/355172308_All_One_Needs_to_Know_about_Metaverse_A_Complete_Survey_ on_Technological_Singularity_Virtual_Ecosystem_and_Research_Agenda
2. How the metaverse is going to change the reality of communication? [Internet]. Accessed 12 May 2022. https://www.c247.com/how-the-metaverse-is-going-to-change-the-reality-of-communication
3. The Gateway Into The Metaverse [Internet]. Accessed 10 May 2022. https://metahero.io/
4. Leica BLK Autonomy | Leica Geosystems [Internet]. Accessed 10 May 2022. https://shop.leica-geosystems.com/leica-blk/autonomy
5. Scanning Sets for Hit Series: 3D Laser Scanning in the VFX Industry | Leica Geosystems [Internet]. Accessed 11 May 2022. https://leica-geosystems.com/case-studies/reality-capture/75mm-studio
6. An Overview of Virtual Tours for Heritage Sites and Museums [Internet]. Mused (2021). Accessed 10 May 2022. https://blog.mused.org/a-guide-to-virtual-tours-and-3d-scans-for-heritage-sites-and-museums/
7. Richardt, C., Tompkin, J., Wetzstein, G.: Capture, reconstruction, and representation of the visual real world for virtual reality. In: Magnor, M., Sorkine-Hornung, A. (eds.) Real VR – Immersive Digital Reality. LNCS, vol. 11900, pp. 3–32. Springer, Cham (2020). https://doi.org/10.1007/978-3-030-41816-8_1
8. Berger, M., et al.: State of the art in surface reconstruction from point clouds, 26. https://hal.inria.fr/hal-01017700/document
9. The Brain Doesn't Like Visual Gaps And Fills Them In. ScienceDaily. Accessed 10 May 2022. https://www.sciencedaily.com/releases/2007/08/070820135833.htm
10. Penn, R.A., Hout, M.C.: Making reality virtual: how VR "Tricks" your brain. front young minds, vol. 6, p. 62 (2018). Accessed 10 May 2022. https://www.frontiersin.org/article/https://doi.org/10.3389/frym.2018.00062/full
11. Map of the Botanical Garden of the University of Coimbra. Universidade de Coimbra. Accessed 27 Dec 2021. https://www.uc.pt/jardimbotanico/visitar/mapa
12. How digital will help us preserve our cultural heritage. European Commission (2021). Accessed 10 May 2022. https://ec.europa.eu/commission/commissioners/2019-2024/breton/announcements/how-digital-will-help-us-preserve-our-cultural-heritage_en
13. Kahn Jr., P.H.: Losing touch with nature | IAI TV - Changing how the world thinks (2020). Accessed 14 May 2022. https://iai.tv/articles/losing-touch-with-nature-auid-1683
14. Gullone, E.: The biophilia hypothesis and life in the 21st century: increasing mental health or increasing pathology? J Happiness Stud. Accessed 1 Sept 2000. https://www.researchg ate.net/publication/23545430_The_Biophilia_Hypothesis_and_Life_in_the_21st_Century_ Increasing_Mental_Health_or_Increasing_Pathology
15. VRO. Mixed Reality with Passthrough. Accessed 12 May 2022. https://developer.oculus.com/blog/mixed-reality-with-passthrough/
16. RubenFro - Memories of Tsukiji. Accessed 11 Dec 2021. https://rubenfro.com/memories-of-tsukiji
17. ROM#001 – Benjamin Bardou. Accessed 11 Dec 2021. https://benjaminbardou.com/megalo polis/rom001
18. In the Eyes of the Animal. Accessed 20 Jan 2022. http://intheeyesoftheanimal.com/
19. Agisoft Metashape. Accessed 3 Jan 2022. https://www.agisoft.com/
20. CloudCompare - Open Source project. Accessed 11 May 2022. https://www.cloudcompare.org/

21. Technologies U. Unity Real-Time Development Platform I 3D, 2D VR & AR Engine. Accessed 11 May 2022. https://unity.com/
22. Tilia tree of the Botanical Garden of the University of Coimbra. Accessed 13 May 2022. https://www.facebook.com/watch/?v=439818210899650
23. Tilia Root System Drawings - Wageningen University & Research - Image Collections. Accessed 14 May 2022. https://images.wur.nl/digital/collection/coll13/search/searchterm/tilia

Game Communities

Predicting Success Factors of Video Game Titles and Companies

Johannes Pfau[1]([✉]) [ID], Michael Debus[2], Jesper Juul[2], Emil Lundedal Hammar[2], Alessandro Canossa[2], and Magy Seif El-Nasr[1]

[1] University of California, 1156 High Street Santa Cruz, USA
{jopfau,mseifeln}@ucsc.edu
[2] Royal Danish Academy, København, Denmark
j@jesperjuul.net, {eham,acan}@kglakademi.dk

Abstract. What strategies, company organisations, and design decisions render video game titles successful and secure the survivability of a game development studio? These are important questions, subject to situational and contextual variation. Nevertheless, different approaches clearly make a major impact on the public reception or economical outcome of a video game project, thereby making the identification of these factors a critical inquiry for both academia, cultural institutions, and the games industry. This work aggregated 137 (ontology-, theory- and experience-driven) variables about 144 games from 76 companies located in the European game industries, and deployed machine learning to predict success criteria on a feasible level. The most important features from these models were extracted, presented, and validated using the expertise of three long-time industry professionals, highlighting the soundness and actuality of these factors. Among others, genre, game engines, business models and protagonist characteristics can highly impact a game's reception and/or economic accomplishments.

Keywords: Video game success · Expert interviews · Industrial survey

1 Introduction

What is the secret sauce that guarantees success for startup game companies? This Gordian Knot has puzzled investors as well as founders and entrepreneurs since the game development became commercialized and industrialized. Researchers from business schools around the world have been wrestling with the broader topic of successful startups for a while, building a decent corpus of knowledge [3, 10, 23, 24, 26]. Most of the work is justifiably focused on tech startups, but the game industry, with its many idiosyncrasies and hit-driven economy has not been especially covered as extensively. To research this topic further, we set out to uncover what makes some teams so effective while others turn into fruitless failures. At the core of our investigation are the design methods and creative processes that set the games industry apart form other

B. Göbl et al. (Eds.): ICEC 2022, LNCS 13477, pp. 269–282, 2022.
https://doi.org/10.1007/978-3-031-20212-4_22

tech startups. To clarify our approach and aim of the paper, we formulated the following research questions:

- RQ1: **Can we predict factors for success and survivability of video game titles and companies using supervised learning?**
- RQ2: **Do these predicted factors and statements align with the opinions of industry experts?**

Tackling this enterprise, we drew inspiration from related work and theoretical literature for the design of the established key features and aggregated a dataset of 43 companies about 144 video games in total, gathering 137 particular variables that might or might not impact a game's or company's success (c.f. Sect. 3.1). As soon as this was populated, we trained predictive machine learning models (i.e. random forest classification and regression, c.f. Sect. 3.2) to identify the most contributing factors for and their correlation with the success criteria of company survivability, player reception (score) and return on investment, among others. As results of these predictions turned out to be promising, we collected the most important factors and validated these in qualitative interviews with long-standing industrial professionals (c.f. Sect. 4). Eventually, we derive general implications from our results and interpret these with respect to the business and experts' opinions.

2   Related Work

Even if some approaches tackle the aggregation of key factors for video game and company success, this field is largely under-represented, especially from an academic perspective, and industrial reports have only produced linear correlations so far. Bornemark investigated seven properties of video games towards success, using six major e-sport games, but did not confirm any theoretical derivations [5]. Cha found higher-level factors for success and funding capital in the specific case of crowdfunded games, which turn out to be particularly risky [6]. Especially with the respect to the qualitative presentation and a company's prior success, Koch et al. support these insights [16]. Aleem et al. observe the impact of team configuration, management, testing, programming practices and other detailed factors on game success from the respective developer's perspective [2]. Marketing decisions and practices for the Turkish game industry were also studied from Scengun et al. [25]. While they deliver descriptive measures about the local market, yet the impact of these metrics onto the (global) success was not discussed. Song et al. used Bass Diffusion Models and Cluster Analyses to identify success factors of Steam games, mainly considering genre, price and minimum system requirements, as they constrain themselves to publicly accessible Steam data [28]. While certain genres were predictive for the reception of games, the price level did not contribute significantly to the prediction. In the endeavor of establishing a framework for the success of video games, Ahmad et al. discuss factors such as concept design, development budget, game engines, marketing, mutiplayer, and downloadable content [1]. Although their approach encompasses an arguably feasible set of key factors, they only evaluated it on a single game, which lacks evidence of scalability and representativeness. Koch and Bierbamer focused on the smaller subset of player contributions and its effect onto video game success [17]. Apart from that, there is plenty of literature on predicting churn or retention to facilitate the longevity of particular games, highlighting game-related and general factors [4,19].

The most ambitious and closely related endeavor considerably was the industry-driven *Game Outcomes project*[1] from 2014, that sought to uncover which features define successful game development teams. The project collected information from 273 teams regarding teamwork, leadership, and culture and correlated this with five measures of success (outcomes): return on investment (profits or losses), critical acclaim (Metacritic score), internal satisfaction (is the team happy with the product), and project delays (from perfectly on schedule to canceled). The team created a survey with 116 questions derived from literature [12,20,30], collecting responses from 273 projects. The analysis consisted of correlating the 116 variables collected with the four outcomes. Some of the results show expected correlations, for example team experience is very positively correlated with success; other results are particularly surprising, for example crunch imposed on the team from management is negatively correlated with successful outcomes, while voluntary crunch is positively correlated with successful outcomes. The Game Outcomes project was a key inspiration for our work, which we strive to extend by investigating potential non-linear relations employing machine learning algorithms as well as expanding the pool of collected variables. We also pursuit to explore the sustainability of development teams as well as the success in terms of revenue and critical acclaim. Therefore, we set out to investigate whether we could predict different types of success metrics (5-year survival rate, players scores and return on investment) based on the variables collected.

3   Approach

In order to predict success criteria of video game companies or their particular products (RQ1), we aggregated a data set including a major sample of Scandinavian video game studios that incorporates a multitude of factors for success, company history, demographic distribution and metadata (delineated in detail in Sect. 3.1). Based on these, we explicitly aimed to predict measures for a company's survivability (as tiered into *"active since more than five years"*, *"active since less than five years"*, *"defunct and lived more than five years"* and *"defunct and lived less than five years"*), return on investment (calculated by the Sharpe ratio [27]), success rating (according to expert assessments) and an individual game title's user perception (based on their percentage of positive Steam reviews or star ratings on the app/play store, respectively). Joining the advantages of high predictive power and intuitive means of explainability, we chose Random

---

[1] http://intelligenceengine.blogspot.com/2014/12/the-game-outcomes-project-part-1-best.html.

Forests to predict the previously listed criteria and identify the most important features that lead to this prediction. Random Forests ensemble large collections of binary decision trees to solve classification or regression problems, suiting the discrete as well as continuous input and target variables of our data set. The decision trees used all operate on slightly different variable decisions along their pathways, which leads, if considering votes from a large number of those, to decently accurate predictions while training in reasonable calculation time and, most importantly, expressing insights and reports about why which factors were chosen, enabling the desired explainability of the approach. The following sections will give an overview about the composition and magnitude of the data set and the prediction accuracy, before validating these outcomes with the help of industry experts (RQ2).

3.1   Dataset and Processing

The dataset is based on interviews that were conducted with companies contacted through a European industry cluster. The list of companies provided was checked against and complemented with a national registry of companies by type. 76 companies were contacted and 43 companies responded. Semi-structured interviews were conducted via online meetings. The interviews covered the broader areas of "Company Information", "Business Metrics", "Success Assessment", "Production", and "Open Remarks". All interviews were conducted by the same researchers, who followed an agreed upon structure, developed by the project's team of four researchers in advance. Due to the semi-structured nature, the interviews lasted between 45 and 90 min. Notes were taken during the interview, and recordings of the interviews were transcribed in the following weeks. Transcriptions were analyzed by two of the researchers with a grounded theory approach, identifying themes and clusters (dimensions), and responses (variables) while cross checking coding regularly. The extracted data was gathered in a shared spreadsheet. This data was then complemented by (1) additional research in public repositories, including revenue and employee numbers, released titles, public funding received, and others, and (2) the analysis of 144 games of the interviewed companies. The game analysis was based on already established game ontologies, classifications, and related research [7–9,14,15]. The dimensions of analysis were chosen based on a mapping onto Jørgensen and Boger's categories [13]. In a survey of Reddit posts where users collaborate to help remember particular games from the past, Jørgensen and Boger identified categories at hand of which games were described and thereby identified. Choosing these categories for the present project is based on the assumption that, as these are the categories that players use to describe forgotten games they want to rediscover, they must be of some importance to the user. As the current project aims to measure game company success criteria, using categories that have importance to consumers was logical. The analysis included - but was not limited to - structural, graphical, and narrative elements of the games, release dates, age ratings, platforms, monetization schemes, as well as public and user reception. For the latter, major game related news websites were targeted with a google search including the game's name. If articles existed they were gathered and analyzed via "review analysis" - a method based on grounded theory - with "focus questions" [21]: 'Does the article mention anything innovative or unique about the game?' - 'Does the article indicate a reason for 'newsworthiness' in the categories of Sensation, Conflict, Identification, Current Interest, or Significance?' The former focus question was also employed on the analysis of user reviews. For this, ten user reviews for each game were collected, using the standard sorting method of each platform (Steam, Google Play Store, the App Store).

Due to the diversity of the selected games, their genres, elements [9], and platforms, and instances of unavailable data, some variables were sparsely populated. In these cases it was necessary to establish comparable values across games. For example, "User Scores" are different between distribution platforms. With an underlying binary system of "Recommended" or "Not Recommended" ratings, Steam rates games according to the amount of positive reviews they received. The App Store and Google Play Store, on the other hand, rate games on a decimal system from 0–5. A sample of games that were rated on both Steam *and* at least one mobile platform showed that transforming percentage of positive Steam reviews into the decimal 0–5 system is viable, with only small deviations of $+-0.2$.

The final data set contains 137 variables covering the topics "Developer Experience", "Organization Culture", "Diversity Metrics", "Business Metrics", "Success Metrics", "Production" and "Product" of those 144 projects. Due to the general data protection regulation (GDPR) conform agreements between research institution and participating companies, the dataset itself cannot be made available, but we report on the outcomes and most impactful features in Results and Appendix.

Table 1. Most important factors for predicting success criteria (indicating Random Forest feature importance in brackets and top positive/negative values below).

Survivability	Player score	Success rating	Sharpe ratio
Genre (0.23)	Business Model (0.09)	Dependencies (0.06)	Genre (0.11)
↑ Adventure Games	↑ Paid	↑ Unreal Engine 4	↑ Action Games
↓ Party Games	↓ Advertisements	↓ Unity	↓ Puzzle Games
Dependencies (0.11)	Realism (0.04)	Genre (0.05)	Retention Metrics (0.06)
↑ Unreal Engine	↑ Abstract	↑ Sport	↑ 7-Day retention
↓ Flash	↓ Realistic	↓ Party Game	↓ Not in development
Play Setting (0.05)	Genre (0.03)	Acquisition metric (0.04)	Protagonist Gender (0.06)
↑ Solo	↑ Adventure	↑ Only for marketing	↑ Female
↓ Social	↓ Idle Game	↓ None	↓ Neutral

3.2   Prediction Outcomes

We chose Random Forest configurations of 1,000 estimators, assessed split quality via Gini impurity, and settled on the square root of the feature size for the number of variables at each split (mtry), based on suggestions by Kuhn and Johnson [18] and own experiments with the data set. Using 5-fold cross-validation (as the established standard measure for the power of machine learning models [29]), 5-year survivability was correctly predicted with a 92.02% accuracy. For the remaining continuous variables, the Random Forest regression predicted Player Score with a mean absolute error (MAE) of 0.48 (with respect to 0 to 5-star ratings), Success rating with a MAE of 0.37 (with respect to 5-point ratings) and Sharpe ratio (commonly ranging from 0 to 3) with a MAE of 0.22. The most important features that lead to these predictions are summarized in Table 1 and are used to compile a set of statements for the following expert validation of the system.

In essence, companies that mainly develop adventure games will have a higher survivability, especially when compared to developers of party games; players rate games higher when they do not display any advertisements even if they have to pay for them; Companies that draw on Unreal Engine are rated as more successful than Unity studios; and female protagonists turn out to produce higher returns on investment than male or neutral ones.

4   Validation

After compiling statements about the (positive or negative) impact that important factors of game companies or titles might have (produced by the proposed system, for a subset see Table 1), we recruited a concise set of experts ($n = 3$) to validate whether these factors are truly important and whether the predictions stand to reason. For that, we implemented a survey that asked 26 questions regarding the direction of impact a factor might have on a target success variable, e.g. *"If a company develops mainly Free to Play games, its 5-Year Survivability will be..."*, so that experts' answers could be compared with the system's outputs. To ensure objectivity, participants were in no way affiliated with the companies approached for establishing the dataset. In a subsequent semi-structured interview, we further evaluated their responses by confronting participants with their answers in contrast to the system's predictions. If these matched, they were asked to briefly explicate their reasoning behind the answer. If these contradicted each other however, we followed up by assessing why the system output might not be the case; or if it still could make sense under some circumstances. Eventually, they were presented their overall agreement percentage and commented on that, listed additional factors that might have been important to predict the mentioned success criteria and expressed their opinion on the factors brought up by our approach.

4.1   Measures

In total, the pre-survey consisted of 26 binary questions (abstaining possible) targeting survivability, player score, success rating and return on investment. Each of those categories presented two to three factors that might impact these criteria and listed two to five sample values each, for which participants indicated if they are positively or negatively impacting the target variable. We computed the agreement between participants and the system as well as an inter-rater reliability between them. For the following interview, we recorded mainly qualitative responses about the match or mismatch between their own and the system's answers and classified them afterwards using structuring content analysis [22].

4.2 Procedure

After recruitment, subjects of the validation were sent online informed consent forms together with the aforementioned pre-survey. Once completed, they scheduled an appointment for the subsequent interview, either via an online video conference tool or in person.

4.3 Participants

Participants were approached based on their expertise in the video games industry. All of them spent considerable amounts of years (10 to 30) within leading game companies (such as Electronic Arts, Sony Interactive Entertainment or SEGA) in the roles of producers, designers, coordinators, consultants, creative directors and/or sole proprietors. In total, one female and two male subjects took part in this validation.

5 Results and Discussion

When asked about their estimation in how far certain factors of game companies and titles influence success outcomes (c.f. Table 1), participants tended to come up with the same answers as our prediction. Following the chance-adjusted Fleiss' Kappa [11], we found moderate ($\kappa_{P1} = 0.54$) to very good ($\kappa_{P2} = 0.87, \kappa_{P3} = 0.84$) agreement. Among themselves, they reached a good inter-rater reliability of ($\kappa_P = 0.61$), leading to a moderate agreement ($\kappa_{all} = 0.55$) when calculating between all participants and the prediction.

5.1 General Findings

In most cases (54%), all experts agreed in accordance to the system, as in the opinion that *"if a game's business model is mainly through advertisements, the player rating will be lower"* (especially as *"people react to the annoyance. [...] Ads have gotten very pushy."* (P2)) or *"if you can choose from multiple protagonists, a game's return on investment will turn out higher"*. Apart from that, for 23% of the statements, the majority of experts agreed with the prediction and only shared some concerns (e.g., two participants confirmed the statement that *"if a company mainly develops Party Games, its 5-year survivability will be lower"*, whereas only one judged the commonly low-risk, low-budget business of Party Games as a robust venture). Only for some (12%) factors, all experts disagreed with our data-driven estimation, such as *"if a company develops mainly education games, its 5-year survivability will be higher"* or *"if a game's protagonist is male, its return on investment will be lower"*.

When confronted with mismatches between their individual answers and the system's predictions, experts commonly expressed that they did not know better and would rather trust data and/or came up with reasons why their initial instinct might be incorrect or only conditionally true. Referring to the previously mentioned example, experts were convinced that education games do not produce higher market values than conventional video games for leisure, yet the higher availability of governmental and research funds for educational games in the European Union (where the data set was collected) might make these studios more likely to survive, which was reported to differ from the North American business (where the validation was carried out). On the other hand, game companies that focus on educational games *"are rather niche [...] and those who exist have low overhead"* (P2).

Only on rare occasions, participants uttered strong opinions against the computed predictions. One of these results states that *"if a company uses Unreal Engine as their main game engine, its 5-year survivability will be higher, whereas using the Unity Engine decreases survivability"*. P3 claimed that *"It is not necessarily the game engine that is important for the company, but it is what they are able to produce. If you go for [First-person shooters] with high-fidelity graphics then you are more likely to use Unreal Engine, but if you are doing something smaller, then its probably going to be Unity. [...] Companies that develop Unity mobile games are more likely to go bankrupt versus high-fidelity games. But not because they make mobile games, but because if you are developing high-fidelity games, you are already an established group, have funding and everything else you need."* This reflects the common misconception of correlation being causation, as this approach can obviously not comprehend causes, but relations between variables always have to be interpreted with context. On another note, P2 added that *"Unity is definitely superior to Unreal for mobile.[...] Apart from that, it might make sense. [...] At the high end of the game market, Unreal has more adoption than Unity. [...] So there is the perception that anyone can do Unity, but Unreal is hard. It makes you more valuable if your skill set is Unreal"*.

With respect to the used data set, the proposed approach produced viable predictions with high classification accuracies and rather low regression errors (c.f. Sect. 3.2). Validating factors with the highest random forest feature importance through an expert assessment, the agreement between industry professionals and the prediction turned out to be reasonably above chance and feasible, especially when compared to the baseline agreement between the participants themselves. A perfect consensus is unlikely to expect, neither between data-driven results and individual opinions, nor between multiple opinions of experts - but as our subsequent qualitative interview suggests, the larger part of disagreements stem from lack of knowledge, personal opinions and preferences, regional differences, and the manifolds of circumstances that a production of a game can entail.

Eventually, participants agreed that the factors highlighted by the system can be critical for the success or survivability of a game or company. Above that, they mentioned further factors that they deemed important for company or game outcome, such as *"having experienced people in the top positions"*, *"management practices"*, the *"competitive landscape"* against similar games that are already out there, the *"platform"* and further economic and quality factors. As the most important factor however, it was stressed that *"having the potential to construct a franchise [...] or sequel"* is a distinctive predictor for success.

5.2 Survivability

For the impact of Party Games on a company's survivability, only one participant mentioned that *"the social aspect is more important than the quality of the game, [...] so they can be developed with lower costs"* (P1), whereas another expert explicitly refuted this, as *"there is an oversaturation of party games on the market. [...] People put out party games without making them good. They expect the* "party aspect" *to carry it and rely on social factors"* (P3), which is in line with our prediction.

Even though P3 argued against the estimation of Unreal resulting in higher survivability than the Unity Engine, they admitted that when it comes to correlation, these results can definitely make sense - it is just not the engine that causes better or worse survivability.

5.3 Player Ratings

All participants agreed that if a game is financed through advertisements, player ratings will definitely be lower than for paid or premium games. As a reason, they stated that *"when people pay for things, they assign value to it. They naturally think its worth more because they paid money for it"* (P3). On the other hand, they don't see this trivially true as *"at the same time, expectations of the demographics changed. Older people don't like ads, younger people even value websites more if they have ads"* (P3). As many games are tailored for and/or targeted at younger populations, the temporal dimension and current zeitgeist are arguably critical for the development of video games - and for the prediction of their success.

5.4 Return on Investment

Overall, experts agreed that game projects with low cost and budget lead to less risky endeavors and thus tend to increase Return on Investment, as with the case of Casual Games and/or Idle Games, yet not for Puzzle Games (as the *"market might be very crowded"* (P2). The impact of a protagonist's gender raised more controversial discussions though. Despite the fact that one participant (P3) admitted that his answer to that was rather subjective, as they prefer to play male characters, they expressed that, when compared to playing a game with a female protagonist, *"males are still the dominant target group for most video games"* (P3) and playing as a female includes *"fantasy fulfillment and suggestive content"* (P3) for the male audience. P2 contested this position as *"the most successful video games of all time are based on male characters"* but acknowledged that there are definitely fewer games with exclusively female main characters and *"companies that create these are also likely to make better games"*. When it comes to neutrally gendered or objects as protagonists, experts agreed that it impacts financial success in a rather negative way, as *"there is little identity in that and players want to feel connected to the protagonist"* (P1). For the contemporary prominent category of games where players can choose from multiple protagonists or create a custom one, predictions and expert opinions all point into a positive influence on ROI.

6 Implications

Returning to the initially posed research questions, we follow from the previously outlined predictions, quantitative and qualitative results that:

- (RQ1) The genre of games typically developed, used engines and software dependencies, as well as the social setting of play are important factors that can facilitate or inhibit the survivability of a game company; the business model, realism and genre are critical for the public reception of the player base; and genre, the type of used retention metrics and the gender of protagonists can highly influence the financial outcome of a video game.

We do not limit the expressiveness of our approach onto these listed factors, but focused on these during the interviews and this paper for the sake of brevity. In order to not neglect the importance of other critical factors, we are going to publish this approach via a web-based interface that produces the same predictions and offers interactive visualizations and analysis of all related variables.

Regarding the second research question, we argue that:

- (RQ2) considerably high agreements between statements produced by the approach of this work and opinions of long-standing industry experts indicate that outcomes of this approach are sound and notably substantial factors for the success of video game titles.

Combining these considerations, we contribute to the fields of games user research and industrial video games market research by developing and publishing an artifact capable of predicting valid critical success criteria. As this is highly dependent on the magnitude, actuality and representativeness of the underlying data set, it will be continuously extended to incorporate appropriate and global information. Powerful data-driven predictions should always be interpreted with respect to temporal, spatial and contextual factors, and cannot replace professional interpretations alone, but uniting expert industrial knowledge and data backed up by sound and expressive approaches can arguably lead to improved predictions and explanations that are essential for both industry and academia.

7   Limitations and Future Work

Although we sought to make the data as representative as possible, the magnitude of the data set used for the prediction and validation of this approach can be seen as a limitation, as it can only reflect a part of the industrial landscape. This becomes even more noticeable with the focus on European game companies, whereas the validation was executed with experts from North America, as some differences in the businesses showed up within the study. Nevertheless, we investigated a set of fundamental factors that are not limited to regional occurrences and arguably transfer to the international market, and the approach proposed in this work is generally independent from the used sample. Thus, we strive to extend the data set to a larger global scope and repeat the experiments to end up with probably similar, but ideally even more factors critical for video game success.

With a limited sample size of three, the variance of opinions is certainly higher than from a larger population. Yet, during our recruitment, we focused on quality before quantity and excluded participants without the necessary in-depth knowledge and experience about industrial processes, decisions and the business. To account for this smaller sample, we deployed subsequent qualitative interviews that gave reason to the expert's decisions, determined how convinced they are on a specific topic and discussed each of the particular factors in detail. This helped explain the majority of mismatches between the data-driven and individual statements and consolidated our findings on the respective factors.

The majority of factors that experts claimed to be of highest importance for predicting success were actually covered in the utilized data set, yet did not turn out as most predictive for the target criteria. This might be due to how the deployed random forest models work, as a limited set of distinctive factors is often enough to classify data and not all critical factors turn reach high feature importance, or due to the difference between the markets, and/or due to the fact that perceived importance might deviate from actual factor contribution in the end. To not lose the insights from either perspective, we recommend to not rely on only a single source of information, but to ascertain expert opinions on a topic and consolidate these with data-driven results when speaking about success factors for video games.

Eventually, participants stated that they would have liked to express their opinion on continuous scales rather than binarily, which adds a measurement of confidence to their estimations and will definitely be considered in the next iteration of this work.

8   Conclusion

The economic success and failure of video games, as well as the survivability of their respective developer companies, are multifarious variables dependent on a high number of qualitative, temporal, societal and strategic factors. In order to derive the importance of particular detailed factors on these outcomes, we aggregated a larger data set from various game companies, describing a host of game projects through myriad qualitative and quantitative measures. These variables were trained on a machine learning approach to estimate survivability, player reception and economical success, which produced decently accurate predictions that were validated from selected experts with long-term industrial knowledge. This work presents a set of important factors that contribute to video game success or failure and illustrates a feasible approach for extracting these.

Acknowledgements. We would like all participants. This research was enabled by a research grant from the Interreg EU project Game Hub Scandinavia 2.0. Other authors were funded by the James S. McDonnell Foundation (grant title: A Methodology for Studying the Dynamics of Resilience of College Students).

A   Appendix

In the following, we list the set of important features for predicting the respective success variable, as used for the pre-survey (in a randomized manner). Participants were asked to estimate in which direction a factor and its value might impact survivability, player rating or Sharpe ratio (or abstain). Answers that correspond to the underlying data set used in this approach are **highlighted**, but not presented to the experts before the following interview. This is not meant as an exclusive list of factors, as many parameters from Sect. 3.1) are significantly correlated with the outcomes, but these turned out as most predictive.

A.1   Survivability

If a company has Phaser in their dependencies, its 5-Year Survivability will be... (lower/**higher**).
If a company has Unreal Engine in their dependencies, its 5-Year Survivability will be... (lower/**higher**).
If a company has Unity in their dependencies, its 5-Year Survivability will be ... (**lower**/higher).
If a company has Java in their dependencies, its 5-Year Survivability will be ... (**lower**/higher).
If a company has Flash in their dependencies, its 5-Year Survivability will be ... (**lower**/higher).
If a company develops mainly Free to Play games, its 5-Year Survivability will be ... (lower/**higher**).
If a company develops mainly Action games, its 5-Year Survivability will be ... (lower/**higher**).
If a company develops mainly Education games, its 5-Year Survivability will be ... (lower/**higher**).
If a company develops mainly Party games, its 5-Year Survivability will be ... (**lower**/higher).
If a company develops mainly Endless Runner games, its 5-Year Survivability will be ... (**lower**/higher).
If a company develops mainly MMORPGs, its 5-Year Survivability will be ... (**lower**/higher).

A.2   Player Rating

If a game's business model is Advertisements, the User Ratings will be ... (**lower**/higher)

If a game's business model is Free To Play (with In-App purchases), the User Ratings will be ... (lower/**higher**)

If a game's business model is Paid/Premium, the User Ratings will be ... (lower/**higher**)

If a game's realism is abstract, the User Ratings will be ... (lower/**higher**)

If a game's realism is realistic, the User Ratings will be ... (**lower**/higher)

If a game is not particularly designed to be newsworthy, the User Ratings will be ... (**lower**/higher)

If a game is particularly designed to be newsworthy, the User Ratings will be ... (lower/**higher**)

A.3   Sharpe Ratio (ROI)

If a game's genre is Puzzle Games, its ROI will be ... (**lower**/higher)

If a game's genre is Idle Games, its ROI will be ... (lower/**higher**)

If a game's genre is Casual Games, its ROI will be ... (lower/**higher**)

If a game features a female protagonist, its ROI will be ... (lower/**higher**)

If a game features a male protagonist, its ROI will be ... (**lower**/higher)

If a game features a neutrally gendered protagonist, its ROI will be ... (**lower**/higher)

If a game features multiple protagonists, its ROI will be ... (lower/**higher**)

References

1. Ahmad, N.B., Barakji, S.A.R., Abou Shahada, T.M., Anabtawi, Z.A.: How to launch a successful video game: a framework. Entertain. Comput. **23**, 1–11 (2017)
2. Aleem, S., Capretz, L.F., Ahmed, F.: Critical success factors to improve the game development process from a developer's perspective. J. Comput. Sci. Technol. **31**(5), 925–950 (2016)
3. Allen, T.J., Gloor, P., Colladon, A.F., Woerner, S.L., Raz, O.: The power of reciprocal knowledge sharing relationships for startup success. J. Small Bus. Enterp. Develop. 23(3), 636–651 (2016)
4. Bertens, P., Guitart, A., Periáñez, Á.: Games and big data: a scalable multidimensional churn prediction model. In: 2017 IEEE Conference on Computational Intelligence and Games (CIG), pp. 33–36. IEEE (2017)
5. Bornemark, O.: Success factors for e-sport games. In: Umeå's 16th Student Conference in Computing Science, pp. 1–12 (2013)
6. Cha, J.: Crowdfunding for video games: factors that influence the success of and capital pledged for campaigns. Int. J. Media Manag. **19**(3), 240–259 (2017)
7. Cho, H., Donovan, A., Lee, J.H.: Art in an algorithm: a taxonomy for describing video game visual styles. J. Am. Soc. Inf. Sci. **69**(5), 633–646 (2018)
8. Davidovici-Nora, M.: Paid and free digital business models innovations in the video game industry. Digiworld Econ. J. **94**, 83 (2014)

9. Debus, M.S.: Unifying game ontology: a faceted classification of game elements. IT University of Copenhagen, Pervasive Interaction Technology Lab (2019)
10. Dellermann, D., Lipusch, N., Ebel, P., Popp, K.M., Leimeister, J.M.: Finding the unicorn: predicting early stage startup success through a hybrid intelligence method (2017)
11. Fleiss, J.L.: Measuring nominal scale agreement among many raters. Psychol. Bull. **76**(5), 378 (1971)
12. Hackman, J.R., Hackman, R.J.: Leading teams: setting the stage for great performances. Harvard Business Press (2002)
13. Jørgensen, I.K.H., Bogers, T.: kinda like the sims... but with ghosts?: a qualitative analysis of video game re-finding requests on reddit. In: International Conference on the Foundations of Digital Games, pp. 1–4 (2020)
14. Juul, J.: Half-real: video games between real rules and fictional worlds. MIT press (2011)
15. Juul, J.: Handmade pixels: independent video games and the quest for authenticity. MIT Press (2019)
16. Koch, J.A., Siering, M.: Crowdfunding success factors: the characteristics of successfully funded projects on crowdfunding platforms (2015)
17. Koch, S., Bierbamer, M.: Opening your product: impact of user innovations and their distribution platform on video game success. Electron. Mark. **26**(4), 357–368 (2016). https://doi.org/10.1007/s12525-016-0230-5
18. Kuhn, M., Johnson, K.: Applied Predictive Modeling. Springer, New York (2013). https://doi.org/10.1007/978-1-4614-6849-3
19. Lee, E., et al.: Game data mining competition on churn prediction and survival analysis using commercial game log data. IEEE Trans. Games **11**(3), 215–226 (2018)
20. Lencioni, P.: The five dysfunctions of a team. Pfeiffer, a Wiley Imprint, San Francisco (2012)
21. Livingston, I.: Post-launch in games user research. In: Drachen, A., Mirza-Babaei, P., Nacke, L. (eds.) Games User Research. Oxford University Press, Oxford, UK (2018)
22. Mayring, P.: Qualitative content analysis: theoretical foundation, basic procedures and software solution (2014)
23. Okrah, J., Nepp, A., Agbozo, E.: Exploring the factors of startup success and growth. Bus. Manage. Rev. **9**(3), 229–237 (2018)
24. Olugbola, S.A.: Exploring entrepreneurial readiness of youth and startup success components: entrepreneurship training as a moderator. J. Innov. Knowl. **2**(3), 155–171 (2017)
25. Şengün, S.: A survey of marketing management for the video games industry in turkey. In: Marketing management in Turkey. Emerald Publishing Limited (2018)
26. Sharchilev, B., Roizner, M., Rumyantsev, A., Ozornin, D., Serdyukov, P., de Rijke, M.: Web-based startup success prediction. In: Proceedings of the 27th ACM international conference on information and knowledge management, pp. 2283–2291 (2018)
27. Sharpe, W.F.: Mutual fund performance. J. Bus. **39**(1), 119–138 (1966)
28. Song, S., Cho, N.W., Kim, T.: Success factors of game products by using a diffusion model and cluster analysis. J. Korean Inst. Indus. Eng. **42**(3), 222–230 (2016)
29. Stone, M.: Cross-validatory choice and assessment of statistical predictions. J. Roy. Stat. Soc.: Ser. B (Methodol.) **36**(2), 111–133 (1974)
30. Wagner, R., Harter, J.K.: 12: The elements of great managing, vol. 978. Simon and Schuster (2006)

The Importance of Dashboard Elements During Esports Matches to Players, Passive-Viewers and Spectator-Players

Stan J. P. van Kempen[1], Erik D. van der Spek[1(✉)] ⓘ, and Günter Wallner[1,2] ⓘ

[1] Department of Industrial Design, Eindhoven University of Technology, Den Dolech 2, 5612AZ Eindhoven, The Netherlands
sjpvankempen@outlook.com, {e.d.vanderspek,g.wallner}@tue.nl
[2] Johannes Kepler University Linz, Linz, Austria

Abstract. The reporting of esports matches is mostly done via dashboards, which contain the main match stream, as well as additional information about the match. Research has shown that these dashboards should be more adaptable to different user demands. However, little is known about the relative importance of the presented information on the dashboards to different individuals and how they should be arranged. In this paper, we report on a study designed to investigate the importance and preferred placements of different dashboard elements, across three spectator types identified in literature. For this purpose, a tool allowing users to individually arrange their own dashboards for *League of Legends* was created. Data from 31 participants was collected with the help of a survey and by recording the positions of the self-arranged elements. Based on the results, this paper formulates more in-depth design recommendations for spectator dashboards with a focus on adaptability and the importance of its elements.

Keywords: Dashboards · Esports · Spectatorship

1 Introduction

Over the years, esports broadcasts have attracted more and more spectators. The reporting of esports matches is mostly done by commentators [1] and via dashboards that provide additional information to support the spectators' interpretation of gameplay [2].

Research has been conducted on dashboards and other ways of enhancing the spectator experience, contributing guidelines, recommendations, and design goals. A theme repeatedly occurring in this line of research is the adaptability of the dashboards (e.g., [2–6]). However, throughout those studies, the importance of the presented information to individuals appears to not have been considered, since little is known about this so far [7–9]. This suggests that important steps within a user-centered design process are missing, such as the identification of the end-users and their needs [10]. While there is an established body of work regarding video game players and their experiences, not all

B. Göbl et al. (Eds.): ICEC 2022, LNCS 13477, pp. 283–295, 2022.
https://doi.org/10.1007/978-3-031-20212-4_23

esports spectators actually play the game themselves, and the experience they seek from spectating may also be different. Based on previous research, we can delineate three different types of esports spectators: players, passive-viewers, and spectator-players [6]. According to Stahlke et al. [6] a 'player' is normally in primary control of the observed gameplay, which in this study represents a player of an esports team, that also spectates to learn. A 'passive-viewer' may be invested in the matches and the competition, but is not actively participating within the esports community and thus not part of a team. The spectators that are interacting with the community are referred to as 'spectator-players' but are also not part of a team.

Inspired by previous design goals regarding adaptability, this study explores how these different types of spectators value different dashboards elements and their preferred placement. To address this, we created a small tool allowing users to individually place dashboards elements in order to investigate the following three questions:

1. What is the importance of individual dashboard elements during esports matches to players, passive-viewers, and spectator-players?
2. What are the preferred placements of the individual dashboard elements for players, passive-viewers, and spectator-players?
3. How far are the individual dashboard elements displaced?

The study is focused on the multiplayer online battle arena game *League of Legends* (*LoL*) [11], one of the biggest esports games. During the study, a three-step research process was followed. First, a survey was conducted to gather demographic information, the spectator type, and ratings on the importance of the individual dashboard elements. Next, the tool was experienced and the dashboards were created through rearranging predefined elements. Finally, a qualitative evaluation in the form of a semi-structured interview was carried out.

The results show significant differences between the importance of the dashboard elements across the different spectator types. This was corroborated by the information that could be perceived from the placement of the dashboard elements from the outcomes of the dashboards designed by the participants. Our results contribute to design recommendations for spectator dashboards that can help researchers and designers with creating adaptable dashboards for esports.

2 Related Work

Several researchers examined the opportunities and challenges presented by spectator experiences in order to propose new design goals or guidelines, to explore research opportunities, and to increase awareness. For instance, Alhamadi [3] identified and investigated the challenges associated with dashboards, what users do in response to those challenges and what adaptions can be applied to mitigate these challenges. Kriglstein et al. [12] hosted a workshop aimed to foster discussion on how technology and HCI can support transforming the act of spectating games from a passive to a more active and engaging experience. With the aim of finding factors that contribute to qualitative spectator experiences, observations and focus-group interviews were conducted by Rambusch et al. [5], leading to the identification of four themes: the need for an overview of game events, exposing hidden objects and highlighting important moments, spectator- and commentator-friendly game pacing, and the importance of professional commentators and casters. Wallner et al. [13] conducted a mixed-methods study exploring the information demands posed by players on post-play visualizations and the goals they pursue with it. Zhu and El-Nasr [14] stated that data is becoming an important central point for making design decisions for most software, including games. By defining the design space for open player modelling and how this can empower players through data transparency, new research opportunities were presented. Kleinman and El-Nasr [15] discussed the notable lack of research exploring how players use their data to gain expertise in the context of esports and argue that there is a need for further research into how players use their data and what they expect from data-driven systems.

Researchers also designed and evaluated different dashboards with experienced esports spectators. Kokkinakis et al. [8] presented a second-screen app for live esports events and discussed implications for the design of such apps by reflecting on the encountered methodological challenges. Aksun [16] focused on investigating the needs and expectations of spectators by considering their motivations and habits in order to reach conclusions on how the experience of spectating esports can be enhanced. The study includes a design intervention regarding improved dashboards to put recommendations into practice and to test their suitability with spectators. This intervention consisted of illustrations indicating how the interfaces could work. However, participants could not experience the design. For Charleer et al. [2], designing and evaluating dashboards resulted in design goals with four themes: adaptability, intelligence, transparency, and glanceability.

Regarding adaptability, a one-size fits-all approach is hard to achieve, as spectators have highly individual ideas and needs [2]. This suggests that a nuanced approach to dashboard design is required, either specifically developing solutions that address individual groups of spectators, or creating flexible solutions that can easily be adapted to a range of viewing settings, preferences, and needs. However, those aspects have not been thoroughly studied yet.

Hence, the present study aims to extend some of the related work. Firstly, design goals were integrated to create an adaptable dashboard. Secondly, this dashboard presented elements with information and statistics demanded by players and spectators. Thirdly, more research was conducted on how individual groups of spectators use their data and how they value this data.

3 Design

A tool with a GUI for creating dashboards was designed with the help of Open Broadcasting Software (OBS) [17]. A user-centered design approach was followed and the final iteration of this process will be reported in this section.

Previous research on the design of dashboards concluded that many participants felt a need to learn how to use the dashboards, since the eye tracking data indicated too much effort was required [2]. We therefore tried to keep the tool as easy to use as possible, and the decision was made to use a simple drag-and-drop function for displacing the dashboard elements with the left mouse button. Before usage, a key on the keyboard had to be bound to the function of (un)hiding elements when selected with the left mouse button. Simply pressing this key hid or unhid the selected element.

The tool has a black background with the gameplay being shown fixed in the middle of the screen. The gameplay shown was a fragment of the first game of the *LEC Spring Finals: MAD vs. RGE* [18]. Around the frame for the gameplay, five different interface elements were placed in predefined positions. The tool was originally designed for a resolution of 2560 × 1440 pixels but could be scaled down to any size with an aspect ratio of 16:9.

Five dashboard elements are part of the tool. These elements were chosen, since they were the most present elements during matches on the eSport website of *LoL* [19] at the time of the study. The different elements are highlighted in Fig. 1.

1) External scoreboard: This element gives an overview of the match and its current state regarding the objectives to achieve. It also shortly presents the current statistics for all 10 players involved in a *LoL* match.

2) Internal scoreboard: This element is from the game itself. In addition to showing statistics for each player, it indicates the current state of the bought items in the game and information on whether a player is alive or not. When a player is not alive, red numbers indicate the seconds until respawn.

3) Direct opponent: Traditionally, during a game, the five players in one team are divided over three 'lanes' and an area in-between, which is called the 'jungle'. Each player has its own role: the *top-laner* plays on the 'top' lane; the *jungler* plays in the 'jungle'; the *mid-laner* plays on the 'middle' lane; and the *ADCarry* and *support* play together on the 'bottom' lane. This interface element provides information about two direct opponents, for example, the opposing *top-laners*.

4) Last teamfight: This element shows a bar chart, with a bar for each player, indicating the damage dealt during the last teamfight for each player involved. A *teamfight* is a fight in which 8 or more players are participating.

5) Webcams: It contains two webcam streams, one for each team. The webcam footage shows one player at a time with their name next to it. The player shown varies, depending on the actions happening during the game.

More, similar, elements are present during the matches, but to avoid split-attention [20], those were left out. One of the main motives to watch esports, is to learn from professional players [6]. To create effective learning environments, designers must avoid the split-attention effect. This occurs when learners are required to split their attention between two or more mutually dependent sources of information, which have been separated either spatially or temporally [20]. Including more elements would necessitate them being placed further apart and could make it difficult to determine whether elements were really determined less useful by the spectator, or simply missed due to cognitive overload.

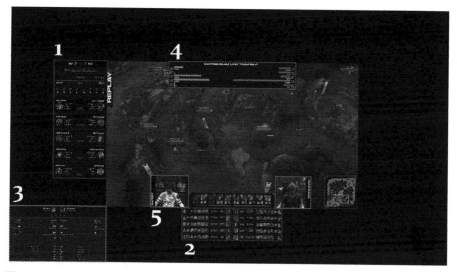

Fig. 1. Example outcome of dashboard with highlighted elements. 1) External scoreboard, 2) Internal scoreboard, 3) Direct opponent, 4) Last teamfight, 5) Webcams.

4   Method

In this section we report how a tool to create dashboards is used by different spectators in order to investigate the values the spectators have towards different dashboard elements.

4.1   Participants

Thirty-one participants (29 male, 2 female) took part in the study. The average age of the participants was 23 years (SD = 3.4), with the youngest spectator being 19 years and the oldest 31 years of age. All participants came from European countries. Recruitment involved sharing the call for participation using personal and professional social networks (including *WhatsApp, Twitter, and Discord*). All participants reported to have more than 10 h experience watching esports. Eight participants saw themselves as players, twelve as passive-viewers, and eleven as spectator-players.

4.2   Procedure

At the beginning, participants were given information about the study, which was conducted online. Each participant was introduced to the definitions of players, passive-viewers, and spectator-players (see Sect. 1) and asked to which one they felt most connected. Afterwards, participants were introduced to the five different dashboard elements and asked to fill out a survey which consisted of two sections. The first section included socio-demographic questions, i.e., gender (male/female/other); age (in years); spectator type (player/passive-viewer/spectator-player). The second one focused on the dashboard elements and asked participants to rate the importance of individual dashboard elements to them on a 7-point Likert scale (ranging from $1 = not\ important\ at\ all$ to $7 = very\ important$).

When the survey was completed, participants were shown a video segment of a *LoL* esports match [18]. The segment lasted 4 min and 27 s and contained a game changing moment in one of the finals as well as a replay of this moment. During the replay, the participants could pause the game and create a dashboard according to their preferences.

During the study, participants were asked to think aloud so the recorded sessions could be transcribed. A screenshot of the created dashboard was saved for each participant. The creation of the dashboard was followed by a semi-structured interview. Notes were taken during the whole session, which on average took 27 min.

4.3 Data Analysis

The data from the survey were analyzed quantitatively. Next to this, the screenshots of the dashboards were analyzed by creating heatmaps out of them. First, the placement of the elements was read in pixels. This enabled the execution of descriptive statistics on the displacement of the elements. The displacement was calculated in pixels in contrast to the resolution of 2560×1440.

With the pixel coordinates, a program could be written in Python to translate the pixel data to heatmaps. Twenty-four heatmaps were created. Four for every individual element: one for each spectator type and one with all participants (Fig. 2). Additionally, four heatmaps were created with all dashboard elements involved. Also, one for each spectator type and one for all participants (Fig. 3).

Statements from the participants are used as qualitative data to support and supplement the quantitative data and the data retrieved from the heatmaps.

Variables. In this study, one independent variable was used: the spectator type (players, passive-viewer, or spectator-player). As dependent variables, two variables were included: (1) importance ratings for each element and (2) the displacement in pixels

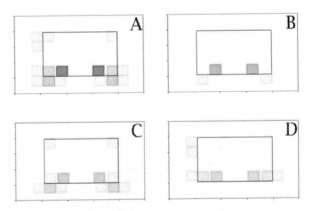

Fig. 2. Heatmaps of webcams for A) all participants, B) players, C) passive-viewers, and D) spectator-players. The outer black rectangle indicates the complete interface area and the inner black rectangle indicates the location of the gameplay.

for each element. All results were analyzed using SPSS 27.0 [21]. First, descriptive statistics (i.e., mean score, standard deviations, minimum and maximum values) were calculated. Visual assessment of normality using QQ-plots showed that the data was normally distributed for which reason the data was analyzed using parametric tests. As such, one-way ANOVAs were conducted to assess differences in the importance ratings of the dashboard elements.

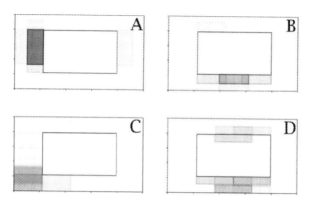

Fig. 3. Heatmaps for each individual element with all participants involved. A) External scoreboard, B) Internal scoreboard, C) Direct opponent, and D) Last teamfight.

5 Results

In the following section, the results are presented separately for each individual dashboard element. Table 1 gives an overview of the importance ratings based on spectator type. We also report the average numbers of displaced pixels of the elements, to give an indication of the strength of disagreement with the original placing, although no strong conclusions should be drawn from this.

5.1 External Scoreboard

The external scoreboard element appears to be the most important for spectator-players ($M = 6.27$, $SD = 1.01$) while it is of similar importance to passive-viewers ($M = 5.33$, $SD = 1.07$) and players ($M = 5.38$, $SD = 0.74$). However, there was no statistically significant effect of spectator type on the importance of the external scoreboard element as determined by a one-way ANOVA ($F(2,28) = 3.170$, $p = .057$, $\eta^2 = .185$).

The external scoreboard element was used by all participants. On average, the element was displaced by 447 pixels ($SD = 302$), with a minimum of 280 pixels and a maximum of 2058 pixels.

Almost all (30 out of 31) participants placed the external scoreboard element on the left side of the streamed match (Fig. 3A). All players put the element on the exact same location, connected to the top left side of the streamed match.

5.2 Internal Scoreboard

There was a statistically significant effect of spectator type on the importance of the internal scoreboard element ($F(2,28) = 8.562, p = .001, \eta^2 = .379$). A Tukey HSD post-hoc test revealed that the importance of the element was statistically significantly higher for spectator-players ($M = 5.09, SD\ p = .018$) and players ($M = 5.63, SD = 1.06, p = .002$) compared to passive-viewers ($M = 3.92, SD = 1.00$). There was no statistically significant difference between spectator-players and players ($p = .463$).

The internal scoreboard element was used by all participants. On average, the element was displaced by 371 pixels ($SD = 242$), with a minimum of 192 pixels and a maximum of 1324 pixels.

All except one participant placed the internal scoreboard element on the bottom of the streamed match (Fig. 3B). Seven out of 8 players placed the element exactly at the bottom-center of the streamed match. For both passive-viewers and spectator-players the placement of the element on the bottom side was slightly more spread out.

5.3 Direct Opponent

There is a statistically significant effect of spectator type on the importance of the direct opponent element ($F(2,28) = 7.481, p = .002, \eta^2 = .348$). A post-hoc Tukey HSD test shows that passive viewers ($M = 3.50, SD = 1.17$) valued the direct opponent element significantly less important than spectator-players ($M = 4.91, SD = 0.83, p = .005$) and players ($M = 4.88, SD = 0.84, p = .012$).

The element was used by 28 participants. One spectator out of every category hid the direct opponent element. On average, the element was displaced by 193 pixels ($SD = 288$), with a minimum of 0 pixels and a maximum of 1261 pixels.

24 out of 28 participants placed the direct opponent element on the bottom left corner of the dashboard (Fig. 3C). 23 out of 24 participants who placed the direct opponent element on the bottom left corner also placed it under the external scoreboard element.

5.4 Last Teamfight

There was a statistically significant effect of spectator type on the importance of the last teamfight element ($F(2,28) = 4.341, p = .023, \eta^2 = .237$). Tukey HSD post-hoc tests revealed that the value of the importance of the element was statistically significantly lower for passive-viewers ($M = 4.08, SD = 1.38, p = .025$) compared to players ($M = 5.63, SD = 1.06$). There was no statistically significant difference between spectator-players and players ($p = .058$) and between passive-viewers and spectator-players ($p = .926$).

The element was used by 28 participants. Three spectator-players hid the last teamfight element. On average, the element was displaced by 987 pixels ($SD = 323$), with a minimum of 523 pixels and a maximum of 1436 pixels.

Eight out of 28 participants placed the last teamfight element on the top side of the interface (see Fig. 3D). Half of them put the element on top of the streamed match (3 players and 1 spectator-player). The other 20 participants placed the element on the bottom side of the interface, all underneath the streamed match. 21 participants placed the last teamfight element together with the internal scoreboard element, either next to each other or on top of each other.

5.5 Webcams

There was a statistically significant effect of spectator type on the importance of the webcam elements ($F(2,28) = 4.530$, $p = .020$, $\eta^2 = .244$). A Tukey HSD post-hoc test revealed that the value of the importance of the element was statistically significantly lower for the spectator-players ($M = 3.36$, $SD = 1.57$, $p = .025$) compared to passive-viewers ($M = 5.00$, $SD = 1.13$). There was no statistically significant difference between spectator-players and players ($p = .071$) and between passive-viewers and players ($p = .979$).

The element was used by 25 participants. One passive-viewer, four spectator-players and one player hid the webcam elements. On average, the element was displaced by 564 pixels ($SD = 187$), with a minimum of 349 pixels and a maximum of 1118 pixels.

The placement of the webcam elements is the most varied one (Fig. 2A). Six out of the seven players placed the elements on top of the streamed match, all at the same place fitting well with existing elements that are in the game. The placement of the element by the passive-viewers and spectator-players is quite diverse. However, none of the spectator-players put the elements underneath the streamed match.

Table 1. Means (Std. Deviations) of importance ratings from each spectator type. Bold values represent the highest ratings per spectator type, italics represent the lowest rating per spectator type. SB = scoreboard.

Dashboard elements	Players (N = 8)	Passive-viewers (N = 12)	Spectator-players (N = 11)	All participants (N = 31)
External SB	5.38 (0.744)	**5.33 (1.073)**	**6.27 (1.009)**	**5.68 (1.045)**
Internal SB	**5.63 (1.061)**	3.92 (0.996)	5.09 (0.831)	4.77 (1.175)
Direct opponent	*4.88 (0.835)*	*3.50 (1.168)*	4.91 (0.831)	*4.35 (1.170)*
Last teamfight	5.62 (0.744)	4.08 (1.379)	4.27 (1.272)	4.55 (1.338)
Webcams	*4.88 (1.553)*	5.00 (1.128)	*3.36 (1.567)*	(1.564)

5.6 Qualitative Feedback

Overall, the players rated the importance of all elements quite high, with the lowest mean of 4.88 for both the direct opponent element and the webcams. The internal scoreboard and last teamfight element were most important to them. One player noted that *"as a player in the game one of the most important aspects is to be aware of the items in the game. Personally, I always like to see the effect of the items on the damage dealt."* (P13).

This may also support the fact that 21 participants placed the last teamfight element together with the internal scoreboard.

Passive-viewers were more interested in the external scoreboard and webcams. One passive-viewer noted: *"I am interested in the state of the game when I am watching. Some elements give a lot of information, which can be very interesting, but I prefer the external scoreboard. It provides simple information which can help me to understand the match even if I did not watch it from the start."* (P4).

Regarding the webcams, a passive-viewer stated that *"although the webcams do not really give information about the game, I still like them. I am not really sure why, maybe because it makes it more personal? I also like it when I recognize a player."* (P20).

For spectator-players, the external scoreboard showed to be particularly important as well, because as one spectator-player noted *"With one glance at the left side, you know what has been done during the game."* (P30). The importance rating for the webcams by the spectator-players was the lowest of all. Another spectator-player reflected that: *"I watch those games for entertainment, but mostly to get better as well. All elements help me to understand what happened and what the result of it can be, except for the webcams. Sometimes it is funny to see which kind of players are behind the screens, but for me, the webcams could be left out."* (P17).

In total, only three elements over all participants have been placed on the right side of the streamed gameplay. When talking about this with the participants, most of them answered similarly as one passive-viewer: *"I think I did not place something there, because normally in that place would be the chat."* (P26).

6   Discussion

The aim of this study was to gain insights into differences of the importance the different spectator types have towards different dashboard elements and how they would place those elements.

Our results show that different spectator types rate the dashboard elements differently with respect to their importance. The different values attached to the elements could also be seen when analyzing the heatmaps. Building on these results, we discuss design recommendations next.

Across all participants, the external scoreboard was considered the most important element. Looking at the placement of the element, designers can position the external scoreboard on the left of the streamed gameplay. Designers might want to consider making the element not adaptable at all since the position is highly favored.

The internal scoreboard was the second most important element across all participants but showed to be the most important one for players. Following the results, it is recommended to position the internal scoreboard underneath the streamed gameplay.

The third most important element was the last teamfight element. It was also the most displaced element, meaning the participants put a lot of time, attention, and effort into finding a suitable place for this element. Although eight participants placed the element on the top side of the interface, the position on the bottom side appears recommended. The reason for this is the number of times this element was connected to the internal scoreboard.

The second to last rated element were the webcams. It is also the element that was hidden the most. Designers should allow users to hide certain elements but should also consider that elements can be placed on top of the streamed gameplay. Using the tool, this happened the most for the webcam elements. It seems to visually fit in well with the interface of the streamed game.

Overall, the direct opponent element was the least important one. Next to this, it was also the element with the lowest mean of displacement in pixels. This can be related to the importance of the element: the participants did not want to spend time on moving the element as it was not important to them. Most of the times, the element was only connected to the streamed gameplay with one corner, meaning this element was placed the furthest away from the streamed gameplay. Designers may want to position this element on the bottom left side of the interface.

To improve the user experience of such dashboards, it is recommended to create an example dashboard or template for each spectator type. All templates should have the external scoreboard placed on the top left side of the streamed gameplay, whether the element is adaptable or not. Regarding the internal scoreboard, for the players it should be placed underneath, but connected to, the streamed gameplay and exactly in the middle of the streamed gameplay. The last teamfight element can be connected to the internal scoreboard by placing it underneath the element.

For passive-viewers and spectator-players it is recommended to place the internal scoreboard element underneath, but connected to, the streamed gameplay. For all templates, it is recommended to place the direct opponent element on the bottom left side of the interface, with only the top right corner of the element connected to the streamed gameplay.

For passive-viewers, the webcam elements should be placed somewhere on the bottom half of the interface. Suggested is a place underneath the streamed gameplay in such a way it fits properly with the internal scoreboard and last teamfight. Afterwards, the passive-viewers can always choose to move it on top of the streamed gameplay. For players and spectator-players it is important the webcam elements are placed on the bottom half of the interface, but not underneath the streamed gameplay. This means the webcams should be placed on top of the streamed gameplay on the bottom side, fitting properly with the interface of the streamed gameplay.

In summary, it can indeed be concluded that a one-size-fits-all approach is hard to achieve. As such, this research supports statements calling for a nuanced approach to dashboard design [2]. The recommendations provide a means to address individual groups of spectators and create solutions that can easily be adapted to a range of viewing preferences.

7 Limitations and Future Work

This study has a couple of limitations, which can be addressed in future work. Firstly, it is important to discuss the designed tool. This research is mainly focused on adaptability, but only on two parts of it: the placement of interface elements, and hiding/unhiding them. Since this study focused on *LoL*, the sizes of the existing elements were used [19], but future research could scrutinize how adaptive size may interact with importance.

Due to the number of participants needed and the time available only one fragment from a single match [18] was used. Future work could research usage over time.

The direct opponent element seemed to fit perfectly in the bottom left corner of the interface, which also was the starting position of this element. This might have biased the participants. Future work may want to circumvent this by, for instance, placing the elements randomly initially. In addition, in this study, relatively few elements have been placed on the right and above the streamed gameplay. This may be the cause of preferences formed by previous designs and the predefined location of other elements such as the chat. Another reason for this could be the preferred script of the participants. Since all participants came from European countries, they most likely are used to left-to-right writing systems. For example, Arabic spectators might have the opposite preferences due to their preference for right-to-left scripts. Generally, because our participants were young and European, it would be interesting to study differences across various target audiences.

Although the five elements were carefully chosen with mitigating split-attention in mind, the effect might still have occurred [2]. Even though the elements represent different kinds of information, the elements connected enhance knowledge acquisition better than separated elements.

Finally, this work only explored an adaptable dashboard tool in the context of *LoL*.

The tool will be developed further in future research, in which previous guidelines and the guidelines from this study will be integrated.

8   Conclusion

As the broadcasting of esports matches attracts more and more spectators, providing well-designed dashboards to support the spectators' interpretation of gameplay becomes more important. This work makes an attempt to address this challenge by providing an adaptable dashboard. Findings suggest those adaptable dashboards will look different depending on the spectator type of the user: player, passive-viewer, or spectator-player. This paper presented design recommendations for the design of adaptable dashboards for esports, related to spectator type and with in-depth information about the dashboard elements.

References

1. Li, L., Uttarapong, J., Freeman, G., Wohn, D.Y.: Spontaneous, Yet Studious: esports commentators' live performance and self-presentation practices. In: Proceedings of the ACM on Human-Computer Interaction, vol. 4, CSCW2, pp. 1–25 (2020). https://doi.org/10.1145/341 5174
2. Charleer, S., et al.: Real-time dashboards to support eSports spectating. In: Proceedings of the 2018 Annual Symposium on Computer-Human Interaction in Play, pp. 59–71 (2018). https://doi.org/10.1145/3242671.3242680
3. Alhamadi, M.: Challenges, strategies and adaptations on interactive dashboards. In: Proceedings of the 28th ACM Conference on User Modeling, Adaptation and Personalization, pp. 368–371 (2020). https://doi.org/10.1145/3340631.3398678

4. Horton, M., Read, J.C., Willitts, C.: InCuDe: heuristics for enhancing spectator experience in streamed games. In: Fang, X. (ed.) HCII 2020. LNCS, vol. 12211, pp. 97–116. Springer, Cham (2020). https://doi.org/10.1007/978-3-030-50164-8_7

5. Rambusch, J., Taylor, A.S.A., Susi, T.: A pre-study on spectatorship in eSports. In: Spectating Play 13th Annual Game Research Lab Spring Seminar (2017)

6. Stahlke, S., Robb, J., Mirza-Babaei, P.: The fall of the fourth wall: Designing and evaluating interactive spectator experiences. Int. J. Gam. Comput.-Mediated Simul. (IJGCMS) **10**(1), 42–62 (2018). https://doi.org/10.4018/IJGCMS.2018010103

7. Block, F., et al.: Narrative bytes: data-driven content production in esports. In: Proceedings of the 2018 ACM International Conference on Interactive Experiences for TV and Online Video, pp. 29–41 (2018). https://doi.org/10.1145/3210825.3210833

8. Kokkinakis, A.V., et al.: Dax: data-driven audience experiences in esports. In: ACM International Conference on Interactive Media Experiences, pp. 94–105 (2020). https://doi.org/10.1145/3391614.3393659

9. Wallner, G., Kriglstein, S.: Visualization-based analysis of gameplay data–a review of literature. Entertain. Comput. **4**(3), 143–155 (2013). https://doi.org/10.1016/j.entcom.2013.02.002

10. Abras, C., Maloney-Krichmar, D., Preece, J.: User-centered design. In: Bainbridge, W (ed.) Encyclopedia of Human-Computer Interaction, vol. 37, no. 4, pp. 445–456: Sage Publications, Thousand Oaks (2004). https://doi.org/10.7551/mitpress/6918.003.0015

11. Riot Games. League of Legends. Game [PC]. Riot Games, Los Angeles, California, USA (2009)

12. Kriglstein, S., et al.: Be part of it: spectator experience in gaming and esports. In: Extended Abstracts of the 2020 CHI Conference on Human Factors in Computing Systems, pp. 1–7 (2020). https://doi.org/10.1145/3334480.3375153

13. Wallner, G., Van Wijland, M., Bernhaupt, R., Kriglstein, S.: What players want: information needs of players on post-game visualizations. In: Proceedings of the 2021 CHI Conference on Human Factors in Computing Systems, pp. 1–13 (2021). https://doi.org/10.1145/3411764.3445174

14. Zhu, J., El-Nasr, M.S.: Open player modeling: empowering players through data transparency (2021). https://doi.org/10.48550/arXiv.2110.05810

15. Kleinman, E., El-Nasr, M.S.: Using data to" Git Gud": a push for a player-centric approach to the use of data in esports. In: CHI 2021: ACM CHI Conference on Human Factors in Computing Systems, pp. 1–4 (2021). https://doi.org/10.1145/nnnnnnn.nnnnnnn

16. Aksun, O.: Enhancing the experience of esports spectating: a design study on competitive gaming and spectator interfaces (Master's thesis, Middle East Technical University) (2022)

17. Bailey, H.: The OBS Project Contributors. Open Broadcasting Software (2017). https://www.obsproject.org/

18. Lol Esports.: LEC Spring Finals Game 1: MAD vs. RGE. https://lolesports.com/vod/105753980949216259/1/lPcDzbbbrRE. Accessed May 2021

19. Lolesports.com.: LoL Esports. https://lolesports.com/. Accessed 28 Apr 2021

20. Ayres, P., Cierniak, G.: Split-attention effect. In Encyclopedia of the Sciences of Learning, Norbert M. Seel (ed.). Springer US, Boston, MA, 3172–3175. https://doi.org/10.1007/978-1-4419-1428-6_19

21. IBM Corp.: IBM SPSS Statistics for Windows, Version 27.0. Armonk, NY: IBM Corp. (2020)

A Reusable Methodology for Player Clustering Using Wasserstein Autoencoders

Jonathan Tan and Mike Katchabaw[✉]

Department of Computer Science, Western University, London, ON, Canada
{jtan97,mkatchab}@uwo.ca

Abstract. Identifying groups of player behavior is a crucial step in understanding the player base of a game. In this work, we use a recurrent autoencoder to create representations of players from sequential game data. We then apply two clustering algorithms–k-means and archetypal analysis–to identify groups, or clusters, of player behavior. The main contribution to this work is to determine the efficacy of the Wasserstein loss in the autoencoder, evaluate the loss's effect on clustering, and provide a methodology that game analysts can apply to their games. We perform a quantitative and qualitative analysis of combinations of models and clustering algorithms and determine that using the Wasserstein loss results in better clustering.

Keywords: Data modeling · Autoencoders · Cluster analysis · Quantitative user studies · Interpretability

1 Introduction

Video games are differentiated by their genres, artistic designs, stories, and gameplay mechanics. In addition, they have varying budgets, team sizes, and production qualities. However, the backbone of all video games is the players, so understanding the player base is critical for a game studio. This has given rise to the discipline of game analytics, the study of play and players to provide insights into making better games and making games in better ways.

Our current work involves clustering players in the popular mobile game *My Singing Monsters*.[1] Creating clusters, or groups, of players based on their in-game behavior can help game analysts identify trends in the player base and better understand the parts of a video game that make it enjoyable or displeasing. Game producers can then use the clustering results to suggest improvements to the game or continue releasing content that players will enjoy. Understanding the player base through clustering is a win-win: the players' experiences improve, and the game studio enjoys increased success.

In Sect. 2, we go over some necessary background for our work. Next, we describe related work in Sect. 3. Then, we walk through the method for our

---

[1] http://www.mysingingmonsters.com.

© IFIP International Federation for Information Processing 2022
Published by Springer Nature Switzerland AG 2022
B. Göbl et al. (Eds.): ICEC 2022, LNCS 13477, pp. 296–308, 2022.
https://doi.org/10.1007/978-3-031-20212-4_24

analysis in Sect. 4 and present the results of the models in Sect. 5. Finally, we discuss the results as a whole in Sect. 6. The source code of our work is available at https://github.com/tanjo3/wae-clustering.

2   Background

2.1   Recurrent Neural Networks

Neural networks are a practical and versatile form of function approximation. However, in their simplest form, they require their inputs to be feature vectors. Unfortunately, many real-life data, such as images or audio sequences, do not fit this description, so either we must adapt the input to the model or the model to the input. Constructing features for this type of data can be laborious, and it is not always clear how to do so. Recurrent neural networks (RNNs) are designed to work with sequential data as their inputs to address this issue. Effectively, a recurrent neural network recursively applies its hidden state over each item in the input sequence.

2.2   Autoencoders

The goal of an *autoencoder* is to recreate its input. Thus, an autoencoder consists of two parts: the encoder, which creates a latent representation, or embedding, of the input, and the decoder, which reconstructs the original input from the embedding. If we implement the autoencoder as a neural network, we can train it end-to-end via backpropagation to learn the weights. We use the standard mean squared error for the loss function, though any reconstruction error is possible. Here, we use an autoencoder as a feature extraction method in our work, creating vector embeddings from sequential player data and using them as input to clustering algorithms.

2.3   Adversarial Training and Generative Adversarial Networks

For autoencoders, the training procedure looks to minimize the reconstruction error. However, there is benefit in adding a secondary, competing criterion that instead seeks to be maximized. *Generative adversarial networks* (GANs) [10] are generative models that use such adversarial training. The discriminator tries to maximize its success rate by separating actual and generated samples, while the generator aims to generate realistic output to minimize it.

2.4   Wasserstein Distance

While GANs are handy and flexible models, they are infamously susceptible to unstable training [2]. Arjovsky, Chintala, and Bottou [3] introduce the *Wasserstein GAN* to fix this instability. They show that optimizing for the Wasserstein-1, or Earth-Mover (EM), distance results in more stable training than optimizing for the Jensen-Shannon (JS) divergence as the original GAN formulation does.

2.5   Clustering Metrics

Clustering is an unsupervised learning task that looks to group similar examples meaningfully. However, without knowing exactly how many clusters there are and to which each player should be assigned, there is no strict way to evaluate the quality of a clustering. However, we can use metrics that evaluate what one would expect from a "good" clustering, such as dense clusters and clear separation between clusters. These are, of course, not necessary nor sufficient criteria for good clustering, but they serve as a qualitative measure without ground truth labels. We use two different metrics: the Calinski-Harabasz index [5] and the Davies-Bouldin index [7]. The Calinski-Harabasz index prefers high values, while the Davies-Bouldin index prefers low values.

2.6   Archetypal Analysis

In this work, we compare the performance of two different clustering algorithms. Both algorithms produce cluster representatives, which we will use to interpret the properties and behaviors of the players in those clusters. The first is the traditional k-means algorithm [12], which produces k centroids representing their cluster. The centroids represent an average over its cluster members. However, the algorithm has a couple of key weaknesses. The first is that the centroids identified by the algorithm do not correspond to an actual member of the data set, which can result in illegitimate values for features, such as fractional values for features like player level. The second weakness is that centroids of similar clusters may be difficult to distinguish. For example, if the centers of mass of two clusters are close, the average values represented by the corresponding centroids could also be comparable.

We also apply archetypal analysis (AA) [6] to our data set for these reasons. AA instead finds k archetypes representing extreme members of each cluster. Since archetypes are members of the original data set, their features will always be valid and directly interpretable. Additionally, they are generally easily distinguishable among other archetypes. For example, consider a data set of all sports athletes. The k-means centroids for tennis and badminton players might be similar, and since they do not represent real players, they are possibly hard to interpret. On the other hand, the archetypes for the same clusters might be Roger Federer and Lin Dan. Comparing these two data points is easier since they are real players and exemplars of their respective sports.

3   Related Work

Understanding player behavior in games is an active area of research. For example, Drachen *et al.* [8] use self-organizing maps (SOMs) to identify four player classes in *Tomb Raider: Underworld*. However, the input to their model uses six hand-crafted features extracted from game data. Our work uses recurrent neural networks to avoid hand-crafting such features. In another study, Drachen *et al.*

[9] compare and contrast k-means and simplex volume maximization (SiVM) for clustering players in *Tera* and *Battlefield 2: Bad Company 2*. SiVM is an algorithm based on archetypal analysis. The authors find that while both methods produce a similar number of clusters, behaviors were easier to distinguish when using SiVM. In our work, we compare k-means to archetypal analysis on the players of *My Singing Monsters*, while also comparing different autoencoder models.

To our knowledge, the Wasserstein loss was first adapted to autoencoders by Tolstikhin *et al.* [15]. They demonstrate the training procedure and provide two different implementations differing in the penalty used in the autoencoder. One of the implementations uses the GAN penalty, which we adapt for our work. Furthermore, we modify the training procedure to use recurrent neural networks and the gradient penalty presented by Gulrajani *et al.* [11]. Our contribution is to evaluate the Wasserstein autoencoder's performance in clustering, providing both a quantitative and qualitative analysis of player data.

Boubekki *et al.* [4] introduce the Clustering Module (CM), which adds a single-layer autoencoder to the existing autoencoder structure. This autoencoder minimizes the reconstruction error on the embeddings and additional loss terms that derive from viewing the k-means clustering algorithm as a Gaussian mixture model. Their autoencoder system demonstrated performance on par with other state-of-the-art deep clustering methods as measured by several clustering metrics that use the true labels of the dataset. Unfortunately, we do not know the true labels for our work, so we cannot use these same metrics. Additionally, optimizing for k-means clustering may not be entirely appropriate for our data. Regardless, we demonstrate the performance of CM-augmented autoencoders with and without the Wasserstein loss in our work.

4   Method

This section describes the process we take to prepare and perform our clustering analysis. Below, we provide an enumerated list of the steps in performing our clustering analysis.

1. **Game Identification and Understanding.** The first step is to identify the game to be analyzed clearly. In our case, we first introduce the core gameplay mechanics for *My Singing Monsters* to better understand what exactly might be the gameplay features we use for analysis. After identifying which gameplay we will accumulate, we need to decide the period during which and the frequency with which we will collect the data. What is appropriate depends on the game that is being analyzed. In our case, we opt to aggregate features by day over 60 days, but being more or less granular may be appropriate for different games.

2. **Data Collection and Preprocessing.** The next step is to collect the data and preprocess it. Ensuring that the data passed to the model makes sense is vital. We want to look at interesting gameplay behavior, and as a result, we only choose to look at players with activity past a certain threshold. Other

analyses may make use of different criteria. It is also important that we do not impose too many biases on the data selection and preprocessing at this stage. We want the sampling of players to be random; otherwise, our inferences will also be biased.

3. **Model Definition and Construction.** The next step is to define and construct the models. Models such as neural networks will have hyperparameters, and it is important to do a hyperparameter search at this stage to compare models as closely as possible. As a result, the optimization criterion needs to be clearly defined. For our work, this would be the reconstruction errors of our autoencoders. A key contribution of this work is the exploration of autoencoder models augmented with the Wasserstein loss. This methodology can also be applied to other models and approaches to data modeling, as we will demonstrate with the Clustering Module [4].

4. **Analysis of Results.** We then compare the clustering performance of the models. Again, the comparison needs to be quantitatively defined. We use two clustering metrics to determine how many clusters we will consider and compare one model against another quantitatively.

5. **Translation Into Actionable Interpretations.** The last step is to visualize both the embeddings and the clusterings. The former helps us understand the distribution of the player base. The latter allows us to infer the representative behaviors of the players in our game. In a game studio, not everyone is familiar with data science. Game analysts can more easily communicate the results to non-technical parties through visualization. Translating the data into actionable interpretations is arguably the most critical step, and so we split this discussion in our work here into its own section below.

4.1   Game Identification and Understanding: My Singing Monsters

My Singing Monsters is a mobile game developed by Big Blue Bubble that is free to download and start playing. It was first released on iOS in 2012 and has since been released on numerous other platforms. It is a world-building game where players buy and breed singing monsters to place on their island. Each monster has a unique timbre and will sing or play a part of a song depending on which islands the player places them. One implicit goal of the game is to collect all the different types of monsters available on an island to get the complete island song. The usual method of obtaining new monsters is to breed two monsters that the player already owns to receive a monster egg. The player must then incubate the egg until it hatches. Both the breeding and incubation processes take real-world time. The player can speed up this process through diamonds or watching advertisements. The primary way to acquire diamonds is to purchase them from the store using real-world currency, but the player can also earn them passively in-game, albeit very slowly.

Additionally, the player can buy decorations using coins to beautify their islands. The singing monsters generate coins at a fixed rate depending on their breed and level. The player can level up a monster by feeding them treats. The player bakes treats at the cost of coins, and baking takes real-world time. Again, the player can speed up this process by using the premium currency of diamonds or watching in-game advertisements.

4.2 Data Collection and Preprocessing

Ultimately, each action that the player makes in the game is anonymized, timestamped, and recorded into a database. Thus, gigabytes of data are collected daily with a large player base. So how should we represent the player? We could look at every player's action since account creation, but that could be thousands of data points to consider. Traditionally, analysts will instead aggregate the data. However, selecting features that represent players well takes time and domain expertise. There is also the risk of human biases leaking through, intentionally or not.

For this reason, we try to adhere to the natural representation of the data as a sequence of events. We aggregate events by day since looking at individual actions might be too much. In particular, for each player, we consider 16 different gameplay features aggregated by day. These features are (1) the number of sessions (i.e., the number of times they log in that day); (2) the number of seconds played; their (3) minimum and (4) maximum player level; the number of (5/6) coins, (7/8) diamonds, and (9/10) treats earned/spent; the number of (11) monsters bred, (12) bought, and (13) sold; and the daily number of (14) ads watched, (15) in-game purchases made, and (16) offers completed. We collect these daily features for each player over the 60 days since account creation. We perform a preliminary filter to include only US players who (a) created their accounts between January 1, 2018, and June 1, 2018; (b) who have at least one game session after 60 days; and (c) who reached a maximum level of at least 4. We also remove players for whom we have incomplete data. From the remaining players, we choose 99,840 of them at random as our training set.

4.3 Model Definition and Construction

We prepare four recurrent autoencoder models. All models are constructed using PyTorch [14] and have hyperparameters as determined by an optuna [1] hyperparameter study over 200 trials. We execute the optimization study on a Linux GPU server consisting of 4 NVIDIA GeForce GTX 1060 6 GB GPUs. We utilize the study's default optuna parameters, and record results locally to a database file. Each trial runs for 16 training epochs, and we select the model with the lowest objective value for the clustering analysis.

In our work, we first construct a basic recurrent autoencoder, the RAE. For our second model, we follow Tolstikhin *et al.* [15] and construct a Wasserstein autoencoder (WAE) that uses the Wasserstein distance. Our third model augments the base RAE model with the Clustering Module [4]; we refer to this model as RAE-CM. Similarly, we augment the WAE with the Clustering Module for our fourth and final model to construct the WAE-CM. We omit details on the hyperparameters of these models here for brevity, but the interested reader can find the code and final hyperparameters at https://github.com/tanjo3/wae-clustering.

We then apply two different clusterings to their learned embeddings with our trained models: k-means and archetypal analysis. To determine the appropriate number of clusters, we first apply these algorithms to the entire data set while varying the number of clusters. We then evaluate the clusterings based on the metrics described in Subsect. 2.5. Finally, we proceed to analyze the composition of these clusters empirically. Note that the number of clusters acts as a hyperparameter for the RAE-CM and WAE-CM models. Regardless, we will select the number of clusters using the same clustering metrics as we use for the RAE and WAE models to unify the selection procedure for the number of hyperparameters.

k-means Clustering. We focus our attention on clustering metrics for k-means. Since we do not know the "true" number of clusters in our data set, we run the k-means algorithm multiple times, varying the number of clusters from 2 to 8. We plot the results of this analysis in Fig. 1. A first observation is that the RAE-CM has quite aberrant values in the Davies-Bouldin index for two clusters. A second observation is that models that use the Wasserstein distance have better values than their non-Wasserstein counterparts, suggesting that the Wasserstein distance helps produce better clusters. Finally, a third observation is that models with the Clustering Module typically perform better than without it. Based on this analysis, we choose three clusters for the RAE, WAE, and RAE-CM models and six clusters for the WAE-CM model.

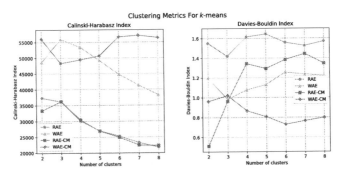

Fig. 1. Clustering metrics for different numbers of clusters using k-means. Recall that a higher value of the Calinski-Harabasz index is better, while we prefer a lower value for the Davies-Bouldin index. Our final determination for the number of clusters is three for the RAE, WAE, and RAE-CM and six for the WAE-CM.

Archetypal Analysis. We perform a similar analysis using archetypal analysis and plot the clustering metrics on these results in Fig. 2. Generally speaking, the RAE performs the worst of the four models. The WAE model performs the best on the Calinski-Harabasz index and improves over the RAE and RAE-CM for the Davies-Bouldin index. On the other hand, the WAE-CM model performs comparably to the RAE and RAE-CM for the Calinski-Harabasz index. The less-noticeable performance improvements of the models that use a Clustering Module may be due to the different clustering criteria that archetypal analysis uses over k-means. Based on these results, we choose three archetypes for the RAE, WAE, and WAE-CM models and five archetypes for the RAE-CM model.

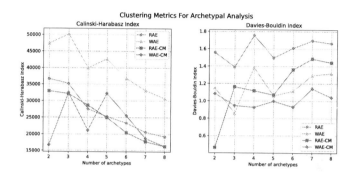

Fig. 2. Clustering metrics for different numbers of clusters using archetypal analysis. Our final determination for the number of clusters is three for the RAE, WAE, and WAE-CM and five for the RAE-CM.

5   Translation into Actionable Interpretations: Clustering Analysis

In the previous section, we found that utilizing the Wasserstein loss in our autoencoders' training can improve the clusterings' performance, as given by our metrics. Furthermore, combining this with the Clustering Module can add further performance. This section performs an empirical analysis of the clustering and interprets some of our formed clusters.

5.1   Player Visualizations

To start, we first project the learned embeddings into 2D space for visualization purposes. To accomplish this, we use UMAP [13]. We then overlay various player metrics to understand if there are correlations between player features and these player metrics.

Day-120 LTVs. A player's day-120 lifetime value (D120 LTV) is defined as the total revenue that the player has generated after 120 days since account creation. We are interested to see if there is any correlation with the gameplay over the first 60 days with long-term LTV. We map the log-transformed D120 LTV of each player with their UMAP embeddings for all four models in Fig. 3.

Immediately, we can see some correlation of D120 LTV with clustering. Players in the sparser parts of the clustering tend to have lower LTVs than those in the denser parts. Further analysis, omitted here for brevity, generally shows that the denser the cluster, the higher the D120 LTV. Additionally, these dense areas are where the smallest cluster of players exists, suggesting that high LTV players have more distinctive playstyles than low LTV players.

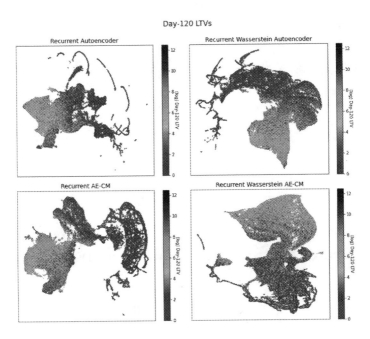

Fig. 3. A scatter plot showing the players and their log-transformed D120 LTVs. We show the color scales for the LTVs to the right of each plot. (Color figure online)

Acquisition Source. Next, we observe how organic vs. non-organic players are clustered. An organic player is one that was not introduced to the game via a user acquisition (UA) campaign. These campaigns are expensive to start and maintain. We plot the players color-coded by their status in Fig. 4. We can see that most of the players are organic and that the distribution of organic players is largely uniform. We can conclude that the game features do not indicate whether a player is organic, contrasting with D120 LTVs. It would seem to suggest that a player acquired through a UA campaign is not predisposed to spend more on the game or that the UA campaigns run in the past did not necessarily attract higher LTV players.

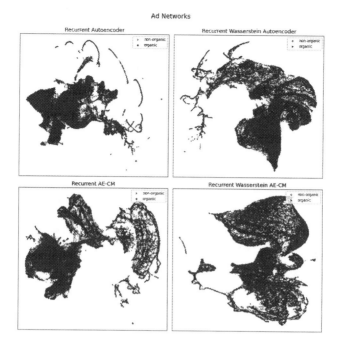

Fig. 4. A scatter plot showing organic and non-organic players.

5.2   Representative Analysis

Finally, we take a look at the daily features of the representatives of some of the clusters. For k-means, we look at the average of all players in the group, as represented by the cluster centroid. For archetypal analysis, we look at the player selected as the archetype of that cluster. We only consider some of the features for brevity and only look at one model each for both clustering algorithms. For k-means, we choose to look at the centroids of the WAE-CM model. For archetypal analysis, we will compare archetypes from the RAE-CM model.

k-Means: WAE-CM Model. We show the plot of a selection of the daily features for the k-means WAE-CM clustering in Fig. 5. There are six centroids in the WAE-CM model, and we can immediately see that the smallest cluster, Cluster 6, is interesting. Because of the extreme early activity in the clusters, the scale of many plots is distorted, making it hard to discern the values for the other centroids. Interestingly, based on the number of sessions and seconds spent on islands, the centroids of all clusters seem to reach similar values after 60 days. Players in Cluster 4 seem to watch more ads in the first 30, but Cluster 6 takes over for the last 30 days. Players in Cluster 5 seem to breed more monsters in the first 30 days before Cluster 6 again takes over.

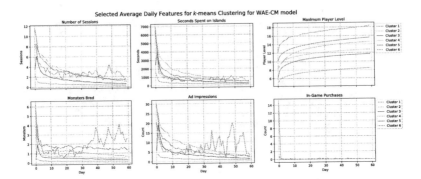

Fig. 5. Line plots showing the 6 of the 16 daily features of the centroids of the WAE-CM model. These values are averages of the values over all players in the cluster.

Archetypal Analysis: RAE-CM Model. Next, we look at a selection of the daily features of the archetypes identified by the RAE-CM model. We plot the daily features in Fig. 6. We can note that with the maximum level feature, the lines are stepwise since these are the features for an actual player. For this reason, the behavior exhibited in these plots is less subdued than with the k-means clustering. We see that the archetype for Cluster 2 gets to level 7 early on but is inactive until after 50 days. The archetype for Cluster 1 is more active but does not progress past level 10 over the 60 days. The remaining clusters have fairly consistent activity. The archetype for Cluster 5 makes many in-game purchases and achieves the highest level but does not log any more sessions than the other active clusters do. The archetype for Cluster 3 almost reaches the same level but with much fewer in-game purchases. They seem to play most of the five archetypes and might represent primarily active free-to-play players.

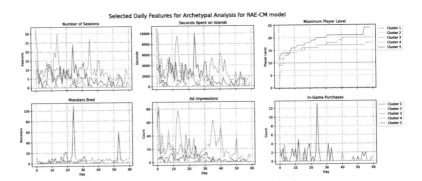

Fig. 6. Line plots showing the 6 of the 16 daily features of the archetypes of the RAE-CM model. Note that these are the features of an actual player, restricting the values to legal values. Note the stepwise appearance of the maximum level feature and the spikiness of the other features.

6   Discussion

This work has provided a reusable methodology for player clustering that game analysts can adapt and follow with their games, giving valuable insight into the game and its players. We demonstrate the methodology's application by an analysis of the players of *My Singing Monsters*. This methodology includes the application of creating player representation from sequential game data, the application of a clustering algorithm, and the evaluation of the results.

We use UMAP to visualize player embeddings, giving us a sense of distance between players. The visualization clearly shows that the clusterings are correlated to D120 LTV but not the player's organic statuses. Displaying this information as text or tables would not be as effective. Through contrasting k-means and archetypal analysis, we also demonstrate differences in conveying player behavior within a cluster. We note that by using archetypal analysis, particularities of a cluster's behavior are more apparent. By not having averaged values, the analysis is more interpretable.

Future work includes drilling down into these clusters to identify more specific trends, possibly even labeling the clusters with player profile names such as "optimizers" and "island decorators". In addition, Wasserstein models add a level of regularization. Exploring other regularization methods could yield better clustering results; we explore the Clustering Module's effect in this chapter. Another avenue for future work includes identifying or developing other metrics for evaluating clusterings. Metrics that do not inherently favor dense clusters could be of particular interest. Finally, we can apply the methodology outlined in this chapter to other games or refine the process further to suit the specific needs of a game studio.

References

1. Akiba, T., Sano, S., Yanase, T., Ohta, T., Koyama, M.: Optuna: A next-generation hyperparameter optimization framework. In: Proceedings of the 25rd ACM SIGKDD International Conference on Knowledge Discovery and Data Mining (2019)
2. Arjovsky, M., Bottou, L.: Towards principle methods for training generative adversarial networks (2017). arXiv:1701.04862
3. Arjovsky, M., Chintala, S., Bottou, L.: Wasserstein GAN (2017). arXiv:1701.07875
4. Boubekki, A., Kampffmeyer, M., Brefeld, U., Jenssen, R.: Joint optimization of an autoencoder for clustering and embedding. Machine Learning **110**(7), 1901–1937 (2021). https://doi.org/10.1007/s10994-021-06015-5
5. Calinski, T., Harabasz, J.: A dendrite method for cluster analysis. Commun. Stat.-Theory Methods **3**(1), 1–27 (1974). https://doi.org/10.1080/03610927408827101
6. Cutler, A., Breiman, L.: Archetypal Analysis. Technometrics **36**(4), 338–347 (Nov 1994). https://doi.org/10.1080/00401706.1994.10485840
7. Davies, D.L., Bouldin, D.W.: A Cluster Separation Measure. IEEE Trans. Pattern Anal. Mach. Intell. PAMI-1(2), 224–227 (1979). https://doi.org/10.1109/TPAMI.1979.4766909

8. Drachen, A., Canossa, A., Yannakakis, G.N.: Player modeling using self-organization in tomb raider: underworld. In: 2009 IEEE Symposium on Computational Intelligence and Games, pp. 1–8. IEEE, Milano, Italy (2009). https://doi.org/10.1109/CIG.2009.5286500

9. Drachen, A., Sifa, R., Bauckhage, C., Thurau, C.: Guns, swords and data: clustering of player behavior in computer games in the wild. In: 2012 IEEE Conference on Computational Intelligence and Games (CIG), pp. 163–170. IEEE, Granada, Spain (2012). https://doi.org/10.1109/CIG.2012.6374152

10. Goodfellow, I., et al.: Generative adversarial nets. In: Ghahramani, Z., Welling, M., Cortes, C., Lawrence, N., Weinberger, K.Q. (eds.) Advances in Neural Information Processing Systems, vol. 27. Curran Associates, Inc. (2014), https://proceedings.neurips.cc/paper/2014/file/5ca3e9b122f61f8f06494c97b1afccf3-Paper.pdf

11. Gulrajani, I., Ahmed, F., Arjovsky, M., Dumoulin, V., Courville, A.: Improved Training of Wasserstein GANs (2017). arXiv:1704.00028

12. Lloyd, S.: Least squares quantization in PCM. IEEE Trans. Infor. Theory **28**(2), 129–137 (1982). https://doi.org/10.1109/TIT.1982.1056489

13. McInnes, L., Healy, J., Melville, J.: UMAP: Uniform manifold approximation and projection for dimension reduction (2020). arXiv:1802.03426

14. Paszke, A., et al.: PyTorch: an imperative style, high-performance deep learning library. In: Wallach, H., Larochelle, H., Beygelzimer, A., Alché-Buc, F.d., Fox, E., Garnett, R. (eds.) Advances in Neural Information Processing Systems 32, pp. 8024–8035. Curran Associates, Inc. (2019). http://papers.neurips.cc/paper/9015-pytorch-an-imperative-style-high-performance-deep-learning-library.pdf

15. Tolstikhin, I., Bousquet, O., Gelly, S., Schoelkopf, B.: Wasserstein Auto-Encoders (2019). arXiv:1711.01558

Towards a Community-Based Ranking System of Overwatch Players

David Staat[1], Günter Wallner[1,2（✉)], and Regina Bernhaupt[1]

[1] Eindhoven University of Technology, Eindhoven, The Netherlands
d.e.staat@student.tue.nl, r.bernhaupt@tue.nl
[2] Johannes Kepler University Linz, Linz, Austria
guenter.wallner@jku.at

Abstract. Competitive games usually feature some sort of ranking system to rank players or teams based on their performance. As such these ranking systems allow to draw comparisons across players. In many cases, however, the details of the ranking system are not made transparent to the player community. On the other hand, the community may have a different opinion on which factors should more or less influence a player's or team's rank.

In this paper, we report on our first steps towards a community-based ranking system for the professional *Overwatch* scene built upon results of a survey conducted among the game's community. Further, we reflect on challenges and discuss possibilities for future work.

Keywords: Esports · Competitive gaming · Player rankings · Community

1 Introduction

Esports viewership has grown tremendously. In 2020, nearly half a billion people watched esports matches or events [8] and generated 947 million US dollars in revenue in 2019 [9]. Like many team-based sports, championships and leagues in competitive gaming are established to find out who the best teams are. A team's success, in turn, is heavily influenced by individual player performances. It is, therefore, important to find out how well players are performing, individually as well as a team.

For this purpose, competitive games apply some ranking system to rank players and teams (see, e.g., [12]). The ranking systems are often defined by the game developer itself according to metrics deemed relevant for capturing the performance. Usually, however, the internal workings of ranking algorithms are not made transparent to the player community, thus making it difficult to fully understand how a ranking was established. In this work we propose a community-based ranking system for professional gaming which is based on how important different performance metrics are judged by the community itself.

© IFIP International Federation for Information Processing 2022
Published by Springer Nature Switzerland AG 2022
B. Göbl et al. (Eds.): ICEC 2022, LNCS 13477, pp. 309–319, 2022.
https://doi.org/10.1007/978-3-031-20212-4_25

As use case, we focus on the *Overwatch League* (OWL)[1], a popular franchised league created to determine the best *Overwatch* teams in the world. At its inception in 2018, team owners paid approximately 20 million US dollars for one of 12 franchise spots [22]. This, and a broadcasting deal with *Twitch* worth approximately 90 million dollars and many other sponsors investing millions [22] shows the importance OWL takes on in contemporary esports. *Overwatch* has its own in-game competitive playlist and ranking. In 2018, game director Jeff Kaplan shared a distribution of players across different ranks, with 1% of players ranked as *Grandmaster* [7]. With 5 million active players each month on average [11], that amounts to about 50,000 people. The number of players, playing *Overwatch* professionally is significantly lower. At the highest rank, it becomes increasingly difficult to differentiate individual players' skill level. Apart from being very popular, we have opted for *Overwatch* for this work because it gathers extensive data from every match – expanding on what the game shows every casual player after a match (eliminations, damage done, healing done, etc.). This dataset is available publicly on the *OWL Statslab* [3].

In brief, this paper reports on the first steps towards a community-based ranking of professional players in the *Overwatch* league. For that purpose a community survey among 139 participants was conducted and performance metrics weighted according to the gathered responses. Lastly, we further discuss challenges and directions for future steps in this direction.

2   Background

Performance analysis on an individual level is extensively studied in traditional sports. For instance, baseball is famous for its data-driven play as discussed by Lewis [13]. Similarly, with football being one of the most popular sports in the world, many studies (e.g., [5,14,21]) attempt to find out who the best players are and why. A comprehensive review of this area is out of scope but two works should be mentioned exemplarily. Robertson et al. [18] developed a method to determine the performance of an individual player in the *2014 Australian Football League*. They studied the correlation of individual performance indicators and match outcome and found multiple significant performance indicators. Barrow et al. [1], on the other hand, compared different sport ranking methods in terms of their predictive power.

In video games, matchmaking heavily relies on player rating models such as *Elo*, *Glicko* and *Glicko-2*, or *TrueSkill* and *TrueSkill 2* which are built upon the outcomes of matches (see [23]). Some other examples of work in this space include but are not limited to the following. For instance, Shim et al. [20] gathered in-game player performance data to evaluate the existing point scaling system of *EverQuest II* to rate player performance. Their findings indicate that while the system is generally well in accordance with player performance, additional in-game performance data can offer potential for fine-tuning such point systems. Cooper et al. [6] proposed a player rating system for human-computation games

---

[1] https://overwatchleague.com/en-us/ Accessed: July, 2022.

(HCGs), considering both player skill and task difficulty, using a bi-partite graph representation (similar to Shim et al. [20]). They concluded that existing multi-player rating systems such as *Glicko* and *TrueSkill* are also applicable for HCGs. Subsequently, Sarkar et al. [19] studied the effects of the *Glicko-2* player rating system on player engagement in HCGs, concluding that player rating systems can contribute to engagement. In contrast to these works, our goal is to build a ranking system based on community perception of performance.

With the proliferation of competitive esports, interest in performance measures and analytics accelerated further. For instance, Railsback and Caprusso [17] studied the importance of human factors such as dedication, concentration, and physical ability for sports and esports players. While this study analyzes players on a more individual level, it is not based on in-game performance measures like ours. Novak et al. [15] explored performances in the 2018 *League of Legends* world championships. They asked three expert coaches how much different variables would influence the outcome of a match. They found two variables to be significant: tower percentage and number of inhibitors. Their methodology is similar to ours in that they relied on human input of which variables are perceived as important.

3 Overwatch and Player Rankings

Overwatch [2] is a 6 vs 6 team-based first-person shooter. Teams are tasked with either attacking or defending different positions on a map. The most efficient method of defending and or attacking is by eliminating the enemy players. Players can select one out of 30 playable characters, all with different abilities and playstyles. Nowadays, a team always consists of two damage characters, who specialize in eliminating enemy players; two support characters, who focus on helping and healing their teammates; and two tank characters, who specialize in absorbing damage, protecting teammates, and creating space. What sets *Overwatch* apart from similar character-based games or shooters is the ability to swap characters midway through a game. This allows players to adapt to opposing team compositions at any time.

However, the amount of research done on competitive *Overwatch* specifically is limited. There are, nevertheless, several informal instances where fans have attempted to make their own team rankings. One example of those is *Plat Chat* [16], a YouTube channel run by OWL casters and producers in which they discuss topics related to the OWL. They, for instance, rank the teams in their own personal rankings based on past and expected results. These rankings are limited to teams though. For a while, likely the closest thing to individual rankings, were the end of the season most valuable player (MVP), rookie of the year, and *Role Star* awards. At the end of the season, the community could vote who they think performed best during the whole season. These observations show that there is interest within the community to rank players based on their perception of performance.

At the opening weekend of the 2021 season, IBM introduced their *Power Rankings* [10], which rates every player individually, while differentiating between the three different roles (i.e. tank, support, and damage) in *Overwatch*. Every week they would update their rankings based on performances in that week and present those rankings on the OWL website [4]. However, the details of the algorithm have not been made public. A similar approach is used in this paper, but the statistics weights are based on a community voting instead of using an AI algorithm. This could be seen as a more 'subjective' approach to rank players as it is influenced by the perception of the community.

4   Method

Three steps were performed to determine how important different statistics are considered by the community and to calculate the ranking. First the in-game performance measures were collected. Second, an online survey was conducted to gauge the importance of the gathered statistics. Third, the statistics and weights were combined into a ranking system.

4.1   Data

Player statistics were gathered from the official datasets provided by the OWL itself through their *Statslab* [3]. For this study, data from the first half of the 2020 season was used as this was the largest dataset publicly available from the most recent season. The league provides this data in files limited to half a season at a time. The 2020 season was the first to introduce role locks (i.e. a team always must play two tanks, two supports and two damage characters). This enforced an even distribution of character playtime, resulting in fairer comparisons between different roles. Additionally, at the start of this project, the 2020 season was the most recently completed season, providing a ranking system which should best match the current implemented practices.

The statistics provided in the dataset are almost all absolute values per map played. To create a fair comparison, these values were converted to relative values. As such, in this study the values were transformed into 'per 10 min' values by multiplying the values by $600 \, sec/time \, played$. This time interval was chosen because the OWL itself uses per 10 min values to present data to viewers as does the in-game statistics page. As such the broadcast audience and study participants are likely familiar with this presentation. Statistics were considered on a per-character basis, not a per-player basis. As *Overwatch* allows players to switch characters mid game, players often switch to a different character on which they likely perform differently. This method allows multiple ratings per map. A character is only taken into account, if it was played for more than 30 s (after which we assume a player can have a significant impact on the match).

4.2   Survey

Second, the importance (weight) of each statistic needs to be determined. Not every statistic is equally important for the different roles. For instance, for a support player the amount of damage done and the number of eliminations are not as important as for a damage player. To determine the weight of every statistic, the competitive *Overwatch* community on r/CompetitiveOverwatch[2] was asked to rate the importance of different statistics. In a survey, they were asked to rate the importance of 14 – in the dataset available – statistics for damage characters, 16 statistics for support, and 17 for tank characters on a 7-point Likert scale (*1 = being not important at all* to *7 = being extremely important*). The responses were then averaged to determine a weight for each statistic. In addition to collecting statistic weights, the respondents were also asked about their gender, age, playing experience, skill level, and investment in the OWL. The survey was posted on the r/CompetitiveOverwatch subreddit with a brief description of the study and the survey.

At the time of the survey their were more than 250,000 registered members on this subreddit. While some of them are likely professional players and coaches it can be assumed that they are greatly outnumbered by casual players and fans and thus should not have skewed the survey results considerable. Responses were gathered over a five day period and were limited to one per registered Google account.

The survey was filled in by 139 participants of which 135 were usable responses. Over two thirds (67.6%) of these participants were relatively invested in the OWL as they engaged in OWL-related content for more than 3 h per week. A majority (66.2%) was over level 500 in *Overwatch*. Table 1 shows the average importance ranking per statistic per role. These values were used as weight for the statistics when calculating the performance rating.

4.3   Rating System

It should be noted that the statistics are captured on different scales which need to be harmonized first to make them comparable. For instance, 'All damage done' can easily exceed a value of 10,000 in one match, while the number of multikills will usually be below 10. To make sure 'All damage done' is not weighted more heavily than other statistics, all statistics were adjusted so that their contribution is independent of their scale before the community weighting factor is applied.

While most statistics follow a higher is better rule of thumb, three do not. 'Time holding ultimate'[3], 'Time elapsed per ultimate earned', and 'Deaths' work the other way around with lower being better. 'Time elapsed per ultimate' has a maximum value per role as an ultimate ability also charges passively while not doing anything. Healing or doing damage speeds up the ultimate charge time. By subtracting the recorded value from the passive charge time, the value is converted into a higher equals better statistic. 'Time holding ultimate' and 'Deaths' can be transformed similarly. However, these statistics have no finite maximum value. Instead, the highest recorded value per role was used to subtract the statistic value from.

---

[2] https://www.reddit.com/r/CompetitiveOverwatch/ (Accessed: July, 2022).

[3] In *Overwatch*, players have one extra powerful ability, a so-called *ultimate*, that they can charge by healing or doing damage.

Table 1. Average weight of statistics for tank, support, and damage players based on the survey results (SD = standard deviation).

Metric	Tanks	SD	Support	SD	Damage	SD
All damage done	3.977778	1.32	3.496296	1.56	5.955556	1.17
Assists	4.096296	1.38	5.222222	1.48	4.992593	1.49
Average time alive	6.303704	0.94	6.503704	0.77	5.311111	1.36
Barrier damage done	2.807407	1.28	2.407407	1.32	4.407407	1.54
Damage blocked	4.777778	1.43	–	–	–	–
Character damage done	4.785185	1.06	3.97037	1.53	6.118519	1.16
Damage taken	5.02963	1.53	4.622222	1.67	4.303704	1.58
Deaths	6.177778	1.15	6.340741	1.13	5.362963	1.44
Eliminations	4.17037	1.39	3.725926	1.40	5.881481	1.18
Final blows	3.718519	1.63	3.192593	1.66	6.037037	1.28
Multikills	2.688889	1.57	2.02963	1.34	4.214815	1.84
Objective kills	3.555556	1.63	2.837037	1.48	4.22963	1.79
Objective time	3.437037	1.80	3.088889	1.68	2.496296	1.44
Time alive	6.222222	0.99	6.348148	0.94	–	–
Time elapsed per ultimate earned	5.6	1.33	5.911111	1.22	5.562963	1.22
Time holding ultimate	4.118519	1.72	4.340741	1.88	4.451852	1.77
Ultimates used	4.718519	1.64	–	–	–	–
Healing done	–	–	6.096296	1.03	–	–

The performance rating (per role) can then determined by the sum of the statistic values, multiplied by their corresponding weight, mathematically

$$rating = \sum_{i=1}^{N} weight_i \cdot stat_i \cdot adjustment_i$$

where $weight_i$ is the weighting factor for $stat_i$ as shown in Table 1. $Adjustment_i$ ensures that all statistics influence the rating equally by default. N is the total number of statistics for a role, with $N = 16$ for support, $N = 17$ for tank, $N = 14$ for damage. Before applying the equation to our dataset we removed all instances of a character being played for less than 30 s (as discussed in Sect. 4.1). Next, the performance rating for each character a player has played was calculated. These instances were then averaged to obtain an overall performance rating per player. Similar, an average team rating was calculated from the individual ratings of its members (taking into account individual players' playtime). In a similar fashion, average performance ratings per playable character were calculated. All roles averaged a score around 1,000. To facilitate comparisons between roles scores were adjusted such that the average performance rating equals 1,000. A rating above 1,000 thus means above average performance, while a rating below 1,000 indicates below average performance.

Table 2. Top three and bottom three performing damage players (players playing less than 40 min have been excluded). Ratings above 1,000 indicate above average and ratings below 1,000 correspond to below average performance in our system.

Player name	Rating	Team name	Rating	Time played [min]
eq0	1172.3	Philadelphia Fusion	1079.1	301.1
Fleta	1120.5	Shanghai Dragons	1068.0	907.4
STRIKER	1118.5	San Francisco Shock	1063.8	474.8
...				
Jaru	857.4	Los Angeles Gladiators	985.4	108.3
Baconjack	852.2	Chengdu Hunters	932.2	210.6
Tsuna	837.2	Vancouver Titans	928.1	151.3

5 Use Cases

In the following, we discuss a few potential uses cases for the rating system. First, Table 2 shows the three top and bottom performing damage players, including the total time played and excluding players who played less than 40 min total. Note that these results are season averages per player and do not represent single map performances.

While some high-ranking players were to be expected, some other high-ranking players were quite surprising. For instance, regular season MVP 'Fleta' and grand finals MVP 'Striker' both scored near the top of the average performance ratings. Others, in contrast, who scored high in our ranking such as 'eq0' are not considered *Role Stars* by the league at the end of the season. The *Role Star* awards were determined by general managers, head coaches, broadcast talent, and members of the media, who were all asked to cast four votes per role at the end of the season. This approach is relatively subjective and more susceptible to being skewed by factors such as recency bias compared to our approach. It shows how players performing well can sometimes go under the radar or get overshadowed by others playing even better.

Overwatch features different characters which can differ drastically in playstyle. While some of these differences are currently not considered in the rating other differences are already captured by the approach. For instance, one of the statistics that contributes to the tank rating is 'damage blocked' with a weight of 4.78. Consequently, a high amount of damage blocked will improve a player's rating. However, while most tank characters are capable of blocking damage, not all of them are. Some excel at it, such as REINHARDT and ORISA, while other tanks such as ROADHOG and D.VA require a playstyle less focused on blocking damage. It might therefore be expected that ROADHOG players are at a disadvantage when it comes to the rating and that their rating would be considerably lower. However, the opposite is the case. ROADHOG happens to be the best performing tank of all (cf. Table 3). This might be attributed to good character balancing. The average performance rating per character is visible in

Table 3. Average performance rating per character. Ratings above 1,000 indicate above and ratings below 1,000 correspond to below average performance in our system.

Support		Tank		Damage		Damage (cont.)	
Hero	Rating	Hero	Rating	Hero	Rating	Hero	Rating
Moira	1156.4	Roadhog	1042.6	Paharah	1112.7	Echo	1018.2
Lúcio	1016.8	D.Va	1034.7	Bastion	1100.6	Tracer	990.0
Baptiste	1015.7	Sigma	1031.8	Junkrat	1098.3	Symmetra	988.3
Brigitte	991.4	Zarya	1016.7	Torbjörn	1086.6	McCree	983.9
Zenyatta	983.5	Orisa	1010.9	Reaper	1067.9	Soldier: 76	959.0
Ana	935.1	Reinhardt	972.5	Genji	1055.1	Hanzo	950.5
Mercy	782.7	Winston	960.8	Mei	1029.9	Sombra	938.8
		Wrecking Ball	915.0	Ashe	1026.3	Doomfist	891.6
						Widowmaker	851.1

Table 3. While all tank characters are somewhat similar in their rating, we see larger discrepancies in the support role. MERCY has a very specific use case as one of her main abilities is to increase the damage done by other players. As this statistic was not used in the calculation of the performance rating, MERCY ratings tend to be lower. MOIRA excels when the entire team is close together. Contrarily, when the team plays further apart, MOIRA becomes less efficient. These nuances are not fully captured by the statistics (see Sect. 6). Other heroes have a broader use, resulting in less inflated ratings.

6   Discussion

This study gives an indication of a community's perception of the best players. This is a more subjective approach compared to more objective methods assessing the impact of a statistic on win percentage. However, what *feels* like a good player and what *is* a good player are not necessarily the same thing. While these players and performances might not actually be the objectively best players in the game, these players are perceived by the community as being the best. Having a rating system which reflects the communities opinions could thus offer an interesting alternative to established rankings to, for instance, discuss performances from different angles. In this sense, one could argue that the knowledge of the average OWL fan about what makes a player a good player can be limited compared to a coach, scout, player, or computer. Having coaches taking the survey would likely result in different weights. Building a similar ranking system based solely on their opinion would allow for further comparisons.

Apart from the occasional 'power ranking' posts on social media from people in the community, there are very little community-based ranking systems publicly available. This lack of comparison material makes evaluating the approach more challenging. The IBM power rankings are inherently different because of the more objective approach. A comparison to that ranking system could be used to evaluate the differences between perceived and actual performance levels, but does not evaluate the community-driven approach used in this study directly. While there are many online communities of OWL fans and spectators, none are as large as the r/CompetitiveOverwatch subreddit. Because of its well known status and size, it was assumed that this community represents well the average OWL spectators.

Developing a performance rating system which takes into account community preferences and fairly compares players is challenging, especially for games such as *Overwatch* where different characters require a different style of play. Currently, the rating only differentiates between the three different roles but does not take into account that even within a role playable characters also fulfill different purposes. Ideally, the community survey would have differentiated between all characters rather than just roles.

Additionally, the "passive ultimate charge" differs between characters. This means that the maximum time to charge is different for every character. An ultimate also differs per character. However, the value used to subtract the "time building ultimate" and "time elapsed per ultimate earned" values were fixed. They were based on the maximum time per role, rather than the maximum time per character. Were these values to be substituted by the per character maximum values, these statistics would have a more representative impact on the player rating. Thus, gathering the relevance of different statistics per character could help to improve the proposed ranking system further.

Apart from considering metrics in a more nuanced fashion, the proposed ranking should be evaluated with the community in the future to gather feedback on its value and how it could be further improved.

7   Conclusions and Future Work

In this work we discussed first steps towards a community-based ranking system of player performance. While we specifically focused on the *Overwatch* league as use case, the approach is general enough to be applied to other games in a similar way. We argue that such a community-based ranking could offer a valuable complement to existing objective measures to, for instance, discuss and reflect on player performance from different angles during live broadcasts. Offering a fair comparison of performance in games with different characters which have different characteristics is not straightforward. Future work will need to focus on tweaking the system further by more closely taking into account these characteristics and should explore the differences between perceived performance as presented in this study and objective performance rankings. This could shed light on why they are different which could further inform player rankings.

As the dataset only contained completed games we focused on post-game summary ratings in this paper. However, if statistics are provided in real-time it could also be applied to calculate live performance ratings. These ratings could then be used to improve viewing experiences by enriching the live feed. Future work may also explore ways to present the player performance ratings in visual form.

References

1. Barrow, D., Drayer, I., Elliott, P., Gaut, G., Osting, B.: Ranking rankings: an empirical comparison of the predictive power of sports ranking methods. J. Quant. Anal. Sports 9(2), 187–202 (2013). https://doi.org/10.1515/jqas-2013-0013
2. Blizzard Entertainment: Overwatch. Game [PC]. Blizzard Entertainment, Irvine, CA, USA, May 2016
3. Blizzard Entertainment: The Overwatch League - Stats Lab (beta) (2021). https://overwatchleague.com/en-us/statslab. Accessed July 2022
4. Blizzard Entertainment: Power Rankings | The Overwatch League (2021). https://overwatchleague.com/en-us/power-rankings?utm_source=owlweb& utm_medium=navigationbar&utm_campaign=general Accessed: July, 2022
5. Boscá, J.E., Liern, V., Martínez, A., Sala, R.: Increasing offensive or defensive efficiency? An analysis of Italian and Spanish football. Omega 37(1), 63–78 (2009). https://doi.org/10.1016/j.omega.2006.08.002
6. Cooper, S., Deterding, C.S., Tsapakos, T.: Player rating systems for balancing human computation games: testing the effect of bipartiteness. In: Proceedings of the First International Joint Conference of DIGRA AND FDG. DIGRA Digital Games and Research Association (2016)
7. Esports Tales: Overwatch competitive rank distribution: Pc and console - updated monthly (2022). https://www.esportstales.com/overwatch/competitive-rank-distribution-pc-and-console. Accessed: July 2022
8. Geyser, W.: The incredible growth of esports [+ esports statistics] (2021). https://influencermarketinghub.com/growth-of-esports-stats/. Accessed: July 2022
9. Gough, C.: Esports market revenue worldwide from 2019 to 2024 (2021). https://www.statista.com/statistics/490522/global-esportsmarket-revenue/.   Accessed July 2022
10. IBM: IBM and the Overwatch League (2021). https://newsroom.ibm.com/Overwatch-League. Accessed: July 2022
11. Knudsen, C.: How many people play Overwatch? Player count tracker (2022). https://www.dexerto.com/overwatch/how-many-people-play-overwatch-player-count-tracker-2022-1643403/#:~:text=future%20of%20Overwatch-,Overwatch %20Monthly%20Active%20Players,around%20500%2C000%2D600%2C000 %20daily%20players. Accessed July 2022
12. Kou, Y., Gui, X., Kow, Y.M.: Ranking practices and distinction in league of legends. In: CHI PLAY 2016, pp. 4–9. Association for Computing Machinery, New York, NY, USA (2016). https://doi.org/10.1145/2967934.2968078
13. Lewis, M.: Moneyball: The Art of Winning an Unfair Game. W. W. Norton & Company, London (2004)
14. McHale, I.G., Scarf, P.A., Folker, D.E.: On the development of a soccer player performance rating system for the English premier league. INFORMS J. Appl. Anal. 42(4), 339–351 (2012). https://doi.org/10.1287/inte.1110.0589
15. Novak, A.R., Bennett, K.J.M., Pluss, M., Fransen, J.: Performance analysis in esports: Part 2 - modelling performance at the 2018 League of Legends world championship. Int. J. Sports Sci. Coach. 15(2019). https://doi.org/10.31236/osf. io/84fmy

16. Plat Chat: Plat Chat (2019). https://www.youtube.com/c/PlatChat/featured. Accessed July 2022
17. Railsback, D., Caporusso, N.: Investigating the human factors in esports performance. In: Ahram, T.Z. (ed.) AHFE 2018. AISC, vol. 795, pp. 325–334. Springer, Cham (2019). https://doi.org/10.1007/978-3-319-94619-1_32
18. Robertson, S., Gupta, R., McIntosh, S.: A method to assess the influence of individual player performance distribution on match outcome in team sports. J. Sports Sci. **34**(19), 1893–1900 (2016). https://doi.org/10.1080/02640414.2016.1142106
19. Sarkar, A., Williams, M., Deterding, S., Cooper, S.: Engagement effects of player rating system-based matchmaking for level ordering in human computation games. In: Proceedings of the 12th International Conference on the Foundations of Digital Games. Association for Computing Machinery, New York, NY, USA (2017). https://doi.org/10.1145/3102071.3102093
20. Shim, K.J., Ahmad, M.A., Pathak, N., Srivastava, J.: Inferring player rating from performance data in massively multiplayer online role-playing games (MMORPGs). In: International Conference on Computational Science and Engineering, pp. 1199–1204. IEEE (2009). https://doi.org/10.1109/CSE.2009.452
21. Tiedemann, T., Francksen, T., Latacz-Lohmann, U.: Assessing the performance of German bundesliga football players: a non-parametric metafrontier approach. CEJOR **19**, 571–587 (2011). https://doi.org/10.1007/s10100-010-0146-7
22. Wolf, J.: Overwatch league expansion will face serious stumbling blocks overseas play (2018). https://www.espn.com/esports/story/_/id/22386533/overwatch-leagueexpansion-face-serious-stumbling-blocks-overseas. Accessed July 2022
23. Zook, A.: Building matchmaking systems. In: Wallner, G. (ed.) Data Analytics Applications in Gaming and Entertainment. Auerbach Publications, Boca Raton, FL, pp. 33–48. Auerbach Publications (2019)

Understanding Stakeholders' Perspectives Towards Serious Games for Vocational Training for People with Intellectual Disabilities in Macau

Choi On Lei[1]([⊠]) 🆔 and Jorge C. S. Cardoso[2] 🆔

[1] University of Saint Joseph, Macau, China
lei.choi.on@usj.edu.mo
[2] University Coimbra, CISUC, DEI, Coimbra, Portugal
jorgecardoso@dei.uc.pt

Abstract. People with intellectual disabilities need vocational training and support in order to be able to get into the work market and maintain their workplace. In Macau SAR, China, the vocational training ecosystem still operates in fully classic, in-person, fashion, which means it is susceptible to pandemic situations such as COVID-19. This causes a big disruption to the training when isolation measures are in place. Our goal is to study the introduction of serious games for vocational training of people with disabilities in Macau. This work presents a study to assess the training benefits of serious games and usability factors, understand the acceptability and adoption factors/benefits of serious games for vocational training for people with intellectual disabilities and associated stakeholders in Macau.

Keywords: Serious games · Vocational training · People with intellectual disabilities

1 Introduction

Intellectual disabilities (IDs) refer to the slow or incomplete development of brain functions, resulting in limited learning ability, and social adaptability difficulties [2]. People with IDs need varied degrees of help and counselling to address their unique physiological and psychological aspects, so that they may smoothly enter the workplace and subsequently remain stable in that workplace. Vocational training (VT) for people with IDs helps them develop their potential and increase their ability to lead independent and normal lives [3]. However, VT for people with IDs in Macau SAR, China, is still reliant on traditional face to face training methods. Additionally, the economic climate of Macau has been continually impacted by the COVID-19, with the emergence of unpaid leaves and layoffs. In the 2020 Vocational Training Survey, during COVID-19, the Department of Statistics and Census Service found that face-to-face training dramatically decreased. All organisations had to stop the training due to the government policy [1]. Service providers will undoubtedly confront difficulties in the future, such as changes in their working environment and occupations, and VT programs will face

© IFIP International Federation for Information Processing 2022
Published by Springer Nature Switzerland AG 2022
B. Göbl et al. (Eds.): ICEC 2022, LNCS 13477, pp. 320–330, 2022.
https://doi.org/10.1007/978-3-031-20212-4_26

several obstacles. Despite this, digital training is not popular in Macau. With this work, our objective is to assess how stakeholders imagine the training benefits of serious games (SGs), understand the main usability factors, understand the acceptability and adoption factors/benefits of SGs for VT for people with IDs. We present the results of the qualitative research (questionnaires and interviews) that brings together the perspectives of various stakeholders.

2 Related Work

Kwon and Lee [7] developed a SG for job training of persons with developmental disabilities and evaluated the effect on hands-on performance. Participants played two SGs related to apple packaging and hydroponics and then performed a hands-on task (real apple packaging and hydroponics task). They compared the results with a control group that did not play any SG. They concluded that gameplay increased speed and accuracy of the hands-on task. However, Kwon & Lee did not investigate the acceptance of the SG by the stakeholders. Our approach is to first try to understand how a SG for VT of people with IDs would be received by the main stakeholders.

Martínez-Pernía et al. [5] studied a novel approach in using a SG authoring platform (eAdventure) for creating screen-based simulated functional assessments. They measured the feasibility of this technology with respect to staffing, economic and technical requirements. They developed a game, applied it in a clinical assessment situation of patients with traumatic brain injury, and followed up with interviews with the patients and clinical staff along with a filling of the Technology Acceptance Model questionnaire [8]. Results indicate that SGs have good acceptability and usefulness for therapists and patients. In this work, we chose to first run interviews and questionnaires before developing the game because we felt there is not yet a good understanding of the requirements or expectations of the various stakeholders regarding the use of SGs in VT for people with IDs.

Our approach is similar to the one by Vieira [4], which studied the development of custom SGs for physical therapy in Portugal. Vieira did the research by questionnaire and interviews, and literature review of related fields. She summarised the result through market analysis, abridging social, economic and technological aspects that resulted in the design of several scenarios. The research showed that SGs for physical rehabilitation in Portugal are still widely unknown among healthcare professionals and there is an underlying stigma against video games. However, it also showed that there is evidence that the paradigm of customised SGs for physical rehabilitation is economically viable.

3 Understanding Stakeholders' Perspectives

3.1 Questionnaires

We designed a questionnaire targeting the service providers in the rehabilitation services fields in Macau (occupational therapist, trainer, social worker, event coordinator, clerk, and management level staff). We approached these service providers by email and phone call. They came from 7 social welfare organisations that provide VT service for people with ID and related companies which had recruited people with ID in Macau. Some of the questionnaire sessions were conducted in group face-to-face. We collected 27 responses within 2 months (full questionnaire can be seen in Appendix A).

These questions focused on characterising the respondents (demographics), on understanding their thoughts on video games and SGs, and their thoughts on the use of SGs as a tool for VT. We also wanted to understand their perspectives on what they consider to be the main barriers for the usage of SGs as a training tool in Macau's VT environment, and the market value of digitalization development of VT.

Demographics

The sample was diverse in terms of the participants' age: 63% were [18–34] years old, 22% were [35–44] years old, 4% were [45–54] years old, and 11% were [55–65] years old.

In terms of work experience, 37% claimed to have 3–5 years of experience in the field, 26% claimed to have 6–10 years, 19% claimed to have over 10 years, and 22% claimed to have 1–2 years of work experience. Eighty-two percent of the participants worked in private organisations, 11% in public organisations, and 7% in other kinds of organisations. The work area of the participants was distributed among occupational therapists (25.9%), social worker (18.5%), trainer (22.2%), a few of them worked in management level (14.8%), activity coordinator (11.1%) and clerk (7.4%).

Characteristics of Vocational Training Services

In terms of channels for providing the service (service centre, school, user's home, phone call, online), most of the channels (28) correspond to the traditional face-to-face way (service centre, school, user's home).

About the time that service users spend in physical activities in VT, they are roughly equally distributed by three time periods: more than 5 h, 3–5 h, and 0–2 h per week (Fig. 1a). The time spent in mental activities varies a bit more with the majority (40.7%) lying in 0–2 h per week (Fig. 1b).

Regarding the importance of different aspects of VT of people with IDs, 85% think that service user's motivation and engagement are the most important part, followed by trainee characteristics (48%), training goal (44%), training tool/technique (37%), evaluation strategy (26%), and other aspects (7%).

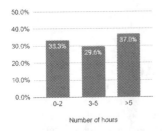

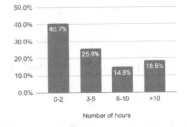

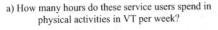

a) How many hours do these service users spend in physical activities in VT per week?

b) How many hours do these service users spend in mental activities in VT per week?

Fig. 1. Hours spent in physical and mental rehabilitation

Serious Games in Vocational Training for People with ID

Eighty-five percent of the participants have never heard about SGs. Only 4 were aware of what SGs were and only 2 of them have used a similar model in VT or other training. However, when asked about whether participants ever played a video game, 93% answered positively. When asked to rate several statements about video games, participants expressed a positive or neutral attitude (Fig. 2a), e.g., regarding the possible improvement of cognitive abilities, eye-hand coordination, thinking and judgement. There were, however, also some concerns regarding the addictiveness, and impact in physical health.

When asked about their support for the use of video games in VT, participants expressed a positive position: 60% would support or very much support the use of video games, while 40% expressed a neutral position. No one expressed a negative position regarding the use of video games for VT.

To better meet the game design of game play time, the questionnaire asked how many hours per week participants considered appropriate for people with IDs to spend in SG training. The majority of participants considered either between 3–5 h or up to 2 h an appropriate amount of time (Fig. 2b).

We also asked what part of VT participants considered could be replaced/complemented by a SG. Forty-four percent of participants stated that the "Learning part", which refers to the theory of vocational skill (knowledge of working tools, working procedure, etc.) could be replaced; 22.2% stated the "Mental support part", which refers to the psychological counselling and construction at training and work; and 18.5% stated the "Physical part", which refers to the practical training (for example, for a cleaning task: twist hand towel); and 14.8% stated "Other".

Question: Video games	Rating				
1. could improve cognitive ability (attention distrib	0%	22%	26%	33%	19%
2. could improve hand-eye coordination	0%	11%	11%	44%	33%
3. could make thinking quicker and improve judgm	0%	7%	19%	41%	33%
4. could improve personal planning and resource r	11%	15%	44%	22%	7%
5. could improve problem-solving skills	4%	22%	37%	22%	15%
6. could improve mood and relax.	7%	11%	37%	19%	26%
7. are easy to be addictive that affects learning	4%	11%	30%	30%	26%
8. could more likely to show impulsive and danger	26%	22%	37%	11%	4%
9. are not good for body health in long time.	4%	15%	22%	30%	30%

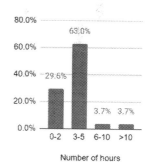

a) Participants perceptions about video games

b) Hours per week that are considered appropriate for SG training

Fig. 2. Perceptions about video games and about the number of hours appropriate for spending in SG training.

Barriers to Adoption

We also asked participants about what they consider could be the barriers to adoption of SGs for VT in Macau. We analysed and classified their answers in the following categories:

Lack of Expertise in SGs in Macau - Participants have little familiarity with SGs, don't understand how they can be used for VT, and have doubts about the transferability to the real work setting.

Adaptation of Service from Traditional Form to New Form - Classical training includes physical encounters with interpersonal communication and flexible adaptation in the workplace. Participants are unsure how SGs could apply to these highly interactive needs in training, they were concerned that SGs would reduce physical interaction and communication.

High Cost of Game Design, Customization, and Support - Participants were afraid of the potential costs of game design, because people with IDs need customised solutions, which may also require providing support to both students and trainers in SGs. Additionally, SGs need hardware/software equipment (tablet, computer, mobile phones, Internet resources), which are costly and affect the training quality.

Future Perspectives

Participants consider that employment opportunities are affected by socioeconomics, employment motivation is affected by the government, and employment stability is affected by workplace support. For example:

Limited Industry in Macau – the gaming sector dominates Macau's economy – there is small variety in job opportunities, thus suitable employment will be lower for people with IDs.

VT for People with IDs in Macau is Non-professionally-led. There is a lack of academic theories and evidence supporting the VT system and equipment is less adequate than other regions & countries. Therefore people with IDs encounter the problem of the reliability of certification and professionalism.

Foreign Labourers' Competition. According to the policy of the Labour Affairs Bureau, importing non-local workers only temporarily supplements the shortage of local human resources. Macau local enterprises were suggested to give priority to hiring local residents, thus local enterprises are willing to hire and provide job opportunities to people with IDs. There is still an optimistic outlook for people with IDs that go through VT.

Regarding the attitude of SGs in the future, most participants think that it could increase the engagement of service users of VT and it would be good to have different training methods for them. However, participants have little confidence in SGs because there are no direct resources from the government for SGs, organisations themselves also have little experience with SGs. In addition, participants have doubts about the adaptability of people with IDs to technology, and they think there is a lack of expertise in SGs in Macau. They are not optimistic that SGs could replace traditional training because of the diversity of people with IDs.

With rapid development of electronic technology nowadays, participants were asked to rate the demand value for VT digitalization in Macau. It is obvious that the result is a positive trend for digitization training and SG future development as shown in Fig. 3a and Fig. 3b.

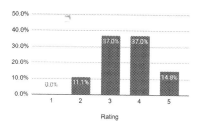 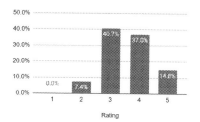

a) VT digitalization in Macau is needed or not (rating)

b) Willingness to use SGs as training tool in the future (rating)

Fig. 3. Perspectives regarding the need for digitization and willingness to use SGs

3.2 Interviews

We complemented the insights of the questionnaires with interviews to get more detailed information about the perspectives from stakeholders. We interviewed 6 professionals (identified here with only the first letters of their names), involved in the rehabilitation services field from Macau Special Olympics (MSO). They all come from different parts of the VT services area (nursing staff, head of VT, training tutor, occupational therapist, managing, director), and have more than 4 years of professional experience. MSO provides specifically tailored courses for mentally retarded/special educational needed students through full-time and systematic VT.

Some of the discussed topics involved understanding the situation of VT in the rehabilitation services field (training contexts, system operation, service users character, government support and perspective about VT), and the acceptability of SGs in specific context. The expectation and the need of game designs and approaches were also discussed. Results are summarised next.

Importance of Training

For the direct service staff, like nurses, occupational therapists and tutors, they are all concerned about the pre-assessment. Because of the varieties of people with ID characteristics, like cognition, body condition and working abilities, the training context and goal will be different for each person and an individual evaluation plan needs to be set up for them to achieve the training goal. They need to understand and analyse the data in order to set the VT goal and provide the suitable service and need to adjust the training strategy depending on different situations they meet. For instance, Mr. L, an occupational therapist, claimed that "*occupational therapists focus on objective data and conduct a thorough diagnostic process that is tailored to the region's culture.*"

Interviewees that were social workers considered that motivation is the most critical factor for people with IDs. Mr. HS, who has been involved in the rehabilitation field for around 37 years, said "*without motivation there is nothing to do for people with intellectual disabilities.".* For Mr. R, a social worker in management level, from the perspective of management *"funds, manpower and venues resources is the biggest concern for organisations to develop vocational training."*

Difficulties in Adopting Serious Games in Macau

Most interviewees were not familiar with the concept of SGs, so we explained and discussed the concept with them. We discussed possible barriers to the use of SGs in VT. In line with previous responses to the questionnaire, interviewees pointed out: resource availability problems like expertise, technology, and equipment; customization difficulties; acceptability for people with ID. Among all the topics, acceptability, seems a particular concern. Mr. H thinks that electronic games can partially replace direct instruction, but *"the most challenging component is demonstrating to trainees how to connect the games to reality."* Mr. L is also mainly concerned with realism: *"it is critical to ascertain their capacity to identify reality from fiction."*

Vocational Training Environment in Macau

Due to COVID-19, services user's learning and training need to be continuous, online training demand has increased. Mr. R claimed that the government pays more attention to VT for the mentally handicapped than in the past decade. Numerous Corporate Social Responsibility policies have been published, and the *"government expected that local corporations hire people with intellectual disabilities."*

Regarding the possible benefit of SGs and future expectations, Mr. R claimed that *"simulation scenarios are an excellent method of training people with intellectual disability in practical skills."* He believed that SGs are better appropriate for early concept and idea training, and it could help to resolve the problem of manpower and lighten the related pressure. For front line staff, they expected that *"Serious games can boost the chances of exercise, monitor the quality of training thought assessment function in the game, and as an additional tool to stimulate service users to be joyful for 'training'"*, but if there are too many exercises, problems may arise. Another problem is being addicted to the game.

3.3 Discussion

The result of questionnaire shown that most of participants have a certain experiences and their specialisation areas were also very heterogeneous and the key personnel/frontline staffs are occupational therapists, social worker and trainer to the VT field, the training of physical is spend more time than mental training in traditional, way, and the motivation is being the most important factor for VT for people with intellectual disabilities.

Unsurprisingly, most of the participants agree that video games can be helpful and could improve related body functions and no one disagrees with the use of video games as a tool. But participants express concern about the game design and since they have never used video games as a vocational tool, they tend to adopt a neutral position.

The interviews allowed us to better grasp the context of VT for people with IDs and relatives and stakeholders' needs in Macau. Motivation, the user's personal characteristics and the transition between the virtual world and the real world are the most concerned elements by all the interviewed professionals. For the implementation of SGs for VT, it is significant to make the training process more motivating for service users, and how service users transfer skills from the video game at the same time. According to the variety characteristics of service users, customization and adjustment of the game are being concerned and cause other problems like cost, manpower, government policy and support, etc. promotion and education of SGs would be an initial step to get into the VT market in Macau due to the lack of knowledge about SGs and the intention of government, organisations and enterprises to invest and get an approach of "Serious Game" to the public.

In order to better understand the SG development in the future: we summarise our findings in a Strengths, Weaknesses, Opportunities, Threats (SWOT):

Strengths	● Supporting policy of employment for people with disabilities ●Early vocational education in high school ●High acceptability for video game and SG
Weaknesses	●Market development capabilities need to be improved (from professionalism, manpower, technologic and funds) ●Limited industry & job variety in Macau ●Small user group
Opportunities	●Demand of Local marketplace for professional skills ●Employment opportunities are higher than other Asian regions ●Demand of online training has increase due to COVID-19 ●Trend of digitise training in the future
Threats	●Irreplaceable for traditional training mode ●Competition with Foreign Labour manpower from Mainland China ●Low social recognition

4 Conclusion

People with IDs already naturally face many challenges and difficulties throughout their lives. The COVID-19 pandemic has impacted Macau's economy and job market and has exacerbated the difficulties in training and in finding them suitable workplaces.

Digital training tools for people with intellectual disabilities are a potential social need and a big market in Macau. In this work, we set out to better understand stakeholders' perspectives towards SGs for VT for people with intellectual disabilities in Macau. Results show there are many opportunities for disseminating the concept of SGs for VT. We also now have a better understanding of the acceptability and benefits of the use of digital SGs for VT of people with IDs, for various related stakeholders. We also have a better understanding of the possibility of implementation of a SG for VT of people with IDs.

In the future, we plan to develop a prototype of a SG and study its introduction into this work practice.

Acknowledgements. Jorge C. S. Cardoso's work was funded by national funds through the FCT—Foundation for Science and Technology, I.P., within the scope of the project CISUC—UID/CEC/00326/2020 and by the European Social Fund, through the Regional Operational Program Centro 2020.

Appendix A

This questionnaire is a part of a student's master dissertation in Design for the Faculty of Arts and Humanities. Its objective is to assess the training benefits of serious games, understand the main usability factors, understand the acceptability and adoption factors/benefits of serious games for vocational training for people with intellectual disabilities (ID people) and associated stakeholders (Services user, Occupational Therapist, Trainer, Welfare organisation, Employer, etc.) in Macau.

A Serious game is a video game that is used for a serious purpose, such as training, while still carrying the defining traits of video games and allowing users to experience positive emotions, such as fun. Serious games could be used for behavioural training: creating a virtual environment in which this pathway is reversed by encountering and solving problems in the game world, the player learns skills and builds knowledge useful for problem-solving in the real world.

The purpose of this questionnaire is to allow us to better understand the current perceptions towards the use of serious games for vocational training for ID people. The last step of this dissertation will design a serious game of vocational training prototype and evaluate the usability and user experience of the game (from function, aesthetics and game control method) and the receptivity of ID people and related stakeholders (from engagement and sustainability), in order to better understand and assess the possibility of development of serious game of vocational training for ID people in Macau.

*Confidentiality and Anonymity:

The participant's anonymity and confidentiality will be protected. The collected data will be kept for the duration of the dissertation and deleted after it has been concluded. It takes around 10–15 min to answer the questions, looking forward to your response and support, thank you!

1. What's your area of expertise?(short answer).
2. What's your age group? (18–34, 35–44, 45–54, 55–65, >65).
3. What kinds of organization are you working for? (Public, Private, Other).
4. What is your working position? (Occupational therapist, Social Worker, Tutor/Trainer, Event coordinator, Officer, Management level, Technician, Clinical staff, Other).
5. How many years of experience do you have in the rehabilitation services field? (<1, 1–2, 3–5, 6–10, >10).
6. What rehabilitation services do you provide? (Short answer).
7. Where do you provide the services? (e.g., online, at home) (Short answer).
8. How many hours do these services' users spend in physical activities in vocational training per week? (0–2 h, 3–5 h, >5 h).
9. How many hours do these services' users spend in mental activities in vocational training per week? (0–2 h, 3–5 h, 6–10 h, >10 h).

10. Which part do you consider as the most important part of vocational training of ID people? (Training goal, Service user's characteristics, Service user's motivation and engagement, Evaluation strategies, Training tool/technique, other).

11. Are you familiar with the concept of "serious game"? (Yes, No).

12. Have you ever used any kind of serious games in any service? (Yes, No (Skip to question 14)).

13. What kinds of services did you use with serious games? (short answer).

14. Have you ever played video games? (Yes, No).

15. If you answered yes to the previous question, what kind of video game you played? (short answer).

16. Please make the rating for the following statement. (1 is lowest, 5 is the highest).

- Video games could improve cognitive ability (attention distribution, visual processing, memory, etc.)
- Video games could improve hand-eye coordination
- Video games could make thinking quicker and improve judgment
- Video games could improve personal planning and resource management
- Video games could improve problem-solving skills
- Video games could improve mood and relax.
- Video games are easy to be addictive that affects learning
- Video games could more likely to show impulsive and dangerous behaviours in life
- Video games are not good for body health for a long time.

17. What do you think about the use of video games for vocational training for ID people? (Very positive, Positive, Neutral, Negative, Very Negative, No opinion).

18. In terms of serious games as a training tool, how many hours per week do you consider it useful for ID people to use? (0–2 h, 3–5 h, 6–10 h, >10 h).

19. Which part of vocational training do you believe could be replaced by serious games? (Physical part, Mental support part, Learning part, other).

20. How many hours of a training session do you believe that could be replaced by serious games? (0–2 h, 3–5 h, 6–10 h, >0 h).

21. What barriers do you think there are in using serious games as a form of vocational training tool? (High cost of game design, Lack of expertise in serious games in Macau, Lack of knowledge in serious games field, Implementation difficulties, Adaptability of service user between traditional form and new form, Lack of interaction and communication with service user, Other).

22. What other difficulties or barriers do you think there could be in using serious games as vocational training tools? (long answer).

23. What do you think about the vocational training environment /market in Macau now? (paragraph).

24. What is your opinion of using video game as a training tool in the future in Macau? (paragraph).

25. With the rapid development of electronic technology nowadays, do you think the trend of the vocational training digitalization in Macau is needed or not? (1–5).

26. Would you be willing to accept the use of serious games as your training tool in the future? (Will, Neutral, Will not, No opinion).

27. Other comments you would like to leave here about serious games in relation to vocational training for ID people: (paragraph).

References

1. Direcção dos Serviços de Estatística e Censos: DSEC - Survey on Vocational Training 2020 (2020). http://www.dsec.gov.mo/Statistic/Social/SurveyonVocationalTraining/2020%e5%b9%b4%e8%81%b7%e6%a5%ad%e5%9f%b9%e8%a8%93%e8%aa%bf%e6%9f%a5.aspx
2. The Mental Health Association of Hong Kong. Understanding Intellectual Disability (2022). https://www.mhahk.org.hk/index.php/event1/
3. Hong Kong Down Syndrome Association: Intellectual Disability (2022). https://www.hk-dsa.org.hk/resources/id/
4. Catarina Matos Vieira: Study and development of custom "serious games" for patients and users (2020). http://hdl.handle.net/10400.14/32910Accessed May 2022
5. Martínez-Pernía, D., et al.: Using game authoring platforms to develop screen-based simulated functional assessments in persons with executive dysfunction following traumatic brain injury. J. Biomed. Inform. **74**, 71–84 (2017). https://doi.org/10.1016/J.JBI.2017.08.012
6. Laamarti, F., Eid, M., El Saddik, A.: An overview of serious games. Int. J. Comput. Games Technol. **2014**. https://doi.org/10.1155/2014/358152
7. Kwon, J., Lee, Y.: Serious games for the job training of persons with developmental disabilities. Comput. Educ. **95**, 328–339 (2016). https://doi.org/10.1016/j.compedu.2016.02.001
8. Davis, F.D.: perceived usefulness, perceived ease of use, and user acceptance of information technology. MIS Q. **13**(3), 319 (1989). https://doi.org/10.2307/249008

Workshop: Digital Arts and Health

SleepHill: Designing an Incrementally Bouncing Pillow as a Comfortable Wake-Up Approach

Wenshu Xun, Pengsong Zhang, Zixuan Liu, Yufei Meng, Yaqi Zheng, Renyao Zou, and Xipei Ren[✉]

School of Design and Arts, Beijing Institute of Technology, Beijing, China
x.ren@bit.edu.cn

Abstract. Healthy sleep is crucial to individuals' health and wellbeing, whereas healthfully waking up from the sleep cycle can significantly improve the sleep quality. Among technologies used as sleep alarms, haptic feedback has been widely adopted to serve as an effective wake-up alarm, yet how it can comfortably wake users up is underexplored. This paper presents a design study of SleepHill, an inflatable sleep pillow that can incrementally bounce its body and softly tilt its surface to create a gentle yet efficient haptic alarm for comfortable wake-up. We prototyped SleepHill and conducted a pilot user study to preliminarily understand the resulted user experiences. Our findings revealed that the wake-up process facilitated by SleepHill allowed participants to be gently awakened without being frightened. Also, we learned that the usage of SleepHill could produce improved sleep and wake-up experiences due to its incremental haptic feedback mechanism. Based on this project, we discuss implications for the future development of embedded tangible interaction design for improving the sleep circle with enriched wake-up experiences.

Keywords: Interactive sleep pillow · Wake-up experience · Inflation-based haptic feedback

1 Introduction

Sleep plays an essential role in the overall health and wellbeing [1] and can significantly impact individuals' mental health [2], as well as supports the self-reliance of human bodies [3]. Particularly, interventions that support people to wake up healthfully from the sleep cycle has been identified one of the contributors to improved sleep quality. Empirical studies have shown that the improper disruption or deprivation of sleep can produce detrimental effects on mood and negatively influence people's cognitive performance during the daytime [4].

Many researchers have investigated using different modalities as health interventions to interrupt users from sleep. For instance, Lee et al. [5] examined the effect of music for sleep induction and wake-up and found certain types of pop songs with lyrics are helpful

---

W. Xun, P. Zhang, Z. Liu and Y. Meng—Contributed equally to this paper as co-first authors.

© IFIP International Federation for Information Processing 2022
Published by Springer Nature Switzerland AG 2022
B. Göbl et al. (Eds.): ICEC 2022, LNCS 13477, pp. 333–341, 2022.
https://doi.org/10.1007/978-3-031-20212-4_27

for sleep induction and wake-up of young adults without sleep disorder. Knufinke et al. [6] attempted to optimize the sleep quality of athletes by the means of light regulation. Oh et al. [7] explored how users show different behaviors over interactive sleep alarms with some inconvenient tasks. Sekiya [8] utilized a robot to nudge an object (in this case, a bed) that in contact with the user as a new type of wake-up notifications.

Additionally, haptic feedback has been widely adopted in the real-life applications (e.g., mobile apps, wearable devices, etc.) as an effective wake-up approach. Dalei [9] applied vibration effects to human bodies to improve their waking up quality. Korres et al. [10] developed an adaptive alarm system to enable a pleasant awakening experience. Duong et al. [11] designed an alarm system based on a smart wristband named Aegis to track sleep patterns with minimal noise disturbance. Nevertheless, how haptic feedback can be experienced to comfortably waking users up is underexplored.

In this paper, we set out an exploratory study to design a sleep alarm system that leverages novel haptic feedback to create a gentle yet efficient approach for comfortable wake-up. As shown in Fig. 1, specifically, we proposed an embedded tangible interaction design concept, called SleepHill, which is an inflatable pillow that can wake the sleeper up through incrementally bouncing its body and softly tilting its surface. We prototyped SleepHill and conducted a pilot user study to preliminarily understand how our design concept has been experienced as a comfortable wake-up alarm.

As a project, this paper makes the following two contributions. First, the design of SleepHill exemplifies a tangible user interface that embodies haptic feedback mechanism to create an experiential sleep alarm for improved wake-up process; Second, this study offers some design insights into future explorations of this type of wake-up alarm clocks that embodies haptic feedback into the bedding accessories.

2   SleepHill

In this project, we propose SleepHill, an inflatable pillow that can gently wake up the user by actively and incrementally changing its shape. Our core idea is to unobtrusively change the user's sleep posture to an undesired head position by slowly controlling the inflation intensity of the inflatable bag embedded in SleepHill. The rest of this section describes the system design and the implementation of the SleepHill prototype in detail.

2.1   System Design

The System Consists of an Inflatable Pillow that Can Deform According to the Situation. There have been several projects integrating the health-related interactive components into the existing objects and infrastructure of the contexts [12, 20]. Similarly, we were interested in combining unobtrusive alarm mechanisms with the bedding. After analyzing the advantages and disadvantages of different bedding accessories, we eventually decided to develop an inflatable pillow that can seamlessly integrate its wake-up alarm into the daily sleep circle of the user without radical changes to the setup of the bedding.

The Inflation Process is Gentle Enough to Avoid Discomfort to the User. Although existing haptic technologies [13] can efficiently serve the wake-up process, we focused on investigating a gentle technique to allow the wake-up to be natural and comfortable. In SleepHill, we leveraged the inflation process to create haptic feedback for waking up users. To make the working mechanism gentle and unobtrusive, we chose to modify the inflation rate of the air pump to be very slow. Similar to several other health-related applications of slow technologies [14, 15], we hoped this kind of design could be helpful to avoid psychological and physiological discomfort to users.

The Inflation and Deflation of the System are Responsible to the USEr's Condition and the Context. Based on the inflatable bag, we also envisioned that SleepHill could trigger its slow inflation mechanism according to the preset sleep alarm. Moreover, SleepHill would be associated with an ultrasonic sensor to detect if the user has left, so as to deflate its air bag.

2.2 Implementation

We developed a proof-of-concept prototype to test the feasibility of our concept. The main components include an inflatable bag (1.5L capacity), a latex pillowcase, and a cotton pillow core for the SleepHill pillow, as well as two air pumps, an Arduino board, and an ultrasonic sensing module for controlling the inflation and deflation process. As shown in Fig. 2, all the electronic components were capsuled into a box, where an LED display and two knobs were added to set and present the alarm and the pump speed.

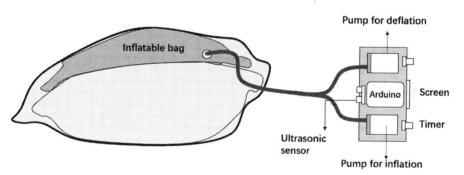

Fig. 1. The technical implementation of SleepHill.

3   The Study

In order to effectively evaluate the design concept of SleepHill, we conducted a preliminary user evaluation with eight participants. The main purposes of this study were: 1) to understand the user experience of the wake-up process facilitated by SleepHill; 2) to examine the efficiency of SleepHill for the wake-up purpose; 3) to identify design opportunities for the future development of this type of wake-up technology.

3.1 Participants

We recruited participants through spreading information via word of mouth. We were interested in recruiting users who were troubled by getting up every day. During recruiting, we also asked them to describe their sleep habits and sleep quality. Finally, a total of eight undergraduate students from the major of industrial design volunteered to participate in the experiment to experience the SleepHill prototype. Their detail is summarized in Table 1. Prior to the experiment we explained the study procedure to the participants without discussing our research hypotheses. All the experiments were conducted upon receiving the consent from the study participants.

Table 1. Characteristics of participants.

ID	Gender	Age	Self-evaluation of sleep habits and quality
P1	Male	21	Poor sleep quality, poor mood after getting up, lack of motivation, and don't like to be awakened by the alarm clock
P2	Male	21	Average sleep quality, poor mood after getting up, don't like to be awakened by the alarm clock
P3	Female	20	Average sleep quality, getting up late and being awakened by the alarm clock is in a bad mood
P4	Female	21	Average sleep quality, forced to wake up will be unhappy
P5	Female	21	Average sleep quality, feel better after getting up and don't stay in bed
P6	Female	21	Good sleep quality, like waking up by self and don't like being woken up
P7	Female	20	Good sleep quality, tangled and painful when getting up
P8	Male	21	Poor sleep quality, tired after waking up and like to stay in bed, don't like to be awakened by the alarm clock

3.2 Apparatus and Setup

We developed a prototype for the user study that could facilitate the user experience of the design concept. To create a bedroom-like environment, the research was carried out in the lounge where we covered sofas with a blanket and placed a SleepHill pillow on top (see Fig. 2(a)). Specifically, Fig. 2(b) shows that the SleepHill prototype is presented as a soft pillow filled with cotton and an inflatable bag, which is covered with a latex pillowcase to ensure different components integrated with each other. As shown in Fig. 2(c), during the experiment the participant needs to use earplugs for sound isolation and an eyeshade to eliminate the interference of sound and light, so as to ensure a quiet and dark context for sleep.

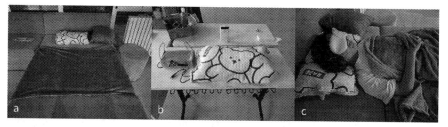

Fig. 2. (a) the experiment setup; (b) the SleepHill prototype used in the experiment; (c) the participant's condition during the experiment.

3.3 Procedure

Before the experiment, we briefly introduced the experimental process and demonstrated the functionality of the SleepHill prototype. Then we started the experiment by instructing the participant to lay on the bed with the designated position and put on the eyeshade and earplugs. During the experiment, the environment was kept quiet and dark to help the participant fall asleep. Upon confirming that the participant was sleeping, we switched the prototype on to initiate the shape-changing of the pillow to wake the participant up. After the user got up, the prototype would automatically deflate at a certain speed to returns to its original state. We wrote observational notes and recorded the time of different phases of the experiment. After the users were fully awake, they would be invited to fill in a post-study questionnaire based on the System Usability Scale (SUS) [19]. Each experiment was concluded with a semi-structured interview in person, focusing on the following five aspects: 1) the usefulness and advantages of our design; 2) opinions towards long-term usage of our prototype; 3) the positive user experience with SleepHill; 4) the negative user experience with SleepHill; and 5) design challenges for the future development.

3.4 Data Collection and Analysis

For qualitative data, we wrote observational notes during each experiment and wrote interview notes afterwards. All the observational and interview data were analyzed together using the thematic analysis approach. For quantitative data, our post-study survey adopted System Usability Scale (SUS) [19], a 10 items 5 points (1–5) Likert scale that has been widely used to measure the user's perceived usability of new technologies and products. All the obtained SUS data were imported into an Excel sheet and calculated the SUS score according to its analysis guideline [19].

4 Findings

4.1 Quantitative Findings

Overall, our participants gave relatively positive feedback on the availability and user experience of SleepHill with an average score of 76.25 (SD = 11.88), which is about eight points higher than the benchmark score of 68.

4.2 Qualitative Findings

Benefits of SleepHill. As described before, all the recruited participants had difficulty with getting up. Furthermore, most of them stated having anxious experiences with using typical alarm clocks for wake-up. In this experiment, we found that the design of SleepHill played a decisive role in waking participants up, and all participants were efficiently waking up. We observed that P1, P2 and P5 woke up within 1–2 min after switching on the prototype, and the others woke up within 2–3 min. During the interview, for instance, P5 mentioned that *"the fully inflated prototype was not suitable for sleep on any longer, then I know I need to get up"*.

Meanwhile, we learned that the prototype was also deemed as a comfortable tool for improving their sleep experiences. This might due to the fact that the incrementally bouncing pillow with the inflatable bag made it ergonomically supportive. As P4 and P6 stated, *"this wake-up experience is obvious and comfortable"*.

Consequently, the participants tended to believe that waking up using SleepHill would lead to enhanced psychological state compared to the traditional alarm clock. They indicated that *"the use of tactile user interface did not reduce its efficiency for wake-up"* (P8), and *"the probability of the so-called repeated sleep also decreased"* (P1). Our findings revealed that this design concept could have potential to provide a comfortable, pleasant, and efficient wake-up experience to end-users.

Design Challenges. In addition to validating the design concept, the study also helped us identify the following design challenges that need to be further addressed in the next design iteration of SleepHill. First, the current prototype has some shortcomings. The ultrasonic module for detecting the presence of the was not accurate, which failed to achieve our goal of *"a prototype that can be bounced back automatically"*. Second, prior to the experiment, several participants expressed their concern over the real usage of our prototype. E.g., P4 said that the shape of the pillow would make it feel too tight for the neck (although the participant said that there was no such discomfort after the test). Similarly, P7 worried about *"whether this shape will lead to stiff neck"*. Although P4 and P7 emphasized that they had positive user experience with our prototype after the experiment, their comments made us reflect on improving the aesthetics of the SleepHill prototype in the next design iteration to enable affective user experience in a real-life setup, such as a longitudinal field study.

5   Discussion, Conclusions, and Future Work

Designing and utilizing persuasive technology to promote various healthy behaviors can greatly improve the quality of daily lifestyles [16]. The appropriate adoption of health-promoting interventions can support individuals to foster healthy sleep patterns and in turn develop healthy life routines [17]. This paper has presented an exploratory design study of SleepHill, a smart pillow that incrementally bounces and tilts its surface to comfortably wake the user up. The core concept of SleepHill was realized in three aspects. First, the system consisted of an inflatable pillow served as an actuator of the haptic sleep alarm. Second, the inflation process was gentle enough to avoid creating discomfort to the user. The inflation and deflation of the system are responsive to the user's condition and the context. Our pilot user study revealed that the wake-up process facilitated by SleepHill allowed participants to be gently awakened without being frightened, resulting to reasonably high user acceptance from the SUS results. In line with [14, 18], this project introduced the slow-intermittent technology [16] into the health domain of sleep promotion. Similarly, we found that the usage of SleepHill could produce improved sleep experience due to its incremental wake-up approach and unique haptic feedback (the bouncing and tilting mechanism). Compared with existing sleep alarm technologies, therefore, SleepHill has potential advantages in supporting healthful sleep and thus healthy lifestyles. Additionally, this study helped us yield the following two design implications for the next development of SleepHill and other similar slow-intermittent sleep technologies.

5.1 Design Implications

Improving the Wake-Up Experience Flow of SleepHill Through Personalizing the Haptic Feedback Mechanisms. In our study, all the parameters of the system feedback, including the inflation speed and the tilt angle, remained identical. Although most participants have made positive comments on SleepHill, they still expressed that the experimental prototype did not well meet the needs of various users, such as their differences in ergonomic demands and the sensitivity to the haptic feedback. For example, some participants (P4 and P7) wanted to increase the maximum tilt angle of the prototype, so that it can be more efficient in waking the user up. Some others (P5 and P3) hoped the inflation speed could be adjusted according to individuals' sleep status, sleep contexts, and even daily schedules. In the future, we should explore the relationship between the wake-up efficiency, the comfortability of the user experiences, as well as the feedback mechanisms such as inflation speed and tilt angle, for various types of users in a diversity of the use scenarios, so that the user-system interactions of SleepHill can be personalized to better meet needs of different users.

Enabling the Application of SleepHill as Personal Nap Companion for Multiple Use Scenarios. From the user study we also learned that SleepHill could be potentially adopted in different sleep scenarios beyond the bedroom. For instance, P6 stated that this prototype could be modified to be easily applied for a nap during the noon break in the office or school or during the long-distance trip, so that SleepHill, as a standalone device, could facilitate a short break, without interfering others in the public space. Yet, at present, the prototype design of SleepHill is only suitable for use in bed. In addition, the current prototype design is relatively rough. It is necessary to further improve its system implementation and appearance design, in order to optimize its shape and usage to be helpful for different use scenarios.

5.2 Limitation and Future Work

As a work-in-progress project, this study has a few limitations. First, we were only able to recruit limited number participants with a lack of diversity in ages, occupations, and culture background, which might lead the results not representative to different usage contexts. Second, the implementations of the prototype for the experiment were relatively simple, with a lack of considerations on the appearance of the interactive prototype, which might have an impact on the effectiveness and the user experience of SleepHill. To obtain consolidated research insights into the embedded tangible user interfaces as the haptic feedback for aiding the wake-up experiences, in the next research step we will further improve the prototype design and implementations following opportunities derived from this study. Based on the new prototype of SleepHill, we will then conduct a control study with increased number of participants and strive to achieve more solid experimental results to enlighten the relevant research area in the fields of health promotion and tangible interaction design.

Acknowledgements. This work was supported by The National Social Science Fund of China (21CG192) and Beijing Institute of Technology Research Fund Program for Young Scholars (XSQD202018002).

References

1. Heng, T.B., et al.: Sleep-wake-behaviour app: towards developing a database for informing e-coaching solutions for neurodevelopmental disorders in children. In: Proceedings of the 12th EAI International Conference on Pervasive Computing Technologies for Healthcare, pp. 371–377 (2018)
2. Meaklim, H., Rehm, I.C., Monfries, M., Junge, M., Meltzer, L.J., Jackson, M.L.: Wake up psychology! Postgraduate psychology students need more sleep and insomnia education. Aust Psychol. **56**(6), 485–498 (2021)
3. Nagele, A.N.: Sleep-mode: on sleeping with wearable technology. In: Proceedings of the Fifteenth International Conference on Tangible, Embedded, and Embodied Interaction, 20211–5 (2021)
4. Liao, W.H., Kuo, J.H., Yang, C.M., Chen, I.Y.: iWakeUp: a video-based alarm clock for smart bedrooms. J. Chin. Inst. Eng. **33**(5), 661–668 (2010)
5. Lee, T., Moon, S., Baek, J., Lee, J., Kim, S.: Music for sleep and wake-up: an empirical study. IEEE Access **7**, 145816–145828 (2019)
6. Knufinke, M., et al.: Dim light, sleep tight, and wake up bright–Sleep optimization in athletes by means of light regulation. Eur. J. Sport Sci. **21**(1), 7–15 (2021)
7. Oh, K.T., et al.: Wake-up task: understanding users in task-based mobile alarm app. In: Extended Abstracts of the 2019 CHI Conference on Human Factors in Computing Systems, 20191–6 (2019)
8. Sekiya, D., Nakamura, T., Kanoh, M., Yamada, K.: Can a robot wake a sleeping person up by giving him or her a nudge? In: Proceedings of the Companion of the 2017 ACM/IEEE International Conference on Human-Robot Interaction, pp. 279–280. (2017)
9. Dalei, N.: Creating a pleasant tactile waking up experience (2010)
10. Korres, G., Jensen, C.B.F., Park, W., Bartsch, C., Eid, M.: A vibrotactile alarm system for pleasant awakening. IEEE Trans. Haptics **11**(3), 357–366 (2018)
11. Duong, L., Andargie, M., Chen, J., Giakoumidis, N., Eid, M.: Aegis: a biofeedback adaptive alarm system using vibrotactile feedback. In: 2014 IEEE International Instrumentation and Measurement Technology Conference (I2MTC) Proceedings, pp. 293–298. IEEE (2014)
12. Ren, X., Yu, B., Lu, Y., Chen, Y., Pu, P.: HealthSit: designing posture-based interaction to promote exercise during fitness breaks. Int. J. Hum.-Comput. Inter. **35**(10), 870–885 (2019)

13. Ornati, M., Cantoni, L.: FashionTouch in E-commerce: An exploratory study of surface haptic interaction experiences. In: Nah, F.F.-H., Siau, K. (eds.) HCII 2020. LNCS, vol. 12204, pp. 493–503. Springer, Cham (2020). https://doi.org/10.1007/978-3-030-50341-3_37

14. Fujita, K., Suzuki, A., Takashima, K., Ikematsu, K., Kitamura, Y.: TiltChair: manipulative posture guidance by actively inclining the seat of an office chair. In: Proceedings of the 2021 CHI Conference on Human Factors in Computing Systems, 20211–14 (2021)

15. Shin, J., et al.: Slow robots for unobtrusive posture correction. In: Proceedings of the 2019 CHI Conference on Human Factors in Computing Systems, 20191–10. (2019)

16. Hallnäs, L., Redström, J.: Slow technology–designing for reflection. Pers. Ubiquit. Comput. 5(3), 201–212 (2001)

17. Hong, J., et al.: Personalized sleep-wake patterns aligned with circadian rhythm relieve daytime sleepiness. Iscience 24(10), 103–129 (2021)

18. Ren, X., Yu, B., Lu, Y., Zhang, B., Hu, J., Brombacher, A.: LightSit: an unobtrusive health-promoting system for relaxation and fitness microbreaks at work. Sensors 19(9), 2162 (2019)

19. Lewis, J.: The system usability scale: past, present, and future. Int. J. Hum.-Comput. Inter. 34(7), 577–590 (2018)

20. Ren, X., Guo, Z., Huang, A., Li, Y., Xu, X., Zhang, X.: Effects of social robotics in promoting physical activity in the shared workspace. Sustainability 14(7), 4006 (2022)

Digital-Pen: An Interactive System for Correcting Writing Posture of Primary School Students

Yousheng Yao[1,2], Jiacheng Lou[3], Guanghui Huang[1(✉)], Xuesong Li[1], and Yingrui Li[2]

[1] Macau University of Science and Technology, Avenida WaiLong, Taipa 999078, Macau, China
120752037@qq.com
[2] Zhongkai University of Agriculture and Engineering, Guangzhou 510225, China
[3] Hubei University of Technology, Wuhan 430068, China

Abstract. People who write for a long time often cause shoulder-neck pain and high-low shoulders because of the unconscious and irregular writing posture, and the problem of myopia which will affect people's eye health because of being too close to the writing carrier. In this paper, we designed an interactive system for Digital-Pen, which can support writing users, especially primary school students aged 6–12, to keep the distance between the head and the writing carrier paper within a reasonable range, thereby promoting eye's healthy and protecting good eyesight, while correcting the writing posture of the writing user. Digital-Pen is a pen (smart hardware) with a sensor, it adopts infrared induction recognition technology and matches an application to record the writing posture, writing time, number of words written and the number of irregular writing behaviors, so as to remind and correct the writing posture of the writing user. Furthermore, the real-time date of writing can feedback score list sharing on the internet to alleviate and improve boredom of writing. We also received preliminary user experience feedback of Digital-Pen. The results showed that most writing users have high interest in and acceptance of the Digital-Pen, and they gain more confidence to correct their writing posture.

Keywords: Digital-Pen · Sensors · User healthy · User testing · Interactive system

1 Introduction

Today or in the future, people's troubles caused by health problems will always entangle our hearts. We feel helpless or even hopeless for many times. And let the health problems rage on and there is nothing we can do. For example, the current COVID-19 has made the world instantly tense, and has greatly changed the way people live and work. Another example is that the various health problems in the process of children's education, training and growth also make many new parents helpless and bring them great psychological

---

Y. Yao and J. Lou—The first two authors contributed equally to the article.

© IFIP International Federation for Information Processing 2022
Published by Springer Nature Switzerland AG 2022
B. Göbl et al. (Eds.): ICEC 2022, LNCS 13477, pp. 342–353, 2022.
https://doi.org/10.1007/978-3-031-20212-4_28

confusion. With the high development of science and technology, more and more digital products have entered people's lives, using technology to change life and improve health will help people solve some of the confusion and problems. Through life experience and observation, it is not difficult to find that most writing users (especially primary school students) have always had a series of health problems in terms of writing willingness, writing strength, writing habits and writing posture. In this article, we introduced the Digital-Pen, a smart module composed of sensors and circuit boards, equipped with an application (the smart module and the application can be connected by Bluetooth or WI-FI), which was combined in the pen tube with the artistic aesthetic, and which was an interactive system designed for communication between people and the pen naturally. In the process of interacting with the Digital-Pen, the user performs face learning and inputs related information on the application, setting the corresponding healthy writing program, such as writing time, writing posture.

and writing ranking. Meanwhile, the intelligent hardware also judges whether the user's posture, the distance between the eyes and the pen, and the writing force are within a reasonable range based on the infrared sensor face image recognition technology learned by the sensor and neural network. If the user performs wrong posture and writing habits, the Digital-Pen will remind the user to correct the posture, control the duration and improve the disgust through indenting pen tip automatically and the real-time feedback from the application. In order to design and create an effective Digital-Pen interactive system, we conducted in-depth interviews, discussions with experts, and made a prototype of the system. Also, In order to evaluate user's views of the Digital-Pen interactive system, we selected 5 pairs of parent-child users and conducted preliminary user tests. The results show that parents are willing to use the Digital-Pen for their children during the writing process, and find that the design of the automatic indentation of the pen tip after infrared recognition of the face can help children correct their writing posture and protect their eyesight, and while providing feedback on the writing time and correcting posture ranking will greatly improve children's aversion to writing. After about 30 days of sample testing experiments, parent-child users generally reported that the Digital-Pen interactive system had greatly improved children's writing posture, writing effect and writing mood. The main contributions of our work are: (1) Created an interactive system, including an intelligent module and an application, which improved users' healthy writing posture and protected their eyesight with real-time feedback when primary school students were writing; (2) Cultivated children's interest in writing through feedback on writing content, writing effect and leaderboard on the internet; (3) In order to demonstrate the effectiveness of the Digital-Pen interactive system, we not only interviewed medical experts and design professors, but also obtained positive feedback from parent-child users in the process of using prototype of the system. (see Fig. 1).

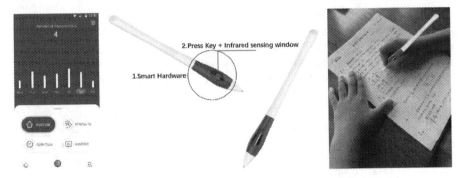

Fig. 1. App, Smart hardware, and Writing posture.

2   Related Work

In this section, we briefly review three relevant studies, including the smart pens, the issue of health hazards in children's writing, and data and explanations on correct writing posture in primary school students.

2.1   Research on Smart Pen

There have been some researches on the application of smart pens in related systems in the world. There are two fields here, one is the field of intelligent technology, and the other is the field of technical application. Goonetilleke R S et al. discussed the impact of pen design on drawing and writing performance, and he believed that speed, comfort and writing ability are important indicators for evaluating a pen [1]. Romat H, et al. designed the Flashpen, a digital pen for VR whose sensing principle provided accurate digitized handwriting and complex drawing, including small, fast turns [2]. Stocco L J, et al. designed a hybrid robot called the Twin-Pantograph. Since the Twin-Pantograph produced the best results, its design has been improved to address practical limitations, and it was implemented as a haptic pen [3]. Heimann-Steinert A, et al. studied digital pen technology for cognitive assessment of older adults, compared the difference in recognition performance between a digital pen and a regular pencil in performing the Trail Making Test [4]. Abidin N R, Anggoro S. studied the impact of Smart-Pen on students who must have the skills on the 21st century, namely collaboration, communication, critical thinking and creativity (4Cs) [5]. Wu P, Fei L, Li S, et al. specialized researched in recognition network on Pen Holding Pose (PHHP) [6]. St-Pierre N R. carried out research, design and analysis of pens in the field of animal science [7]. Shintani M, et al. designed the handwritten letter recognition digital pen, which is a new digital pen that contains multiple miniature force sensors, the force information, accelerometer and gyroscope sensors applied around the tip of the pen during the writing process are used for real-time recognition character, measured the force vector of the pen tip [8]. On the basis of previous work, we further explored the benefits of sensor technology for smart hardware pens. The interactive system is designed to provide real-time feedback to correct posture and share the function of writing grades, so as to help primary school students solved the hidden health risks in the writing process.

2.2 Research on the Hidden Health Problems in the Writing Process of Primary School Students

Focusing on the writing posture of primary school students, the research team randomly collected and investigated about 300 writing samples of primary school students in primary schools in Guangzhou and Shenzhen, and conducted a certain number of interviews with primary school students, parents and teachers. When observing the writing process of primary school students repeatedly, there were general problems for most of them, which are that the eyes are too close to the surface of the paper, that may lead to myopia, the wrong posture of writing and sitting, skeletal deformities, and psychological problems such as boredom and resistance to writing behavior. Lin Wenjian, vice-principal of Binhai Primary School in Bao'an District, Shenzhen, believed that the long-term incorrect writing posture of primary school students was prone to myopia, sloping shoulders, hunched back, and curvature of the spine, which affected the eyesight, bone health and learning efficiency of primary school students [9]. From the perspective of writing and reading, myopia may be caused by the interaction between poor habits on eyes and poor reading posture when reading and writing [10]. Dutta S. believed that the ergonomic design of writing desks may pose health hazards to primary school students in classroom activities [11]. A review of the literature found that there is almost still a blank in the related research fields on that poor writing habits will affect the eye health and skeletal deformities of primary school users. Inspired by the above-mentioned articles by experts and scholars, this paper aimed to explore the possibility of design and technology of Digital-pen to solve the hidden health problems in children's writing process, so as to support parents to guide their children to write more comfortably in a healthy sitting posture, as well as to improve children's healthy habits of writing and develop their interest in writing, etc. (see Fig. 2).

Fig. 2. Health hazards in children's writing process.

2.3 The Data and Explanation of the Correct Writing Posture of Primary School Students

According to the content of the first grade Chinese textbook and writing songs of the Chinese Education Edition, the writing posture is emphasized: when writing, pay attention to sitting upright, and the stroke order rules are from top to bottom, first horizontal and then vertical [11]. Lin Wenjian suggested that the correct writing posture can refer to the method of calligraphy educator Hu Yifan: (1) While reading and writing, keep your eyes one foot away from the book. (2) The finger holding the pen should be one inch away from the tip of the pen. The tip that is too short should be discarded. (3) Readers and writers must sit upright, and keep a one-punch distance between the chest and the desk [9]. (see Fig. 3).

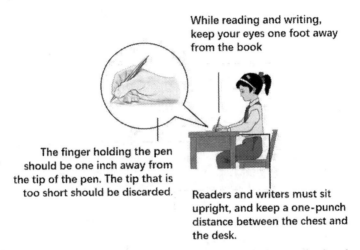

Fig. 3. The explanation of the correct writing posture of primary school students.

3   Design Process of the Digital-Pen Interactive System

In the process of designed and built the Digital-Pen interactive system, we invited ophthalmologists, orthopaedics and design experts to jointly conduct the design exploration.

3.1   Design Exploration with Experts

We conducted in-depth discussions with 3 experts (1F, 2M, average age = 45) who are Ophthalmologist D1 from China Guangzhou Eye Center, Orthopedics Center Doctor D2 and Design Professor D3 from Zhejiang University, there were many years of work experience in related fields for them. Design study sessions usually lasted more than 90 min, starting from the introduction of preliminary design concepts, to discussions and exchanges with experts, sharing their previous work experience and their views on our design prototypes, one by one. They agreed with the starting point of the design: "The impact of primary school students' writing posture on vision and bone health is an objective problem, and it will be more feasible and effective to design and practice through the way of technology and interaction." and made recommendations as follows: (i) D1 and D2 recommended to carry out education and training for primary school students on the correct posture for writing. (ii) D1, D2 and D3 all proposed that when primary school students writing with too much force and their eyes being too close, error correction feedback should be given timely. (iii) D1, D2, and D3 all found that children were resistant and bored with writing. (iv) D3 stated that parents expect to know the data related to children's writing, and suggested that we reduce the production cost of the product system and improve the design aesthetics. (v) D1, D2 and D3 expressed how to improve the interest of primary school students in writing behavior will become a difficult point in the interactive system, because parents often require children to write while children always have resisting behaviors.

3.2 Design Goals

In order to solve the hidden health problems of primary school students in the process of writing, based on the problem discussion meeting with experts and previous related work, we set several key goals for the design of an interactive system: (1) Real-time feedback of data during the writing process to avoid constant wrong postures that affect children's vision and bone health. As shown in (ii) in 3.1, timely error-correcting feedback may be an important means of guiding children's writing posture and eyes health. (2) More intuitive interaction, data presentation and game-style leaderboards in the application, which not only enhance parent-child interaction, but also help to enhance children's interest in writing. As proposed in (iii) and (v) in 3.1, the conflicting psychological interaction between parents and children about writing behavior is an important innovation way, because it improves children's psychological health problems caused by resistance to writing. (3) It is an important issue for reducing the production cost of the product system and improving the design aesthetics, because it involves the manufacturing and acceptance from market of the interactive system.

4 System Design

Based on in-depth discussions with experts, we developed the prototype of Digital-Pen. The Digital-Pen consists of both hardware and software (see Fig. 4). The hardware was a pen with infrared sensing, force point detection, duration detection functions, pressing structure and the appearance of small tadpole design. The software was an application that provides real-time feedback on correctly writing habits, wrong behaviors and writing rankings. Software and hardware are connected via Bluetooth or Wi-Fi.

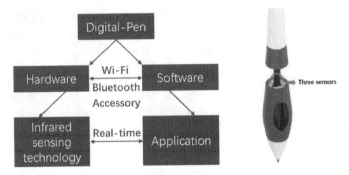

Fig. 4. Conceptual framework of Digital-Pen.

4.1 Application Design of the Software System

The application (APP) sets the parent terminal and the actual running terminal to work together. The parent sets the goal through the parent terminal, and the child completes the goal through the actual running terminal, thereby realizing the behavior of guiding the child to start writing (posture, strength, duration, and sharing the ranking page) by using the application (APP) to select the smart hardware mode (see Fig. 5).In addition, the app works in conjunction with smart hardware, and when the parent operates, the app will display real-time data and pop-up error times reminders according to the parent's request (see Fig. 5a). For example, if the smart hardware recognizes a wrong gesture from a child's writing, it will send a signal to the app, showing real-time reminders of the problem and corrections. At the same time, after the child's writing is completed, both parents and children can use the application (APP) to grasp the transcript of the writing time and the number of times of correcting wrong postures, and obtain the Internet score ranking list and publish it to the personal self-media platform for sharing, so as to improve adverse mental health emotions caused by children's resistance to writing(see Fig. 5d).

Fig. 5. Interface of Digital-Pen APP (a) Number of Posture Errors (b) Writing Strength Chart (c) Writing Times of the day (d) Your Ranking.

4.2   Design of Smart Hardware Pen

The smart hardware of Digital-Pen is entirely made of silicone material that satisfies relative hardness, and integrates a force sensor, an infrared sensor (when the wrong posture occurs, the pen tip will automatically retract to stop writing) and a mechanical pressing structure (re-pull the pen tip out)) to achieve the functionality of multiple components (see Fig. 6a). At the same time, we have carried out ergonomic considerations for the correct posture of holding the pen. The thumb, index finger and middle finger clamp the holding position of pen, and the pen holder rests on the tiger's mouth of the hand to fix the pen state (see Fig. 6b). In terms of the shape of the smart hardware of Digital-Pen, we took inspiration from small tadpoles, which are unique, smart, cute, round and soft to meet children's emotional and psychological demands (see Fig. 6c).

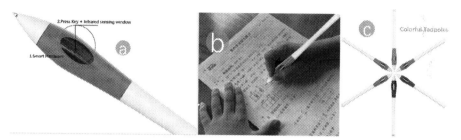

Fig. 6. Design of Smart Hardware Pen (a) Smart hardware of Digital-Pen (b) Correct posture for holding a pen (c) Colorful Tadpoles.

4.3   Communication and Data Processing of Hardware and Software

We used KEEP-REAL Sensors (Guangzhou KEEP-REAL Digital Technology Co., Ltd.) to provide miniature custom board-mounted digital output pressure sensors and infrared sensors as development boards, which can collect and transmit sensor data and infrared sensor face recognition. After KEEP-REAL Sensors sent digital conversion signals to the back-end server through the Wi-Fi module, and the front-end page on the mobile phone obtained the digital conversion signals on the back-end server through HTTP requests, the smart hardware and application started to work. As the infrared sensor face recognition in smart hardware, we used KEEP-REAL Sensors customized miniature infrared sensors on both the left and right sides of the mechanical buttons (which can meet the writing habits of users written by left and right hands).When the user was too close and exceeded the threshold, the infrared sensor recognizes the face and the pen tip will automatically retract and stop writing. The real-time state outputted was switched to an electrical signal. We can judge whether the user's face was recognized according to high level or low level, so as to remind the user whether the writing posture was corrected. It will be fed back to the app to display the number of wrong postures for both parents and children to learn and reference.

5 Preliminary User Research

We conducted a preliminary user study to confirm how parents and children interacted with the Digital-Pen interactive system and their perceptions of the Digital-Pen. We randomly invited 5 groups of parents and child users A, B, C, D, E (3F, 2M, average age = 30.5) in the local community, and all parents who evaluated the design of interactive systems(pA, pB, pC, pD, pE) had the experience of accompany the child to write. All steps were carried out under the guidance of designers and experimenters.

5.1 Procedure

Experiments were conducted in a writing scene. First, we introduced the situation and design prototype of this study and how to use the system to the participants briefly. Next, participants had 60 min to experience and learn using the Digital-Pen interactive system. During this 60-min period, participants were observed fully. After Experiment, we supported participants to take the Digital-Pen home to continue the experience for 30 days. A month later, we used the Likert Scale Questionnaire (Table 1) to summarize the opinions and the experience of the participants focusing on several aspects: (1) the relationship between them and the Digital-Pen interactive system; (2) Suggestions for improvement of the Digital-Pen interactive system; (3) The difference between the traditional writing method and the Digital-Pen interactive system; (4) Whether the Digital-Pen interactive system enables users to develop correct and healthy writing habits.

5.2 Results

As the Table 1 (five-point Likert scale) showed, all participants were willing to use the Digital-Pen interactive system during writing and showed a high willingness to use the Digital-Pen interactive system. However, they showed little confidence in using the Digital-Pen interactive system to improve children's eye health and correct writing posture while writing. For example, all of A, C, D, and E indicated that the effective evaluation of a new product requires a larger base of user testing and market information feedback. A, C, and E gave 4 points in Q(ii), that they think the interaction mode of Digital-Pen is too complicated. Five groups of parents and children noted that real-time feedback was valuable during the writing process (The average score is 4.8). At the same time, They confirmed it will be particularly interesting to share the ranking of writing information on the self-media platforms (The average score is as high as 4.6). However, A and D indicated that it needs more testing and feedback to verify the effect of improving children's resistance to writing. When the participants were asked about their relationship with the Digital-Pen and suggestions for improvements, B said the Digital-Pen will be a particularly interesting new thing to remind him when making a wrong writing posture, and he can't wait to use it to record daily writing. But D was worried that the child may be curious to the real-time data of the application during the writing, which will affect the development of good writing habits. A, C and E confirmed that it was really good to remind in time, and suggested us to make more comfortable for the ergonomics of intelligent hardware. They also worried that it may be some problems in the battery life of the interactive system. Overall, all participants were willing to use the Digital-Pen interactive system during writing, and Digital-Pen interactive system had improved the children's writing posture, writing performance and writing mood during the 30-day user test period. (See Fig. 7) The results of the study showed that the Digital-Pen interactive system was a feasible and effective way for parents to effectively obtain real-time data on children's writing and for children to develop healthy writing habits.

Table 1. Results of user questionnaire.

Questions	Female A	Female B	Female C	Male D	Male E	Average
i. Are you willing to use Digital-Pen interactive system while writing? (1:unwilling-5:willing)	5	5	5	5	5	5
ii. Is it easy for you to understand how to use Digital-Pen interactive system? (1:difficult-5:easy)	4	5	4	5	4	4.4
iii. What do you think of Digital-Pen's real-time feedback and error correction reminder when you make an incorrect action? (1:useless-5:helpful)	5	5	4	5	5	4.8
iv. Do you think writing data rankings can improve children's resistance to writing? (1:useless-5:helpful)	4	5	5	4	5	4.6
v. Do you have confidence that you can improve your child's eye health and correct writing posture by using Digital-Pen interactive system while writing? (1:unconfident-5:confident)	4	5	4	4	4	4.2

Fig. 7. Digital-Pen interactive system enabled users to develop correct and healthy writing habits during the 30-day user test period.

6   Current Limitations and Future Work

Within the presented study, we found some limitations: (1) For the cause of the epidemic, we only invited three experts as the sample to take part in our discussion. In the future, it is necessary to invite more experts to collect more important information and health knowledge; (2) It is possible that the system cannot make further design revisions based on users' feedback, because the duration of the experiment and the base of users are not enough, which may be unable to keep Long-term experience and observation of the Digital-Pen interactive system. In the future, we will improve the design of system and collect more users' experience and feedback to the Digital-Pen interactive system to make the users' experience more natural and effective. It is expected that the system production cost will be further reduced, the system functions will be simplified, and the battery life will be lengthened in the future design. We will continue to apply digital art to solve the health risks of more users who will use the product, and we will try to recruit more users to participate in the research.

7   Conclusion

A interactive system used for the Digital-Pen is studied and introduced in this paper. The system can help parents to encourage their children of primary school to form healthy writing posture when they are writing, and has real-time data feedback function to achieve Internet interaction and sharing. The Digital-Pen provides real-time feedback and error-correction based on children's writing behavior, to improve their writing habits in real-time when they are writing homework, thereby protecting vision and bone health. A preliminary study on the Digital-Pen user show that interactive system for the Digital-Pen is an important tool for parents to effectively obtain children's writing data and children to form healthy writing habits. Compared with previous work, the prototype is based on real-time data feedback and score list sharing on the internet, which supports the identification of users unhealthy writing posture and call their attention to correct. The work would provide more references for the health research of primary school students. It can be believed that the Digital-Pen can play an effective role to primary school students in solving more physical health problems such as myopia and skeletal deformities, and mental health problems caused by the new crown epidemic (COVID-19).

Acknowledgement. We are grateful to all the experimenters who taken part in the project, as well as the experts who shared us the information of primary school students' writing and the design and development of technology and products.

References

1. Goonetilleke, R.S., Hoffmann, E.R., Luximon, A.: Effects of pen design on drawing and writing performance. Journal **40**(2), 292–301 (2009)
2. Romat, H., Fender, A., Meier, M., Holz, C.: Flashpen: a high-fidelity and high-precision multi-surface pen for virtual reality. In:2021 IEEE Virtual Reality and 3D User Interfaces (VR), pp. 306–315. IEEE (2021)
3. Stocco, L.J., Salcudean, S.E., Sassani, F.: Optimal kinematic design of a haptic pen. Journal **6**(3), 210–220 (2001)
4. HeimannSteinert, A., Latendorf, A., Prange, A., Sonntag, D., MüllerWerdan, U.: Digital pen technology for conducting cognitive assessments: a cross-over study with older adults. Psychol. Res. **85**(8), 3075–3083 (2020)
5. Abidin, N.R., Anggoro, S.: Development of Smart Paper Engineering (SMART-PEN) Thematic Media using the RADEC model to train creative skills and critical thinking elementary school students. In: ICONESS 2021: Proceedings of the 1st International Conference on Social Sciences 2021, pp. 329. Purwokerto, Central Java, Indonesia (2021)
6. Wu, P., Fei, L., Li, S., et al.: Towards pen-holding hand pose recognition: a new benchmark and a coarse-to-fine PHHP recognition network. Journal (2022)
7. St-Pierre, N.R.: Design and analysis of pen studies in the animal sciences. Journal **90**, E87–E99 (2007)
8. Shintani, M., Lee, J.H., Okamoto, S.: Digital pen for handwritten alphabet recognition. In: 2021 IEEE International Conference on Consumer Electronics (ICCE), pp. 1–4. IEEE (2021)
9. Lin, W.: Investigating the causes of large deviations in primary school students' writing posture and improving strategies. Journal 212–213 (2010–11)
10. Shi, H., Fu, J., Liu, X., et al.: Influence of the interaction between parental myopia and poor eye habits when reading and writing and poor reading posture on prevalence of myopia in school students in Urumqi, China. Journal **299** (2021)
11. Dutta, S.: Evaluation of health hazards during classroom activities and an ergonomic approach for designing a writing desk for the children of rural primary school. Vidyasagar University Midnapore INDIA, Dissertation (2014)
12. People's Education Edition Primary School Chinese Grade 1 Chinese Textbook, p. 16. People's Education Press, Beijing (2018)

The Study on Digital Art Generation of Health Data for the Elderly

Shuyao Li[1] ⬡, Yahi Shuai[1] ⬡, Ran Wan[1(✉)], Jianxin Jin[2], Shuqi Wang[1], Zepeng Yu[1], Qianqian Hu[1], Feifei Liu[1], and Yijia Wang[1]

[1] Nanchang University, Nanchang 330031, JinangXi, China
w13807085763@163.com
[2] Hangzhou BaMai Technology LTD, Hangzhou, China

Abstract. With the aging of the population becoming severe, the elderly's health has become a concern. The survey shows that the main providers of voluntary services for the elderly are college students, who help to improve the quality of life of the elderly and alleviate their psychological problems. In this paper, digital art generated from health data were assessed through interview to verify their correlation with the health of the elderly. We selected ten college student volunteers with the aesthetic basis to view 100 digital artworks generated by the health data from the elderly. Volunteers were asked to score these digital artworks and assess their emotional state before and after the experiment. The relationship between digital art and health and mood was examined by analyzing interview results. Finally, we found that the score was associated with the health data (X^2 = 15.174, $\rho < 0.001$). Of these, 60% of the volunteers could understand the expressive intention of the images in the digital artworks, and 70% thought they could perceive the emotions expressed in those artworks. In conclusion, the digital artworks generated from different health data have different features, forms, and colors. They bring different emotional experiences to volunteers and provide a scientific method for them quickly identify the health of the elderly.

Keywords: Elderly · Health data · Digital art · Health recognition

1 Introduction

In recent years, with the progress of science and the improvement of living standards, the life expectancy of human beings has been gradually extended, and the ageing of the population has become one of the common social development issues around the world.

At the same time, mental health problems among the elderly are also severe. Zenebe Yosef et al. [1] used Stata-11 to determine the average prevalence of the elderly's depression was 31.74%. Sharma Muna et al. [2] collected data through face-to-face interviews using Geriatric Depression Scale - 15 and Geriatric Anxiety Scale - 10. They found that senior citizens having physical health problems or being physically dependent are likely to have poor mental health. According to a Chinese survey in 2001 [3] 769 million Chinese residents over 18 participated in voluntary service, with a rate of 85.2%. Youth,

© IFIP International Federation for Information Processing 2022
Published by Springer Nature Switzerland AG 2022
B. Göbl et al. (Eds.): ICEC 2022, LNCS 13477, pp. 354–362, 2022.
https://doi.org/10.1007/978-3-031-20212-4_29

especially college students, have higher quality and are more willing to contribute to society. They form the most prominent volunteer team in China and are eager to participate in the elderly care community to broaden their vision and enrich their experience. Seniors can also feel cared for and respected. So it is essential for volunteers to quickly understand the physical health and emotional state of the elderly.

In the research of Christina R Davies et al. [4] A framework was developed on the relationship between artistic participation and population health. A thematic analysis using QSR - NVivo10 revealed the potential of art to help promote health and rehabilitation. And in another study [5], they provide a measurement of exposure for use in studies investigating the relationship between arts engagement and health. Lily Martin et al. [6] found that 81.1% of the included research reports, Creative Art Therapies, and art intervention can significantly reduce the psychological stress of participants. With the development of technology, digital art has widespread influence and rich and diversified ways of expression as one art form. Lin Hua et al. [7] summarized a variety of benign interactions between digital art and medical science. As for medical theory, Jiao Dongliang et al. [8]. Western medicine believes that emotional changes lead to the occurrence of diseases through the Neuro-Endocrine-Immune network system. They also found that traditional Chinese medicine believes that emotional changes lead to diseases by affecting the functions of the viscera.

Therefore, digital art as an expression of health attracted our attention. It has the potential to help volunteers better understand the health and emotional state of the elderly.

2 Related Work

We examine the work of other scholars in data visualization and the use of digital algorithms to generate digital art to provide feasibility for the idea of generating digital art from health data.

In health data visualization research, Peter Groves et al. [9] proposed that in the era of connected health, data extracted from various health care institutions, payers, research entities, and pharmaceutical industries, as well as patient-generated health data (PGHD), are being used to create the lifelong electronic health record (EHR) Collins describes. In the study of Vivian L West et al. [10], they investigate the use of visualization techniques reported between 1996 and 2013 and evaluate innovative approaches to information visualization of EHR data for knowledge discovery.

In terms of digital art algorithm research, Zhang Zefang proposes [11] that programming software is the soul of interactive works in digital media, where the input, output, and conversion of signals are all achieved by the programming language. The advent of visual programming has dramatically improved the efficiency of artists and designers. Zhao Yang et al. [12] introduced the theory of fluid dynamics to study the transport and transmission patterns of ink particles in shallow water layers. A fast, interactive ink painting coloring algorithm was designed by solving the ink motion model based on the Navier-Stokes system of partial differential equations through Helmholtz-Hodge decomposition. Wu Yuxuan [13] realized the visual design of Chinese classical music through digital program design and *Processing, Max*, and other software based on existing digital media and music visualization research and design. Siyu Zhou et al. [14] used information and communication technology (ICT) equipment to collect and record pulse data of the elderly, understand the health condition of the elderly, and assist doctors in simple diagnosis.

3   System Design

3.1   The Analysis of Health Data Generates Digital Art

Our experimental method is a new and creative attempt, combining the above theoretical and technical achievements. It aims to construct digital artworks from health data through combinatorial algorithms in an attempt to identify the health status and emotional state of the elderly in a new way. In the system design, We clarify our work to build an algorithm model and framework for the digital art generation from health data and create a visual correspondence system. Through the products invented by BaMai technology LTD, the health data are calculated from the collected Surface Electromyographic (sEGM) of the human body.

3.2   The Description of Visual System Design

See Fig. 1 for the conceptual framework of the visual design.

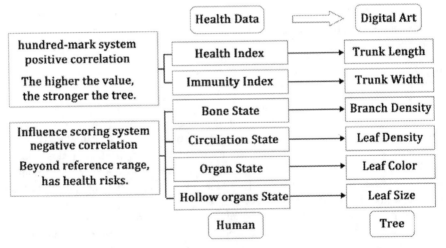

Fig. 1. Conceptual framework of the design (The prototype of digital art is the tree)

3.3   The Construction of Algorithm Model and Framework

We use the software named *Processing* as a programming mapping tool. See Fig. 2 for the Conceptual flow of digital art algorithm. The new value is available in the visual system by inputting the health data.

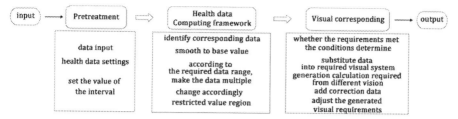

Fig. 2. Conceptual flow of digital art algorithm

3.4   Final Visual Presentation

See Fig. 3 for 16 digital artworks extracted from 100 final visual presentations. See Fig. 4 for the corresponding health data.

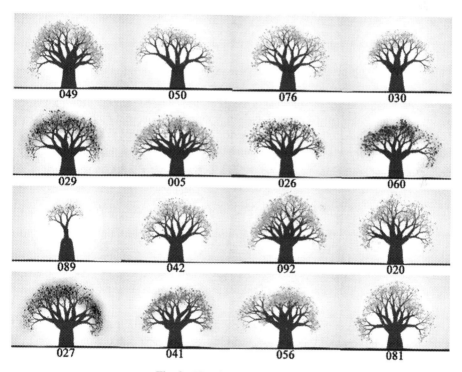

Fig. 3. The visual presentations

As shown in Fig. 3, the branches of No. 050 are thin, and the leaves are sparse. We can see that its Immunity Index in Fig. 4 is low, and the Gallbladder item reaches 210.17. The leaves in No. 060 are deep blue and purple. We can see that the Spleen and Heart of Organ State in Table 5 are 73.60 and 83.02, both of them exceed the normal reference range.No. 089 has only one branch. We can see that the Bone State in Fig. 4 is 801.99,

Sequence	Immunity Index	Health Index	Circulation State	Bone State	Organ State					Hollow organs State				
					Spleen	Lungs	Liver	Kindey	Heart	Bladder	Large intestine	Stomach	Small intestine	Gallbladder
049	86.00	85.00	0.35	0.81	0.49	0.38	0.99	0.38	0.59	0.63	0.85	0.26	0.51	0.99
050	16.00	50.00	32.55	18.87	4.42	0.00	3.93	1.60	7.07	3.79	7.32	0.00	6.15	210.17
029	23.00	59.00	15.34	195.89	0.00	0.77	1.13	0.39	203.70	13.83	0.77	0.40	0.00	220.11
005	63.00	82.00	0.85	1.76	0.92	1.59	0.27	0.70	1.27	0.47	0.85	0.91	0.95	1.62
069	37.00	68.00	91.57	801.99	1.23	0.60	5.02	1.21	1.32	0.62	1.85	1.80	2.57	0.61
042	74.00	83.00	1.62	0.46	0.60	1.04	1.00	1.40	0.64	0.00	0.84	0.32	0.23	0.76
076	83.00	86.00	1.25	0.55	0.76	0.97	0.17	0.68	0.48	1.05	0.88	0.84	0.77	0.00
030	20.00	48.00	32.44	391.24	4.42	0.00	3.93	1.60	6.03	3.90	6.33	0.00	7.14	210.27
026	47.00	67.00	3.42	0.95	69.29	0.91	0.00	0.95	0.92	1.12	0.88	1.93	5.32	3.76
060	34.00	64.00	2.43	26.51	75.62	0.65	27.58	2.56	83.02	0.00	28.40	0.61	0.64	1.19
092	77.00	85.00	0.00	0.63	0.20	0.00	0.25	0.22	0.53	0.86	0.69	2.56	1.39	0.56
020	68.00	78.00	1.30	139.01	2.67	0.83	28.15	0.51	0.45	0.15	8.86	0.90	0.47	0.91
027	47.00	67.00	3.42	0.95	69.29	0.91	0.00	0.95	0.92	1.12	0.88	1.93	5.32	3.76
041	34.00	59.00	12.73	55.64	2.65	4.76	5.05	60.47	0.16	1.97	0.42	1.47	4.50	0.58
056	52.00	72.00	2.43	5.18	1.28	3.22	0.50	0.30	3.66	5.20	0.81	4.95	0.54	2.66
061	78.00	87.00	3.77	2.57	0.13	0.81	1.13	0.13	0.33	0.00	0.46	0.53	6.64	0.44

Fig. 4. The corresponding health data.

far beyond the reference range (The reference range is 0–34 according to the 5% worst results, beyond which there may be health risks).

4 Analysis

4.1 Study Methods

In the four million health database of BaMai technology, we divided them into four kinds of health groups: Substandard (under 50 points), reach the standard (50–65 points), good (66–80 points), and excellent (81–100 points). We randomly selected 25 health data from each group of people over 60 years old for a total of 100 health data and made label records on them.

In this experiment, ten volunteers were selected. They are 20–25 years old and have some artistic basis. Before the experiment, we asked the volunteers to fill out the Emotion measurement Scale (Classifies emotions into two standards: positive and negative; Six types: excitement, joy, ease, anger, sadness, and decadence; 1 to 5 points to express the intensity of emotion, positive takes the positive number, negative takes the negative number) to gain their current emotional experience before viewing the artwork. After that, we started the experiment. They were asked to fill the Digital artwork evaluation Scale (Scores 1 to 5 indicate the degree of normality of different features) according to the random ten digital artworks from the same health group to obtain their perceptions of the artwork. After the experiment, the volunteers were asked to fill out the Emotion measurement Scale again, to record their emotional changes after appreciating digital artworks and interview their opinions on the digital artworks. There are four experiment rounds, and each round adopts artworks from different health groups. In order to eliminate the emotional interference that remained after each experiment, every round was carried out at 3 pm each day.

4.2 Study Results

Through the analysis and arrangement of the scale data, we calculated the average score of the scores of different health condition groups, as shown in Tables 1, 2 and 3. See the statistics of the evaluation and emotion measurement results of digital artworks of different health condition groups in the experiment.

Table 1. Evaluation results of digital art in different health condition groups

Health groups/average score	Trunk length	Trunk width	Branch density	Leaf density	Leaf color	Leaf size	Average
Substandard	2.6	2.4	3.0	2.3	1.4	1.8	2.3
Reach the standard	3.3	3.5	3.6	3.3	3.8	3.2	3.5
Good	3.5	4.1	4.3	4.2	5.0	3.5	4.1
Excellent	4.2	4.6	4.8	4.5	5.0	4.4	4.6

Table 2. The results of emotion measurement before the experiment

Health groups/average score	Excitement	Joy	Ease	Anger	Sadness	Decadence	Average
Round 1	4.3	4.2	3.6	−1.0	−1.0	−1.1	1.5
Round 2	4.0	4.2	3.8	−1.0	−1.1	−1.0	1.5
Round 3	3.8	4.0	3.5	−1.1	−1.0	−1.2	1.3
Round 4	3.5	3.8	3.6	−1.0	−1.0	−1.1	1.3
Average	3.8	4.1	3.5	−1.0	−1.0	−1.1	1.4

Table 3. The results of emotion measurement after the experiment

Health groups/average score	Excitement	Joy	Ease	Anger	Sadness	Decadence	Average
Substandard	2.6	2.2	2.3	−2.4	−3.6	−3.4	−0.4
Reach the standard	3.2	3.4	3.5	−1.6	−1.5	−2.1	0.8
Good	4.0	3.6	3.8	−1.7	−1.3	−1.4	1.2
Excellent	4.4	4.2	3.6	−1.8	−1.2	−1.1	1.4

Then we interviewed the volunteers to understand their views on these digital works. See Table 4 for the perceptions of digital artworks after the experiment.

Table 4. Volunteers' perceptions of digital artworks after the experiment (n = 10)

Variables	Yes	No
	N(%)	N(%)
Experience before the experiment can affect judgment	3(30.0)	7(70.0)
Can understand the expressive intention of the corresponding image in the painting in the experiment	6(60.0)	4(40.0)
Can evaluate the exact score in the experiment	5(50.0)	5(50.0)
Can sense the emotion of the digital artworks in the experiment	7(70.0)	3(30.0)
Can sense the emotional changes that occur when view the digital artworks in the experiment	8(80.0)	2(20.0)
Can evaluate the exact emotional perception score in the experiment	6(60.0)	4(40.0)

5   Result

See Table 1. The healthier date also has a higher score. The comparison between Tables 2 and 3 reflects that before every round of the experiment, the volunteers' emotion was stable. See Table 3. We can find that these digital artworks did bring different emotional experiences, in general. Furthermore, we can see from Table 4 that the majority of volunteers can understand the intentional associations and emotional visualizations of the artworks.

By the end of the experiment, through interviews with volunteers, we knew that slight differences in their observations made it challenging to determine the score. Moreover, they felt different emotions from different random forms, even similar data. In addition, due to different people's different cognition, part of the volunteers felt that over-exuberant trees and developed trunks could be aggressive, while dense foliage could be depressing, and that sparse branches were instead relaxing and pleasant.

Regarding association, in our study, the chi-square test was used to calculate the statistical results. According to the health groups from 100 health data, the "substandard" and "reach the standard" groups were divided into the sub-health group and the "good" and "excellent" groups into the health group.

See Tables 5 and 6. In this study, the proportion of "well" digital art was 80%, and the proportion of "positive" emotional evaluation was 84% in the healthy group. Both were higher than that of the sub-health group, and the data difference was statistically significant. ($X^2 = 15.174$, $p < 0.001$; $X^2 = 14.439$, $p < 0.001$) The results show that digital artworks generated based on health data correlate with human health and emotional experience. The higher the health score, the better the positive rating of the artworks, and the more positive emotions the artworks bring to people, and vice versa.

Table 5. Comparison of works' scores from different health groups (In the digital art scoring system, the average of the total full scores in Table 2, i.e. 3, is used as the passing line, with greater than being "Well" and less than or equal to being "Poor")

Items	Number	Well N (%)	Poor N (%)
Health group	50	40(80.0)	10(20.0)
Sub-health group	50	21(42.0)	29(58.0)
x^2	15.174		
ρ	<0.001		

Table 6. Comparison of emotion's scores from different health groups (In the emotion measurement system, the average score in Table 5 can define the emotions before and after the experiment, with greater than 0 being "Positive" and less than or equal to 0 being "Negative")

Items	Number	Positive N (%)	Negative N (%)
Health group	50	42(84.0)	8(16.0)
Sub-health group	50	24(48.0)	26(52.0)
x^2	14.439		
ρ	< 0.001		

6 Conclusion

This paper is based on the technique for generating digital art from the elderly's health data to assess their health state. It is intended to provide a scientific method to assist volunteers in the identification of the elderly's health.

However, the limitations of our method make these results, on the one hand, small in sample size, and the volunteers of study are not broad enough. On the other hand, the emotional feedback and cognitive judgment of the volunteers are generated from their subjective cognitive volunteers. The participants' aesthetic perception influences the experiment results. Nevertheless, the results show that digital art can help volunteers understand the elderly's health, which may raise concerns among the elderly about their health and psychological issues. We hope that through this study, people will understand that digital art can also generate value in the health field.

At present, the influence of digital art on the elderly's psychological feedback, quality of life, emotion, behavior and other disruptive factors is not clear yet. The guiding principles of digital art need to be regularised by further research. Future studies could focus on appropriate samples, different digital art forms targeted mediation, and digital art variables. It has a specific practical value for the mental health of the elderly and helps study the practical significance and effect of digital art intervention in the health field.

References

1. Zenebe, Y., Akele, B., W/Selassie, M., Necho, M.: Prevalence and determinants of depression among old age: a systematic review and meta-analysis. Ann. General Psych. **20**(1), 55–55 (2021)
2. Muna, S., Tilarupa, B., Prafulla, S.: Anxiety and depression among senior citizens. J. Nepal Health Res. Council. **19**(2), 305–310 (2021)
3. Wang, Z.: A Study on Current Status Function and Problems of Voluntary Service in China. MA thesis. Huazhong Normal University (2005)
4. Davies, C.R., Knuiman, M., Wright, P., Rosenberg, M.: The art of being healty: a qualitative study to develop a thematic framework for understanding the relationship between health and the arts. BMJ Open **4**(4), e004790 (2014)
5. Davies, C.R., Rosenberg, M., Knuiman, M., Ferguson, R., Pikora, T., Slatter, N.: Defining arts engagement for population-based health research: Art forms, activities and level of engagement. Arts Health **4**(3), 203–216 (2012)
6. Lily, M., et al.: Creative arts interventions for stress management and prevention—a systematic review. Behav. Sci. **8**(2), 28 (2018)
7. Lin, H., Gao, L.: Telemedicine visualization and digital art design. Ind. Des. **6**, 65–68 (2015)
8. Jiao, D., et al.: J. Comparison and reflection on the theory of emotional pathogenicity in Chinese and Western medicine. J. Beijing University of Trad. Chinese Med. **33**(10), 656–658,663 (2010)
9. Groves, P., Kayyali, B., Knott, D., Van Kuiken, S.: The "BigData" Revolution in Healthcare: Accelerating Value and Innovation. McKinsey and Company, New York (2013)
10. West, V.L., David, B., Ed, H.W.: Innovative information visualization of electronic health record data: a systematic review. J. Am. Med. Inform. Assoc. JAMIA. **2**, 330–339 (2015)
11. Zhang, Z.: A pilot study on the use of visual programming in digital media art: the example of TouchDesigner. Times Rep. **6**,140–141 (2019)
12. Yang, Z., Ruan, Y., Yang, J.: Research and design of an algorithm for ink painting based on fluid dynamics. J. Liaoning University. (Nat. Sci. Edn.) **39**(02), 144–148 (2012)
13. Wu, Y.: Study on the visualization design of Chinese classical music. MA thesis, Jiaotong University, Beijing (2020)
14. Zhou, S., et al.: Analysis of health changes and the association of health indicators in the elderly using TCM pulse diagnosis assisted with ICT devices: a time series study. Eur. J. Integr. Med. **27**, 105–113 (2019)

Effects of Color Tone of Dynamic Digital Art on Emotion Arousal

Qiurui Wang[1]([⊠]), Zhenyu Liu[2], and Jun Hu[1]

[1] Department of Industrial Design, Eindhoven University of Technology, Eindhoven, The Netherlands
wwqrr@126.com, j.hu@tue.nl
[2] College of Computer Science and Technology, Zhejiang University, Hangzhou, China
liuzhenyu0713@zju.edu.cn

Abstract. The fast-paced life of contemporary society increases people's psychological stress, and a piece of creative digital art may help relieve the stress. Color has a certain contribution to adjusting a person's emotion. The interactivity and dynamics of digital art bring different experiences to our vision. This article was to present our work on the topic of whether different tones of still and dynamic digital art could make an impact on the emotion arousal. Over two experiments, 106 participants were invited to transfer the styles of 8 abstract images by adding blue and red tones. The dynamic creation processes were recorded to be used as stimuli, and three-dimensional valence-arousal-enjoyment model was used to measure emotions. The result of the experiment showed that adding different tones to digital art had no significant impact on the emotion arousal, however some participants expressed certain interests in the dynamic presentation of the creation process. The insights from this work could provide input to the design of digital art in emotion intervention and stress management.

Keywords: Emotion · Digital art · Color tone · Interactivity

1 Introduction

While humans are born with creativity in their most active minds, art is able to nourish the spirit of humans by its abundant spiritual nourishment in return, which enriches the human experience [1]. The wide variety of painting art does not only give various inspiring philosophies, but also gives people leisure and satisfaction. The painting art therapy [2] has enabled abstract art to become a communication bridge between art and the psychology field, which can help people to deal with stress and anxiety.

In paintings, color gives people the most direct and effective intuitive feelings. Paul Cézanne states that "First of all, a painting is and shall present color" [3]. The painters have combined cultures by practices, explorations on the application and expression of color, giving the color a wider range of expression. This article focused on the integration

---

Q. Wang and Z. Liu—Contributed equally to the article.

© IFIP International Federation for Information Processing 2022
Published by Springer Nature Switzerland AG 2022
B. Göbl et al. (Eds.): ICEC 2022, LNCS 13477, pp. 363–371, 2022.
https://doi.org/10.1007/978-3-031-20212-4_30

of digital technology and art, where much was to be explored for emotion intervention and stress management.

Researchers are exploring and researching on digital art [4] in the area of emotion cognition from the visual dimensions. One of such dimensions is for example motion. The interpretation of motion quoted in the book *Art and Visual Perception*, "Motion is the strongest visual appeal to attention…Human beings are similarly attracted by movement" [5]. The article was to look into another dimension, namely, color, to experiment with the features of digital art, to explore how the process of changing color tone in abstract art dynamically could increase people's attention on tone change and whether the sensation of interactive experience would be increased.

French philosopher, Hippolyte Adolphe Taine, states that "The interaction between different colors will give us different impressions, so the combination of colors will have different expressions [6]". One of the mentioned "the interaction between different colors" is color tone, and "different expressions" suggests that different interactions could affect people's emotions. A lot of research has been done to investigate the impact of color on emotion, mostly focused on red and blue tones [7]. The work presented in this article was to verify whether the addition of blue and red tones in digital art via still and dynamic ways would have different effects on emotion arousal.

2   Related Work

Tone is a term originated from music. It refers to pitch in musical works. Color tone refers to the tint in paintings, and it is the tonal key of a picture. Color connection is formed by dominant color and color schemes, and it is responsible for the overall color effect of all colors in a picture [8]. The color tones vary in hue, shade, purity, and temperature. In terms of hue, there are green, blue, red, yellow tones, etc.

Henri Matisse said, "The main function of color should be to serve expression [9]". Different applications of color bring different feelings to people. For example, the Man Golden Helmet by Rembrandt in brown tones conveyed an atmosphere of majesty and sorrow; By using light and pleasant tones, the Gypsy Girl by Frans Hals depicted a young gypsy wench who seemed happy with her life; The Massacre at Chios by Eugène Delacroix described the cruelty of the killing by intense brownish red; Henri Matisse used blue in his paintings to neutralize the emotions incurred by the colorful paintings, bringing people fancy purity and serenity. Art can satisfy people's aesthetic needs and stimulate people's inner emotions and awareness.

The effect of color on emotional perception has been found in internet web page design [10] and physical space [11]. Space where its dominant color was red, would be more possibly described as "stimulus induction", and this was identical to the viewpoint of Birren [12]. Birren believed that warmer colors (e.g. red and yellow) were more capable of further evoking emotion from an individual compared with cool colors (e.g. blue and green). In industry, the color psychology has broadly applied to use color tone to influence human behaviour. In the application areas of interior design and architecture, a systematic impact of color on emotion was often assumed [13]. For instance, in comparison to the medium and short wavelength of lights (blue or green), the light mainly consisting of a longer wavelength (red) would raise a higher arousal [14].

In comparison with traditional painting art, the strength of digital art is apparent. The emergence of dynamic media, e.g. animation, audio, video etc., has broken the monotonous traditional painting art, further enriched the visual sensation, and increased the interactivity and entertainment. As the main visual element of painting art, color can effectively convey emotion, combine with dynamic effect display, and more effectively convey information, which can be used as an effective way to attract viewers. In our work we tried to compare the process of presenting the image style transfer process in a dynamic way to the process with still images. We hypothesized that the presentation of the process of adding color tones by this approach would have certain effects on human emotion. The three-dimensional valence-arousal-enjoyment emotion model was adopted to conduct emotion analysis based on collected data.

3   Study Design

3.1   Stimuli

The experiment applied the open data set of abstract artworks established in 2010 by Machajdik and others, including 280 pieces of abstract artworks that contains only color and texture, with no identified objects to evoke emotion without simulating any specific objects. In this article, 8 images (Fig. 1) were selected from the data set, 4 of them were with a low arousal level (Sad and Content), and 4 with a high arousal level (Angry and Excited).

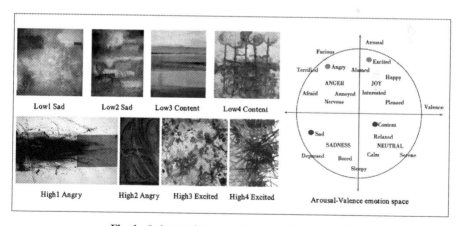

Fig. 1. 8 abstract images with low and high arousal

Each image was added stylish pictures manipulated with red and blue tones. They were displayed in 2 ways, one was in still motion (16 images, see Fig. 2), using the PowerPoint (PPT) format. The other was in dynamic way (16 videos, see Fig. 3 for production process).

The production process was captured in 16 videos (see Fig. 3). The style transfer processes were visually recorded and edited, that each image creation lasts for 30 s in

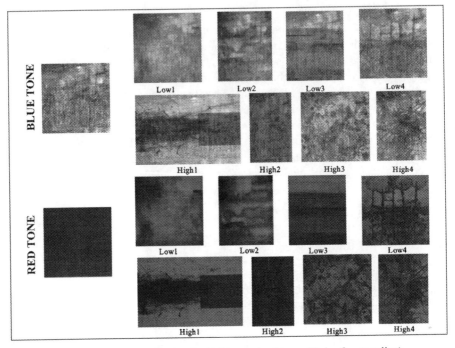

Fig. 2. 8 images manipulated with blue and red tone. (Color figure online)

motion. As a type of art language, oil painting is a rich one. It has plenty of color relations and expressions. Therefore, oil painting was adopted in the style transfer process. ALab and SmartPainting were used. These two software tools are developed by the Engineering Research Center of Computer Aided Product Innovation Design, the Ministry of Education, China. They were used to carry out algorithm techniques to realize image style transfer methods meanwhile showcase the process of image manipulation with brushwork.

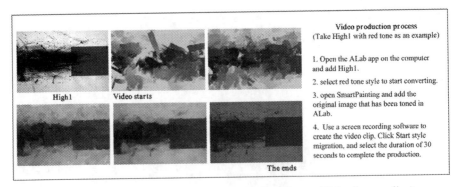

Fig. 3. Video production process of High1 with red tone. (Color figure online)

3.2 Participants

We recruited 106 participants from Zhejiang University for 2 experiments. They were at the education level of college or above, and with computer literacy. The test was arranged during the pandemic period, and the videos and questionnaires were sent to participants for the online experiments. The participants watched the videos on a computer, and filled out the questionnaires following the intervals of the process.

3.3 Experiment Design

Experiment 1

Participants
There were 53 participants in Experiment 1 (31 women and 22 men; Aged between 18 to 35, M = 21.4, SD = 4.1). All participants reported good vision, no color feebleness, nor color blindness.

Stimuli
Blue and red tones were added in each of the 8 images, which were divided into 2 sets, and played in order, see 1-A and 1-B of Fig. 4. 26 participants were in Group A (blue tone) and 27 participants in Group B (red tone).

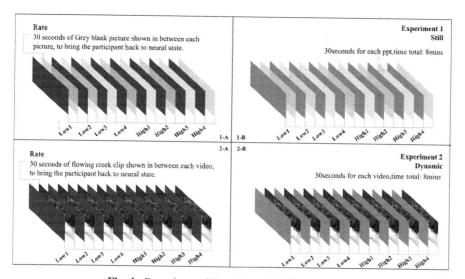

Fig. 4. Procedures of Experiment 1 & Experiment 2.

Procedure
An online survey was created at www.wjx.cn, an online survey and questionnaire platform. Participants were divided into two groups randomly. Group A watched the slides in blue tone, and Group B watched the slides in red tone. The participants were asked

to evaluate the levels of arousal, valence, and enjoyment for each image or video. The 0–10 rating scale was applied to evaluate arousal, valence, and enjoyment. To evaluate arousal, a rating of 0 (no arousal, e.g. calm) to 10 (the highest arousal, e.g. excitement) was scaled; To evaluate valence, a rating of 0 (negative) to 10 (positive) was scaled; To evaluate enjoyment, a rating of 0 (no enjoyment) to 10 (full of enjoyment) was scaled.

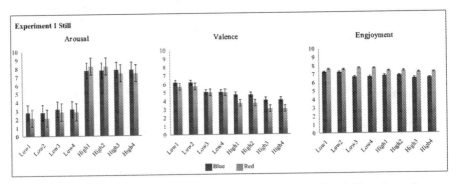

Fig. 5. Bar plots of mean arousal, valence and enjoyment ratings in Experiment 1.

Result and Discussion
The results showed that, regardless of the conditions, there was no significant difference in the level of arousal with of the 8 stimuli images. Figure 5 showed the results of arousal, valence and enjoyment levels. Among the 53 participants, 45 claimed that they had watched all of the slides, and none of them said they had not watched any slides. As a result, all participants had at least a glance at blue or red toned images, which shall be enough to trigger color association.
   Experiment 2

Participants
There were 53 participants in Experiment 2 (30 women and 23 men; Aged between 18 to 64, M = 25.8, SD = 10.8). All of them reported good vision, no color feebleness, nor color blindness.

Stimuli and Procedure
Blue and red tones were added in each of the 8 images, which were divided into 2 sets. The image style transfer process was edited and recorded as videos, see 2-A and 2-B of Fig. 4. 26 participants were in Group A (blue tone), and 27 participants in Group B (red tone).

Result and Discussion
The average ratings of arousal, valence and enjoyment under each condition were calculated, see Fig. 6. Regardless of the conditions, there was no significant difference between the arousal of the original images and the arousal of the images with additional tones. There was also no significant difference in arousal in dynamic conditions. The

blue group recognized the Low arousal images with the addition of blue tone as more pleasant than the High arousal image with the addition of red tone in the red group. In addition, in the same condition, minimal changes were observable in all conditions (Figs. 5 and 6). Moreover, the result stayed the same with the data of valence. We combined data from 2 experiments and made an analysis of the impact of still and dynamic conditions (n = 53 per condition). Again, arousal ratings were not significantly different in the red compared to the blue condition. The a priori statistical power of this analysis was better than 0.8 (N = 106, single-tailed, independent-sample t-test).

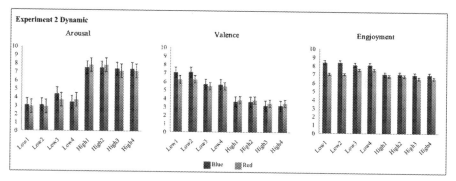

Fig. 6. Bar plots of mean arousal, valence and enjoyment ratings in Experiment 2.

4   Discussion and Future Work

The result did not support the assumption of the effect of digital art with the addition of tones on emotional arousal, whether in still or in dynamic conditions. In contrast, many researches have indicated that the emotional attribute of color is irreplaceable in any visual art form. The nature of color is an electrical signal formed by the retina struck by different wavelength of lights and then identified and processed by the brain. The research focused more on hue to emotional arousal. The settings of unadjusted saturation and brightness etc., might have been the reasons for not having an expected effect.

The article combined the features of digital art [15], presenting the process of changing color tone of images in a still or dynamic way. The transformation process of the formation of an image, starting from painting the outline with an oil painting brush, was artistic and rhythmical. It was a transformation of color in a flow, by presenting to the participants in the dynamic way, making the conveyance of a flat image to integrate with the characters of motion. However, only little change was made to people's emotional arousal, and it might be because of the video duration or other factors in the formation of the final image.

Furthermore, as a result of human mental activities, the digital art image implies rich affective semantics and messages. Kang et al. [16] conducted a research on different affections generated by different colors, and used quantization of 3-dimensional space to estimate the affection of color; Machajdik et al. [17] extracted the color, texture, layout and content feature from drawings and paintings; Zhao and the team [18] discussed about the concept of art principle and its impact on images and emotions. Our work merely focused on emotional intervention by the color of low-level features, which may be one of the causes of the results.

The concrete objects which may cause specific emotions for the participants had been removed from the selected abstract paintings in the article. It was primarily consisted of visual features: line, color, texture, space, color block etc. [19]. By the applications of these type of visual features, it brought certain stimulation to human senses, affection resonance could be produced while people were watching abstract paintings [20]. Hence, only focusing on the change of hue may not be able to influence the affection towards the abstract paintings.

Another limitation was the physical experiment environment. As it was the pandemic period, it was not applicable to arrange for all participants to be tested in one single laboratory and use the same screens in the same environment. It was out of our control to collect data in a reasonably controlled physical space. We were unable to confirm whether different sizes of screens may influence the effect of tone on arousal. On the other hand, the article presented abstract still paintings with the addition of tones with the adoption of a dynamic way, which may also have a certain impact on participants.

Moreover, we will recruit more participants for the reliability and validity of the experiment. Last but not least, physiological data collection could be added in the future research [21], e.g. measurements of skin conductance, myoelectricity, electrocardio etc., to coordinate with the surveys for a comprehensive observation on the impact of arousal.

5 Conclusion

The research has indicated that, changing the color tone of digital art in either still or dynamic way had little effect on people's emotion arousal. We need to consider integrating other features in digital art to achieve the goal. Such features are, for instance, music and animations, and we could add these features into digital art stimuli so as to increase interactivity. Nevertheless, this research provided insights into using color tone for emotion intervention, that could lead to more explorations in the innovative use of digital art for emotion intervention and as one of the interesting directions, for managing stress and anxiety.

References

1. Case, C., Dalley, T.: Handbook of Art Therapy. Routledge, London (2006)
2. Hagood, M.M.: Art therapy research in England: impressions of an American art therapist. Arts Psychother. 17, 75–79 (1990)
3. Tian, Y.: The application and study of subjective color expression and emotion expression in Chinese and western oil paintings. Liaoning Normal University (2020)
4. Xu, B.: Digital art: an integration of technology with art. J. Ningbo Univ. (Liber. Arts Edn.) 5, 123–126 (2015)
5. Arnheim, R.: Art and Visual Perception: A Psychology of the Creative Eye. University of California Press, Oakland (2004)

6. Taine, H.A.: Lecture on Art. People's Literature Publishing House, Beijing (1963)
7. Kao, W., Chen, L.-Y., Wang, S.: Tone reproduction in color imaging systems by histogram equalization of macro edges. IEEE Trans. Consum. Electron. **52**(2), 682–688 (2006)
8. Arsenault, H., Hebert, M., Dubois, M.C.: Effects of glazing color type on perception of daylight quality, arousal, and switch-on patterns of electric light in office rooms. Build. Environ. **56**, 223–231 (2012)
9. Li, L.: Henri Matisse. Hebei Fine Arts Publishing House, Heibei (2008)
10. Demir, Ã.: Investigation of color-emotion associations of the university students. Color Res. Appl. **45**, 871–884 (2020)
11. Kurt, S., Osueke, K.K..: The effects of color on the moods of college students. SAGE Open. **4**, 1–12 (2014)
12. Birren, F.: Color Psychology and Color Therapy: A Factual Study of the Influence of Color on Human Life. McGraw-Hill, New York (1950)
13. Adams, F.M., Osgood, C.E.: A cross-cultural study of the affective meanings of color. J. Cross-Cult. Psychol. **4**(2), 135–156 (1973)
14. Jacobs, K.W., Hustmyer, F.E.: Effects of four psychological primary colors on GSR, heart-rate and respiration rate. Percept. Motor Skills **38**(3), 763–766 (1974)
15. Zhongxiang, L.: Digital Art Theory. China Broadcasting and Television Press, Beijing (2006)
16. Kang, D., Shim, H., Yoon, K.: A method for extracting emotion using colors comprise the painting image. Multimed. Tools App. **77**(4), 4985–5002 (2018)
17. Machajdik, J., Hanbury, A.: Affective image classification using features inspired by psychology and art theory. In: Proceedings of the 18th ACM International Conference on Multimedia, pp. 83–92. ACM Press, New York (2010)
18. Zhao, S., Gao, Y., Jiang, X.: Exploring principles-of-art features for image emotion recognition. In: Proceedings of the 22nd ACM International Conference on Multimedia, pp. 47–56. ACM Press, New York (2014)
19. Bai, R., Guo, X., Jia, C.: Research on emotion of abstract painting based on multi-feature fusion. App. Res. Comput. **40**(8), 2207–2213 (2020)
20. He, X., Zhang, H., Li, N.: A Multi-attentive pyramidal model for visual sentiment analysis. In: 2019 International Joint Conference on Neural Networks (IJCNN), pp. 1–8. IEEE (2016)
21. Haag, A., Goronzy, S., Schaich, P., Williams, J.: Emotion recognition using bio-sensors: first steps towards an automatic system. In: André, E., Dybkjær, L., Minker, W., Heisterkamp, P. (eds.) Affective Dialogue Systems. LNCS (LNAI), vol. 3068, pp. 36–48. Springer, Heidelberg (2004). https://doi.org/10.1007/978-3-540-24842-2_4

Personalized Synchronous Running Music Remix Procedure for Novice Runners

Nan Zhuang[1], Shitong Weng[2], Song Bao[1], Xinyi Li[1], Jingru Huang[2], and Pinhao Wang[1($\boxtimes$)]

[1] Zhejiang University, 38. Zheda Road, Hangzhou, China
wangpinhao0409@gmail.com
[2] South China Agricultural University, 483. Wushan Road, Guangzhou, China

Abstract. Running music, which refers to background music for running, plays a crucial part in various mobile applications for running. Existing solutions for presenting running music cannot simultaneously address runners' preferences, physical conditions, and training goals, resulting in lower running efficiency, higher injury likelihood, and significant mental fatigue. We proposed a novel running music adaptation method to address this problem. Specifically, the adaptation starts with a trial run, where the runner's running statistics are sampled. Then, with parameters identified from the trial run, cadence goals are set accordingly. The song list provided by the runner is augmented with recommendation systems and later tagged, screened, sorted, and split. Finally, the music parts are rearranged and adjusted to match the cadence goals before being mixed with the training instructions. Unlike previous running music interventions, our method introduces a way to blend different music parts, giving runners unprecedented pleasure in running. Quantitative and qualitative results have shown that the crafted remix can reduce perceived effort, boost the pleasures, run more safely, and help the runners reach their second wind, providing novice runners with a passion for following the training programs.

Keywords: Digital art · Health · Preferred music · Synchronous music · Remix

1 Introduction

Music-related interventions have been an inseparable part of many athletes' daily and training routines for decades [1]. It is associated with almost all sports forms and is considered one of the most significant occurrences in athletic competitions [2]. Meanwhile, running is a popular physical activity worldwide, and music has always been a companion [3]. Listening to music before, during, or after exercise is common [4]. Runners with musical intervention usually find it easier to distract themselves from physical stress, maintain a steady pace, keep their spirits up, and thus stimulate overall performance [4, 28, 29, 31].

N. Zhuang, S. Weng, S. Bao, X. Li——Contributed equally to this work.

© IFIP International Federation for Information Processing 2022
Published by Springer Nature Switzerland AG 2022
B. Göbl et al. (Eds.): ICEC 2022, LNCS 13477, pp. 372–385, 2022.
https://doi.org/10.1007/978-3-031-20212-4_31

Despite the widespread adaptation to music-related interventions in running and music apps, existing solutions either lose sight of users' personal music choices or do not provide personalized training goals. Specifically, most running apps use a fixed, generic training music template - users cannot cut, select, customize, or even choose their songs, which is unsuitable for runners with various fitness levels. These solutions ignored the user's personalized indicators, but they are essential [23, 27]. On the other hand, most running apps provide music recommendations based on real-time performance measured by sensors [50, 51]. These experiences cannot be customized to users' real-time needs and cannot be combined with training goals, resulting in a low incentive effect [52].

Addressing the gaps, we contribute a synchronously running music remix scheme to help the novice runners reach their second wind [55]. The experimental results revealed that the music remixed through the scheme may raise running beginners' performance, motivate them, evoke a positive emotional response, and increase the enjoyment of running music to a greater extent than randomly selected synchronous music in existing applications. This is because the music remixed through the scheme can meet the runner's music preferences and adapt to the runner's cadence.

2 Related Work

2.1 Music, Health, and Sports

Second wind is a common phenomenon whereby a runner suddenly finds the strength to keep running instead of quitting. In the second wind, runners can reach the period of peak physical activity performance and conquer exercises that previously caused muscle fatigue, palpitations, and shortness of breath [55]. One explanation for the second wind is the switch from impaired anaerobic to normal oxidative metabolism [10].

Much literature holds that music is widely recognized and used for its positive psychological, physical, and psychophysiological properties [17]. First, from a psychological point of view, people often use music to regulate their emotions [7]. Music influences psychological aspects by arousing and stimulating emotions in daily life through induction mechanisms [6]. This includes the basic emotions of happiness, sadness, fear, and sameness [8, 9]. Moreover, music can reduce negative emotions and feelings such as fear, anxiety, and nervousness [12]. And it also promotes the effects of positive emotions [10]. At the physiological level, the health benefits of physical activity are well accepted. Statistics show that people who engaged in an average of 15 min of moderate-intensity exercise per day had significant health benefits compared to those who did not [16]. Meanwhile, listening to music during exercise is undoubtedly a way to make exercise more enjoyable and pleasant [18, 19, 32]. Furthermore, previous studies indicate that music can increase sports enjoyment and increase physical performance in various physical activities [13]. Additionally, listening to music has been shown to increase stamina and motivation [13–15]. Some studies have used music as therapy in the exercise environment, and music beats per minute (BPM) has also been considered an essential factor in exercise [17, 20, 21]. From the psychophysiological dimension, the enjoyment of exercise is thought to be a key determinant of exercise adherence [30]. And studies have shown that audiovisual stimuli can reduce feelings of perceived exertion [31] and increase feelings of pleasure. Moreover, music leads to dissociated thinking and altered attention, which improves athletic performance [28, 29].

2.2 Intervention of Music on Sports Performance

Previous research has proposed a model of musical intervention in the field of sports [33], which has referred to synchronous and asynchronous music [17, 21, 22]. It has been proposed that central pattern generators or pacemakers in the brain may respond to regulate and control the rhythm. In other words, humans naturally tend to synchronize their movements with musical rhythms [34, 41]. Synchronous music is often used in endurance-based sports, where synchronous music allows athletes to feel a stronger stimulus and work longer [17, 25, 35]. Experiments show that synchronous music has ergogenic effects on the treadmill and in the 400-m run [3, 24]. In running, synchronous music can make endurance activities more energy-efficient [36]. Synchronous music has been shown to reduce the energy cost of exercise because it increases neuromuscular metabolic efficiency [26].

In addition, music preference has been identified as an essential mediator of the functional benefits of listening to music during exercise [23]. In a variety of different forms of exercise, listening to preferred music has been shown to improve athletic performance [37–40]. Self-selected stimulating music appears to have an entrainment effect [27] and has been shown to improve resistance training performance [23], and familiar music may even elicit psychological and physiological responses without the athlete being aware of it [13].

3   Proposed Method

Based on the problem and related work, we propose a procedure for creating customized running music.

3.1 Trial Run

Trial runs are required to ensure that the running music fits the physical and health conditions of novice runners.

Trial Run Setup. For the trial run, novice runners are asked to wear comfortably. Before the test, runners do 3 min of warm-up exercises. They will then complete a base run on a 400 m standard track at a minimum speed of 9 min per kilometer. Runners run until their self-reported perceived exertion exceeds a score of 8 on the Borg's Perceived Exertion (RPE) scale CR-10 [42, 43], a scale ranging from 0 to 10.

Retrieval of Statistics. To obtain data from the test runs, runners will wear a commercial electronic sports wristband that integrates heart rate monitor (HRM), global positioning system (GPS), and accelerometer to measure heart rate (HR), pace, and cadence. The data should be sampled every 5 s to ensure granularity.

3.2   Data Analytic and Goal Establishment

All HR, pace, and cadence data collected during the test run will be smoothed by a moving average of $n = 6$ to perform the following analysis.

Parameter Identification. The term parameter refers to the observed statistical data of the test run. Three types of parameters should be observed: 1) Warm-up Point - the first starting point for the periods when HR oscillates in the range of ± 5 for 2 min, or the time when HR peaks if no such HR oscillation is observed; 2) Tiring Point - the starting point for all continuous 2-min periods when HR decreases by more than 5, or cadence decreases by more than 5, or pace decreases by 40 s per kilometer; 3) Platform Cadence - the cadence before each fatigue period.

Cadence Goals. Cadence goals Ct refer to the target cadence (steps/minute) for each second t of running. Cadence is 150 at $C0$ and then increases linearly until it reaches the first platform cadence at the warm-up point. Ct will begin to decrease linearly 30 s before each Tiring Point, reaching Ct - 2.5 at the tiring point. Ct will never be lower than 155.

3.3   Music Retrieval and Pre-processing

Music Retrieval. A favorite song list is collected from the runner. Then similar songs will be retrieved from a music recommendation platform (e.g., Musiio). All collected music will be tagged (e.g., Pop, Korean, Male, Rap, Powerful) and downloaded.

Music Screening. To ensure the beat of each song matches the step and the song not to be stretched too much in the mixing process, songs with the following identity will be excluded: 1) BPM between 90 and 140; 2) BPM lower than 70; 3) Beat not obvious; 4) Syncopation too obvious. Then the songs will be sorted by BPM and grouped by tags and pitch.

Splitting. Each of the song is split into intro, verse, chorus, bridge, outro [53]. All collected audios are separated by four sources with DEMUCS [54], in particular, vocal, bass, drum, and other components.

3.4   Mixing

Music Rearrangement. Using the song list, generate the song sequence and rearrange all music parts according to cadence goals. For example, strong choruses are saved for the tiring point and low volume bridges are removed. Then, similar verses, choruses, and outros are swapped, layered, or repeated throughout the songs to keep the music engaging.

Speed Matching. To ensure that the BPM of the track matches the cadence goals, speed adjustment algorithms (e.g., iZotope Radius) are applied to the rearranged music track so that the BPM at time t matches the Ct.

Chaining and Adding Instructions. The beats for each song in the track are synchronized and matched to ensure consistency throughout the track. Then the metronome sound is superimposed over the beats. To refrain the runners from injury, voice instructions on postures, time, step, breathing, and stride are added to the track at specific time spans and fatigue points (see Appendix 1).

Mastering. Minimalist mastering operations are performed on the target track: Vocals are lowered when it is not on the beat; bass and drums are boosted when it is not obvious; volume is adjusted to a comfortable, consistent level. Finally, equalizers, compressors, and limiters are applied to the track to ensure that the dynamic and tonal balance is correct.

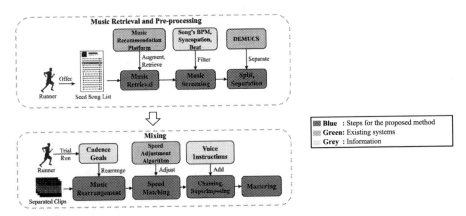

Fig. 1. The overview of proposed method processes

4   Experiment

4.1   Experiment Design

Participants. 12 Zhejiang University students (6 men, 6 women; $M = 23.83$ years) were recruited. They were all amateur runners who ran less than 4 times a month, half of whom hardly ran for years. They were aware of the importance of exercise and had a certain level of performance and fitness improvement goals (On a five-point scale, $M = 3.83$, $SD = 0.986$). The gender, age, height, and weight information are shown in Table 1. All participants provided informed consent before the experiment.

Equipment. Huawei Watch GT 2 was used to measure the participants' heart rate, distance, cadence, and pace during the tasks. It was proved that the measurements could be reliably made through the mainstream devices [45].

Table 1. Demographics of participants.

	Group 1 (n = 6)	Group 2 (n = 6)	Overall
Gender	$N_M = 3, N_F = 3$	$N_M = 3, N_F = 3$	$N_M = 6, N_F = 6$
Age (years)	23.17 ± 1.67	24.50 ± 0.76	23.83 ± 1.46
Height (cm)	168.33 ± 7.25	170.83 ± 6.28	169.58 ± 6.90
Weight (kg)	58.17 ± 7.27	60.67 ± 10.13	59.42 ± 8.90
BMI (km/m^2)	20.44 ± 1.24	20.61 ± 2.15	20.53 ± 1.76

Tasks and Groups. Participants were randomly divided into two groups. A repeated-measures design method was employed where both groups were asked to complete two running tasks. The tasks had three conditions, including no music (NM), personalized synchronous music (PSM) remixed in our procedure, and random synchronous music (RSM) recommended by QQ Music Running Radio. Both groups completed the first task under NM condition during the trial run. In the second task, participants in group 1 were conditioned on PSM, and those in group 2 were conditioned on RSM.

Test Setup. Running tasks were carried out on a 400 m circular track. While running, the runners are required to report their feelings. Participants were asked to maintain their eating and sleeping habits and avoid vigorous activities on their task day.

Measures. Total running distance, total running duration, average pace, and fastest pace were measured to evaluate running performance. The Feeling Scale (FS) and the Felt Arousal Scale (FAS) were used to measure Affective Valence and Arousal [42, 44]. The Physical Activity Enjoyment Scale (PACES) adaptation was included to quantify enjoyment ratings [46, 47]. Borg's rating of perceived exertion (RPE) scale was adapted to assess perceived exertion during running [42, 43]. Participants' heart rate (HR) was recorded continuously via wristband throughout the experiment. In addition, three single-item 5-point scales, including Music Liking, Music Motivation, and Music Dissociation, were adapted and used to evaluate runners' music experience [48, 49]. Semi-structured interviews were carried out for more information.

4.2 Procedure

Participants conducted a questionnaire prior to the experiment, which includes their basic information, running experience, running goals, and views on running music.

Before the first task, both groups of participants were informed about the detailed experimental procedure and the use of scales. Participants wore their wristband when they arrived. After a 3-min warm-up, participants began the first running task until their perceived exertion reached a score of 8. The first run was conducted under the conditions of NM. Participants had to report some subjective indicators during the run. After completing the run, participants filled out a questionnaire about the run.

The second running task was performed after participants had been fully rested for approximately 72 h. The procedure of the second task was similar to that of the first but under different conditions. Group 1 participants ran under the PSM condition, and Group 2 participants ran under the RSM condition. After completing the run, participants completed questionnaires and were given semi-structured interviews to obtain further information.

5 Results

5.1 Quantitative Analysis

Quantitative analysis was conducted using SPSS. Levene's test and Shapiro-Wilk test were used to evaluate the homogeneity of variance and the normality of the distribution. The analysis of variance with two-way repeated measures (RM-ANOVA) was conducted. A series of 2 (Condition: PSM, RSM) $\times$ 2 (Time: Task 1, Task 2) RM-ANOVA was conducted to determine whether significant differences existed between the two conditions throughout the tasks. For a more detailed comparison in task 2, a series of 2 (Condition: PSM, RSM) $\times$ 6 (Time: Arrival, Warm-up, First Half, Second Half, End, Post) RM-ANOVA was conducted. Independent samples t-test and Mann-Whitney test were used to compare participants' differences in Music Liking, Music Motivation, and Music Dissociation between the two conditions.

In contrast to no music, the results showed that both types of synchronous music enhanced beginner runners' performance, especially their total running distance and duration. Furthermore, compared to random synchronous music, personalized synchronous music had better effects in stimulating the beginner's running motivation, promoting positive emotions, and distracting attention, leading to better performance.

Above all, listening to synchronous music has a significant effect on the running performance of novice runners, especially in total running distance ($p = .043$, $\eta_p^2 = .348$) and duration ($p = .018$, $\eta_p^2 = .443$). Simple effects indicated that the changes between two tasks are more significant under the PSM condition ($p = .004$, $\eta_p^2 = .583$). Participants listening to PSM ran 7.48 min longer and for 0.82 km further on average than those listening to RSM in task 2.

There was no difference in pace and heart rate between groups. Participants' perceived exertion changed significantly over time but not across music types. Music conditions did not cause a measurable difference in RPE.

For the psychological response, both types of synchronous music may trigger positive emotions. The mean scores of affective valence and total PACES scores in task 2 were higher than those in task 1 (for FS, $p = .007$, $\eta_p^2 = .534$; for PACES, $p = .009$, $\eta_p^2 = .512$). The simple effect of FS through time on the PSM condition was more significant ($p = .001$, $\eta_p^2 = .665$), indicating the importance of music preference and adaption.

In addition, the results of the T-test and Mann-Whitney test showed that the scores of music experience, including Music Liking, Music Motivation, and Music Dissociation about PSM, were significantly higher than NSM.

5.2 Qualitative Analysis

We used grounded theory [56] to extract qualitative conclusions from Semi-structured interviews and questionnaires - 12 open coding were collected, then they were theorized into 4 axical coding. (See Appendix 3).

"*Music's effect towards running*" indicated that compared to the No Music condition, participants in both groups stated a more motivative, enjoyable, and relaxing running experience under the synchronized music condition.

For "*synchronized music's effect towards running*" and "*experiences towards synchronized music*", opinions are varied between the groups. Half of the RSM participants reported the feeling of inconsistency between the music beats and their cadence, while subjects in the PSM group felt the beat matched their cadence seamlessly. They also believed that the voice instructions regulated their postures and stride, while the beats and metronome sound provided them with reasonable cadence and pace control. The PSM group is confident that the music produced with our proposed method allowed them to avoid unnecessary injuries, got through the exhaustion of running, and reach their second wind. Furthermore, some of the RSM participants negatively viewed the songs in their running, and some indicated RSM's negative impact on mental feelings and cadence control. Nevertheless, runners in group the PSM group favored the music provided and were thrilled about the remix and transitions in their familiar songs, and it is possible that the preference consideration plays a key role in the improvements.

In the "*shifts in attention*" coding, we also revealed a shift in attention while running with PSM. We suspect that the role of PSM in the running may be phased - In the early stage of running, PSM mainly helps adjusting cadence, and the hearing enjoyment become dominate in PSM running experience. This conjecture deserves further study.

6 Discussion

This article presented a method for synchronous remixing of running music. This study features the contributions from several aspects: 1) We propose a running music customization scheme that simultaneously considers the music preference, the runner's physical condition, and the training goals. 2) This is the first running music customization scheme on the scale we are aware of and the first attempt to integrate remix - an art form - into running music. 3) We demonstrate through experiments that remix of playlists, cues, and metronomes can raise the interest levels in the running. 4) By proposing a novel method for presenting running music, we outperform existing running music platforms on runners' objective indicators. The results suggest that the music remixed can improve novice runners' performance, motivate them, elicit positive emotional responses, and increase their enjoyment of running music. This is because the PSM can respond to the runner's music preferences and adapt to the runner's cadence.

There are also some limitations: 1) The music remix is not a real-time generation. It assumes the status of the subsequent run based solely on the trial run, so it cannot change instructions based on real-time physical conditions. Future research may focus on adaptive remix music generated in real-time based on sensors. 2) All remixes are generated manually, which is delicate but involves high production costs and a large amount of time. Since our proposed method includes many qualified indicators, it offers the possibility of using batch playlist creation programs in the future. 3) Although the result shows that our experimental design is simple and effective, the specific method for setting cadence targets is relatively unscrupulous. Future studies may address generating more specific cadence goals according to different physical conditions.

Appendix 1. Power Words List

Power words (translated from Chinese)	Type	Key time point
Let's adjust our pace, get relaxed and start our [time] minutes of rhythmic running today! Let's start with a simple warm-up run!	General instruction	Warm-up point
If you're feeling okay but still struggling to keep up with the music, try leaning forward and taking smaller steps	Step instruction	Tiring point
Watch your breath! Your cadence is now [BPM] steps per minute. Two steps in and two steps out is the right rate! Remember, never breathe through your mouth!	Breathing instruction	Warm-up point
Now let's listen to something more energetic! Let's adjust the pace from [BPM] to [BPM] in the following [time] seconds! Follow the music!	Cheering words	Warm-up point
Remember to keep your body straight and stable! It is helpful to prevent injury in the long run!	Posture instructions	Warm-up point
Feeling okay? If you are feeling exhausted, try taking smaller steps, no need to rush, let's listen to more awesome songs together!	Step instructions	Tiring point
Bravo! Your steps match the rhythm like a clock! Run as if you are immersed in the music, you're perfect! [favorite singer]'song is waiting for you!	Cheering words	Tiring point
You may feel tired now, but trust me, you're doing great! Let's focus on the music and try to forget about the physical exhaustion! Let's get through this phase and feel your second wind!	Cheering words	Tiring point
Remember to step as light as a hare! Don't dump your feet on the ground! This is good for your joint and can help you preserve your stamina!	Posture instruction	Tiring point
Your pace is now [BPM] steps per minute, stepping on the beats to give the run a more rhythmic feel and make it easier on your body!	Step instruction	Platform Cadence
Rotate Your Arms harder! Think of your arm as a pendulum swinging back and forth over your shoulder	Posture instruction	Platform Cadence
Take it easy! Don't strain your body! keep going! You are fabulous	Cheering words	Platform Cadence

Appendix 2. Descriptive Statistics for the Two Tasks

Measurements	Group 1 (NM + PSM)		Group 2 (NM + RSM)			Total
	Mean	SD	Mean	SD	Mean	SD
Distance 1	1.65 km	0.68	1.97 km	0.74	1.81	0.73
Distance2	2.66 km	1.11	1.84 km	0.75	2.25	1.04

(continued)

(*continued*)

Measurements	Group 1 (NM + PSM)		Group 2 (NM + RSM)			Total
	Mean	SD	Mean	SD	Mean	SD
Duration1	10.77 min	4.88	13.32 min	4.77	12.05	4.99
Duration2	20.08 min	7.43	12.60 min	5.13	16.34	7.40
aPace1	6.39 min/km	0.57	6.79 min/km	1.12	6.59	0.91
aPace2	7.11 min/km	0.78	6.87 min/km	1.39	6.99	1.14
fPace1	4.71min/km	0.48	4.74 min/km	4.70	4.73	0.63
fPace2	5.27 min/km	0.57	4.70 min/km	0.80	4.99	0.75
aHR1	167.33	5.50	168.17	7.80	167.75	6.76
aHR2	169.33	5.41	170.17	11.95	169.75	9.28
fHR1	180.33	4.92	185.67	5.59	183.00	184.75
fHR2	185.83	5.01	183.67	11.97	5.90	9.24
FS1	+ 0.36	2.18	+ 1.28	0.98	0.82	1.75
FS2	+ 2.56	1.17	+ 1.44	1.84	2.00	1.64
FAS1	3.98	0.69	3.54	1.00	3.74	0.89
FAS2	4.26	0.64	3.68	0.42	3.97	0.62
RPE1	4.96	0.82	4.06	0.95	4.51	0.99
RPE2	4.56	0.79	4.24	0.36	4.40	0.63
EE1	49.86	9.17	58.50	11.87	54.17	11.46
EE2	68.83	5.40	62.83	7.65	65.83	7.27
ML	4.50	0.50	2.83	1.07	3.67	1.18
MM	4.50	0.50	3.50	1.12	4.00	1.00
MD	4.33	0.47	3.00	0.82	3.67	0.94

Appendix 3. Qualitative Results

Axical coding	Open coding	PSM (Persons)	RSM (Persons)	Total (Persons)
Music's effect towards running	Music motivates me	6	6	12
	Music guides me	6	0	6
	Music makes my mood better	6	6	12
Synchronized Music's effect towards running	Instructions guided me	5	0	5
	Synchronized Music guided me	6	2	8

(*continued*)

(*continued*)

Axical coding	Open coding	PSM (Persons)	RSM (Persons)	Total (Persons)
	Synchronized Music not meet pace need	0	3	3
	Synchronized Music affects running	0	2	2
	Synchronized Music makes running safer	6	0	6
Experiences towards synchronized music	Synchronized Music is powerful	6	5	11
	Looking forward to the next song	3	0	3
	Synchronized Music is boring	0	4	4
	Synchronized Music is similar	0	2	2
	Synchronized Music help reach 2nd wind	4	1	5
	Liked the Synchronized Music	6	2	8
Shifts in attention	Attention shifts between instructions and enjoyment of the music	5	1	6

References

1. Mithen, S., Morley, I., Wray, A., Tallerman, M., Gamble, C.: the singing neanderthals: the origins of music, language, mind and body. Camb. Archaeol. J. **16**, 97–112 (2006). https://doi.org/10.1017/s0959774306000060
2. Goehr, L.A.: Sporting sounds: relationships between sport and music edited by Bateman, Anthony and John Bale. J. Aesthet. Art Critic. **69**, 233–235 (2011). https://doi.org/10.1111/j.1540-6245.2011.01465_2.x
3. Karageorghis, C.I., Mouzourides, D.A., Priest, D.-L., Sasso, T.A., Morrish, D.J., Walley, C.L.: Psychophysical and ergogenic effects of synchronous music during treadmill walking. J. Sport Exerc. Psychol. **31**, 18–36 (2009). https://doi.org/10.1123/jsep.31.1.18
4. Karageorghis, C., Kuan, G., Schiphof-Godart, L.: Music in sport: From conceptual underpinnings to applications. Essentials of exercise and sport psychology: An open access textbook, pp. 530–564 (2021). https://doi.org/10.51224/b1023
5. Clarke, E., DeNora, T., Vuoskoski, J.: Music, empathy and cultural understanding. Phys. Life Rev. **15**, 61–88 (2015). https://doi.org/10.1016/j.plrev.2015.09.001
6. Juslin, P.N.: From everyday emotions to aesthetic emotions: towards a unified theory of musical emotions. Phys. Life Rev. **10**, 235–266 (2013). https://doi.org/10.1016/j.plrev.2013.05.008

7. Sloboda, J.: Everyday uses of music listening: A preliminary study. Exploring the Musical MindCognition, emotion, ability, function, pp. 318–331 (2004)
8. Ekman, P.: Basic emotions. Handbook of Cognition and Emotion, pp. 45–60 (2005)
9. Quintin, E.-M., Bhatara, A., Poissant, H., Fombonne, E., Levitin, D.J.: Emotion perception in music in high-functioning adolescents with autism spectrum disorders. J. Autism Dev. Disord. **41**, 1240–1255 (2010). https://doi.org/10.1007/s10803-010-1146-0
10. Haller, R.G., Vissing, J.: Spontaneous "second wind" and glucose-induced second "second wind" in McArdle disease. Archives of Neurology 59 (2002). https://doi.org/10.1001/arc hneur.59.9.1395
11. Thompson, W.F., Schellenberg, E.G., Husain, G.: Arousal, mood, and the Mozart effect. Psychol. Sci. **12**, 248–251 (2001). https://doi.org/10.1111/1467-9280.00345
12. de Witte, M., Pinho, A.da, Stams, G.-J., Moonen, X., Bos, A.E.R., van Hooren, S.: Music therapy for stress reduction: A systematic review and meta-analysis. Health Psychol. Rev. **16**, 134–159 (2020). https://doi.org/10.1080/17437199.2020.1846580
13. Terry, P.C., Karageorghis, C.I., Curran, M.L., Martin, O.V., Parsons-Smith, R.L.: Effects of music in exercise and sport: a meta-analytic review. Psychol. Bull. **146**, 91–117 (2020). https://doi.org/10.1037/bul0000216
14. Karow, M.C., Rogers, R.R., Pederson, J.A., Williams, T.D., Marshall, M.R., Ballmann, C.G.: Effects of preferred and nonpreferred warm-up music on exercise performance. Percept. Mot. Skills **127**, 912–924 (2020)
15. Laukka, P., Quick, L.: Emotional and motivational uses of music in sports and exercise: a questionnaire study among athletes. Psychol. Music **41**, 198–215 (2011)
16. Wen, C.P., et al.: Minimum amount of physical activity for reduced mortality and extended life expectancy: a prospective cohort study. The Lancet. **378**, 1244–1253 (2011). https://doi.org/10.1016/S0140-6736(11)60749-6
17. Terry, P.C., Karageorghis, C.I., Saha, A.M., D'Auria, S.: Effects of synchronous music on treadmill running among elite triathletes. J. Sci. Med. Sport **15**, 52–57 (2012)
18. Brand, R., Ekkekakis, P.: German Journal of Exercise and Sport Research **48**(1), 48–58 (2017). https://doi.org/10.1007/s12662-017-0477-9
19. Greco, F., Grazioli, E., Cosco, L.F., Parisi, A., Bertollo, M., Emerenziani, G.P.: The effects of music on cardiorespiratory endurance and muscular fitness in recreationally active individuals: A narrative review. PeerJ. **10** (2022). https://doi.org/10.7717/peerj.13332
20. Rodriguez-Fornells, A., Rojo, N., Amengual, J.L., Ripollés, P., Altenmüller, E., Münte, T.F.: The involvement of audio-motor coupling in the music-supported therapy applied to stroke 678900000patients. Ann. New York Acad. Sci. **1252**, 282–293 (2012). Doi: https://doi.org/10.1111/j.1749-6632.2011.06425.x
21. Williams, D., Fazenda, B., Williamson, V., Fazekas, G.: On performance and perceived effort in trail runners using sensor control to generate Biosynchronous Music. Sensors. **20**, 4528 (2020). https://doi.org/10.3390/s20164528
22. Karageorghis, C.I.: Music-related interventions in the exercise domain. In: Handbook of Sport Psychology, pp. 929–949 (2020). https://doi.org/10.1002/9781119568124.ch45
23. Ballmann, C.G., Maynard, D.J., Lafoon, Z.N., Marshall, M.R., Williams, T.D., Rogers, R.R.: Effects of listening to preferred versus non-preferred music on repeated Wingate Anaerobic Test Performance. Sports. **7**, 185 (2019). https://doi.org/10.3390/sports7080185
24. Simpson, S.D., Karageorghis, C.I.: The effects of synchronous music on 400-M sprint performance. J. Sports Sci. **24**, 1095–1102 (2006). https://doi.org/10.1080/026404105004 32789
25. Ramji, R., Aasa, U., Paulin, J., Madison, G.: Musical information increases physical performance for synchronous but not asynchronous running. Psychol. Music **44**, 984–995 (2016). https://doi.org/10.1177/0305735615603239

26. Zatorre, R.J., Halpern, A.R., Perry, D.W., Meyer, E., Evans, A.C.: Hearing in the mind's ear: a pet investigation of musical imagery and perception. J. Cogn. Neurosci. **8**, 29–46 (1996). https://doi.org/10.1162/jocn.1996.8.1.29

27. Lingham, J., Theorell, T.: Self-selected "favourite" stimulative and sedative music listening – how does familiar and preferred music listening affect the body? Nord. J. Music. Ther. **18**, 150–166 (2009). https://doi.org/10.1080/08098130903062363

28. Lopes-Silva, J.P., Lima-Silva, A.E., Bertuzzi, R., Silva-Cavalcante, M.D.: Influence of music on performance and psychophysiological responses during moderate-intensity exercise preceded by fatigue. Physiol. Behav. **139**, 274–280 (2015). https://doi.org/10.1016/j.physbeh.2014.11.048

29. Bigliassi, M., Karageorghis, C.I., Nowicky, A.V., Orgs, G., Wright, M.J.: Cerebral mechanisms underlying the effects of music during a fatiguing isometric ankle-dorsiflexion task. Psychophysiology **53**, 1472–1483 (2016). https://doi.org/10.1111/psyp.12693

30. Stork, M.J.: Music enhances performance and perceived enjoyment of sprint interval exercise. Med. Sci. Sports Exerc. **47**, 1052–1060 (2015). https://doi.org/10.1249/mss.0000000000000494

31. Chow, E.C., Etnier, J.L.: Effects of music and video on perceived exertion during high-intensity exercise. J. Sport Health Sci. **6**, 81–88 (2017). https://doi.org/10.1016/j.jshs.2015.12.007

32. Bigliassi, M., Karageorghis, C.I., Hoy, G.K., Layne, G.S.: The way you make me feel: psychological and cerebral responses to music during real-life physical activity. Psychol. Sport Exerc. **41**, 211–217 (2019). https://doi.org/10.1016/j.psychsport.2018.01.010

33. Karageorghis, C.I.: The scientific application of music in exercise and sport: Towards a new theoretical model. Sport and Exercise Psychology. 288–334 (2015). https://doi.org/10.4324/9781315713809-21

34. Schneider, S., Askew, C.D., Abel, T., Strüder, H.K.: Exercise, music, and the brain: Is there a central pattern generator? J. Sports Sci. **28**, 1337–1343 (2010). https://doi.org/10.1080/02640414.2010.507252

35. Karageorghis, C.I., Priest, D.-L.: Music in the exercise domain: a review and synthesis (part I). Int. Rev. Sport Exerc. Psychol. **5**, 44–66 (2012). https://doi.org/10.1080/1750984x.2011.631026

36. Bacon, C. J., Myers, T. R., Karageorghis, C. I.: Effect of music-movement synchrony on exercise oxygen consumption. J. Sports Med. Phys. Fitness, 359–365 (2012)

37. Ballmann, C.G.: The influence of Music Preference on exercise responses and performance: a Review. J. Funct. Morphol. Kinesiol. **6**, 33 (2021). https://doi.org/10.3390/jfmk6020033

38. Silva, N.R., Rizardi, F.G., Fujita, R.A., Villalba, M.M., Gomes, M.M.: Preferred music genre benefits during strength tests: Increased maximal strength and strength-endurance and reduced perceived exertion. Percept. Mot. Skills **128**, 324–337 (2020). https://doi.org/10.1177/0031512520945084

39. Ballmann, C.G., McCullum, M.J., Rogers, R.R., Marshall, M.M., Williams, T.D.: Effects of preferred vs. nonpreferred music on resistance exercise performance. Journal of Strength and Conditioning Research. Publish Ahead of Print (2018). https://doi.org/10.1519/jsc.0000000000002981

40. Meglic, C.E., Orman, C.M., Rogers, R.R., Williams, T.D., Ballmann, C.G.: Influence of warm-up music preference on anaerobic exercise performance in Division I NCAA Female Athletes. J. Funct. Morphol. Kinesiol. **6**, 64 (2021). https://doi.org/10.3390/jfmk6030064

41. Karageorghis, C.I.: run to the beat: Sport and music for the Masses. Sport Soc. **17**, 433–447 (2013). https://doi.org/10.1080/17430437.2013.796619

42. Hardy, C.J., Rejeski, W.J.: Not what, but how one feels: the measurement of affect during exercise. J. Sport Exerc. Psychol. **11**, 304–317 (1989). https://doi.org/10.1123/jsep.11.3.304

43. Foster, C.L., et al.: A new approach to monitoring exercise training. J. Strength Conditioning Res. **15**, 109 (2001). https://doi.org/10.1519/00124278-200102000-00019
44. Svebak, S., Murgatroyd, S.: Metamotivational dominance: a multimethod validation of reversal theory constructs. J. Pers. Soc. Psychol. **48**, 107–116 (1985). https://doi.org/10.1037/0022-3514.48.1.107
45. Xie, J., Wen, D., Liang, L., Jia, Y., Gao, L., Lei, J.: Evaluating the validity of current mainstream wearable devices in fitness tracking under various physical activities: Comparative study. JMIR mHealth and uHealth. **6** (2018). https://doi.org/10.2196/mhealth.9754
46. Kendzierski, D., DeCarlo, K.J.: Physical activity enjoyment scale: two validation studies. J. Sport Exerc. Psychol. **13**, 50–64 (1991). https://doi.org/10.1123/jsep.13.1.50
47. Motl, R.W., Dishman, R.K., Saunders, R., Dowda, M., Felton, G., Pate, R.R.: Measuring enjoyment of physical activity in adolescent girls. Am. J. Prev. Med. **21**, 110–117 (2001). https://doi.org/10.1016/S0749-3797(01)00326-9
48. Karageorghis, C.I., Jones, L.: On the stability and relevance of the exercise heart rate–music-tempo preference relationship. Psychol. Sport Exerc. **15**, 299–310 (2014). https://doi.org/10.1016/j.psychsport.2013.08.004
49. Stork, M.J., Karageorghis, C.I., Martin Ginis, K.A.: Let's go: psychological, psychophysical, and physiological effects of music during sprint interval exercise. Psychol. Sport Exercise. **45**, 101547 (2019). https://doi.org/10.1016/j.psychsport.2019.101547
50. Sarda, P., Halasawade, S., Padmawar, A., Aghav, J.: Emousic: Emotion and activity-based music player using Machine Learning. Advances in Intelligent Systems and Computing, pp. 179–188 (2019).
51. Ayata, D., Yaslan, Y., Kamasak, M.E.: Emotion based music recommendation system using wearable physiological sensors. IEEE Trans. Consum. Electron. **64**, 196–203 (2018). https://doi.org/10.1109/TCE.2018.2844736
52. Deshmukh, P., Kale, G.: Music and movie recommendation system. Int. J. Eng. Trends Technol. **61**, 178–181 (2018). https://doi.org/10.14445/22315381/ijett-v61p229
53. Wright, C.M.: Listening to music. Schirmer/Cengage Learning, Boston (2014)
54. Défossez, A., et al.: Demucs: Deep Extractor for Music Sources with extra unlabeled data remixed. ArXiv abs/1909.01174 (2019)
55. Pearson, C.M., Rimer, D.G., Mommaerts, W.F.H.M.: A metabolic myopathy due to absence of muscle phosphorylase. Am. J. Med. **30**, 502–517 (1961). https://doi.org/10.1016/0002-9343(61)90075-4
56. Martin, P.Y., Turner, B.A.: Grounded theory and organizational research. J. Appl. Behav. Sci. **22**, 141–157 (1986)

Design for Connecting People Through Digital Artworks with Personal Information

Rui Wang[1,2(✉)] and Jun Hu[1]

[1] Department of Industrial Design, Eindhoven University of Technology,
Eindhoven, The Netherlands
r.wang1@Tue.nl
[2] School of Design, Jiangnan University, Wuxi, China

Abstract. Nowadays, people often experience physical separation in daily life. The level of social connectedness between people is declining gradually, but social connectedness is much important for human well-being. Communication techniques for people connecting remotely are most aimed at verbal information communication. However, during physical interaction, there is still a lot of non-verbal personal information other than direct verbal information we can perceive that contributes to social connectedness. Therefore, we try to explore if combining non-verbal personal information into digital artworks in a daily context, would influence connectedness between people. In this paper, we present VizArt, a channel that helps people connect through digital artworks with non-verbal personal information. A functional prototype was implemented and a pilot experiment was conducted.

Keywords: Social connectedness · Personal information · Digital artworks

1 Introduction

Nowadays, people often experience physical separation in their daily life [1, 2]. Especially in their relationships with family, friends, colleagues, and others. This is mainly because more and more young adults have to stay in a city far away from their hometown for education and other personal ambitions. Moreover, due to the pressure and stress from people's work and study, there is limited time for individuals to connect with their colleagues. Also, technological development, such as the use of various self-service machines and online social media, while bringing convenience to people makes interaction opportunities get fewer and fewer between people in real life. Because of these separations, the level of social connectedness between people, which is quite important for human well-being, is declining gradually [3].

At present, communication techniques are used for people connecting remotely, which are mostly aimed at verbal information communication, such as sending e-mail, sending messages and talking through the telephone, and interacting through various social media [4]. However, other than direct verbal information during physical interaction. However, during physical interaction, there is still a lot of non-verbal personal

© IFIP International Federation for Information Processing 2022
Published by Springer Nature Switzerland AG 2022
B. Göbl et al. (Eds.): ICEC 2022, LNCS 13477, pp. 386–397, 2022.
https://doi.org/10.1007/978-3-031-20212-4_32

information other than direct verbal information we can perceive that contributes to social connectedness [5] and can make people feel a strong connection with each other and positive emotion of "co-existence" and "we are being together".

The nonverbal information, including body movements, expressions, emotional states, activity information and accompanying noises with activities [6], can be collected through quantified-self technology [7] and made available for transferring personal information through communication channels. As for the visualization of individuals' information, we want to try the digital media art form. The advantages of the digital media art form are that it has the potential to be merged into the peripheral scenes of daily life without being abrupt with the quality in both functionality and aesthetics.

We try to provide a new channel for helping people connect remotely through nonverbal personal information that could naturally integrate into daily context. Therefore, in this paper, we explore if combining personal information into digital artworks in a daily context would influence connectedness between people.

2 Related Work

2.1 Social Connectedness and Health

Social connectedness plays an important role in human health and well-being [8, 9]. Social connectedness is defined as the sense of belonging and subjective psychological bond that people feel in relation to individuals and groups of others [10] Social connectedness and social support that emerges from it provide the individual with core psychological benefits such as a sense of meaning, self-esteem, a sense of belonging and companionship, and an overall positive effect [11]. Lacking social connectedness is always associated with depression, loneliness, and other mental health disorders. These negative emotions are tied to ill-health, such as, it may affect the immune system by buffering the impact of stress [12].

2.2 Work for Social Connectedness Enhancement Remotely

Quantified-self technology is a tool to collect personal information for different purposes [13]. Most research about quantified-self data is currently aimed at gaining self-knowledge and self-health management, such as sleep [14] and blood pressure [15] monitoring, and also for behavior changes, such as physical activity promotion [16, 17] and weight loss [18]. Quantified-self technology can also be used to enhance social connectedness. When used properly, it can not only provide rich nonverbal information about an individual through online communication but also help people stay connected without occupying people's attention at the same time.

Several studies have explored quantified-self data sharing in a daily social context. HeartLink [19] is a system that collects real-time personal heart rate and broadcasts this data to social networks through numbers and mathematical graphs. Empathy Amulet [20] is a wearable for strangers, and it is anonymously connected for experiencing shared warmth. PiHearts [21] is a tangible heart display that is shaped like a real heart to visualize data of the individual's heartbeats. Social Flower [22] is a tangible system that presents the high activity level with a green light color. These studies present personal information in the mathematical form, wearable devices and tangible systems. However, few studies explored digital media art visualization of data sharing in a daily social context.

A few studies have explored digital media art visualization with personal data for improving social connectedness. JeL [23] is a bio-responsive immersive installation art for interpersonal synchronization through a breathing sensor and a VR device to tackle social isolation and disconnectedness in our society. Blobulous [24] is a visualization system shown on a public display that generates visuals according to users' biological data through wearable devices and thereby movements, aimed at improving social connectedness. These studies focused on art installation in public spaces and provided contemporary interaction through wearable devices.

To the best of our knowledge, there is no work yet that aims to explore how to visualize non-verbal personal information with digital artworks in daily scenes for social connectedness enhancement. Thus, we created VizArt.

3   Design

3.1   Proposed Design

VizArt is an interactive and connecting channel that helps people who work in the same building to enhance social connectedness. It aims to the physical separation situation in the workplace. Due to the modern work style and architectural workspace arrangement, people usually work in an independent space in separate seats, rooms, and on different floors. On the other hand, they need to spend most of their time on various and numerous work tasks, so that they have little time for communicating face to face, in many cases except the coffee time during the whole day's work. The VizArt provides a common occasion in public space, a digital art display that presents the real-time personal information collected from individuals working in the same building (Fig. 1).

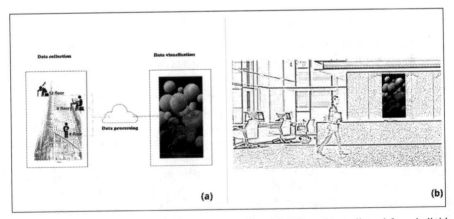

Fig. 1. "VizArt" system: (a) The digital art display with real-time data collected from individuals working in the same building. (b) Application scenario: The data visualization in a public workspace.

3.2   Design Considerations

VizArt is designed for social connectedness enhancement by showing individuals' data through digital artworks in the public workplace. There are three criteria that we need to consider: meaningful data, non-intrusiveness, and privacy concerns.

Meaningful Data. The design should make sense for workers: (1) The design should collect the data that workers are curious and concerned about. (2) Data visualization should be easy to understand. Only when users want to know the data and understand the data successfully can the design work on enhancing social connectedness.

Non-intrusiveness. The design should keep low interference for users: (1) The design should help people keep connecting with the group in the same building, but at the same time integrate into workers' daily routine and not occupy their time from their busy work schedule for reporting data. (2) The design should be integrated into the daily environment while conveying personal information naturally.

Privacy Concerns. The design should protect the privacy of personal data. It is because when personal data are shown in a public space, most people will worry about the problem of privacy leaks naturally. So only when design makes sure that personal data can be protected do users be willing to accept and use it.

3.3   Design Components

VizArt has two parts: data collection and data visualization (Fig. 2). Data collection includes two components: data selection and data input. Data visualization includes two components: data presentation and data output.

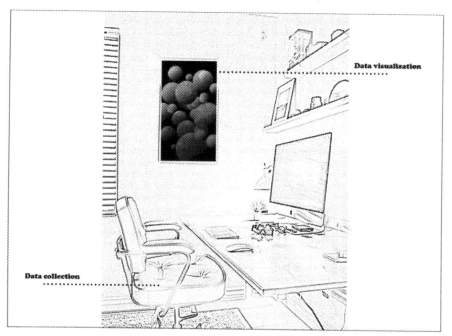

Fig. 2. The design components in VizArt.

Data Selection: Which Types of Data Are Suitable?

VizArt is designed for connecting workers through visualizing personal information recorded when they are working. There is a lot of real-time information in the workplace we can use, such as heart rate, breath, movement, water intake, mood, environment temperature, etc. These sources of information about individuals can be classified into the following categories: physiological, psychological, activity and context. For meaningful design, data should be selected such that workers who are curious and concerned about themselves and others.

Data Input: Which Types of Collection Devices Are More Convenient for Users?

In the workspace context, workers need to spend most time concentrating on their work tasks. So data collection devices should be integrated into their work routine, and workers should not spend extra time and attention on the devices. So individual data should be collected automatically and non-obtrusively. In order to achieve this goal, a convenient way is to integrate the input device into daily work objects and scenarios naturally. Daily objects, such as office chairs, office desks, and water cups that workers usually use in the office are suitable. These daily objects are usually peripheral so as to keep the lowest interference for users.

Data Presentation: How to Present Personal Data with Digital Artworks in Public?

To show individuals' data in public, the problem that users may worry about is privacy leaks. When presenting the personal data in digital artworks, it can be realized in an implicit manner so that the personal identity is not revealed to protect privacy. As for the type of digital art, different forms could be used, such as abstract painting, natural landscape painting, surrealist painting, etc.

Data Output: What Kinds of Presentation Devices Could Be Integrated into the Work Context?

In this work, we decided to use a display that can be integrated into the office environment to show a decorative digital painting, which has aesthetic value and is not abrupt while conveying personal information.

4 Pilot Study

In order to explore whether digital artworks with personal information in a daily context have an impact on users' social connectedness, a pilot study was conducted.

4.1 Experiment Setup and Place

We create two digital artworks as the experiment setups (Fig. 3), "Walk into Broccoli" and "VizArt Bubbles". One is without personal information, and the other is with personal information included.

"Walk into Broccoli" is one of the "Food and Environment" series digital artworks. It is a general digital artwork without personal information. The design of "Walk into Broccoli" was inspired by vegetable waste which has the highest waste rate among all kinds of food waste. The main reason is that the slow growth mode of vegetables reflects that people may ignore their vitality easily. Therefore, this digital artwork chooses

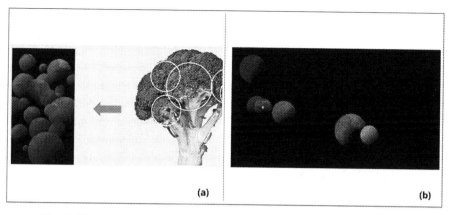

Fig. 3. The experiment setups: (a) "Walk into Broccoli". (b) "VizArt Bubbles"

broccoli as the design object, emphasizes the symbiotic relationship between people and plants on the earth, and simulates the breathing state of plants to show their vitality. The design elements use noise to express the granular sense of broccoli, abstract the form of broccoli one by one, and develop with the sphere as the primary figure.

"VizArt Bubbles" is a digital artwork with personal information included. The design elements are developed based on the digital artwork "Walk into Broccoli". It visualizes personal information that is most relevant to the workers collected from a smart cushion on a TV screen. Personal information includes total sitting time today, recent sitting time, heart rate, breath, sitting on the chair or not sitting on the chair, and fatigue state. The study was performed using the smart cushion for office chairs from BOBO Technology. A piece of Polyvinylidene Fluoridefilm is integrated into the smart cushion to capture the BCG signals from the users. Typically for the smart cushion, the output includes heart rate, respiratory rate, and heart rate variability. The heart rate variability index is usually treated as a valued indication of stress. The graphical expression and description of visualization associated with personal information are as follows (Table 1). The X and Y coordinate of the bubble indicates total sitting time today and recent sitting time, respectively. The dynamic change of the bubble's outer ring size indicates the frequency of heart rate per minute of the participant. The Dynamic change of the bubble's contraction speed indicates the frequency of breathing per minute. The bright and dark bubbles indicate people are sitting and not sitting on the office chair, respectively. As for fatigue state, there are green, green and grey, and grey bubbles, which indicate not tired, slight and severe tired, respectively. The color center point is used for the participant to identify themselves in many bubbles, but it won't show when the bubble turns dark. This is because all real-time personal information is only present when people are sitting on their chairs. All the other personal information data except the participant were collected from part of the workers in advance in the same building to make participants believe that this personal information is real-time between them and the others who are working in an independent workspace of the same building when they attend the experiment and also to keep the consistency of experiment setup in each experiment.

Table 1. "VizArt Bubbles": the graphical expression and description of visualization association.

Graphical Expression	Description of Visualization Association
	X coordinate of bubble – total sitting time today Y coordinate of bubble – recent sitting time
	Dynamic change of bubble's outer ring size – Frequency of heart rate per minute
	Dynamic change of bubble's contraction speed – Frequency of breathing per minute
	Bright bubble – People is sitting on office chair Dark bubble – People isn't sitting on office chair
	1: Green bubble – State well and not tired 2: Green and a little grey bubble – Slight tired 3: Grey bubble – Severe tired
	Color center point – Each participant's representative color

The experiment was conducted in a laboratory room (Fig. 4) located on the second floor of the Design Department Building at Jiangnan University.

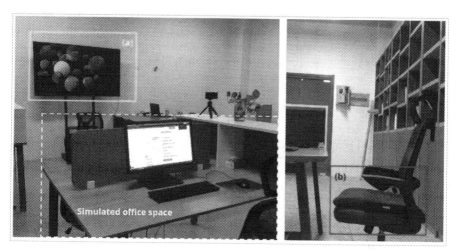

Fig. 4. Experiment room: (a) Digital artworks presentation (b) Personal information collection: smart cushion

4.2 Participants, Procedure and Measurements

We recruited 25 participants (16 females, nine males, age range from 25–38) from workers who work in the same design department building at Jiangnan University of China. Participants' backgrounds were distributed to different aspects of design, including User Experience Design (3), Design Strategy (1), Design Education (1), Design History and Theory (8), Architectural Art Heritage Protection and Utilization (2), Fashion Design (6), Interface Design (1), Digital Media Design (3).

Each participant attended the experiment individually with the independent workspace in the experiment room. The experiment was carried out in three steps (Table 2). The whole experiment lasted for about one hour:

Firstly, the participant needs to fill out a questionnaire with basic personal information, like gender, age, etc. Then before coming to the experiment, the participant was requested to do a questionnaire to fill out a questionnaire to measure their initial level of social connectedness.

Secondly, the participant was requested to complete the assigned task of browsing the introduced web page for 40 min. During this period, the participant needed to perceive and experience two different digital artworks, visualization A: "Walk into Broccoli" and visualization B: "VizArt Bubbles", each for 20 min, respectively. The researcher will give an introduction about the design background and details of each visualization to help the participant understand the digital artworks before experiencing the process and the description text of each artwork will also be put on their desk in order to help participants know more clearly of the artworks during experience process. In order to avoid the interference of the fixed experience order of the experiment, the order of presentation of digital artworks A and B was changed during each experiment. After every 20 min of the experience, the participant was requested to fill out the same questionnaire as they filled in the first step to measure the participant's feeling of social connectedness.

Thirdly, After experiencing two different digital artworks, researchers conducted semi-structured interviews with participants to obtain more information from the user experience, perspectives, and suggestions for this design.

Table 2. Experiment procedure

Experiment Steps		Duration
First	Basic information questionnaire + Initial questionnaire	10 min
Second	Browse web page + Experience (A) or (B) + questionnaire	20 min
	Have a break	10 min
	Browse web page + Experience (B) or (A) + questionnaire	20 min
Third	Semi-structured interviews	10 min

This experiment chose the Social Connectedness Scale-Revised (SCS-R) questionnaire [25] and the Inclusion of community in Self Scale (ICS) questionnaire [26] to measure the level of social connectedness of participants.

SCS-R consists of 20 items (10 positive and 10 negatives), asking people to grade from 1 to 6 depending on whether they agree or disagree with the statement. Then, the mean score is calculated using 10 positive scores and 10 negative reverse scores. A higher mean score of the SCS-R indicates a stronger feeling of social connectedness. ICS has six options, each option composed of two circles, the S (Self) circle and the C (Community) circle. The different part is the changes in the intersection surface. The more intersection surface indicates a closer feeling of Inclusion between self and people in their environment.

4.3 Preliminary User Feedback

Quantitative results (score of SCS-R and ICS) and complete qualitative results are being analyzed. So in this paper, we only present preliminary user feedback. Results are summarized as follows:

Perspectives for design: Some participants think the design with personal information is novel and interesting. *"This design is really novel and interesting (P13)."* *"I have never seen a design like this which is quite interesting (P14)."* The other participants hold the view that this design is useless. *"I don't care about other coworkers at all (P2)." "I don't think people have the requirement for this design because social and strong connections make me feel tired in my point of view (P5)."*

Feeling of social connectedness: Some participants had a strong feeling of connectedness changes when experiencing two different digital artworks. *"Even though I didn't do anything and didn't take the initiative to contact others, I felt a strong sense of connection with others. I think this design is very successful (P7)." "I just feel like I'm being with the people around me (P19)."* The other participants thought the impact on connectedness was weak and even had no impact. *"It has only a little impact on my feeling of connection, probably because of anonymity (P23)." "It doesn't impact my feeling of connection, probably because the experience time is too short (P2)."*

Data privacy concern: Some participants are worried about privacy. They are mainly worried about what if their boss uses this design to monitor them. *"I feel that the employers will use this design to check their employees' attendance and post (P2)." "I always feel like I'm being watched by my boss when I use this (P21)."*

5 Discussion

This paper tried to explore how to help people connect remotely and influence connectedness between people through combining non-verbal personal information into digital artworks in a daily context. As highly social animals, all human beings have a fundamental need and desire to belong, so it is important for people to feel a connection with others, just as the famous line says "No man is an island".

The VizArt aims to provide an interactive and connecting channel to help the people who are working in the same building, but in a different workspace to enhance their social connectedness. In the work space, most people are experiencing stress because they are under too much pressure from busy kinds of tasks during work time. But it will be helpful for releasing stressful state if we can have good relationships and strong connections with colleagues, those people we can have a chance to meet in the workplace.

However, people don't have many opportunities in the workplace for face-to-face communication which usually needs both space and time consistency between people. VizArt provides a common space in public which includes real-time personal information collected from individuals who worked in the same building, to help people keep the feeling of connecting without occupying their time from their busy work schedule at the same time.

The pilot study explored whether digital artworks with personal information in a daily context have an impact on users' social connectedness, by keeping in touch with knowing other people's real-time information remotely. The result of preliminary user feedback shows opposite perspectives from the participants. It may be because the feeling of social connectedness is entirely subjective, and it has a great difference between individuals' different personalities and social attitudes. Regarding experiment design, the reason why those participants felt little feeling changes in social connectedness could be that the experiment was conducted in a laboratory rather than in a real daily work environment, and maybe the experience time is too short for the participants to have the feeling of changes in social connectedness.

6 Conclusion and Future Work

In this paper, we explored the influence of social connectedness by combining non-verbal personal information into digital artworks. VizArt was presented as a new channel for people who work in the same building to connect non-intrusively. An experiment was conducted with VizArt system with 25 participants. We found that the VizArt system indeed influences the feeling of social connectedness, although it is quite different from person to person as far as preliminary user feedback can tell.

The system needs to be further developed according to the quantitative and complete qualitative results. Moreover, the information-sharing perspectives of target users are found to be very important in this system, so we plan to understand the target user group and their daily context better for further design and development.

Acknowledgement. The first author of this paper is supported by China Scholarship Council (CSC).

The design of "Walk into Broccoli" in the experiment setup is from the Digital Art Class outcomes. Thanks to my team member Yingxia Li, Xinyi Xu, Mengyao Chen, and Xuan Lu.

The smart cushion for office chairs is from BOBO Technology. Thanks to BOBO Technology for providing the smart cushions and related technical support in this experiment.

References

1. Banerjee, D., Rai, M.: Social isolation in Covid-19: the impact of loneliness. Int. J. Soc. Psychiatry **66**, 525–527 (2020)
2. Cornwell, E.Y., Waite, L.J.: Measuring social isolation among older adults using multiple indicators from the NSHAP study. J. Gerontol. Ser. B Psychol. Sci. Soc. Sci. **64**(Suppl. 1), 38–46 (2009)
3. Bailey, M., Cao, R., Kuchler, T., Stroebel, J., Wong, A.: Social connectedness: measurement, determinants, and effects **32**(3), 259–280 (2018)
4. Burnett, M.: CHI 2008: The 26th Annual CHI Conference on Human Factors in Computing Systems, Florence, Italy, 5–10 April 2008. Conference Proceedings. Association for Computing Machinery (2008)
5. Phutela, D.: The importance of non-verbal communication (2015)
6. Mandal, F.B.: Nonverbal communication in humans. J. Hum. Behav. Soc. Environ. **24**(4), 417–421 (2014)
7. Kido, T., Swan, M.: Know thyself: data driven self-awareness for understanding our unconscious behaviors-Citizen Science Genetics for sleep and wellness research
8. Stavrova, O., Luhmann, M.: Social connectedness as a source and consequence of meaning in life. J. Posit. Psychol. **11**(5), 470–479 (2016). https://doi.org/10.1080/17439760.2015.111 7127
9. Kawachi, I., Berkman, L.F.: Social ties and mental health. J. Urban Health Bull. N. Y. Acad. Med. **78**, 458–467 (2001). https://doi.org/10.1093/jurban/78.3.458
10. Haslam, C., Cruwys, T., Haslam, S.A., Jetten, J.: Social connectedness and health. In: Pachana, N. (ed.) Encyclopedia of Geropsychology, pp. 1–10. Springer, Singapore (2015). https://doi.org/10.1007/978-981-287-080-3_46-2
11. Thoits, P.A.: Mechanisms linking social ties and support to physical and mental health. J. Health Soc. Behav. **52**(2), 145–161 (2011)
12. Hudson, R.B.: Lack of social connectedness and its consequences. Public Policy Aging Rep. **27**(4), 121–123 (2017)
13. Swan, M.: The quantified self: fundamental disruption in big data science and biological discovery. Big Data **1**(2), 85–99 (2013)

14. Vandenberghe, B., Geerts, D.: Sleep monitoring tools at home and in the hospital: bridging quantified self and clinical sleep research. In: Proceedings of the 2015 9th International Conference on Pervasive Computing Technologies for Healthcare, PervasiveHealth 2015, pp. 153–160. Institute of Electrical and Electronics Engineers Inc. (2015)
15. Georgi, N., Kuchenbuch, M., Corvol, A., Jeannes, R.L.B.: An overview of blood pressure measurement in telemonitoring context. IEEE Consum. Electron. Mag. **9**(5), 42–49 (2020)
16. Dulaud, P., di Loreto, I., Mottet, D.: Self-quantification systems to support physical activity: from theory to implementation principles. Int. J. Environ. Res. Public Health **17**, 1–22 (2020)
17. Yang, N., van Hout, G., Feijs, L., Chen, W., Hu, J.: Facilitating physical activity through on-site quantified-self data sharing. Sustain. (Switz.) **12**(12), 4904 (2020)
18. del Río, N.G., González-González, C.S., Toledo-Delgado, P.A., Muñoz-Cruz, V., García-Peñalvo, F.: Health promotion for childhood obesity: an approach based on self-tracking of data. Sens. (Switz.) **20**(13), 1–28 (2020)
19. Curmi, F., Ferrario, M.A., Southern, J., Whittle, J.: HeartLink: open broadcast of live biometric data to social networks. In: Proceedings of Conference on Human Factors in Computing Systems, pp. 1749–1758 (2013)
20. Brueckner, S.: Empathy amulet: a wearable to connect with strangers. In: Proceedings of International Symposium on Wearable Computers, ISWC, pp. 248–253. Association for Computing Machinery (2018)
21. Aslan, I., Seiderer, A., Dang, C.T., Rädler, S., André, E.: PiHearts: resonating experiences of self and others enabled by a tangible somaesthetic design. In: ICMI 2020 - Proceedings of the 2020 International Conference on Multimodal Interaction, pp. 433–441. Association for Computing Machinery, Inc. (2020)
22. Wallbaum, T., Heuten, W., Rauschenberger, M., Boll, S.C.J., Timmermann, J.: Exploring social awareness: a design case study in minimal communication. In: Proceedings of Conference on Human Factors in Computing Systems. Association for Computing Machinery (2018)
23. Desnoyers-Stewart, J., Pasquier, P., Stepanova, E.R., Riecke, B.E.: JEL: connecting through breath in virtual reality. In: Proceedings of Conference on Human Factors in Computing Systems. Association for Computing Machinery (2019)
24. Funk, M., Le, D., Hu, J.: Feel connected with social actors in public spaces (2013)
25. Lee, R.M., Draper, M., Lee, S.: Social connectedness, dysfunctional interpersonal behaviors, and psychological distress: testing a mediator model. J. Couns. Psychol. **48**, 310 (2001)
26. Mashek, D., Cannaday, L.W., Tangney, J.P.: Inclusion of community in self scale: a single-item pictorial measure of community connectedness. J. Community Psychol. **35**(2), 257–275 (2007)

Research on the Design of the Pre-hospital Emergency System Based on Kano-QFD

Di Lu[1,2(✉)], Guanghui Huang[1], Fangtian Ying[1], and Yu Jiang[3]

[1] Macau University of Science and Technology, Macau 999078, China
984350790@qq.com, ghhuang1@must.edu.mo, group318@zju.edu.cn
[2] Beijing Normal University, Zhuhai 519000, China
[3] Southwest University of Science and Technology, Mianyang 621000, China

Abstract. To effectively obtain the requirements for and their weights in the construction of the pre-hospital emergency system, quantify the determined requirements into key design elements, and thereby effectively improve the efficiency and reasonableness of the emergency procedures as a whole. To propose a new system scheme for the routine "blank period" before the arrival of the pre-hospital personnel so as to save the lives of the rescued in the most efficient manner. Methods: First of all, the user requirements were summarized through in-depth interviews with senior practitioners of emergency rescue. Secondly, based on the Kano model, the priority of the requirements was analyzed qualitatively from the perspectives of user satisfaction and the level of importance of the requirements, on top of which important design requirements were analyzed and quantified with the help of quality function deployment (QFD). Results: According to the functional priority in practice, the sequence of the pre-hospital emergency system procedures was sorted out and determined, i.e. receiving emergency tasks (initiating pre-hospital emergency), waiting for the medical team to arrive (performing pre-hospital emergency treatment), and the arrival of the medical team (emergency tasks completed). The design practice was also completed. Conclusion: By analyzing the actual requirements of the users and building the Kano model and "QFD", the pre-hospital emergency system was established and implemented based on the design elements, the priority of relative importance, and the principle of interface design. The research provides a theoretical and practical reference for the construction and design practice of systems of the same type.

Keywords: Pre-hospital emergency · Kano · QFD

1 Introduction

Healthcare is the most common and fundamental issue in human society. People all over the world attach great importance to pre-hospital emergency treatment for the public. With the rapid industrialization, urbanization and population aging and changes in the ecological environment and our lifestyle, trauma and public health events have increased every day, as well as the number of people in need of emergency treatment

© IFIP International Federation for Information Processing 2022
Published by Springer Nature Switzerland AG 2022
B. Göbl et al. (Eds.): ICEC 2022, LNCS 13477, pp. 398–411, 2022.
https://doi.org/10.1007/978-3-031-20212-4_33

[1]. In cases of acute and severe illness, the "golden rescue time" is only the first 4 min. Despite some common factors like "120" line busy, time spent describing the location and the patient condition when calling for rescue, information transmission across medical emergency departments, and traffic jams, in most cities in China, it costs pre-hospital medical emergency personnel 10–15 min on average (about 30 min in villages and towns) from departure to arrival at the scene [2]. Currently, the popularity of common first-aid knowledge and skills among the public in China is less than 1% [3]. In such a context, an inescapable core issue to address is how to improve system efficiency and maximize the right of life and health of the citizens through persistent practice.

In the event of a medical emergency, the rescue action performed in the "blank" period from the moment of the call for rescue to the arrival of the ambulance is pre-hospital emergency treatment. Currently, the vast majority of the people at the scene do not know what to do and how to help in the face of emergencies, for which many patients have missed the best time for rescue [4]. This seriously affects the effectiveness of pre-hospital emergency treatment. The period from the moment of the call for rescue to the arrival of the ambulance is called the "wait-for-rescue period of pre-hospital emergency". During this period, the patient's self-rescue or timely help from others will effectively improve the survival, reduce disability and mortality, and facilitate early recovery of the patient [5].

According to survey and data analysis, most developed countries have established advanced systems of emergency medical rescue, with a preliminary urban (local) emergency rescue chain of three closely-linked segments as "site conditions and self-rescue and mutual rescue initiated by the people at the scene—pre-hospital emergency treatment—in-hospital emergency treatment" [6]. The development of technology and 5G communication has brought about the rapid development of information dissemination. In such a context, UAV-carried first-aid devices are introduced to shorten the time to arrive at the scene because of such advantages of UAVs as high mobility and being unconstrained by traffic jams. This effectively reduces the probability of death due to behind-time rescue. By developing UAVs as carriers of information and further bridging the scene of rescue and the medical center, both the reasonableness and efficiency of the rescue process are significantly improved [7].

Therefore, by building the pre-hospital emergency platform to guide UAVs and reasonably coordinating and visualizing the tripartite information from the patient, the ambulance and the medical department, we may replace traditional "waiting" with efficient interconnection. This is of great significance from the perspective of vulnerable emergency personnel.

2 Pre-hospital Emergency System

With a more systematic pre-hospital emergency system, we may (i) distribute and handle emergency information in a more scientific way, (ii) more effectively integrate resources to deal with emergency tasks, and (iii) more effectively dispatch UAVs to the scene to communicate. Through management of unmanned transport of simple measuring devices and from the most professional perspective of emergency doctors, emergency rescue information is extracted as much as possible from the surrounding environment;

in the meantime, the most professional advice is given on emergency rescue. This paper studies the use of the pre-hospital emergency system and platform with UAVs as carriers combined with communication and Internet technology in guiding self-rescue and mutual rescue of people at the scene, for the purpose of minimizing losses and saving lives.

3 Explanation of the Kano-QFD Method

The Kano model is proposed by Noriaki Kano, a Japanese scholar. The model reflects the relationship between product performance and user satisfaction. It is widely used in many fields. In the design field, it helps designers to sort user needs and thereby improve products and user experience in a targeted manner. To better translate user needs into functional requirements, QFD is introduced to quantify the ratio of user needs to product features. On such a basis, Matzler and Hinterhuber proposed a method integrating the Kano model and QFD in 1998 [8]. On top of their research, Duan Liming proposed an improved algorithm to enhance the accuracy of the measurement [9]: first, collect user requirements through questionnaires, interviews, etc., then work out the weights of the requirements based on the Kano model, and form the matrix of user requirements and functional requirements, in the end, obtain the weights and order of functional requirements. This paper adopts this method to further analyze user requirements.

4 Research Process of Pre-hospital Emergency System Design Based on Kano-QFD

Since the pre-hospital emergency system is an auxiliary system established and used in medical emergency institutions, it involves directly ① the medical personnel in the hospital with a role in emergency treatment, ② the medical staff participating in the treatment at the scene outside the hospital, and ③ the people providing assistance at the scene. Therefore, this system regards in-hospital medical staff and pre-hospital medical staff on the scene as the primary system users and operators.

4.1 User Requirement Elicitation

To further identify user needs, on top of those collected from the questionnaire survey, in-depth interviews were given to target users. Nielsen pointed out in the research on user experience that, 80% of the problems were identified by testing 5 users on average [10]. Considering that the actual operators of the system are the medical personnel to perform the rescue, 6 practitioners still engaged in medical and emergency treatment-related work and 2 experts in user experience were selected for the in-depth interviews. By interpreting the original interview text, and sorting out words and sentences of the same meaning, the user needs were eventually summarized, see Table 1 in the Appendix.

4.2   Analysis of Interactive Requirements for the Pre-hospital Emergency System

Kano Questionnaire Analysis

The Kano questionnaire here includes 20 secondary needs from the previous section as the questions to determine the users' attitudes toward each need. Their specific feelings are described as five levels: very dissatisfied (1 point), dissatisfied (2 points), indifferent (3 points), satisfied (4 points), and very satisfied (5 points). Through preliminary analysis, this questionnaire survey included professionals with experience in medical emergency rescue. To enhance the accuracy of the survey and facilitate the interviews, the questionnaires were distributed offline. A total of 60 questionnaires were collected, of which 56 were valid. The obtained Kano questionnaire data were tested for reliability and validity. Generally, if Cronbach's alpha is above 0.7, the questionnaire data are considered highly reliable. The validity, on the other hand, is measured by KMO and Bartlett's test—KMO > 0 and p in Bartlett's test < 0.05 indicate that the research data are great for extracting information.

The questionnaire data were imported to SPSS for analysis. The obtained Cronbach's α for forward problems was 0.922, and that for reverse problems, 0.916. KMO of forward problems was 0.793, p = 0.000; KMO of reverse questions was 0.799, p = 0.000. Therefore, the questionnaire is of good reliability and validity, and very suitable for extracting information.

Kano User Requirement Analysis

The collected questionnaire data were then analyzed statistically. According to the table of Kano model scores (see Table 2 in the Appendix), the attribute of each requirement was obtained.

In the table, A = Attractive, O = One-dimensional, M = Must-be, I = Indifferent, R = Reflected, and Q = Question.

Percentages of A, O, M and I in a requirement were worked out:

$$X_i = \frac{A_i + O_i}{A_i + O_i + M_i + I_i} \tag{1}$$

$$Y_i = \frac{O_i + M_i}{A_i + O_i + M_i + I_i} \tag{2}$$

Here: X_i is the increase of user satisfaction with this requirement met; Y_i is the decline in user satisfaction when this requirement is not met. Therefore, the relative weight w_i of each secondary requirement is:

$$w_i = max\left(\frac{X_i}{\sum_{i=1}^{n} X_i}, \frac{|Y_i|}{\sum_{i=1}^{n}|Y_i|}\right) \tag{3}$$

Here, i = 1, 2, ..., n, n being the number of secondary requirements.

X_i, Y_i and the relative weight w_i of each requirement were obtained from formulas (3-1), (3-2) and (3-3), as well as the attribute and weight of each requirement, see Table 3 in the Appendix.

The weight and attributes of each requirement were worked out. There were 1 must-be requirement, 13 one-dimensional requirements, and 6 indifferent requirements, to be satisfied as the specific function settings may be.

4.3   QFD-Based Functional Transformation and Sorting

Building the Mapping Between User Requirements and Design Elements
With QFD, the user secondary requirements summarized may be converted into functional requirements; meanwhile, the priority of the functions was analyzed quantitatively. First of all, the functional requirements to meet the user requirements were obtained based on the mapping of user requirements, see Table 4 in the Appendix. Functional transformation of user requirements by using the mapping ensured the rationality of the functional requirements. Realizability decomposition of the requirements guaranteed maximum functionality while meeting user requirements.

House of Quality and Priority of Design Elements
Next, a panel of three experts rated the relevance of the functional requirements to user needs. The scores were 0, 1, 3, 5, representing no relevance, weak relevance, relevance, and strong relevance.

On such a basis, the matrix of the relationship between user needs and functional requirements was obtained, see Table 5 in the Appendix.

The weight of each functional requirement was worked out:

$$R_j = \sum_{i=1}^{n} w_i r_{ij} \tag{4}$$

Here, r_{ij} is the coefficient of relevance between the ith user need and the jth functional requirement, $j = 1, 2, ..., m$, m being the number of functional requirements. The obtained weights and order of functional requirements are see Table 6 in the Appendix.

The weights of the functional requirements R_j were ranked to reveal their level of importance. The results are see Table 7 in the Appendix.

The priority of the functions obtained from the table provides a reference for the architecture of the pre-hospital emergency system. It also provides feasible plans for the visualized display of the system.

5   Design of the Pre-hospital Emergency System

5.1   Manual for and Structure of the Pre-hospital Emergency System

Possible operation procedures of users were analyzed on top of the determined interface function modules [11]. The interface layout was reasonably designed according to the operation procedures—continuous procedures were placed together to reduce unnecessary operations and the memory load for users. The pre-hospital emergency system would follow the user interface operation procedures in chronological order: receiving emergency tasks (initiating pre-hospital emergency), waiting for the medical team to arrive (performing pre-hospital emergency treatment), and the arrival of the medical team (emergency tasks completed), see Fig. 1, 2 and 3 in the Appendix.

5.2 Design of the Scheme

Characteristics of the developed pre-hospital emergency system:

Accurate: The "golden rescue period" before the arrival of the pre-hospital rescue team is usually the best timing for rescue. However, due to the poverty of medical first-aid knowledge in people at the scene of the accident, the decisive opportunity for rescue is often wasted. The pre-hospital emergency system adopts UAVs as carriers to acquire information. It supports the direct observation of the situation and the patient's illness through video and audio; it also provides direct guidance for people around the scene of the rescue. The entire process of rescue is under the accurate control of the medical staff. In this way, the doctors may reach further in a more scientific way to save the life of the patient.

Effective: The physical charging and collection platforms of UAVs can be set up near metro stations and other public facilities across the city. After receiving the emergency tasks, the pre-hospital emergency system will dispatch UAVs to arrive at the scene as quickly as possible under the control of the medical personnel, thus examining the situation on-site and guiding the rescue. Conventional ambulances are limited by public transport. UAVs, on the other hand, are more flexible; moreover, the entire process will be displayed on the interface.

Adaptive: Emergency situations are very random and uncontrollable events. The security level at the scene can be classified as low risk, medium risk, and high risk [12]. ① Low risk: Common diseases mostly occur under normal circumstances, usually in the patient's home, other everyday life places or general workplace. These places are relatively safe and won't endanger the safety of the emergency responders in most cases. ② Medium risk: Common diseases occur in non-living areas like the wilderness, in which cases the emergency responders should be more careful and formulate a safety plan according to the specific situation. ③ High risk: Natural disasters, accidents, major public health events and other high-risk environments. The emergency responders should be vigilant and complete self-assessment and environmental risk assessment before entering the field [13]. The pre-hospital emergency system helps judge the situation on-site as quickly as possible at a distance and facilitates the development of rescue measures adapted to the environment.

Real-time: The dictated state of illness might be different from the actual situation. Therefore, real-time observation with UAVs can help doctors to understand the situation in a clearer and more accurate manner without getting to the scene. Via the pre-hospital emergency interface, the medical staff may adapt the rescue methods and strategies to the environment or other factors of the patient, thus saving the patient's life as much as possible.

Scalable: With the development of modern technology, more functions can be introduced to UAVs and other hardware devices to supplement their rescue function. With respect to the pre-hospital emergency system, its scalability and sustainability are very promising. Through the platform of the pre-hospital emergency system, more function modules can be mounted to the media (UAVs). In the near future, more forms of media will be developed to fulfill emergency tasks. Therefore, the platform is of bright prospects.

For details of the system's design interface, see Fig. 4 in the Appendix.

6   Conclusion

To begin with, through preliminary research on emergency rescue and interviews with practitioners of emergency rescue, the requirements of target users are classified by nature and type based on the Kano model, thus obtaining the importance of the requirements. Then, the requirements are converted quantitatively into functional importance based on QFD. In the end, it is converted into visual interface design through hierarchical analysis. Such a qualitative-quantitative method effectively avoids the subjective bias held by the relevant designers. It should also be noted that all preliminary user requirements require the attention of designers; but in practice, limited by resources, the priority must be given to more important requirements. This paper only briefly discusses the design method. The priorities are to be further studied over a long period.

Appendix

Table 1. User requirements table.

Level 1 requirement	Level 2 requirement
C_1 Patient condition	S_1 Real-time heart rate of the person in need S_2 Real-time blood pressure of the person in need S_3 Local details of the body of the person in need S_4 Body temperature of the person in need for the reference of the medical staff
C_2 Environmental conditions	S_5 Temperature at the scene for the reference of the medical staff S_6 Oxygen concentration at the scene for the reference of the medical staff
C_3 Real-time monitoring	S_7 Display of time passed since the call S_8 Display of the usual golden rescue time for the disease S_9 Display of remaining distance of the ambulance to the scene S_{10} Display of estimated time of arrival of the ambulance at the scene S_{11} Display of the remaining distance for the ambulance to take the patient to the hospital S_{12} Display of estimated time of arrival of the ambulance at the hospital
C_4 Operating the drone	S_{13} Display of UAV remaining battery and remaining time S_{14} Basic control (lock, hover, move up, down, left and right, rotate up, down, left and right, zoom in and out, land, return) of UAVs S_{15} Display of use of UAV-mounted accessories
C_5 Drone functions	S_{16} UAV equipped with detachable secondary lens S_{17} Support real-time calls between medical staff and rescue scene S_{18} Support real-time video calls between medical staff and rescue scene S_{19} Supplemental lighting on the rescue of rescue S_{20} Sharing of rescue audio, video and required information within medical rescue related institutions (for the convenience of subsequent emergency treatment in a hospital)

Table 2. Kano model comparison table.

		Negative topics				
	Function/service	Very unsatisfied (1 score)	Unsatisfied (2 score)	Indifferent (3 score)	Satisfied (4 score)	Very satisfied (5 score)
Positive topics	Very unsatisfied (1 score)	Q	R	R	R	R
	Unsatisfied (1 score)	M	I	I	I	R
	Indifferent (1 score)	M	I	I	I	R
	Satisfied (1 score)	M	I	I	I	R
	Very satisfied (1 score)	O	A	A	A	Q

Table 3. Attributes and weights of requirements table

Requirement	A	O	M	I	R	X_i	Y_i	w_i	Attribute
S_1 Real-time heart rate of the person in need	9	26	11	10	0	0.6250	0.6607	0.061	O
S_2 Real-time blood pressure of the person in need	10	25	13	7	1	0.6364	0.6909	0.064	O
S_3 Local details of the body of the person in need	12	17	13	13	1	0.5273	0.5455	0.050	O
S_4 Body temperature of the person in need for the reference of the medical staff	12	19	6	19	0	0.5536	0.4464	0.049	I
S_5 Temperature at the scene for the reference of the medical staff	10	6	2	38	0	0.2857	0.1429	0.025	I
S_6 Oxygen concentration at the scene for the reference of the medical staff	9	13	5	29	0	0.3929	0.3214	0.035	I
S_7 Display of time passed since the call	10	19	15	12	0	0.5179	0.6071	0.056	O
S_8 Display of the usual golden rescue time for the disease	15	22	1	18	0	0.6607	0.4107	0.058	O
S_9 Display of remaining distance of the ambulance to the scene	12	23	10	11	0	0.6250	0.5893	0.055	O
S_{10} Display of estimated time of arrival of the ambulance at the scene	15	21	4	16	0	0.6429	0.4464	0.057	O
S_{11} Display of the remaining distance for the ambulance to take the patient to the hospital	10	22	8	16	0	0.5714	0.5357	0.050	O
S_{12} Display of estimated time of arrival of the ambulance at the hospital	12	21	2	21	0	0.5893	0.4107	0.052	I

(continued)

Table 3. (*continued*)

Requirement	A	O	M	I	R	X_i	Y_i	w_i	Attribute
S_{13} Display of UAV remaining battery and remaining time	8	15	18	15	0	0.4107	0.5893	0.054	M
S_{14} Basic control	9	24	19	4	0	0.5893	0.7679	0.071	O
S_{15} Display of use of UAV-mounted accessories	9	10	6	31	0	0.3393	0.2857	0.030	I
S_{16} UAV equipped with detachable secondary lens	9	15	3	29	0	0.4286	0.3214	0.038	I
S_{17} Support real-time calls between medical staff and rescue scene	7	36	11	2	0	0.7679	0.8393	0.077	O
S_{18} Support real-time video calls between medical staff and rescue scene	9	34	12	1	0	0.7679	0.8214	0.076	O
S_{19} Supplemental lighting on the rescue of rescue	8	27	11	10	0	0.6250	0.6786	0.062	O
S_{20} Real-time shared information of related units	11	34	8	3	0	0.8036	0.7500	0.071	O

Table 4. Functional requirements table

Secondary requirements (S)	Functions (D)
S_1 Real-time heart rate of the person in need S_2 Real-time blood pressure of the person in need S_3 Local details of the body of the person in need S_4 Body temperature of the person in need for the reference of the medical staff	D_1 Heart rate monitoring D_2 Blood pressure monitoring D_3 Separate shooting D_4 Remote body temperature monitoring
S_5 Temperature at the scene for the reference of the medical staff S_6 Oxygen concentration at the scene for the reference of the medical staff	D_5 Ambient temperature measuring D_6 Oxygen concentration measuring
S_7 Display of time passed since the call S_8 Display of the usual golden rescue time for the disease S_9 Display of remaining distance of the ambulance to the scene S_{10} Display of estimated time of arrival of the ambulance at the scene S_{11} Display of the remaining distance for the ambulance to take the patient to the hospital S_{12} Display of estimated time of arrival of the ambulance at the hospital	D_7 Real-time timing D_8 Real-time monitoring of vehicle running

(*continued*)

Table 4. (*continued*)

Secondary requirements (S)	Functions (D)
S_{13} Display of UAV remaining battery and remaining time S_{14} Basic control (lock, hover, move up, down, left and right, rotate up, down, left and right, zoom in and out, land, return) of UAVs S_{15} Display of use of UAV-mounted accessories	D_9 Low battery warning D_{10} Basic control of UAVs D_{11} Prompt of use of UAV accessories
S_{16} UAV equipped with detachable secondary lens S_{17} Support real-time calls between medical staff and rescue scene S_{18} Support real-time video calls between medical staff and rescue scene S_{19} Supplemental lighting on the rescue of rescue S_{20} Sharing of rescue audio, video and required information within medical rescue related institutions (for the convenience of subsequent emergency treatment in a hospital)	D_{12} Real-time picture and voice transmission D_{13} Lighting function D_{14} Real-time picture and voice sharing

Table 5. Matrix of user requirements and functions

Requirement	Weights	D_1	D_2	D_3	D_4	D_5	D_6	D_7	D_8	D_9	D_{10}	D_{11}	D_{12}	D_{13}	D_{14}
S_1	0.061	5	0	1	0	0	0	1	0	0	0	3	3	1	0
S_2	0.064	0	5	1	0	0	0	1	0	0	0	3	3	1	0
S_3	0.050	1	1	5	1	1	1	0	0	0	1	3	5	5	1
S_4	0.038	0	1	0	5	5	0	3	0	0	0	3	1	0	0
S_5	0.025	0	0	0	3	5	0	0	0	0	0	3	3	0	0
S_6	0.035	1	1	0	0	0	5	0	1	0	0	3	1	1	0
S_7	0.056	1	1	0	0	0	0	5	3	3	0	1	3	0	3
S_8	0.058	1	1	1	1	1	1	5	5	0	0	1	3	0	3
S_9	0.055	0	0	0	0	0	0	5	5	3	0	3	5	0	5
S_{10}	0.057	1	1	0	1	0	0	5	5	0	0	0	5	0	5
S_{11}	0.050	0	0	0	0	0	0	5	5	0	0	0	5	0	5
S_{12}	0.052	1	1	0	1	0	0	5	5	0	0	0	5	0	5
S_{13}	0.054	0	0	0	0	0	0	1	0	5	1	5	0	0	0
S_{14}	0.071	0	0	3	1	0	0	0	0	0	5	3	0	0	0
S_{15}	0.030	1	1	1	1	1	1	1	0	3	3	5	3	3	3
S_{16}	0.049	0	0	5	0	0	0	0	0	0	3	5	5	1	5
S_{17}	0.077	0	0	3	0	0	0	0	0	0	3	5	5	3	3
S_{18}	0.076	0	0	5	0	0	0	0	0	3	3	3	5	3	5
S_{19}	0.062	0	0	0	0	0	0	1	0	0	3	5	3	5	3
S_{20}	0.071	0	0	0	5	0	0	0	0	3	3	3	5	1	5

Table 6. Function weighting table

Weight	D_1	D_2	D_3	D_4	D_5	D_6	D_7	D_8	D_9	D_{10}	D_{11}	D_{12}	D_{13}	D_{14}
R_j	0.643	0.696	1.532	0.938	0.453	0.313	2.025	1.563	1.134	1.554	3.112	3.826	1.389	2.949

Table 7. Function sorting table

No.	Functions	No.	Functions
1	Real-time picture and voice transmission	8	Lighting function
2	Prompt of use of UAV accessories	9	Low battery warning
3	Real-time picture and voice sharing	10	Basic control of UAVs
4	Real-time timing	11	Blood pressure monitoring
5	Real-time monitoring of vehicle running	12	Heart rate monitoring
6	Basic control of UAVs	13	Ambient temperature measuring
7	Separate shooting	14	Oxygen concentration measuring

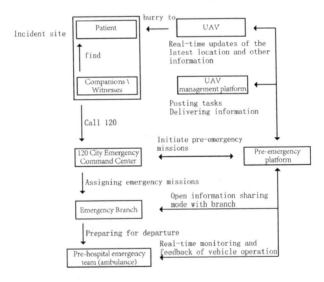

*UAV: Unmanned Aerial Vehicle

Fig. 1. Pre-hospital emergency system start

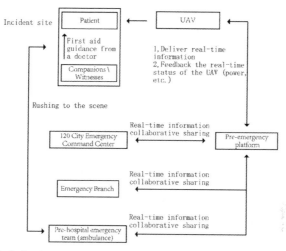

2

**The "gap" period of waiting for the medical team
(pre-emergency implementation in progress)**

Fig. 2. "gap" period of waiting for the medical team (Pre-hospital Emergency System implementation in progress)

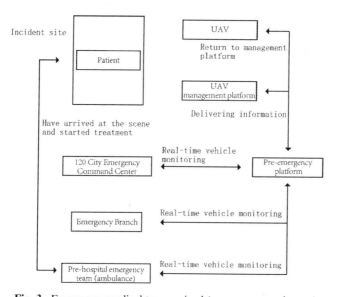

3

**Emergency medical team arrived
(pre-emergency is over)**

Fig. 3. Emergency medical team arrived (pre-emergency is over)

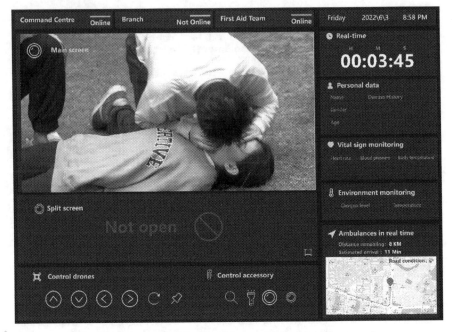

Fig. 4. Interface design details of the pre-hospital emergency system

References

1. Taymour, R.K., Abir, M., Chamberlin, M., et al.: Policy, practice, and research agenda for emergency medical services oversight: a systematic review and environmental scan. Prehosp. Disaster Med. 33(1), 89–97 (2018)
2. Lu, L.B., Zhang, S.S.: Investigation on the current situation of pre-hospital care for patients with cardiac arrest: epidemiological investigation and analysis of outcomes of patients with out-of-hospital cardiac arrest in Zhengzhou. HeNan Med. Res. 28(8), 1356–1362 (2019)
3. Chen, M.: The method of popularizing first aid knowledge among Chinese residents. Chin. J. Hyg. Rescue (Electron. Ed.) 5(1), 34–35 (2019)
4. Zhang, W.W., Xu, J., Yu, T., et al.: Discussion on the construction of public first aid training system in China. Chin. J. Crit. Care Med. 39(4), 309–312 (2019)
5. Wu, X.K.: From waiting for rescue (nursing) to participating in rescue (nursing)–development and application of first aid priority hierarchical scheduling system. Chin. Hosp. Manag. 31(3), 13–14 (2011)
6. Fan, M.Y., Zou, L.H., Liu, X.L., et al.: Analysis of first responders' demands and willingness for first aid knowledge in Hunan. J. Clin. Emerg. 17(8), 606–609 (2016)
7. Qiao, R.: Research on first aid System based on unmanned aerial vehicle. Technol. Wind 06, 11–12+15 (2017)
8. Matzler, K., Hinterhuber, H.H.: How to make product development projects more successful by integrating Kano's model of customer satisfaction into quality function deployment. Technovation 18(1), 25–38 (1998)
9. Duan, L.M., Huang, H.: Integration and application of Kano's model into quality function development. J. Chongqing Univ. (Nat. Sci. Ed.) 31(5), 515–519 (2008)
10. Nielsen, J.: Why you only need to test with 5 users. Weblog Measuring Usability, pp. 5–8 (2011)

11. Deng, X.Y., Liu, L., Zhang, R.Q.: Optimal design of fitness game system based on Kano-QFD. Packag. Eng. **42**(14), 148–154 (2021)
12. Yue, M.X., Wang, L.X., Li, Q.L., et al.: Expert consensus on disaster emergency and emergency response. J. Chin. Res. Hosp. **4**(6), 37–49 (2017)
13. Zhang, H., Cheng, S.W., Wang, P., et al.: Expert consensus on public response measures during pre-hospital emergency waiting for aid. Chin. J. Crit. Care Med. **42**(05), 380–386 (2022)

Student Game Competition

The Public Transport Stress Test (PTST) at Bogotá: A Perceived Reality and Handling Anxious Situations with a Cool Mind Through Preparation

Juan Pablo Romero, Juan Diego Rueda, José David Tamara, and Pablo Figueroa(✉)

Universidad de los Andes, Cra 1E #18A 40, Bogotá, Cundinamarca, CO, USA
{jp.romero12,jd.ruedaa,jd.tamara,pfiguero}@uniandes.edu.co

Abstract. Making use of the public transport system in Bogotá is a stressful and even daunting experience for many yet given the lack of safe and accessible alternatives there aren't many ways to avoid it. As part of a software development project the team decided to create a 2D survival, point-and-click videogame set on communicating the prior sensations to the player and providing a small aid in reducing stress through preparation. An MVP (minimum viable product) is disclosed amid early development stages to gather valuable feedback. The game's implementation is then continued based on the collected comments, suggestions, and data.

Link to Playable Game. https://kiroe.itch.io/the-public-transport-stress-test

Keywords: Public transport · Stress · Theft

1 Motivation

Having experienced the stark contrast between the public transport systems of other countries and Colombia's, regarding the feelings of trust, safety and carefreeness that can be experienced when making use of them, it became a driving issue for the team to communicate the highly stressful and unsafe experiences that the people in Bogotá have on a daily basis when taking the buses.

1.1 Problem Statement

It is commonly reported by Colombian news outlets that yearly thousands of robberies take place in the public transportation system, combining this with the fact that a great part of the population doesn't believe in Bogotá's justice institutions (and hence many don't report theft cases even when they're the victims) (Rodríguez, Rodríguez 2022), feelings of uneasiness, distrust and insecurity have become a constant for a majority of the citizens who often take the buses because there aren't any other safe and accessible options to move around Bogotá (Cortés, Cortés 2019). As a result of the prior, commuting in the capital through public means can be an extremely stressful and daunting experience and even more so for first timers.

Published by Springer Nature Switzerland AG 2022
B. Göbl et al. (Eds.): ICEC 2022, LNCS 13477, pp. 415–420, 2022.
https://doi.org/10.1007/978-3-031-20212-4_34

1.2 Goals

To portray the stories of firsthand experiences and daily news regarding stolen items, and to communicate the stressful nature of taking the public transport system in Bogotá, all in the form of a serious videogame as part of a software development project seeking to also provide a small aid in reducing the stress incurred when participating in this routine activity.

2   Game Experience

The game experience that the game is designed to provide is a stressful yet interesting challenge to the player where they will have to experience a normal day in Bogotá's public transport system. During the trip different minigames are presented to the player, all based on everyday stories of theft. There are some variables the player will need to always have in mind, like the progression of the stress bar and the constant attempts of others to steal his cellphone in his pocket. In the case the player losses his cellphone he will lose the game, the same happens if he lets himself get to the maximum stress level or if he loses all the objects in his backpack.

2.1   Abstraction

The problem of security in the public transport system of Bogotá is the root of plenty of health and psychological issues, for a lot of citizens. On the same note, insecurity causes a lot of stress due to the risk of getting robbed being present all the time. As such, there are tons of stories that can be extracted from users' experiences while taking the buses, from each of those stories different minigames could be created. Our team's mission was to imprint those experiences in the different mechanics of the game, so it feels like the player faces the most common challenges of Bogotá's public transport (most prominently stress and insecurity). To abstract that feeling, the team designed different minigames, each of them taking part of the player's concentration and time with each of the prior having their own abstraction process: key aspects of methods of theft were analyzed and thought into a simple game, maintaining the simplicity and essence. When put together these games form an overwhelming (and stressful) experience of day-to-day Transmilenio.

2.2   Game Structure

The game is composed of a level selector and a shop that helps with the game's progression.

Level Selector. Composed of 5 levels and a tutorial level, each level is planned to have different mechanics and difficulty, each simulating different scenarios in which the player must react to avoid losing their belongings. The idea in each level is that the player will have to embark on harder trips in the later levels making them such that even in places that might be considered safe the player could lose their objects if (s)he is careless.

Each level takes a combination of pre-selected minigames which will occur in random intervals, each interval being longer if the player gets the upgrade related to that minigame. When the player finishes a level, they will be rewarded with points, which they can spend in the shop.

2.3 Aesthetics

The art of PTST was mostly made by the members of the team, at first the basic sprites for each character and for all the objects were created. After that the team found a background sprite for the city, which was made to move and loop, so it seemed like the bus was moving through the city. During the development of the different minigames more sprites were created to complete them and give them a better aesthetic. Additionally, a few of the sprites in the minigames, like the cellphone and some of the objects in the backpack, were taken from the internet (and credited). The main menu and the results screen were also made during development, to help introduce the player to the context of the game.

2.4 Minigames and Mechanics

Stress Bar Mechanic. Throughout each level there is a stress bar which gets filled as time passes, the player needs to combat the bar's progress using relaxation mechanics such as the window or store consumables like the chocolate. If the bar becomes full the player will lose since their character will decide to leave the bus before their destination due to accumulated stress.

Fig. 1. Stress bar (red) located at the top of the main screen along with a stress counter. (Color figure online)

Phone Minigame. In this minigame the player has their phone in their pocket and through events such as notifications and the theft method cosquilleo (pickpocketing) the phone will start to move out of the pocket until it reaches a threshold, when the limit is reached it becomes stealable and steal attempts will begin to occur. Due to the prior, the player will have to check their pocket constantly as they travel (by hovering on the blue bar that appears on the lower portion of the main screen) in order to move the phone away from the threshold. Losing the phone will lead to a game over.

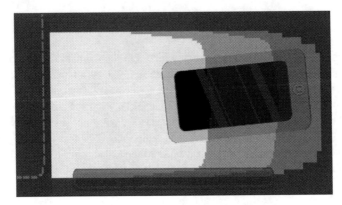

Fig. 2. Phone Minigame: Phone at starting position within the pocket screen.

Backpack Minigame. Whenever the backpack falls due to the bus's movement, or other reasons, the items inside fall to the floor and a timer start for the player to pick them up. The prior happens regardless of whether the player is on another screen meaning that by the time the player notices that the backpack fell it is possible that a certain amount of the time for the minigame has passed. Once the player enters the minigame, multiple items will be on the ground and the player will have to drag them into their backpack before the time limit ends (and they are taken by others). The player may lose a few items during the trip, but they will earn less points if they beat the level, also if they lose more than 2 backpack items, that will mean game over.

Fig. 3. Backpack minigame: Fallen items with timer ticking.

Window Mechanic. The main way to combat stress, by looking out the window the player can relax and reduce or even reverse the progress of the stress bar, however entering this screen will also leave the player's belongings vulnerable (since the player won't be interacting with them) so they will have to switch screens repeatedly (in a sort of a dance) to combat stress while protecting their items.

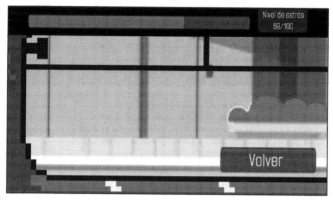

Fig. 4. Window mechanic: Relaxing moving view of the outside from within the bus.

2.5   Additional Content

Store and Upgrades. At the end of each level the player will earn points according to how much stress they accumulated during the ride and how many items they managed to save, these points can then be spent in the shop which is accessible from the main menu. There are three permanent upgrades available for the phone and the backpack, each taking the form of recommendations to protect said items (for instance, anti-theft bags) these will help in their related minigames. In addition, there's also consumables such as chocolate bars which (as the name implies) can be used with immediate effects like reversing stress progression by a certain amount, these are limited to 3 per store visit and level.

Difficulty Selection. The starting menu of the game features a button to access difficulty selection, there the player will be able to (as the name implies) choose a difficulty to play in. There's easy, medium and hard, each with a description of what kind of player they are intended for: the first one being for new comers and people who don't play many games, the second being the default difficulty, and hard being for players who are doing a replay and/or wish for a greater challenge. All difficulty options have positive or negative effects on almost all aspects of the game including (but not limited to) stress bar progress speed, effectiveness of the window on reducing stress, backpack timer duration, etc.

Fig. 5. Upgrade store (WIP)

3   Proposed Solution

By creating a serious game, the team means to communicate and critique the overwhelming and stressful everyday experiences that one can encounter while using Bogotá's public transport system. It is also intended to create further awareness about the prior issue and to provide useful tools (in the way of in-game upgrades) for people to use in order to reduce the dreadful feeling of insecurity in the buses through preparation.

3.1   Results

A demo of the game was publicly released as well as a survey to collect player feedback, the second was mostly positive and suggestions are still (as of May 16th, 2022) being taken into account for the development of the full release.

References

1. Cortés, L.: Bogotá: La ciudad en la que los medios nos están llevando al fin. https://plazacapital.co/ciudadania/4086-transporte-y-salud-mental-en-la-capital. (2019)
2. Rodríguez, J.: Denuncian que aumentaron cifras de robos en TransMilenio. https://www.wradio.com.co/2022/02/08/ojo-a-las-cifras-denuncian-que-aumentaron-cifras-de-robos-en-transmilenio/. (2022)

Corruptio: An Interactive Insight on City Management

Andrés Sánchez, Santiago Gamboa, Nicolas Fajardo$^{(\boxtimes)}$, and Pablo Figueroa

Universidad de Los Andes, Bogotá, Colombia
{af.sanchezr1,se.gamboa,n.fajardor,pfiguero}@uniandes.edu.co
https://sistemas.uniandes.edu.co

Abstract. One of the biggest problems seen in Colombia and Latin America, if not the biggest, is corruption. Due to this, and with the objective to raise awareness of it and encourage young people to take a bigger role in politics, an interactive videogame was developed. This game puts the player as the mayor of a city, where they must perform tasks such as budget management and decision making on specific events, all while keeping a positive popularity score to avoid being impeached. During development time, an MVP (Minimum Viable Product) was developed and published online to get feedback from players to release a second MVP, improved by this information.

Keywords: Corruption · Young people · Politics · Simulation game · Serious games

1 Introduction

For a long time, Colombia has been troubled with corruption. Stealing money from the public meal plan for schools [1], the 'disappearance' of more than 17 million dollars that were destined to provide internet connection to schoolchildren during the Covid 19 pandemic [2], and the Odebrecht scandal in which Novonor, known before as Odebrecht, bribed several politicians in Colombia, and several countries of Latin America and Africa, to get contracts on public works [3], are just some of the many corruption scandals that damage Colombia and other third world countries.

Since the participation of youth is proven to be a critical factor in politics in Colombia, as demonstrated by the movement known as *"séptima papeleta"* (seventh ballot) in 1990, where university students of the time pushed for a reform to the constitution that had been legitimate since 1886 [4].

With this in mind, and to both encourage young people to participate in politics and be aware of the corruption problem that affects Colombia and several other countries across Latin America, the idea of *Corruptio* was conceived. *Corruptio* is a videogame in which players can manage the budget of six different city departments (healthcare, public transportation, amenities, education, security and *"mermelada"*) and make decisions on certain events that occur naturally in the game.

© IFIP International Federation for Information Processing 2022
Published by Springer Nature Switzerland AG 2022
B. Göbl et al. (Eds.): ICEC 2022, LNCS 13477, pp. 421–426, 2022.
https://doi.org/10.1007/978-3-031-20212-4_35

1.1 Development Process

For the development of *Corruptio* the SCRUM methodology was used, in this methodology we wrote a Game Design Document (GDD) that acted as a Product Backlog, where every idea, game mechanics, and details of the videogame were stated.

In total, the development process consisted of two sprints of approximately eight weeks each. The first sprint was centered around the development of an initial MVP that has the main characteristics of the proposed game, and its release to gather valuable feedback. The second sprint was centered around using that information to improve the initial MVP into a second one, which was released to gather more feedback. This feedback was gathered to both evaluate the improvements made and get more information on how to improve the game in the future.

2 Game Experience

To accomplish the objectives via the use of a videogame, it must be both interactive and entertaining, so that it catches the interest of players. To do this, a base model of a city was initially developed and further improved by the implementation of several systems that made it more appealing to players.

2.1 Base City

The base city consists of two components: logic and visualization. The logic component was centered around the definition and modeling of six city departments: healthcare, public transport, education, amenities, safety and '*mermelada*' (a word used in Colombia that refers to corruption). The representation of these departments can be seen on the sidebar on the left of Fig. 1.

The visual component refers to a 3D model of a city that is fully explorable via the use of two cameras: a 'first person' camera that can move and rotate, and a top-view camera that shows the whole city from the sky. Figure 1 shows a part of the city.

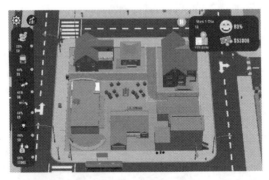

Fig. 1. Screenshot taken from the game. Here, the city can be seen along with the graphic user interfaces that indicate the current state of the city and its departments.

2.2   Match System

This system is centered around the definition of endgame conditions that, as the name indicates, define the end of a playthrough. In the end, two conditions were defined: a negative one, in which the player gets 'impeached', and a positive one, in which the player manages to complete their electoral period.

To allow the possibility of impeachment, an acceptance value was defined. This value can range between 0 and 100% and can be seen at the top right corner of Fig. 1. At the start of the game, the acceptance starts at 100% and gets decreased overtime and because of decisions made by the player or random events. If this value reaches zero, the player gets automatically impeached and 'loses' the game.

On the other hand, for the player to 'win' the game by completing their electoral period, they only must withstand a playthrough of about 3 min (without counting time on menus) without getting impeached.

Additionally, a game over screen was implemented. This screen shows some data to the player regarding their playthrough over different slides (See Fig. 2), like a score, endgame condition applied and graphs of popularity over time and budget invested.

Fig. 2. First slide of the game over screen. This slide includes the endgame condition reached, total game duration, score, and the mandate's efficiency. The arrow button takes the player to another slide.

2.3   Budget System

The main interaction of the player with the game is via the budget management menu (See Fig. 3), which can be accessed via the 'TAB' key or the button at the right of the 'settings' button on the top left corner of Fig. 1. In this menu, the player can assign a set amount of money from the total budget (shown both in the menu on Fig. 3 and below the acceptance on Fig. 1) to each department. The player can also go over the budget, at the cost of their acceptance value.

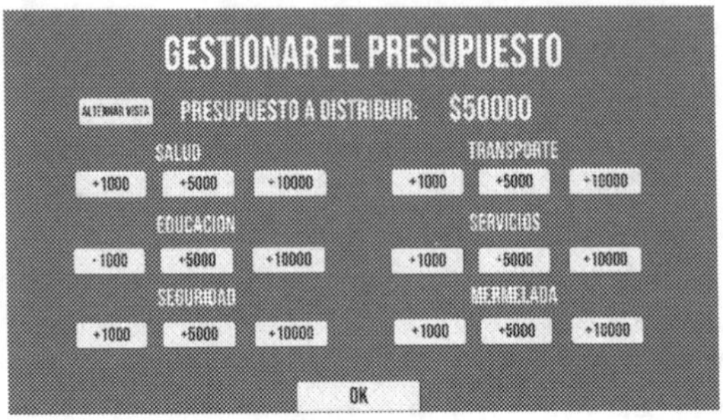

Fig. 3. Budget management menu

2.4 Adaptative City System

This system contains two subsystems: Needs-Based AI (NBAI) selection system, and an event visualization system.

The NBAI selection system is based on the explanation given by Robert Zubek on his paper 'Needs-Based AI' [5]. Before attempting to implement it, a satisfaction value was added to each of the departments that measures their quality, so if a department has a high satisfaction value, the player's acceptance value will increase, or decrease if the value is low enough. The exception to this last rule is the *'mermelada'* department, since a high satisfaction value in it would indicate that the corruption levels are high. With that being said, the implementation of this system in *Corruptio* consisted of modeling the city as an agent that must fulfill the necessity of keeping each of the department's satisfaction level as high as possible by using the budget each of them is assigned.

The event visualization system consists of the implementation of a series of events that occur when the departments satisfaction gets either too high or too low. A high satisfaction value will generate a positive event, while a low value will generate a negative one. The exception to this rule is the *'mermelada'* department, for which a high satisfaction value will generate a negative event, while a low one would generate a positive event.

In general, the events selected for each department are related to a challenge regarding it. For example, the access of a quality service for the healthcare and amenities department, while the education's quality and opportunities for the education department.

2.5 Notifications System

This system was implemented to help the player understand the changes the city goes through every time one of the events from the event visualization system occurs. To help the player with this understanding, this system uses a couple of tools. First, a pop-up notification on the right, below the total budget, that gives a message regarding the department and the event type that occurred. Then, the player can click on the pop-up to focus on the second tool: a balloon-like indicator with some particles that indicates the place of the event that is happening at the moment. Both tools can be seen on Fig. 4.

Fig. 4. Notification pop-up and balloon like indicator

2.6 Decision-Making System

The decision-making system was implemented to give another point of interaction between the player and the game. This new player-game interaction has a possibility to occur every few seconds and consist of presenting the player with a situation in which they must make a decision that may affect both the city (the acceptance or total budget) or one or more departments (their satisfaction or budget). An example of a situation and choices available for the player is shown in Fig. 5.

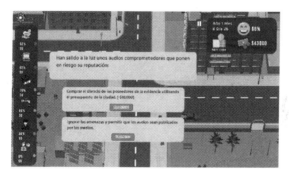

Fig. 5. Example of a situation exposed by the game so that the player decides on what to do

2.7 Random Events System

This last system was put in place to try and make every game different for the player. In a similar manner to the decision-making system, the random events system allows for a possibility (given that at that moment in time no situations are presented to the player) to expose a random event that occurred and influenced the city or departments. The player has no choice on how to act when these events occur, other that adjusting the budget to try and improve the satisfaction of negatively affected departments. An example of a random event is shown in Fig. 6.

Fig. 6. Example of a random event exposed by the game. The player does not have a possible action further than closing the event and adjusting the budget afterwards.

3 Results

As mentioned above, we released a total of two MVPs that were used to get feedback on the current state of the game and make improvements upon it. These MVPs were uploaded on itch.io, where they were publicly accessed and helped us receive several reviews that we used to improve the quality of the game.

The most recent MVP can be accessed via the following url: https://paco-democratico-devs.itch.io/corruptio-mvp-2.

References

1. Gutiérrez, H.: Prisión a responsables de proveer carne de caballo y burro a contratistas del PAE en Santander. RCN Radio (2021)
2. Contreras, C: Centros Poblados, un año después: ¿dónde están los $70.000n millones (2021)
3. Rodríguez, M., Castro, B: Odebrecht, el gigantesco escándalo de corrupción que derriba líderes políticos en América Latina (2019)
4. Pardo, D.: Qué fue la Séptima Papeleta, el movimiento que cambió Colombia hace 30 años (y por qué sus demandas aún están insatisfechas). BBC News Mundo (2020)
5. Zubek, R.: Needs-Based AI. http://robert.zubek.net/publications/Needs-based-AI-draft.pdf, pp. 1–11 (2010)

Workshops and Tutorials

Workshop on Social and Ethical Issues in Entertainment Computing

Roderick McCall[1]([✉]), Jethro Shell[2], Celina Kacperski[3], Stanley Greenstein[4], Nicola Whitton[5], and Jo Summers[6]

[1] Luxembourg Institute of Science and Technology, L-4362 Esch-Sur-Alzette, Luxembourg
roderick.mccall@list.lu
[2] De Montfort University, Leicester LE1 9BH, UK
jethro.shell@dmu.ac.uk
[3] University of Mannheim, 68131 Mannheim, Germany
celina.kacperski@uni-mannheim.de
[4] University of Stockholm, 106 91 Stockholm, Sweden
Stanley.Greenstein@juridicum.su.se
[5] University of Durham, Durham DH1 3LE, UK
nicola.j.whitton@durham.ac.uk
[6] Unity Software, Brighton BN1 4RB, UK
jo.summers@unity3d.com

Abstract. Entertainment computing spans anything from a single player game on a console through to large-scale multiplayer online virtual worlds. This workshop focuses on a range of issues which impact on the design, use and adoption of entertainment computing systems from an ethical and social perspective. Issues to be explored include the composition of those working in the industry from the perspectives of diversity and inclusion, how this impacts on design and how groups are represented within games and other entertainment platforms. We will further explore issues relating to monetization, incentives, and potential addiction. We will explore how to design for ethical and social issues while also looking at problems which have arisen and the potential challenges of the future.

Keywords: Ethics · Legal · Games · Serious games · Virtual worlds

1 Introduction

Early computer games such as River Raid, had a relatively short play cycle and may have involved a few players at the same time packed around a console or (what is now) a relatively basic computer. Beyond the tactics and play styles of players, it is unlikely they would have had any social or ethical implications, beyond perhaps some angry children. Today's games are entirely different beasts. They are often highly complex, explore ethical and social issues, involve monetization and play can go beyond the boundaries of digital space into the real world itself. They may also offer persistent experiences which span long periods of time. Therefore, ethical and social issues within today's computer

© IFIP International Federation for Information Processing 2022
Published by Springer Nature Switzerland AG 2022
B. Göbl et al. (Eds.): ICEC 2022, LNCS 13477, pp. 429–435, 2022.
https://doi.org/10.1007/978-3-031-20212-4_36

games span many aspects. Ranging from diversity issues within the game development sector, through to how in-game purchases may become harmful for players. They can also include aspects such as stigmatizing groups in society due to their portrayal in games, through to how player behavior in large-scale multiplayer online games (and increasingly digital worlds) may have impacts outside of the game. Therefore, while players may play games inside the framed magic circle (see Sect. 2.2), their impacts may go far beyond the game itself. This workshop will explore the range of ethical and social issues within the computer games industry, across game types and entertainment computing systems.

2 Background

2.1 Foundations

Table 1. APA ethical principles (2010)

Principle	Summary
Beneficence and nonmalefeance	The participants should benefit and no harm should be done to any persons involved
Fidelity and responsibility	There should be no gain from the person undertaking the study
Integrity	The work should be open, transparent and honest
Justice	The benefits of taking part should be spread across the individuals involved and society as a whole
Respect for people's rights and dignity	Respect for gender, race, sexual orientation and other related aspects. Privacy and use of data must be considered

The American Psychological Associated [1] defined a set of core ethical principles outlined in Table 1. Although these relate to the undertaking of psychological studies, they are also relevant when exploring issues relating to computer games. For example, games should not harm either the players or those represented in the games. Clearly, aspects such as no gain are more problematic, as games companies wish to sell their products and thus it opens up the debate as to who is really benefiting from playing a game and where the benefits rest.

In contrast with participating in a psychological or scientific study, game players are often not made specifically aware of any risks they may face. For example, while minimum ages ratings may indicate violent content, there is little in the way of an informed consent procedure which outlines risks and rewards. Given the context of playing games, this is to be expected as few players already read data privacy policies in full and are probably less likely to read informed consent documents should that need ever arise. Yet, as noted later, players face several hidden ethical and social issues which may not be clear when they buy or play a game. Thus, integrity, or the openness and transparency aspects of ethics, becomes problematic.

Adopting codes from outside of computer science and applying them to aspects of computing is as Brey [2] notes is potentially problematic. Rather, we argue in common with work by Floridi et al. [3] that we should seek to build on a range of values which are derived from aspects including (but not limited to) professional practice.

2.2 Ethics While Playing Computer Games

Games are "a formal set of rules that project a fictional world that a player has to experience" ([4] p14). According to Sicart, the game world only exists when it is played and the act of playing is voluntary. Within this game world, Huizinga [5] defines the magic circle, which comprises rules, objects, locations, people and a time period. This brings us to the first problem area, that we would normally expect that players play within the letter and spirit of the rules. Salen and Zimmerman identify five types of player while Bartle explored player types in single and multi-player games, and identified four types. Broadly speaking, Salen and Zimmerman [6] can be viewed as how the players interpret and enact the rules, and how this impacts their behavior. While Bartle [7] explores player behavior almost from the perspective of the player objective (e.g. exploring), which may or may not rely on adherence to rules. A summary can be found in Table 2.

Table 2. Player Types from Salen and Zimmerman and Bartle

Salen and Zimmerman	Bartle
Standard	Achievers
Dedicated	Explorers
Unsportsmanlike	Socializers
Cheater	Killers
Spoilsport	

A standard player is one who follows the rules but is not overly passionate about the game. A dedicated player is more passionate and seeks to win. An unsportsmanlike player will strictly interpret the rules with the pure intention of winning, even if the interpretation is seen as unfair by others. In common with Salen and Zimmermann, Bartle also identifies some more extreme player types in his taxonomy. From those whose primary interest is socializing through gaming (socializers) rather than the game itself, through to Killers (who are highly competitive and seek to win). In contrast, explorers seek to discover the game at their own pace.

For games which are played over a short time, different play styles coupled with unethical conduct may become frustrating and annoying, but little else. However, in digital worlds where game play could last for days, weeks, months or even years, behaviour which complies with the rules but is ethically dubious could be problematic. Examples of such worlds include the World of WarCraft, Metaverse and Second Life. Although

Metaverses such as Second Life have existed for many years and allow a persistent life and habitat for those who inhabit them. The Metaverse launched by Meta (previously Facebook) perhaps poses the largest challenge and most interesting case study in terms of long-term ethical issues within online worlds, mainly because Facebook can bring 2bn potential users to the platform. In some ways, online long-term worlds and games share aspects and problems of legacy games which are played over a long time period.

Pervasive, expressive, and persuasive games bring in further ethical and social issues. For example, pervasive games seek to break the magic circle by allowing play across time and potentially locations. Persuasive games seek to persuade people to undertake certain actions. They may share some elements of gamified applications which also seek to encourage certain behaviors. In common with Metaverse type environments, pervasive games have the potential to significantly impact behaviors over a longer term, and when combined with more persuasive elements, there is a risk that overall behavior of individuals even in everyday contexts may be impacted. This is similar to the challenges faced by gamified applications and serious games, where certain behaviors may be encouraged, for example, by an employer. While the behaviours may meet organizational targets, they may lead to unethical conduct by those taking part. In contrast to persuasive games, expressive games seek to put people in the shoes of someone else who is experiencing ethical and moral choices, with the intention of letting the player experience the impact of those choices. Thus, in themselves, expressive games, while not seeking to persuade people, could inform the moral and ethical behavior of players long after the play session.

2.3 Social Issues While Playing Computer Games

While there are recognized benefits to playing digital games for learning [8] social facilitation and community building [9] there are potentially several negative social issues associated with their use. Moral panics in the media have highlighted the relationship between video games, real-life violence and addiction, but the evidence on both issues is unclear. Some research evidence supports the theory that playing violent video games can lead to aggressive thoughts and behaviors, but there is also evidence that this depends on the content of the game, moderated by age, and magnified by environmental factors. Shliakhovchuk et al. [10] found that video games have the potential to help gain cultural knowledge, including among other facets, thus helping to improve personal awareness and reinforcing or weakening stereotypes. In, a review of research by Halibrook et al. [11] summarized a range of on the positive and negative impacts of gaming on wellbeing and social interaction. Across the various sources they cite, they show that moderate game play can help reduce psychological symptoms. However, excessive gaming could be seen as addiction, with consequential effects such as depression. Also, the motivation for playing the game impacts wellbeing, such as whether this is driven by enjoyment, achievement or obsession. The latter two can overshadow the benefits of social activity. Despite the limited evidence of the negative impacts of video games, these strong negative narratives permeate popular discourse, thus creating an additional ethical dimension to the use of digital games.

2.4 Legal Issues

As society becomes more digitalized, the law as a mechanism for regulation is changing from being reactive to being more proactive and with this development, so too is its form changing, from traditional natural language texts to actual code embedded in the systems. In addition, legal frameworks demand that certain legal values are considered already at the stage of system design and that they be built into these systems. For example, the European Union GDPR (General Data Protection Regulation) in Article 25 promotes the notion of Privacy by Design. Consequently, as computer systems are developed, they will increasingly be required to take cognizance of the legal values that must be embedded in their code for them to be legally compliant.

2.5 Digital Game-Based Learning

Two aspects of digital game-based learning stand out in relation to ethics. First, the ethical implications of using any form of games and play in educational settings, and the 'paradox of play' that highlights the ethical implications of 'forcing' play, which then (by definition) cannot be play. Second, there are considerations relating to the use of digital games, both commercial games and those designed for specifically learning. Commercial games require levels of gaming literacy (understanding the conventions of the genre and modes of interaction) that means that all learners may not start on a level playing field. Many commercial games also use sexist and racist tropes that could be unethical if used in an educational setting without time to discuss and contextualize. In contrast, the development of bespoke digital games for learning is expensive, often niche, and could be difficult to ethically justify as an alternative to cheaper and more flexible game formats such as traditional non-digital games, escape games, or collaborative game-building.

2.6 Monetization

According to Markropolis [12], games can be monetized in several ways, including subscriptions, in-game advertising, in-game micro-transactions and data orientated monetization. The latter includes the use of crowdsource data to drive sales. From the perspective of in-game reward based micro-transactions, Neely [13] concludes that "fixed, cosmetic rewards are ethically permissible" while "random rewards of all types are ethically problematic", and "fixed functional rewards can be acceptable but only under certain conditions". This is because random rewards prey on self-regulation issues (e.g. gambling); while gameplay rewards disadvantage players without access to the items if they are not attainable through effort (i.e. are exclusive). Furthermore, deceptiveness in presentation of micro-transactions plays a major role in ethical considerations, for example, existence of patience paywalls (players having to overcome absurd hurdles to achieve what others can buy with money) are ethically problematic.

Data collection in video games is usually used in game and level design and for bug fixing and improving the game experience. However, video game companies might employ tactics such as behavioral tracking and base data manipulation/price manipulations on this tracking data to incentivize continuous spending. However, this raises privacy issues as players have no control over what type of data is sold and are often not even told. Often, it is unclear what the data is being used for, an extreme example would be that unethical prediction models can fuel addition and personalized or micro-targeting algorithms that have been shown to marginalize certain already disadvantaged groups. Therefore, the use of data drive monetization may fuel these problems.

2.7 Diversity

Diversity remains challenging in three ways. Within the industry itself, for example, by having an inclusive policy towards different groups within society, avoiding stigmatization of groups via their representation in games (i.e., from an ethnicity and heritage perspective), and supporting users with disabilities. For example, within the industry itself, Baird and Harrer [14] noted that there may be unconscious values (biases) during the game design process which need to be more transparent. For more information on these and related issues please see [14–16].

3   Conclusions

Games are now a more pervasive part of life and have moved on significantly from the early days of the 1970s and 80s where play was relatively simple, and the implications limited. This workshop addresses the social and ethical challenges of modern computer games as they move away from being isolated play experiences with little impact on players and society, to experiences which increasingly must draw on external social and ethical practices while at the same time are also shaping social and ethical behavior. These issues span aspects of game development, through playing and the impacts on wider society. Therefore, a more thorough dialogue on the challenges facing the industry and society is required.

Acknowledgements. This workshop is organized by the IFIP Working Group 14.5 on Social and Ethical Issues in Entertainment Computing.

References

1. American Psychological Association: Ethical Principles of Psychologists and Code of Conduct (2017). https://www.apa.org/ethics/code/. Accessed 16 July 2022
2. Brey, P.: Method in computer ethics: towards a multi-level interdisciplinary approach. Ethics Inf. Technol. **2**, 125–129 (2000)
3. Floridi, L., Sanders, J.: Mapping the foundationalist debate in computer ethics. Ethics Inf. Technol. **4**, 1–9 (2002)
4. Sicart, M.: Game, player, ethics: a virtue ethics approach to computer games. Rev. Inf. Ethics **4**, 13–18 (2005)
5. Huizinga, J.: Homo Ludens: A Study of the Play Element in Culture. Beacon Press, Boston (1955)
6. Salen, K., Zimmerman, E.: Rules of Play: Game Design Fundamentals. MIT Press, Boston (2004)

7. Bartle, R.: Hearts, clubs, diamonds, spades: Players who suit MUDs. J. MUD Res. **1**(1) (1996)
8. Whitton, N.: Digital Games and Learning. Routeledge, New York (2014)
9. Steinkuehler, C., Williams, D.: Where everybody knows your (screen) name: online games as "third places." J. Comput.-Mediat. Commun. **11**(4), 885–909 (2006)
10. Shliakhovchuk, E., Muñoz García, A.: Intercultural perspective on impact of video games on players: insights from a systematic review of recent literature. Educ. Sci. Theory Pract. **20**(1), 40–58 (2020)
11. Halbrook, Y.J., O'Donnell, A.T., Msetfi, R.M.: When and how video games can be good: a review of the positive effects of video games on well-being. Perspect. Psychol. Sci. **14**(6), 1096–1104 (2019)
12. Markopoulos, E., Markopoulos, P., Liumila, M., Almufti, Y., Aggarwal, V.: Mapping the monetization challenge of gaming in various domains. In: Ahram, T. (ed.) AHFE 2019. AISC, vol. 973, pp. 389–400. Springer, Cham (2020). https://doi.org/10.1007/978-3-030-20476-1_39
13. Neely, E.L.: Come for the game, stay for the cash grab: the ethics of loot boxes, microtransactions, and freemium games. Games Cult. **16**(2), 228–247 (2021)
14. Baird, J., Harrer, S.: Challenging systems of play: towards game design ethics for transgender allyship. In: The 16th International Conference on the Foundations of Digital Games (FDG) 2021 (2021)
15. Stafford, P.: The dangers of in-game data collection, Polygon (2019)
16. Dergousoff, K., Mandryk, R.L.: Mobile gamification for crowdsourcing data collection: leveraging the freemium model. In: Proceedings of the 33rd Annual ACM Conference on Human Factors in Computing Systems, Seoul (2015)
17. King, D.L., Delfabbro, P.H., Gainsbury, S.M., Dreier, M., Greer, N., Billieux, J.: Unfair play? Video games as exploitative monetized services: an examination of game patents from a consumer protection perspective. Comput. Hum. Behav. **101**, 131–141 (2019)
18. Moura, D., El-Nasr, M.S., Shaw, C.D.: Visualizing and understanding players' behavior in video games: discovering patterns and supporting aggregation and comparison. In: ACM SIGGRAPH 2011 Game Papers (2011)

Digital Arts and Health

Mengru Xue[1,2](✉) [ID], Cheng Yao[1,2] [ID], Jun Hu[3] [ID], Yuqi Hu[1,2] [ID],
and Hui Lyu[1,2] [ID]

[1] Zhejiang University, Ningbo, 1 Xuefu Road, Ningbo, China
{mengruxue,yaoch,yuqihu,lvhui}@zju.edu.cn
[2] Zhejiang University, 866 Yuhangtang, Hangzhou, China
[3] Eindhoven University of Technology, 5612 Eindhoven, AZ, The Netherlands
j.hu@tue.nl

Abstract. Digital arts refer to artworks that use digital technology as part of the creative or presentation process. Different components of art activities are known to be health-promoting. These components can trigger psychological, physiological, social, and behavioral responses that are linked with health and well-being. The emerging forms of digital arts and new ways of interacting with these arts enable a new area of research and practice in promoting health and well-being. This workshop is intended to bring together researchers, designers, artists, and practitioners involved in the design and use of systems combining digital arts and health to build on an understanding of emerging digital art interventions in health and well-being.

Keywords: Digital arts · Health · Well-being

1 Arts and Health

Art activities are considered as interventions that combine components that are known to be health promoting [7]. For instance, art activities can involve social interaction, physical activity, cognitive stimulation, emotion evocation, and engagement with themes of health [15]. These components can trigger psychological, physiological, social and behavioral responses linked with health and well-being [9–11,40]. Numerous disciplines attempt to apply arts for health and well-being. **Arts in health** is a multidisciplinary field dedicated to transforming health and healthcare experiences through the arts [30]. This discipline advocates the participation of arts in maintaining and promoting health in healthcare and community context. **Creative arts therapy** is defined as "the use of art modalities and creative processes for the purpose of ameliorating disability and illness and optimizing health and wellness" [1], which has been applied for a variety of life-threatening illnesses [18,20,33]. The therapists specialize in one of

An event of the IFIP TC14 working group Art and Entertainment (https://ifip-tc14. org/working-groups/14-7/).

© IFIP International Federation for Information Processing 2022
Published by Springer Nature Switzerland AG 2022
B. Göbl et al. (Eds.): ICEC 2022, LNCS 13477, pp. 436–442, 2022.
https://doi.org/10.1007/978-3-031-20212-4_37

the six creative modalities: visual art, dance, music, poetry, drama, and group psychotherapy and psychodrama [35]. **Expressive arts therapy** applies one or several expressive modalities to "foster deep personal growth and community development" [12,26].

2   Digital Arts and Health

Digital arts refer to artworks that use digital technology as part of the creative or presentation process. They take forms of digital imaging, digital music, digital animation, digital installation, virtual reality, NFT (Non-Fungible Token), and so on [19]. Digital art is a multidisciplinary intersection where art and technology are highly integrated. Technologies bring new possibilities to arts, which are recognized as a "vast expansion of the creative sphere" [4].

Following the therapeutic nature of arts, incorporating the ubiquitous digital technologies, an emerging number of studies implement **Digital art therapy** [3] in clinical sessions [5,27]. For instance, visual arts-based therapy can improve communication for people with social and emotional difficulties [14]. Darewych et al. explored digital technology as a new art medium and clinical intervention in art therapy for adults with developmental disabilities. They found their participants favored creating arts on the "compact and mess-free" touchscreen devices over the traditional messy art materials in the therapeutic environment [8]. However, Choe et al. considered the lack of tactility, smell, and messiness in art making process as a disadvantage in using digital media in art therapy [6]. Other modalities such as digital music had been claimed by scholars and therapists as beneficial for clients' **music therapy** sessions [32]. **Animation therapy** uses visually and verbally within the process of recording and editing over a period of the therapeutic process [2,22]. **Virtual reality therapy** provides clients with a computer-generated virtual environment with fear-provoking stimuli that mimic their real-life experiences, which had been practiced in cognitive therapy and psychological disorders [31]. A growing number of works demonstrate the use of **digital technology in art therapy**. Zubala et al. structured current practices in this field and captured art therapeutic practices from the perspective of both therapists and clients [48].

Other than the potential to be a promising clinical intervention tool, digital arts in health have been applied to wider scenarios. Emerging modalities of digital arts brought opportunities and challenges in terms of interactivity and health-promoting impacts. As mentioned above, these modalities have been practiced not only for illness prevention but also commonly applied in health promotion in the context of health and well-being. The most popular digital modality used in health is digital visual arts. A subbranch of **health data visualization** uses diverse health data coming from various sources and transforms them into artistic visual content. Unlike bar graphs, tables, and pie charts that are often used in **health informatics** [42], health data visualization helps people to view simplified information at a glance, resulting in a better understanding and higher engagement [34]. For example, Yao et al. designed an aesthetic arousal-awareness tool using light media to discuss the possibilities to interact with arts using fashion wearables [45]. Tao et al. design situated-based affective communication art to express emotion [36]. Yu et al. implement ambient lighting as an intervention to inform people about their stress levels to assist in relaxation training [46]. Similarly, stress-related health data visualization using digital artworks has scaled up for a larger group of users [44] on a larger scale [47] in order to explore social interactions in health improvement. Digital music is interdisciplinary by nature that weaved acoustics, psychoacoustic, electronics, noise, environmental sound, and so on [25]. Previous research found that musical activities can enhance the emotional competence of children to promote class performances [37].

Origin from net art, which is made using the internet and presented on the internet, **NFT digital art** stands out to solve authenticity, ownership, and transferability problems existing in the digital art field, which brings a revolutionary change to digital artworks in terms of interactivity and privacy. NFT is a type of cryptocurrency, encoded within smart contracts in Ethereum [41]. Unlike traditional digital arts, NFT arts find a way to confirm the copyright of digital artworks that were originally reproducible and difficult to trace. By using NFT, creators can easily prove the existence and ownership of specific digital assets, such as artworks [17]. With the burgeoning amount of electronic health data, it becomes significant to manage a large amount of data innovatively and effectively [39]. With blockchain technology, health data can be visualized into digital artworks and transformed into unique, verifiable, and tradable digital assets. A team from the University of California, Berkeley created an NFT digital artwork based on Nobel laureate Jennifer Doudna's gene-editing work as a revolutionary mechanism for memorializing these breakthrough discoveries[1]. George Church, a professor of Genetics at Harvard Medical School, will be auctioning off his full genome as an NFT[2]. Similarly, Sinso technology[3] launched the world's first medical data NFT project. Sinso creates a unique NFT for each user, which can be used as a personal biometric ID card. It allows users to transfer specific data parts to NFT, such as fingerprints and medical images. On one hand, as data producers, patients and doctors can get permanent benefits from the data trade in the future. On the other hand, the huge amount of shared health data can be used in countless research, which can be pivotal in science and human history [17]. Although trading personal health assets got practiced in the industry, there are remaining ethical concerns. As demonstrated in [24], whether any individual truly owns their genome, given that it is shared with family members.

Overall, technology is influencing the way art therapy practices in a variety of aspects. The emerging modalities of digital arts not only open up possibilities in handling personal health data, but also provide broader potentials to promote health [21], prevent diseases [28], manage mental [43] and physical illness [29], and facilitate end-of-life care [38].

---

[1] https://news.berkeley.edu/2021/05/27/uc-berkeley-will-auction-nfts-of-nobel-prize-winning-inventions-to-fund-research/.

[2] https://nebula.org/genomic-nft/#about.

[3] https://www.sinso.io/index.html.

3   Opportunities and Challenges

Previous research has demonstrated the benefits digital arts bring to health and well-being. However, digital art-based interventions are complex and challenging, since they operate simultaneously on the individual and social, as well as mental and physical levels [16]. It is essential to understand the possibilities, challenges, and limitations of digital arts bring to health and well-being.

The benefits digital arts brought to health and well-being are lack of structured exploration in this field. Summarized from previous cases in digital arts for health, the benefits of digital arts brought to health can be structured from the following aspects: the digital art per se, digital art activities [23], and interactions with the digital art media [13]. Future research can explore further how digital arts affect health and well-being from these aspects and how to evaluate the effects in therapeutic or non-therapeutic contexts respectively.

Limitations and concerns have been brought up in the field of digital art therapy, which affords us lessons that merit attention in the field of digital arts for health in general. For instance, equipment cost, study efforts for the practitioners, lack of tactile stimuli, and technical breakdowns are unavoidable barriers in digital art making or presenting [48]. Moreover, a large amount of work in the field of digital arts for health demonstrates positive findings over negative effects. The potential harm that digital arts might bring to health is also essential for us to reduce the risks of overusing such technologies. Last but not least, different cultures devote differently to arts for health domain. To assure the good effects of art interventions be replicated across cultures challenges scholars and therapists in this field.

4   Workshop Goals

For implementing previous approaches and maximizing the potential value digital arts bring to health and well-being worldwide, research papers on (but are not limited to) the following topics are of mutual interest to this workshop:

- Explore the mechanisms on how digital art interventions affect health;
- Sharing cases of digital arts and health in practice;
- Explain where the digital arts can and where they cannot facilitate health;
- Sharing knowledge on scaling up the applications of successful digital art interventions.

5   Summary

This paper presents a systematic elaboration of digital arts bring to health and well-being from the current state of research, which our workshop is built upon. One keynote speaker whose expertise is in the digital arts and health domain will be invited to give a speech at the workshop and join a panel discussion. The workshop is intended to bring together researchers, designers, artists, and practitioners involved in the design and use of systems combining digital arts and health to build upon an understanding of emerging digital art interventions in health and well-being. The desired outcome of this workshop is to gather people in this field through the academic event, as a starting point to make efforts in one place. This could set the stage for designing digital arts for health, and transfer knowledge for practitioners in scaffolding their experiences.

Acknowledgement. This is an event of the IFIP TC14 working group Art and Entertainment, organized by researchers from Ningbo Research Institute, Zhejiang University, Ningbo; School of Software Technology, Zhejiang University; Department of Industrial Design, Eindhoven University of Technology. We would like to express great thanks to our sponsors: China Institute of Eco-design Industry; Computer Aided Product Innovation and Design Engineering Center (Ministry of Education); World Eco-Design Conference (WEDC); Meta-Creation Arts (MCA).

References

1. National Coalition of Creative Arts Therapies Associations, Inc. (2018). https://www.nccata.org/
2. Ashworth, J., Reg, H.: Animation in therapy: the innovative uses of haptic animation in clinical and. Assist. Technol. **5**(1), 40–42 (2010)
3. Barber, B., et al.: Digital art Therapy: Material, Methods, and Applications. Jessica Kingsley Publishers, London (2016)
4. Bessette, J., Fol Leymarie, F., W. Smith, G.: Trends and anti-trends in techno-art scholarship: the legacy of the arts "machine" special issues. Arts **8**(3), 120 (2019)
5. Carlton, N.R.: Digital culture and art therapy. Arts Psychother. **41**(1), 41–45 (2014)
6. Choe, S.: An exploration of the qualities and features of art apps for art therapy. Arts Psychother. **41**(2), 145–154 (2014)
7. Craig, P., Dieppe, P., Macintyre, S., Michie, S., Nazareth, I., Petticrew, M.: Developing and evaluating complex interventions: the new medical research council guidance. BMJ **337** (2008)
8. Darewych, O.H., Carlton, N.R., Farrugie, K.W.: Digital technology use in art therapy with adults with developmental disabilities. J. Dev. Disabl. **21**(2), 95 (2015)
9. Davies, C., Pescud, M., Anwar-McHenry, J., Wright, P.: Arts, public health and the national arts and health framework: a lexicon for health professionals. Aust. N. Z. J. Public Health **40**(4), 304–306 (2016)
10. Davies, C.R., Knuiman, M., Wright, P., Rosenberg, M.: The art of being healthy: a qualitative study to develop a thematic framework for understanding the relationship between health and the arts. BMJ Open **4**(4), e004790 (2014)
11. Davies, C.R., Rosenberg, M., Knuiman, M., Ferguson, R., Pikora, T., Slatter, N.: Defining arts engagement for population-based health research: art forms, activities and level of engagement. Arts & Health **4**(3), 203–216 (2012)
12. Dewey Lambert, P., Sonke, J.: Professionalizing arts management in healthcare facilities. J. Arts Manag. Law Soc. **49**(3), 155–170 (2019)
13. Edmunds, J.D.: The applications and implications of the adoption of digital media in art therapy: a survey study. Masters dissertation, Drexel University, Philadelphia, PA (2012)

14. Edwards, B.M., Smart, E., King, G., Curran, C., Kingsnorth, S.: Performance and visual arts-based programs for children with disabilities: a scoping review focusing on psychosocial outcomes. Disabil. Rehabil. **42**(4), 574–585 (2020)

15. Fancourt, D.: Arts in Health: Designing and Researching Interventions. Oxford University Press, Oxford (2017)

16. Fancourt, D., Finn, S.: What is the evidence on the role of the arts in improving health and well-being? A scoping review. World Health Organization, Regional Office for Europe (2019)

17. Franceschet, M., et al.: Crypto art: A decentralized view. Leonardo **54**(4), 402–405 (2021)

18. Ganim, B.: Art & Healing: Using Expressive Art to Heal Your Body, Mind, and Spirit. Echo Point Books & Media (2013)

19. García, L., Vilar, P.M.: The challenges of digital art preservation (2007). http://www.e-conservationline.com/content/view/884/296

20. Graham-Pole, J.: Illness and the art of creative self-expression: stories and exercises from the arts for those with chronic illness. New Harbinger Publications Incorporated (2000)

21. Hallam, S., Creech, A.: Can active music making promote health and well-being in older citizens? findings of the music for life project. Lond. J. Primary Care **8**(2), 21–25 (2016)

22. Hani, M.: Defining animation therapy: the good hearts model. Animat. Pract. Process Prod. **6**(1), 17–51 (2017)

23. Hartwich, P., Brandecker, R.: Computer-based art therapy with inpatients: Acute and chronic schizophrenics and borderline cases. Arts Psychother. **24**(4), 367–373 (1997)

24. Jones, N., et al.: How scientists are embracing NFTS. Nature **594**(7864), 481–482 (2021)

25. Kahn, D.: Noise, Water, Meat: a History of Sound in the arts. MIT Press, Cambridge (1999)

26. Knill, P.J., Levine, E.G., Levine, S.K.: Principles and Practice of Expressive Arts Therapy: Toward a Therapeutic Aesthetic. Jessica Kingsley Publishers, London (2005)

27. Malchiodi, C.A., Johnson, E.R.: Digital art therapy with hospitalized children. In: Art Therapy and Health Care, pp. 106–121 (2013)

28. Martin, L., et al.: Creative arts interventions for stress management and prevention-a systematic review. Behav. Sci. **8**(2), 28 (2018)

29. Moghimian, M., Akbari, M., Moghaddasi, J., Niknajad, R.: Effect of digital storytelling on anxiety in patients who are candidates for open-heart surgery. J. Cardiovasc. Nurs. **34**(3), 231–235 (2019)

30. National Organization for Arts in Health: Arts, health, and well-being in America. Author, San Diego (2017)

31. North, M.M., North, S.M.: Virtual reality therapy. In: Computer-Assisted and Web-Based Innovations in Psychology, Special Education, and Health, pp. 141–156. Elsevier, London (2016)

32. Partesotti, E., Peñalba, A., Manzolli, J.: Digital instruments and their uses in music therapy. Nord. J. Music. Ther. **27**(5), 399–418 (2018)

33. Puig, A., Lee, S.M., Goodwin, L., Sherrard, P.A.: The efficacy of creative arts therapies to enhance emotional expression, spirituality, and psychological well-being of newly diagnosed stage i and stage ii breast cancer patients: a preliminary study. Arts Psychother. **33**(3), 218–228 (2006)

34. Skiba, D.J.: The connected age: big data & data visualization. Nurs. Educ. Perspect. **35**(4), 267–269 (2014)
35. Sonke, J., et al.: Arts in health: considering language from an educational perspective in the united states. Arts & Health **10**(2), 151–164 (2018)
36. Tao, Y., Chen, H., Meng, F., Zhang, X., Ying, F., Yao, C.: Situated apparel: designing to reinforce affective communication. In: Proceedings of the Ninth International Conference on Tangible, Embedded, and Embodied Interaction, pp. 529–532 (2015)
37. Theorell, T.P., Lennartsson, A.K., Mosing, M.A., Ullén, F.: Musical activity and emotional competence-a twin study. Front. Psychol. **5**, 774 (2014)
38. Vesel, T., Dave, S.: Music therapy and palliative care: systematic review. J. Pain Symptom Manage. **56**(6), e74 (2018)
39. West, V.L., Borland, D., Hammond, W.E.: Innovative information visualization of electronic health record data: a systematic review. J. Am. Med. Inform. Assoc. **22**(2), 330–339 (2015)
40. White, M.: Arts Development in Community Health: A Social Tonic. Radcliffe Publishing, Oxford (2009)
41. Wood, G., et al.: Ethereum: a secure decentralised generalised transaction ledger. Ethereum Project Yellow Paper **151**(2014), 1–32 (2014)
42. Wu, D.T., et al.: Evaluating visual analytics for health informatics applications: a systematic review from the American medical informatics association visual analytics working group task force on evaluation. J. Am. Med. Inform. Assoc. **26**(4), 314–323 (2019).
43. Xue, M., Liang, R.H., Hu, J., Feijs, L.: Clockviz: designing public visualization for coping with collective stress in teamwork. In: Proceedings of the Conference on Design and Semantics of Form and Movement-Sense and Sensitivity, DeSForM 2017. IntechOpen (2017)
44. Xue, M., Liang, R.H., Yu, B., Funk, M., Hu, J., Feijs, L.: AffectiveWall: designing collective stress-related physiological data visualization for reflection. IEEE Access **7**, 131289–131303 (2019)
45. Yao, C., Li, B., Ying, F., Zhang, T., Zhao, Y.: VisHair: a wearable fashion hair lighting interaction system. In: Streitz, N., Konomi, S. (eds.) DAPI 2018. LNCS, vol. 10921, pp. 146–155. Springer, Cham (2018). https://doi.org/10.1007/978-3-319-91125-0_12
46. Yu, B., Hu, J., Funk, M., Feijs, L.: Delight: biofeedback through ambient light for stress intervention and relaxation assistance. Pers. Ubiquit. Comput. **22**(4), 787–805 (2018)
47. Yu, B., Hu, J., Funk, M., Liang, R.H., Xue, M., Feijs, L.: Resonance: Lightweight, room-scale audio-visual biofeedback for immersive relaxation training. IEEE Access **6**, 38336–38347 (2018)
48. Zubala, A., Kennell, N., Hackett, S.: Art therapy in the digital world: an integrative review of current practice and future directions. Front. Psychol. **12**, 595536 (2021)

Current Opportunities and Challenges of Digital Game-Based Learning

Jannicke Baalsrud Hauge[1,2], Heinrich Söbke[3], Heiko Duin[1], Ioana Andreea Stefan[4], and Barbara Göbl[5,6(✉)]

[1] BIBA – Bremer Institut für Produktion und Logistik GmbH, Hochschulring 20, 28359 Bremen, Germany
{baa,du}@biba.uni-bremen.de
[2] Royal Institute of Technology, Kvarnbergagatan 12, Södertälje, Sweden
jmbh@kth.se
[3] Bauhaus-Universität Weimar, Bauhaus-Institute for Infrastructure Solutions (b.is), Goetheplatz 7/8, 99423 Weimar, Germany
heinrich.soebke@uni-weimar.de
[4] Advanced Technology Systems, Str. Tineretului Nr 1., 130029 Targoviste, Romania
ioana.stefan@ats.com.ro
[5] University of Vienna, Centre for Teacher Education, Porzellangasse 4, 1090 Vienna, Austria
barbara.goebl@univie.ac.at
[6] Faculty of Computer Science, University of Vienna, Währinger Straße 29, 1090 Vienna, Austria

Abstract. Digital game-based learning (DGBL) has been discussed for over 50 years. Despite countless studies over several decades, DGBL is still the exception rather than the standard in most educational contexts. A workshop at the 21st International Conference on Entertainment Computing 2022 (IFIP ICEC) in Bremen, Germany, prepares an overview of the current state of DGBL. This article provides a systematic overview of the fundamental concepts of DGBL. For this purpose, a life cycle model for learning games is proposed for structuring the overview. At each phase of the life cycle model, opportunities and challenges are identified and discussed through a literature review. Overall, the result is an overview serving as a framework for the workshop and as an orientation for the design, development, and deployment of learning games.

Keywords: Digital games · Game-based learning · Advantages · Disadvantages · Learning games · Life cycle model · Serious games

1 Introduction

Serious games have another purpose beyond entertainment, such as learning [1]. The term serious games does not limit the characteristics of games and subsumes both analog games, such as board games, digital games, and hybrid games. In the following, serious digital games for learning are considered, and the term digital learning games is used.

© IFIP International Federation for Information Processing 2022
Published by Springer Nature Switzerland AG 2022
B. Göbl et al. (Eds.): ICEC 2022, LNCS 13477, pp. 443–450, 2022.
https://doi.org/10.1007/978-3-031-20212-4_38

Closely related to digital learning games is the term digital game-based learning (DGBL) [2]. DGBL has a long-term history and has been discussed for over 50 years [2–4]. Learning games have numerous positive effects, including unique learning experiences, immersion, and interest capturing [5]. Despite decades of dedicated commitment from the research and education communities, learning games are not among the most widely taken-for-granted media in educational contexts, such as texts. Issues that might inhibit the establishment of games in educational contexts include uncertain findings on actual learning effects [6], special requirements for educators [7], specific skill sets required in design [8], and high efforts in developing serious games [9]. Discussions on whether mandated gaming is harmful for motivation [10] or even the phenomenon of game ageing [11], i.e. digital games losing their technical operability over time due to lack of maintenance or no longer meeting the learning goals in terms of subject matter, are also issues that impact the uptake. Another challenge is the widespread application of DGBL across various disciplines, rendering DGBL a fractured field of research [12]. Additionally, the alignment of learning games as a medium and the respective learning objectives must be ensured [13] - an insight that has to be considered as a fundamental principle in multimedia learning [14].

For specifically addressing all challenges to be solved for the establishment of DGBL and for appreciating all potentials, an inventory of the state of the art of DGBL research and practice is missing. This article aims to assemble a substantiated foundation in preparation for the workshop. With this as a basis, a life cycle model for digital learning games is proposed in the next section. In the following section, opportunities and challenges from the literature are arranged according to this life cycle model.

2   Life Cycle Model for Digital Learning Games

A framework will be provided to explore the potential and challenges of learning games systematically. A life cycle model of games seems suitable to provide this framework. Various life cycle models are described in the literature. The majority of these models refer to digital games per se. Life cycle models for learning games have to consider the purpose beyond entertainment, in this case, learning. In addition to digital games for entertainment, learning content has to be integrated, and the learning effectiveness has to be evaluated. In the following, some life cycle models are presented, followed by a proposed life cycle model for digital learning games.

Game Development Software Engineering (GDSE) [15]. GDSE includes three phases: pre-production, production, and post-production. Aleem et al. [15] discuss key work areas for each phase. The pre-production phase focuses on management, requirements specification, game system description language, reusability, game design document (GDD), game prototyping, design tools, and risk management. The production phase focuses on asset creation, storyboard production, development platform, formal language description, programming, game engine, and implementation. In the post-production phase, quality assurance, beta testing, heuristic testing, empirical testing, testing tools, and marketing are mentioned. The priorities in the work mentioned above are certainly not conclusive in terms of chronology but may be used as a checklist for identifying the challenges of game-based learning.

Game Development Life Cycle (GDLC) [16]. Ramadan & Widyani [16] describe a GDLC as a synthesis of various previous GDLCs and name six phases: the first phase is initiation resulting in a simple game description. The second phase is pre-production, in which the game design is completed, a prototype and the GDD are created. The result of the third phase, production, is a complete prototype. The fourth phase is testing, which decides whether a further cycle of the production phase is essential or whether it is possible to move on to the next phase. The fifth phase, Beta, contains the handover of the game to selected end-users. In case of severe deficits, the result is the entry into a different production phase or the change to the sixth phase, Release. In the release phase, the game is made available for public use, a project retrospective is conducted, and maintenance is planned.

Serious Gaming in Medical Education [17]. Based on a literature review, Olszewski and Wolbrink [17] have developed a framework for developing learning games specifically for application in the field of medicine. They distinguish between the three phases: Preparation and Design, Development and Formative Evaluation, each comprising specific tasks. The tasks Team Assembly, Medical Concepts Transfer, Content Production and Learner Experience Mapping, are mentioned for the Preparation and Design phase. The tasks of the Development phase are Iterative Mapping, Prototype and Wireframes. In the Formative Evaluation phase, Multiple Rounds of Testing and Final Product Delivery are performed.

Approaches for Serious Game Design [18]. In a systematic literature review of methods, frameworks and models used in serious game design, Ávila-Pesántez et al. [18] identified 11 approaches for designing serious games. Among these approaches, 31 different stages can occur in the development of learning games. The stages were assigned to four different phases. In the first phase *Analysis* the stages *Identification of the problem, teaching objective, teaching competence, learning tools, user profiles, quality assurance, specification document, therapeutic techniques* and *instructional activities* were grouped. The second phase *Design* consists of the stages *pattern design, narrative, game mechanisms, requirements specification, architecture, design prototype, quality assurance, document specification, evaluation design* and *risk analysis*. The third phase *Development* includes the stages *game programming, application prototype, quality assurance, specification document* and *game integration*. In the last phase *Evaluation* the stages *goal validation, quality assurance, testing, feedback, maintenance* and *continuous improvement plan* are included.

The brief presentation of the development frameworks and life cycle models shows similarities on the one hand, but also different aspects in the life cycle of (learning) games on the other hand. Based on this, Table 1 shows the proposal of a life cycle model for learning games that we intend to take advantage of to situate the opportunities and challenges of DGBL systematically. The six phases are presented sequentially. However, it is likely that in applying this model, the sequence might not be adhered to in its pure form. As in the underlying models, jumps back to earlier phases are conceivable, e.g., from the evaluation phase to the design phase if the game is ineffective, or parallel phases such as operation and maintenance.

Table 1. Life cycle model for digital learning games

Phase	Description
Ideation	In the ideation phase, the idea for the learning game is developed, the requirements for implementation are formulated, and the implementation team is specified
Design	Game design is developed based on the learning objectives and further requirements in the design phase, and playability is ensured via prototypes
Implementation	The game is fully developed in the implementation phase, usually with several development iterations and playability tests
Evaluation	After the game is made available to external users, it is evaluated to determine whether it achieves the intended learning objectives
Operation	The game is used in the designated didactic scenarios in the Operation Phase
Maintenance	In the maintenance Phase, the game is adapted based on discovered defects, new requirements, or changing technologies to ensure continued usability

3   Opportunities and Challenges

This section provides a selection of the respective opportunities and challenges for each phase of the proposed learning games life cycle model.

3.1   Ideation

A decision in the ideation phase is whether to develop a learning game independently, use a commercial off the shelf (COTS) game, use freely available learning games, or purchase learning games. COTS games offer the advantage that they have been optimized for entertainment purposes and are thus usually more motivating than dedicated learning games [19–21]. The use of COTS games implies that various phases, such as the development phase, do not have to be processed, and that there is no influence on other phases, such as the design phase. When developing dedicated learning games, significant resources must be devoted to integrating learning content and game mechanics [22, 23]. Also considered challenging is the multidisciplinary project team required for learning game development [17].

3.2   Design

The design of learning games is supported by various guidelines, such as [24] and frameworks, such as the Design, Play and Experience (DPE) framework [25]. Guidelines and frameworks provide formal guidance but must be enlivened in the design process.

Balancing game fun and learning content are considered a key objective of learning game design [12]. Guidelines assist in selecting game mechanics that support specific learning objectives [26]. Also chosen in the design phase is the game medium to be used: In addition to games that are playable on desktop PCs or consoles, virtual reality games strongly influence immersiveness, which in turn may lead to improved learning experiences [27]. Augmented reality games [28, 29] and location-based games [30–32] are other categories of games offering unique characteristics for learning. Ethical constraints must be considered as well. A significant amount of data might be collected from gaming behaviors, but it is also essential to ensure that the use of these data in adaptive settings, for example, complies with ethical principles [12, 33].

3.3 Implementation

A current overview of the implementation of learning games for the subject domain of Software Engineering, but also beyond, is given in [34]. In particular, it points out that efficiency still needs to be increased. A particular challenge of efficient implementation is tools for test automation [15, 35].

3.4 Evaluation

So far, only slight effects of DGBL on learning outcomes have been confirmed [6]. In contrast, Boyle et al. [36], in a new edition of their 2012 study [37], have found a significant increase in studies confirming improved learning outcomes. They call for a more detailed analysis of the factors of DGBL that are conducive to learning. Questionnaires are often used to evaluate learning games. The quality of the questionnaires is currently debated, and the reproducibility of the results is questioned [38].

3.5 Operation

The didactic scenario for the use of games is to be defined. For example, it is to be defined whether games are played at lecture times guided by lecturers or freely chosen by the learners. Previous work also taps into recent developments in gaming culture and suggests the creation of gameplay-based videos by learners, i.e. "Let's Plays", to present new game-based learning experiences [39].

Another distinction is whether the game is played in groups or individually. If lecturers guide the game, lecturers may exploit their expertise to contribute to a sustainable learning experience e.g. [19]. However, the synchronous play also requires lecturers' skills as game facilitators-skills that are essential but currently rarely trained systematically [7]. Also seen as challenging are educational scenarios characterized by, for example, across disciplines longer learning times, and social learning [12]. On the other hand, these challenges also provide one of the opportunities of DGBL, namely enhanced learning experiences [5].

3.6 Maintenance

The post-production phase is yet underrepresented in research and deserves further attention [15]. One challenge that needs to be addressed is game ageing, i.e., the limitation of the usability of games due to domain or technical obsolescence [11]. A related research topic is the preservation of games, i.e. the maintenance of playability while the technical environment is constantly innovating [40–42].

4   Conclusion

Digital Game-based Learning (DGBL) has been a medium for teaching knowledge and skills training for over 50 years. Nevertheless, in a few cases only, DGBL has reached the maturity level of other educational media such as textbooks. This article compiles several fundamentals and has analyzed the current opportunities and challenges of DGBL. It will be a starting point for further discussions and collaborative research in the upcoming year. To structure the compilation, a life cycle model for digital learning games, which are the basis of DGBL, was previously derived from various existing life cycle models and guidelines for developing digital games in different game categories. The article provides an extendable basis for the structured analysis of the current opportunities and challenges of DGBL.

Acknowledgements. This work has been partly funded by the German Federal Ministry of Education and Research (BMBF) through the projects DigiLab4U (No. 16DHB2113) and AuCity2 (No. 16DHB2131) and by the Austrian Research Promotion Agency (FFG) within the Call "Talente regional 2019" (No. 878696 – "StreamIT!: Streaming als pädagogisches Tool zur Interessenvermittlung & zum Kompetenzerwerb").

References

1. Ratan, R., Ritterfeld, U.: Classifying serious games. In: Ritterfeld, U., Cody, M., Vorderer, P. (eds.) Serious Games: Mechanisms and Effects, pp. 10–22. Routledge, New York (2009)
2. Prensky, M.: Digital Game-Based Learning. Paragon House, St. Paul (2007)
3. Abt, C.C.: Serious Games. University Press of America (1987)
4. Gee, J.P.: Reflections on empirical evidence on games and learning. In: Tobias, S., Fletcher, J.D. (eds.) Computer Games and Instruction, pp. 223–232. IAP (2011)
5. Squire, K.R.: Video Games and Learning: Teaching and Participatory Culture in the Digital Age. Teachers College Press, New York (2011)
6. Wouters, P., van Nimwegen, C., van Oostendorp, H., van der Spek, E.D.: A meta-analysis of the cognitive and motivational effects of serious games. J. Educ. Psychol. **105**, 249–265 (2013)
7. Baalsrud Hauge, J., et al.: Current competencies of game facilitators and their potential optimization in higher education: multimethod study. JMIR Serious Games **9**, e25481 (2021)
8. Engström, H., Backlund, P.: Serious games design knowledge - experiences from a decade (+) of serious games development. EAI Endorsed Trans. Serious Games (2021). https://doi.org/10.4108/eai.27-5-2021.170008
9. Söbke, H., Streicher, A.: Serious games architectures and engines. In: Dörner, R., Göbel, S., Kickmeier-Rust, M., Masuch, M., Zweig, K. (eds.) Entertainment Computing and Serious Games. LNCS, vol. 9970, pp. 148–173. Springer, Cham (2016). https://doi.org/10.1007/978-3-319-46152-6_7
10. Rockwell, G.M., Kee, K.: Game studies - the leisure of serious games: a dialogue. Game Stud. Int. J. Comput. Game Res. **11** (2011)
11. Söbke, H., Harder, R., Planck-Wiedenbeck, U.: Two decades of traffic system education using the simulation game MOBILITY. In: Göbel, S., et al. (eds.) JCSG 2018. LNCS, vol. 11243, pp. 43–53. Springer, Cham (2018). https://doi.org/10.1007/978-3-030-02762-9_6
12. de Freitas, S.: Are games effective learning tools? A review of educational games. Educ. Technol. Soc. **21**, 74–84 (2018)

13. Burn, A.: Liber ludens: games, play and learning. In: Haythornthwaite, C., Andrews, R., Fransman, J., Meyers, E.M. (eds.) The SAGE Handbook of E-learning Research, pp. 127–151. SAGE Publications Ltd (2016)

14. Kerres, M.: Mediendidaktik: Konzeption und Entwicklung digitaler Lernangebote. De Gruyter (2018)

15. Aleem, S., Capretz, L.F., Ahmed, F.: Game development software engineering process life cycle: a systematic review. J. Softw. Eng. Res. Dev. 4(1), 1–30 (2016). https://doi.org/10.1186/s40411-016-0032-7

16. Ramadan, R., Widyani, Y.: Game development life cycle guidelines. In: 2013 International Conference on Advanced Computer Science and Information Systems (ICACSIS), pp. 95–100 (2013)

17. Olszewski, A.E., Wolbrink, T.A.: Serious gaming in medical education: a proposed structured framework for game development. Simul. Healthc. 12, 240–253 (2017)

18. Ávila-Pesántez, D., Rivera, L.A., Alban, M.S.: Approaches for serious game design: a systematic literature review. Comput. Educ. J. 8, 1–11 (2017)

19. Arnold, U., Söbke, H., Reichelt, M.: SimCity in infrastructure management education. Educ. Sci. 9, 209 (2019)

20. Squire, K.R.: Replaying History: Learning World History through playing Civilization III (2003). http://website.education.wisc.edu/kdsquire/dissertation.html

21. Holmes, W.: Digital games-based learningTime to adoption: two to three years? In: Education and New Technologies, pp. 196–212. Routledge (2017)

22. Harteveld, C., Guimarães, R., Mayer, I., Bidarra, R.: Balancing pedagogy, game and reality components within a unique serious game for training levee inspection. Technol. E-Learn. Digit. Entertain. 128–139 (2007)

23. Habgood, M.P.J., Ainsworth, S.E.: Motivating children to learn effectively: exploring the value of intrinsic integration in educational games. J. Learn. Sci. 20, 169–206 (2011)

24. Pereira de Aguiar, M., Winn, B., Cezarotto, M., Battaiola, A.L., Varella Gomes, P.: Educational digital games: a theoretical framework about design models, learning theories and user experience. In: Marcus, A., Wang, W. (eds.) DUXU 2018. LNCS, vol. 10918, pp. 165–184. Springer, Cham (2018). https://doi.org/10.1007/978-3-319-91797-9_13

25. Winn, B.M.: The Design, Play, and Experience Framework. In: Handbook of Research on Effective Electronic Gaming in Education, vol. 5497 (2011)

26. Arnab, S., et al.: Mapping learning and game mechanics for serious games analysis. Br. J. Educ. Technol. 46, 391–411 (2015)

27. Dinis, F.M., et al.: Development of virtual reality game-based interfaces for civil engineering education. In: 2017 IEEE Global Engineering Education Conference, EDUCON 2017, Athens, Greece, 25–28 April 2017, pp. 1195–1202 (2017)

28. Li, J., van der Spek, E.D., Feijs, L., Wang, F., Hu, J.: Augmented reality games for learning: a literature review. In: Streitz, N., Markopoulos, P. (eds.) DAPI 2017. LNCS, vol. 10291, pp. 612–626. Springer, Cham (2017). https://doi.org/10.1007/978-3-319-58697-7_46

29. Pallavicini, F., Pepe, A.: Comparing player experience in video games played in virtual reality or on desktop displays: immersion, flow, and positive emotions. In: CHI Play 2019 - Extended Abstracts of the Annual Symposium on Computer-Human Interaction in Play Companion Extended Abstracts, pp. 195–210 (2019)

30. Ribeiro, F.R., Silva, A., Silva, A.P., Metrôlho, J.: Literature review of location-based mobile games in education: challenges, impacts and opportunities. Informatics 8 (2021)

31. Laato, S., Pietarinen, T., Rauti, S., Sutinen, E.: Potential benefits of playing location-based games: an analysis of game mechanics. In: Lane, H.C., Zvacek, S., Uhomoibhi, J. (eds.) CSEDU 2019. CCIS, vol. 1220, pp. 557–581. Springer, Cham (2020). https://doi.org/10.1007/978-3-030-58459-7_27

32. Schaal, S.: Location-based games for geography and environmental education. In: Walshe, N., Healy, G. (eds.) Geography Education in the Digital World: Linking Theory and Practice, p. 54. Routledge (2020)

33. Sandovar, A., Braad, E., Streicher, A., Söbke, H.: Ethical stewardship: designing serious games seriously. In: Dörner, R., Göbel, S., Kickmeier-Rust, M., Masuch, M., Zweig, K. (eds.) Entertainment Computing and Serious Games. LNCS, vol. 9970, pp. 42–62. Springer, Cham (2016). https://doi.org/10.1007/978-3-319-46152-6_3

34. Cooper, K.M.L.: Software Engineering and Serious Games for K-20 Education A Summary of Recent Literature (2022)

35. Politowski, C., Petrillo, F., Gueheneuc, Y.G.: A survey of video game testing. In: Proceedings - 2021 IEEE/ACM International Conference on Automation of Software Test, AST 2021, pp. 90–99 (2021)

36. Boyle, E.A., et al.: An update to the systematic literature review of empirical evidence of the impacts and outcomes of computer games and serious games. Comput. Educ. **94**, 178–192 (2016)

37. Connolly, T.M., Boyle, E.A., MacArthur, E., Hainey, T., Boyle, J.M.: A systematic literature review of empirical evidence on computer games and serious games. Comput. Educ. **59**, 661–686 (2012)

38. Law, E.L., Brühlmann, F., Mekler, E.D.: Systematic review and validation of the game experience questionnaire (GEQ) – implications for citation and reporting practice. In: CHI PLAY 2018 The Annual Symposium on Computer-Human Interaction in Play Extended Abstracts, pp. 257–270. ACM, New York (2018)

39. Denk, N., Göbl, B., Wernbacher, T., Jovicic, S., Kriglstein, S.: StreamIT!-towards an educational concept centred around gameplay video production. In: European Conference on Games Based Learning, pp. 196–202. Academic Conferences International Limited (2021)

40. Lee, J.H.,et al.: Challenges in preserving augmented reality games: a case study of ingress and Pokémon GO. In: iPRES (2017)

41. Brown, S., Lowrance, S., Whited, C.: Preservation Practices of Videogames in Archives. https://ssrn.com/abstract=3174157

42. Guay-Bélanger, D.: Assembling auras: towards a methodology for the preservation and study of video games as cultural heritage artefacts. Games Cult. **17**, 659–678 (2022)

Author Index

Printed in the United States
by Baker & Taylor Publisher Services